EARLY AMERICAN HISTORY

An eighteen volume series reproducing
over three hundred of the most
important articles on all aspects of the
colonial experience

EDITED WITH INTRODUCTIONS BY
PETER CHARLES HOFFER
UNIVERSITY OF GEORGIA

A Garland Series

THE MARROW OF AMERICAN DIVINITY

Selected Articles
on Colonial Religion

EDITED WITH AN INTRODUCTION BY
PETER CHARLES HOFFER

Garland Publishing, Inc.
New York & London
1988

Introduction copyright © 1988 by
Peter Charles Hoffer

Library of Congress Cataloging-in-Publication Data

The Marrow of American divinity : selected articles on colonial
religion / edited with an introduction by Peter Charles Hoffer.
p. cm.—(Early American history)
Reprint of previously published articles.
ISBN 0-8240-6241-8 (alk. paper)
1. United States—Church history—Colonial period,
ca. 1600–1775.   I. Hoffer, Peter C.   II. Series.
BR520.M365   1988
277.3—dc19   87-17208
CIP

The volumes in this series are printed on
acid-free, 250-year-life paper.

Printed in the United States of America

CONTENTS

PREFACE

In 1970, Darrett Rutman reminded us that colonial theology must be studied in the context of a pervasive religiosity.[1] Religion reached out from pew and pulpit, past creeds and liturgies, to all facets of local life. Later scholars agreed: religion suffused family, ethnicity, and culture.[2] At the same time, there were many other stimuli competing for the colonists' attention. The task for the historian of American religion thus has been to define the boundaries of his or her field as much as to probe the marrow of worship, piety, and church-making. For Rutman's Puritans, that boundary was defined by the personal relationship of preachers to congregants. In colonial society, where the meeting house was a vital social as well as religious center, and so much of social life depended upon face to face contacts, this relationship between minister and flock was characteristic of all sects. Ritual observance was balanced by personal obligation to the pastor as well as to the diety. Study and preparation seemed to outweigh mere faith. Voluntary adherence and periodic shifting of allegiances confuted central religious authority.

Rutman's marvelously succinct essay was meant as a corrective to Perry Miller's massive and learned treatment of Puritanism. Miller speaks briefly for himself throughout the volume and needs no defense, but it must be admitted that religious history has moved away from the dichotomies of piety versus intellect and prophecy versus memory that Miller stressed and Rutman redressed. More recent studies have taken far more interest in the forms of religion than in theology. Scholars have not lost their appreciation of intel-

ix

lect, nor their recognition of the crucial role of the ministry, but they have discovered that religion in America was far more flexible and open than earlier generations of scholars believed. Compromises in liturgy, church organization, and even the language of the sermon were more common than not. There was a renaissance of sorts in the sacramental forms in the late seventeenth century, a counterpoint to the renaissance of piety in the 1730s and 1740s. Historians now stress popular religious movements and their connections to similar strivings among the common people of western Europe. They have rediscovered a radical strain in the Anglo-American religious connection. In all, they have found that religion was more varied in the colonies than they had heretofore thought.

Lest lay readers join earlier generations of historians in claiming this vitality, voluntarism, and variety as proof of American religious exceptionalism, recent scholarship has demonstrated that much the same process was transforming European religion. In the eighteenth century, new protestant sects, many of them pietistic, were emerging across the continent. England and Scotland were the home, and remained the base, for many of the sects—Quakers, Methodists, Presbyterians—that were agitating for greater religious toleration in America. The Great Awakening, which spurred denominationalism, and, perhaps ironically, led to broader religious toleration, was a transatlantic movement from its inception, part of a revival sweeping across the Western World. Throughout this world, religion mirrored the strains upon older, corporate forms of belief and organization. The new institutions of worship that emerged from this revolution of enthusiasm were more individualistic.

The essays in this collection illustrate the fruitfulness of the field and the many changes through which it has gone. They also illustrate the connection that religion had to the colonists' politics, social beliefs, and migration patterns. Rutman was right: religiosity was important *because* of its place among all the other demands upon the colonists' allegiance.

Peter Charles Hoffer
University of Georgia

Notes

1. Darrett Rutman, *American Puritanism, Faith and Practice* (Philadelphia, 1970), 5.

2. Jon Butler,"The Future of American Religious History," *The William and Mary Quarterly*, 3d ser. 42 (1985), 167.

HEBREW LEARNING AMONG THE PURITANS OF NEW ENGLAND PRIOR TO 1700.[1]

By Rev. D. de Sola Pool, Ph. D.

The following paper is an attempt at estimating the nature and extent of Hebrew learning among the New England Puritans of the seventeenth century, and at ascertaining in how far this learning was a native growth, and to what extent it could claim originality. In the treatment of these qualitative questions, a quantitative heaping of literary material becomes of secondary importance; and the temptation to multiply names and quote extracts from the tedious doctrino-theological literature of the period has been indulged in only so far as has been necessitated for substantiating the results to be arrived at.

1

[1] When this paper was finished, Dr. Cyrus Adler called my attention to an article by Professor G. F. Moore in *Zeitschrift für die alttestamentliche Wissenschaft*, Vol. VIII (1888), pp. 1-47, on " Alttestamentliche Studien in Amerika." Only the first six pages deal with the period up to 1700, and the treatment is necessarily very brief. Professor Gottheil, writing in the *Rivista Israelitica*, Vol. V (1908), p. 68, on " Gli studi ebraici in America," has made use of this article for the earliest period, as has also Rabbi William Rosenau in his paper, " Semitic Studies in American Colleges," " Year Book of the Central Conference of American Rabbis" (1896), p. 101. Dr. Rosenau devotes about a dozen lines to the seventeenth century. There is a slight popular sketch of Semitics at Harvard College in *The Menorah*, Vol. XXXIV (1903), by Joseph Lebowich. The first two paragraphs touch on the early period. A. W. McClure, in his " Life of John Cotton," Boston (1846), p. 151, makes some general remarks on Hebrew knowledge among the New England Puritan divines. Another reference that must now be added is to the *Publications of the American Jewish Historical Society*, No. 19, p. 108, where Mr. Hühner, in his paper on " Jews in Connection with the Colleges of the Thirteen Original States prior to 1800," devotes a few lines to the study of Hebrew in the early years of Harvard University.

The story of Hebrew culture in Massachusetts begins with
the very foundation of the Plymouth colony, for the first
Hebraists to settle in New England came over in the *Mayflower.* Governor Bradford (1590-1657), one of the *Mayflower* Pilgrims, was a man' whose ability, character, and
comparative culture raised him above his fellow settlers. Particularly his knowledge of languages is praised by Cotton
Mather in the *Magnalia,*[2] for he was conversant with Dutch,
French, Latin, and Greek,

> but the Hebrew [tongue] he most of all studied, because he said
> he would see with his own eyes the ancient oracles of God in
> their native beauty.

Bradford's own words to this effect have been preserved.
They occur in the original MS. of his valuable "History of
Plymouth Plantation." In this MS. are some eight pages of
Hebrew roots with English explanations, and quotations from
the Hebrew Old Testament written in Bradford's hand. To
this he has prefixed the following:

> Though I am growne aged, yet I have had a longing
> desire to see with my own eyes, somthing of that most
> ancient language, and holy tongue, in which the law
> and Oracles of God were write; and in which God
> and angels spake to the holy patriarchs of old
> time; and what names were given to things
> from the creation. And though I cañot
> attaine to much herein, yet I am refresh-
> ed to have seen some glipse hereof
> (as Moyses saw the land of Ca-
> nan a farr of). My aime and
> desire is, to see how the words
> and phrases lye in the
> holy texte; and to
> discerne somewhat
> of the same
> for my owne
> contente.[3]

---

[2] Vol. I, p. 105.

[3] *Proceedings of the Mass. Hist. Soc.*, Series I, Vol. XI, p. 402;
Collections of the Mass. Hist. Soc., Series IV, Vol. III, p. xiv.

To Bradford, the Old Testament was never truly itself in a translation, and his quotations from it are made by preference from the original Hebrew. These Hebrew quotations are numerous in his MSS.;[4] but, "though an angel should write, still 'tis devils must print," and the printer of these MSS. has in most cases obscured this Hebraic coloring simply by omitting the Hebrew quotations. Thus, in the *Proceedings of the Massachusetts Historical Society* (Series I, Vol. XI), Bradford's third "Dialogue" is printed, and in the printed reproduction of the title-page, no Hebrew is found. But reference to the photographic plate of the original MS. title-page shows that three separate lines of Hebrew head it. These Hebrew lines are made up of Psalm xxvi, 8, the first three words of Psalm xvi, 5, and the first half of the distich Psalm xxvi, 5, all the Hebrew being punctuated. We are told further[5] that:

Two pages at the beginning of this Dialogue contain both the Hebrew and the Greek alphabet, in Bradford's hand, expressed in the original characters, with the names also of each letter spelled out in the Roman character, with some additional illustration as to long and short vowels, to aid in pronunciation. Eight pages at the end (and possibly some leaves may be wanting) contain passages from the Old Testament, in Hebrew, with English translation written underneath, from the Genevan version.

All this Hebrew is omitted in the printed reproduction, the only Hebrew that is reproduced being the word אֲדֹנִי *adoni*, p. 434, which Bradford explains as being the equivalent of Monsieur, Dominus or Mr.

A poem composed by Bradford entitled "Some observations of God's merciful dealings with us in this wilderness . . . ." is preceded by the apt quotation in Hebrew of Psalm xlvi, 12.

---

[4] *E. g., Proceedings, ibid.,* p. 466, note.
[5] *Ibid.,* p. 402.

Bradford was not the only Hebraist on the *Mayflower,* for
Elder William Brewster also had some knowledge of the
sacred tongue. This we judge from the inventory of the
books in his library made by Bradford and others in May,
1644. In the list, the following items of Hebrew interest
occur:

> (10) Tromellius and Junius, *Biblia Sacra, i. e.,* the Bible trans-
> lation of Tremellius, a converted Jew who will be mentioned
> later; (31) *Psalm Pagnii, i. e.,* possibly the Psalms with the
> commentary of Sanctes Pagninus, a pupil of Savonarola; (59) a
> book registered as *Hebrew Gramat,* which has been identified
> (for what reason I know not) with J. Avenarius, *Grammatices
> Hebraicae tres partes 1586;* (63) Buxtorf, *Lexicon, i. e.,* Hebrew
> Lexicon; (103) Waimes, *Christia Synagogue,* which refers to a
> book by Jo. Weemes, called " The Christian Synagogue, wherein
> is contayned the diverse reading, the right pointing, translation,
> and collation of Scripture with Scripture; with the customs of
> the Hebrewes and Proselytes . . . ." [4]

Brewster, whose library contained about four hundred separate books, probably learned the rudiments of Hebrew during
his short stay at Peterhouse College, Cambridge.

The religious character of the early settlers in New England is the determining factor in early colonial history. But
an influential feature of colonial life that is often overlooked,
is the fact that a considerable number of these settlers were,
at least in the first half of the seventeenth century, men of
classical education and broad culture. The laws against heresy
and the uniformity legislation, in a word, the religious unrest
and growing intolerance in England in the time of the first
two Stuart kings, especially under the reforming activity of
Archbishop Laud, drove many of the better-educated laymen,
and a larger proportion of the non-conformist clergy over the
ocean to seek religious freedom in the young Puritan colony.
Cotton Mather has put on record the names of seventy-seven
of these ministers who began their church life in England,

---

[4] *Proceedings Mass. Hist. Soc.,* Series II, Vol. III, p. 265; Vol.
V. p. 37 *et seq.*

and who later became ministers in the churches of New England. These men brought with them the tradition of learning that flourished in the church of Old England after the Reformation, and transplanted it in New England like a Minerva birth in its full development.

Therefore it is that the sun of Hebrew scholarship in New England rose suddenly to its apogee, and then slowly but steadily declined throughout the seventeenth century. For academic Hebrew learning that flourished indigenously in the sequestered cloisters of Oxford and Cambridge, often under the care of converted Jews, could not thrive so fruitfully in the ruder atmosphere of the unfashioned colony. Indeed, our wonder and admiration are excited at finding the study of Hebrew pursued at all in the rugged little colonies subject to all the harshness and privation that fall to the lot of a pioneer settlement in a virgin land, among an unfriendly people. And this admiring wonder is heightened when we remember the perilous and haphazard nature of communication with the motherland, the consequent isolation of the little band of scholars from all centres of learning, the extreme difficulty and inordinate expense of procuring books, the complete lack of patrons of learning, at first the absence of a local printing press, and later its inadequacy; and finally the apparent remoteness of Hebrew knowledge from the bluff, rough and ready conditions of life in the young colony.

Typical of these English-trained scholars who introduced the study of Hebrew into Massachusetts is John Cotton (1585-1652). Cotton arrived in Boston in 1633, having been induced to leave England through the disfavor shown by Laud to his Puritanic views. This divine had entered Trinity College, Cambridge, at the early age of thirteen, and had subsequently become a Fellow of Emmanuel College.[a] Cotton

[a] Cambridge University, especially Emmanuel College, was a great stronghold of Puritanism, and there were about three Cambridge graduates to every one Oxford graduate in New England in the first half of the seventeenth century.

Mather tells us in the *Magnalia*[7] of John Cotton's examination for his fellowship,

wherein 'twas particularly remarked, that the Poser trying his Hebrew skill by the third chapter of Isaiah, a chapter which, containing more hard words than any one paragraph of the Bible, might therefore have puzzled a very good Hebrician, yet he made nothing of it.[8]

Further he writes:[9]

The Hebrew he understood so exactly and so readily that he was able to discourse in it.

To judge what value we may assign to this statement, we must remember that a modicum of Hebrew knowledge was the common possession of every university-trained cleric of the time; and although this knowledge was in some cases, such as in the men who prepared the Authorized Version of 1611, very considerable, in the majority of cases it must have been conventionally fragmentary and rudimentary. Only rarely would this Hebrew learning have been extensive enough to have allowed of free translation from English into Hebrew. The basis of credible fact in Cotton Mather's statement, therefore, when all allowances have been made for his pious enthusiasm for the good name of his grandfather, seems to be that John Cotton understood Hebrew unusually well, and was even able on occasion to put Hebrew sentences together into a connected discourse with comparative ease.

Another representative Hebrew scholar of the time was Richard Mather (1596-1669) who, fleeing from England for non-conformity, became pastor of the Congregational Church in Dorchester in 1635. His chief contribution to Hebrew

---

[7] Book III, chap. I, p. 233.
[8] In this account, Mather is simply reproducing Samuel Whiting's (1597-1679) words with some alterations. See Whiting's " Life of John Cotton " in Alexander Young's " Chronicles of the First Planters of the Colony of Massachusetts," p. 421.
[9] *Magnalia*, III, 1, p. 249.

learning—besides his son Increase—was his work as one of, if not actually the chief of, the editors of the "Bay Psalm Book." In this work he was associated with other scholars, among whom were John Eliot, to whom we must refer later, and Thomas Welde (1590-1662)."

All three men were educated in England, Mather at Oxford, Eliot and Welde at Cambridge.

The "Bay Psalm Book," issued in 1640 by the Cambridge press, which had been set up in the preceding year, was the third publication of that press—a broadside, "The Oath of a Free-Man," and a small work, Pierce's "Almanac for 1639," being the two small publications which antedate it. It is therefore the first book of importance printed in English America, although not the first book printed on the continent, for the Spanish press in Mexico had been in existence many years earlier.

From every point of view, the "Bay Psalm Book" is a notable achievement for the time, consisting, as it does, of an original, metrical translation of the Psalms made directly from the Hebrew. Fittingly enough, in this thoroughly Hebraic first triumph of the American press, there are to be found in the preface several Hebrew words, the crude block type for which was probably specially cut for the book. It

7

" This Thomas Welde returned to England a year after the publication of the book of Psalms. We find him again on the periphery of Jewish interest in 1653, when he appears as part author of the pamphlet, "A False Jew; or a Wonderful Discovery of a Scot, baptised at London for a Christian, circumcised at Rome to act a Jew; rebaptised at Hexham for a Believer, but found out at Newcastle to be a cheat." The first edition was issued in Newcastle, 1653; the second in London, 1654. (Jacobs and Wolf, "Bibliotheca Anglo-Judaica," p. 50, No. 268; also Nos. 266, 267.) The Scotch "Jew" was Thomas Ramsay, of whom the "Dictionary of National Biography," Vol. XLVII, p. 260, gives a good account.

is worth while quoting these passages, owing to the extreme rarity of the first edition. They are as follows:

David's psalmes, some being called by himselfe מזמורים: psalms, some תהילים Hymns; some שירים, spirituall songs .... The word ו which we translate *and* .... Lastly, Because some Hebrew words have a more full and emphaticall signification then (*sic*) any one English word can or doth sometime expresse, hence wee have done that sometime which faithfull translators may doe, viz. not only to translate the word but the emphasis of it; as אל *mighty God* for *God.* ברך *humbly blesse* for *blesse;* *rise to stand* psalm 1, for *stand, truth and faithfullness* for *truth.*

This preface is said to be the work of Richard Mather. The alphabetical divisions of the 119th Psalm are marked in this edition by the Hebrew letters and their names in English transliteration, the two Hebrew letters ׳ and כ through some oversight being omitted.

In the same year that this historic Psalm book was issued, Henry Dunster (*circa* 1612-1659) became the first president of the recently founded Harvard College. From this date, the cause of Hebrew learning in New England is associated with Harvard College, where the first promise was given that the colony would not long have to depend exclusively upon imported scholarship. " New England's First Fruits," 1643, tells us of the far-seeing hopes which made the foundation of the college possible.

After God had carried us safe to *New England* and wee had builded our houses, provided necessaries for our livell-hood, rear'd convenient places for God's worship, and setled the Civill Government: One of the next things we longed for and looked after, was to advance *Learning* and perpetuate it to Posterity; dreading to leave an illiterate Ministery to the Churches, when our present Ministers shall lie in the Dust.

Henry Dunster had been educated at Cambridge University (B. A., 1630; M. A., 1634) and had then gone into the English ministry. But being obliged, as Cotton and Mather had been before him, to leave England on account of his non-conformist views, he fled to New England. There he was hailed as a scholar, and, soon after his arrival in the new continent, he was chosen president of Harvard.

This choice fell upon him in his clerical capacity, for the spirit and the purpose of the new seat of learning were rigidly theological. In the sequel, fourteen years later, in 1654, Dunster had to resign his position as president of Harvard on account of his outspoken views on infant baptism.

Upon Dunster devolved much of the work of building up the college system on a firm basis. How the studies were organised we know in some detail, for the scheme of work is preserved for us in " New England's First Fruits " (London, 1643, p. 28). It reads in part as follows:

> The fift day reads Hebrew, and the Easterne Tongues.
> Grammar to the first yeare, houre the 8th.
> To the 2d. Chaldee, at the 9th houre.
> To the 3d. Syriack at the 10th houre.
>
> Afternoone.
>
> The first yeare practice in the Bible at the 2d. houre.
> The 2d. in Ezra and Danel at the 3d. houre.
> The 3d. at the 4th houre in Trostius New Testament.[11]

The qualifications for the first degree, which were commendably ambitious for the young colony, were as follows:

> Every Schollar, that on proofe is found able to read the Originalls of the Old and New Testament in to the Latine tongue, and to resolve them Logically; withall being of godly life and conversation; And at any publick Act hath the Approbation of the Overseers, and Master of the College, is fit to be dignified with his first degree.[12]

It was the president who

> inspected the manners of the students thus entertained in the College, and unto his morning and evening prayers in the hall,

---

[11] This refers to the Syriac and Latin New Testament, edited by Martin Trost, 1621-22.
[12] " New England's First Fruits," *ibid.*

joined an exposition upon the chapters which they read out of Hebrew into Greek from the Old Testament in the morning, and out of English into Greek, from the New Testament in the evening,

and it was the fellows resident on the place who

became Tutors to the several classes, and after they had instructed them in the Hebrew language, led them through all the liberal arts 'ere their first four years expired.[13]

10

At the completion of the first four years of study, in 1642, the first commencement exercises ever held in America took place. On September 26, of that year, the governor of the colony wrote back to England that the exercises for

The Students of the first classes that have beene these foure years trained up in University learning

included

Hebrew Analasis, Grammaticall, Logicall Rhetoricall of the Psalms.[14]

Among the theses offered by this first class of Harvard graduates in 1642 were

Hebraea est Linguarum Mater.
Consonantes et vocales Hebraeorum sunt coaetaneae.
Punctationes Chatephatac syllabam proprie non efficiunt.[15]
(Hebrew is the mother of languages.
The Hebrew consonants and vowels are of equal age.
The chateph vowel sign does not constitute a syllable.)

A thesis similar to this last one was offered by a member of the class of 1643.[16]

It is especially noteworthy that of six linguistic theses, one is devoted to a Latin subject, two deal with Greek subjects and three with Hebrew. The orations that marked the exercises

[13] *Magnalia*, IV, 1, p. 9.
[14] " New England's First Fruits," p. 31.
[15] *Ibid.*, p. 34.
[16] Sibley, " Harvard Graduates," I, p. 75.

were made not only in Latin, but sometimes in Greek and in Hebrew also."

From these early records, we may fairly assert that no element of instruction figured more largely or made more show in the educational course at Harvard College during the first few decades after its foundation than did Hebrew. This state of affairs was due to the Puritan spirit and to the especial enthusiasm for Hebrew shown by the first president, Dunster, and his successor in office, Charles Chauncy.

11

Dunster seems to have kept himself in touch with European scholars during his presidency of the college, and a letter, written by him, presenting many points of interest for this study, has been preserved." The date of the letter is apparently 1648. In this

coppy of my lr. to Dr. Christianus Ravius Orientaliū linguarū pfessor Londini,"

Dunster first replies to Ravius' questions about the pronunciation of the Indian language, incidentally referring to the pronunciation of the letter ח, which he pronounced as ch in the English " chose," so as not to confound it with ה or ע on the one side, or with כ or ק on the other. He queries whether the pronunciation of ק should be as q or as k. He asks Ravius why he pronounces ט as th and ת as t. He tells us that he distinguished between ס, שׂ and שׁ, pronouncing

" *Magnalia, l. c.*

" *Coll. Mass. Hist. Soc.*, Series X, Vol. I, p. 251.

" Christian Rau (Ravius) was born, 1613, at Berlin and died, 1677, at Frankfort-on-the-Oder. He travelled much in the East collecting MSS., and he published many works on Semitic languages. In London, he taught Oriental languages between 1647 and 1651. It is noteworthy, from a Jewish point of view, that in 1651 he bought the Hebrew printing outfit of Menasseh ben Israel for a thousand florins given him by Queen Christina of Sweden, herself an accomplished Hebraist and a friend of Menasseh.

them as ß, sh, and sch, respectively, in the English words
" sew," " shew," and " eschew." Finally, he questions whether
ע should be pronounced as gn or y. He proceeds:

> To yor 8th and 9th. The students in the Colledge to whom I
> have imparted as occasion requireth, yor Hebrew sheet Grammar,
> wth yor Conjugationall, Hebrew Table doe return you hearty
> thanks, as I myselfe doe for yor notes on Udall's Grammar, and
> yor Orthographicall delineation.
>
> Lastly wee professe orselves unable to answer the Tender of
> your good will and propensity of spirit towards us. Our Infant
> Colledge compared wth the Academyes in Europe, being like
> Mantua unto Rome, and as unworthy to confine a man of your
> parts and place, as that small Town the Prince of the Latin
> Poets. Yet neverthelesse, if Divine providence should waft you
> over the Atlantick Ocean, or if yor Spirit desire to see what
> sons of Seth wander in these woods, then Harvard Colledge
> would think itselfe honourd in yor visit.

From these words it would appear that Ravius, who spent
many years of his life travelling in the East making a comparative study of Oriental languages and collecting MSS.,
wished to be invited over the ocean by Harvard College, in
order to have the opportunity of studying the language of the
Indians, doubtless hoping to find in it some Semitic affinities.
This was a wish that Dunster delicately says the college was
unable to gratify.

Further on in the letter, Dunster thanks Ravius for a box
of Oriental books sent out to the college, and proceeds to
name the books that they would be most glad to receive, mentioning especially Buxtorf's [Hebrew] Concordances and the
Bible, and " what soever Hebrew, Caldee, Syriack or Arabick
authors " should be sent. He concludes:

> A wonderfull impulse unto these studies lyes on the spirits
> of our students, some of wch can wth ease dextrously translate
> Hebrew, and Caldee, into Greek.

Dunster, as president of Harvard, was looked upon as the
best Hebraist of his time; so that when it was decided to

subject the version of the Psalms in the "Bay Psalm Book" to a literary revision,

they were committed unto Mr. Dunster, who revised and refined this translation; and (with some assistance from one Mr. Richard Lyon, who being sent over by Sir Henry Mildmay as an attendant upon his son, then a student in Harvard College, now resided in Mr. Dunster's house) he brought it into the condition wherein our churches ever since have used it.[20]

This revised edition was issued in 1651.

For the reason stated in the opening paragraph, it is not necessary to devote any detailed or lengthy attention to the minor figures of the period. Yet, before proceeding to the second president of Harvard, it may be mentioned, as a characteristic sign of the general interest in Hebrew shown at the time, that a New England work published in London in 1648 entitled "The Cleare Sun-shine of the Gospel Breaking Forth upon the Indians in New England," by Mr. Thomas Shephard, is prefaced by an epistle to the reader signed by twelve ministers, in which the quotation of a Hebrew word from Isaiah xxvi, 16, is made in Hebrew characters, and in which the following sentence occurs:

13

Where are the churches of Asia, once famous for the gospel, for general Councels, now places for *Zim* and *Ochim*,[21] their habitation desolate? where are those ancient people of the Jews who were (*segulla micol hagnâmim*) his peculiar and chosen people of all nations?

The reason for the frequent extraneous quotations of Hebrew words in the literature of the period will be clearer in the sequel.

We are told of the Rev. Samuel Whiting,[22] another divine educated at Cambridge University, England, that

especially he was accurate in Hebrew, in which primitive and expressive language he took much delight.

---

[20] *Magnalia*, III, xii, p. 367 *et seq.*
[21] Hebrew for wild cats and jackals, Isaiah xiii, 21.
[22] *Magnalia*, III, xxviii, p. 456.

In his *Oratio quam Comitiis Cantabrigiensibus Americanis
Peroravit* .... 1649, occur three lines of Hebrew at the end
of page 16.[23] This rare tract, preserved in the library of the
Massachusetts Historical Society, is not in the Lenox Library,
New York, and I have not been able to examine a copy. Mr.
Saxton, a Yorkshireman who died in England, but who was
for a time minister in Scituate and in Boston, is described
as " a great Hebrician." [24]

One other figure that may delay us for a moment is that of
the pious Michael Wigglesworth (born in England, 1631;
died, 1705), best known as the author of the appalling poem
" The Day of Doom." He graduated at Harvard under Dunster in 1651, and acted as fellow and tutor there from 1652
to 1654. We may fairly assume, therefore, that in knowledge
he represented the best that Harvard produced at the time.
Moreover, although the president of Harvard was later chosen
sometimes for his character rather than for his learning, it
must be some tribute to Wigglesworth's reputation for learning as well as to his saintliness of character that, in 1684, when
he was minister at Malden, Massachusetts, he was approached
in regard to the presidency of his *alma mater.* This offer
he could not consider on account of ill health. Perhaps it is
as well for the college that he could not accept the office of
president; for, in spite of his minute and touching devotion
and his profound and childlike religious spirit, his early teaching seems to have met with very poor success—at least in his
own eyes. His diary is filled with sad reflections on the
contumaci∙ and disrespective negligēt carriages of my pupils.

We read some of the entries in his diary of 1653 with sympathetic interest:

August 30th. God appear'd somewt in inclining yᵉ spt [spirit]
of my pupils to yᵉ study of Hebrew as I had pray'd yᵗ god would
do.

---

[23] *Proceedings Mass. Hist. Soc.*, Series II, Vol. IX, p. 414.
[24] *Magnalia*, III, iii, p. 536.

1653-4. February 14: Upon yᵉ obstinate untowardn. of some of my pupils in refusing to read Hebrew, god brings to mind & ashameth me of my own pversn herefore both to my naturall parẽts & Achademical: & also I see that this is yᵉ spt & I fear if yᵉ Lord prvẽt not wil be yᵉ ruin of yᵉ whole cõutry A spt of unbridled licẽtiousn, Lord in mercy heal, or I know not wt wil become of N. England.

March 7: I was much pplexed in mind wᵗʰ many thoughts to & fro, about leaving yᵉ colledge, one while ready to resolv upõ it almost, and quite another way: & I know not wt to do, how to live here & keep a good cõsciẽce bec. my hands are bound in point of reforming disorders; my own weakness & pupils froward negligẽce in yᵉ Hebrew stil much exercise me.[ᶻ]

15

When, in 1654, Henry Dunster had to give up his position as president of Harvard College, owing to his views on infant baptism, he was succeeded by Charles Chauncy, or Chauncey, who held office until his death in 1672. Chauncy, like Cotton, Richard Mather, and Dunster, was a non-conformist refugee. In his youth in England he had enjoyed the benefit of a training at Cambridge University, graduating B. A. in 1613 and M. A. in 1617. He had later been nominated Hebrew professor at Trinity College, although he was actually elected to the professorship in Greek.

He was indeed a person incomparably well skilled in all the learned languages, especially in the Oriental, and eminently in the Hebrew; in his obtaining whereof his conversation with a Jew for the space of a year was no little advantage to him.[ᵃ]

Who was this Jew? Mather's statement presumably refers to the time when Chauncy was studying at Cambridge,[ᵇ] and

[ᶻ] Sibley, "Harvard Graduates," Vol. I, pp. 265, 267, 268. A similar entry under August 29, 1653, is given in the *Publications of the American Jewish Historical Society*, No. 19, p. 108, note 25.

[ᵃ] *Magnalia*, III, xxiii, p. 419.

[ᵇ] Joseph Lebowich in his popular sketch, " Semitics at Harvard College " in *The Menorah*, Vol. XXXIV (1903), makes the statement that " the students (at Harvard) may have been helped by a Jew who lived in the same house with President Chauncy." This inference from Mather's words seems hardly justifiable. We know of no Jews in New England at this date.

it may well be correct. For, although theoretically there were
no Jews in England between 1290 and the time of Cromwell,
we know from many sources that during the whole period
individual Jews lived practically unmolested in England. Besides such well-known examples as Roderigo Lopez, we find
Jews, nominally converted, teaching Hebrew at the universities. Tremellius, a converted Italian Jew, who perhaps returned to Judaism before his death in 1580,[*] taught Hebrew
at Cambridge in the middle of the sixteenth century. Philip
Ferdinand, a Polish Jew, born in 1555, was professor of Hebrew first at Oxford, later at Cambridge. In the year 1598,
shortly before his death, he obtained a pension from the
Domus Conversorum. Chauncy, born in 1592, could not have
studied with either of these two men, who moreover passed
as Christians.

But it is not impossible to suppose that his Hebrew intercourse may have been with one Jacob Barnett, who gave instruction in Hebrew at Oxford early in the seventeenth century. Lucien Wolf, in " Papers of the Anglo-Jewish Historical Exhibition, 1888 " (p. 73), reproduces from the " Life
of Isaac Casaubon " a lively account of Barnett and the manner in which he hoaxed the university with his promised conversion. He writes in part:

When Casaubon visited Oxford in 1613, [the year in which
Chauncy graduated from Cambridge] he met Barnett, and was
at once struck by his profound learning and his great natural
capacities. He was particularly pleased to find that he was not
only well read in Hebrew literature, but that he also knew Latin.
Casaubon seized the opportunity of reading Hebrew with one so
well informed, and when he bade farewell to the University,
carried off Jacob with him to London and installed him in his
own house. He found profit, he says, not only in the lessons of
the young Jew but also in his conversations . . . .

[*] Increase Mather, however, quotes his dying words as " *Vivat
Christus et pereat Barabas,*" preface to Judah Monis' " Nothing
but the Truth . . . . ," and in Tremellius' will, dated July 31,
1580, two months before his death, he reaffirms his Christianity.

These words are almost identical with those Cotton Mather uses of Chauncy. What Casaubon did Chauncy may also have done. But against the supposition that Barnett was the Jew mentioned by Mather, stands the fact that Chauncy graduated from Cambridge in 1613, and at that time Barnett was connected with Oxford.

We know, however, of a Jew resident about this time in Cambridge who may have been Chauncy's instructor. The English " Calendar of Domestic State Papers, 1623-1625," p. 517 (quoted by Mr. Wolf, *ibid.*, p. 76), mentions a pension of £40 granted to a Jew at Cambridge in 1625. This Jew may have been Antonio de Verona, also called Maria Antonio de Verona. He received £2 from King's College, Cambridge, in 1623, appearing in the account books as Jew, and on his behalf Queen Henrietta Maria wrote to the authorities at Oxford University on January 19, 1625.[*] Chauncy was still a figure in Cambridge in these years—in 1624 he took the degree of B. D.—as is shown by the fact that in 1626 this Antonio de Verona wrote a Hebrew panegyric on him. The original of this Hebrew panegyric on Chauncy by de Verona seems to be lost; but Ezra Stiles has preserved the English translation of it, made in 1712, in his diary under the date of December 31, 1779 (Vol. II, pp. 399-400).

These facts, that this Antonio de Verona was a Jew, that he was a contemporary of Chauncy at Cambridge University, that he knew Chauncy, as appears from the encomium he wrote on him, and that the encomium was written in Hebrew, are strong grounds for identifying de Verona with the Jew mentioned by Mather as having aided Chauncy in the study of Hebrew.

---

[*] *The Athenaeum*, London, 1887, pp. 279, 311, 341. This name *Maria* Antonio de Verona, under which he appears in the letter of the Queen, has misled G. A. Kohut in " Ezra Stiles and the Jews " (p. 71 *et seq.*), into thinking him a woman.

Whether the Jew who was Chauncy's teacher was de Verona or not, Chauncy's knowledge of Hebrew seems to have been at least as good as, and probably better than, that of his predecessor Dunster. Matching Cotton Mather's superlatives of praise is Ezra Stiles' judgment of Chauncy's scholarship. Stiles looked upon Chauncy as

the most truly & extensively learned of all the N. Engld Fathers, especially in the Sciences, ... and the Knowledge of the learned Languages, particularly Greek & besides Hebrew, its several Dialects as Syriac, Arabic, Samaritan . . . .[20]

Every day in the college hall at Harvard, Chauncy " expounded a chapter (which was first read from the Hebrew) of the Old Testament." [21] How this was done, we know from "The Lawes of Harvard College" of the year 1655.[22] Section 2, paragraph 2, reads as follows:

It is appointed that part of the holy Scripture be read at morneing and evening prayer, to wit some part of the Old Testament at morneing and some part of the new at evening prayer on this manner: Thatt all Students shall read the old Testament in some portion of it out of Hebrew into Greek, and all shall turne the new Testament out of English into greeke, after which one of the Bachelors or Sophisters shall in his course Logically analyse that which is read, by which meanes both theire skill in logick, and the Scripture's originall language may be Increased.

This custom, which had been introduced by Dunster, was later neglected, perhaps in the time immediately after Chauncy's death. For Cotton Mather's special mention of the practice under Dunster and Chauncy seems to imply that it was not the custom of the college when he wrote the *Magnalia.* We know further from Leverett's diary that in January and May, 1708, this " ancient and laudable practice was revived."

[20] Diary, Vol. I, p. 133, quoted in G. A. Kohut, " Ezra Stiles and the Jews," p. 71.

[21] *Magnalia,* III, xxiii, p. 423.

[22] *Proceedings Mass. Hist. Soc.,* Series I, Vol. XIII, p. 210.

At morning prayers all the undergraduates were ordered, beginning with the youngest, to read a verse out of the Old Testament from the Hebrew into Greek, except the Freshmen, who were permitted to use their English Bibles in this exercise.[23]

The order of studies under Chauncy, as revealed in the copy of the laws for 1655, was much the same as under Dunster. Section 2, paragraph 5, reads:

In the first yeare after admission for foure dayes of the week all Students shall be exercised in the Studies of the greek and Hebrew tongues, onely beginning logick in the morneing towards the latter end of the yeare . . . .

The qualifications for the first degree began (paragraph 10):

Every Scholler that upon proofe is able to read extempore the pentateuch of [or] the new testament into latine out of the originall tongues, and be skilled in logick . . . .

One stray notice, preserved in the diary of the Rev. William Adams (1650-1685), gives us another glimpse of the college at work under Chauncy. On May 5, 1671, Adams entered in his diary:

Our class declaimed their last declamations upon ye foure languages Hebr. Gr. Lat. Eng. and ye 5 senses with an oration salutatory and valedictory.[24]

We know little of the progress, or retrogression perhaps we should say, of Hebrew studies in the college in the thirteen years that intervened between the death of Chauncy and the election of Increase Mather as president of Harvard in 1685. One event only stands out. John Lightfoot, one of the finest Christian Hebraists of his day, whose *Horae Hebraicae et Talmudicae* are read still in Christian circles, died in 1675, and bequeathed his Oriental books to the library of Harvard College. Gibbon tauntingly says of Lightfoot that " by con-

---

[23] Quincy, " History of Harvard University," I, p. 439.

[24] *Mass. Hist. Soc. Coll.*, Series IV, Vol. I, p. 13. There is also a Latin and Hebrew entry in this diary under Dec. 1, 1670.

stant reading of the rabbis he became almost a rabbi himself ";
and the accession to Harvard's young library of the library of
a man who loved to read rabbinical literature in its original
language, must have given a great impetus to a more original
study of Hebrew than before had been possible, if we may
assume, as we probably may, that the men into whose hands
it fell were capable of making good use of it.

Before considering the last two representatives of Hebrew
learning in New England in the seventeenth century, we must
take passing notice of the Semitic attainments of one of
Chauncy's best scholars—Thomas Thacher. Thacher was born
in England in 1620, and came to Boston as a lad'of fifteen.
He entered the family of Chauncy, then minister at Scituate,
and

under the conduct of that eminent scholar, he became such a
one himself . . . . He was not unskilled in the tongues, especially in the Hebrew, whereof he did compose a Lexicon; but
so comprized it, that within *one sheet* of paper, he had every
considerable word of the language . . . . And to all his other
accomplishments there was this added, that he was a most incomparable scribe . . . . there are yet extant monuments of
Syriac and other oriental characters of his writing, which are
hardly to be imitated."

We need not regard this dictionary as being the first American
work in Hebrew scholarship. It cannot have been more than
a student's MS. vocabulary. Ezra Stiles also describes
Thacher as " Very learned in the Oriental Languages." "

Scholastically, the most important figures in New England
during the closing years of the seventeenth century were undoubtedly Increase Mather and his son Cotton. These two
men brilliantly continued the family tradition of Hebrew
scholarship derived from Richard Mather and John Cotton.

Increase Mather (1639-1723), sixth son of Richard Mather

" *Magnalia,* III, xxvi, p. 442.
" Ezra Stiles, " Diary," II, 332. See also p. 73, note 69.

(whose work on the "Bay Psalm Book" has already been noticed), was called in 1685 to act as president of Harvard College, a post which had not been worthily filled since Chauncy's death in 1672. The man who now took the helm was the first native American to become president of Harvard, a position he held until 1701. He had graduated from the college under Chauncy in 1656, and then had gone to study in Europe, graduating again at Trinity College, Dublin, in 1658. Throughout his life he devoted the major portion of his days to his library, in which works in and on Hebrew figured in a not inconsiderable number. In the diary of Judge Sewall, the following entry occurs under the date of Wednesday, July 1, 1685:[37]

21

Commencement Day .... Besides disputes there are four orations. One Latin by Mr. Dudley; and two Greek, one Hebrew by Nath Mather, and Mr. President [Increase Mather] after giving the Degrees made an Oration, in Praise of Academical Studies and Degrees, Hebrew Tongue.

This sort of learned show, which in the case of Hebrew was kept up in Harvard until 1817,[38] was common at the time in Europe. We find, for example, under the date of April 29, 1689, in Sewall's diary, kept while he was in England:

In the morning saw the Westminster Scholars; three of them made Orations in Hebrew, Greek, and Latin before the Dean and Delegates.[39]

A digression may here be permitted to take note of Sewall's Hebrew scholarship and his interest in affairs Jewish. He is described by Sibley[40] as "a diligent student of the Bible in the original languages." His Hebrew knowledge was prob-

---

[37] *Mass. Hist. Soc. Coll.*, Series V, Vol. V, p. 85.
[38] E. J. Young, *Proceedings Mass. Hist. Soc.*, Series I, Vol. XVIII, p. 122.
[39] *Mass. Hist. Soc. Coll.*, Series V, Vol. V, p. 86. 328
[40] "Harvard Graduates," Vol. II, p. 354.

ably of the same character as that of the average graduate of
Harvard in his day. We find recorded in his diary under
the date of August 8, 1689, the expenditure of eighteen
shillings for Leusden's Hebrew Bible, and under January 30,
1701-2:

Cousin Moodey of [New] York comes to see me; upon enquiry
about a Hebrew word, I found he had no lexicon; and I gave
him my Buxtorf.

22

Sewall was a wealthy man, and could afford to buy and
give away books. On June 10, 1700, he wrote " to John Love,
Merch^t in St. Lawrence Lane, London," ordering many books.
On July 1 he added a further list of desiderata. This second
list included:

Account of a Jew lately converted, and baptised at the Meetinghouse near Ave-Mary-Lane: Four [copies] of them."

This probably refers to a pamphlet written by a certain
Shalome Ben Shalomoh, entitled " A true Narrative of God's
gracious dealings with the soul of Shalome b. Shalomoh, of
the circumcision after the flesh; as delivered to the Church
of Christ assembled at their Meeting House, Rosemary Lane,
Sept. 29th, 1699." " Another time when ordering books from
London, Sewall specifies among them " Dr. Lightfoot's Works
in Volums." "

There are several items of Jewish interest in his diary.
While in London, he writes under the date of Monday, July
29, 1689:

This 29th July the Jews have great joy by reason of a Priest
come to Town in the Harwich Coach, they having not had one a
long time.

The " Priest " mentioned is the Haham Solomon Aylion, who
was appointed Haham of the community on the 19th of Sivan,
corresponding with June 7, 1689. The previous Haham,

" *Coll. Mass. Hist. Soc.*, Series VI, Vol. I, p. 239.
" This title is listed in Jacobs and Wolf, *supra*, No. 793, p. 117.
" *Coll. Mass. Hist. Soc.*, Series VI, Vol. II, p. 11.

Jacob de Joseph Abendana, had died on Rosh Hashana in
1685. Another notice of his London sight-seeing, written by
Sewall in an interleaved almanac of 1689, reads:

Monday March 18, 1689. Went and saw the Jews' burying
Place at Mile-End: Some Bodies were laid East and West: but
now all are ordered to be laid North and South. Many tombs.
Engravings are Hebrew, Latin, Spanish, English, sometimes on
the same stone. Part of the ground is improv'd as a garden,
the dead are carried through the keeper's house. First Tomb is
abt the year 1659. Brick wall built abt part. Ont's two sides
5444, Christi 1684, Tamuz 21, June 23, as I remember." I told
the keepr afterwards wisht might meet in Heaven: He answerd,
and drink a Glass of Beer together, which we were then doing."

An item of indirect Jewish interest is contained in the
diary under the date of Friday, January 13, 1687-8. Joshua
Gee called to see him, and

said Gee presents me with a pair of Jerusalem garters which
cost above 2 pieces ⁸ [Spanish dollars] in Algiers: were made
by a Jew.

This notice of a skilful Jewish artisan recalls a remark made
by Increase Mather in his " Cases of Conscience " (1693,
p. 247) :

There is newly published a book (mentioned in the *Acta
Eruditorum*) wherein the Author (Wiechard Valvassor) relates

" Sewall's memory was not quite accurate. The earliest burial
seems to have been that of Isaac Brito in Ellul 5417, 1657. There
was another interment the following year, and two in the year
5420. One of these two was that of Antonio Fernandez Carvajal,
who was buried 26th Heshvan, 5420, 12th November, 1659. It may
well be that the tombstone of this prominent man was pointed
out to Sewall as being the oldest in the ground. Furthermore
Sewall's synchronization is not quite correct. Tammuz 21, 5444,
corresponded with July 3, 1684, and June 23, therefore, with
Tammuz 11. He also seems to confuse the *Metaher* house with
the cemetery keeper's house. The cemetery in question is the
old Sephardic Beth Holim cemetery, leased by Carvajal and
Simon de Caceres in 1657. This de Caceres is the one who en-
ters into the history of Barbados and Chili.

" *Coll. Mass. Hist. Soc.*, Series V, Vol. V, p. 301.

that a Venetian Jew instructed him (only he would not attend
his instruction) how to make a Magical Glass which should
represent any Person or thing according as he should desire.*

Two other notices of Jewish interest in Sewall's diary, one
under February 5, 1704, chronicling the death of a Jew
named Frazon or Frazier, whom Cotton Mather had unsuccessfully attempted to convert to Christianity, and the other
under September 13, 1702, taking note of the baptism of a
Jew named Simon, have already been referred to in Mr.

24

* At this period, the Jews were widely credited with using
both black and white magic. *En passant* it may be noted, now
that the pranks and antics of the New England witches are so
often explained as spiritualistic phenomena, that in the seventeenth century Jews seem to have dabbled in the medium's art.
Frederick Brentz, a converted Jew, wrote a work in which he
claimed to explain, "How the Jews raised tables with stones
of several hundredweights on them by means of black magic."
A Jew Dsalman, with the surnames of Solomon and Zebi, published a reply or apology, entitled *Theriok*, in which he said:
"We are accused of raising tables by black magic; whilst we
whisper hellish names into each other's ears the tables ascend.
We do not deny the raising of tables, but it is effected by practical cabala, which is founded on holy names, and is no devilish
work. We sing holy songs during the performance, which is
intended to glorify God's power." Christopher Arnold, a German
astronomer (died 1695), wrote, in 1674, to a friend that a Jew
of Fürth on a certain occasion showed hospitality to some
Jewish students from Würzburg, and that as an acknowledgement of his kindness they showed himself a marvellous sight:
They placed heavy weights on a table, on which the servants
also sat down, and then pronouncing a sacred name, the table
with all the weights and men on it rose high into the air, and
by the power of the same name, slowly came down again. See
"The Gaming World," by *Rouge et Noir*. This wonder working
by the power of the *Shem Hameforash* is well known in Jewish
legend, and subsequently created the fame of the various Baal
Shems.

Hühner's paper on "The Jews of New England prior to 1800," " and by Rev. G. A. Kohut."

Sewall took great interest in Jews, his interest springing from the millenarian hope of their speedy conversion to Christianity. He even composed a poem on this theme." This interest reveals itself further in a letter written by him on March 12, 1701-2, to his cousin Jeremiah Dummer, then at Leyden, in Holland. He writes therein:

> You will pleasure me if you send me word, when the Jews observed their last Jubilee: and whether with them, a Jubilee do not contain Fifty years. And whether the Jews in Holland and elsewhere doe begin their weekly Sabbath in the evening."

25

To return to Sewall's notice of the commencement exercises at Harvard College in 1685, at which Nathanael Mather made a Hebrew oration, and Increase Mather, the newly appointed president, made another. This Nathanael Mather was a son of Increase Mather. He was born in 1669, and as a lad he showed unusual mental precocity.

> When he was but twelve years old he was admitted into the Colledge by strict examiners; and many months after this passed not, before he had accurately gone over all the Old Testament in Hebrew as well as the New in Greek .... He commenced bachelour of arts at the age of sixteen, and in the act entertained the auditory with an Hebrew oration which gave a good account of the academical affairs among the ancient Jews. Indeed the

---

"*Publications of the American Jewish Historical Society*, No. 11, p. 79. In note 3 the words "The forgery was so plainly detected that Mr. Cotton Mather confest it, after which Mr. Frasier would never be persuaded to hear any more of Christianity," are attributed to Judge Sewall. This is inaccurate. They are the words of the anonymous author of the pamphlet, "A Modest Enquiry into the Grounds and Occasions of a late Pamphlet Intituled a Memorial of the Present Deplorable State of New England." *Coll. Mass. Hist. Soc.*, Series V, Vol. VI, p. 80*.

" "Ezra Stiles and the Jews," p. 42.
"*Proceedings Mass. Hist. Soc.*, Series II, Vol. II, p. 41.
"*Coll. Mass. Hist. Soc.*, Series VI, Vol. I, p. 268.

Hebrew language was become so familiar with him, as if (to
use the expression which one had in an ingenious elegy upon his
death) he had apprehended it should quickly become the only
language which he should have occasion for . . . . Rabbinick
learning he had likewise no small measure of; and the questions
referring unto the Scriptures which philology is conversant
about, came under a very critical notice with him.

So wrote his elder brother Cotton." This early promise
never reached fulfilment; for, before Nathanael Mather completed his twentieth year, overstudy, added to the austere
self-mortification and morbid religious torture which he practiced on himself, brought on his death.

The appointment of Increase Mather as president of Harvard marks a revival of activity in the college. The college
could not but gain from the scholarly enthusiasm and eminently practical energy of its new president. For Increase
Mather was, besides being a scholar, a man of the world. His
literary activity was remarkable, at least 136 works of his
being known. Many of these contain citations of Hebrew.
For example, in his " Remarkable Providences . . . ." (London, 1856, a reprint of the 1684 Boston edition), he quotes
(p. 77) two Hebrew words from Job xxxvii, 5. On page 80
he argues rightly that the word רשפים in Psalm lxxviii, 41,
translated by the Authorized Version " hot thunder-bolts,"
really means " lightning." The same meaning he gives (p.
88) to אש אלהים of Job i, 16. On page 130 he speaks of
" teraphims," giving a quotation from Rashi. On page 178
he refers to some Talmudic and cabbalistic ideas of devils
called *Shedim*, dismissing the subject with the remark that
" such Jewish fables are so foolish as that they need no confutation." He quotes from Josephus a method of exorcism,
and a description of the fabled plant, the mandrake, adding:

He speaketh untruly in saying that they learned such ne-
farious arts from Solomon for they had them from the heathen
who received them from the devil himself.

---

[31] *Magnalia*, IV, x, p. 133.

What Isaac D'Israeli might have called a curiosity of literature is recorded on page 212. Increase Mather there writes:

Not long since Fran. Mercur. Helmont designing to teach a deaf man to speak, concluded it would be more easily practicable if the experiment were made with an eastern wide-mouthed language which does remarkably expose to the eye the motions of the lips, tongue and throat. Accordingly he tried with the Hebrew tongue, and in a short time his dumb schollar became an excellent Hebrician.

Finally, at the end of the book, he quotes Psalm iii, 2, in the original Hebrew, and adds over the word *finis* its Hebrew equivalent םת.

27

It may be noted *en passant,* that the love for Hebrew shown by so many Puritan divines, did not necessarily imply a love for Jews. Increase Mather, however, shows a praiseworthy fairness of mind towards Jews, of whom he must have known at this period more from books than from life. For avowed Jews were rare in the British Isles at the time when Mather was there, and much rarer in Massachusetts in the seventeenth century. This fact is brought out by a letter written to Joseph Dudley,[33] that has been overlooked by Mr. Hühner in his paper on "The Jews of New England (other than Rhode Island) prior to 1800," *Publications,* No. 11, and by Mr. Lebowich in his paper on "The Jews in Boston till 1875," *Ibid.,* No. 12. Increase Mather denies authorship of this letter which purported to be written by him. In the letter, which Mather claims was a forgery, occurs the sentence:

This comes to you by way of Barbados, a Jew going thither. and so for your place [Amsterdam] has promised to deliver it in your hands.

Of this sentence Mather writes:

He pretends in the close of his forgery, as if I had sent the letter by a Jew by way of Barbados. This doth more fully demonstrate the forgery; for I knew not that there was any

---

[33] *Mass. Hist. Soc. Coll.,* Series III, Vol. VIII, p. 102.

Jew in Boston the last winter, nor did I learne that any Jew
did go from thence to Barbados: to be sure, I saw none, nor did
I ever send a letter by any Jew in my life.

This forged letter, although it makes clear the fact that
Jews were not settled in Boston at the time, allows us to
assume that transient Jews now and again came to New England at this period. The Marranos, as is well known, had
extensive business relations in Barbados and the West Indies,
and it is not improbable that Marranos, not recognisable as
Jews, passed through Boston from time to time on the way
from Europe to the West Indies.[53]

Mather's open-minded attitude towards Jews is shown further in his " Mystery of Israel's Salvation," London, 1669.
In this, constant reference is made to Jewish authorities, *e. g.*,
Abarbanel, Benjamin of Tudela, Ibn Ezra, Saadya, Kimchi,
Rashi, etc., and Hebrew words are repeatedly quoted. Further,
he denies (p. 173) that the Jews have falsified the Hebrew
text of the Bible with malicious corruption:

I believe that this is a very false and injurious charge against
them.

He doubts (p. 175) the blood accusation and the charge
that the Jews poison wells to create epidemics of plague. He
wonders, and this seems to be the "Mystery" of his title,
how the Jews who blaspheme Jesus in the synagogues—this
charge he does not doubt—and who call the gospel און גליון.
Aven gillaion (Evangelion) " a volume of lies," can ever be
saved; nevertheless, he has full faith that, through a Divine
Mystery, Christian salvation will eventually come to Israel.

To multiply citations from the specimens of Hebrew learning which bristle in some of Increase Mather's writings would

---

[53] Sewall's letter to Dummer, written in 1702, from which quotation has been made above, showing how Sewall sought for
information from Europe about Jewish customs, might also be
taken to indicate that a professing Jew was truly a *rara avis*
in Massachusetts in the second half of the seventeenth century.

be of casual interest. But a correspondence which he conducted in 1687 with John Leusden must be dealt with more
fully, because of its incidental bearing on the Indian-Israel
theory, and because it resulted in two editions of the Hebrew
Psalter which are of unique bibliographical character. John
Leusden, one of the most learned Hebraists of his day, was
professor of Hebrew at Utrecht " from 1650 until his death
in 1699. He had as a young man, after finishing his university course, proceeded to Amsterdam, where he had deep-
ened his knowledge of Hebrew and of Jewish literature and
customs by learning directly from the Jews. His interest is
heightened further from the Jewish point of view by his cooperation with the famous Amsterdam rabbi-printer, Joseph
Athias, in the preparation of the 1660 Amsterdam edition
of the Hebrew Bible. Leusden, like many others in Europe
at the time, and like Ravius in 1648, was curious about the
Indians, their evangelisation, and the theory that they might
prove to be the lost ten tribes of Israel; and in this connection, Increase Mather was drawn into correspondence with
him, more especially about the missionary work of John Eliot,
the " apostle to the Indians."

To understand the correspondence which passed between
Leusden and Increase Mather, we must go back a little, and
explain how Eliot's missionary work among the Indians came
about. John Eliot (1604-1690) was born in England and
educated at Cambridge University. He arrived in Boston in
November, 1631, a refugee from Laud's persecution. He has
already been noticed in this paper as one of the three ministers who prepared the " Bay Psalm Book." Cotton Mather
says of him: "

He was a most acute grammarian: and understood very well
the languages which God first wrote his Holy Bible in.

" Not Leyden as " The Jewish Encyclopedia " says, Vol. II,
p. 268.
" *Magnalia*, III, iii, p. 494.

In the middle of the seventeenth century, a wide interest was aroused in the American Indians. In September, 1644, Menasseh ben Israel had taken down a deposition of Aaron Levi, otherwise known as Antonio Montezinos, declaring that the Peruvian Indians recited the *Shema'* and observed Jewish customs. Menasseh was spurred on by this story to write his *Esperança de Israel,* Amsterdam, 1650. The account therein set forth created a great sensation, and, in the following years, was translated into Latin (by Menassch himself), Dutch, English, Judaeo-German, and Hebrew. In 1646, the saintly Eliot had turned his attention to the conversion of the Indians to Christianity, being encouraged in his heroic missionary efforts, as Cotton Mather tells us, through the belief

that our Indians are the posterity of the dispersed and rejected Israelites, concerning whom our God has promised that they shall yet be saved by the deliverer coming to turn away ungodliness from them. He saw the Indians using many parables in their discourses; much given to anointing of their heads; much delighted in dancing, especially after victories; computing their time by nights and months; giving dowries for wives . . . . and accustoming themselves to grievous mournings and yellings for the dead; all which were usual things among the Israelites. They have, too, a great unkindness for our swine, but I suppose that is because our hogs devour the clams which are a dainty with them. He also saw some learned men looking for the lost Israelites among the Indians in America, and counting them that they had *thorow-good* reasons [84] for doing so. And a few small arguments, or indeed but conjectures meeting with a favourable disposition in the hearer will carry some conviction

---

[84] Cotton Mather's pun. Dr. Thomas Thorowgood wrote in 1648, and published in 1650, a work called "Jewes in America, or Probabilities that the Americans are of that Race." This work called public attention in Europe to Eliot's efforts, and appealed for support for them. As an appendix to this book, Thorowgood printed, through the instrumentality of John Durie, the deposition of Montezinos. Sir Hamon L'Estrange issued a rejoinder called "Americans no Iewes . . . ." To this, in 1660, Thorowgood replied with another work, "Jews in America, or Proba-

with them; especially if the report of a Manasseh ben Israel be to back them.⁵⁷

The excitement over the Indian-Israel possibilities did not repidly die away, and therefore it is that we find John Leusden, in 1687, in correspondence with Increase Mather about Eliot's work among the Indians.

Mather's letter to Leusden, the original of which was written in Latin, opens as follows:

> Written by Mr. Increase Mather, Minister of the Word of God at Boston, and Rector of the Colledge at Cambridge in New England to Dr. John Leusden, Hebrew Professor in the University of Utrecht. Translated [by Cotton Mather] out of Latin into English.
>
> Worthy and much honoured Sir: Your letters were very grateful to me, by which I understand that you and others in your famous University of Utrecht desire to be informed concerning the converted Indians in America; take therefore a true account of them in a few words.

31

Mather then related in some detail how John Eliot took up the work of evangelisation among the Indians. He enumerates the different assemblies and churches of Christianised Indians, describing their simple service of song, scripture, and prayer. He names the white ministers who were devoting themselves to the spiritual care of the Indians and also the baptised Indian ministers, summing up in the following words:

> In short, there are six Churches of baptised Indians in New England and eighteen assemblies of Catechumens professing the name of Christ. Of the Indians, there are four and twenty who are preachers of the word of God, and besides these, there are four English ministers who preach the Gospel in the Indian tongue.

---

bilities that those Indians are Judaical, made more probable by some Additionals to the former Conjectures." One of the many prefaces to this work is a letter from Eliot, filling twenty-eight closely printed pages. Albert M. Hyamson, *Jewish Quarterly Review*, Vol. XV, 1903.

⁵⁷ *Magnalia*, Vol. I, p. 506 *et seq.*

He ends with the following words:

I salute the famous professors in your University, to whom
I desire you to communicate this letter, as written to them also.
Farewel, worthy sir, the Lord preserve your health for the
benefit of your country, his church and of learning. Yours ever,
Increase Mather."

This letter, which is dated Boston, New England, July 12,
1687, stirred up a profound sensation in Europe, and it was
soon published in Latin, in English, in German, in Dutch,
and in French. Cotton Mather follows his " Englishing " of
the letter with this note:

After the writing of this letter, there came one to my hands
from the famous Dr. Leusden together with a new and fair
edition of his Hebrew Psalter dedicated unto the name of my
absent parent. [Increase Mather was at the time in England on
a mission on behalf of the colony and Harvard College.]

This reply of Leusden's has also been preserved; it runs
as follows:

Translation of a letter from John Leusden to Increase Mather
[in the handwriting of Nathaniel Mather of Dublin and London].

Most Reverend, much to bee Respected Sr,—I sought you in
America, and thither on the 30th of March I sent some books,
vizt a New Lexicon, a Compendium of the Greek New Testament,
two Psalters in Hebrew and English and one in Hebrew and
Latine. The Psalmes in Hebrew and English I dedicated to Mr.
Eliot, & those four and twenty Preachers, lately heathens, now
christians. The Psalmes in Hebrew and Latine I have inscribed to
your Revd name. Whether you received those books in America I
know not. That letter of yours, written frõ London on the 24th
of December I received the 16th of January. That letter which
you had written to mee from America concerning the Conversion
of the Indians, hath been read here with great rejoysing, &
translated into the French language, & published in print. I will
send you a Copy of it in French with the books. I lately received moreover two American Bibles, 2 American Grammars
and other American books, as also the Indian's A. B. C. & some

---

" *Ibid.*, p. 508 *et seq.*

others, all which our Netherlanders look on with great admira-
c̄on. . . ."⁰ I have written you largely unto America, and that
in the name of our University, in answer to your letter concerning the conversion of the American Indians. You now
desyre fifty Hebrew Psalters for the use of the students in Harvard Colledge, which I would now have sent, but because you
doe not express what kind of Psalters it is you desyre, whether
Hebrew and Latine, or Hebrew and English, therefore I have
not sent them. For I have already put forth three sorts of
Psalters, vizt Hebrew and Latine, Hebrew and English and
Hebrew & Dutch. As soon as you shall write back what sort
of Psalters it is you desyre, I will forthwith send them over to
you. Much honored Sr, Farewell. frō Yours, John Leusden.
Utrecht ;i of January, 168 ί.⁰⁰

The Hebrew and English and the Hebrew and Latin Psalters mentioned in this letter deserve description on account
of their combination of American and Hebrew interest, the
unique character of their dedications and their rarity. They
are both small-sized volumes of about 500 pages each. The
Hebrew and English Psalter (I transcribe from a copy in my
possession) is entitled "ספר תהילים" The / Book of Psalmes /
With the New English / Translation / Published By / John
Leusden / Professor of the Hebrew Tongue in the / University of Utrecht / London / Printed by Samuel Smith, and
are to / be sold by him at his Shop in the sign of the /
Princes Armes in S. Paul's Church-Yard 1688." The dedication on the first page runs:

This Hebrew-English Psalter is intituled To the very Reverend
and pious JOHN ELIOT. The Indefatigable and faithfull Minister of the Church of Ripon, (being now in the Eighty fourth
year of his age) and Venerable Apostle of the Indians in America; Who hath translated into, and published in, the American
tongue, by an Antlaean Labour, the Bible and several English
practical Tractats, together with Catechisms; being the first
who preached the word of God to the Americans in the Indian

⁰⁰ American here means American-Indian and refers to works
translated by Eliot into Algonquin.
⁰⁰ *Coll. Mass. Hist. Soc.*, Series IV, Vol. VIII, p. 678.

33

tongue, and gathered a Church of Indian Converts, and administrat the Holy Supper to them.

This is followed on the second page by:

As also TO the Reverend and pious the TWENTY FOUR AMERICAN MINISTERS. Lately Gentiles, but now converted to the Christian Religion (by the Grace of God, and labour of the Reverend John Eliot and other Ministers) and publishing the Word of God and the Gospel of Christ in the American tongue (with four English Ministers) in great fervour, among the Americans in twenty four American Churches (both of baptised persons, and such as are Catechised in order to their Baptisme) lately Gentiles, but now converted Christians, I Wish you all and every one of you, all prosperity and happiness with fortunat success in converting the Americans. John Leusden, Professor at Utrecht.

These dedications are followed by a preface, dated Utrecht, March 15, 1688, which opens in the following words:

John Leusden to the Christian Reader. Having occasion to publish the Hebrew Psalter with the Latine and Dutch version, I resolved to adde the English likewise; if so be I might excite the English nation to jealousy, which is commonly very zealous to read Gods word; I have the rather done it at this time, when there is a great door of the Gospel opened in New-England by means of the Illustrious School at Boston: for at present they have there four and twenty Churches and Meeting-places of Indians; over whom four and twenty Indian Ministers are placed, who exercise their publick worship on the Lords-day, in praying, preaching, reading of Gods word, singing of Psalms, and that, in the Indian language. All this was written to me and our University in a letter, which I receivd on the 3 of February this present year 1688. from the worthy and Reverend INCREASE MATHER, Minister of the Gospel and President of the Colledge or Illustrious School at Boston.

And because that it's troublesome to learn the Hebrew without a Grammar; I have publishd a short Hebrew and Chaldaick Grammar, written in the English, printed for Mr. Samuel Smith, Book-seller at London, and for Francis Halma at Utrecht.

The Hebrew-Latin edition is of the same date as this Hebrew-English one, the preface being dated *Ipsis Kal. Aprilis,* MDCLXXXVIII, and it contains the following dedication:

Sit hoc / Psalterium Hebraeo-Latinum / inscriptum / Maxime Reverendo & Clarissimo / Viro / D. Crescentio Mathero / Verbi Divini Ministro Vigilantissimo, atque Collegii Harvardini, quod est Cantabrigiae Nov-Anglorum Rectori & Doctori Celeberrimo ac Honorandissimo, conversionem Indorum, in America (unâ cum viginti quatuor, nuper Gentilibus sed jam Christianis Pastoribus) feliciter promoventi, cui omnia fausta & felicia in convertendis Gentilibus precatur Johannes Leusden. [Translated in the style of the dedications in the Hebrew-English Psalter, this would run: This Hebrew-Latin Psalter is intituled to the very Reverend and eminent Doctor Increase Mather, the zealously vigilant minister of the Divine word, and the illustrious and highly to be honoured Doctor and Rector of Harvard Colledge, which is in Cambridge of New England, there prays for whom happily spreading the conversion of the Indians in America (together with 24 ministers, lately Gentiles but now Christians), all auspicious fortune for the converting of the Gentiles, John Leusden.]

35

These two Hebrew volumes, lastingly associated with the names of John Eliot and Increase Mather, must be among the earliest, if not actually the earliest Hebrew works directly connected with America.

From Increase Mather,[a] the last president of Harvard College in this century, we pass to his son and colleague Cotton Mather (born 1662). Cotton Mather is the last and the most remarkable figure of the period. This incurably vain prodigy and learned and productive pedant began the study of Hebrew while yet a child. In the manuscript which he left his son (Paterna), he writes:

. . . . at the age of little more than eleven years I had . . . . made some entrance in my Hebrew grammar. And I think before I came to fourteen, I composed Hebrew exercises.

---

[a] Mather's comment on the occasion of the baptism of Judah Monis should be mentioned here, as being of Jewish interest. But as it belongs to the eighteenth century (1722), and as it has been already dealt with by Mr. Kohut ("Ezra Stiles and the Jews," p. 40 *et seq.*), and others, this mention must satisfy the claims of completeness.

At the childish age of twelve, he was admitted to Harvard
College, and in 1678, when sixteen years of age, he graduated
Bachelor of Arts.   In the list of *Quaestiones* of this class of
1678, the second thesis is entitled *An Puncta Hebraica sunt
Originis Divinae. Affirmat Respondens Cottonus Matherus.*
[Whether Hebrew punctuation is of divine origin.   Cotton
Mather maintains the affirmative.]   It should be noted, *en
passant,* that later, with increasing knowledge, he modified
his views, and held that Hebrew punctuation had not the same
divine origin as the Hebrew consonants.

Although in 1642 we found that Hebrew theses figured in
almost disproportionate number among the linguistic *Quaestiones* propounded at the commencement exercises, one looks in
vain for another Hebrew theme in such commencement lists
as are preserved until this year 1678, when Cotton Mather
essayed a Hebrew subject.   Moreover, in the years immediately following this year, the disputations almost invariably
neglected Hebrew themes, with the exception that in 1684
Gurdon Saltonstall chose the same Hebrew theme as Cotton
Mather had selected, and in the list of 1693 occurs the thesis
" Is the Hebrew language the oldest of all ? "   This does not
allow us to infer that Hebrew learning did not figure in the
commencement exercises, for we have seen that on many occasions Hebrew orations were made at the giving of degrees.*
But it does seem to imply that the devoting of three theses
to Hebrew, and only one to Latin and two to Greek in 1642,
was a spectacular effect contrived to impress the New England
public attending these first commencement exercises of the
new college with the erudite nature of the studies there
pursued.

A full consideration of the Hebrew learning displayed in

* A Hebrew oration was annually delivered at Commencement
at Harvard until the year 1817. E. J. Young, *Proceedings Mass.
Hist. Soc.*, Series I, Vol. XVIII, p. 122.

Cotton Mather's publications is, within the limits of this
paper, neither possible nor desirable. For, besides the fact
that most of his works appeared after 1700, there is a daunt-
ing consideration which would make the most painstaking
historian pause, namely, that the list of his works compiled
by Sibley reaches the formidable number of 456 entries. In
these circumstances, the purpose of this paper will best be
served by a brief notice of that invaluable agglomeration of
facts and supposed facts, pedantry and puns which makes
up the *Magnalia Christi Americana, or The Ecclesiastical
History of New England.**

37

In spite of the entertaining character of many of the passages of Hebrew interest in this work, it is impossible to
quote them all here. But some notice must be given to some
of the more characteristic of Mather's unnecessary outbreaks
into Hebrew. The introduction to the whole work is headed
א ׳ ה. the Hebrew acrostic abbreviation for " God willing " !
Chapter six of the second book is entitled "בעלי נפש id est
Viri Animati or assistants," and the third book opens with
a list of ministers called "חסידים ראשונים or our First Good
Men." The second part of the third book is named " Sefer
Jereim, *i. e.,* Liber Deum Timentium " [the book of God-
fearing men]. Chapter seven of the third book is introduced

* The edition of this monumental work to which reference
is made throughout this paper is the first American edition,
printed in 1820. There are altogether over half a hundred passages of Hebrew interest in this work. In order that the curious
reader, and he who wishes some learned amusement, may make
easy reference to them, the list of the more interesting is here
given. They will be found in the first volume on pages 39, 63,
105, 120, 124, 128, 204, 212, 213, 218, 228, 232, 233, 289, 320, 367,
379, 388, 419, 423, 428, 434, 442, 456, 467, 494, 495, 533 and 536;
and in the second volume on pages 7, 9, 12, 17, 21, 33, 34, 37,
73, 76, 89, 91, 100, 133, 158, 209, 228, 291, 317, 335, 388, 427, 450,
451, 480, 500, 559, 572, 582 and 583.

by a Jewish proverb. Similarly book six is labelled " Thau-
maturgus vel ספר דכרניא, *i. e.*, Liber Memorabilium " [book
of the records], a phrase taken from the Aramaic text of Ezra
iv, 15. Mather often essays original derivations involving
Hebrew, perhaps the most curious being his derivation of
Parnassus from פרע and נחש, " Parai-nahas," *i. e.,* " Hiatus
Divinationis " (ii, 451), and his Midrashic attempt to derive
from the word Azazel the

38   two properties that have signalized the devil; his being first
a powerful and then an apostate spirit עז Fortis, אול Abiens,
fugiens (II, 308).

He attempts, usually successfully, translations of I Samuel
xv, 12 (i, 120), Malachi iv, 6 (i, 212), Isaiah ii, 22 (ii, 335),
and Amos ii, 13 (ii, 583), which differ from the rendering
of the Authorized Version of 1611. It should be mentioned
that what Cotton Mather considered the chief work of his
life is the *Biblia Americana,* a manuscript commentary on
the Bible in six large volumes preserved in the library of the
Boston Historical Society. To this work, which must be a
mine of curious and outworn learning, I have not had access.

The rabbinical, exegetical device of *Temurah* (anagrams)
is familiar to him (i, 289), and he knows of the " daughter
of the voice " (ii, 317), and of the scarecrow on the temple
roof (ii, 209). We are surprised to find that Mather knows
that practically the earliest Bible concordance ever made was
" that of R. Isaac Nathans in Hebrew " (i, 388), the reference being to the Hebrew concordance *Meir Netib* of Isaac
Nathan b. Kalonymos of Arles, compiled 1437-1447. He
quotes the *Midrash Bereshit Rabbah* (i, 232), Onkelos (ii,
582), and Biblical comments of Ibn Ezra (i, 428), Rashi
(i, 424), Kimchi (*ibid.*), and Bachya (i, 456), and sayings
of Abraham Zacuto (ii, 450) and Maimonides (ii, 572). He
often quotes from the Talmuds, and is familiar with Talmudic
stories, such as Bar Kappara's parable on the death of Rabbi

(i, 379), and with facts in the lives of the Rabbis, such as that R. Eleazar ben Azariah was made president of the Sanhedrin at sixteen (ii, 34), and that R. Tarphon was known as הכהן העשיר (the wealthy priest, ii, 427). His note on the Hebrew character of the Indian name of Salem has been quoted by Mr. Hühner.** A passage characteristic of Cotton Mather's style of recklessly displayed learning is that (i, 124) in which he speaks of the varying estimates of Sir Harry Vane, introducing the subject (in part) as follows:

39

There has been a strange variety of translations bestowed upon the Hebrew name of some animals mentioned in the Bible: *Kippod*, for instance, which we translate a bittern, R. Solomon will have to be an owl, but Luther will have it to be an eagle,

---

** *Publications of the American Jewish Historical Society*, No. 11, p. 75, note 4. Mather's note is neither accurate nor original. He writes, speaking of Salem, " Of which place I have somewhere met with an odd observation that the name of it was rather Hebrew than Indian; for נחום signifies comfort and חיק signifies an haven." This observation he found in Joshua Scottow's " Narrative of the Planting of the Massachusetts Colony," Boston, 1694, p. 51, as follows: " Its original name was Naumkek, the Bosom of Consolation, being its signification, as the learned have observed." The remark had been made, however, much earlier. It occurs in the rare tract, " The Planter's Plea," London, 1630, p. 14, attributed to the Rev. John White. In this White mentions the possibility that the Indians may have had intercourse with Jews. He proceeds: " Howsoever it be, it falls out the name of the place which our late Colony hath chosen for their seat, proves to be perfect Hebrew, being called *Nahum Keike*, by interpretation, The Bosom of Consolation." (Alexander Young, " Chronicles of the First Planters of the Colony of Massachusetts Bay from 1623-1636," p. 12, note.) The earlier writers were accurate in giving to the word חיק the meaning " bosom," Mather's " haven " is hardly correct. This early reference by White (1630) to the possible connection of the Indians with Jews, preceding Menasseh ben Israel's " Hope of Israel " by twenty years, is in itself a fact of interest.

while Paynim will have it to be an hedg-hog, but R. Kimchi will have it a snail . . . ."[46]

Mather has a theory (ii, 26), which, it seems, was not original with him, that the connection of the Druids with oak trees goes back to Noah and to Abraham's dwelling by the oaks of Mamre. But there occurs in the *Magnalia* a prodigious theory (ii, 500), which was all Mather's own. It is so typical of the erudition of the day, that its quotation may be allowed in order to acquaint the reader with the nature of the broadest Hebrew scholarship of the New England divines. He writes:

> I make no question that the story of Og, the king of the woody Bashan, encountered and conquered by Joshua, the Lord General of Israel with his armies passing into Canaan, was the very thing which the Gentiles in after ages did celebrate under the notion of the serpent Python (which is the same with Typhon) destroyed by Apollo. Og signifies a burner, as well as the name of Typhon whom the poets make a Theomachous giant; and the Hebrews for good causes affording the name of Pethen, or a serpent unto such an enemy, we need not wonder that he is also named Python. The land where the gods gave battel to Typhon, was according to Homer ἐν Ἀριμοις. And as we know Syria was the land of Aram, so Strabo tells us that the Arimi are the Syrians; which with the river Orontes, called Ophites as well as Typhon in Coelo Syria, designates the very country of Og unto us. The seat of the transaction related by Homer

---

[46] This is not quite accurate. R. Solomon, *i. e.*, Rashi, translates *Kippod* as owl in Isaiah xxxiv, 11, and Zephaniah ii, 14; but in Isaiah xiv, 23, and in *Talmud Shabbath*, 54b, he gives it the meaning "hedgehog." Kimchi quotes in explanation of *Kippod* the Arabic *kanafid* which means hedgehogs, and at the same time the Provençal *tortuga*, meaning tortoise or turtle, adding that the animal, whichever he means, is found always where there is water. In the middle ages, the tortoise or turtle was sometimes referred to as a snail, for instance in Maundeville's "Travels." It is not quite clear, therefore, how Kimchi translates *Kippod*. But Mather blunders in translating Luther's rendering *Igel* as eagle, the German *Igel* meaning, of course, hedgehog.

40

to have been in ιϐιη, which learned men have so long sought in
vain, that at last they said it was in Cimmeria, that is to say
no man knows where; it is doubtless by a long mistake of the
scribes put for Ιοδια or the land of Judaea, but when he adds
that it was χωρω ενι διρυοεντι, in a region abounding with oaks,
the region of Bashan is unquestionably pointed at.

When Homer sings about the Τυφωεος ευναι, Typhonis Cubilia
was not understood by Virgil when he made a sepulchre thereof
in his translating the matter into his ninth Aeneid because he
had not read the account which the scripture gives about Og's
bedstead of iron. Tis as clear that Apollo who was anciently
called Paean or an healer, is the same with Joshua whose name
is of a like signification. And Apollo was called Anacaeus, likewise, but in commemoration of Joshua's exploits against the
Anakim, the Phoeniciaei being also but Bene Anak or the sons
of Anak in the first original. They by whom Typhon was combated, came out of Egypt, and so did the armies of Joshua, an
hero, of whose mother, because we read nothing, she must be
called Δηλω or Latona a Latendo. Cadmus the Gibeonite carrying a colony in Graecia, did use there to remember the victories
of Joshua, in such hymns as they had learned from their new
masters in Canaan: and of those hymns it is probable the 135th
Psalm in our Psalter might be one, yea the Grecian ελελευ Ικ Ικ
used in their Paeanisms might be but rude remembrances of
the Hallelujahs anciently used in these hymns of Israel.

41

We cannot withhold our admiration from the facile jug-
gling with learning that this theory shows, notwithstanding
its naively uncritical nature. Indeed, *mutatis mutandis,* we
might almost imagine ourselves reading the pages of some
modern representative of the Aryo-Semitic school of myth-
ology.

Two references to Cotton Mather's *Magnalia* will show that
his inveterate habit of punning was not restricted by any
narrow linguistic limits. *Jonathan* Mitchel, we are told (iv,
4, p. 76),

made a most entertaining exposition on the book of Genesis and
part of Exodus: (an evangelical *targum* of *Jonathan*).

The second example is less easy to condone. In 1694-5, Tom
Maule wrote a book, protesting against the persecution of the

Quakers, and filled with what was to the authorities of the
time pernicious heresy. In this connection, Cotton Mather's
quick brain reverted to a demon mentioned in the Talmud
under the name of Ben Temalion (Bartholomew), and he
wrote (ii, 559) of this book of Tom Maule's,

> None but he whom the Jews in their Talmuds call *Bentamalion*
> could have inspired such a slander,

and, we may add, such a pun.

Cotton Mather's valuation of a knowledge of Hebrew was
of the highest. He writes:

> I know that the Hebrew tongue as an exception to the general
> rule *Difficilia quae Pulchra*[⁵⁶] is more easily attained than any
> that I have yet observed: and hence we see even our English
> women sometimes in a little while, and with a little pains, grown
> as expert at it as the ladies Pausa or Blasilla, by Jerom there-
> fore celebrate;[⁵⁷] and I have wished that many in the world,

---

[⁵⁶] The most beautiful things are the most difficult to attain.

[⁵⁷] Does he mean women of *New* England? Professor Moore, in
Zeitschrift für die alttestamentliche Wissenschaft, VIII (1888),
p. 5, assumes that he does. This is very doubtful. I know of
only one New England woman of the time to whom this might
possibly apply. In the diary of Ezra Stiles, under the date of
April 3, 1772 (Vol. I, p. 220), the following notice occurs: "There
was one woman in New England who was an Hebrician, perfectly understanding the Hebrew Bible which she used to carry
with her to meeting: and also would frequently have Recourse
to it in Conversation with Ministers. She was taken off a wreckt
Vessel, as I understand near Plymouth in New England. After
this she returned to England while a Girl, and there lived in a
Jew Family and was taught Hebrew. After this she returned
to New England and settled and died here. She married Mr.
Parker, by whom she had a daughter *Paltah Parker*, whom she
named Paltah or the *Deliverance of God* in memory of her being saved from the Wreck . . . . She died about 1772. This is
a loose Memoir I pencilled from the Mouth of Miss Molly Brown
of Boston, a Maiden Lady and Descendant from &c. I suspect
there is some defect in the story—but I conclude so much is true,
that she had an Ancestor brought up in a Jew Family and able
to read the Hebrew Bible."

42

were more moved by the words of a worthy author *'Ausim spondere, illos qui Studiis Hebraicis, tantum temporis impenderent, quantum Tubulo Nicotianae imbibendo (quo nunc pars bona Studiosorum pro Hydragogo uti consuevit) tum Mane, tum Vesperi impendi solet, progressus in hujusce Linguae Cognitione, haud Vulgares brevi esse facturos, adeo ut mirentur, se esse tum dictos, antequam didicerint.*⁶⁸ Nevertheless this tongue is as easily forgotten. But being once attained and therewith preserved and improved, good men will find as our Mr. Chancey did that the conjunct of profit and pleasure of it were inexpressible, and that the talents wherewith it would furnish them to do so many services for the Church of God were such as to make them join with Luther in his protestation that he would not part with his knowledge of Hebrew for many thousands of pounds.

43

The Latin quotation with its contemptuous reference to tobacco smoking, and indeed, the whole paragraph, is a typical Puritan utterance, which may be paralleled by a sentence in the preface to Leusden's Hebrew English book of Psalms described above, running as follows:

I would not stir up the Young men and women, who have other necessary affairs, to the study of the Hebrew: but I exhort such only who spend their time only with idleness and vanity.

These quotations from Cotton Mather's *Magnalia,* which was written between 1697 and 1700 and published in London in 1702, bring us to the end of our period, and it remains now only to draw what conclusions we may from the facts that have been passed in review.⁶⁹

⁶⁸ I dare promise, that those who would spend as much time morning and evening in Hebrew studies as is given up to smoking tobacco (which many students use nowadays for imbibition), would quickly make such exceptional progress in the knowledge of this language that they would marvel at having gained so much knowledge, so to speak, unawares.

⁶⁹ Timothy Cutler can hardly be regarded as belonging to the seventeenth century. He was born in 1683 and graduated at Harvard College in 1701. He was later Rector of Yale. Ezra Stiles writes of him (Diary, II, 339), ... " he was a great

It will be clear from what has gone before that the men who represented Hebrew learning in New England in the first half of the seventeenth century were all, as we should expect, English-trained men. John Cotton, Richard Mather, John Eliot, Thomas Welde, Henry Dunster, Charles Chauncy, and Samuel Whiting gained their knowledge of Hebrew at Oxford or Cambridge. Native Hebrew scholarship can be looked for only some time after the foundation of Harvard College, where Hebrew stood in the curriculum almost on the same level as Greek and Latin. And then it appears in the person of Michael Wigglesworth, Thomas Thacher, Judge Sewall, Increase and Cotton Mather. But it must be confessed that the Hebrew knowledge of the 77 ministers enumerated by Cotton Mather, who received their training in English universities, was greater in quantity and superior in quality to that of the 110 ministers of the latter half of the century listed by him who had graduated from Harvard College. It may well be doubted whether the men in New England in 1690, apart from Increase and Cotton Mather, would have been able to issue an original translation of the Book of Psalms, had one been called for, as had been done fifty years previously. The theologico-political and learned activities of the two Mathers, father and son," throw a bright light over the period which must not blind us to the failing light in other learned circles. In fact, when proportionately valued, it casts into strong relief the unilluminating nature of the learning of their contemporaries.

This again is a result that we would anticipate, when we remember the pioneer nature of the struggling colony, the lack of incentives to Hebrew scholarship, the remoteness from the

---

Hebrician & Orientalist. He had more know. of the Arabic than I believe any man ever in N. England before him, except President Chauncy and his Disciple the first Mr. Thatcher."

" It must not be forgotten that Increase Mather received part of his training in Europe.

world of learning and the sudden check given to the immi-
gration of university-trained Puritan clergymen into New
England by the triumph of Puritanism in England under
Cromwell. The inadequacy of the local printing press must
also not be overlooked. Many of the evidences of Hebrew
learning that were to be found, and in some cases are still
to be found in the MSS. of the time, would be suppressed by
the Cambridge Press printer, whose font of Hebrew type in
the seventeenth century could never have been equal to the
demands made on it by New England scholars of the type
of Cotton Mather." In fact, most of their larger works,
whether involving Hebrew type or not, were printed in
London.

But above all, we must make allowance for the lack of
books. Again and again in letters we come across utterances
deploring the lack of books, followed by requests for gifts to
the library of Harvard College. This we have met with in
Dunster's letter to Ravius in 1648 and in Increase Mather's
letter to Leusden forty years later. On December 13, 1672,
Leonard Hoar, only a few weeks after his inauguration as
president of Harvard College, wrote to Sir Robert Boyle as
follows:

If I durst, I would beg one of a sort of all your printed monuments, to enrich our library and encourage our attempts this

---

" Even in modern times, the evidences of Hebrew scholarship
that appear in MSS. are often unhesitatingly suppressed when
the MSS. are published. Thus the copyist of the all important
MS. of Governor Bradford's " History of Plymouth Plantation "
writes (1855): " Everything has been copied except the Hebrew
quotations from the Old Testament Scriptures and a Collection
of Hebrew Roots." (*Coll. Mass. Hist. Soc.*, Series IV, Vol. III,
p. x.) We have seen in the beginning of the paper how other
examples of Bradford's Hebrew knowledge have been expunged
by modern printers. This fact must be reckoned with in estimating the extent of Hebrew culture, as evidenced in the printed
books of the time.

45

way. I know nothing so stunting our hopes and labours in this
way, as that we want one of a sort of the books of the learned,
that come forth daily in Europe, of whose very names we are
therefore ignorant."

Lightfoot's library of *Orientalia,* bequeathed to the college
in 1675, which was especially complete in Hebrew works, must
have enriched the college library considerably; and as time
went on, the college library of Hebraica must have become
reasonably adequate. The public library of Boston also possessed at least one book of Jewish interest. For when this
library was burnt in 1711, the Polyglot Bible was one of the
valuable books lost in the fire."

But private possession of books in and on Hebrew seems
to have been rare. Thomas Dudley (*c.* 1634-1655) bequeaths
in his will his " Hebrew Lexicon y^t Paynin made." " The
Pilgrim Father Brewster possessed, as we have seen, two Hebrew books, a Hebrew grammar and Buxtorf's " Lexicon,"
and Governor Bradford must have possessed at least a Hebrew
Bible, and probably the inevitable Buxtorf's " Hebrew Lexicon." In an inventory made in 1700 of the books of Michael
Perry, a book-seller in Boston, we find entered one Hebrew
book—a small Hebrew Bible, valued at sixpence. A fact
that is suggestive of the scarcity of books of Hebrew learning
in New England, is that in the list of books belonging to
Michael Wigglesworth, a man who had been tutor of Hebrew
at Harvard College, we find only two entries of Hebrew books,
namely Buxtorf's Hebrew Grammar valued at one shilling and

" Sibley, " Harvard Graduates," Vol. I, p. 590.

" *Coll. Mass. Hist. Soc.,* Series VI, Vol. I, p. 422.

" Either the *Thesaurus Linguae Sanctae* of 1529 or a later
edition; or the *Epitome* of the same work in 1570, or a later
edition by Sanctus Pagninus. See Steinschneider, *Handbuch,*
Nos. 1510 and 1511. (Steinschneider's remark that the first edition of the *Epitome,* 1570, seems to be unknown, was corrected
by Porges, *Centralblatt für Bibliothekswesen,* 1898, p. 568, in
whose library there is a copy. A second copy is in my possession.)

a Hebrew Bible valued at six shillings. The Rev. Samuel
Phillips (1625-1696), a graduate of Harvard in 1650, inherited his Hebrew books from the library of his father, the
Rev. George Phillips of England.[17] Even in the orders given
to London book-sellers by a wealthy man and Hebraist like
Judge Sewall, we find hardly a book of Jewish interest specified, although we know that he possessed the indispensable
Buxtorf's "Lexicon," before he gave it away to his cousin,
Leusden's Hebrew Bible, and Lightfoot's works. The representation of Hebrew works in the library of the average graduate of Harvard College in this time, therefore, seems to
have been limited to a copy of the Hebrew Bible, Buxtorf's
"Lexicon," and Buxtorf's Grammar, and this minimum seems
seldom to have been exceeded.

47

But already in 1675 the library of Increase Mather was
large. On November 27th of that year, his house was burnt
down, and in the fire he lost "not an Hundred Books from
above a Thousand." The loss was made up, probably with
additions, through the kindness of the widow of Dr. Leonard
Hoar, president of Harvard College from 1672 to 1675; after
Mather's fire, she gave him free choice to take what he would
from the library of her deceased husband. Therefore Cotton
Mather's library, partly inherited, partly collected by himself, we may suppose contained a representative sprinkling
of works in or on Hebrew. Of this library, John Dunton, in
"The Life and Errors of John Dunton," London, 1705,
tells us

His library is very large and numerous, but had his books been
fewer when he writ his history 'twould have pleased us better.

Cotton Mather himself describes his library already on October 20, 1683, as "exceeding any man's in the land."[18]

[17] Sibley, "Harvard Graduates," Vol. I, p. 221.
[18] Cotton Mather's Diary, *Proceedings Mass. Hist. Soc.,* Series
II. Vol. XVII, p. 71.

7

In view of this almost complete lack of Hebrew and Rabbinic books in New England at this time, we are faced with
the question as to the source of the knowledge of Hebrew and
Rabbinic literature so frequently displayed in the writings
of the period. The answer to this question is simple, but un-
favorable to our estimate of the Hebrew learning of the New
England divines. They derived their quotations from Hebrew
and Rabbinic literature from the *Latin* works written by
Christian European scholars on the Old Testament and on
Hebrew literature. The astonishing familiarity with Rabbinic literature and the Hebrew Bible commentaries displayed by the Mathers, for instance, astounds us less when we
realise that it in no wise represents immediate acquaintance
with the Talmud, Midrash, and later Hebrew writings. This
learning was derived entirely from secondary sources. For
example, in Increase Mather's " Mystery of Israel's Salvation," the quotation of Hebrew words, and the references to
the Talmud and Targum, to Abarbanel, Benjamin of Tudela,
Ibn Ezra, Saadya, Kimchi, Rashi, and other mediaeval Hebrew
writers, are all borrowed from the Latin works of Christian
European scholars. We have only to remember the large
number of original Christian Hebraists who sprang up after
the Renaissance and who published the fruits of their learning
freely, to understand how little originality can be credited to
the paraded Rabbinic learning of the Mathers and their New
England contemporaries. In the seventeenth century alone
there were, in England, Lightfoot, Pococke, Selden, John
Spencer, Hyde, Hody, Henry More, Archbishop Usher, Cas-
tell, and Samuel Clark, and, of lesser importance, Hugh
Broughton, Thomas Smith, Ainsworth, Cartwright, Fuller,
Guisius, Sheringham, Francis Taylor, Bernard, and Whee-
locke; and this list takes no account of profound Hebrew
scholars of the stamp of William Bedwell, Saravia, Lancelot
Andrewes, Richard Kilbye, John King and Miles Smith, and
the score of scholars associated with these men in the prepara-

tion of the Authorised Version of 1611. Germany, in the same century, claimed a large number of learned and original Christian Hebraists, the most notable of whom were the Buxtorfs, Eisenmenger, Wagenseil, Carpzov, Hottinger, Schudt, Breithaupt, the two Eberts, Baron Knorr von Rosenroth, Ravius, Gentius, Schickard, and Schwenter. Holland, too, at this time, boasted of an equally distinguished number of Christian Hebraists, chief among whom were Surenhuys, Vossius, Leusden, Drusius, Vitringa, L'Empereur, de Dieu, and Coccejus, the last of whom was of German birth. In Italy, Bartolocci was at work, and in France, Richard Simon and Bochart should be mentioned. As an indication of the extent to which Hebrew was studied at the time, it may be instanced that while we have here quoted only two French Hebraists of the first rank, Paulus Colomesius in his *Gallia Orientalis,* 1665, gives the biographies of 150 Christian Frenchmen and two Christian French women (Maria Molinaea and Anna Rohania) who were known as Hebraists. Not a few Christian women of the time were able to read Hebrew, and sometimes even to correspond in Hebrew. The best known of these are Queen Christina of Sweden, Anna Maria Schurmann, Dorothea Moore, Maria Dorothea, consort of the Duke of Saxe-Weimar; Maria Eleanora, wife of Charles Ludovic of the Palatinate, and the Princess Antonia of Wurtemburg.[77]

In consideration of the ample evidence of the wide extent of Christian Hebrew learning in Europe in the seventeenth century, the large number of Latin works published by these scholars devoted to Rabbinic learning, the paucity of these works in the libraries of the New England scholars, the fact that some Hebrew knowledge was expected of every university-trained cleric of the time, our evaluation of the Hebrew knowledge of the New England divines must conclude

[77] Steinschneider, *Hebräische Bibliographie,* Vol. XX, p. 66 *et seq.*

49

that this learning was confined to familiarity with the Hebrew
Old Testament. The New England scholars knew little or
nothing of Rabbinic literature in the original. It is significant, too, that they did not produce a single book of Hebrew
learning, with the possible exception of the " Bay Psalm
Book." Moreover, if we may judge from slight indications,
their acquaintance with the work of European Christian Hebraists in philology, archaeology, and exegesis was not as
up to date as it would have been had they had the ready
access to books so much desired by Leonard Hoar in his letter
to Robert Boyle. For instance, in 1642 a thesis was offered
at the closing exercises at Harvard College maintaining that
the Hebrew vowels and consonants are of equal antiquity.
Again, in 1678, Cotton Mather attempts to prove that Hebrew punctuation is of Divine origin, and in 1684 Gurdon
Saltonstall maintained the same theme. Had Hebrew knowledge in Harvard College been more nearly abreast of the times,
we should not hear of these men pleading a cause, which by
their time was regarded by the best European scholars as lost.
For, already in 1538 Elias Levita had proved that the Hebrew
vowel points dated back only to about the fifth century of
the Christian era; and this contention had been made known
to the Christian world by Sebastian Münster in 1539, by
Buxtorf in 1620, by Capellus in 1650, and by others. However, Levita's work was not quite unknown in New England;
for, in Increase Mather's diary for 1675, we read under the
date of the 21st of October:

A. M. read in Elias Levita. P. M. Read Buxtorf Lex. Thalmud.[76]

Furthermore, Dunster's letter to Ravius cited early in this
paper, does not reveal a high standard of knowledge of Hebrew phonetics, when all mitigating considerations have been
adduced.

[76] " Diary of Increase Mather," ed. by Samuel A. Green, p. 21.
The same: *Proceedings Mass. Hist. Soc.*, Series II, Vol. XIII, p.
356.

50

Although this conclusion, that the seventeenth century New England Hebrew scholarship has no original value, robs the whole subject of much of its importance, there are two further points revealed by the inquiry that are deserving of special mention. The theory that identified the Indians of America with the lost ten tribes of Israel produced on both sides of the Atlantic Ocean a shower of pamphlets and tracts, as has been pointed out. But the stimulus that this theory gave to the study of Hebrew has not been noticed. Scholars in Europe were daily expectant of hearing of the discovery of some Indians whose vernacular should contain elements recognisable as Hebrew. The letter of Dunster to Ravius indicates that Ravius wished to be invited over the ocean by Harvard College, in order to have the opportunity of acquainting himself personally with the Indian language. We may assume with great probability that Ravius, who wrote a comparative grammar of Semitic languages, cherished the hope of being able to discover Semitic elements in the Indian tongue. Eliot, again, was encouraged in his mission to the Indians and in his master work of translating the Bible into the Indian language, through the belief that the Indians were the outcast tribes of Israel. Leusden, we have seen, dedicated a Hebrew Psalm book to Eliot and the converted Indians; and another to Increase Mather and the converted Indians. In many ways, therefore, the Indian-Israel theory reacted directly and indirectly to stimulate Hebrew study.

Finally, this inquiry may help to show from a fresh point of view how deeply Hebraic was the Puritan colony in New England. The Old Testament spirit of the Puritan has repeatedly been demonstrated. But it has not been recognised to how great an extent this was a *Hebrew* Old Testament spirit. This fact is brought vividly before us by the love of the Hebrew Old Testament that we found in the Pilgrim Father, Governor Bradford. Indicative of this also is the curriculum at Harvard College with its emphasis on Hebrew,

51

and the daily readings in the College Hall from the Hebrew
Bible. But perhaps the most striking and significant fact of
all, although it is one of apparently minor importance, is the
occurrence in the "Bay Psalm Book" of Hebrew words and
letters. That an *original* translation of the book of Psalms
should be practically the first product of the Massachusetts
colonial printing press is alone an eloquent tribute to the
Hebrew Old Testament spirit of the settlers. But the assertion may be hazarded, that in no other country in the world
would conditions have made it possible for an experimental,
infant press to print Hebrew words in Hebrew type in its
first publication. Similarly, the apparently unnecessary citation of Hebrew, common in New England works of the seventeenth century, is to be explained, not so much through the
desire of the authors to vaunt their learning, as by the Hebrew Old Testament atmosphere in which the colonists lived.
The citation of Hebrew was unconsciously looked for, even
by readers ignorant of the sacred tongue, as a cachet of the
Hebrew Old Testament spirit.

The confession of faith assented to at the Synod of Boston
on May 12, 1680, laid down the following dictum regarding
the Bible:

The Old Testament in Hebrew (which was the native language
of the people of God of old) and the New Testament in Greek
(which at the time of writing of it was most generally known
to the nations) being immediately inspired by God and by his
singular care and providence kept pure in all ages are therefore authentical: so as in all controversies of religion the Church
is finally to appeal unto them. But because these original
tongues are not known to all the people of God who have the
right unto and interest in the scriptures, and are commanded in
the fear of God to read and search them; therefore they are
to be translated into the vulgar tongue of every nation in which
they come . . . ."[77]

---

[77] *Magnalia*, v. 1, §8.

It may be objected that this pronouncement, including the
Greek New Testament with the Hebrew Old Testament, proves
nothing for the Hebrew Old Testament character of the Puritan colony in New England. But when this standpoint, which
regards the Hebrew Old Testament as the ultimate authority,
and any translation as a concession to ignorance, is compared
with the earlier attitude that regarded the Latin Vulgate as
the supreme authority for the Old Testament, this article of
faith bears eloquent and triumphant witness to the comparatively Hebraic character of the New England colony, which
made possible and encouraged the labors of the many Christian
Hebraists in New England in the seventeenth century.

53

THE HALF-WAY COVENANT

PERRY MILLER

AMONG a vast array of safe assertions, safest of all are wide generalizations concerning the abiding qualities of a nation or a people. While historical principles which seem universally applicable invite deserved suspicion, yet any rule not too good to be true gathers strength by surviving the exceptions which "prove" it. We should have no fears, for instance, that a lack of contradictory testimony will ever compel us to abandon our ancient belief that the English are a pragmatic race, with an innate propensity for compromise and a congenital aversion to clear thinking — that they prefer always to muddle through with muddled logic. To this good platitude a host of convenient exceptions clamor for attention, and of these the conduct of Englishmen in the early and middle seventeenth century is surely the most gratifying.

Up and down the land were men with utopias in their brains and the voice of God in their ears. Whatever else can be said of these worthies, it must be generally agreed that all in their several fashions comprehended the meaning of "thorough." Puritan and prelate alike were prepared to make of their ideals a Procrustian bed upon which society would be stretched or hacked to fit the predetermined dimensions, and both were sublimely indifferent to what might be the practical consequences. Strafford would make an Anglican satrapy of Catholic Ireland, and Laud would do likewise with Presbyterian Scotland; the Scotch in turn would fasten the solemn league and covenant upon the English, and the Massachusetts-Bay Company would bend the wilderness to a Bible commonwealth. Much of the character of American Puritanism is to be attributed to its having been formulated by Englishmen in a day when too many Englishmen were behaving themselves in a manner which Britons have usually considered bad form. Of all examples of this un-English *a priori-ism*, New England Congregationalism is probably the most extreme.

It should be added, however, that the most spectacular form in which this quality of preconception was manifested in New England was not that which is most often singled out for comment and disparagement. The notion that Biblical ethics should dominate the life of a community was indeed an important item in the New England creed, but it was not the central doctrine, nor was it peculiar to the new world. The fate of such diverse persons as Servetus and Mary Stuart is a reminder that the notion was not unfamiliar to Geneva and Scotland. But the sanguine colonials went far beyond this elementary stage and dedicated themselves to an even more rigorous program, which they called Congregationalism. They had accepted Protestant theology. Very well then, they would conform their world to that theology. For a century Protestant reformers had preached regeneration and faith; New Englanders would make regeneration and faith the touchstones of an ecclesiastical and even of a political system. In this spirit they dared to make a deduction which Calvin had explicitly declared was inadmissible,[1]

[1] Ernest Troeltsch, *The Social Teaching of the Christian Churches* (New York, 1931), I, 598.

they dared to assume that if there was any truth in predestination, then the predestined elect could be distinguished in the flesh from the predestined reprobate. Upon this conclusion they proceeded to act. They turned over the government of the churches to congregations made up exclusively of the regenerate. They reasoned, with flawless logic, that saints, being sanctified, needed no supervision of bishops or classical bodies, that the Word of God was for them sufficient check upon their portion of human depravity. Up to this time no orthodox Protestants had contemplated putting the principle of salvation by faith into anything like so extensive a practice. Compared with the blithe assurance of the New England divines, Luther and Calvin appear downright skeptics; they would have recoiled in horror at the prospect of giving any groups of human beings, even hand-picked groups of the evidently righteous, such breath-taking powers as those of electing their own ministers and enjoying local ecclesiastical autonomy.

The marvel is that this super-logical system actually worked. There were slight modifications, but the essential idea was completely carried out. After overriding antinomianism, expelling Roger Williams, circumventing Dr. Child, and crushing the Quakers, the clergy and magistrates could boast with pardonable pride that in all the world New England alone had succeeded in living up to the Word of God, and at that when the Word had been most exactingly interpreted. And then, at this very moment of satisfaction, events threatened to get out of hand. The ministers confronted what Artemus Ward would have called "a darned uncomfortable reality" to which it seemed that they had to make concessions, or else the whole system would go to pot. The problem came, as problems generally do, from an unexpected quarter—not from any frontal attack, which they could have withstood, nor from an outburst of heresy, which they had demonstrated they were competent to deal with, but from the simple fact that time moved on and that even the chosen people of God married and had the customary issue. It was their children, and then their children's children, who by doing nothing but allowing themselves to be born constituted a threat to the marvellous perfection of New England Congregationalism.

57

It was not that the original theory had failed to provide for these children. The Bible taught that churches were to consist only of visible saints, of adults who had experienced regeneration, but it also declared, in passages too numerous to mention, that whenever God extended the covenant of grace to His saints, He included their "seed" in the grant. On such authority Congregationalists had provided for the baptism of the children of church-members, and for no other children whatsoever, as a symbol that God had taken them into the covenant. Of course, everybody assumed that these baptized children would grow up to become somehow saints themselves; whereupon their own children could be baptized, and so *ad infinitum*. Thus, the theory had confidently expected, the churches would be perpetuated through the ages by a continual and unfailing succession of the elect.

The fault lay not in a lack of provision or foresight. It was rather that the provision was not of the right

sort, that what was foreseen was precisely what did not
happen.   Incredible though it might be, there were a
vast number of the second generation who were earnest
and sober and had immaculate reputations, who sincerely
desired to partake of the Lord's Supper, but who, try as
they might, "could not come up to that experimental
account of their own regeneration, which would sufficiently embolden their access to the other sacrament."[2]
And when we reflect that at almost their earliest opportunity, they generally became parents themselves, not
once but frequently, we can understand how the problem of an ecclesiastical status for the descendants of
the original saints did "come on with some importunity
and impetuosity."[3]   In 1646 the General Court summoned a synod to frame a platform of discipline; it
had various motives, but the most insistent was a fear
that unless the question of baptism were settled, the
various apprehensions of the matter then rampant
would "begett such differences as will be displeasing
to the Lord, offensive to others, and dangerous to ourselves."[4]   At the Cambridge gathering the subject was
warily introduced, discovered to be "difficultly circumstanced"—which is putting it mildly—and dropped
with unanimous alacrity.   But within a very few years
Puritan fecundity made it impossible to stall any longer.
At the suggestion of Connecticut an assembly of divines
met at Boston in 1657, drew up a statement which at
once caused a furor and divided New England into
two violently opposed theological camps.   In 1662 an

[2] Cotton Mather, *Magnalia Christi Americana* (Hartford, 1855), II,
277.

[3] *Ibid.*, 98.

[4] *Records of Massachusetts*, II, 155; III, 70-73.

official synod was found necessary, and the conclusions of this body, reached after a stormy session by a majority of about seven to one, were promulgated as the official opinion of the churches.

The issue in these gatherings was simplicity itself: "The children of the parents in question, are either children of the covenant, or strangers from the covenant."[5] The unregenerate heirs of what Cotton Mather called the "good old generation" had to be frankly kept in the churches or else turned out. On this crucial point the ministers had no mind to compromise, and the simple truth of the matter is that they did not. In spite of the label which their solution has borne ever since, there really was no "half-way." In no uncertain tones the majority responded in the affirmative. Baptized children were held to be members, even if unregenerate. This membership was qualified and hedged about, it was distinguished from "full" membership which entitled to communion, but it remained essentially membership, and as such gave the baptized members the right to present their own children for baptism.

There is not the slightest obscurity about the motives for this decision. If the constrictive operation of the polity had been permitted to force the posterity of the saints outside the pale, then presently the whole community would be left "at a loose end without the Discipline of Christ, the Means to prevent sin, or to reduce them to Repentance unto life."[6] Since "even the children of the godly" were making a "woful proof,"

59

[5] [Jonathan Mitchel], *Propositions Concerning the Subject of Baptism and Consociation of Churches. . . .* (Cambridge, 1662), 12.

[6] John Allin, *Animadversions upon the Antisynodalia Americana* (Cambridge, 1664), 6.

Ezekiel Rogers in 1658 trembled to think what would "become of this glorious work that we have begun, when the ancient shall be gathered to their fathers."[7] Intrusions of irreligion and apostasy would be bound to emanate from so large a number ejected beyond the limits of control. "Church-way for the good of these there is none, if they be not under Church-government and Discipline."[8] Damned or saved, the children had to be made subject to the watch and ward of the church, or the Bible commonwealth was ruined.

To the modern mind motives as good as these might be deemed sufficient, and we may pardonably wonder what all the pother was about. But unhappily the seventeenth-century mind did not work in this fashion. It was not that New Englanders considered the gaining of happiness or the satisfaction of ulterior motives sinful; they decidedly approved of getting what one wanted if one could. But in their scheme worldly profit was incidental to serving the will of God. To aim merely at the continued prosperity of the churches would be in their view to put the cart before the horse. A church system had been decreed once and for all in the Bible. To patch up the divine constitution in response to some mere mechanical urgency was to make "innovation," most heinous of sins and of crimes. Biblical polity did not depend upon sociological considerations, but solely upon the immutable decree of God. The New England fathers had known this when,

60

---

[7] Cotton Mather, *Magnalia*, I, 413.

[8] Richard Mather, *A Defence of the Answer and Arguments of the Synod met at Boston in the Year 1662* (Cambridge, 1664), 18. Jonathan Mitchel's *An Answer to the Apologetical Preface Published in the Name and Behalf of the Brethren that Dissented in the Late Synod*, was issued together with Mather's pamphlet under one title-page.

rather than sacrifice one jot or iota of that polity, they had betaken themselves to the wilderness. The synod could not get away with its doctrine unless it could somehow show that it had enacted "no Apostacy from the first Principles of New England, nor yet any declension from the Congregational way,"[9] but only "a progress in practising according thereunto, as the encrease of the Churches doth require."[10] If baptized but unregenerate persons were members, then somebody had to prove that the idea had been implicit in the system from its very origins.

Nor was this all. New Englanders had a theology as well as a polity. The leaders of Massachusetts and Connecticut had always insisted upon their complete doctrinal concord with the reformed churches of the world. They had accepted without reservation that system of thought which in its main outlines was the creed of English Puritanism and which is generally, though somewhat loosely, spoken of as Calvinism. To prove this the synod at Cambridge in 1648 had enthusiastically endorsed the *Confession of Faith* which the Westminster assembly had just published. Heresy was as black a sin as innovation, and the synod of 1662 could not issue its *Propositions* without first reassuring the world that these did no violence to the inherited theology.

To generalize about this theology has ever been a dangerous undertaking, and nowadays is certainly a thankless one. Engaging as one may find the laby-

[9] Increase Mather, *The First Principles of New England, Concerning the Subject of Baptisme And Communion of Churches* (Cambridge, 1675), A4, *verso*.
[10] Allin, *Animadversions*, 5.

rinthine involutions of this creed outworn, inflicting
them too heavily upon the reader would be like boring
a guest with a favourite cross-word puzzle. But considering the fashion in which the New England intellect operated, one must notice certain features of that
primitive philosophy in order to trace the history of
this movement. A moderately extensive reading of
New England authors suggests the thought that the
predestinarian aspect of its theology has been rather
overemphasized. Popular impressions to the contrary,
it is not altogether accurate to declare that New Englanders interpreted their creed to require complete
passivity of man in the face of an absolute and arbitrary God. They were not given over irreparably to
fatalism and paralysis of the spirit.[11] True, they did
conceive the cosmos to be pure determinism, and they
did hold that the sole moving force therein was the
will of God, a will unfettered by aught but the divine
pleasure. True, they did believe that when God
saved a man, He did it out of His lofty condescension, "without any fore-sight of Faith or good Works,
or perseverance in either of them or any other thing
in the Creature, as Conditions or Causes moving him
thereunto, and all to the praise of his glorious
Grace."[12] So, until a man experienced effectual calling, he did dwell in impotency of spirit, prostrate before God, unable either to lift or to wish to lift a finger
for his own salvation. To this extent there can be no
doubt that Calvinism succeeded in stifling human effort

[11] Cf. Frank Hugh Foster, A Genetic History of New England Theology.

[12] Williston Walker, The Creeds and Platforms of Congregationalism
(New York, 1903), 371.

and initiative, but even so it did not entirely suppress them. Even among the unconverted, New Englanders understood that a certain activity, or at least semblance of activity, could go on: the unregenerate could be offered the "means" of conversion. The Gospel and its ordinances, the ministry and the sacraments, could be held out as an inducement to sinners. The clergy were "Ambassadors" of Christ, and their "great business is to make the offers of, and invite sinful Men to embrace Reconciliation with God, through Christ."[13] Of course, these sinful men could make no response, logically they could not be supposed even to make sense out of what was preached to them, until the spirit came to their assistance. Until then they might have ears but they would hear not. "The power to discern the excellency of the Truth, and so to approve and embrace it, and to chuse and close with Christ . . . must come from a superior agent; because in doeing it, the blind mind must be illuminated, and the rebellious heart subdued."[14] But then no one could tell in advance where the superior agent, like lightning, would strike. The only thing to do was continually to stand by, offering the means of conversion to all the unregenerate. Any one of them might suddenly discover himself able to take advantage of his opportunities. None of them could therefore be deprived of a chance. The clergy would sleep ill of nights if they faltered in offering the objective means of grace, not only in spite of, but in the very midst of human inability.

63

[13] Samuel Willard, *A Complete Body of Divinity* (Boston, 1726), 431.
[14] *Ibid.*, 427.

Once the soul became infused with the regenerating spirit, the whole situation was gloriously changed. As soon as the sinner had authentically experienced effectual calling, justification, and adoption, he was freed. Then he could, he inevitably would, commence to strive against sin and the flesh. He was no longer a supine recipient of grace; he was a warrior penetrated with the active spirit of Christ. The *Westminster Confession*, which New England synods endorsed in 1648 and in 1680, emphasized again and again that a sinner translated to a state of grace was a man emancipated from natural bondage to sin, who could, albeit imperfectly, will to do good. He had not only a choice but a duty "to give all diligence to make his calling and election sure."[15] He was voluntarily to coöperate with the divine spirit in striving for sanctification, saving faith, good works, and true repentance. Best of all, the church could exhort and incite him. As long as natural man could contribute positively nothing to his own salvation, so Samuel Willard wrote, then it must be that "a Christians real work begins, when he is Converted."[16]

Thus we can perceive that the existence of these recalcitrant children posed a delicate theological problem. Because they could not even in "the judgment of charity" be accounted saints, they had then to be held incapable of spiritual exertions. What could be the use of exhorting them to moral conduct or making them memorize a catechism? Even if they did the things which God had commanded, they would not do them with a heart purified by faith and their deeds would be

[15] Walker, *Creeds and Platforms*, 385.
[16] Willard, *Complete Body of Divinity*, 503.

of no avail. Good works done by the unregenerate "cannot please God, nor make a man meet to receive grace from God."[17] But though the church could not undertake to convert the children, there was no impropriety in its offering them the "means" of conversion. A great many of them were expected to be ultimately chosen; they had all therefore to be constantly called, and called as loudly as possible. The seed of believers "are successively in their Generations to be trained up for the Kingdome of Heaven," to which "the Elect number shall still be brought in the way of such means."[18] The difficulty was that mere providing of means could not be permitted to become anything more. Opening chances to those who might some day utilize them was one thing, but evangelizing among those who betrayed no signs of a circumcised heart was quite another. The merely baptized could not be treated as though elected nor expected to behave as if regenerate. The temptation was great to demand regenerate actions from sinners, to transform, unwittingly but none the less sinfully, "means" into goads, opportunities into provocations. If their concern for the future led the clergy to push or entice the baptized into actions to which they knew men could really be aroused only by the divine summons, they would make a ghastly mockery of the Congregational principle of regenerate membership.

The majority report in the synod of 1662 has so often been indicted by church historians for being the initiation of precisely such a treason, and that indict-

65

---

[17] Walker, *Creeds and Platforms*, 384.
[18] *Propositions Concerning the Subject of Baptism*, A3, recto.

ment has become so much the accepted verdict, that some further explanation is necessary. The principle of regenerate membership presents at least as many difficulties as any other Puritan conception. It was based upon a postulate, upon a belief in the reality of a super-sensual realm in which a converted individual could encounter a definite series of spiritual experiences. In the Congregational plan, before a man became a member of the church militant, he must have had these experiences, he must have become by divine election a member of the church triumphant. This meant that in the inner recesses of his soul there must have been engendered a new life, he must have undergone a subjective, incomprehensible, but recognizable transformation. Upon the foundation of this subjective experience was reared the objective church; correlated with the spiritual realm, with the emotional life, was the ecclesiastical realm, the organized system. The external church was not primarily an evangelical organization to carry the gospel to the heathen, but a brotherhood for the cultivation and intensification of grace in those who already had it. It was designed, as we have just seen, to offer "means" to those who were some day to be converted, but its more important function was to direct the already converted towards larger achievements in the way of sanctification, repentance, and saving faith. The greatest of the early prophets of Congregationalism, William Ames, who was a master among other things of the Aristotelian terminology, defined the "essential" form of the true church to be invisibility, the "accidental" form to be visibility: "the accidental forme is visible, because it is nothing else then an outward profession of inward Faith."[19] As Thomas Hooker expressed it with less jargon, "the Covenant of Grace is ever included and presupposed in the Covenant of the Church."[20] The organization followed upon the fact that certain persons were predestined to salvation; the ecclesiastical realm assumed the previous occurrence of conversion in the spiritual, and without maintaining that assumption the whole theory of Congregationalism would have collapsed.

67

To make an assumption is easy. To maintain it in the presence of facts is to invite trouble. The trouble here was that this spiritual realm remained a closed book to human comprehension. God alone could know with certainty what happened there. We, poor creatures, could merely follow the motions of the spirit from afar, and endeavor to read the language of the spirit as it was translated in the language of sense. Naturally we would make mistakes. Hence Congregationalists hovered always upon the verge of an exciting predicament: they created an ecclesiastical system based upon the objective reality of election, and at the same time recognized that in practical life it was impossible to be absolutely certain just who was elected and who was not. They desired the membership of their churches to approximate as closely as possible to the membership of the church invisible. But they could discover no method for guaranteeing that the two realms would be more than remotely identical. So the best they could do was to go upon evidences, to pass

[19] William Ames, *The Marrow of Sacred Divinity* (London, 1643), 137-138.

[20] *A Survey of the Summe of Church Discipline* (London, 1648), Part III, 24.

no judgment upon the thing-in-itself, but to be concerned with its attributes. He who *seemed* regenerate must for practical purposes be treated as such. The individual was to search for faith within the trackless hinterland of the soul, but it remained his own problem to establish his sincerity. The church wished only to know what evidences justified its accepting the individual into the ecclesiastical realm on the assumption that he had probably already been received into the spiritual.

Thus Congregational theorists had progressively recognized that the ecclesiastical realm was based, properly speaking, not upon the *terra incognita* of actual faith and regeneration, but upon externalities, upon evidences, upon probabilities. Whether we were members of the invisible church, said Hooker, "we for the present doe not know: and its certain, you can neither see, nor know, for truth of grace is invisible to man."[21] We judged on the basis of actions and professions, as best we might, but in the end we called him a Christian who stood up under such fallible tests as we could devise.

The Profession is to be judged of by Men who cannot know the Heart, but must judge according to Appearances. . . . God hath put it into the hands of Men to dispense the Gospel-Ordinances, and hath told them who are the Subjects, and by what Rule they are to determine them, and that is by their Profession, or outward demeanure of themselves.[22]

The two realms overlapped, but they would always remain separate and distinct. "There is a twofold Dispensation of the Covenant of God in his visible Church," wrote John Allin in reply to President Chauncy; there is the "Inward, Spiritual, and Saving Dispensation of

[21] *A Survey of the Summe of Church Discipline* (London, 1648), Part I, 37.
[22] Willard, *Complete Body of Divinity*, 854.

the Covenant to such as truly Believe, and perform the conditions of the Covenant," but quite a different matter is the other dispensation, "Outward and visible, by which the Lord bestows upon his Church, and all the members thereof, the outward Priviledges of the Covenant, his Ordinances, and Means of Grace."[23]

Specific individuals who presented instances either of notorious unregeneracy or of conspicuous holiness caused no confusion between the dispensations. He who in every respect conducted himself as a man of God could safely be supposed truly elect; whereas an equally obvious limb of Satan was presumably not among the saved. But by no means were all persons such clear-cut cases of black or white. As time went on, the divines kept finding a surprising number who did not fit readily into either category. Some who were far from vicious were yet not ostensibly regenerate, and many who seemed in some respects to be called were in other respects palpably deficient. Worse than that, some who gave the most convincing exhibitions, who made "a more than ordinary profession of religion," came to bad ends, created "prodigious and astonishing scandals."[24] It did the bewildered clergy no good to pray to God for an answer to the enigma; no answer was forthcoming, nor could one be expected. God knew His own mind, and He had made no pledge to reveal accurately the secret transactions of the spiritual realm. Congregationalists had undertaken a mighty task: they had set out to embody the infinite will of God in a finite church. They had admitted from the beginning that there might be discrepancies, but when these became too

[23] Allin, *Animadversions,* 18-19.
[24] Cotton Mather, *Magnalia,* II, 493.

flagrant, they put on a bold face and determined to save their own consistency in default of their parishioners' sincerity. They had aspired to capitalize the hidden energies of conversion, but when they perceived how hidden those energies were, they made shift to be content with evidences. More and more the clergy dodged the responsibility, took refuge in the reflection that the life of the spirit was beyond human ken. It was not their fault if their technique of examination worked injustices or was sometimes inadequate.

> To make a person a Member of the visible Church, the matter is not whether he hath Faith and Grace really, or not; if he hath such qualification as the Rule of the Word accepteth for Faith in the visible Church, we can go no further.[25]

It was enough if a man seemed to possess the qualifications; the clergy declared him as good a Christian as any, unless later on he gave overwhelming evidence to the contrary. To say church-members were regenerate, said John Cotton, was to speak of what "they ought to be *de jure* . . . rather then what they are, or are want to be *de facto*."[26]   Evidence, not reality, was the bailiwick of the churches, and their evaluation of evidence was confessedly faulty. Clearly they would frequently admit some who would seem satisfactory but who would be in God's eyes reprobate, who were, in short, hypocrites. "It is clearer then the day, that many who are inwardly . . . the children of the *Devil*, are outwardly, or in respect of outward Covenant, the children of God."[27]   To this anomalous conclusion the fathers of

[25] Allin, *Animadversions*, 25.

[26] *A Defence of Mr. John Cotton From the Imputation of Selfe Contradiction* (Oxford, 1658), 71.

[27] Thomas Shepard, *The Church-Membership of Children and their Right to Baptisme* (Cambridge, 1663), 1-2.
    (1649)

New England themselves had come, quite independently of the problem of children. They had already made it a part of the Congregational tradition by 1662.

Into the ecclesiastical realm, the fellowship of the evidently righteous, a person could get admitted in one of two ways. The first was to make a personal profession of faith and regeneration before the congregation. Hypocrites could do this, yet it still was the most reliable method for detecting the elect. Any one who passed this inspection became for official purposes one of the chosen, and therefore was entitled to all the privileges of the church, especially the communion. Hence the Lord's Supper came to be the crucial link between the spiritual and the ecclesiastical realms. Everybody agreed that the sacrament should be confined to those who not merely had private assurance of salvation, but who could offer public evidence, who could show "historical faith," blameless lives, and the ability "to examine themselves and to discern the Lords body." The most stalwart advocates of the half-way covenant were as much resolved as their opponents that satisfactory personal confession should be a prerequisite to partaking of the communion, because that ceremony was instituted, "not for regeneration, but for nourishment and confirmation" of those already regenerate.[28]

The second way was baptism. Because the ecclesiastical realm was not necessarily identical with the spiritual, God by His arbitrary fiat could, if He so pleased, set up another standard besides visible holiness. As

71

---

[28] Richard Mather, *A Disputation Concerning Church-Members and their Children, in Answer to XXI Questions.* . . . (London, 1659), 17. MS. in The American Antiquarian Society, Worcester, Massachusetts.

New Englanders read the Bible, they found that He
would permit no heathen to come in before making a
profession, but that after an erstwhile heathen became
converted He counted that man's children among His
flock. There was, possibly, very little rhyme or reason
in this entailing of the covenant, but there was no
getting around it. So the children were baptized. But
of infants nothing could be demanded, not even evidences. They became church members solely and simply
because God so ordered it, and for no better reason.
Presumably He would some day elect them. Apparently He desired them in the church, where the means
of conversion could be set before them. "Others hear
the word, but these in outward Covenant enjoy it by
Covenant, and promise; and hence these in the first
place, and principally, are sought after by these
meanes."[29] To most of the children, it was believed,
God would not say, "If thow believest thow shalt be
saved," but instead, "I will enable to believe;" they
would have the means "unless they refuse in resisting
the means," and even if they refused, God would
probably be especially patient with them:

. . . he will take away this refuseing heart from among them indefinitely, so that though every one cannot assure himself, that
he will do it particularly for this or that person, yet every one,
through this promise, may hope and pray for the communication of this grace, and so feel it in time.[30]

Thus the normal development of the baptized child
ought to cause no trouble. At the age of discretion he
would discreetly reveal signs of regeneration, be taken
into full membership, and seated at the Lord's Supper.

[29] Shepard, *The Church-Membership of Children*, 3-4.
[30] *Ibid.*, 5-6.

In that case the church would have to regard him as
having been chosen in the divine mind from all eternity. Had it been able to decipher his destiny at birth,
it would have received him into full standing at once.
For obvious reasons that had been impossible, but there
had been good grounds to presume that he would grow
in grace and become saved; therefore he had to be considered as having been a legitimate member of the
ecclesiastical realm even in his probationary period. He
had made progress in his ability to furnish evidences,
but he had not come from non-membership into membership. He had been included within the church
covenant at birth by the explicit statement of God and
now his inclusion was simply made good. *Ergo*, the
child had been a true member from the very day of
his baptism.

That much was clear. But any system of education
has to reckon with abnormal children. Abnormality was
expressed in this case by a growing up without a concomitant ability to prove regeneration. What should the
church do with such intractable youths? How should
it account for them? Whom should it blame? The
only certainty was that they could not be allowed to
approach the communion table, but that still left much
to be determined. For example, did every member
necessarily have to be a communicant? If so, the children who did become regenerate had not been members
before their conversion. Then where was the point in
baptism at all? That way anabaptist madness lay. But
if all baptized children were held to be members, could
those who failed to make the expected progress be
thrown out of the fold when they came of age on the

grounds that they had secured no foothold in the spiritual realm, when the two realms were held to be altogether separate, when happenings within the spiritual realm were unfathomable by man, and when every one acknowledged that beyond a doubt many who were received into the church were a stench in the nostrils of God?   In determining who should participate in the ecclesiastical system, was the blanket promise of God to extend the covenant to the seed of believers less valid evidence than that offered by the individual through his own profession, when all evidence at best was purely presumptive and apt to be fallacious?   It was the core of Calvinistic theology that God saved men by His arbitrary condescension, but what if in one case He did it through contact with the individual and in another through the parent, without apparently touching the individual at all?   Such a prospect would even seem a challenge to the faith of a people who believed that the Deity customarily performed His wonders in mysterious ways.   In fact, in their minds it might take on a decided tinge of probability as they reflected that the danger of getting hypocrites into the church was about as great one way as the other.   But on the other hand, if these children continued to flood the churches, would not that be the end of Congregationalism in New England?   Congregationalism, we must recollect, was based on the theory that church-members were at least evidently regenerate. About these unfortunates not even a supposition could be made. Could this system, founded as it had been upon the attributes of sincere religion, continue in existence at all when a great percentage of the generations who were to perpetuate it obviously and conclusively failed to acquire any such attributes?

The dissenters at the synod of 1662, ably represented by President Chauncy, John Davenport, Increase Mather, and Nicholas Street, found the last question unanswerable. They decided that if the system was to survive, it could not stomach baptized but unregenerate children, no matter who their parents were. The churches might indeed be founded upon appearances, but nevertheless these were appearances of spiritual realities. Children who grew up unable to muster any such manifestations should get no better treatment than any other incapable persons. So far as the world could judge, they were essentially unbelievers; they might not have committed open immoralities, but they would have shown their true colors by "neglecting the means of Grace, or non-manifestations of making profession of the Faith, and the fruits thereof."[31] If the adult children could not manage a personal and immediate confederation, said Davenport, they were in a state of sin, they were naturally incapable of good, and in their hearts "these despise the Church of God."[32] Thus, though they may have been members during their minority, when they came of age and made no professions, "then they do not retain their Membership which they had in minority."[33] They were automatically to be expelled. The dissenters waxed so hot upon this point that they actually insinuated that the children were in

75

[31] Charles Chauncy, *Anti-Synodalia Scripta Americana* (London, 1662), 24.

[32] John Davenport, *Another Essay for Investigation of the Truth* (Cambridge, 1663), 45.

[33] *Ibid.*, Increase Mather in Preface, A2, *recto*.

some fashion responsible for not having made a better showing. They declared their failure made them *felones de se.* Davenport argued that the children had been pledged to God in their infancy, whereby they had become "engaged and excited the more to give themselves to God in Christ . . . not by constraint but willingly;" consequently they had only themselves to blame if their sinful hearts did not surrender. Amusingly enough, Davenport went on to say that such a willing surrender to Christ would have had to come about "through the operation of God working Faith in their hearts, by the Spirit, who is a voluntary Agent, and therfore likened to the wind which bloweth where it listeth." But though his reasoning was a trifle confused, Davenport came to an unequivocal conclusion: "The Church must make a difference of children grown up, where God makes a difference . . . and receive onely such whom Christ receiveth."[34] Here the dissenters took their stand, and demanded that the churches of New England unchurch the helpless children, expel the grandchildren, and consign the lot of them to everlasting torments. And the dissenters, it should be remembered, were still Englishmen.

The majority of the divines recognized that the dissenters' position was sincerely taken, but they felt that it was altogether too rash and precipitous. They had an armory of careful theorizing to draw upon, and they were grateful to the fathers who had meticulously distinguished and divided the realms of the spirit and the church. They had no mind to minimize the epistemological speculations which already had brought home

[34] Davenport, *Another Essay for Investigation of the Truth,* 6.

the impossibility and the danger of identifying manifestations of regeneration with the thing itself. The
minority were zealous, the majority more circumspect.
A machinery was needed for rationalizing the pursuit
of a practical objective in terms of a divinely pre-
ordained system, and they saw that the way to achieve
it was to interpret the whole problem as pertaining only
to the realm of organization. They remained within
the letter of Congregational tradition by the strange
device of insisting that the spirit was not concerned, that
the issue was not whether the children "have true Faith,
or not, in the act or habit, so they have such qualifications as God accepts of, to receive their persons into his
Covenant, and to be Members of the Body of Christ."
If they had the qualifications, "this sufficeth, though
they have no Faith or Grace really."[35] The church
realm was, at best, one of probabilities, and God alone
specified how the probabilities should be gauged; therefore if He said that simply by being the progeny of
church-members persons were fit to become members,
that would constitute good qualification. It was enough
to warrant their formal, legal inclusion within the
group, enough to invest them with evident righteousness, with "federal holiness," if not with inner virtue.
To treat them as confederated believers and to keep
them within the church did not mean, Thomas Shepard
had written,

. . . that they are alwaies in inward Covenant, and inward
Church-Members, who enjoy the inward, and saveing benefits
of the Covenant, but that they are in external, and outward
Covenant, and therefore outwardly Church-Members, to whom

[35] Allin, *Animadversions*, 25.

77

belongs some outward privileges of the Covenant for their inward and eternall good.[36]

Hence the synod boldly determined that "meer membership" was its province, a matter quite distinct from ability to make professions, "as in the children of the Covenant, that grow up to years is too often seen."[37] Children could not inherit a right to Heaven or to the communion table, but they could succeed to citizenship in a body politic. "Only the confederation, not the condition or conversation of the Parent is imputed to the Child."[38] The church as a society was concerned only with the legality of their title within the corporate group; if they did not profit by the opportunities it offered for becoming genuine converts, that was their loss. They might secure no standing in the church triumphant, but they would lose none in the church militant. If they did not prove regenerate,

. . . we may say their Covenant and Church-relation is as none in respect of any Spiritual saving benefit to their souls . . . and yet it can no more be said, that in respect of their Church-relation and external visible state, they are not in the Church . . . then in other particulars it can be said, that they are not . . . baptized.[39]

Just as soon as membership was defined in these terms, as being a formal relationship to a specific commonwealth, a number of interesting consequences followed. In a commonwealth an individual had to be either completely a member or none whatsoever. No one could be half citizen and half alien. He might be

[36] Shepard, *The Church-Membership of Children*, 2.
[37] *Propositions Concerning the Subject of Baptism*, 11.
[38] Increase Mather, *First Principles*, 19.
[39] Richard Mather, *A Defence of the Answer*, 33.

a good member or a bad one, he might be entitled to communion or not, but once in, he was altogether in, "Even as a childe of the family is not so perfect to do the work, and enjoy all the Priviledges of the Family, as a grown person is, but yet he is as perfectly a Member of the Family as a grown man."[40] The difference between a non-communicating and a communicating member was not a distinction of kind, but merely one of the methods by which each had entered the compact. One was a citizen by birth, the other had been naturalized. "The Free-grace of God in his Covenant, extended both to Parent and Childe. . . . The way of entring into this Covenant on mans part is onely a differing *modus* or manner of Covenanting with God."[41] Once the essential membership of the children was thus established, the thing clearly could be extended through the generations; the grandchildren were members by the same token. Adults who had not been baptized and had been reared outside the church could not be admitted to the covenant until examined for the visible signs of piety,

. . . yet this concerns not the Parents of the children here spoken of, because they are not now to be admitted into the Covenant and Church membership, but are therein already, and have been long afore now, even from their minority or birth.[42]

The whole dispute, as the apologists persisted in viewing it, had nothing to do with the admission of adults through personal profession; it was only concerned "About persons already in the Church, and Baptized,

79

---

[40] Allin, *Animadversions*, 28.
[41] *Ibid.*, 29.
[42] Richard Mather, *A Defence of the Answer*, 30.

whether in such, the grounds of Baptizing their seed, be Faith and Grace made visible in some manner, or their Interest in the Covenant?"[43] Through "interest in the covenant" these children obtained only a political and not necessarily a religious status; therefore political maxims applied to their condition. It was already a platitude of Puritan political dogma that a compact was irrevocable as long as both parties lived up to it. Therefore, unless these children and grandchildren broke the compact of federal holiness by some overt act of scandal, how in God's name could they be dropped from the society? The idea of their becoming *felones de se* was absurd. A church-member "cannot be outed, till God out him."[44] "In Admitting Members into the Church," said John Allin, "we justly work for such positive Qualifications as the Word of God requireth," but once we have determined that certain persons have the qualifications, either by virtue of their own profession or by virtue of their parentage, then "to cast out such as are *Regularly admitted*, we must have positive Impenitency in sin."[45]

This much of its doctrine the synod attained merely by accentuating already accepted opinions concerning the necessarily objective character of a corporate church. Thus it managed to enter the substance of its decision without apparently doing violence to the inherited theology or creating innovations in the discipline. Indeed, the distinguishing mark of the *Propositions* might be said to be precisely too rigorous a consistency, too in-

[43] Allin, *Animadversions*, 22.

[44] Jonathan Mitchel, *An Answer to the Apologetical Preface* (Cambridge, 1664), 12. See *note* 8.

[45] Allin, *Animadversions*, 19.

genious a fidelity to tradition and creed. It has been
noted that there was a marked trend towards formalism in the New England of the forties and fifties, but
the resolution in 1662 of the status of children on the
grounds solely of visibility put a finishing touch to the
transformation of Congregationalism from a religious
Utopia to a legalized order. Religion was practically
confined to the inner consciousness of the individual.
He alone needed to be concerned about the assurances
of election. The churches were pledged, in effect, not
to pry into the genuineness of any religious emotions,
but to be altogether satisfied with decorous semblances.
The apologists concentrated upon the letter of the law,
and so solved their problem without noticeably reno-
vating the divine scheme, but they did so at the cost
of ignoring the spirit. This came out most clearly when
they drew a lengthy analogy between the rite of baptism and the Old Testament rite of circumcision. They
refused altogether to recollect that Israel had been a
tribe first and a church only secondarily, and that conversion as a basis for membership was utterly foreign
to the spirit of Judaism. Even though the Jewish
church was "National," argued Richard Mather, while
ours is "Congregational," still in each church the covenant runs to members and their seed; "now as well as
then, if the Parents continue in covenant, the Children
do so also, and so are part of the Church."[46] If an increase of hypocrites had threatened the churches even
when men became members only through profession,
how much greater was the threat when generation after
generation could continue in church compact with con-

81

---

[46] Richard Mather, *A Defence of the Answer*, 56.

fessedly no more grounds to distinguish them from the heathen than the negative virtue of avoiding open scandal! Thomas Shepard had foreseen this possibility, and the synodalists confessed they perceived it too, for they published his letter in 1663:

God knowes what Churches we may have of them, even heaps of hypocrites, and prophane persons, for I know not what can give us hope of their not apostatizing, but only Gods promise to be a God to them, and to preserve them.[47]

This was a melancholy prospect for good Christians to contemplate. It is not surprising that at this point the apologists betrayed an uneasy sense that perhaps they had gone too far; and they turned once more for reassurances to logic, which generally worked such wonders in the seventeenth century. Was it after all necessary, they mused, to assume that baptized children who lived and died soberly and morally within the church were damned just because they had undergone no emotional convulsion? If, for instance, a baptized child experienced effectual calling on his twentieth birthday, he was considered to have been all along a legitimate member of the church. But another who did not have the experience until his fortieth year still enjoyed his membership on trust every bit as legitimately for a score of years longer. Now it was conceivable that this one, instead of living to become obviously regenerate at forty, might be cut off at thirty-nine. If God had chosen him, would not God save him anyway? And since no one could even begin to comprehend what went on in the realm of spirit, and since that realm had been divorced completely from the

---

[47] Shepard, *The Church-Membership of Children*, 15.

physical world, might not some men become truly regenerate without ever anybody in this world suspecting it, least of all themselves? There might exist a sort of state of grace half-way between demonstrable reprobation and demonstrable regeneration in which men would become saved, as it were, subconsciously. The half-way members, baptized but not communicating, actually might be construed as the worldly embodiment of this intermediate condition. The apologists knew that at this point they skated upon very thin ice indeed. They were dangerously close to pleading for some species of "Universal Baptism Grace," to declaring that baptism was not a means of grace but a vehicle — which Davenport pointed out was a damnable error of the Arminians. Strangely enough, Richard Mather, one of the older generation, handled the notion most daringly. He did not say baptism made children regenerate, but he did go so far as to assert that baptized children who grew up respectable but unconverted need not be pronounced to lack "the very being of Faith." May there not, he asked, be real saving grace "even there where the exercise of it is much wanting? . . . Notwithstanding all this weakness, there may be the being and truth of the thing in such Souls." Even though the children did not have the ability to examine themselves, as required by the Lord's Supper, yet they "are in a latitude of expression to be accounted visible believers" because "Being in covenant and baptized, they have Faith and Repentance indefinitely given to them in the Promise, and sealed up in Baptism . . . which continues valid, and so a valid testimony for them, while they do not reject it."[48] "Surely," Jonathan Mitchel

83

---

[48] Shepard, *The Church-Membership of Children*, 51-52, 13.

pleaded, suddenly shifting from ecclesiastical metaphysics to *argumentum ad hominem,*

> . . . the Lord does not make so light a matter of his holy
> Covenant and seal . . . as to enter into a solemn Covenant with
> Children, take them into his Church, and seal up their taking
> in before Men and Angels, and then let them goe out so easily,
> or drop off we know not how.[49]

One strange and — for the future — pregnant result
of having made the realm of spirit a mystery unde-
cipherable to man seems to be here revealing itself
almost immediately: New Englanders had practically
surrendered the attempt to make positive assertions concerning the real workings of predestination, they had
decided that election was an impenetrable "secret with
God"; then, paradoxically, they began to prefigure the
operations of the decree in a more lively and human
fashion than when their imaginations had been weighed
down by their original respect for authentic evidences.
Once the realm of spirit and the eternal decrees of God
were decided to be unintelligible to the flesh, they became susceptible of description in terms of human emotions. The perennial anthropomorphic tendency of the
race reasserted itself in the statement that God's attitude toward the baptismal covenant would "surely" be
influenced by men's standards of justice. To proclaim
the divine mind incomprehensible might become in
reality the first step for projecting humanity into it.
Samuel Willard, an earnest exponent of the synod's
doctrine, would shortly be expressing the orthodox
opinion of New England when he wrote:

[49] Shepard, *The Church-Membership of Children,* 15.

We conceive of Gods decrees in a rational way, or according to the manner of men in their purposing and decreeing, in which we design one thing for another; hence first one thing and then another . . . because else we could entertain no conceptions at all about this glorious mystery, but must be wholly ignorant of it.[50]

But in 1662 these were yet undeveloped implications. For the moment the immediate effect was the supplying of a program by which the churches could treat the children as something better than passive onlookers. The children were only formal members, but members of any sort could be incited to good works. Should they by any chance happen to be regenerate without even knowing it, their good deeds would be acceptable to God. In any event they could be disciplined by church censure and excommunication, though they never on earth achieved the ability to warrant "full" membership. As members of a body politic they were subject to its legislation.

Baptism leaves the baptized . . . in a state of subjection to the authoritative teaching of Christs Ministers, and to the observation of all his commandments . . . and therefore in a state of subjection unto Discipline . . . otherwise Irreligion and Apostacy would inevitably break into Churches, and no Church-way left by Christ to prevent or heal the same; which would also bring many Church-members under that dreadful judgement of being let alone in their wickedness.[51]

As a purely ecclesiastical matter, baptism was "in the Nature of a Covenant . . . a Mutual Obligation between two Parties upon terms;" to the baptized, therefore, it ought to be "as a strong bond upon them, carefully to keep it;" it would "be a Witness against them, if they

[50] Willard, *Complete Body of Divinity*, 255.
[51] *Propositions Concerning the Subject of Baptism*, 10.

violate it."[52] Since there had been shown to be "no certain, but onely a probable connexion between federal Holyness . . . and Salvation," persons could be required to become federally holy without implying that they were required to undertake their own conversion. The baptized had promised to do their best on the ecclesiastical plane; they could always be reminded what a compact they had entered into,

86

> . . . and by what promise of gratitude they have likewise obliged themselves unto obedience to God. . . . And they are seriously to be exhorted . . . that they abide in that Covenant of peace, and endeavour to fulfill that obligation, by mortifying sin, and setting upon newness of life, and that they do this freely, and sincerely.[53]

The response which the baptized were expected to make to these exhortations was institutionalized by the synod in a ceremony called "owning the baptismal covenant." This rite comes the nearest to being an innovation of anything the synod proposed, and it was what earned for the whole doctrine the sobriquet of "halfway;" yet the establishment of this ritual was simply a gesture necessary to the thinking which had reached the point we have described. The children were members of the church, they had accepted a covenant by becoming baptized, and were to live up to their pledge. When they came of age and desired to have their own infants baptized, the churches would need some overt sign that they had done and would continue to do their duty. They could not make a full profession of faith, for they still lacked "ability," but they could acknowl-

[52] Willard, *Complete Body of Divinity*, 848, 855.

[53] Quotation from Chemnitus, printed in Shepard, *Church-Membership of Children*, A1, *verso*.

edge their ecclesiastical obligations. They could pledge obedience, make a formal agreement with the church, which at the same time was understood to imply no profession of any Christian experience.[54] They could make "an orderly and Church profession of our Faith ... in an Ecclesiasticall way," if not in a spiritual way.[55] The objectives of the visible church would be obtained if the baptized fulfilled their contract, voluntarily pledged a continuation of their endeavors, and put themselves under discipline. As for the objectives of the invisible church — well, by owning the covenant the children offered evidence of a sort, they demonstrated they had enough freedom of will to undertake at least ecclesiastical responsibilities, and that was something more than impotent passivity. Who could say what this might really mean?

87

If Faith be taken for the grace of Faith in the heart, why may they not be said to have Faith in this sense also, seeing it is required of them, that besides their understanding the Doctrine of Faith, and their professing their Assent thereto, that they must also not be Scandalous in Life, but solemnly own the Covenant. . . . And does not this imply some beginning of Faith? Can persons have all these Qualifications, and yet for this be utterly destitute of the grace of Faith? . . . And in as much as men have neither Faith, nor any thing that good is by Nature, therefore they that have it may be said to be converted to it.[56]

The church could confidently risk working with this material. It could not only require the children to own this covenant in order to have their offspring baptized,

[54] Leonard Bacon, "Historical Discourse," in Contributions to the Ecclesiastical History of Connecticut (New Haven, 1861), 21.

[55] A Disputation Concerning Church-Members, 15.

[56] Richard Mather, quoted in Increase Mather, First Principles, 14.

it could even take the initiative: "It is the duty of the Church to call upon them for the performance there-of."[57] The apologists had traveled a difficult dialectical road, and it is to be suspected some of them made a wry face when they had to swallow such stuff as the analogy between baptism and circumcision; but they emerged with their objective gained and their scruples laid at rest. The theology of New England remained as deterministic as it had been, the structure of the ecclesiastical system was not disturbed; yet the churches possessed a clear-cut program for keeping youth within bounds. They had grounds upon which they could meet the problem and do something about it.

The success of the majority on the score of practical effectiveness overwhelmed the dissenters. On the whole the minority argued the matter with a finer logic and certainly with a greater concern for the sincerities. They riddled the apologists' picture of a state of grace that could not become evident, they recognized the ridiculousness of setting out to separate the sheep from the goats and then including a number of goats because, although they did not look like it, they might possibly be sheep. "The Children in question," said President Chauncy, "are in a state of Neutrality for the present;" that was the best that could be said of them, but all such in the final analysis "Christ accounts to be against him."[58] The dissenters clearly saw through the parallel between circumcision and baptism: "the similitude runs not upon four feet."[59] They perceived that "owning

[57] *A Disputation Concerning Church-Members*, 20.
[58] Chauncy, *Anti-Synodalia*, 34.
[59] *Ibid.*, 14.

the covenant" was an affair of the head and not of the heart — that devils, if necessary, could go through with it. To cause unregenerate persons to profess subjection was, as they saw it, to embody a contradiction in terms; "it is but an obligation to an impossibility; neither can there be obedience without faith."[60] Unless the churches preserved healthy faith against contagion by lopping off unhealthy tissue, the dissenters predicted a future of decay. They forecast that the churches would become pervaded with pharisaism.

89

> It is apparent unto all what a corrupt masse of Unbelievers shall by this change throng into the fellowship of Gods People, and the children of strangers, uncircumcised in heart, shall be brought into Gods Sanctuary to pollute it.[61]

But all these excellent arguments were not powerful enough to compensate for the crucial weakness in the dissenters' position: by ruling out the oncoming host of baptized but unregenerate children as *felones de se* they would have reduced the churches to a wraith. They argued that if persons were admitted without due regard for spiritual fitness "the application of Church-Censures to them, will be disregarded and slighted by them,"[62] but they could suggest no method for dealing with such persons. And yet they, too, confessed that if children were not put under watch and government, the regime would not survive. To the apologists this was enough; "the whole Cause was given up in that Proposition."[63] So the ultimate moral would seem to be that though our seventeenth-century forbears would do

---

[60] Chauncy, *Anti-Synodalia*, 31.
[61] *Ibid.*, 10.
[62] Davenport, *Another Essay*, 34.
[63] Allin, *Animadversions*, 34.

nothing without proofs from Holy Writ, yet as between one array of proofs and another, they could find it convenient to choose that which was the more compatible with their mundane interests.

The truth of this observation is aptly illustrated by the history of Increase Mather. To him the rigorous position of the dissenters had at first seemed more attractive, and he had entered the lists against his father, writing the preface for old John Davenport's *Another Essay*. But soon after, largely through the ministrations of Jonathan Mitchel, he came to realize that though the dissenting position might be theologically right, it was ecclesiastically all wrong. Whereupon he came over to the other side with such a vehemence that he soon out-apologized the apologists. He pushed to extremes every argument he had formerly opposed. He refused to acknowledge that the question could be anything but an ecclesiastical affair. "That Faith which giveth right to Baptism . . . *as to us* is not invisible faith. But the visibility of faith is that which we must proceed upon."[64] Accepting this doctrine wholly, Mather quoted Mitchel to inform his former allies that they had been headed up an ecclesiastical blind-alley. "In the way your self and some others go, the bigger half of the people in this Country will in a little Time be unbaptized."[65] When he had been in the opposition, he had implied that the New England experiment had better fail utterly than survive by transforming its character; thereafter, he seems to have decided that the idealistic position was too quixotic, that the cause of

[64] Increase Mather, *A Discourse Concerning the Subject of Baptisme* (Cambridge, 1675), 9.

[65] Mitchel, in Increase Mather, *First Principles*, Appendix, 5.

religion was bound up with the continuation of the New England regime in any circumstances. It would be, he now agreed, "subversive to Religion," it would be "absurd," that a people "of a more reformed temper then ordinarily the world hath known . . . should so soon be the body of them unbaptized, as if they were not a Christian, but an Heathen People."[66] As soon as the standard of the synod was taken up by this practical and dynamic man, the intricacies of theological rationalization became a bit superfluous. Once Increase Mather had made up his mind, he brushed aside all the debate, *pro.* and *con*, in which his elders had indulged; and, with the instincts of a statesman rather than a theologian, placed his greatest emphasis upon an out-and-out emotional appeal, an argument decidedly *ad hominem*:

91

> There are many godly Souls in *New-England*, that the great motive which prevailed with them to come into this wilderness, was that so they might leave their Children under the Government of Christ in his Church. . . . Have we for our poor Childrens sake in special, left a dear and pleasant Land, and ventured our Lives upon the great waters, and encountered with the difficulties and miseries of a wilderness, and doth it at last come to this, that they have no more Advantages as to any *Church care* about them, then the *Indians* and *Infidels* amongst whom we live? O this is sad![67]

Sad indeed, and the synod of 1662, with its provision of a half-way arrangement for baptized but unregenerate church-members, preserved Massachusetts and Connecticut from such a fate. But it preserved "church care" for "our poor Children" at the cost of interpreting it to mean care for only their ecclesiastical well-

[66] *First Principles*, Appendix, 5.
[67] Increase Mather, *A Discourse Concerning the Subject of Baptisme*, 30-31.

being. Yet I can not altogether sympathize with the church historians who have unanimously condemned the synod for having guided Congregationalism into compromise and legalism. The leaders of the day faced their task manfully and intelligently, they brought to bear upon it all the learning and insight of their generation. The fault, if it can be called a fault, lay not in themselves but in their stars. They were committed by their inheritance and their characters to the well-nigh hopeless task of bolstering up a system founded on the courageous but ill-considered conviction that the wayward, subjective mysteries of regeneration could be institutionalized in an ecclesiastical system. All over Christendom the intricate, top-heavy structures of Reformation theology were sagging; the age was turning away from them to more comfortable, if less logical, views; it was groping toward the greater simplicity and utility which were to characterize the eighteenth century. The divines were unwittingly caught between a dying age and one striving to be born, and the halfway covenant controversy is simply the New England counterpart to what was taking place in other guises throughout the western world. It is conceivable that had there existed in Boston at the time some great religious and philosophical mind, some Jonathan Edwards, let us say, enough in advance of his day to proclaim that the emotional life should not be strangled in the coils of an ecclesiastical system, such a mind might have profited by the experience of the preceding decade, remodeled the system and infused it with a revivified faith. But no Edwards appeared. Instead, a man paced forth from the ranks of the dissenters to become, as much as any, the leader of New England orthodoxy for at least the next thirty years, and he was a statesman and a politician before he was a theologian or a priest. He embodied the decision already reached by the majority of the clergy when he assumed leadership in the name of the doctrines of externality, of visibility, of formalism. It was only when the churches had gone the limit in these directions that either Edwards or the rationalists could abandon the preoccupation with polity and get back to the first principles of religion itself.

93

JONATHAN EDWARDS' SOCIOLOGY
OF THE GREAT AWAKENING

PERRY MILLER

JONATHAN Edwards believed that in the Great Awakening
of 1740 he was witnessing—that he had actually recalled
to life—the same piety that had inspired the founders of New
England. He was a close student of Thomas Hooker and Thomas Shepard, the preëminently "evangelical" writers of the first
generation, whom he cited repeatedly, whereas he showed
little interest in the more scholastic John Cotton. George
Whitefield made no criticism of the opponents of the revival
more stinging than that they and the Harvard faculty neglected Hooker and Shepard out of their preference for Tillotson. When the opponents rallied their forces and went over to
the offensive, in 1744-1745, they scored most heavily by denying that the Awakening, with its "enthusiasm" and "bodily
effects," resembled the sober, controlled spirituality of the
founders, which even in its most ravishing moments had always
held firm to the vision of an ordered, disciplined society.

Edwards and Charles Chauncy were the chief spokesmen for
the two wings into which the New England Way divided during the fateful 1740's. It is striking testimony to the immensity
of the silent revolution wrought in the New England mind between 1640 and 1740 that they conducted their great debate
with practically no reference to any theory of society or any
function of the state. The issue on which they joined was wholly one of psychology; in both *Seasonable Thoughts* and the *Religious Affections*, the individual exists in a social vacuum.
In Chauncy's case we know from his famous election sermon
and from other utterances that he did have an articulated philosophy of politics, essentially that of the Whig tradition which
was soon to become the doctrine of the American Revolution.
Yet he confronted Edwards and the revivalists solely on the
question of whether the revival was generated by the Spirit of
God or the emotions of man. True, he was concerned about

some consequences that had social implications, such as the divisions and separations in the churches or the "censoriousness" of the new lights, and his code of manners was shocked by the revivalist's uncouth antics, but he discussed these things as the effects of an inflamed subjectivity rather than as errors against an objective order. The remedy he proposed was not, as the first Puritans would have held, an appeal to the civil authority, but a therapeutic treatment of sick personalities.

In the seventeenth century the issues of personal conversion could not have been so separated from the external system. The founders sought, in their ecclesiastical and political structure, to institutionalize phases of the inner life. The forms of the church and the procedures of the state, the very lay-out of the town fields, were arranged to accommodate the processes of the spirit. Theologians, Hooker and Shepard no less than Cotton and Norton, always came from their psychological analyses, through the stages of preparation, justification, exaltation, and sanctification, to a social program which for them was inherent in the stuff of divine grace. The results were such social institutions as the Congregational discipline, the restricted membership, the church covenant, the social covenant, the limited franchise, and the sumptuary legislation—all the practices, in short, which embodied the doctrine of Winthrop's speech on liberty.

95

Although Chauncy argued the psychological issue of the Awakening apart from his social theory, we know that he did have one. In Edwards, social theory seems conspicuous by its absence. For him the only problem that concerned mankind seemed to be the "distinguishing marks" of a work of grace. Even the ecclesiastical issue on which he split with his church in Northampton, his effort to reinstate the profession of faith as a prerequisite to membership, he no longer conceived in the terms of Hooker's *Survey*, as a feature of the archetypal platform of polity, but only as a way of testifying to a private, inward experience. Edwards' attitude toward society, it has been generally concluded, was detachment or downright indiffer-

ence. He appears to have had no more sense or even understanding of the social environment than he exhibited in such
a passage as this:

We ought wholly to subordinate all our other business, and all
temporal enjoyments to this affair of travelling to heaven. Journey-
ing towards heaven, ought to be our only work and business, so that
all we have and do, should be in order to that. When we have
worldly enjoyments, we should be ready to part with them, whenever they are in the way of our going toward heaven. . . . When we
use our worldly enjoyments and possessions, it should be with such
a view and in such a manner as to further us in our way heavenward.
Thus we should eat, and drink, and clothe ourselves. And thus
should we improve the conversation and enjoyment of friends.[1]

He did at times stoop to castigate the business practices of New
England, condemning him who gets his neighbor's money "by
falsely commending what he hath to sell, above what he knows
to be the true quality of it," or those who use "some advantages
which they have over their neighbor, in their dealings with
him, to constrain him to yield to their gaining unreasonably of
him,"[2] but these admonitions sound like the moralizings of a
soul so wrapped in a vision of the otherworld that he could not
comprehend a canny people who made fortunes out of wooden
nutmegs. In the contrast between Edwards and Franklin,
which becomes every decade a more trenchant symbol of the
American dilemma, as against the man who in his youth resolved to keep his shop so that, as soon as possible, his shop
would keep him, Edwards comes off a poor second because of
his supposed blindness to economic realities.

For this reason Edwards is often called, and rightly, a
"Pietist." The whole evangelical movement of the eighteenth
century, whether Quietism in France, Pietism in Germany,
Methodism in England, or Revivalism in America, exhibits
this curious indifference, even studied aversion, to social concerns. Consequently it generally played into the hands of re-

[1] *Works* (New York, 1844), IV, 577.
[2] *Works*, IV, 604.

action. The moral appears to be that in the history of ideas omissions are as significant as inclusions. When men cease, as by a tacit conspiracy, to talk about something which has long been central in their tradition, the historian must begin to ask certain questions which are the most difficult of all questions, because answers can be found only amid silences or at best in indirect revelations that require for their interpretation the most exacting tact.

We may be certain of one thing, that Jonathan Edwards did not grow up in a social vacuum. He was a product of the Connecticut Valley, which by the eighteenth century was a peculiar culture, anthropologically speaking. Even his most abstruse metaphysics must be understood, in part at least, as something of which only a mind nurtured in the Valley and at Yale was capable, which a Boston childhood and a Harvard education would have inhibited. And then, for over two decades he was the foremost citizen in one of the most dynamic towns in Massachusetts. His career in Northampton was every bit as intense a social experience as that of Aristides in Athens, and the conflict which resulted in his defeat and ostracism was no holy improvement of the conversation of friends along the journey to heaven. Consequently I have been interested to discover among his papers indications that even while he had his eyes fixed on heaven, his feet were on the earth. The danger is that I may read into him things that I imagine must be there, but the three sermons from which these extracts are made seem to me, granting that Edwards was not writing a *Middletown* or a *Winesburg, Ohio,* to be full of acute observations about the Northampton community, and also to show, in the organization of the remarks, a sense of a pattern of human relations.

If they be taken as documentation for social history, they must, of course, be read primarily for what they reveal indirectly. Only when Edwards turned on the town to berate it for its sins, or made specific application of a theological doctrine to the sorts and conditions of men, did he have occasion to show, even by implication, that he possessed a system of ideas about

97

the commonwealth. More than any of his published works, the three sermons here quoted are revealing. They are long and repetitious, so that I am offering only the crucial sections, and to score the point more clearly I have taken the liberty, perhaps unwarranted, of giving them headings in the. language of today. Especially in the third selection, the structure of the discourse corresponds to Edwards' conception of the structure of society.

The first and third of the sermons exist only in the transcriptions now at Andover-Newton Theological Seminary; the second survives among the Edwards Manuscripts in Yale University Library. Permission has been graciously given by both institutions for the publication.

I.

COLONIAL CULTURE

[During one of the revivals, whether that of 1734-1735 or of 1740-1741 is not clear, Edwards delivered a sermon on *Matthew* 25. 24-28; the doctrine, derived from the parable of the talents, is an exhortation to all to improve the occasion. In the applications, Edwards enumerates the signs of the times "that seem to look with a very threatening aspect upon us"; as he points out how English manners and modes are aped in America, he is led into a brief disquisition upon the cultural dependence of the colonies on the mother country.]

1. The prodigious prevalency of infidelity and heresy in this nation at this day. It is surprising and almost amazing to hear what a pass the nation is got to at the present day, and what a swift progress Deism and heresies have lately made in the nation. Those that deny all revealed religion, that deny Scripture to be the word of God, that deny all the Gospel, deny that Christ was any thing but a mean cheat, and deny all that is said about the way of salvation by him, they are vastly multiplied of late years, yea, even so as to threaten to swallow up the nation, and to root the very name of Christianity out of it;

they are become the fashionable sort of men. Never was there any nation that any history gives an account of that lived in the enjoyment of the [advantages] of the Gospel as our nation does, and that did so great part of it cast off the name of Christians, and despise and ridicule the very name.

It is a very common thing now for Christ to be openly blasphemed, and mocked, and scoffed, and laughed at in the streets in our nation, and this alteration is chiefly come upon the nation of a sudden, in a few years. And besides, [among] the remaining part, that have not openly cast off all pretence to any Christianity, Arianism, and Socinianism has prodigiously prevailed. And among those that still remain, the far greater part are Arminians. And vice and immorality has as much prevailed as those errors. Men are not ashamed to be open in their vices, and vice and sensuality even in gross acts is pleaded and stood up by great men and learned men, as well as others, and the corruption seems to have infected all sorts, all [conditions] and degrees of persons.

99

Now I say this has a very threatening aspect upon this land. We are [a] country dependent on them, we are such to their government, we have our books, and our learning from thence, and are upon many accounts exceeding liable to be corrupted by them. This country is but a member of the body of which they are the head, and when the head is so sick, the members, it is to be feared, will not long be in health. We are a branch of which they are the stock, and shall naturally derive, be assimilated, and likened to them.

2. Another thing that more immediately threatens us is the very great prevalency of corrupt opinions here among ourselves in this land. The corruption of the nation not only naturally tends to corrupt us that are dependent on them, but has already that effect, and that exceedingly, and that more than the generality of persons are aware. . . . It seems as though the anger of God were so much [aroused] against this land as it does at this day, however little [we are] sensible of it. Our case is the more doleful for our insensibility of it; that is one of the great-

est judgments, a spirit of deep sleep, and a perfect insensibility of their own misery. It is the nature of spiritual judgments that they stupify, and so are not lamented.

There was never so great an appearance of God's withdrawing His presence from the land. God seems to be taking away our light from us, and turning [it] into darkness, taking away the truth, and sending us delusions instead of it. It is surprizing what a swift [change] has made in this land in the course of a few years, a general despotism seems to be threatened.

Errours have for some time crept as it were underground, but now begin to appear open and barefaced. We have been asleep, we have made pretences of repentance and reformation from year to year, but we have but mocked God; we have not at all reformed, but rather grown worse and worse, and so we have gone on for a long time, and God's spirit will not always strive with men, He will not bear with our declensions always, and He seems to be coming forth in a most awful manner, though it may be it is not much taken notice of.[3]

II.

THE COLONIAL TOWN

[By May, 1737, the wave of the first revival in Northampton was receding, and Edwards faced the problem of an emotional let-down in which certain of the less agreeable but abiding qualities of the New England community, momentarily transcended during the fervor, were appearing with renewed vigor. Edwards preached this sermon on 2 *Samuel* 20.19, from which he derived the doctrine, "Persons in times of strife do greatly provoke God, especially a visible people of God, a people who are favoured with distinguishing privileges." Northampton from the beginning had been a tumultuous pioneer outpost, and it had taken the iron will of Edwards' grandfather, "Pope"

[3] The blanks in the transcription undoubtedly indicate imperfections in the original manuscript; that Edwards had not only the cultural but political dependence of the colony in view is indicated by the fragments of the next paragraph in which he argues that "If God should bring persecution on us, and our charter taken away from us," this would cause great noise and be much lamented, but that it would be less lamentable and doleful than the loss of our souls.

Solomon Stoddard, to keep the populace in order. Edwards was losing his hold upon them, and the lashing he gave them in this sermon helps to explain why he was capable of cowing them for several years longer and even of driving them again up the heights of the spirit in 1740, and also why, after the ebb of that excitement, the issue between him and the town could be resolved only by the town's abject submission or by his expulsion. In the course of berating them, Edwards manages to give, to the modern reader, an exhaustive if somewhat terrifying picture of a rural community in eighteenth-century New England. The extracts convey the fury of his passion; the whole sermon, which continues in the same vein for what must have taken two hours to deliver, suggests its extent, as also the extent of the incurable malady he chastizes. Whatever light these denunciations may shed upon the mores of Northampton, their right to a place in American literature cannot be denied. We have been rather too poor in authentic utterances of God's angry men.]

101

I appeal to the experience of all who are now my hearers, whether at such times as when their spirits have been heated with a spirit of opposition and a desire of disappointing others, or the like, their souls have not been destitute; and instead of flourishing in grace and comfort, and the light of God's countenance, all has not gone down and languished. . . .

It is most notorious that there has been much of a spirit of strife in this town of late. Contention and party spirit is the old iniquity of this town. It has been a remarkably contentious town. I suppose for these thirty years people have not known how to manage scarcely any public business without dividing into parties. Though it be a great disgrace to a town, yet it is too notorious to be denied of this town. When the Spirit of God was of late so remarkably poured out, this spirit seemed to cease. But as God has withdrawn, this hateful spirit has again put forth his head; and of late, time after time, that old party spirit has appeared again, and particularly this spring. Some persons may be ready to think, that I make too much of things, and think worse of them than they are. However, though I do not suppose that the town in general have actually been engaged in a malicious, envious, or hateful spirit; yet so much is notorious, that some hot-spirited, contentious persons have been. I do not determine who they are. God knows who they are. They have industriously stirred up strife, so that great numbers have been foolishly heated in their spirit, which they have in many ways manifested; and so that there has been a manifest, open division into two parties, with much heat in many of them, one against another. And these things are undeniable. He who would hide them, must hide the wind. Many men have shown an edge and grudge one towards another, and have had their spirit enraged to disappoint one another. And however they may have restrained themselves in open and public town meetings, yet there has been much backbiting. Persons have given themselves a liberty in slandering each other; much time has been spent in it. Yea, and much ridicule has been employed against those of opposite parties. Possibly in time of it, they might think of no harm. But if two parties do so, one against another, that is contention, if any thing be contention, and a very bad degree of it. And persons have given themselves a great liberty in judging and surmising things one against another only from conjecturing things which they did not certainly know. And thus some have been fierce and violent, and shown spirit in their representations of each other. And there has been much secret contrivance and caballing one against another. These things are too evident to be denied. . . .

God has of late put great honour upon this town. He has most remarkably honoured us by the great things which He has done for us. The great work, which He has lately wrought in this part of the country, began here and was principally seated here. This has given us honour abroad in other places, in the eyes of good men, who have heard what God has wrought. For they have entertained very honourable thoughts of this town on account of the peculiar favours which God has shown us. They have been ready to say, What people are so great, who have God so near them? We have had great honour put upon us on that account by wise, pious, and learned men beyond the seas, who have taken great notice of what has been done. And they account us a happy people, and look upon us as a sort of chosen people above all others, and have very high thoughts of the blessings which God has bestowed upon us, as appears by their letters. But doubtless they are expecting to hear of a walk and conversation very distinguishing from other people, as well they may. But the divisions which we have had in all probability will turn greatly to their disappointment and our dishonour. And so much the more abundantly, for the very high and great professions we have made. Those things which are wrong, which could not be noticed in other people, will be noticed in us with surprise. There have been many who have reproached us for the professions we have made, and have called us a parcel of hypocrites and enthusiasts, and a whimsical, deluded people. But good men have been for us, and opposed those who reproached us, and have pleaded that it must be a work of God, and that we are certainly a wise and truly Christian people. . . . But when such things as these are heard of us, it will weaken their hands, and will cover them with shame and confusion, and in a great measure stop their mouths. It will put an argument into the mouths of our adversaries, which our friends will not know how to answer. . . .

103

While their mouths have been filled with praises, our mouths have been filled with backbitings. No town in America is so much like a city set on a hill, to which God has in so great a degree entrusted the honour of religion. He has committed to us the honour of His great name, by putting honour upon us and by blessings bestowed upon us. It has also been very much noticed by pious and learned persons in other parts of the land. And they have been greatly affected by it. They have spoken of it, how wonderfully God makes Northampton a place of wonders. But when they hear, after all that has been done for us, that we have strifes and contentions, what a wound will this be to the honour of this kind of religion, which we profess? . . .

It is probable that some may say that I have been instigated by others thus to preach at this time. I have observed to my surprise that I have scarcely ever, since I have been in the town, in my preaching reproved any public disorders or iniquities, but I have heard that this has been surmised; though it has at every time been without ground. Such surmises seem to proceed from the same jealous and evil surmising spirit which prevails among us. . . .

104

As to those persons that are of contentious spirits and that have had a hand in our former and late contentions, it is to be feared they will be contentious still. There is no prospect from any thing which appears in men, or any circumstances at present, but there will be still from time to time contentions in the town, notwithstanding all which may be said to persuade to the contrary. When men's outward interests or their pride is touched, I have no reason to think from any thing which at present appears but they will contend, and create strife and division in the town. I confess that I have had great hopes in times past, that the people would be persuaded, and that the consideration of the great things which God has done for the town would have such an impression upon them, as would be an effectual restraint; but soon saw that it had not so great an effect as I expected. Then I flattered myself, that when the town knew what great notice was taken of these things abroad, that that would have effect. And when I set home the consideration of those things, I must confess I thought we were not so bad, but that it would have a lasting effect upon the town in general. But still I found myself disappointed. People still appeared apt on every little difference of opinion to contend. Then came this surprising providence, and so wonderful a reformation, which was so exceedingly remarkable and affecting, and so many families were immediately concerned in that providence, that I thought, surely providence had put such an advantage into my hands, that which I said in public as applying that Providence, and warning them from it, would be effectual; not imagining so soon after it contention would return among us. I do not know but I have trusted too much in men, and put too much confidence in the goodness and piety of the town. I have seen all external means and all strength of men fail, as to preventing this. It is very likely there may be some men in this town, that there has scarcely been a public strife in the town this twenty years, or ever since they came to act in public affairs, but they have been on edge and their mouths open in evil speaking, in fierce and clamorous talk and backbitings and evil surmising; though it may be they condemn quarrelling, and cry out against it in others. As to such persons, I have now no hope but that they will quarrel still, unless God takes their hearts in hand and makes them much better men than ever yet they have been....

105

I have no reason to expect that the town will be in circumstances where it will have more powerful obligations and external inducements to avoid contention than it has now, and of late has had, especially this spring, since so wonderful a providence, and such warnings on that occasion given from the pulpit. I am unable to bring more powerful arguments to persuade them than I have already done, to peace and to avoid contention. I have sought out acceptable words, and those which I thought most likely to have that effect. I have used my utmost skill, and I have seen it all ineffectual. There are many men in the world who, when they are opposed and crossed, will contend, let what will become of the honour of religion; yea, though heaven itself should go to wreck. Nero, the Roman Emperor, wished that all the people of Rome had one neck, that he might cut it off at one blow. So there is a sort of men who, if the honour of religion had, as it were, but one neck, and their contending would cut it off at one blow, yet they would contend, rather than not get their wills.

III.

THE STRUCTURE OF SOCIETY

[During the Awakening of 1740 Edwards preached a sermon on *Matthew* 22. 9-10; from the parable of gathering in the guests from the highways, Edwards reached the doctrine, "The saving mercy of God in Christ extends to all sorts of persons," and logically divided the application into addresses to the several sorts in his audience. He was endeavoring to urge each group into the experience of grace, yet in so distinguishing them, he inevitably generalized their characteristics. The result is that this section of the sermon becomes in effect a sociological analysis of Northampton. It ought to modify the notion that Edwards was oblivious of social realities; if anything, it shows a highly developed sense of the groups and types that make up the community. Edwards did not need to speculate about the nature of society, as he did about the will or original sin, because rather than having none, he had all too clear a conception of how it was constituted. Implicit in his conception is the assumption that the social pattern is status, in which all persons are types determined by their position in the community, exactly as in their inward life they are determined by their moral ability. Edwards, having studied Locke, was evidently content to surrender the political covenant to nature and reason, so that it no longer was a department of theology, but he still conceived of grace as operating within a social setting, just as it operated in particular persons through a psychological mechanism. This assumption, we may safely conclude, is a major premise, in all his thinking.]

Classification by age-groups:

1. *Children.*

You are all of you naturally the children of God's wrath. If you are not converted, God is angry with you every day; if you should die in the condition you are now in, you would surely go to hell. . . . Many children die, and all those of them that

are not converted, go down to the pit of hell into everlasting
burnings, to dwell there forever and ever. So that you must be
converted and get an interest in Christ. You cannot bear hell,
there is none of you can bear it; you could not bear to lie in
such a fire as is made every day upon the hearth for one quarter
of an hour; how then will you bear to lie in the dreadfull fire of
hell forever and ever? For those that are cast into that fire
never shall be delivered out of it. . . .

You do not know but that you may die now, while you are
children; it may be, there is but a very little while before the
time will come when you must die; for ought we know the
threatening distemper may in a little time come into the town,
and carry off multitudes of children, as it has lately done in
many other towns. There are some towns where the greater part
of the families in the whole town have died with that distemper,
so that though the town before was full of children, yet in a
little time, but few have been left. In some families where there
has been a considerable number of children, all the children
have died with that distemper. We have had but little of that
distemper in this town hitherto, but we do not know that our
turn to have it is at hand; for ought we know, in a little time
it may come and make as dreadful work here, as it has in many
other towns. . . .

107

If you are converted, you need not be afraid to die, you need
not be afraid of the threatening distemper. Let it come when
it will, it will not do you any hurt: no distemper, no death,
can do them any hurt who have an interest in Christ. . . .
How will you bear hereafter to see other children shining in
robes of glory, standing at the right hand of Christ, and rejoicing in the love of Christ, while you stand a poor, wicked,
miserable hateful creature, among devils, going to be cast into
hell along with them forever and ever?

2. The youth.

The devil has had your tender age; your childhood has been
spent in his drudgery, and you have been learning of him all

the days of your life, ever since you were infants and have been capable of learning anything. . . . You were foolish and perverse like wild asses' colts, and you acted like a child of the devil. . . .

Let the time past of your life suffice that you have served your lusts, and served Satan. Now give up all the remaining part of your life to an earnest striving in religion. Do not think now for a little while to be serious and religious, and by and by to turn again to frolicking and vain mirth. If there be no hurt in frolicking, and it has no tendency to any hurt, and if it is in no respect contrary to the increase of religion in the soul,— then frolick now. Why do you leave it off? Why should not that which is harmless, and which in no way hinders the good of the soul, be as much in fashion in a time of awakening and religious concern as at any other time? The best way is to be consistent with yourself. . . . Therefore do not avoid this practice now under a notion of its hindering your soul's good, and by and by change your tone and say there is no hurt in it, and plead that there is time for all things. . . . If it be a thing of no ill tendency, then there is no sin in it at all. Go on frolicking in a time of awakening, keep on in this way, and see if ever you come to good in this way.' Be consistent with yourself one way or the other; either always practice it or else always avoid it. Do not sometimes avoid it, as if you yourself were convicted in your own conscience that it was a thing of ill tendency, and then at the same time plead that there is no manner of hurt in it.

3. *The middle-aged.*

Thus your best is gone; you have it not now to offer to God, if you had never so great a mind to it. It has all been spent and wasted in the service of the devil. . . . The hardness of persons' hearts grows as fast as their age; as they grow older and older in a Christian state, their condition grows more and more dreadful. . . .

Instead of your seasons becoming more convenient, have not you found on the contrary that they have grown more and more inconvenient? Do not you find now that you are much more in-

cumbered with the business and concerns of the world than
when you were young, your heart more and more charged with
those things, and less and less at liberty, and less and less disposed to mind the affairs of your soul? . . . Is it not now high
time to set about the work, without any more putting off? When
you have been pursuing a shadow thirty or forty years together
without overtaking it, is it not then high time to give over? . . .

What times have you seen and passed through, what seasons
of remarkable mercy of the Spirit of God! You have seen several
such seasons, wherein many have been brought in; there has
been a harvest of souls for Christ, but you have always been as
the barren heath in the wilderness. Others have had their eyes
opened, but you have remained blind. Others have flourished
like the palm tree, but you have remained like a dead dry tree
among them. In the late, remarkable, and wonderful time of
awakening, six years ago, when Christ so gloriously appeared
and rode forth in the chariot of salvation, and so many had a
new song put into their mouths, you had no part or lot in the
matter. And since that, God has wrought great things in other
countries, in England and in Germany, in Scotland and Wales,
and in Pennsylvania and New York and the Jerseys, in Carolina
and Georgia; but still your soul has remained dead. And now
lately God has revived His work here again, and has revived
the work of conversion amongst us, and some have been
brought home to Christ; but still you are left behind. And
will you still delay, will you let slip this opportunity also, as
you have all others that you have had? Consider how swiftly
you are going down the hill of life; the state of your soul does
not remain at a stand, five or six years make a great alteration.
As for instance, you are now under far greater disadvantage,
since this last time of the outpouring of the Spirit of God, your
heart is very much hardened, and your guilt vastly increased
since that time, and your advantage far less than it was then.
But yet Christ invites you now, and now there is a blessed opportunity for all that are alive; and though the opportunity
you now have is not so great as you have had heretofore, yet

109

it is greater in all probability than you ever will have again.

4. *The aged.*

If there are any here who are come to old age, and yet are in a Christless condition, I would now call on them, though it be at the eleventh hour. . . . You have nothing left but your withered old age to offer to God, a few days in the decay and latter end of your life. . . .

Indeed, to behold one in your circumstances, an old grey headed man or woman going about stooping with age, and yet in a Christless condition, is one of the most awful sights in the world. Your soul is every whit as precious as the souls of young persons, you are under as much necessity of salvation as they, and in some respects under much greater necessity; for if you perish, you will have a vastly more dreadful damnation than those that die in youth, for you have spent all your life in nothing but sin. . . .

You have lived under a former minister, and though he lived long, yet your love to your idols and your unbelief, blindness, and obstinacy in rejecting Christ, have outlived him, and live to this day. . . . The whole life of man is given to prepare for eternity, and all is short enough; but you have spent most of it, and are ten times further from a preparation for eternity than when you were a little child. Instead of preparing for heaven, you have all your days been preparing for hell. . . . You have as it were gone through the world, and made thorough proof of the service of sin, and now look back, and consider what fruit you have had of all, what have you got by it?

Classification by sex:

1. *The men.*

Possibly the male sex, by reason of their superior strength and influence, are more exposed to a roughness of spirit, less easily affected and subdued, more ready to stand out against what is affecting and awakening; and so your superior place and your superior power may be a snare to you, and probably are the undoing of the male sex, and are one reason why there commonly are so many more converted of the female sex than of the male. Also the circumstances of the affairs and business of the male sex does in some respects expose them to many more temptations than those of the female. Their business leads them more into the world, to be concerned abroad with more persons and to be concerned more extensively with the affairs and business of the world, when they have more worldly objects in their view to tempt them. They are in some respects more in danger of being much involved in those things that are earthly, and it is more difficult for them to keep unspotted from the world, and you are in some respects more in the way of the snares of the god of this world, and particularly are more in the way of publick contentions and broils, wherein men are wont to divide into parties and set up their wills, and envy one another and hate one another and plot against one another. . . . Doubtless it is the undoing of many men that they were born of that sex: the business in which they by that means have been concerned and the temptation to which they have been exposed have proved their ruin. . . . And of this you may be assured, that the greater your strength is and the larger your sphere of action, the more God requires and expects of you; and if you continue in a way of wickedness, the greater will your guilt be and the more dreadful your condemnation at last. . . .

111

And as the men of this town have long been divided into two parties, I would now earnestly call upon both parties to improve the present season to seek the good of their souls. Let who will be right in those affairs about which you have been so divided and in which your spirits have been so often heated and ruffled, and in the management of which has been so much grudging and backbiting one another; let who will be chiefly in fault. Christ this day invites you both. . . . If you of both parties will hearken to the call and invitation of Christ this day, and will throw by all those contentions with which your minds have been so much taken up, and will apply yourselves with one mind to seek and serve Christ and make your calling and election sure, it is to be hoped that both of you will hereafter meet together in heaven and there dwell forever in everlasting peace and love. There are no parties, no secret jealousies, one of another, no gathering together in distinct companies to judge and backbite others, no plotting and contriving one against another; but there you shall be united in the same interest, and shall be of one mind and of one heart and one soul forever.

2. *The Women.*

Though in the fall of man, the female sex falls under peculiar dishonour in that woman first eat of the forbidden fruit and tempted the man, yet this sex has peculiar honour in the affair of the redemption of the second, . . . and all you, if you are converted, will become mothers of Christ in a more honourable and blessed sense than the virgin Mary was, for it is more blessed to have Christ conceived in the heart than in the womb.

As the male sex has some particular disadvantages, so also has the female. Through their weakness they are in some respects more easily prevailed upon by the temptations of the devil. The devil, knowing this, craftily began with Eve when he attempted to seduce man from his first integrity. You have therefore the more need of watchfulness and care, lest as the serpent beguiled Eve through his subtilety, so he should seduce and ruine you.

Let young women this day harken to the invitation of Christ. If you will do so, this glorious person will be your lover, yea, he will be your glorious bridegroom. You are invited this day to the marriage feast of the king's son, not only as a guest, but as a bride. He is your suitor, he courts you; importunately he stands at your door and knocks, saying, "Open to me, my sister, my spouse, my head is wet with the drops of the night." And let me, in Christ's stead, beseech you to give him your hearts; let him have your love who is fairer than the sons of men and is the most excellent, lovely, and honourable lover; come to him and spend your youth, yea, your whole life, in his love, in communion with him. Yield yourselves to Christ and he will

112

adorn you with excellent ornaments. Your adorning shall not be that outward adorning of the wearing of gold and putting on fine and rich apparel, but it shall be the ornament of a meek and quiet spirit that is in the sight of God of great price.

Let those women that have the care of families this day harken to the call of Christ. Many of you may be ready to think that your disadvantages are peculiar by reason of the care and cumbrance you have in your families, and the many hindrances you have from religious duties. And doubtless you have many temptations and difficulties which may justly make you lament and bewail the loss of past opportunities when you were young. But yet if you have a heart engaged to do the utmost that lies in your power, according to your opportunities and as your circumstances and necessary business of your families will allow, if you make the concern of your soul your great concern and make all temporal affairs give place to it, and attend to the outward concerns of your families in no other way than that to which the duty of your place obliges you, and improve what advantages and opportunities remain to you, to your utmost, and continue so to do, begging of God His help, I say, if you do thus, there is yet hope that you may obtain mercy.

113

Classification by class:

1. *Those of low rank.*

However you may be had in but little esteem, may be despised and slighted and accounted of no great consequence in the world, and have not that respect shewn to you that many of your neighbours have, yet the great king sends forth his messengers to invite you to come. . . . In the high ways we shall meet many that are very low in the world, many poor and despised. Christ sends his ministers to gather up such, and such as being poor vagrants sleep under hedges like the beasts as having no house of their own, and being so despised that none will take them in.

Christ himself, when he was upon earth, confined himself to your condition. He did not appear in the world in the cir-

cumstances of a man of note, but in the state of the poor and
despised. He was of low parentage: his mother was a young
woman of low degree, her husband Joseph was not one of their
men of influence, but an obscure person. . . .

The great God has a greater respect for one saint, though
mean and despised among men, than He has for the greatest
wicked monarch on the earth, and will show a thousand times
greater regard to him in what He will do for him. The saints
are His jewels, but the wicked men, however rich, learned, and
great, are of no account with Him. . . .

114

But if you refuse and will neglect your salvation, then you
will not only be low and despised in this world, but so will you
be forever; you will not only be despised of men, but you will
forever be despised of God also. You will not only continue
to be lightly esteemed as you now are, but you shall be thrust
down into an immensely greater degree of contempt. . . .

1. So you that are weak in understanding and are comparatively ignorant, and are upon that account not much accounted
of, you see that your judgment of things is not much regarded,
what you say in conversation is not so much taken notice of,
your voice is not so much heard as others on publick affairs.
Hearken this day to the call of Christ, and set yourself with all
your might to seek and follow him. If you will give up and do
so, Christ will make no objection of your weakness and your ignorance; you shall be as freely and as readyly accepted as if you
excelled in human learning and wisdom. Christ does as much
invite you as any of the politicians, philosophers, or divines of
the world. Christ is able savingly to enlighten you; he does not
stand in need of great abilities or acquired knowledge in order
to his imparting that knowledge that is saving; he has chosen
the foolish things of the world to confound the wise, and the
weak things of the world to confound the mighty, and the base
things of the world, and things which are despised, hath God
chosen, yea, and things which are not, to bring to nought things
that are. . . . The least beam of the light of the knowledge of
the glory of God in the face of Jesus Christ is worth more than

all the human knowledge that is taught in all the most famous colleges and universities in the world. . . .

2. So you that are poor and have a much smaller part of the good things of this life than the greater part of your neighbours and are hard put to it to provide things necessary for yourself or family, and are often reduced to straits and difficulties that your neighbours about you, who have a greater fullness, know nothing of, hearken to the call of Christ this day, and look to him and follow him. . . . If now you are meanly clad and forced to wear that which is coarse and homely, Christ has white raiment to clothe you. . . . If you live upon mean fare and sometimes are pinched with hunger, come to Christ and you shall not have mean fare. . . . And besides, if you mostly seek heavenly riches, this is the surest way for you to be provided for with those temporal good things that you need.

115

And when you have done with the world, when those things fail, you shall be received into everlasting habitations, where you shall hunger no more nor thirst anymore, but the lamb that is in the midst of the throne shall feed you. . . .

But if you refuse to hearken to Christ and will neglect your salvation or seek it in but a poor, indifferent, unsteady manner, then as you are poor here, so you are like to be poor forever; here in this world you have little, and in another world you shall have nothing. How hard will be your lot: you will neither have a portion in this world nor in that which is to come; you will get neither heaven nor earth. While you stay here, you will go without those comforts and enjoyments of life that others have, suffering many hard things; and when you die, then you will be cast out to perish in everlasting famine. . . . You will make but a hard shift to get through the world, and when you have finished your course, then you must go away into everlasting perdition. You are some of the meanest and lowest in this world, and many of the afflictions and hardships, and difficulties of the world fall to your share here; and when you have done with the world, then you must be thrust down infinitely lower, you shall be trodden down as the mire of the streets.

How much better then would it have been for you that you had never been born, than to be born to meet with so much difficulty and trouble in this life, and to have eternal misery in the life to come, and never, never to see any good?

3. So you that are servants and poor negroes. You are of those who are poor in the world, but harken to the call of Christ, and improve the present opportunity earnestly to seek your salvation. . . . Though you are a servant, yet if you will come to Christ, and heartily give up your life to his service, you shall be the Lord's freeman. . . . If you refuse to hearken to Christ, and live in the neglect of your salvation, then you will not only be the servant of men, but the servant of the devil, and will hereafter fall into his hands, and be in his possession forever.

2. *The middle class.*

I would apply myself to those that possess a greater measure of this world's goods, and are in higher circumstances in the world.

If you are more regarded than some of your neighbours and have greater respect shewn you, if your words are looked upon as of greater weight than theirs, yet if you are in a natural state, you are contemptible in God's eyes. . . . If you have more land than some of your neighbours, a larger stock, and more comfortable and plentiful accommodations, yet none of those things can make you any other than a miserable creature if you are not of Christ. . . . If you had the favour of God with your worldly enjoyments, they might well be sweet to you, you might eat your meal with gladness; but instead of that, you eat and drink under the wrath of God, you lie down and rise up under His wrath. When you look upon your buildings, your cattle, your stores that you have laid up, you may consider that brimstone is scattered upon them all.

When you sit down at a full table, yet there is God's bow bent, His arrows ready, the dart pointing at your heart all the while you are satisfying your appetite. You eat and drink, and sleep and walk, and march over this part of hell, in slippery places. The ground you are upon is not solid ground, but is as it were hollow ground, and there is the dreadful pit of hell underneath. The covering is very thin and weak, men are continually dropping through into the pit, and lost irrecoverably; but one in many escapes, and you are in danger every moment.

Men are apt to rely much on their worldly possessions and advantages, and to be much pleased to be themselves so much higher in the world than others, and to be greatly taken with it that they have so much more than they. . . . Men's worldly possessions and worldly honour with which they are so taken very commonly prove their undoing; setting their hearts so much upon them occasions them to neglect God, and so they have their portion in this life, and when they have enjoyed all that comfort that they have to enjoy in those things, they have ruined their soul's salvation, there remains nothing else for them.

117

If you continue in a Christless condition, all that you have in the world will prove only to have fatted you for the slaughter, and ripened you for the wine press. . . . And though now you sit forward in the meeting house, and have a higher seat than your poor, inferiour neighbours, yet hereafter you shall have no place at all in heaven. . . . And not only so, but you shall be set in a lower place in hell than those wicked men who now sit behind you in the meeting house. Therefore now hearken to the calls brought you from God, do not let your worldly possessions be a weight to hinder you.

Therefore do not make excuse, and go away, one to his farm and another to his merchandize; but go and sell all that you have, and buy the pearl of great price. . . . As to the world, you have already a considerable measure of it; but as to the good things of another, if you that are in a Christless condition have nothing of them, you have no part in the good of God's chosen in the inheritance of God's children. How many earthly things soever you have, you have not Christ, and so are aliens from the commonwealth of Israel, and strangers to the covenant of promise, having no hope, and are without God in the world, and therefore are miserably poor, and have nothing of your precious and immortal souls.

Now God is opening His grand treasure among us, His treasure of spiritual blessings; He has been letting open a fountain for the supply of the wants of poor souls. Therefore now improve your time, and put in for a share that you may not continue famishing, and perish in the midst of plenty.

Classification by moral condition:

118

1. Those that have been guilty of immoral and wicked practices, against the light and convictions of conscience.

Are there not some here who have, with considerable deliberation and forethought of the sinfulness of an act, gone abreast against all that conscience could say?

Have not some of you thus been guilty of acts of uncleanness against the convictions of your consciences, has not there been some lascivious vile acts that you have been guilty of by yourself alone, actions not fit to be named, unfruitful works of darkness, or some lewd, immodest, lascivious behavior that you have been guilty of with some other person, contrary to the conviction of your own conscience? And so are there not some that have been guilty of gratifying of other lusts, as a grinding spirit after gain, or a spirit of pride, or a spirit of ill will against the conviction of your consciences?

2. Such sinners as have formerly been awakened and prompted to seek salvation and have been guilty of backsliding.

There are some such here; there are some here who were in a measure awakened in the last time of the pouring out of God's spirit in this place, and sought salvation, who afterwards quenched the convictions of the spirit of God. It is an exceedingly great and dangerous sin of which you have been guilty, and very provoking to God. . . . You have greatly wounded your own soul, so foolish have you been; when you had a precious opportunity in your hands, you would not improve it. If you had gone on earnestly seeking, in all probability you might before this time have been rejoicing with the gladness of God's nation; but by quenching your conviction, you have had great blocks in the way to your salvation. . . . Now it is a time of awakening amongst us, many are stirred up and are much affected; but how few, how very few of them, are those that were come to years of discretion in the last time of the outpouring of the spirit of God here, and were then awakened and lost their convictions. They looked back when flying out of Sodom, and there they stood like pillars of salt, or statues of stone, on the very spot where they were when they looked back; there they are still, they have not stirred out of the spot to this day. Warnings of fire and brimstone from God out of heaven do not move them any more, the flash of the lightnings, and the noise of the thunders in Sodom and Gomorrah do not move them at all. And how little do they seem to be moved by all that they now see of the world of God upon others?

But yet you must be converted: you cannot bear everlasting burnings; you are in absolute infinite necessity of conversion, and therefore you must improve what opportunity you have. It may be you will never be converted; but if ever you are, it is most likely to be in some such season as this, a time of the outpouring of the spirit, a time of gracious visitation. . . . Therefore improve this opportunity, now rouse up yourself to lay hold on God; . . . as you have made your work more difficult, so double your diligence. . . . But only take heed you do not lose this second opportunity, and that you do not quench convictions a second time.

3. Those who have been long seeking conversion, and have never yet obtained [it], that have been for many years uneasy about your being in a natural condition, and have been after a sort seeking to enter in at the strait gate. . . .

You have had the spirit of God long striving for you, God has been nigh to you, and has long been calling, and knocking and waiting; and what a wretched use have you made of such an advantage? . . . And how often have you grieved the spirit of God by your slothfulness, and by your unsteadiness, and by

119

your worldliness, and innumerable corrupt workings of heart
and unsuitable unchristian thoughts, words, and deeds? How
often have you been exhorted to be more in earnest, and how
obstinate have you been in your slothfulness? . . . If you saw
your behavior since you have been in the wilderness in the true
light, you would not think that God dealt hardly with you,
that He has not yet comforted you; you would not think it a
strange thing that others who have till of late been secure sinners are converted, and you left behind still. . . . It is time to
alter your course, and to leave off dreaming, and to wake thoroughly out of sleep, and apply yourself in real earnest to your
great work; and not only to seek as you have done, but to strive
to enter in at the strait gate, and to be violent for the kingdom
of heaven.

120

4. All such as have lately been awakened and are now under
awakenings.

To all such as do thus, . . . I now apply myself and would call
upon them to improve the present opportunity. . . . It may be,
if you do not harken to those calls and strivings, they will
prove the last knocks and calls that ever you will have of that
nature; and if it should be so, then all external calls will forever be in vain. . . . Commonly the time when a person is under
the first convictions that ever he has is by far the best opportunity that ever he has to obtain salvation in his whole life;
and if such an opportunity be diligently and thoroughly improved without backsliding, there is an exceedingly great
probability of success.

5. Those living in a state of sinfulness and security.

How brutishly selfish and stupid are you who have had so
much to awaken you, and have seen such awakening providence of late, instances of sudden and surprising death, and
have seen, and do now see, such works of an invisible power in
the hearts of others, and hear so much of what is done in other
parts of the world, and know that you are in a natural condition, and yet are secure in your sins? . . . If you think the wrath
of God is not so terrible that persons need to be so much con-

cerned to escape it, then go on and see how you will conflict with the wrath of an almighty God; see if your hand can be stronger, or your heart endure, in the day when God rises up and girds Himself with His omnipotence to glorify His justice and magnify His mighty power upon you; try and see what it is to fall into the hands of almighty God; see whether you can bear the devouring fire or swell with everlasting burnings.

Conclusion to the whole society:

So let all hearken to the call of Christ, by his word, and in his providence, and by his spirit, this day: young men and maids, old men, middle aged, and little children, both male and female, both black and white, high and low, rich and poor together; great sinners, sinners against great light, against convictions of conscience, backsliders, old sinners and old seekers, self-righteous murmurers, and quarrellers with God; those that are under convictions, and those that are senseless and secure, moral and vicious, good and bad, poor, maimed, halt, and blind, prodigals eating husks with swine, vagabonds and beggars in the highways and hedges, persons of every condition, and all parties, and every denomination whatsoever.

121

FROM COERCION TO PERSUASION: ANOTHER LOOK AT THE RISE OF RELIGIOUS LIBERTY AND THE EMERGENCE OF DENOMINATIONALISM

Sidney E. Mead, *University of Chicago*

I

So far as religious affairs are concerned, the colonial period of our history begins with the planting of the first permanent English colony in 1607, guided by the intention to perpetuate in the new land the religious patterns to which the mother country had grown accustomed. Chief of these for our purposes was uniformity enforced by the civil power. The period culminates just 180 years later with the complete rejection of this central intention in the provisions for national religious freedom in the Constitution (1787) and First Amendment (1791).

Regarding these provisions Philip Schaff said, "Congress was shut up to this course by the previous history of the American colonies and the actual condition of things at the time of the formation of the national government."[1] In brief, it was recognized at the time that if there was to be a *United* States of America, there had to be religious freedom on the national scale. The following interpretation of developments during the colonial period is therefore guided by two questions: 1), what was this "actual condition of things?" and 2), how had it come to be?

II

All the original ventures in settlement in the new world—including the English—were guided by the intention to establish for whatever reasons outposts of European empires where the general social, religious, and political patterns of the homelands would be perpetuated. By the time that English colonization got underway early in the 17th century, the Reformation movement had shattered the once tangible unity of European Christendom in one church. Inevitably the spiritual re-formation of the church had found affinities with the rising national consciousnesses, and had found protective power in the new states to oppose the physical power controlled by Rome. Thus the one re-formation of the church found diverse expressions in the new nations—Lutheranism in the realms of the German princes and in the Scandinavian countries. Anglicanism in England, Reformed in Geneva and Scotland. These are the so-called "right-wing" churches.

With differences unimportant at this point, these groups agreed with Roman Catholics on the necessity for religious uniformity in doctrine and practice within a civil state, and enforced by the civil power. This view of more than ten centuries' standing in western Christendom they accepted as axiomatic.

Meanwhile in the social crevices created by universal upheaval certain "sects" or "left-wing" groups were emerging, as blades of grass soon thrust themselves up through the cracks once a cement sidewalk is broken. Throughout Europe both Catholics and Protestants universally tried to suppress these groups by force as heretics and schismatics who constituted a threat to the whole structure of Christianity and civilization as then conceived.

All the first settlements on that part of the continent that was to become English were made under the religious aegis of right-wing groups, with the exception of Plymouth where a handful of separatists "made a small, bustling noise in an empty land."[2] But Anglicans who were making a bigger noise on the James, as were Dutch Reformed on the Hudson, Swedes on the Delaware, and Puritan Congregationalists on the Charles, all assumed that the pattern of religious uniformity would of necessity be transplanted and perpetuated in the colonies. And all took positive steps to insure this—even the Pilgrims. For as Plymouth colony prospered it made support of the church compulsory, demanded that voters be certified as "orthodox in the fundamentals of religion," and passed laws against Quakers and other heretics.[3]

123

The first Charter of Virginia of 1606 provided that "the true word and service of God and Christian faith be preached, planted, and used. . . . according to the doctrine, rights, and religion now professed and established within our realm of England," and from the beginning laws provided for the maintenance of the church and clergy and for conformity.

Orthodox ministers of the Dutch church came early to New Netherlands, and the new charter of freedoms and exemptions of 1640 stated that

> no other religion shall be publicly admitted in New Netherlands except the Reformed, as it is at present preached and practiced by public authority in the United Netherlands; and for this purpose the Company shall provide and maintain good and suitable preachers, schoolmasters, and comforters of the sick.[4]

When John Prinz was sent as Governor to the struggling Swedish colony in 1643 he was specifically instructed to

> labor and watch that he render in all things to Almighty God the true worship which is his due . . . . and to take good measures that the divine service is performed according to the true confession of Augsburg, the Council of Upsala, and the ceremonies of the Swedish church. . . .

After a brief stay he was happy to report that

> Divine service is performed here in the good old Swedish tongue, our priest clothes in the vestments of the Mass on high festivals, solemn

prayer-days, Sundays, and Apostles' days, precisely as in old Sweden,
and differing in every respect from that of the sects around us.[5]

That the New England Puritan's holy experiment in the Bible
Commonwealth required uniformity hardly needs documentation.
"There is no Rule given by God for any State to give an Affirmative
Toleration to any false Religion, or Opinion whatsoever; they must
connive in some Cases, but may not concede in any," was Nathaniel
Ward's dictum. And although the forthright clarity of this "simple
cobler" was not typical of the usually more discreet apologists for
the New England way, who perhaps did not welcome him as their
self-appointed spokesman, nevertheless his sentiment was one of the
stones in the foundation of their "due forme of Government both
ciuell & ecclesiastical."

124

With these beginnings, it is notable that in contrast to the success in this respect of Roman Catholics in New France and the
Spanish settlements in South and Central America, the intention
to perpetuate uniformity in the several Protestant colonies that were
gathered under the broad wings and "salutary neglect" of mother
England during the 17th and 18th centuries, was everywhere frustrated, and the tradition of thirteen centuries' standing given up
in the relatively brief time of 180 years. By around the middle of the
18th century "toleration" was universally, however reluctantly, accepted in all the colonies, and within fifty years complete religious
freedom was declared to be the policy of the new nation.

The importance and significance of this change can hardly be
overestimated. Professor W. E. Garrison has rightly called it one
of "the two most profound revolutions which have occurred in the
entire history of the church"—"on the administrative side"—and
so it was.

Detailed historical explanation of this momentous change is
not a primary purpose of this article. There have been many studies
of the rise of religious liberty in America. They range all the way
from the sentimental to the cynical, with a large number of very
substantial works by careful scholars in between. There would seem
to be fairly wide consensus on Professor Schaff's view that "Congress was shut up to this course." In explaining why this was so
two factors are to be weighed and balanced. The first is that of
the positive thrust for such freedom represented for example by the
Baptists and given voice by individual leaders in most of the other
groups. The second factor is that represented by Perry Miller's thesis
that "by and large Protestants did not [willingly] contribute to religious liberty, they stumbled into it, they were compelled into it, they
accepted it at last because they had to, or because they saw its strategic value."[7]

It is my impression that Protestant writers have commonly stressed the first factor. And if in this article I stress the second factor, it is primarily for the purpose of bringing into the discussion what I hope will be a salutary and corrective emphasis. This emphasis necessarily somewhat discounts the historical importance among Protestants of a positive, self-conscious and articulated aspiration for religious freedom for all, such as gained a place in their popular folklore through such gems as Felicia Heman's poem on the landing of the Pilgrims. It does not deny the existence of the important seminal ideas among "left-wingers" and other outcasts such as the Roman Catholics who established Maryland, or even among the respectable Puritans and Presbyterians. Nor does it underestimate the long-term symbolic value of the halting steps taken along this road by the Baltimores, and the surer steps of Roger Williams, William Coddington and that motley collection of the banished in Providence, Portsmouth, and New Port, or those of William Penn and his Quakers in the Jerseys and Pennsylvania. But it should also be kept in mind that the freedom extended to all in early Maryland was connived in only so long as was necessary. Rhode Island was the scandal of respectable New England precisely because of its freedom, and was commonly referred to by the Bay dignitaries as the sewer and loathsome receptacle of the land, that was not cleansed because they could not. And by the time that Penn launched his holy experiment in Pennsylvania, coerced uniformity had already broken down in the neighboring colonies, and England herself, having experimented extensively with toleration between 1648 and 1660, and unable to forget it with Restoration, was trembling on the verge of toleration.

125

Accepting the view that the original intention of the dominant and powerful groups was to perpetuate the pattern of religious uniformity, the thesis here developed is that the intention was frustrated primarily by the unusual problems posed by the vast space with which the Planters had to deal in coming to the new land, by the complex web of self interest in which they were enmeshed, and the practical necessity which these imposed to "connive in some cases," and finally by effective pressures from the motherland. This thesis, which is merely a summary of common knowledge, need not be extensively documented here, but only briefly illustrated.

The web of self-interest was complex indeed, the strongest strands being Protestant, national and personal. At a time when in England Protestant was synonymous with patriot, and the first feeble English settlements were encircled by the strong arms of French and Spanish Catholicism, whose fingers touched on the Mississippi, it is small wonder that all the early writings and charters stressed the planting of *Protestant* outposts of empire, and that a sentiment came to prevail that almost any kind of Protestantism was preferable to Catholicism. Perhaps this is why Dutch and English policy differed radically from French, in that the Protestant countries after a few random gestures such as the provision in the second Virginia Charter of 1609 that "none be permitted to pass in any Voyage .... to be made into said Country but such as first shall have taken the Oath of Supremacy," let their dissenters go. Civil and ecclesiastical pressures ranging from slight disabilities to active persecution thus added an external push from the rear to the lure of land and of economic and social betterment operating in the colonists' minds. And this, coupled in many of them with a religious fervor that was always in danger of crossing the boundary into self-righteousness, pushed them out with the intention to become permanent settlers, to possess the land, and perchance to be an example for all mankind—as witness the Bay Puritans.

126

It is notable also that from the beginning the one outstanding Roman Catholic proprietor had to tolerate a majority of Protestants in his colony, and that eventually the heirs of the first Baltimore probably retained their lands and prerogatives only by becoming Protestants.

National self-interest merged of course with Protestant and hatched a desire for strong and profitable colonies that tended to overcome squeamishness about the religious complexion of the settlers. Thus when Peter Stuyvesant, the new Director General, came to New Netherlands in 1647, he immediately took steps to put the religious house in order by limiting the sale of liquor on Sundays, instituting preaching twice rather than the former once a day, and compelling attendance thereon. When Lutherans, Jews and Quakers arrived he tried to suppress them, finally shipping one notorious Quaker back to Holland. The Directors' reaction to this move is eloquent testimony to the mind that prevailed among them. They wrote in April 1663 that

> .... although it is our cordial desire that similar and other sectarians might not be found there, yet as the contrary seems to be the fact, we doubt very much if vigorous proceedings against them ought not to be discontinued, except you intend to check and destroy your population; which, however, in the youth of your existence ought rather to be encouraged by all possible means: Wherefore, it is our opinion, that some connivance would be useful; that the consciences of men, at least, ought ever to remain free and unshackled. Let everyone be unmolested, as long as he is modest; as long as his conduct in a political sense is irreproachable; as long as he does not disturb others, or oppose the government. This maxim of moderation has always been the guide of the magistrates of this city, and the consequence has been that, from every land, people have flocked to this asylum. Tread then in their steps, and, we doubt not, you will be blessed.[8]

So on another occasion Stuyvesant argued that "to give liberty to the Jews will be very detrimental . . . . because the Christians there will not be able at the same time to do business." And besides, "giving them liberty, we cannot refuse the Lutherans and Papists."[9]

At the time he was backed by the doughty Reformed Minister, Megapolensis, who thought the situation was already bad enough since there were "Papists, Mennonites and Lutherans amongst the Dutch, also many Puritans or Independents, and various other servants of Baal among the English under this government," all of whom "conceal themselves under the name of Christians."[10] Nevertheless the desire of the Directors not to "check and destroy" the population overruled the desire of both magistrate and clergy for semblance of religious uniformity and Jews had to be granted permission to reside and traffic in New Netherlands only "provided they shall not become a charge upon the deaconry or the Company."[11]

127

Finally, from the beginning the ruling geniuses of the new age of expansion managed to mingle strong personal self-interest with the more abstract Protestant and national by making trading companies and proprietaryships the instruments of planting. Dutch, Swedish, and English companies made possible the plantings in Virginia, Plymouth, New Netherlands, Massachusetts Bay, and Delaware, while proprietors instrumented the founding of Maryland, New Hampshire, New Jersey, the Carolinas, Pennsylvania, and Georgia. And it might be argued that William Coddington and his commercially minded cohorts were the real backbone of Rhode Island, while obviously Theophilus Eaton the merchant was hand in hand with John Davenport the minister in the founding of the ultra-theocratic New Haven.

By 1685, says Greene, "more territory along the seaboard than New England and Virginia combined" was under proprietary control, and there "governmental policies in relation to religion were radically different from those prevailing either in New England or Virginia." From the viewpoint of the proprietors, he continues, "it was obviously not good business to set up religious tests to exclude otherwise desirable immigrants." Hence, "the proprietors tried to attract settlers by promising, if not full religious equality, at least greater tolerance than was allowed elsewhere."[12]

But if self-interest dictated in more or less subtle and devious ways a kind of connivance with religious diversity that helped to spell out toleration in the colonies, the efforts even of the most authoritarian groups to enforce uniformity on principle were dissipated in the vast spaces of the new land.

The Anglicans tried it in Virginia, even resorting in 1611-12 to the savage "Lavves Diuine, Morall and Martiall &c." which threatened the death penalty for speaking "impiously or maliciously. against the. . . . Trinitie," or "against the knowne Articles of the Christian faith," or for saying or doing anything which might "tend to the derision, or despight of Gods Holy Word," and threatened loss of the "dayes allowance," whipping, "a bodkin thrust through his tongue," six months in the "Gallies," or other punishments "according to the martiall law in that case provided" for failing, among other things, in respect for the clergy, for failing to attend "diuine Service" twice daily, for breaking the "Sabboth by any gaming, publique or private, or refusing religious instruction."[13]

128   No one supposes that such laws were enforced during the horrendous years between 1607 and 1624 when thirteen of the fourteen thousand people sent over died from exposure, disease, starvation, and the weapons of the savages. By that time the remaining settlers were scattered on plantations along the rivers and even honest clergymen despaired of conducting the routine affairs of the English Church in parishes that might be 100 miles in length. In 1661 an acute observer argued in *Virginia's Cure* . . . . that the chief difficulty was due to the "scattered Planting" for which there was "no other Remedy . . . . but by reducing her Planters into towns." He proposed, therefore, to raise money in England to send workers to Virginia to build towns in every county, and then to make the planters bring their families and servants in to these centers on week ends and there submit to regular catechetical instruction and church attendance.[14] Obviously this was the counsel of despairing, albeit ardent, churchmen who were beginning to realize that the snug parish life of settled England could not be duplicated in the wilderness.

The Puritan theocrats on the Charles early grasped one important aspect of the meaning of the great space available for all. Nathaniel Ward, presuming to speak for Massachusetts Bay, proclaimed that "all Familists, Antinomians, Anabaptists, and other Enthusiasts, shall have free liberty to keep away from us, and such as will come to be gone as fast as they can, the sooner the better."[15] Back of this of course was the thought that there was plenty of room "to be gone" in, and John Cotton but took the next obvious step when in partial justification for forcing some to leave he blandly stated that

> The Jurisdiction (whence a man is banished) is but small, and the Countrey round about it, large and fruitful: where a man may make his choice of variety of more pleasant, and profitable seats, than he leaveth behinde him. In which respect, Banishment in this countrey, is not counted so much a confinement, as an enlargement.[16]

Cotton probably never understood just how much of an "enlargement" it might be, and how it would help to undermine the Puritan citadel itself. For while the Puritans were intent on protecting their own religious absolutism by inducing Antinomians, Baptists, Quakers and other dissenters "to be gone as fast as they can," they overlooked the implications of the fact that they could neither keep them from settling in neighboring Rhode Island where "Justice did at greatest offenders wink,"[17] nor prevent every wind from the south carrying the contagion of their ideas back into the Puritan stronghold. They could not foresee that the same inscrutable Providence that gave Puritans the opportunity to build their kind of Bible commonwealth on Massachusetts soil, would offer dissenters the opportunity to build whatever kind of commonwealth they wished on Rhode Island soil. But when they saw that happen in spite of all their efforts to bring Providence and the Islanders under their godly control, they came to see that they had to connive in it.

Meanwhile, the zeal of the dissenters, far from being dissipated by banishment, was truly "enlarged" by the knowledge thus forced upon them that even the long arms of civil and ecclesiastical authority could not encompass the vast spaces of the new land. Although four stubborn Quakers, who refused to accept the "free liberty to keep away," were effectively and permanently suppressed in Boston with the hangman's noose, the majority of dissenters in America soon learned to escape the deadly vertical pressures of entrenched authority by the simple expedient of moving horizontally in the free space. In rather short order, belief in the effectiveness of suppression by force, and hence the will to use it to maintain uniformity, was undermined by the obvious futility of attempts to land solid and decisive blows on the subversive little men and women who were seldom there when the blows fell. Samuel Gorton, after being forced to attend church in the Bay, wrote that the sermonic fare seemed adapted to the digestive capacities of the ostrich. But in spite of such supposed capacities, the residents seem to have been unable to stomach the savage proceedings against the Quakers, and finally even the magistrates and ministers had to connive in their existence.[18]

In the process the dissenters waxed strong and saucy—a development that could not go unnoticed by those within the traditional folds, where many citizens began willy-nilly to nourish within themselves a desire to emulate this exhibition of a new kind of freedom made possible in the wilderness. They began to people all neighboring colonies.

There was of course another aspect of space—the distance from the motherland, which, relative to existing means of movement and communication, was immense. The Puritans began with the idea that

....God hath provided this place to be a refuge for many whome he meanes to save out of the generall callamity, and seeinge the Church hath noe place to flie into but the wildernesse, what better worke can there be, then to goe and provide tabernacles and foode for her against she comes thither.[19]

129

They early sensed the protection inherent in the great distance, as is evidenced by their ingenious idea of taking the Charter and the Company bodily to New England. Thereafter they perfected a system of sanctified maneuvering within the time granted by distance that frustrated all attempts of English courts and crown to control them for about three generations.

The same factor militated against any effective control and discipline of the transplanted Church of England in the southern colonies. From the beginning oversight fell somewhat accidentally to the Bishops of London, who during the last quarter of the 17th century sought to instrument their supervision through representatives called commissaries. But failing to secure resident bishops, effective supervision proved impossible, and the church languished under too many second rate and even fraudulent clergymen and fell increasingly under the control of parochial vestries made up of local citizens.

Turmoil in England at times reinforced distance in frustrating effective ecclesiastical control of the colonies. In 1638, after a series of reports and proclamations beginning in 1632, Archbishop Laud made arrangements to send a bishop to New England with sufficient forces if necessary to enforce conformity and obedience. But the outbreak of troubles in Scotland sidetracked this interesting project, and "there are no records of any official connection between the Anglican Episcopate and the Colonies during the period 1638-1663."[20]

Meanwhile through revolution, Protectorate and Restoration, England was moving toward its rendezvous with the kind of toleration made manifest in the famous Act of 1689. Already in 1652 Dr. John Clarke had published in London his *Ill Newes from Newe England or a Narrative of New England's Persecution,* in protest against the fining and whipping of three Baptists in Massachusetts under the aegis of a law passed in 1644. His telling thesis was that in matters of religious tolerance, "while Old England is becoming new, New England is become Old."[21] From about that time the mother country did interfere increasingly and effectively to curb intolerance and persecution in the colonies. Perhaps this should be seen as an aspect of national self-interest.

Thus the King "having got a book written by George Bishop containing a relation of the cruel persecution [of Quakers] in New England,"[22] and having learned from Edward Burrough of the execution of William Leddra in Boston and "the danger that others were in of going the same way," there being "a vein of innocent blood opened in his dominions, which if it were not stopped would overrun all," declared " 'But I will stop it' "—and he did. "A mandamus was forthwith granted" and carried to New England by Samuel Shattock, a resident of Salem who had been banished on pain of death. Shattock

130

and his fellow Quakers made the most of the occasion, which resulted
in a suspension of the laws against the Quakers as such in November,
1661.

Meanwhile, John Clarke's *Ill Newes from New England*....
had resulted in a protest to the Governor of Massachusetts from ten
Congregational ministers in London, who, seeking for more toleration in England, were embarrassed by this show of intolerance on
the part of their New England brethren. Sir Richard Saltonstall
added his protest in a letter to Cotton and Wilson of Boston's First
Church, and their reply that it was better to have "hypocrites than
profane persons" in their churches and domain sounded outmoded.[23]

In 1663 the Crown, in giving its consent to Rhode Island's "livelie
experiment" with "full libertie in religious concernments" in the new
Charter,[24] gave official sanction to the scandal of Massachusetts Bay
and forestalled all future attempts on the part of the Bay Puritans
to impose their kind of theocratic order on the neighboring chaos.

But probably the most spectacular case of royal interference
that worked for the broadening of toleration in the colonies was the
revocation of the Massachusetts Bay Charter in 1684 and the coming
of Sir Edmund Andros as the Royal Governor in 1686. For Andros
brought an Anglican chaplain with him, and after trying persuasion
on the taciturn Puritan ministers he finally took over one of their
meeting houses with force and had the English services conducted
therein while King's Chapel was being built. The new charter of 1691,
in which the New Englanders themselves had a part through the person and work of Increase Mather, wrote "the end" to the Puritan
chapter on the preservation of uniformity in the new land.

131

III

By around 1720, then, the original intention to perpetuate religious uniformity had been almost universally frustrated in the
colonies by the strange rope of circumstances woven from various
kinds of self interest and the problems growing out of the great
space confronted. Effective interference from the motherland
in the interests of broader toleration served only to hasten the process.
When the two Mathers, father and son, took part in the ordination
of a Baptist minister in Boston in 1718, they thereby indicated that
some churchmen sensed that a new day was dawning. But it is probably not to be wondered at that most of them adhered to the inherited
standards and conceptions of the church with religious fervor sometimes bordering on desperation. It took the prolonged upheavals associated with the great revivals to break the hold of the old patterns,
give the new an opportunity to grow, and inextricably to scramble
both with others emerging out of the immediate situation.

Once it was seen that uniformity was impracticable, two possible paths lay open before the churches: toleration, with a favored or established church and dissenting sects—the path actually taken in England—or freedom, with complete equality of all religious groups before the civil law. In this situation it is important to note that transplanted offshoots of Europe's state churches were clearly dominant in all but two of the colonies, and indeed remained so until after the Revolution. Further, nine of the colonies actually maintained establishments—Congregationalism in New England, Anglicanism in the south and, nominally, in part of New York—while none of the other dominant churches as yet rejected the idea on principle, and indeed, as witness Presbyterians in the south and Anglicans in New England, were willing to acknowledge the prerogatives of establishments by assuming the role of dissenters. On the eve of the great revivals, then, the prevailing sentiment in these churches is probably best described as tolerationist based on necessary connivance.

132

Meanwhile in Rhode Island and the stronger middle colonies religious freedom prevailed—in New York practically, ambiguously, and largely because of necessity, in Rhode Island and Pennsylvania actually and more clearly on principle and experience. Further, as has been intimated, the factors that had confounded the uniformitarian intentions of the churches originally established in the new land, had also encouraged the numerical growth, geographical expansion and bumptious self-confidence of the dissenting and the free groups in all the colonies. However, these were as yet largely unconscious of their real strength for facing the future, which lay in their necessary espousal of voluntaryism as the basis for a church, and their consequent experience with dependence upon persuasion alone for recruiting members and maintaining their institutions in competition with other groups. An entry in Henry M. Muhlenberg's *Journal*, November 28, 1742, suggests how rapidly a minister, transplanted from a European state church might size up the realities of the new situation in America and come to terms with them. Sent over to bring some order into the scrambled Lutheran affairs, he immediately ran into a squabble in one of the churches, and recorded:

> The deacons and elders are unable to do anything about it, for in religious and church matters, each has the right to do what he pleases. The government has nothing to do with it and will not concern itself with such matters. Everything depends on the vote of the majority. A preacher must fight his way through with the sword of the Spirit alone and depend upon faith in the living God and His promises, if he wants to be a preacher and proclaim the truth [in America].[25]

Such espousal of voluntaryism by these American offspring of Europe's right-wing state churches meant, of course, that they accepted one aspect that of necessity had been common to the left-wing sectarian groups of Europe from their beginnings. But this was a triumph of a left-wing influence in America, as is sometimes held, only in a "guilt by association" sense.

Much more important for the future than left-wing influence was the movement called Pietism, which had originated in the European right-wing state churches during the last quarter of the seventeenth century under leaders who sought to provide more palatable spiritual food for the hungry souls of the common folk who were then languishing on Protestant scholasticism and formalism. Conceived and projected by its leaders as a movement *within* churches aimed at the revitalization of the personal religious life of the members and a restoration of Christian unity, Pietism did tend to develop its own patterns of doctrine and polity. While assuming the validity and continuance of traditional standards and practices, Pietists tended to make personal religious experience more important than assent to correctly formulated belief and the observance of ecclesiastical forms —which was to intimate that the essence of a church was the voluntary association of individuals who had had the experience. Stress on the intuitive religion of the heart "strangely warmed" by "faith in Christ," as John Wesley was later to put it, was of course a possible seed bed for the dreaded religious "enthusiasm." However, in Europe the movement was always somewhat constrained by the sheer existence and accepted forms of the powerful state churches.

But, sprouting indigenously in their American counterparts, or transplanted thereto by such leaders as Freylinghuysen, Muhlenberg, Zinzendorf, and the great Whitefield, where such constraining ecclesiastical forms were already weakened, Pietism, cross-fertilized by other movements, grew rankly and blossomed in the spectacular phenomena associated with the Great Awakenings that swept the colonies from the 1720s to the Revolution, transforming the religious complexion of the land.

Jonathan Edwards' experience in Northampton indicates how short was the step from preaching even the most traditional doctrines out of a heart "strangely warmed," to the outbreak of a surprising revival in the church that soon led to "strange enthusiastic delusions" which threatened to disrupt established parish customs.[26] And to a modern student the emotional upheavals created by George Whitefield's preaching seem to be out of proportion even to that noted evangelist's reputed powers that so impressed Benjamin Franklin.

Back of this was the peculiar religious situation that had been developing in the colonies for a century. Concurrent with the frustration of the ideal of uniformity had come the obvious decline of vital religion and morality which so concerned religious leaders throughout the colonies during the twilight years of the seventeenth century, and turned so many of their sermons and official pronounce-

133

ments into lamentations for the departed glory of the founders. Apparently the churches were not reaching the masses of the people effectively or with power, and they confronted a greater proportion of unchurched in the population than existed in any other country in Christendom.

Closely related of course was the breakdown of the traditional pattern of church membership by birth into a commonwealth and baptism into a church that was coextensive with it, together with the passing of support encouraged by the persuasive inducement of coercion—while as yet no new, effective and acceptable method for recruiting and holding members had emerged.

134 Over all was the general cultural attrition associated with living on the frontier of western civilization, which consumed so much of the vital energy of the prosperous in practical affairs—usually related to immediate profits—and of the poor in the even more engrossing problem of survival. The end of the seventeenth century has been called with reason the lowest ebb tide of the cultural amenities in America. Here was fertile soil for the growth of the kind of fearful and superstitious religiosity later so vividly pictured by Crevecoeur in the twelfth of his *Letters from an American Farmer*. Hence, to change the figure, at the very time when the tried old dams of civil and ecclesiastical law and custom were crumbling, there was building up behind them in the population a religious yearning waiting to be released in floods of religious "enthusiasm." And the revivals came, doing just that.

Most of the early revivalists were pietistically inclined ministers who more or less unwittingly stumbled upon this technique that so perfectly met the immediate needs of the churches as plausibly to be looked upon as a direct answer to their prayers and a sign of the divine approbation of their doctrines.[27] They were obviously successful in carrying the claims of the gospel to the masses of indifferent people, in recruiting members from among the large body of the unchurched, and in filling the pews with convinced and committed Christians. While thus checking the ominous drift toward religious decline, the revivals demonstrated the unimagined effectiveness of persuasion alone to churches recently shorn, or rapidly being shorn, of coercive power. This helped to relieve their present confusion, and raised their languishing hopes for the future.

In the context of our general interpretation it is important to note two things. The first is that the revivals took place largely within the entrenched and dominant churches of right-wing tradition. The second is that everywhere, whether among Dutch Reformed and Presbyterians in the middle colonies, Congregationalists in New England or Anglicans in the south, they resulted in a head-on clash between the pietistic revivalists and the powerful defenders of the traditional authoritarian Protestant patterns of doctrine and polity. For the latter correctly sensed that the revivalists, in keeping with their pietistic sentiments, stressed religious experience and results—namely conversions—more than correctness of belief, adherence to creedal statements, and proper observance of inherited forms, and hence that their work in the churches tended to wash out all traditional standards.

When the revivals broke out, traditionalists were largely in control in all these churches. Their attitude is fairly reflected in the Old Side Presbyterian condemnation of the revivalists for

> preaching the terrors of the law in such a manner and dialect as has no precedent in the Word of God....and so industriously working on the passions and affections of weak minds, as to cause them to cry out in a hideous manner, and fall down in convulsion-like fits, to the marring of the profiting both of themselves and others, who are so taken up in seeing and hearing these odd symptoms, that they cannot attend to or hear what the preacher says; and then, after all, boasting of these things as the work of God, which we are persuaded do proceed from an inferior or worse cause.[28]

135

And as for the greatest of the revivalists, the Rev. John Thompson wrote that he was "almost fully persuaded" that George Whitefield was either "a downright Deceiver, or else under a dreadful Delusion," and his publications "nothing but mere confused inconsistent religious jargon, contrived to amuse and delude the simple."[29]

Feeling a strong sense of responsibility for order and decency in the churches, and still being powerful enough to do so, these men in every area used every civil and ecclesiastical weapon they could against the revivalists and their ways.

The revivalists defended themselves primarily on the basis of their sense of the importance of personal religious experience, which they thought the traditionalists neglected. Gilbert Tennent struck their key note in his sermon of March 8, 1740 which he called "The Danger of an Unconverted Ministry." Such ministers, he asserted, are "Pharisee-teachers, having no experience of a special work of the Holy Ghost, upon their own souls. They are merely "carnal," and have

> discover'd themselves too plainly to be so, in the Course of their lives; some by Ignorance of the Things of God, and Errors about them, bantering and ridiculing of them; some by vicious Practices, some both Ways, all by a furious Opposition to the Work of God in the Land; and what need have we of further Witnesses?

Of course, he added, "God, as an absolute Sovereign, may use what Means he pleases to accomplish his Work by," but "we only assert this, that Success by unconverted Ministers Preaching is very improbable, and very seldom happens, so far as we can gather."[30]

Here was the revivalists' most telling argument—they were obviously more successful than their traditionalist brethren and, for example, the experience of the divided Presbyterian churches between 1745 and 1758 amounted to a demonstration. At the time of the separation the Old Side party numbered 25 ministers, at its close only 22. Meanwhile the New Side revivalist party which began with 22 ministers, had 72 in 1758—and churches and members were proportionately in keeping with these figures. The success of the re-vivalists could be made very tangible, and nicely measured merely by counting ministers, churches and converts. Thereafter the emphasis upon it was to play havoc with all traditionally rooted standards of doctrine and polity in the American churches. One hundred and fifty years later Dwight L. Moody was to declare that it makes no difference how you got a man to God, just so you got him there—and there is a direct line of descent from the colonial revivalists to their nine-teenth century heir.

136

At this point it is worthwhile to note specifically that the battle was not one between tolerant "left wing" sectarian revivalists riding the wave of the democratic future, and anachronistic "right-wing" churchmen stubbornly defending the past and their own present pre-rogatives. It is important to stress this, because even Professor W. W. Sweet, dean of the historians of Christianity in America, gave the prestige of his name to the thesis that "it was the triumph of left-wing Protestantism in eighteenth century colonial America which underlay the final achievement of the separation of church and state."[31] This thesis has difficulties, chief of which is the plain fact that the left-wing, whether defined institutionally or ideologically, never "tri-umphed" during the colonial period in America.[32]

To be sure the pietistic revivalists everywhere belabored what Tennent had called "The Danger of an Unconverted Ministry," and Jonathan Edwards was dismissed from his Northampton church in 1750 primarily for insisting in that stronghold of right-wing sentiment locally known as "Stoddardeanism," that a conversion experience was the prime requisite for full communion in a Christian church—some-thing he had perhaps learned in the revivals. Further, under the wide-spread harassment and persecution emanating from the traditionalists, the revivalists naturally developed a kind of anti-clericalism and anti-ecclesiasticism that helped to blur the lines between them and those of more authentic left-wing tradition. And from the time of Münster every departure from accepted order in the Protestant churches was apt to conjure up visions of an imminent upsurge of familism, anti-nomianism, anabaptism, and enthusiasm—terms that the traditionalists used loosely in the heat of controversy, further compounding the con-fusion between their opponents and the left-wing.

But actually all the outstanding revivalists belonged to churches of right-wing tradition, and it might cogently be argued that what

growth accrued to left-wing groups as a result of the revivals came
largely through their ability to reap where others had sown. Thus,
for example, the Baptists in New England apparently took little part
in the Awakenings there, looking upon them as a movement within the
churches of their Congregational oppressors.[33] But when conflict led
to a separatist movement, and Separate Congregationalists were treated even more harshly than Baptists by their erstwhile brethren who
remained in the established churches, many separatists became Baptists.

Once this point is clear, we may note that during the clash between traditionalists and revivalists, the latter were thrown willy-nilly
—but somewhat incidentally—on the side of greater toleration and
freedom. It was not that they developed clearly formulated theories
about religious freedom—in fact the striking thing about the whole   137
pietistic movement, as A. N. Whitehead pointed out, was that it "was
singularly devoid of new ideas," never appealed to any "great intellectual construction explanatory of its modes of understanding," and
its sweep in the churches marks the point at which "the clergy of the
Western races began to waver in their appeal to constructive reason."[34]
What they appealed to was religious experience and feeling, and as
John Wesley said of his Methodists, they spread "scriptural religion
throughout the land, among people of every denomination; leaving
every one to hold his own opinions, and to follow his own mode of
worship."[35] Methodists, he said,

> do not impose in order to their admission, any opinions whatever.
> Let them hold particular or general redemption, absolute or conditional
> decrees; let them be churchmen or dissenters, Presbyterians or Inde-
> pendents, it is no obstacle. Let them choose one mode of baptism or
> another, it is no bar to their admission. The Presbyterian may be a
> Presbyterian still; the Independent and the Anabaptist use his own wor-
> ship still. So may the Quaker and none will contend with him about it.
> They think and let think. One condition and only one is required — a
> real desire to save the soul. Where this is it is enough; they desire no
> more; they lay stress upon nothing else; they only ask, "Is thy heart
> herein as my heart? If it be, give me thy hand."[36]

Although seldom so clearly expressed, this is the kind of outlook
that the revivals tended to sponsor in the churches. Obviously men of
such sentiments could be expected to have little interest in the continuance of uniformity or of establishments. But by the same token,
neither can they be expected to have had, or to have developed, any
well rounded theories about anything, religious freedom included. Hence
such freedom as the revivalists came to represent during the controversies was not generated by a theoretical consideration of its ultimate
desirability on principle, but by a practical desire for freedom from the
immediate restraints and oppressions imposed by the dominant churchmen. What they fought for at the time was the freedom to publish
their own point of view in their own way, unmolested by traditional

civil and ecclesiastical customs and laws—which to their mind served primarily to prevent getting the show on the road. Traditionalist spokesmen, such as the Rev. John Thompson, snorted at the inadequacy of this conception, and with some insight wished the revivalists "freedom from their captivating Delusion."[37] But here the revivalists *were* riding the wave of the future, and theirs was to become in Protestant America, the most prevalent conception of the meaning of religious freedom.[38]

Meanwhile the rationalist permeation of the intellectual world during the eighteenth century meant that any man or group that appeared to be fighting for wider toleration of religious differences would attract the sympathetic attention of "enlightened" men in positions of social and political leadership. Furthermore, these men *were* interested in giving such freedom rational theoretical justification.

The rationalist, as befitted the learned, found that "the essentials of every religion" could be summarized in a set of intellectual propositions regarding God, immortality, and the life of virtue. And, as Benjamin Franklin suavely put it, these being

> found in all the religions we had in our country, I respected them all, tho' with different degrees of respect, as I found them more or less mix'd with other articles, which, without any tendency to inspire, promote or conform morality, serv'd principally to divide us, and make us unfriendly to one another.

Back of this genial but discriminating respect for all, was "the opinion that the worst had some good effects."[39] What "good effects" these men had in mind, Thomas Jefferson made clear. Surveying his "sister states of Pennsylvania and New York" in 1781 or '82, he noted that there were religions "of various kinds, indeed, but all good enough; [because] all sufficient to preserve peace and order."[40] This, he thought, amounted to a practical demonstration that uniformity of religious belief and practice in a civil commonwealth was not essential to the public welfare, as had been assumed in Christendom for many centuries.

The rationalists' theoretical defense of freedom was based on the view that since religion is one's "opinion" about the "duty which we owe to our creator, and the manner of discharging it," and "the opinions of men" depend "only on the evidence contemplated in their own minds" and "cannot follow the dictates of other men,"[41] therefore, true uniformity is impossible except insofar as it can be achieved through persuasion alone. Coercion, in the interests of uniformity, said Jefferson, had served only "to make one half the world fools, and the other half hypocrites."[42] So while the pietists, stressing religious experience, were feeling their way to a lack of interest in uniformity, the rationalists were thinking their way toward religious freedom, and concluding by the way that "uniformity of opinion" is no more desirable "than of face and stature."[43]

138

Here, as in other areas, rationalists and pietists were closer together in practical interests and conclusions than is many times supposed. Very important in this respect was the rationalists' high regard for the teachings of Jesus, whom they considered the first great Deist. His teachings, Jefferson held, constituted "the most sublime and benevolent code of morals which has ever been offered to man"[44] and on them he and his cohorts based their attack on existing ecclesiastical institutions, arguing that in the light of them the story of the church through the ages was largely a history of the corruptions of Christianity "for the purpose of deriving from it pence and power"—as Joseph Priestley attempted to demonstrate in his two volumes published in 1793.[45]

Men of this mind, however much they might abhor "enthusiasm," could take a sympathetic view of the practical moral application of the revivalists' gospel, and the concomitant pietistic appeal to the teachings and simple religion of Jesus. Naturally, then, as rationalists observed the controversies in and between the religious "sects" occasioned by the revivals, and the attempts of entrenched traditionalists to preserve order through the use of all possible means, including coercion, their sympathies were with the revivalists who appeared to be on the side of freedom. Hence rationalists many times in effect became in the legislatures the spokesmen for and defenders of the revivalistic "sectarians"—as, for example, Thomas Jefferson and James Madison in Virginia.

Hence came that apparently strange coalition of rationalists with pietistic-revivalistic sectarians during the last quarter of the eighteenth century that provided so much of the power that lay behind the final thrust for national religious freedom that was written into the fundamental laws of the new nation. This coalition seems less strange if we keep in mind that at the time religious freedom was for both more a practical and legal problem than a theoretical one, and that they agreed on the practical goal.

IV

Finally then, to hark back to Schaff's thesis, we have traced the "previous history of the American colonies" that is pertinent to our understanding of the consequent "condition of things at the time of the formation of the national government." This "condition of things" can now be briefly summarized.

First, the churches of right-wing background were still dominant in every area. But no one of them, and no possible combination of them, was in a position to make a bid for a national establishment plausible, although those of the Calvinistic tradition were numerous and powerful enough to give Jefferson reason to fear the possibility.[46] Meanwhile, the sweep of pietistic sentiments through these churches during the revivals had undermined much of their desire for establish-

139

ment. On the question of religious freedom for all, there were many shades of opinion in these churches, but all were practically unanimous on one point—each wanted freedom for itself. And by this time it had become clear that the only way to get it for themselves was to grant it to all others.

Second, the situation had actually made all previous distinctions between established churches and sects, between right and left-wing groups, practically meaningless. In the south all but the Anglican Church were dissenting sects, as in New England were all but Congregational churches, and in this respect there was no difference between historically right-wing groups such as Presbyterians, Lutherans, and Anglicans, and historically left-wing groups such as Quakers and Baptists. The latter, of course, had traditionally held for religious freedom on principle, while the former had recently come to accept it of necessity. But since the immediate problem of such freedom was practical and legal, all worked together for it—each for his own complete freedom to publish his own point of view in his own way.

Hence the true picture is not that of the "triumph" in America of right-wing or left-wing, of churches or sects, but rather a mingling through frustration, controversy, confusion, and compromise forced by necessity, of all the diverse ecclesiastical patterns transplanted from Europe, plus other patterns improvised on the spot, to form a complex pattern of religious thought and institutional life that was peculiarly "American," and is probably best described as "denominationalism."

Meanwhile, most of the effectively powerful intellectual, social and political leaders were rationalists, and these men made sense theoretically out of the actual practical situation which demanded religious freedom, and gave it tangible form and legal structure. This the churches, each intent on its own freedom, accepted in practice but without reconciling themselves to it intellectually by developing theoretical defenses of it that were legitimately rooted in their professed theological positions. And they never have. Anson Phelps Stokes' massive three volume work on *Church and State in the United States,* which proceeds over the historical evidence like a vacuum cleaner over a rug, is notable for the paucity of positive Protestant pronouncements on religious freedom that it sweeps up.

It thus appears that the religious groups that were everywhere dominant in America throughout the colonial period seem to have placed their feet unwittingly on the road to religious freedom. Rather than following the cloud and pillar of articulated aspiration in that direction and to that consummation, they finally granted it (insofar as any can be said to have "granted" it) not as the kind of cheerful givers their Lord is said to love, but grudgingly and of necessity.

140

Meanwhile, by the time that the original intention to preserve religious uniformity was seen to be impossible of fulfillment in the new land, there had been incubated, largely within the dissenting groups (which were not necessarily "left-wing"), ideas, theories, practices that pointed the way toward a new kind of "church" in Christendom consistent with the practice of religious freedom. During the upheavals of the Great Awakenings in the colonies, these dissenters' patterns of thought and practice infiltrated the dominant churches, and through confusion and compromise there began that historical merging of the traditional patterns of "church" and "sect," "right" and "left" wings as known in Europe into the new kind of organization combining features of both plus features growing out of the immediate situation. The resulting organizational form was unlike anything that had preceded it in Christendom, and for purposes of distinctive clarity it is best known as the "denomination."[47]

141

1. Philip Schaff, *Church and State in the United States.* New York: G. B. Putnam's Sons, 1888. p. 23.
2. Stephen Vincent Benet, *Western Star.* New York: Farrar & Rinehart, Inc., 1943. p. 144.
3. Evarts B. Greene, *Religion and the State: The Making and Testing of an American Tradition.* New York: N. Y. University Press, 1941. p. 37. See also Joseph P. Thompson, *Church and State in the United States.* Boston: James R. Osgood & Co., 1873. p. 55.
4. As quoted in Frederick J. Zwierlein, *Religion in New Netherland.* Rochester, N. Y.: John P. Smith Printing Co., 1910, pp. 140-41.
5. As quoted in *ibid.,* pp. 117, 118-19.
6. Perry Miller and Thomas H. Johnson. *The Puritans.* New York: American Book Company, 1938. p. 231.
7. See the article, "The Contribution of the Protestant Churches to Religious Liberty in America," *Church History,* IV (March 1935), pp. 57-66.
8. As quoted in William Warren Sweet, *Religion in Colonial America.* New York: Charles Scribner's Sons, 1942. pp. 151-52.
9. Zwierlein, *Religion in New Netherland,* p. 261.
10. *Ibid.,* p. 257.
11. *Ibid.,* p. 256.
12. Greene, *Religion and the State,* pp. 52-53.
13. *For the Colony in Virginea Britannia. Lavves Divine, Moral and Martiall, &c.* Printed at London for Walter Burre, 1612. In Peter Force, *Tracts and Other Papers,* vol. III, #ii. Washington: Wm. Q. Force, 1844, pp. 10-11.
14. *Virginia's Cure: Or an Advisive Narrative Concerning Virginia. Discovering* the True Ground of That Churches Unhappiness, and the Only True Remedy. As it was presented to the Right Reverend Father in God *Gvilbert* Lord Bishop of London, September 2, 1661. London: W. Godbid, 1662. In Peter Force, *Tracts and Other Papers,* vol. III, #xv. Washington: Wm. Q. Force, 1844.
15. Miller and Johnson, *The Puritans,* p. 27.
16. "A Reply to Mr. Williams His Examination and Answer of the Letters Sent to Him by John Cotton" (*Publications of the Narragansett Club,* 1st Series, Vol. II [Providence, 1862], p. 19), quoted by Karl H. Hertz, "Bible Commonwealth and Holy Experiment" (Ph. D. dissertation, University of Chicago, 1948,) p. 148.
17. Miller and Johnson, *The Puritans,* p. 638.
18. For the general factors at work, see the article by Roland Bainton, "The Struggle for Religious Liberty," *Church History,* X (June 1941), 95-124. Professor Winthrop S. Hudson has suggested that English Independents had developed a "denominational" conception of the Church, which in spite of the rigors of the New England way tended always to make its leaders inherently uncomfortable with persecution of dissenters. See his article, "Denominationalism as a Basis for Ecumenicity: A Seventeenth Century Conception," *Church History,* XXIV (March 1955), 32-50. This suggests a fruitful area for further exploration.
19. As quoted in Charles M. Andrews, *The Colonial Period of American History.* New Haven: Yale University Press. 1934. I, 386.

20. Arthur Lyon Cross, *The Anglican Episcopate and the American Colonies*. Cambridge: Harvard University Press, 1924. p. 22.

21. In the *Massachusetts Historical Society Collections*, Series 4, vol. 2, 1854, pp. 1-113.

22. William Sewel, *The History of The Quakers, Intermixed with Several Remarkable Occurrences*. Written originally in low Dutch, and translated by himself into English. 2 vols. Philadelphia, 1856. I, 354-55. This history first appeared in English in 1722.

23. See Sanford H. Cobb, *The Rise of Religious Liberty in America*. New York: The Macmillan Co., 1902, p. 69.

24. Green, *Religion and the State*, p. 51.

25. *The Journals of Henry Melchior Muhlenberg*, trans. Theodore G. Tappert and John W. Doberstein. Philadelphia: Muhlenberg Press, 1942. I, 67.

26. See Edwards' "A Faithful Narrative of the Surprising Work of God, in the Conversion of Many Hundred Souls, in Northampton. . . ." in *The Works of President Edwards*. New York: S. Converse, 1830, IV, 70-71.

27. As, for example, Jonathan Edwards' words: "The Beginning of the late work of God in this Place was so circumstanced, that I could not but look upon it as a remarkable Testimony of God's Approbation of the Doctrine of Justification by Faith alone, here asserted and vindicated: . . . . And at that time, while I was greatly reproached for defending this Doctrine in the Pulpit, and just upon my suffering a very open Abuse for it, God's Work wonderfully brake forth amongst us, and souls began to flock to Christ, as the Saviour in whose Righteousness alone they hoped to be justified; So that this was the Doctrine on which this work in its Beginning was founded, as it evidently was in the whole progress of it."
Discourses on various Important Subjects, Nearly Concerning the Great Affair on the Soul's Eternal Salvation. Boston: S. Kneeland and T. Green, 1738. p. ii.

28. As quoted in Wesley M. Gewehr, *The Great Awakening in Virginia, 1740-1790.* Durham: Duke University Press, 1930. p. 16.

29. In *ibid.*, p. 65.

30. From Leonard J. Trinterud, *The Forming of an American Tradition, A Reexamination of Colonial Presbyterianism*. Philadelphia: The Westminster Press, 1944. pp. 90-91.

31. William Warren Sweet, *The American Churches, an Interpretation*. New York: Abingdon-Cokesbury Press, 1948. pp. 30-31.

32. See for example Winthrop S. Hudson's review of Sweet's *The American Churches*, in *The Crozer Quarterly*, XXV (Oct. 1948), pp. 358-60.

33. See Isaac Backus, *A History of New England, with Particular Reference to the Denomination of Christians called Baptists*. 2d ed., with notes by David Weston. Newton, Mass.: The Backus Historical Society, 1871. II, 41.

34. *Adventures of Ideas*. New York: The Macmillan Co., 1933. pp. 27-28.

35. John Wesley, *Sermons on Several Occasions*. New York: Lane and Scott, 1851. I, 392.

36. Quoted in Sweet, *The American Churches*, pp. 46-47.

37. Quoted in Gewehr, *The Great Awakening in Virginia*, p. 65.

38. See in this connection my article, "American Protestantism During the Revolutionary Epoch," *Church History*, XXII (Dec. 1953), 279-297; Wilhelm Pauck, "Theology in the Life of Contemporary American Protestantism," *The Shane Quarterly*, XIII (April, 1952), 37-50; J. L. Diman, "Religion in America, 1776-1876," *North American Review*, CXXII (Jan. 1876).

39. From the Autobiography, in Frank Luther Mott and Chester E. Jorgenson, *Benjamin Franklin, Representative Selections . . . .* , New York: American Book Company, 1936. p. 70.

40. Saul K. Padover (ed.), *The Complete Jefferson*, New York: Duell, Sloan & Pearce, Inc., 1943. p. 676.

41. James Madison, "A Memorial and Remonstrance on the Religious Rights of Man," as printed in Joseph L. Blau (ed.), *Cornerstones of Religious Freedom in America*. Boston: The Beacon Press, 1949. p. 81.

42. Padover (ed.), *The Complete Jefferson*, p. 676.

43. *Ibid.*, p. 675.

44. As quoted in Henry Wilder Foote, *Thomas Jefferson: Champion of Religious Freedom, Advocate of Christian Morals*. Boston: The Beacon Press, 1947. p. 52.

45. Joseph Priestley, *An History of the Corruptions of Christianity*, Birmingham: J. Thompson, 1793.

46. See Ralph Barton Perry, *Puritanism and Democracy*. New York: The Vanguard Press, p. 80.

47. In a previous article in this Journal (December 1954) I discussed the nature of the denominational organization and the almost complete triumph of denominationalism during the first half of the nineteenth century.

142

PURITANISM AS A REVOLUTIONARY IDEOLOGY

MICHAEL WALZER

I

Ideas, like men, play many parts. They are used casuistically to justify behavior; they rationalize interests; they shape character; they inspire fanaticism
and presumption. No unified theory is likely to explain all the possible
connections of thought and action. The connections are different at different
moments in history and at any single moment they are different for different
men. Recent studies of revolutionary movements and totalitarian governments clearly suggest the shifting role of ideas during periods of crisis and
relative stability. To reduce all this to a single formula would be to im-
poverish our historical and sociological speculation. This was probably the
initial effect of Marxism upon the history of ideas, even though the theory
of ideology was surely the most subtle and valuable contribution yet made
to that history. The Marxist epigone, ignoring the master's metaphysics,
explained the creation, spread and decay of ideological systems in terms of
a unilinear economic history and a theory of "reflection" never satisfactorily
developed in either psychological or epistemological terms. His was a view
obviously inadequate to the understanding of religious thought (where the
original Marxist idea of alienation might be fruitfully applied) and artistic
creativity.[1] But it was also inadequate precisely where he claimed it to be
most useful – in the interpretation of revolutionary ideology.

The Marxist insisted, correctly enough, upon the catastrophic character
of social change; but he never studied the effects of catastrophe upon the
mind and spirit of men. He tended, instead, to view revolutionary thought
as the rational expression of the interests of a rising class, and he imagined
interests to be objective, narrowly based in economic life, and more or less
automatically expressed.[2] This sort of analysis seems best suited to post-

143

[1] This is not only or most often because political judgments interfere with intellectual
or aesthetic judgments. Rather, it is because the crude employment of Marxist methods
(as of Freudian ones) makes the analysis of abstraction, allusion, metaphor and allegory
all too easy. A prime example, which will be referred to again, is Jack Lindsay, *John
Bunyan, Maker of Myths* (London, 1937); see the critique of this book by F. R. Leavis,
The Common Pursuit (London, 1953), 204 ff.

[2] More or less automatically: because Marxist critics have revelled in the discovery
of "confusion" – which is usually interpreted as a wavering between two well-established
class positions and is usually deplored.

revolutionary periods; it hardly reaches beyond the conventional forms of selfishness, self-deception and hypocrisy. Thus the Marxist historian "understands" the Puritans after 1660 far better than he understands Oliver Cromwell; and similarly, the enthusiasm of a Robespierre is far less comprehensible to him than the everyday vulgarity of a Balzac bourgeois.[3]

Of the Dissenting businessman and the nineteenth-century bourgeois, it has often enough been said that their ideas determine only the character of the lies they tell. Selfishness moves these men, but they call it enterprise; success rewards them, but they call it salvation, or happiness. An acute insight into these forms of self-justification – at times very witty and at times a little misanthropic – underlies the Marxist theory of ideology. But the theory moves beyond this insight; even the epigone is not content merely to expose lies, but seeks to understand the strange and complex process by which men become prisoners of the lies they tell. There comes a time when the mind is no longer open to the free play of interests, when opportunity is missed, or even pridefully disdained. At such a time, the casuistry of morality or honor cannot simply be equated with hypocrisy; it also sets limits, finds some lies acceptable, others not. Thus ideologies "harden" and fasten the men who believe them to a conventional mode of thinking and behaving, a mode which is increasingly irrational the more it lags behind the on-going forces of history. Were it not for this irrationality, old ruling groups might readily adapt themselves to the opportunities offered by social change and there would be no revolutions.

There is a corollary to this view of the imperviousness of established ideological systems which Marxists have rarely drawn. Revolutionary ideologies must, in their turn, be intensely negative and destructive. They must foster what Max Weber has called "an unusually strong character", a kind of fanaticism, if they are to help men break through the hardened structure of convention and routine. Now, human beings are open to fanaticism only at certain moments in history; more often they are closed to it, safe from whatever it is that inspires devotion, dogmatism and presumption, and then disdainful of all "enthusiasm" – as for example, in eighteenth-century England. This openness is not made comprehensible by the casual invocation of a "rising" class, although it may well coincide with certain moments in a class history. Nor can the character of the fanaticism be explained solely in terms of the economic interests of a class.

The purpose of this paper is to suggest another explanation and to explore in some detail the part played by ideas during a period of rapid social change

[3] See Bernstein on Cromwell, *Cromwell and Communism*, trans. H. J. Stenning (London, 1930). In similar fashion, orthodox Marxists neither anticipated nor understood Leninism, for even while criticizing it they still imagined it to be a class ideology; see Rosa Luxemburg, *Leninism or Marxism* (Ann Arbor, 1961). Marx is better than his best disciples on this point: see his discussion of Robespierre in *The Holy Family* (Moscow, 1956), 163-165.

and revolution. The startling spread of Puritanism in England during the late sixteenth and early seventeenth centuries will provide a case history and suggest in dramatic form the (often ugly) kinds of discipline and self-control which revolutionary ideology can develop in men and the strength of character it can inspire. And since Puritanism has already been the subject of so many explanations, the English example will provide the opportunity for a critique of several earlier views of the significance of the Calvinist faith, and of various methods of studying revolutionary ideology.

II

Puritanism has twice been assigned a unique and creative role in Western history. Neither of these assignments was made by a Marxist historian; it was rather the Whigs and the Weberians who found modernity in the mind of the saints. But in a curious fashion, Marxists have been driven to adopt the insights of both these groups of writers, since both have defended and elaborated the historical connection which the Marxists themselves have so persistently sought to establish – that is, the connection of Puritanism with capitalism and liberalism.

Whig historians of the nineteenth and twentieth centuries saw in Protestantism in general, but more particularly in English Calvinism, the seed-bed of liberal politics. The purely individualistic relationship of the saint to his God, the emphasis upon voluntary association and mutual consent to church government among the saints themselves, the extraordinary reliance upon the printed word, with each man his own interpreter – all this, we have been told, trained and prepared the liberal mind.[4] And then the natural alliance of Puritans and parliamentarians created the liberal society. It is a clear implication of this view, though one not often expressed by Whig writers, that Puritanism *is* liberalism in theological garb, that is, in a primitive and somewhat confused form.[5]

Max Weber credited Puritanism with a rather different character and a different but related contribution to Western development. Writing in a more modern vein and free, up to a point, from Whig prejudices, he suggested that Calvin's ideas – again, especially in England – played a decisive part in

---

[4] A classic example of this argument is to be found in A. D. Lindsay, *The Modern Democratic State* (Oxford, 1943), 115-121; also G. P. Gooch, *English Democratic Ideas in the Seventeenth Century* (New York, 1959). The argument appears in a more sophisticated form in the introduction of A. S. P. Woodhouse's edition of the army debates, *Puritanism and Liberty* (London, 1951).
[5] That ideas are merely "clothed" in religious fashion for convenience, out of force of habit, or because other clothing was somehow not available is, of course, a Marxist argument. See Perez Zagorin, *A History of Political Thought in the English Revolution* (London, 1954). It presupposes a very awkward theory of expression according to which content and form have little intrinsic connection.

the creation of the "spirit of capitalism". His views are so familiar that they need not be described in any detail here. But it should be said that they involve two rather distinct arguments, which will be considered separately below. Weber thought that Puritanism had sponsored a significant rationalization in behavior, especially in work: it had trained men to work in a sustained, systematic fashion, to pay attention to detail, to watch the clock. In this sense, the Calvinist ethic is related to that long-term process which culminates, but does not end, in a rational-legal (bureaucratic) society. Weber argued in addition to this that Puritanism had produced an extraordinary and apparently *irrational* impulse toward acquisition, which is more directly connected with the rise of a capitalist economy. The source of both impulses, toward rationalization and endless gain, lay in the anxiety induced by the theory of predestination – but the two are not the same and it is at least plausible to imagine the first without the second.[6]

A Marxist historian would obviously deny the views of historical causation expressed or implied by both Whigs and Weberians, but he would defend ardently the close connection of Puritanism with the liberal and capitalist worlds. So ardently, indeed, would he do so, that he would probably concede, for the sake of the connection, a kind of "interaction" between economics, politics and religion, and thus open the way for an eclectic amalgamation of the three different points of view. Thus, contemporary Marxist writers tend still to describe Puritanism as the reflection of a rising bourgeoisie, though not necessarily its direct reflection (and this point – suggested, for example, by Tawney's notion of a "magic mirror" – is none too clear). But they then go on to argue that the reflection reacts somehow upon the original subject, reinforcing latent, perhaps underdeveloped class characteristics, meeting psychic needs, and generally accelerating the progressive evolution.[7] This second argument is made in terms with which Whigs and Weberians would hardly disagree – especially since it constitutes a Marxist appropriation of their own insights. Such an eclecticism may incidentally make more sophisticated the history of all who adopt it; but it does not necessarily do so, for it provides no new insights and often involves the suspension of criticism for the sake of coherence. Giving up the hapless debate over whether Puritanism or capitalism came first would be, perhaps, no such loss. However, it would be a great loss indeed if no one called the union itself

[6] Max Weber, *The Protestant Ethic and the Spirit of Capitalism*, trans. Talcott Parsons (New York, 1958), esp. 26-27, 53. When Herbert Marcuse analyzes Soviet Marxism, he discovers a "protestant ethic" – but this is clearly a rationalist ethic and not an acquisitive one; *Soviet Marxism: A Critical Analysis* (New York, 1961), 217, 222-23.
[7] This view is most clearly argued by Christopher Hill, *Puritanism and Revolution* (London, 1958), esp. chapters 1 and 7; compare this with Hill's earlier pamphlet, *The English Revolution: 1640* (London, 1940).

into question and sought to work out in a new way the historical experience of the saints.

The resemblance between the Calvinist covenant and the capitalist contract – often invoked and elaborated by Marxist writers – will serve to suggest the kind of questions which need to be raised. The voluntarism of both covenant and contract clearly distinguish them from earlier traditionalistic relationships; but they are also distinguished from one another by two facts which the Marxists have surely underrated. First, they are based upon very different, indeed, precisely opposite, views of human nature. The contract assumes trust, a mutual recognition of economic rationality and even of good will. The covenant, as will be argued below, institutionalizes suspicion and mutual surveillance. If it is true that sober-minded capitalists preferred to do business with members of the Puritan brotherhood, this may well have been because they knew that the brethren were being watched. Secondly, the two forms of association serve very different human purposes. Puritan godliness and capitalist gain have, perhaps, something to do with one another, though they have little enough in common. The suggestion that they are *really the same thing,* or one the mere reflex, in thought or in action, of the other, has long distorted our understanding of the saints and their English enterprise. In order to grasp the precise nature of this distortion it is necessary not only to point out the basic incompatibility of Puritanism with both liberalism and capitalism, but also to discuss the various methods by which their similarity has been discovered and to attack the attitude toward historical experience which these methods imply.

147

A number of recent writers have gone so far as to describe the Puritan saints as traditionalists in both politics and economics, a description which has the virtue of standing the older theorists neatly on their heads, but which also makes the revolution incomprehensible.[a] This is not the view which will be argued here; it describes at best only the cautious conformity of Puritan preachers in dealing with such conventional topics as monarchy, rebellion, usury and charity. On the other hand, it is not difficult to detect the sharply anti-traditionalist ideology of these same men working itself out in their attacks upon hierarchy, their new views of ecclesiastical organization, their treatises on family government, their almost Manichean warfare against Satan and his worldly allies, their nervous lust for systematic repression and control. The last two of these are obviously not compatible with liberal thinking (or with entrepreneurial activity). They point directly to the revolution, when the struggle against Anti-Christ would be acted out and, for a brief moment, the repressive Holy Commonwealth established. In the

[a] See Perry Miller, *Orthodoxy in Massachusetts, 1630-1650* (Boston, 1959), chapter I; Charles H. and Katherine George, *The Protestant Mind of the English Reformation, 1570-1640* (Princeton, 1961), chapter 6; Richard Schlatter, *Richard Baxter and Puritan Politics* (New Brunswick, 1957), introduction.

64

MICHAEL WALZER

years before the actual revolution, the nature of Puritanism was best revealed in the endless discussions of church government and in the practices of such Puritan congregations as already existed. These practices can by no means be called liberal, even though they were founded upon consent. Precisely because of this foundation, however, they cannot be called traditionalist either. The experience of the saints suggests something very different.

III

148

It was, perhaps, not without a certain malice that the early Puritans were called "disciplinarians". But malice has its insights and this one is worth pursuing. The association of the brethren was voluntary indeed, but it gave rise to a collectivist discipline marked above all by a tense mutual "watchfulness". Puritan individualism never led to a respect for privacy. Tender conscience had its rights, but it was protected only against the interference of worldlings and not against "brotherly admonition". And the admonitions of the brethren were anxious, insistent, continuous. They felt themselves to be living in an age of chaos and crime and sought to train conscience to be permanently on guard against sin. The extent to which they would have carried the moral discipline can be seen in the following list of offenses which merited excommunication in one seventeenth-century congregation:[9]

– for unfaithfulness in his master's service.
– for admitting cardplaying in his house . . .
– for sloth in business.
– for being overtaken in beer.
– for borrowing a pillion and not returning it.
– for jumping for wagers . . .
– for dancing and other vanities.

Had the saints been succesful in establishing their Holy Commonwealth, the enforcement of this discipline would have constituted the Puritan terror. In the congregation there was already a kind of local terrorism, maintained by the godly elders as the national discipline would have been by an elite of the saints. Thus, Richard Baxter reported that in his Kidderminster parish the enforcement of the new moral order was made possible "by the zeal and diligence of the godly people of the place who thirsted after the salvation of their neighbours and were in private my assistants".[10]

It was for this moral discipline that the saints fought most persistently, and it was over this issue that Baxter and his colleagues left the Established Church in .1662. Their failure to win from Charles II's bishops the con-

---

[9] Quoted in Horton Davies, *The Worship of the English Puritans* (Westminster, 1948), 235.
[10] Richard Baxter, *Reliquiae Baxterianae*, ed. M. Sylvester (London, 1696), 87.

gregational rights of admonition and excommunication finally forced them –
as the political Restoration had not done – to acknowledge the failure of
their revolutionary effort to turn "all England into a land of the saints". By
that time, however, the effort had had a certain prosaic success – not at all
of the sort which Puritan preachers once imagined.

The crucial feature of the Puritan discipline was its tendency to transform
repression into self-control: worldlings might be forced to be godly, but
saints voluntarily gave themselves to godliness. Liberalism also required
such voluntary subjection and self-control but, in sharp contrast to Puritanism, its political and social theory were marked by an extraordinary confidence in the possibility of both a firm sense of human reasonableness and
of the ease with which order might be attained. Liberal confidence made
repression and the endless struggle against sin unnecessary; it also tended to
make self-control invisible, to forget its painful history and naively assume its
existence. The result was that liberalism did not create the self-control it
required. The Lockeian state was not a disciplinary institution, as was the
Calvinist Holy Commonwealth, but rather rested on the assumed political
virtue – the "natural political virtue" [11] – of its citizens. It is one of the
central arguments of this essay that Puritan repression has its place in the
practical history, so to speak, of that strange assumption.

It is not possible, of course, to judge the effectiveness of this repression
or the extent of the social need for it. For the moment it can only be said
that Puritans knew about human sinfulness and that Locke did not need to
know. This probably reflects not only different temperaments, but also
different experiences. The very existence and spread of Puritanism in the
years before the Revolution surely argue the presence in English society of
an acute fear of disorder and "wickedness". The anxious tone of Tudor
legislation – which Puritan leaders like William Perkins often vigorously
seconded – is itself a parallel argument. On the other hand, the triumph of
Lockeian ideas suggests the overcoming of that anxiety and fear, the appearance of men for whom sin is no longer a problem. In a sense, it might
be said that liberalism is dependent upon the existence of "saints" – that is,
of men whose good behavior can be relied upon. At the same time, the
secular and genteel character of liberalism is determined by the fact that

[11] The term "natural political virtue" is that of Locke's latest editor; see Peter
Laslett's edition of the *Two Treatises* (Cambridge. 1960), 108 f. The extraordinary
difficulty with which self-control is learned is best described – that is, described with
some sensitivity to human pain – by Nietzsche, in *The Genealogy of Morals*. He is
writing of a very early period in human history, but his insights have some relevance
to the sixteenth and seventeenth centuries. How free Locke was from any sense of the
dangers of *uncontrolled* men is evident in his "Letter on Toleration". Compare his
description there of voluntary association in religious matters with Jean Bodin's demand
a century earlier for a strict moral discipline enforced by elders, *The Six Books of the
Republic*, trans. M. J. Tooley (Oxford, n.d.), 184-85. On this point, as on many others,
Bodin is very close to the Calvinists.

these are men whose goodness (sociability, self-discipline, moral decency, or mere respectability) is self-assured and relaxed, entirely free from the nervousness and fanaticism of Calvinist godliness.

This, then, is the relationship of Puritanism to the liberal world: it is perhaps one of historical preparation, but not at all of theoretical contribution. Indeed, there was much to be forgotten and much to be surrendered before the saint could become a liberal bourgeois. During the great creative period of English Puritanism, the faith of the saints and the tolerant reasonableness of the liberals had very little in common.

Roughly the same things can be said about the putative connection of Calvinism and capitalism. The moral discipline of the saints can be interpreted as the historical conditioning of the capitalist man; but the discipline was not itself capitalist. It can be argued that the faith of the brethren, with its emphasis upon methodical endeavor and self-control, was an admirable preparation for systematic work in shops, offices and factories. It trained men for the minute-to-minute attentiveness required in a modern economic system; it taught them to forego their afternoon naps – as they had but recently foregone their saints' day holidays – and to devote spare hours to bookkeeping and moral introspection. It somehow made the deprivation and repression inevitable in sustained labor bearable and even desirable for the saints. And by teaching self-control, it provided the basis for impersonal, contractual relationships among men, allowing workmanlike cooperation but not involving any exchange of affection or any of the risks of intimacy. All this, Calvinism did or helped to do. Whether it did so in a creative fashion or as the ideological reflection of new economic processes is not immediately relevant. The saints learned, as Weber has suggested, a kind of rational and worldly asceticism, and this was probably something more than the economic routine required. They sought in work itself what mere work can never give: a sense of vocation and discipline which would free them from sinfulness and the fear of disorder.[12]

But Weber has said more than this; he has argued that systematic acquisition as well as asceticism has a Calvinist origin. The psychological tension induced by the theory of predestination, working itself out in worldly activity, presumably drove men to seek success as a sign of salvation. The sheer willfulness of an inscrutable God produced in its turn, if Weber is correct, the willfulness of an anxious man, and set off the entrepreneurial pursuit of better business techniques and more and more profit. At this point his argument breaks down. If there is in fact a peculiar and irrational quality to the capitalists' lust for gain, its sources must be sought elsewhere than among the saints. For Puritanism was hardly an ideology which encouraged con-

[12] Weber's most recent critic, Kurt Samuelsson, hardly discusses the idea of rationalization which is so central to his argument; *Religion and Economic Action*, trans. E. G. French (Stockholm, 1961).

tinuous or unrestrained accumulation. Instead, the saints tended to be narrow
and conservative in their economic views, urging men to seek no more wealth
than they needed for a modest life, or, alternatively, to use up their surplus
in charitable giving. The anxiety of the Puritans led to a fearful demand for
economic restriction (and political control) rather than to entrepreneurial
activity as Weber has described it. Unremitting and relatively unremunera-
tive work was the greatest help toward saintliness and virtue.[13]

The ideas of Puritan writers are here very close to those of such proto-
Jacobins as Mably and Morelli in eighteenth-century France, who also
watched the development of capitalist enterprise with unfriendly eyes, dreaming of a Spartan republic where bankers and great merchants would be unwelcome.[14] The collective discipline of the Puritans – their Christian Sparta
– was equally incompatible with purely acquisitive activity. Virtue would
almost certainly require economic regulation. This would be very different
from the regulation of medieval corporatism, and perhaps it was the first
sense of that difference which received the name *freedom*. It was accompanied by a keen economic realism: thus the Calvinist acknowledgement of
the lawfulness of usury. But Calvinist realism was in the service of effective
control and not of free activity or self-expression. Who can doubt that, had the
Holy Commonwealth ever been firmly established, godly self-discipline and
mutual surveillance would have been far more repressive than the corporate
system? Once again, in the absence of a Puritan state the discipline was
enforced through the congregation. The minutes of a seventeenth-century
consistory provide a routine example: "The church was satisfied with Mrs.
Carlton," they read, "as to the weight of her butter." Did Mrs. Carlton
tremble, awaiting that verdict? Surely if the brethren were unwilling to grant
liberty to the local butter-seller, they would hardly have granted it to the
new capitalist. The ministerial literature, at least, is full of denunciations of
enclosers, usurers, monopolists, and projectors – and occasionally even of
wily merchants. Puritan casuistry, perhaps, left such men sufficient room in
which to range, but it hardly offered them what Weber considers so essential
– a good conscience. Only a sustained endeavor in hypocrisy, so crude as to
astonish even the Marxist epigone, could have earned them that. The final
judgment of the saints with regard to the pursuit of money is that of Bunyan's

[13] For a detailed criticism of Weber on these points, see George, *op. cit.*, chapters 2
and 3; also Samuelsson, *op. cit.*, esp. 27 ff. Samuelsson's first chapter discusses the
men who have accepted or been significantly influenced by this aspect of Weber's
argument; these are the men who are called "Weberians" in this essay. It should be
said that Weber himself – if not always his followers – was very conscious of the
savage repression which Calvinism sponsored; the question of why bourgeois men
should accept such discipline is central to his book (*op. cit.*, 37). Nevertheless, the
particular forms of repression and control described above are not considered in *The
Protestant Ethic*.
[14] The restrictionist attitudes of Mably and Morelli are discussed in J. L. Talmon,
The Origins of Totalitarian Democracy (New York, 1960), 58 ff.

pilgrim, angry and ill-at-ease in the town of Vanity, disdainful of such companions as Mr. Money-love and Mr. Save-all.

The converse is equally true: to the triumphant bourgeois sainthood, with all its attendant enthusiasm and asceticism, would appear atavistic. And this is perhaps the clearest argument of all against the casual acceptance of the Whig or Weberian views of Puritanism. It suggests forcefully that the two views (and the Marxist also, for surprisingly similar reasons) are founded upon anachronism. Even if it is correct to argue that Calvinist faith and discipline played a part in that transformation of character which created the bourgeois – and too little is known about the historical development of character to say this without qualification – the anachronism remains. The historical present is hopelessly distorted unless the tension and repression so essential to the life of the saint are described and accounted for. Even more important, the effort to etablish a holy commonwealth (to universalize the tension and repression) is rendered inexplicable once liberalism and capitalism are, so to speak, read into the Puritan experience. For then Puritanism is turned into a grand paradox: its radical voluntarism culminates in a rigid discipline; its saints watch their neighbors with brotherly love and suspicion; its ethic teaches sustained and systematic work but warns men against the lust for acquisition and gain. In fact, of course, these seeming contrasts are not paradoxical. The saints experienced a unity, common enough among men, of willfulness and repression, of fanatical *self-control*. Latter-day historians do the Puritans little honor when they search among the elements of the Puritan faith for something more liberal in its political implications or more economically rational. Indeed, the methods of that search invite in their turn the most searching criticism.

IV

Whigs, Weberians and Marxists have reconstructed Puritanism in terms of two other constructs which they know far better and love far more: liberalism and capitalism. The Whig reconstruction is the most crude and the least historical. Whig historians describe liberalism as if it were a kind of Community Chest to which nations, groups of men, and particular thinkers have made contributions. History is a catalogue of the contributors, whose actual intentions and circumstances count for little. The contributions mount up; the world perfects itself. This is a view obviously close to that of the French progressists of the eighteenth century who saw history as a (more or less) steady accumulation of facts, of moral and scientific truths. But the French thinkers at least regarded religious fanaticism as an enemy, a sign that they had some acquaintance with it. Revolutionaries that they were, the very fervor of their attack upon priestly and monkish zeal suggested the coming cult of progress – the new fanaticism. The Whigs, on the other hand, were altogether free from zeal and could neither understand nor even hate the zealot; they did not recognize in him a fellow creature. Thus, at the same time as they described the saints as their own (somewhat lusty) progenitors, they expelled Oliver Cromwell from the moral universe and called the millenarians "insane".[15] But Cromwell was surely a representative figure and the millenarians achieved little more than a logical extension of ideas basic to all Puritan thinking. If they cannot be included in the world the liberals recognize and understand, then that world is false.[16]

Whig writers continually fail to achieve historicity – the quality of truly engaging the past. Perhaps this is because they are so unwilling to criticize, even retrospectively, potential contributors to the liberal consensus. Such moral trepidation makes virtually impossible honest, that is, comprehensive and virile, characterizations of men whose historical labor is deemed valuable. Thus, liberal historians, under the impact of Marxism, have tentatively suggested the connection of Puritanism with the rising middle class, but have been entirely unable to describe realistically the human experience of "rising" – again, perhaps, because it is not always an ennobling experience.[17] They fail to make the complex connections of the new religion with the new men in any way specific. They merely suggest vaguely that an enlightened class embraced an enlightened faith . . . and left us all an inheritance of enlightenment. So we know the past only by its contribution, as if nothing had been lost in the giving. As for the men who, like the millenarians, had nothing to give – had it not been for our own experience with totalitarian movements they might have vanished from history.[18]

153

Nor did Max Weber reconstruct the historical reality of the Puritan saint. His real interests, like those of the Whigs, lay elsewhere. Studying the psychological effects of Puritan faith, he created a new *deus absconditus* for the capitalist world – Calvin's God. But like all mortals, he learned the attributes of that God (and of his human instruments) by studying his creation. Weber

[15] Eighteenth-century Whigs shared Hume's attitude toward Cromwell: they hated his fervor and "the uncontrollable fury of his zeal"; see Hume's *History* (Boston, 1853), V, 437. Oliver was rescued in the nineteenth century, chiefly by Carlyle, who admired precisely his fury. But a sympathetic Whig historian like Gooch can write about him only by avoiding fury and zeal altogether: his discussion of Cromwell's politics, for example, omits all mention of his enthusiastic, almost millenarian speech to the Barebone's Parliament; Gooch, *op. cit.*, 192 ff. (Gooch certainly misinterprets both Carlyle and Cromwell when he writes that since the publication of the *Letters and Speeches*, "no rational being . . . believes the Protector to have been either a hypocrite or a fanatic". *History and Historians in the Nineteenth Century* [Boston, 1959], 306.) It is Gooch also who calls the millenarians insane, 225.
[16] This critique of the Whigs obviously owes much to Herbert Butterfield's sustained polemic, *The Whig Interpretation of History* (New York, 1951).
[17] See Marshall M. Knappen, *Tudor Puritanism: A Chapter in the History of Idealism* (Chicago, 1939).
[18] Contemporary experience provides the occasion for Norman Cohn's study of medieval millenarianism, *The Pursuit of the Millenium* (New York, 1960).

constructed Puritanism as a composite of capitalist (specifically, economically rational) elements, very much as the Marxists do, for all his criticism of their monistic historiography. This obviously required a selection, in which the restrictionist attitudes described above – as well as all that is irrational in Puritan thought – were necessarily ignored. Thus it matters very little whether the saint is the creator of the capitalist or merely his reflection; in the work of the historian the known determines the unknown – and the saint is an unknown man.

Indeed, it seems at times that Weber turns Puritanism into a virtual equivalent of the capitalist spirit. He argues, for example, that among the saints rational labor (conceived by Weber exclusively in economic terms) is a form of worship and worship itself a strenuous and systematic labor. The spirit of capitalism is *first embodied in a religious ideology,* and from this ideology it derives the moral force necessary to break through convention and routine. Without Puritanism, Weber believes, the capitalist spirit might never have taken a historically viable form. Calvinist theology was somehow the crystallizing agent, but at the same time, Puritanism was the crystallization. For nothing is added, according to Weber's account, by the subsequent secularization of capitalist endeavor; hence it must be said that the original form was complete. What existed at first exists still, more ugly, perhaps, as its theological meaning gradually is forgotten.[19] But this virtual confusion of the Puritan and capitalist spirits, which inevitably follows from Weber's work, points to a radical defect in his argument. Briefly put, the defect is this: Weber's explanation of acquisitive behavior – in terms of anxiety over salvation and the desperate need to win some conviction of grace – will serve as well to explain Puritan saintliness. Granted the connection, at best incomplete, the psychological mechanisms which shape the two seem identical. In history, the salvation panic, the concern and self-doubt which Weber describes, is quite common. It is the psychological crisis which culminates in conversion; out of it emerges the self-confident, austere and zealous saint. The saint's anxiety does not begin *after* his conversion, though it may in some manner be maintained by his new religious ideology – "a man at ease is a man lost", wrote the Puritan minister Thomas Taylor. And thus the saint does not become a capitalist through any subsequent psychological process; his acquisitiveness – given Weber's point – is only an aspect and in no historical sense a result of his saintliness. But it is not possible to explain capitalism in terms of Puritanism (that is, Puritanism can be neither a cause nor even a "decisive factor" in the development of capitalism) if both are generated by the same experience. Looked at in this light, Weber hardly raises the problem of causation, for he never asks what are obviously the crucial questions: Why did men become Puritans? Why did they make the experience of anxiety so central to their lives? Why were they

[19]   Weber, *op. cit.,* 180 ff.

open to the extraordinary character change which their new faith presumably effected?

The argument can be put differently. Weber assumes that the cause of anxiety is an anxiety-inducing ideology. He never concerns himself with the origins of Calvinist faith or with that "elective affinity" which its converts presumably experienced. Now ideologies are modes of perceiving the world, and one perceives, up to a point, what one needs to see. That is, ideologies organize and sharpen feelings and sensitivities which are already present. The future saint who "elects" Calvinism is not in utter ignorance of the salvation panic it may induce. He chooses Calvinism, and not some other religious ideology, precisely because it explains a world in which he is already anxious – worried, confused, neurotic or whatever – and it is this original anxiety which must be explained if his eventual conversion and salvation are, so to speak, to be anticipated.[20] The terms and character of the conversion are conditioned by Calvinist thought, but not explained by it. Indeed, a later generation of Puritans, without losing their beliefs, would find conversion enormously difficult.

All this is really a Marxist critique of Weber, but no Marxist has yet undertaken a description of the state of mind of the men who became Calvinist saints, or even of their historical experience. The reason undoubtedly is that the Marxist knows the beginning of Puritanism as well as Weber knew the end: at the beginning and the end is capitalism.

There is another defect in Weber's argument, and it also stems from a failure to ask historical questions about the saints. Neither Weber nor any of his followers have ever demonstrated that the men who actually became Puritans, for whatever reasons – who really believed in predestination and lived through the salvation panic – went on, presumably for the same reasons, to become capitalists. They have not immersed themselves in the history of the period. This by no means precludes all insight: Weber's discussion of the activity of the saint and the energizing effects of predestination – despite a logic which seems to lead to passivity and quiescence – is a triumph of psychological speculation. But his particular judgments are guesswork at best. There is, for example, considerable evidence to show that many of the most sensitive of the saints went on, after the crisis of their conversion, to become ministers, and very little evidence that many went on to become capitalist businessmen. Among lay Puritans, the weight of the diaries, letters and memoirs clearly suggests that the most significant expression of their new faith was cultural and political rather than economic. The saints were indeed activists and activists in a far more intense and "driven" fashion than the men who came after: Scottish peasants learned to read; English

---

[20] This is not to suggest that anxiety about salvation – the fear of hellfire – was *really* anxiety about something else. It will be argued below that the Puritans *said* it was about something else.

weavers worked with a book propped up over the loom; gentlemen attended to parliamentary affairs with a new assiduousness; godly mothers trained their sons to a constant concern with political life.[21] In their sermons, Puritan ministers urged many forms of activity, from methodical introspection to organized philanthropy to godly warfare. Addressing the gentry and their urban associates, the ministers spoke most often of *magistracy* and described a kind of political commitment and zeal which would have its effects in the revolution. Of business, apart from general injunctions to avoid idleness and work hard, they said very little.

But of business they are made to say a great deal through the anachronistic historiography not only of Weber but of the Marxists as well. Both, for example, place an emphasis on the Calvinist acceptance of usury which is totally unwarranted by the texts themselves.[22] Marxists understand this acceptance as a reflection of changing economic conditions. If so, it is a weak reflection indeed of such a common practice, and one which could hardly have brought much comfort to the new man staring hard and moodily into his ideological mirror. The difficulty with the theory of reflection is that one can see in the mirror only what one already sees in front of it. And here is an opening for the endless anachronistic errors into which Marxists fall. In front of the mirror-image of Puritanism they firmly set the capitalist man, a figure who has, for anyone familiar with the nineteenth century, the odd quality of being *déjà vu*. Inevitably, what results is a distortion – the mirror is "magic" indeed! Thus the extraordinary, intense, and pervasive seventeenth-century concern with personal salvation is hardly noticed by Marxist students of the mirror-image, and the scanty texts on usury are brought into the forefront of historical vision. The Puritan covenant is glimpsed in the mirror and all too quickly understood; the intentions and aspirations of the signers themselves are not studied, for real historical motives exist, so to speak, only on this side of the glass. The Puritan hatred of the economic vices, like laziness and profligacy, is sharply reflected, but the vast depths of sin and demonism are obscured. In the Marxist world of economic reason, beggars are duly whipped, witches untouched by the flame. It would be possible, of course, to put a different man in front of the mirror. But in order to know what man to choose, one would first have to look at the image – that is, to reverse the procedures of the usual Marxist methodology. This reversal will be taken up below.

[21] On the last of these, see the fascinating (and moving) *Letters of Lady Brilliania Harley*, ed. T. T. Lewis (London, 1854).
[22] Thus Christopher Hill: "[Calvin] abandoned the traditional absolute prohibition of usury (which theologians had whittled away by allowing exceptions) and permitted it in principle (though restricting it very stringently in a great many particular instances). So revolutions of thought are initiated. This slight shift of emphasis ... was enough." (*op. cit.*, 219). One can only comment that intellectual revolutions of this sort are not revolutions. On the question of usury, see the interesting discussion in Samuelsson, *op. cit.*, 87 ff.

Engels himself, aware up to a point of these difficulties, suggested a some-what different epistemology in an effort to explain the Calvinist theory of predestination. This invocation of God's arbitrary willfulness, he wrote, was the "religious expression" of the functioning of a market economy, where a man's fate depends on impersonal forces over which he has no control. The method of the "expression" is analogical reasoning and not mere reflection. The particular analogical leap from market forces to divine decree is com-prehensible, says Engels, given the general religious atmosphere.[23] This presumably explains the upward direction of the leap, but it is somewhat more of an explanation than is logically necessary. In fact the idea of analogy opens the way for a virtually indeterminate individual creativity. What are the limits of the analogical imagination? Men see shapes in clouds and ink-blots and while the shapes they see undoubtedly tell us something about the men, the historian or the psychologist has extraordinary license in inter-preting what that something is. And this is a license which works both ways: one may well wend one's way back from the theory of predestination and discover some material counterpart other than the market economy. The truth of the discovery cannot be judged formally; it will depend on how well the men who did the original thinking or imagining are known by the his-torian. At the very least the unraveling of such complex modes of thought as analogy or, in the seventeenth century, allegory, should not be prejudged. It is easy to see in Bunyan's *Pilgrim's Progress,* for example, a working out of such bourgeois themes as mobility, calculation and individualism, but not of accumulation, thrift or even sustained work in a calling. And it is never easy to say who are the Christians of this world.

157

V

To make Christian a petty-bourgeois is to ignore the fact that he was . . . Christian, a pilgrim bound for the heavenly city, and that many of the readers of *Pilgrim's Progress* were in some sense his colleagues.[24] Indeed, the Marxists are no more committed than are Whigs or Weberians to the world of experience which this pilgrimage represents. They are as disinclined to encounter the saints in history; but in their case the disinclination has a methodological reason. They tend to treat such an experience as Christian's journey as an epiphenomenon of objective existence, of what Marx called

[23] Marx and Engels, *Basic Writings on Politics and Philosophy,* ed. Lewis S. Feuer (New York, 1959), 55-56.
[24] The difficulties of describing Christian's pilgrimage and yet maintaining his class character are illustrated by Jack Lindsay, *op. cit.,* 5: "He is a writer of the transition, proletarian in that he writes from the viewpoint of the dispossessed, pre-industrialist in that he still clings to a medieval concept of reconciliation, petty bourgeois in that he is tied down to an individualistic ethic."

"real life". This is not to say that the pilgrimage was not actually made. Rather, it involves the assertion that it can only be understood by putting aside Christian's ideology – his perceptions, feelings, thoughts, aspirations – and confronting directly those economic and social processes which somehow underlie and cause the actual journey. But the distinctions presupposed by this kind of explanation are hopelessly precise. Many critics have pointed out that ideas play a vital role in what Marxists call the objective world: no economic relationship is conceivable, for example, which does not involve some shared notions of profit and loss, of security, trust, love or interest.[25] Ideas are intrinsic to any relationship among men, as they are to any perceived sequence of events. It is simply not possible to treat them as reflections or epiphenomena because one can't imagine or satisfactorily construct "reality" without them.

Thus there is, so to speak, no journey but *only* a pilgrimage. One cannot separate the physical motion from the sense of destination and describe the one as an example of increased social mobility and the other as an illusion, a piece of religious confusion, the result of Bunyan's failure to understand social change.

In sharp contrasts to the pilgrim Christian, Defoe's Moll Flanders is something of a Marxist heroine, an economic woman; despite her ideology she is never confused. Defoe at least suggests that ideas and "real life" can easily be distinguished. But this is only true when ideas have become conventional – like Moll's moralizing – and even then it is not entirely true. For ideology is a way of perceiving and responding to the experienced world, so it is always itself an aspect of experience. In relatively peaceful or stable times (when no-one is a pilgrim), perceptions may be widely shared, even inherited, and responses predictable. For ordinary men, ideology may indeed become a reflex, automatic and inescapable, and then the way be opened for all sorts of evasion, hypocrisy, and platitudinizing. Writing about such periods, Marxists have had their greatest success: thus have they struck off the bourgeois ideology. They have done much less well in confronting sharp discontinuities of perception and response. For all his concern with revolution, Marx was himself the product of the same world which produced the great social novels, those elaborate, many-volumed studies of manners, status and class relationships in which the fundamental stability of the society as a whole and of character (what would today be called "identity") within the society was always assumed.[26] And Marx never questions the second of these assumptions: bourgeois and proletarian appear

[25] See H. B. Acton, *The Illusion of the Epoch: Marxism-Leninism as a Philosophical Creed* (London, 1955), 141 ff.
[26] By the end of the nineteenth century, of course, novelists were discussing precisely the problem of character: see the discussion of the social novel and its decline in Irving Howe, *Politics and the Novel* (New York, 1957), 18, 19.

in his work as *formed characters*, free at least from psychological instability even while their struggle with one another tears apart the social order. But in a time like that of the Puritans, Christian's colleagues, there is an enormous range in perception and response, and – more important – an enormous range in the clarity of perception (even if it be the clarity of madness) and in the intensity of response. Ideology cannot be consistently linked with class experiences because those experiences no longer take place in a regular and predictable order. Hence character is not stable; its very formation, so to speak, is problematic.

It is obvious that Bunyan's pilgrim would hardly set out on his strange journey in such a stable bourgeois society as that of nineteenth-century England. Nor, since Christian is everyman and no medieval saint, would he set out from a stable feudal society. He "corresponds" to what can roughly be called a time of transition. But the time of transition, a time of instability and chronic danger, is only the *condition* of his journey – its cause is ideological. And it is the journey in its ideological setting, complete with purpose and meaning, which constitutes the experience and needs to be explained.

In order to get at the world of experience, it may well be necessary to construct some highly abstract model of economic processes and social change. But this construct is not "real life". It is only an intellectual approach to reality and only one among several possible approaches. The Marxist historian seeks to reconstitute the world which is perceived, while at the same time detaching himself from the particular perceptions of historical men. But it ought to be those very perceptions which direct his work. Reality is too complex, too detailed, too formless: he can never reproduce it. He must seek, instead, to reproduce only those aspects of historical existence which were, so to speak, absorbed into the experience of particular men. And if he is to avoid anachronistic reconstructions, his guide must be the men themselves. It would be absurd to assume *a priori* that what is of central importance in late sixteenth- and early seventeenth-century history is, for example, the growth of the coal industry. One must look first to see what impact such a phenomenon had upon the lives of men. It is not, of course, only a question of whether they talked about it, but of whether they *felt* it, directly or indirectly, consciously or unconsciously. If they did not, then its significance must be sought in the future.

Marxists become the victims of the very alienation they claim to understand so well when they reverse this procedure and make experience dependent upon what is originally only a creation of the mind. When Tawney writes that Puritanism is the "magic mirror" in which the middle-class man saw himself ennobled and enhanced, he is in no sense enlightening us as to the historical process by which Puritanism developed and spread. For the Puritan is a real man, who can be encountered in history. But the middle-class man is made up, and it is sheer anachronism to describe him as a historical

159

figure, articulate, already in search of an enhanced image. It has been suggested above that Puritanism is a part of the process (the long succession of perceptions and responses) by which men *become* middle-class. But to know the particular perceptions upon which it is based or the responses it prescribes, it is necessary to know the Puritan. There is, in fact, no magic mirror; sainthood is no mere enhancement of an already established (even if worrisome) identity. It is a far more active thing than that; it is indeed what Weber suggests – a way of forming an identity.[27]

What must be studied, then, is a mind, or a group of minds, coping with problems and not passively reflecting them. For the mind mediates between the "objective" situation and the human act and if the act is to be understood, the mind must first be known. The problems it faces are posed by an environment which can of course be analyzed in some objective fashion – for example, statistically. But different aspects of this environment are experienced by different men with different results in consciousness and behavior. Hence the "objective" construct is of no independent value and has no prior significance in explanation. The first task of the historian is to establish his familiarity with the experience of particular men, with their difficulties, aspirations and achievements, and with the styles in which all these are expressed. This is not to suggest that the historical record should be taken at face value, or the assumption casually made that men always mean what they say. There is, for example, false piety and evasion among the saints which the historian must expose. There is caution and conformity which he must respect, but not too much. For hindsight is also insight into the concealments of respectability and of "Aesopian" prose; and it is often insight as well into purposes half-understood and patterns of thought not yet fully worked out. Hence the methods of the historian must be sceptical, devious and experimental, even while his general approach is open and sympathetic. But ultimately his sympathy is the key to all else: the best judgment of face value will be made by men with some intuitive understanding of other levels of thinking and feeling.

The problem of the Puritan belief in witchcraft and demonology has already been suggested and may profitably be developed at greater length as an illustration of the above argument. One sees in the mirror (that is, in experience and thought) images which have no easy or readily explained connection with the supposed subject, middle-class man. Witchcraft indeed suggests a world altogether apart from the Marxist universe of interest. In his book *Navaho Witchcraft*, Clyde Kluckhohn has analyzed the psychological basis of the belief in terms of the concepts of hostility and anxiety and has sought to give these concepts some precision. He has discussed the

---

[27] Weber, *op. cit.*, 119. See also the interesting, occasionally exasperating, book by Zevedei Barbu, *Problems of Historical Psychology* (New York, 1960), chapters V and VI.

possible ways in which historical events or particular social structures may generate those anxious or hostile feelings which presumably lead to the perception of witches (or of oneself as a witch) and to the responses of persecution and cruelty.[28] Now the history of the persecution of witches in England (also the history of the practice of witchcraft) directly parallels the career of the Puritans. The first enactments were produced by the returning Marian exiles; the persecution reached its height during the revolutionary period and in the centers of Puritan sentiment; interest in and fear of witches declined after the Restoration.[29] Perhaps Marxists have paid so little attention to witchcraft precisely because it had no future; it was neglected in that final process of selection which constituted the bourgeois world. The point here is that this piece of knowledge about Puritan feeling and behavior suggests certain possibilities in the "objective" environment to which Marxists have been singularly blind.

161

Anxiety seems to appear in acute form only among men who have experienced some great disorder or who are caught up in a process of rapid, incomprehensible change: the breakdown of some habitual system of conventions and routines, a departure to an unaccustomed world, the aftermath of epidemic or war. Events of this sort leave men without customary restraints upon their behavior and no longer responsible to revered authorities. The result often is that extraordinary panic which Erich Fromm has somewhat misleadingly called a "fear of freedom."[30] In human experience, this is more likely a dread of chaos, and one of its aspects is a sharp, if often delusory perception of danger and of dangerous men.

If Puritanism is studied with these ideas in mind, a new light is thrown on sixteenth- and seventeenth-century history. One searches more deeply in the life experience of the saints for those feelings of fearfulness which parallel the belief in witches – and for the sources of such fear. One searches for sudden changes in environment, habits, authorities. The result is a hypothesis which is in striking contradiction to that of the Marxists: Puritanism appears to be a response to disorder and fear, a way of organizing men to overcome the acute sense of chaos. With this hypothesis it becomes possible to understand,

[28] *Navaho Witchcraft* (Cambridge, Mass., 1944), esp. 50 ff and 64-66.
[29] Wallace Notestein, *A History of Witchcraft in England from 1558 to 1718* (Washington, 1911), 14-15, 195 ff.
[30] Much of the argument of this essay was first suggested by Erich Fromm's book, *Escape from Freedom* (New York, 1941), but the author cannot accept Fromm's easy distinction between two aspects of modern freedom: freedom *from*, which by itself leads to anxiety and the search for authority; and freedom *to*, which presumably is realized in a sense of dignity and a creative life. That the two are not distinct in history, that is, not always embodied in different people – Fromm clearly recognizes. He seems, however, to believe that their manifestations can be readily distinguished and judged. Thus, for example, he writes that the Puritans, when fighting against the old order, were expressing positive freedom ("strength and dignity of self" – *Escape*, 122). Since that fight involved an effort to establish the repressive holy commonwealth, this seems rather dubious.

for example, the as yet fragmentary evidence which suggests that the Calvinist faith, especially in its more radical forms, appealed most of all to men
newly come to London and not, as Marxists have always assumed, to experienced city dwellers.[31] For coming to the city was an event in a man's life
which might well sharpen his sense of danger and even lead him to seek that
discipline which has been described above as central to Puritan association.
Thus, the sudden increase in London's population between roughly 1580 and
1625 takes on new significance: it may well be that London did not so much
prepare men to become "saints" as that sainthood helped them, through the
hard transition period, to become Londoners. Once they had become *urbane*,
they were in fact unlikely to remain faithful to the original Calvinist creed;
they became revisionists. Similarly, it is somewhat less of a paradox than
Marxists might suppose that witchchraft should range more widely in the
southeast of England, where economic development was most advanced. For
it may be – and this, perhaps, can be investigated – that witchcraft helped
solve, in the minds of the people, some of the problems raised by that very
development and by its impact upon traditional ways of doing things. (This
is, of course, only speculation, but it is speculation which begins at the right
place: with a concern for the concerns of the Puritans themselves.)

162

It seems likely that certain modes of perception and response parallel
certain basic historical experiences; if so, comparison is possible and one
might arrive at general propositions. But the relationship between, for
example, urbanization and some ideological response to urbanization (once
again, it must be said that these are not distinct "spheres") must be understood in dynamic terms. Perhaps it would be best to figure to oneself an
energetic man continually struggling to understand and cope with the surrounding world. Undoubtedly, energy and struggle are not universal in
history: ways of thinking quickly become habitual, as does experience itself.
But it is the creative moments which require explanation and at such moments
ideology is never a mere habit or reflex, but a willful activity. For perhaps
a hundred years after the original creative achievement of Calvin, the spread
of Puritanism can still be described in the active tense: men, with their own
problems and aspirations, continually rediscovered for themselves, with all
the enthusiasm which must have attended the first discovery, the truths of
the new faith. The historian who begins with these ideology-producing men
may then work outward, so to speak, re-experiencing their world and only
after this subjecting that world to such further analysis as will improve his
own understanding of it.

The Puritan saints are such men, making their ideology, and making

---

[31] On the growth of London, see the figures in F. P. Wilson, *The Plague in
Shakespeare's London* (Oxford, 1927), appendix. That members of Puritan conventicles were often newcomers to the city is suggested by the court records reprinted in
Champlin Burrage, *The Early English Dissenters in the Light of Recent Research
1550-1641* (Cambridge, 1912), II.

themselves. The sources and nature of this creativity must next be considered.

VI

The study of the Puritans is best begun with the idea of discipline, and all the tension and strain that underlies it, both in their writing and in what can be known of their experience. It is strange that theorists have had so little to say on this topic, especially since the rebellion against Puritan repression, or rather against its ugly remnants – devoid, as Weber's capitalism is, of theological reason – is still a part of our own experience. The persecution of witches, of course, was not a vital aspect of Puritan endeavor, but the active, fearful struggle against wickedness was. And the saints imagined wickedness as a creative and omnipresent demonic force, that is, as a continuous threat. Like Hobbes, they saw disorder and war as the natural state of fallen men, out of which they had been drawn by God's command and by the painful efforts of their own regenerate wills. But they lived always on the very brink of chaos, maintaining their position only through a constant vigilance and, indeed, a constant warfare against their own natural inclinations and against the devil and his worldlings.

163

The goal of this warfare was repression and its apparent cause was an extraordinary anxiety. It is by no means necessary to argue that these two constitute the "essence" of Puritanism, only that their full significance has not been realized. In Calvin's own work anxiety is presented as central to the experience of fallen man: this is anxiety of a special sort; it is not the fear of death and damnation, but rather the fear of sudden and violent death. Hobbes would recognize it as the dominant passion of man in his natural state. Thus Calvin: [32]

Now, whithersoever you turn, all the objects around you are not only unworthy of your confidence, but almost openly menace you, and seem to threaten immediate death. Embark in a ship; there is but a single step between you and death. Mount a horse; the slipping of one foot endangers your life. Walk through the streets of a city; you are liable to as many dangers as there are tiles on the roofs. If there be a sharp weapon in your hand, or that of your friend, the mischief is manifest. All the ferocious animals you see are armed for your destruction. If you endeavor to shut yourself in a garden surrounded with a good fence, and exhibiting nothing but what is delightful, even there sometimes lurks a serpent. Your house, perpetually liable to fire, menaces you by day with poverty, and by night with falling on your head. Your land, exposed to hail, frost, drought and various tempests, threatens you with sterility, and with its attendant, famine. I omit poison, treachery, robbery and open violence, which partly beset us at home and partly pursue us abroad ... You will say that these things happen seldom, or certainly not always, nor to every man, [and] never all at once. I grant it; but we are admonished by the examples of others, that it is possible for them to happen to us. ...

[32] *Institutes of the Christian Religion* (Allen translation), Book, I, chapter XVII, x.

Among the saints such terrible fearfulness was overcome, and that was the great benefit of sainthood: it did not so much promise future ecstasy as present "tranquillity". "When the light of Divine Providence," wrote Calvin, "has once shined on a pious man, he is relieved and delivered not only from the extreme anxiety and dread with which he was previously oppressed, but also from all care." [33] But relief was not rest in the Calvinist world; it was rather that security of mind which might well manifest itself as self-righteousness – or as fanaticism.

In Puritan literature this same fearfulness is made specific in social terms. Once again, it is a fear which Hobbes would understand: the fear of disorder in society. It is apparent in the nervous hostility with which Puritan writers regarded carousal, vagabondage, idleness, all forms of individualistic extravagance (especially in clothing), country dances and urban crowds, the theater with its gay (undisciplined) audiences, gossip, witty talk, love-play, dawdling in taverns – the list could be extended. [34] The shrewdest among their contemporaries sensed that this pervasive hostility was a key to Puritanism – though they could hardly help but regard it as hypocritical. Ben Jonson's Zeal-of-the-land Busy is a caricature based, like all good caricatures, on a kernel of truth. Zeal-of-the-land is, for all his comical hypocrisy, insistently and anxiously concerned about the world he lives in – and the aim of his concern is supervision and repression. [35]

At times, Puritan preachers sounded very much like Hobbes: " ... take sovereignty from the face of the earth," proclaimed Robert Bolton, "and you turn it into a cockpit. Men would become cut-throats and cannibals ... Murder, adulteries, incests, rapes, robberies, perjuries, witchcrafts, blasphemies, all kinds of villainies, outrages and savage cruelty would overflow all countries." [36] But secular sovereignty was not their usual appeal. They looked rather to congregational discipline, as has been argued above. Thus Thomas Cartwright promised that the new discipline would restrain stealing, adultery and murder. Even more, it would "correct" sins "which the magistrate doth not commonly punish" – he listed lying, jesting, choleric speeches. [37] It need hardly be said that John Locke, a century later, was not terribly worried about such sins. Walsingham's spies reported in the 1580's and '90's that Puritan agitators were promising "that if discipline were planted, there should be no more vagabonds nor beggars". John Penry foresaw the

[33] *Ibid.*, xi.
[34] Alfred Harbage has pointed out that Puritans objected more to the audience at the theaters than to the plays: see his *Shakespeare's Audience* (New York, 1951).
[35] Jonson, *Bartholomew Fair*; see also his characterizations of two Puritans in *The Alchemist*.
[36] Bolton, *Two Sermons* (London, 1635), I, 10. The passage is a curious one since it opens with a paraphrase of Hooker, *Ecclesiastical Polity*, I, iii, 2; but Hooker says nothing about the effects of disobedience *among men*, which is the Puritan writer's chief concern.
[37] John Whitgift, *Works*, I, 21.

"amendment" of idleness and hence, he thought, of poverty.[38] Now none of
these concerns was unusual in Tudor or early Stuart England, but the intensity and extent of Puritan worry and the novelty of the proposed solution
have no parallel among statesmen or traditional moralists. These latter
groups also watched with apprehension the growth of London, the increasing
geographic and social mobility, and the new forms of individualistic experimentation. It must be said, however, that the tone of their writings rarely
reached a pitch of anxiety and fearfulness comparable to, for example, the
diary of the Puritan minister Richard Rogers, endlessly worried about his
own "unsettledness". Nostalgia was a more common theme, satire and
mockery a more frequent defense among moralists like Thomas Dekker.[39]
And the world they would have substituted for Renaissance England was an
already romanticized version of medieval England. Not so the Puritans.
Their discipline would have established dramatically new forms of association: the anxiety of the minister Rogers led him to join with his brethren
in a solemn covenant – and these brethren were neither his immediate
neighbors nor his kinfolk.[40]

165

What Rogers sought from his covenant was a bolstering of his faith, a
steeling of his character. "The sixth of this month [December, 1587] we
fasted betwixt ourselves," he reported in his diary, "... to the stirring up of
ourselves to greater godliness." The need for this "stirring up" is so pervasive
among the Puritans that one might well imagine that what they feared so
greatly was rather in themselves than in the society about them. In fact,
what they feared was the image in themselves of the "unsettledness" of their
world. Puritan fearfulness is best explained in terms of the actual experiences
of exile, alienation, and social mobility about which the saints so often and
insistently wrote.[41] Discipline and repression are responses to these experiences, responses which do not aim at a return to some former security, but
rather at a vigorous control and a narrowing of energies – a bold effort to
shape a personality amidst "chaos". Thus might be explained the extraordinarily regimented life recorded in Margaret Hoby's diary. Mrs. Hoby
was a merchant's daughter, married to a gentleman (the son of the Elizabethan
ambassador Sir Thomas Hoby, translator of Castiglione) and carried off to
a country estate in Yorkshire where all her neighbors were Catholic and, in
her eyes, rowdy and sinful men. There she spent her time in earnest con-

[38] The report to Walsingham is quoted in Hill, *Puritanism and Revolution*, 234. John
Penry, *An Humble Motion with Submission* (Edinburgh, 1590), 72.
[39] The views of the moralists are described in L. C. Knights, *Drama and Society in
the Age of Jonson* (London, 1937).
[40] *Two Elizabethan Diaries*, ed. M. Knappen (Chicago, 1933), 69.
[41] They wrote about more than these themes, of course, and even here described
more than their own experience, for the outsider is an archetypal figure realized with
especial force in Christian thought. The Puritans still lived within a cultural tradition
which shaped their expression as it undoubtedly still shaped their experience. On the
dangers of reductionism, see Leavis, *op. cit.*, 208-10.

versations with her minister, reading and listening to sermons and laboriously copying them out in her notebook, adhering to a strict routine of public and private prayer, assiduous in her daily self-recrimination: [42]

> I talked of some things not so as I ought when I had considered of them, but I find what is in a man if the Lord's spirit do never so little hide itself . . . but this is my comfort, that my heart is settled to be more watchful hereafter. . . .

How many men have settled since for the same "comfort"!

Undoubtedly, Margaret Hoby's behavior might be differently explained, but not so as to account so well for the similar behavior of her brethren. These people felt themselves exceptionally open to the dangers about them and this must have been, in part, because they were cut off, as were the men who succumbed to chaos – beggars and vagabonds – from the old forms of order and routine. It is this sense of being cut off, alien, that is expressed in the endless descriptions of the saint as a stranger and pilgrim which are so important in Puritan writing.[43] Pilgrimage is, perhaps, one of the major themes in all Christian literature, but it achieves among the Puritans a unique power, a forcefulness and intensity in its popular expression which culminates finally in Bunyan's classic. Over and over again, with the detail which only experience or, perhaps, a continually engaged imagination can give, Puritans describe life as a journey (or, in the image which Hobbes later made famous, as a race) through alien country. And yet, at the same time, they write of the vagabond with venomous hatred: he is a dangerous man because he has not disciplined and prepared himself for his journey. "Wandering beggars and rogues," wrote William Perkins, "that pass from place to place, being under no certain magistracy or ministry, nor joining themselves to any set society in church or commonwealth, are plagues and banes of both, and are to be taken as main enemies of [the] ordinance of God . . ." [44] The bitterness of this passage suggests the self-hatred of the Puritan pilgrim, pitying and worrying about his own "unsettledness". When the famous preacher Richard Greenham told a Puritan audience "Paradise is our native country", some of his listeners surely must have winced to think: *not England*. "We dwell here as in Meshech and as in the tents of Kedar, and therefore we be glad to be at home." It was painful, but inevitable, that the saints should live in tents. Perkins himself wrote in the same vein, for all his hatred of the wanderer: "Alas, poor souls, we are no better than passengers in this world, our way it is in the middle of the sea." [46] For many Puritans, if not for Perkins himself, who grew old in Cambridge, these words

---

[42] *Diary of Lady Margaret Hoby, 1599-1605*, ed. D. M. Meads (London, 1930), 97.
[43] See the comments of William Haller on Puritan wayfaring: *The Rise of Puritanism* (New York, 1957), 147 ff.
[44] William Perkins, *Works* (London, 1616), III, 539; the passage is quoted in Hill, *op. cit.*, 228.
[46] Greenham, *Works* (London, 1605), 645; Perkins, *op. cit.*, I, 398.

must have had a meaning both literal and poignant. Since the days of Mary, exile had been a common experience for the saints. And a generation after Perkins wrote, the "middle of the sea" would become a path for tens of thousands.

The fanatical self-righteousness of that first Puritan John Knox, a Scottish peasant's son, set loose in Europe by war and revolution, is surely in some sense a function of his exile: righteousness was a consolation and a way of organizing the self for survival. The "unsettledness" of Richard Rogers was due in part to his devious struggles with the corporate church and its bishops; but Rogers, who remembered his Essex birthplace as a "dunghill", was ever an outsider, and Puritanism his way of stirring up his heart. When William Whitgift, the future archbishop, cruelly taunted the Puritan leader Thomas Cartwright for "eating at other men's tables", he was perhaps suggesting an important source of Cartwright's vision of congregational unity and holiness. Margaret Hoby's life would have been different indeed had she been raised in a traditional country family: there would, for example, have been dancing at her wedding, and her life thereafter would hardly have allowed for time-consuming religious exercises. Deprived of such a life, because of her social background (and the ideas which were part of it) or, perhaps, because of basic changes in rural life, she willfully sought new comforts.[46] Country gentlemen like John Winthrop and Oliver Cromwell, educated at Cambridge, knowledgeable in London, suddenly turned upon the traditional routine of English life as if it were actually vicious. Half in, half out of that routine, they anxiously sought a new certainty. "Oh, I lived in and loved darkness and hated light; I was a chief, the chief of sinners", wrote Cromwell of his seemingly ordinary and conventional life before conversion. But now, he went on, "my soul is with the congregation of the first born, my body rests in hope; and if here I may honor my God either by doing or by suffering, I shall be most glad." [47]

All this suggests once again the view of Puritanism as a response of particular men to particular experiences of confusion, change, alienation and exile. Now Calvinism obviously made men extremely sensitive to disorder in all its forms. It is more important, however, that it gave meaning to the experience of disorder and provided a way out, a return to certainty. It was an active response, and not a mere reflection of social confusion, for indeed other men responded differently. There is no rigid pattern in these responses. It seems probable that members of a rising middle class most sharply experienced that alienation from old England which drove men to the exercises of sainthood. On the other hand, there were both gentlemen and citizens

167

---

[46] *Two Elizabethan Diaries*, 17; A. F. Scott-Pearson, *Thomas Cartwright and Elizabethan Puritanism* (Cambridge, 1925), 66; *Diary of Margaret Hoby*, 32 – at their wedding, the Hoby's sought "only to please the beholders with a sermon and a dinner."
[47] *Cromwell's Letters and Speeches*, ed. Carlyle (London, 1893), I, 79-80. On Winthrop see E. S. Morgan, *The Puritan Dilemma: The Story of John Winthrop* (Boston, 1958).

who certainly enjoyed the new freedoms of mobility, extravagance, individuality and wit, and eagerly sought entrance to the Renaissance court, where freedom was cultivated. And from among these men undoubtedly came many future capitalists. It would not be easy to explain in particular cases why the court held such attractions for some men, while it was vicious and iniquitous in the eyes of others. No more is it readily comprehensible why some of the newcomers to the burgeoning city of London merged into the mob or explored the exciting underworld, while others hated the wickedness of the city and sought out virtuous brethren in the radical conventicles. What is important for the present is that Puritanism was a response to an experience which many men had; it provided one way of understanding the experience and of coping with it.

Coping with it meant being reborn as a new man, self-confident and free of worry, capable of vigorous, willful activity. The saints sometimes took new names to signify their rebirth. If alienation had made them anxious, depressed, unable to work, given to fantasies of demons, morbid introspection or fearful daydreams such as Calvin had suggested were common among fallen men, then sainthood was indeed a transformation.[48] Cromwell's pledge to honor his God "by doing" was no idle boast: he was obviously capable of just that. Perhaps this transformation gave businessmen the confidence necessary for innovation or freed them from the necessity of feeling guilty about routine connivance, usury, extortion. Thus argue Marxists and Weberians alike. But innovation was more likely due to the recklessness of the speculator than to the self-confidence of the saint; indeed, the saints hated the "projectors" who lived in and about the court, currying favor and waiting for opportunity. The congregational discipline, as has been seen, would have established controls hardly compatible with businesslike hard dealing. Cromwell's "doing" was obviously of a different order, and Cromwell was a representative man. His life suggests that the Puritan experience produced first of all a political activist.

The Puritan new man was active not so that success might reinforce his self-esteem, but in order to transform a world in which he saw his own ever-present wickedness writ large.[49] In a sense, his was a struggle to free

[48] Indeed, Calvin thought that commercial competition, with its attendant anxiety, was an aspect of the life of *fallen* man; he pictured him nervously murmuring to himself: "I must use such a mean, I must practise such a feat. I must look into such a business, or otherwise I shall be behindhand in all things. I shall but pine away, I shall not get half my living, if I proceed not in this manner ...". *Sermons upon the Fifth Book of Moses* (London, 1583), 821. Presumably the saint would be free from such anxiety.
[49] Most of the calls for activity in Puritan sermons are put in terms of the struggle against social disorder; activity is rarely described as a way of overcoming the fear of damnation. The clear emphasis of the preachers is on the social effects of hard work, and not, as Weber thought, on success as a spiritual sign. See, for example, the discussion of work in Robert Cleaver and John Dod, *A Godly Form of Household Government* (London, 1621), Sig. P 6 and 7.

himself from temptation by removing all alternatives to godliness, by organizing his own life as a continuous discipline and society as a regiment. His activity was political in that it was always concerned with government – though not only or, perhaps, not most importantly, at the level of the state. Puritans often imagined the congregation as a "little commonwealth", replacing the organic imagery of Anglicans and Catholics with expressions deliberately drawn from the world of coercion and sovereignty. Thus they made manifest their own pervasive concern with *control* rather than with harmony or love.[50] Their treatment of the family was similar: they saw it as a field for the exercise of discipline by a godly father usually described as a "governor". Puritan interest in the family parallels that of Jean Bodin (though, in contrast to Robert Filmer, also a Bodinian, the saints had little to say about paternal affection and benevolence) and probably has the same source. The insistence upon the absolute sovereignty of the father and upon the family as an institution for repressing and disciplining naturally wicked, licentious and rebellious children derives in both cases from an extraordinary fear of disorder and anarchy. Thus two Puritan preachers in a famous treatise on "family government":

169

> The young child which lieth in the cradle [is] both wayward and full of affections: and though his body be but small, yet he hath a great heart, and is altogether inclined to evil.... If this sparkle be suffered to increase, it will rage over and burn down the whole house. For we are changed and become good, not by birth, but by education.... Therefore parents must be wary and circumspect, that they never smile or laugh at any words or deeds of their children done lewdly ... naughtily, wantonly ... they must correct and sharply reprove their children for saying or doing ill....[51]

The father was continually active, warily watching his children; the elders of the congregation were ever alert and vigilant, seeking out the devious paths of sin; so also the godly magistrate. "In you it is now to cleanse, to free your country of villainy," a Puritan minister told the judges of Norwich, " ... consider your power to reform ... if you be faithful, and God's power to revenge if you be faithless."[52] In Puritan writings, political activity was described as a form of work: it required systematic application, attention to detail, sustained interest and labor. Much that the godly magistrates undertook might be called, in Marxist terms, progressive; some of their activity, however, would clearly impede free economic activity. But description in these terms is valuable only if one seeks to understand those aspects of Puritan activity which, through a subsequent process of selection, became permanent features of the modern world. In the seventeenth century, Puritan

---

[50] See Walter Travers, *A Full and Plain Declaration of Ecclesiastical Discipline out of the Word of God* (n. p., 1574).
[51] Cleaver and Dod, *op. cit.*, Sig. S 8; Bodin, *op. cit.*, 9-13.
[52] Thomas Reed, *Moses Old Square for Judges* (London, 1632), 98-99.

politics obviously had an interest rather different from that suggested by the term "progress". Its immediate purpose was to regain control of a changing world; hence the great concern with method, discipline, and order, and the frequent uneasiness with novelty. When the saints spoke of reform, they meant first of all an overcoming of social instability and all its moral and intellectual concommitants. Godly magistracy was a bold effort to seize control of society, much as sainthood had been an effort to control and organize the self. And the first of these followed from the second: in this way did Puritanism produce revolutionaries. In much the same way, it may be suggested, did the Jacobin man of virtue become an *active citizen*, and the hardened and "steeled" Bolshevik first a *professional* revolutionary and then, in Lenin's words, a "leader", "manager", and "controller".[53]

These revolutionary men do not simply attack and transform the old order – as in the Marxist story. The old order is only a part, and often not the most important part, of their experience. They live much of their lives amidst the breakdown of that order, or in hiding or exile from it. And much of their rebellion is directed against the very "unsettledness" that they know best. The analogy with the Bolsheviks is worth pursuing. Lenin's diatribes against "slovenliness ... carelessness, untidiness, unpunctuality, nervous haste, the inclination to substitute discussion for action, talk for work, the inclination to undertake everything under the sun without finishing anything" were intended first of all as attacks upon his fellow exiles – whatever their value as descriptions of the "primitive" Russia he hated so much.[54] The first triumph of Bolshevism, as of Puritanism, was over the impulse toward "disorganization" in its own midst: here, so to speak, was Satan at work where he is ever most active – in the ranks of the godly. And it must be said that this triumph was also over the first impulses toward freedom. Thus the Puritans vigorously attacked Renaissance experimentation in dress and in all the arts of self-decoration and hated the free-wheeling vagabonds who "crowd into cities [and] boroughs ... roll up and down from one lodging to another", never organizing themselves into families and congregations.[55] Similarly, the Jacobin leader Robespierre attacked the economic egotism of the new bourgeoisie and spitefully connected the radical free thought of the Enlightenment with anti-revolutionary conspiracy. Atheism, he declared, is aristocratic.[56] And again Lenin, preaching with all the energy of a secular Calvinist against free love: "Dissoluteness in sexual life is bourgeois, [it] is a phenomenon of decay. The proletariat is a rising class ... It needs clarity,

---

[53]   Lenin, *The Immediate Tasks of the Soviet Government* (1918) in *Selected Works* (New York, 1935-1937), VII, 332-33.
[54]   *How To Organize Competition* (1917, reprinted Moscow, 1951), 63; also see *Letters* trans. and ed. by Elizabeth Hill and Doris Mudie (New York, 1937), 161.
[55]   Henry Crosse, *Virtue's Commonwealth* (London, 1603), Sig. L₁ vers; Perkins, *Works*, III, 191.
[56]   Quoted in A. Aulard, *Christianity and the French Revolution* (Boston, 1927), 113.

clarity and again clarity. And so, I repeat, no weakening, no waste, no destruction of forces." [57]

In fact, Lenin's morality had little to do with the proletariat, and the "dissoluteness" he attacked had little to do with the bourgeoisie. He might as well have talked of saints and worldlings as the Puritans did. The contrast he was getting at was between those men who had succumbed to (or taken advantage of!) the disorder of their time – speculators in philosophy, vagabonds in their sexual life, economic Don Juans – and those men who had somehow pulled themselves out of "unsettledness", organized their lives and regained control. The first group were the damned and the second the saved. The difference between them was not social but ideological.

Puritans, Jacobins and Bolsheviks did tend to come from the same social strata – that is, from the educated middle classes, preachers, lawyers, journalists, teachers, professional men of all sorts. But this is not because such men are representatives of larger social groups whose interests they defend. It has already been shown that the connection between Puritan theory and bourgeois interests is at best a difficult one, which is in no sense implicit in the theory, but is rather worked out later in a long process of corruption, selection and forgetting. Men like the godly ministers speak first of all for themselves: they record most sensitively the experience of "unsettledness" and respond to it most vigorously. For reasons which require further investigation, such men seem less integrated into their society – even in the most stable periods – and more available, as it were, for alienation than are farmers or businessmen. This is not, of course, to reduce their moral discipline (or their radical politics) to the psychological therapy of alienated intellectuals. The alienation which John Knox or Richard Rogers experienced, with all its attendant fearfulness and enthusiasm, sometimes disfiguring and sometimes ennobling, was only a heightened form of the feelings of other men – in a sense, of all men, for ultimately the sociological range of the Puritan response was very wide.

But the historian must also record that "unsettledness" was not a permanent condition and that sainthood was only a temporary role. For men always seek and find not some tense and demanding discipline, but some new routine. The saints failed in their effort to establish a holy commonwealth and, in one way or another, their more recent counterparts have also failed. What this suggests is not that the holy commonwealth was an im-

171

---

[57] Quoted in Klara Zetkin, "Reminiscences of Lenin", in *The Family in the U.S.S.R.*, ed. Rudolf Schlesinger (London, 1949), 78. It should be said that in all the revolutions discussed above, there were men who did not follow the Puritan saints or the vanguard Bolsheviks in their attacks upon human freedom. These men, radical sectarians, secularists, anarchists, libertarians of many sorts, were the products of the same society and the same experience which produced the others. They rarely made good revolutionaries, however, precisely because they never felt the intense need to yield to an organization and a discipline.

practical dream, the program of muddled, unrealistic men. In fact, Puritan
ministers and elders (and fathers!) had considerable political experience and
the holy commonwealth was in a sense achieved, at least among those men
who most needed holiness. Nor is it correct to argue from the failure of the
saints that Puritanism in its revolutionary form represents only a temporary
triumph of "ideas" over "interest", a momentary burst of enthusiasm.[58] For
such moments have their histories, and what needs to be explained is why
groups of men, over a fairly long span of time, acquired such an intense
interest in ideas like predestination and holiness. Puritan ideology was a
response to real experience, therefore a practical effort to cope with personal
and social problems. The inability of the saints to establish and maintain
their holy commonwealth suggests only that these problems were limited in
time to the period of breakdown and psychic and political reconstruction.
When men stopped being afraid, or became less afraid, then Puritanism was
suddenly irrelevant. Particular elements in the Puritan system were transformed to fit the new routine – and other elements were forgotten. And only
then did the saint become a man of "good behavior", cautious, respectable,
calm, ready to participate in a Lockeian society.

VIII

The argument of the preceding section may now be concluded: Puritanism
was not a revolutionary ideology in the Marxist sense, reflecting the interests
of a rising class. Such interests are in the seventeenth century better represented by parliamentarians and common lawyers who had their own ideology.
The faith of the saints was rather a peculiarly intense response to the experience of social change itself, an experience which, in one way or another, set
groups of men outside the established order. It should be obvious that this
may be the result of either "rising" or "falling" in economic terms; mobility
itself is the key, especially if the old social order is traditionalist, dependent
for its stability upon popular passivity. The Puritan response produced
revolutionaries, that is, saints, godly magistrates, men already disciplined
(before the revolution begins) for the strenuous work of transforming all
society and all men in the image of their own salvation. Such men, narrow,
fanatical, enthusiastic, committed to their "work", have little to contribute to
the development of either liberalism or capitalism. To expect freedom from
their hands is to invite disappointment. Their great achievement is what is
known in the sociology of revolution as the *terror*, the effort to create a holy
commonwealth and to force men to be godly.

[58] This is the view of revolutionary enthusiasm suggested in Crane Brinton's book on
the French Revolution, *Decade of Revolution* (New York, 1934) and again in his
Anatomy of Revolution (New York, 1938). The analogy with religion argued in both
books is, however, a very suggestive one.

The contribution of these men to the future is the destruction of the old order. Alienated from its conventions and routines – from its comforts – they feel no nostalgia as they watch its slow decay. They are capable not only of establishing, underground, an alternative system, but also of making a frontal assault upon the old order itself, in the case of the Puritans, upon hierarchy and patriarchy, the central principles of traditional government. Their extraordinary self-confidence, won at some cost, as has been seen, makes them capable finally of killing the king. Here Weber's analysis is undoubtedly closer to the truth than that of the Marxists: the saints are entrepreneurs indeed, but in politics rather than in economics. They ruthlessly (and anxiously) pursue not wealth or even individual power – never rely on great men, warned a Puritan preacher – but *collective control* of themselves, of each other, of all England.

The Puritan struggle for collective control is not unique in history. The illustrations already drawn from Jacobin and Bolshevik experience suggest at least the possibility of a comparative study of revolutionary ideology. To "set up" such a comparison has been one of the purposes of the foregoing argument. It remains only to defend its usefulness: it is useful primarily, of course, because the encounter with sainthood is a part of our own experience.

On the level of ideology, of perception and response, comparisons of the Calvinist elect with the Jacobin men of virtue and the Bolshevik vanguard would not provide any test of the hypothetical description of Puritanism as a response to breakdown, disorder, and social change. They would demonstrate only that the hypothesis can be extended to cover other cases: other men have also lived through the experience of exile and alienation and have shaped their characters in opposition to their environment. Other men have won a self-assurance akin to that of the saints, and it has permitted them similar forms of activity – radical, ruthless, experimental. This extension of the range of analysis is useful even if it does not permit scientific testing of the hypothesis. Comparison always brings new insight: the additional examples often require elaboration and correction of the original hypothesis, and at the same time the discovery of significant differences in similar cases defines its limits. Working back and forth between, say, Puritans and Bolsheviks may also avoid some of the dangers of anachronistic judgment which are probably inherent in a commitment to a single progress – to English history, for example, with its solemn advance from precedent to precedent. For if the foregoing argument is at all correct, then the saints are likely to be similar not to the men who came before or after them in English history, but to other men in other countries who lived through a similar time and shared some of the same experiences.

The conditions of these experiences obviously may be compared in a more systematic fashion. Measurements of social mobility of various sorts and careful studies of economic change both might be useful here, though it

173

must be said again that recording such measurements or carrying out such studies does not bring one face to face with "real life". Mobility, for example, is a different experience for different men. Nevertheless, it can surely be argued that urbanization under more or less similar conditions – which can be investigated and the details quarrelled over – makes a limited number of ideological responses likely, the appearance of a limited variety of new men probable. All these men may not be present in every case, but on a broad enough national scale and over a sufficient span of time, they are all likely to appear: the lost worldling whom the Puritans called damned, the exciting (and often creative) speculator in freedom, the fearful man who desperately seeks authority, and the saint himself.

174

But it is probably not possible in any particular place, at any moment in time, to predict the appearance of the last of these men – though it can be suggested, on the basis of the argument outlined above, that he will not be absent in a time of full-scale revolution. The ideas which shape his character are not automatic products of some objective development – indeed, very little is yet known about their production – and it is not easy to guess when they will take hold or what their precise nature will be. And here comparative work can only serve to increase the sensitivity of the student. If a science is not possible, then one must resort to an older form of knowledge, to that intuition which comes, above all, from the practice of history.

Princeton University

Piety and Intellect in Puritanism

Robert Middlekauff*

WHAT the Puritans knew as common sense about the mind
has survived to be enshrined by historians as a theory of
psychology. Puritans grew up thinking of the mind in terms
of the faculties, such as "reason" and "will." Today we recognize that the
Puritans had accepted the faculty psychology, a theory much older than
they were. We have long since rejected this theory and have exhausted
several others; yet we have not managed to divest ourselves of its vocabulary nor have we shaken off its underlying assumptions. Like the Puritans we still describe the mind's functioning with the familiar terms
reasoning and willing. And, like them, we separate thought and feeling
and ascribe a duality to the mind.

175

The assumption that the mind is a duality has proved especially important in the interpretation of Puritanism. If the Puritan mind was a
duality the problem is one of establishing the relationship of the two
parts—the religious emotion, or piety, and the ideas that historians agree
informed the mind. Historians have approached this question with the
familiar suppositions that emotion somehow produces ideas or, phrased
in another way, that religious ideas are the articulations of piety. This
proposition seems to defy more explicit statement and it does not exclude
a second assumption, which may appear to be in conflict with it, that
piety and intellect were historically in opposition to one another. Both
assumptions may contribute to a disposition among historians of Puritanism to think of the psychic process in mechanistic terms—in this case as
entailing "movement" from feeling to thought. Both hold that the mind
was duality; and both imply that piety and intellect were separate.

With its descriptions of images shuttling back and forth among the
faculties, the traditional Puritan psychology had obvious mechanistic
overtones. If historians have found much of the old language antiquated,
they have insensibly made use of the notion of a mechanical movement in

* Mr. Middlekauff is a member of the Department of History, University of
California, Berkeley.

which piety somehow yielded intellect. This view pervades Perry Miller's *New England Mind* where it is summed up in a splendid metaphor: "The emotional propulsion was fitted into the articulated philosophy as a shaft to a spear-head."[1] And Alan Simpson, declaring that Miller has told us too much about the Puritan mind and not enough about the Puritan's feelings, reveals a similar mode of thinking: "If the seventeenth-century Puritan, with his formal training in scholasticism, usually tries to give a rational account of his faith, it is the stretched passion which makes him what he is. They are people who suffered and yearned and strived with an unbelievable intensity; and no superstructure of logic ought to be allowed to mask that turmoil of feeling."[2]

176

The use of terms such as "superstructure," which have mechanical connotations and the conception of the mind as a duality operating on a sequential basis, with emotion first in the sequence, gives the psychic process a deceptive neatness. These mechanical terms, after all, are abstractions which may establish relationships but they do not convey a state of mind. Rather they seem to suggest that emotions may be understood as any mechanical force can, perhaps even as uniformities. In this notion piety is an entity whose inception and expression parallel the action of any physical force.

Perhaps we cannot avoid thinking of the mind as a duality. The idea is embedded in our vocabulary, and we can in fact make meaningful distinctions between emotion and thought. But if we must acknowledge that thinking and feeling are different modes of the psychic process, perhaps we should give full importance to their connections, for these two modes do not exist apart from one another. Whatever else it is, the psychic process is not simply the sum of thinking and feeling; it is in some peculiar way their interaction. Men think within some emotional disposition and feel in a context that in part has been ordered by thought.

Perhaps, too, we should consider the possibility that creativity in the relationship of Puritan intellect and emotion may have arisen in the intellect. Puritanism, after all, offered an explicit philosophy covering all aspects of human existence. This philosophy defined man's place in the world with absolute clarity: it told him who he was and what he might become; and it told him what God expected of him.

[1] Perry Miller, *The New England Mind: The Seventeenth Century* (New York, 1939), 67.
[2] Alan Simpson, *Puritanism in Old and New England* (Chicago, 1955), 21.

But if man's fate was clear, the fate of individuals was not. In its doctrines of predestination and election, Puritanism offered a man the assurance that his future had been decided. But it gave him no infallible indication of the nature of the decision. All he could know with absolute
certainty was that God in his justice had predestined some men for salvation and others for damnation.

These ideas reinforced a bent towards self-awareness in men eager to
determine whether or not they were of the elect. Puritanism achieved the
same result in yet another way—by explicitly demanding a self-conscious-
ness that made a man aware of his emotions and sensitive to his attitudes
towards his own behavior. It accomplished this by describing in elaborate
detail the disposition of a godly mind. Sin, it taught, might be incurred
as surely by attitudes as by actions. In the process of performing his religious duties a man might sin if his feelings were not properly engaged.
Prayer, for example, was commanded of every Christian; but prayer without inward strain, even agony, is mere "Lip-labour," a formality that of-
fends God.[3] Prayer for spiritual blessings without faith that those blessings will be granted implies a doubt of God's power and is equivalent to
unbelief. Ordinary life, too, must be lived in a Christian habit of mind.
A man getting his living in a lawful calling, though staying within
the limits imposed by the state, might nevertheless violate divine impera-
tives by overvaluing the creatures, as Puritans termed excessive esteem for
the things of this world. The "*manner* of performance," a Puritan divine
once said, was the crucial thing in fulfilling the duties imposed by God.[4]

Puritanism thus bred a deep concern about a state of mind. The
norms of good thought and feeling were clear, and every Puritan felt the
need for effort to bring his consciousness into harmony with these
norms. The most familiar figure among Puritans is the tormented soul,
constantly examining his every thought and action, now convinced that
hell awaits him, now lunging after the straw of hope that he is saved, and
then once more falling into despair. He wants to believe, he tries, he fails,
he succeeds, he fails—always on the cycle of alternating moods.

177

[3] Increase Mather, *A Discourse Concerning Faith and Fervency in Prayer* . . .
(Boston, 1710), 82.
[4] Increase Mather, *Practical Truths Tending to Promote the Power of Godli-
ness* . . . (Boston, 1682), 200. See also Urian Oakes, *New-England Pleaded With* . . .
(Cambridge, Mass., 1673), 11-13; Urian Oakes, *A Seasonable Discourse Wherein
Sincerity and Delight in the Service of God Is Earnestly Pressed Upon Professors of
Religion* . . . (Cambridge, Mass., 1682), 4-5, 9, 17; William Stoughton, *New-Eng-
lands True Interests* . . . (Cambridge, Mass., 1670), 20-25.

460   WILLIAM AND MARY QUARTERLY

Consider, for example, Cotton Mather. By his own account he seems to have been completely at the mercy of his emotions: his *Diary* reverberates with his groaning, sighing, and panting after the Lord. From youth until death, his spirit fluctuated from despair to ecstasy. Between these emotions lay a vast number of others but for Cotton Mather few brought peace and repose.

If Mather's piety was more intense than most—in part because his familial heritage and his conception of his profession were unusual—its sources were similar to that of other Puritans. Mather lived in a world of ideas where God reigned, and man, diseased with sin, craved His dispensation. Only the Lord could save man and the Lord made His decisions about man's fate without consulting anyone. Man, helpless and sinful, did not deserve to be consulted. Evoking a world of uncertainty, these ideas engendered an anxiety in him that could be eased only by a conviction that he was somehow acceptable to God.

Cotton Mather never questioned the view of himself and of the world that these conceptions imposed. His description of himself would have satisfied any Puritan, for any Puritan would have recognized himself in it. All his life Cotton Mather accused himself of sin that rendered him indescribably filthy. He was a "vile" sinner, "feeble and worthless," suffering, he once told the Lord, from spiritual "diseases . . . so complicated, that I am not able so much as distinctly to mention them unto thee; much less can I remedy them."[5] He employed these terms in describing himself when he was an adolescent, apparently in the midst of an agonizing crisis of the soul. He survived this crisis and though years later he sometimes appeared complacent, he never lost his sense of sin. As an old man he confessed in a characteristic way his "Humiliation for my . . . Miscarriages" and called himself "as tempted a Man, as any in the World."[6]

The classic Puritan failures, idleness and waste, did not often contribute to his anxiety. He knew that he was rarely idle, that the little money he earned was not squandered; and he indulged in no false contrition on these scores. But he did recognize in himself pride and sensuality, the habits of mind that Christians had always considered evil.[7]

Mather's anxiety arose when he found himself unable always to bring

[5] Cotton Mather, *Diary of Cotton Mather* (New York, [1957?]), I, 5, 9.
[6] *Ibid.*, II, 483.
[7] See, for example, *ibid.*, I, 15, 79-80, 224-225, 475.

his behavior and his state of mind into harmony with his ideas. A true Christian, he knew, was humble—not swelled with pride. A true Christian did not prize this world: he was to live in it and he was to give his best but at the same time the attention of his heart should be fastened upon God. Mather was pained by his failure to live up to this ideal. In his pride and in his sensuality, he disappointed both the Lord and himself. Falling short of the divine imperative rendered him ugly in the sight of God: truly Cotton Mather was a filthy creature.[8]

This conception of himself must certainly have helped induce the massive anxiety he endured for so long. From an early age Cotton Mather had learned of his sin; and by the time he reached maturity he did not have to be reminded of it, though he reminded himself often. After a few years of life he seems not to have required the specific accusation of sin to experience the unease; it probably was always there—a part of his consciousness or not far from it. The most trivial incident could set his fears in motion. When he had a toothache he asked: "Have I not sinned with my *Teeth*? How? By sinful, graceless excessive *Eating*. And by evil Speeches, for there are *Literae dentales* used in them?"[9]

179

The doctrine of predestination intensified Mather's anxiety. Mather knew that God, in a moment of power and justice, had resolved the eternal fates of all men. He knew too that all men were sinners deserving damnation; only those selected by the Lord would escape a punishment all merited. God had made His choice, nothing could be done to alter it, for predestination was a fact, not a theory.

He responded to this knowledge in several ways. Occasionally he achieved resignation, resolving "to resign all my Conserns unto Him, *without whom not* a little Bird falls unto the Ground." But more frequently he felt compelled to inventory his soul, to tabulate his worth. His *Diary* in one sense is an extended ledger of his merit and his failings. He longed to discover that the balance was on the side of his election.[10]

Just as conventional Puritan ideas about human nature and predestination evoked Mather's feeling about himself, so other related ideas helped him to cope with his anxiety. One set of ideas incited another: Cotton Mather was a sinful, helpless soul, but he could take comfort from the knowledge that God used the sinner for His own purposes. God chose

---

[8] *Ibid.*, 24, 38, 62, et passim.
[9] *Ibid.*, 24.
[10] *Ibid.*, 60.

him, Cotton Mather, for his vileness and used him for divine purposes. The choice demonstrated God's power: even a wretch like himself could be used in the Lord's work. In this way when Mather recognized the fact of his sin he was disconsolate and then when he remembered the power of the Lord to use even a vile sinner his anxiety was converted to joy. It was wonderful but the Lord worked in wonderful ways.[11]

Received ideas about God stimulated strong emotion. He longed for the Lord's blessing, begged for His aid, and strained to think, act, and feel in ways he imagined would earn His favor. "My highest Acquisition," Mather wrote in his *Diary*, "I will reckon to bee, a Likeness unto God. To *love* that which *God* loves, and *hate* that which God hates; to be *holy as God is holy*. . . . O That I may be conformable unto the *communicable* Attributes of God; and agreeable unto his *Incommunicable*."[12]

He would be like Christ. This idea proved to be psychically useful in a life filled with abuse from the external world. As the world grew increasingly hostile to Mather's values, he rejoiced in his suffering: "Yea, a Conformity to Him, in Sufferings, Injuries, Reproaches from a malignant World, makes me, even to rejoice in those Humiliations." He should not sorrow at attacks by evil men—had not evil men attacked Christ? He should glory in their abuse, for they were Satan's agents, and their enmity made him more like Christ.[13]

This mechanism did not always operate with perfection. Robert Calef's "Libel" nine years after the outbreak of witchcraft at Salem left Mather with an anger that smoldered. The best that Mather's attempt to "imitate and represent the Gentleness of my Savior" could achieve was a temporary "sweet calm" seven years after Calef's attacks.[14]

He was more successful in handling his emotions when he faced a twenty-year-old widow who set her cap at him after the death of his first wife in December 1702. The young widow informed him in February 1703 that she had long valued his ministry and now wanted to share his life. The "highest Consideration" in her desire for marriage with Cotton Mather, she told him, "was her eternal Salvation, for if she were mine, she could not but hope the Effect of it would be, that she should also be Christ's." Mather was delighted—and suspicious; he clearly found her

[11] *Ibid.*, 8-12, et passim.
[12] *Ibid.*, 61.
[13] *Ibid.*, 515.
[14] *Ibid.*, 172.

sexually exciting—she was of a "Comely Aspect," he said—but her reputation was not unblemished.[15]

During the next two months he writhed in a confusion marked by desire and despair. He wanted the woman but he feared that her flattering offer was a snare laid by the Devil, who had long plotted to destroy Cotton Mather. He needed the comfort of his family and friends but they, evidently fearing that he was about to make a fool of himself, refused to listen to him talk of the widow. He would like to have had Boston's sympathy in his suffering but all he was likely to get—he sensed—was disapproval. Family, friends, the community, all proved interested but unwilling to come to his aid. The widow was hardly more helpful: when he warned her of the difficulty of life with a man who spent much of his time in fasting and praying, she replied that his way of living was precisely what had attracted her to him.[16]

181

Through his confusion Mather realized that neither his friends nor his family could help him. But within two weeks after the young widow approached him, the way out of his dilemma began to appear. In mulling over what to do Mather decided that he would have to be especially gentle. He admitted to himself that the girl's physical appeal "causes in me a mighty Tenderness" toward her; and of course good breeding demanded that she be treated with respect. "But Religion, above all, obliges me, instead of a rash rejecting her Conversation, to contrive rather, how I may imitate the Goodness of the Lord Jesus Christ, in His Dealing with such as are upon a Conversion unto Him." The problem was to find a Christ-like solution. Within three weeks he was to decide that rejection of the widow was a Christ-like action.[17]

During these three weeks his family and the community urged him toward action by impressing their disapproval upon him. They told him that bad company was often at the house of the widow's father, presumably visiting her. What was more frightening was a "mighty Noise" around the town that he was courting the widow. The rumor was false; all he aimed at—he told himself—was "conformity to my Lord Jesus Christ, and Serviceableness to Him, in my Treating of her."[18]

Cotton Mather could not bear to have his name besmirched, and he

[15] *Ibid.,* 457.
[16] *Ibid.,* 458.
[17] *Ibid.,* 467.
[18] *Ibid.,* 470.

craved the approval of the community. But he could not reject the widow simply because Boston was outraged at his courtship. He would rebuff the widow but he would not be moved by "popular Slanders." Rather he discovered when he made his decision that he was moved "purely, by a religious Respect unto the Holy Name of the L[ord] Jesus Christ, and my Serviceableness to his precious Interests; which I had a Thousand Times rather dy, than damnify." His decision in fact was a victory, a victory over "Flesh and Blood," and suggested that he was regenerate. The girl was his "sacrifice" to Christ.[19]

The language Mather employed to describe this brief episode suggests how Christian values enabled him to act: the whole affair is cast into a conventional Christian form. He—the servant of the Lord—is tempted; he is denied resort to the ordinary comfort supplied by family and friends; his enemies in the community revile him. But strengthened by his conception of conforming to Christ, he disregards his enemies, overcomes the promptings of the flesh, and acts, sacrificing what is dear to him in the service of the Lord.

Phrasing his action in sacrificial terms eased the agony of rejecting in yet another way. His last entry in the *Diary* about the widow conveys a sense of the violence of his inner struggle. "I struck my Knife, into the Heart of my Sacrifice, by a Letter to her Mother." It also suggests that rejection in these terms, especially in the use of the word "knife" and the action described by the phrase "struck my Knife, into the Heart," released at least some small portion of his sexual urges.[20]

Christian ideas, for example the imperative to conform to Christ which had saved him from disaster in this extraordinary affair, also affected Cotton Mather in less spectacular ways. Problems of ordinary scale seemed less annoying when one considered Christ's responses to similar ones. Was his salary insufficient and was he reduced to wearing rags? Poverty presented the temptations of uncharitable anger and self-pity, but he resisted them. Christ's condition in the world had been distinguished by poverty and Christ was robbed of his garments. Why then should Cotton Mather complain of a poverty that left him and his children in want? "Anything that makes my Condition resemble His, tis acceptable to me!" Besides he had another, more desirable kind of garment, the robe of Christ's righteousness. The Lord had also used him to help clothe the poor. He gave

[19] *Ibid.*, 473-474.
[20] *Ibid.*, 474.

182

from his own purse to the needs of the poor; he was honored by the Lord as "the happy Instrument of cloathing other people." This knowledge, he reported, left him "cheerful"; humiliation was banished, and he was strengthened to the point that he resolved to bear his trials with "the Frames of true, vital, joyful, Christianity."[21]

Not even Cotton Mather could keep the divine model constantly in mind; he, like most Puritans, sometimes experienced periods of "deadness," periods when neither ideas of sin nor of God could evoke emotional responses. This paralysis of thought and feeling never lasted long for it gradually built up anxiety until he was desperately searching for revived spirits. When in "an idle Frame of Soul," he found himself "filled with *Fears,* that the Spirit of God was going to take a sad *Farewell* of mee." In this state he would begin to pray. But his prayers were usually not answered immediately; the lethargy continued and he would find himself unable to believe in God. This feeling might persist for as long as a week, though he usually managed to dispel it in a few days. Horror and confusion filled these days; hope and joy returned only after Mather succeeded in completely humbling himself.[22] Following this state, which was reminiscent of the stage of humiliation in the conversion process, Mather began to feel hope once more. Hope arose when he found himself able to believe that the Lord would heed his plea if only he really believed. After all, God wanted to help him, and would; but he had to trust the Lord.

Although Cotton Mather did not ever comprehend the workings of his psyche, he did understand to some extent that his ideas might affect his emotions. The relationship of thought and feeling appeared most clearly in the case of a "particular faith." A particular faith was a promise given by God about future events. It was not given to everyone, rather "but *here* and *there,* but *now* and *then,* unto those whom a *Sovereign* GOD shall Please to Favour with it." All Christians of course may receive general reassurance when praying but a particular faith is granted only to a chosen few who approach the Lord with a specific request. The favored believer who goes to the Lord with his request receives, after strenuous prayer, assurance that he will get his wish. "The Impression is born in upon his mind, with as clear a Light, and as full a Force, as if it

183

---

[21] *Ibid.,* II, 4-5.
[22] See *ibid.,* I, 7-12, an early example of "deadness."

were from Heaven *Angelically,* and even *Articulately* declared unto him."[23]

Convinced that the particular faith came from without, Mather insisted that "the Devout Believer cannot cause himself to Believe *What* and *When* he will"; but the fact is that he developed in the particular faith a technique to induce belief and feeling. At the same time he described the change wrought by a particular faith: the believer's feelings were altered. For example, he was sad and anxious before he pleaded for reassurance from God; afterwards, he lost his sadness and anxiety and his spirits revived. This was the theory; Cotton Mather's *Diary* reveals that he achieved the ideal in practice. He used such words as "afflatus" and "raptures" in describing his renewed feelings; at times his ecstasy became indescribable. More often his anxiety dropped away, and he found himself full of confidence and even joy. Not surprisingly he also felt physically rejuvenated.[24]

A typical experience with a particular faith occurred in April 1700 when he was to deliver the Thursday lecture, an important occasion when a minister strove to give his best. On this day he found himself "tired, and spent, and faint; especially with torturing Pains in my *Head."* Surely, he reasoned, on a day when he was to do work "to glorify my Lord Jesus Christ," the Lord would help him. And so he prayed for a particular faith—and received it: "I felt a wonderful Force from Heaven, strengthening, and assisting, and enlarging of mee."[25]

Psychologically, the conception of a particular faith was a way of expressing man's dependence upon God. Man required reassurance of the Lord's favor; to obtain it he must grasp the immensity of God's power in contrast to his own helplessness. Once he achieved this sense, usually after a prolonged period of humbling himself, the Lord might choose to speak. Man did not coerce the Lord, yet the Lord's response came only after man's extended plea. The answer confirmed God's power.[26]

Cotton Mather's inner life was peculiar and, in several ways, unique. His was a psychology of the extreme. If his peers felt a deep piety, he

---

[23] Cotton Mather, *Parentator . . .* (Boston, 1724), 189-190.
[24] *Ibid.,* 189; Mather, *Diary,* I, 343, 355, 400, et passim.
[25] Mather, *Diary,* I, 344.
[26] I have learned much from Perry Miller's account of Mather's use of the idea of a particular faith in *The New England Mind: From Colony to Province* (Cambridge, Mass., 1953), 403-404. See also Cotton Mather, *Magnalia Christi Americana . . .* (London, 1702), Bk. IV, Pt. II, Chap. I.

ached for union with Christ. When they were complacent, he was self-righteous. If they were filled with a mild dread, he was tormented by agonizing visions. If they enjoyed contemplating the divine, he experienced raptures. They gained reassurance by praying to the Lord, he received direct communication from an angel.

Samuel Sewall, a friend of Cotton Mather, lived a life in no way extravagant but one which revealed almost as clearly as Mather's, the role of Puritan ideas in creating piety. Like Mather, Sewall recognized that man was sinful and helpless and that only the Lord could save him. Like Mather, Sewall craved God's love; and he too wished to make his life conform to Christ's as closely as possible.[27]

185

Sewall did not comment on these convictions extensively or on any of the great ideas of Puritanism. Rather his ideas were masked by a life of placid success. There was his work, which followed an upward course after his marriage to the daughter of wealthy John Hull, and a long period as a Superior Court judge and a councillor, two positions he filled with dignity and skill. There was his service to family and friends and to his church which he performed with loving concern. And there was his interest in New England, an interest that propelled him into beliefs that some of his sophisticated contemporaries considered absurd: opposition to wigs, for example, and to the keeping of Christmas.[28]

The record of this life is set down in Sewall's *Diary*. It is a record largely unadorned by reflection, containing little more than his notes on his actions and the events of his world. Even dreadful accidents such as this one of August 10, 1686, stand unremarked: "Ridd to Braintrey in Company of Mr. Pain, and Mr. Joseph Parson, and home agen. 'Tis said a Groton Man is killed by 's cart, Bowells crushed out; and a Boy killed by a Horse at Rowley; foot hung in the Stirrup and so was torn to pieces; both about a week ago."[29] In Cotton Mather's feverish *Diary* such episodes were improved for all they were worth.

Sewall's emotional detachment was probably as great as the spare entries in the *Diary* indicate. His piety burned slowly and evenly throughout his life: it rarely flared as Cotton Mather's often did. Although Sewall knew that he should love God and reproached himself when he felt

[27] Samuel Sewall, *Diary of Samuel Sewall, 1674-1729* (Massachusetts Historical Society, *Collections*, 5th Ser., V-VII [Boston, 1878-82]), I, 46-47; II, 98, 212; III, 200.
[28] *Ibid.*, passim. For a modern account see Ola Elizabeth Winslow, *Samuel Sewall of Boston* (New York, 1964).
[29] Sewall, *Diary*, I, 146.

deadness to God's claims, neither his sense of sin nor his belief in divine power left him deeply anxious.[30]

Despite the absence of intensity in feeling, Puritan ideas patterned Sewall's responses in the approved way. In Sewall's uncomplicated mind ideas were applied simply and literally—in contrast to Cotton Mather's intricate, even tortured, use. They served to suppress doubt and inquiry and to provide reassurance that things were what they seemed to be, that God's universe was ordered and reliable. The lines that attitudes and emotions and behavior should follow were clear—God had traced them in the Scriptures, and Sewall never doubted for a moment that he, or one of Massachusetts's ministers, could follow them out to the Lord's satisfaction. Even the meaning of death, the worst that the world offered, was comprehensible, or at least man could know all he required about it in this life. Death should not become the occasion of wracking grief, or of philosophical speculation. Death was an affliction sent by God to make the living aware of their sin and to prepare them for their own ends. And death contained the promise of union with Christ. Sewall fronted death hundreds of times and though when relatives or close friends died he felt a grief we would recognize as a sense of loss, his emotions assumed other forms in response to his ideas. When a son died he told himself that God had chosen this way of humbling him; he had overvalued his son; his son had become an "Image" to him.[31] The death of his first wife prompted the reflection that "God is teaching me a new Lesson; to live a Widower's Life"; the death of his second left him "ashamed of my Sin."[32] In all these notions there was the assurance that death was a "righteous sentence upon one's self" and that it led ultimately to conformity to Christ.[33] This elaborate rationale controlled emotion, and made it supportable.

Emotional reactions to ordinary events were no less patterned by Puritan ideas. When he reacted, Sewall's response invariably reflected his conviction that all things occurred through the workings of Providence. Happenings in the world around him drew his comment because he detected God's hand in them. Almost any incident could move him to connect the seemingly trivial to the divine: one day a child's ball clogged a rain spout on the roof causing a leak into a room; Sewall tried to clear the drain and failing put his servant to it. When the ball was poked out

[30] For an example of "deadness," see *ibid.*, II, 189.
[31] *Ibid.*, 114.
[32] *Ibid.*, III, 144, 256.
[33] *Ibid.*, II, 212. See also *ibid.*, 172, 176.

Sewall reflected, "Thus a small matter greatly incommodes us; and when God pleases 'tis easily removed." Spilling a can of water, he remarked "that our Lives would shortly be spilt."[34]

Long before Sewall's time making such connections became a Puritan convention. We are most familiar with it in the Puritan penchant for allegory. Cotton Mather, who made more out of the technique than anyone else in New England, saw in it a grand means of stimulating piety. "Daily spiritualizing," as he called it, could be done by anyone, in contrast to a particular faith which was reserved for a qualified few.[35]

The process served Sewall and Puritans like him in a manner they did not comprehend: it routinized their emotions. Savoring the divine was the end the technique proposed to make habitual, but the beginning point had to be the concrete and the immediate. This world must be pondered before the next was approached; and this world, as Sewall's record indicates, was endlessly intriguing. The shift to cosmic meaning was made but too often in perfunctory and spiceless terms. This world remained so fascinating that, instead of a renewed piety, Puritans found that they were still prone to complacency and even deadness in the face of the Lord's claims. The irony of such experience eluded Puritan ministers who had insisted that in a well-disposed mind the intellect must "frame, and shape, and mould" the emotions.[36] Ruminations on the things of the world were supposed to yield a new spirit, not a growing preoccupation with the creatures.

187

The failure did not arise from the convention but from the emotional framework in which it was exercised. Sewall and those Puritans who in their complacency resembled him were not fully self-conscious. They had not learned to examine every thought and every feeling for godliness. They had forgotten that sin inhered in attitude as well as in behavior. In their unthinking conformity to creed they were "secure," to use the seventeenth-century word that described an absence of tension.

Different as they were from Cotton Mather, men like Sewall were hardly less Puritan. Both types of Puritan felt what their ideas instructed them to feel. In both the intellect's application of a highly articulated

---

[34] For the comment on the ball see *ibid.*, 388; for the comment on the spilled water, 404.

[35] Cotton Mather's *Diary* is filled with his attempts at daily spiritualizing. See also his *Winter Meditations. Directions How to Employ the Liesure* [*sic*] *of the Winter for the Glory of God* . . .(Boston, 1693); *Agricola, Or, the Religious Husbandman* . . . (Boston, 1727).

[36] Oakes, *New-England Pleaded With*, 11.

moral code displaced certain kinds of emotion. At times raw, spontaneous feeling burst through—Mather's seething anger at Calef provides one such instance. But most of the time such spontaneity was absent: the model of what a Christian should be and how he should think and feel was too clear to escape. Even love of one's wife had to be carefully controlled: it should not become so absorbing as to divert one's attention from God. Knowing how they were supposed to respond as Christians, Puritans, at some level of their being, transmuted raw feeling into feeling sanctioned by their code.

The experience of Mather and Sewall suggests the great range in the quality of the emotional lives of Puritans. In these two men even the periods of "deadness" must have differed in tone. Yet both recognized deadness as a state of mind and both felt guilty while they endured it. And in each of them the Puritan conception of man served first to intensify the feeling and then to stimulate the guilt that enabled them to dispel it. Whatever the variation in quality of the feeling of each in these, and similar, periods, the process of emotional development was the same. This process involved a complex interaction of thought and feeling initiated by traditional Puritan ideas.

If this peculiar relationship of piety and intellect existed in Puritans as different as Mather and Sewall were, it probably should be regarded as one of the determinants of Puritan character. Certainly the Puritan was not born with a peculiar emotional bias, nor was his character defined somehow more basically by emotion than by intellect. If "stretched passion" made the Puritan what he was, ideas did much to evoke and control that passion. The traditional notion of the mind as a duality has obscured the connections of emotion and intellect and of the unity of the psychic process itself. This process was incredibly complex; and the interplay of ideas and feelings in Puritans can never be wholly reconstructed. This should not deter us from making the attempt, however. Once it is made, I suspect that it will reveal the pre-eminence of the intellect in Puritan mind and character.[87]

[87] For other examples of Puritans whose minds reveal the relationship of piety and intellect discussed in this article see John Hull, "The Diaries of John Hull," in American Antiquarian Society, *Transactions and Collections*, III (Worcester, 1857), 109-316; M. G. Hall, ed., "The Autobiography of Increase Mather," in Amer. Antiq. Soc., *Proceedings*, N.S., LXXI (Worcester, 1962), 271-360; Edmund S. Morgan, ed., "The Diary of Michael Wigglesworth," in Colonial Society of Massachusetts, *Publications*, XXXV (Boston, 1951), 311-444; *Winthrop Papers* (Boston, 1929——). John and Margaret Winthrop's letters in volumes I and II are especially revealing.

188

S A C V A N   B E R C O V I T C H
Brandeis University

Typology in Puritan New England: The Williams-Cotton Controversy Reassessed

WHEN IN 1635 THE GENERAL COURT OF MASSACHUSETTS BANISHED ROGER Williams for heresy, it provoked perhaps the most basic controversy of colonial New England. In the ensuing seventeen years, in a series of letters and books directed against John Cotton, the outcast denounced the magistrates' "bloody tenent of persecution" and, attacking the very concept of a theocracy, advocated the absolute separation of church and state. For promulgating this doctrine he has become something of a legendary American hero, acclaimed through the eighteenth and nineteenth centuries as "the founder of the democratic form of government in the new world."[1] Recently, however, Perry Miller has presented the whole conflict in a new perspective. "The secular interpretation of Roger Williams," he finds, "is a misreading of his real thought. . . . To understand him we must recognize that his slant was theological, not political"; that, specifically, his radicalism consisted in his uncompromising

---

[1] Reuben A. Guild, "Biographical Introduction" (1866) to *The Complete Writings of Roger Williams* (New York, 1959), I, 4. (This evaluation, though dominant throughout the period, was not universally accepted: see, for example, John Quincy Adams, "The New England Confederacy of MDCXLIII," *Massachusetts Historical Society Collections*, 3rd ser., IX [1844], 206-9). Persecution was, of course, only one of four charges which Williams made against the colony, but it became the central issue in the controversy; the other charges concerned Separatism, the Indians' rights of ownership to the land and the unlawfulness of compelling the "unregenerate" to take oath. All references to the controversy are from the edition cited above, except for those to Cotton's *Bloody Tenent, Washed;* the works involved are listed hereafter by the following abbreviations: Cotton, "A Letter" (1643), in vol. I: *CL;* Williams, "Mr. Cotton's Letter . . . Answered" (1644), in vol. I: *WL;* Williams, *The Bloody Tenent of Persecution* (1644), in vol. III: *BT;* Cotton, "A Reply . . . " (1646), in vol. II: *CR;* Cotton, *The Bloody Tenent, Washed* (London, 1647): *BTW;* Williams, *The Bloody Tenent Yet More Bloody* (1652), in vol. IV: *YM.*

reliance upon typology,[2] the historiographic-theological method of relating the Old Testament to the life of Christ (as "antitype") and, through Him, to the doctrine and progress of the Christian Church. Miller's view obviously improves over the earlier one in that it refers us to the writings themselves. No one who attempts to follow Williams' arguments (rather than treating certain catch phrases out of context) will deny that they depend largely upon various "figures and fulfillments." But to say that the heresy *was* typology is in its way equally misleading. The controversy reveals not a clash between a typologist and a Puritan, but an opposition between two different typological approaches. It is an opposition which has behind it a long tradition, and which holds important consequences for seventeenth-century New England.

Professor Miller's position rests on the premise that the early Puritans "eschewed" typology. He contends that Luther and Calvin "had been very explicit in their condemnation of the typological method" and that, accordingly, "Puritan divines [were] . . . resolved to expunge [it] . . . from Biblical exegesis." Its anti-historical bias, he continues, further alienated the New Englanders from the method: "typologists . . . held that the historical Israel was a 'type' that had been absorbed into the timeless a-historical 'antitype' of Jesus Christ. Cotton and his friends . . . founded their social and historical endeavor upon the reality of . . . [humanity's] temporal and organic development." For practical as well as ideological reasons, therefore, "Williams' resort to typology was [to them] a relapse into a fever which the Reformation believed it had nursed to health. He was a dog returning to the vomit of a decadent [medieval Catholic] scholasticism."

How did Williams, a Cambridge graduate, friend of Winthrop and of Cotton himself, arrive at this "black magic," this "esoteric system" which few of his contemporaries "were even equipped to follow"? In his biography of Williams, Miller declares it all "something of a mystery"; in later essays, he suggests that the Separatist may have "fallen upon some tract [by Henry Ainsworth] . . . which circulated surreptitiously" in England and Holland, or, more likely, that he was writing in real or feigned ignorance of the new order. "Williams was so intense a Biblicist that he made little use . . . of secondary sources, of the works of the Fathers, or of Protestant theologians. He simply presented his own reading of the Testaments, whether out of cunning or bland innocence."[3]

2 "Roger Williams: An Essay in Interpretation," in *Williams' Complete Writings,* VII, 10.

3 *Roger Williams* (New York, 1953), pp. 34-35; Introduction to Jonathan Edwards, *Images or Shadows of Divine Things* (New Haven, 1948), p. 8; "Roger Williams," pp. 10-11, 23, 12; *Williams,* p. 36; "Roger Williams," p. 14.

This analysis is patently wrong in several essentials. In the first place, Williams has constant recourse to the standard authorities. In one work alone, *The Bloody Tenent Yet More Bloody*, he quotes from Puritan contemporaries like Robinson and Eliot, and alludes again and again to the Reformation classics of Fox, Beza, Calvin and Luther as well as to the works of Augustine, Tertullian, Hilary and Jerome.[4] The discrepancy between this list—which could easily be drawn out to tedious length—and Miller's statement is worth recording because the latter is meant to equate Williams' "cunning or bland innocence" with the obsolescence of typology. His display of learning testifies that, on the contrary, he felt himself to be writing within the tradition of his Puritan readers, and that he fully expected John Cotton to understand what Miller calls "his fantastic windings." Indeed, he says so explicitly several times. Explaining, for example, that Israel was a type of Christ, he comments: "Mr. *Cotton* is not ignorant of this, and hath often taught of these *Types* from *Passages* on *Genesis* and other bookes of *Moses*, &c." (*YM*, p. 319); or again, on the same question, "Master Cotton . . . grants that *national church* under the *Jews* . . . did type out the *Christian Church* or *churches* in the *Gospel*" (*YM*, p. 276); or once more, in a summation at the close of his last exchange in the debate: "I doubt not but Mr. *Cotton* doth sometimes give an *heavenly* and *spirituall signification*, to all these *figurative* . . . *Mysteries* [of which I have spoken]" (*YM*, p. 452). Evidently, Williams knew of his adversary's deep interest in the subject. Cotton's discourse on baptism which Williams at one point cites in order to clarify his own position (*YM*, p. 73) is only a minor instance of the Boston minister's persistent application of typology;[5] well before the debate began, he had completed a number of notable "expositions" of the "figurative mysteries," at least two of which far surpassed in this respect Henry Ainsworth's philological *Annotations*.[6]

In his use of typology (as in numerous other ways) Cotton was representative of the New England orthodoxy. Among the first settlers, John Harvard owned typological works by Puritan contemporaries like Francis Bridges, William Guild, John Speed and Thomas Taylor; John Norton and James Noyes, *inter alia*, composed detailed figural studies; and

---

[4] See respectively: pp. 317, 323, 373; 115, 182, 264, 266, 296, 383; 232-33, 298, 355-56, 359, 368, 376-79, 434.

[5] The passage on Canaan as a type which Williams quotes—from Cotton's *Grounds and ends of Baptism* (London, 1647), p. 40—reiterates Cotton's views in, for example, *The Keys of the Kingdom of Heaven* (London, 1644), pp. 28-30, 58-60; and *A Treatise . . . of Grace* (London, 1654), pp. 3 ff., 17, 41 ff., 115-26.

[6] *A briefe exposition . . . of Ecclesiastes* (London, 1654), and *A brief exposition . . . of canticles* (London, 1655). Larzer Ziff dates these works in Cotton's "English ministry," i. e., prior to 1633, in *The Career of John Cotton* (Princeton, 1962), pp. 262-63.

Thomas Hooker (who Miller claims "saw in typology only a fantastic creation of the imagination which had no place in sound scholarship or in orthodox society") discussed the "saints dutie" in terms of "the *type* . . . of the land of Canaan," for "what Moses once said to the children in Israel . . . was *typical* . . . a *type* of Christ's redeeming thee that art a believer."[7] The Mathers particularly distinguished themselves in this area. When in the late 1650s Samuel Mather, the first member of Harvard's Society of Fellows, exclaimed "how full . . . of gospel light and glory" were "the types and shadows of the Old Testament,"[8] he was not reporting a discovery but maintaining a family tradition. His brother Increase had often preached by that "gospel light," as had his father Richard before him, a founder of the Massachusetts theocracy. By the time Samuel completed his massive volume on *The Figures and Types* (London, 1683), his nephew was busy accumulating data for an even larger compilation. "When I applied my mind unto . . . serving of the Lord JESUS CHRIST," says Cotton Mather of his *Biblia Americana*, ". . . I considered that the *treasures of* illustration for the Bible . . . might be fetched all together . . . to have all the *typical* men and things in our Book of Mysteries, accommodated with their Anti-types . . . [and] the *histories* of all *ages*, coming in with punctual and surprising *fulfilments* of divine Prophecies."[9]

Typology pervades all branches of early American writing, secular as well as religious. Its impress upon the New England mind may be seen

---

[7] Alfred C. Potter, "Catalogue of John Harvard's Library," *Publications of the Colonial Society of Massachusetts*, XXI (1919), 215, 222, 224 (Bridges' *Gods Treasurie* [London, 1630] is listed as having been written by "F. B."); Norton, *The Evangelical Worshipper*, in *Three . . . Sermons* (Boston, 1664); Noyes, *The Temple Measured* (London, 1647); Hooker, *The Saints . . . Dutie* (London, 1651), pp. 38, 33. The quotation from Miller is from "Roger Williams," p. 37.

[8] Quoted in Cotton Mather, *Magnalia Christi Americana*, ed. Thomas Robbins (Hartford, 1853), II, 55.

[9] *Magnalia*, I, 33. The result, an immense twenty-year compilation running through almost the whole Bible, is now in manuscript form in the Massachusetts Historical Society. Miller speaks of "Cotton Mather's wish that some apothecary could have administered a purge to cure Williams of typology" ("Roger Williams," pp. 22-23). The passage to which he refers concerns Hooker's cross-examination of Williams about the lawfulness of calling "an unregenerate person to pray," and Mather comments that he wishes Williams had been cured of "making singular and fanciful expositions of Scripture" (*Magnalia*, II, 498). Mather's view of typology is represented in an anecdote which he tells earlier in this work (II, 55) about a "Mr. Rothwel" who, "falling upon the study of *types* . . . found no part of his ministry more advantageously employed for himself or others." The *Magnalia* itself is suffused with typology, both implicitly and explicitly; and its author informs us in a treatise written at the age of twenty-six that he had always been in the habit *"of Treating on the Types."* Introduction to *Work upon the Ark. Meditations upon the ARK as a type of the CHURCH* (Boston, 1689). The use of typology by his father, Increase, and grandfather, Richard, will be shown later.

in the treatises of the logician John Eliot, in the "Commonplace Book"
of a humble divine like Joseph Green, or in the rhetorical flights of Michael Wigglesworth's diary.[10] The poetry of the period demonstrates its
strong influence upon the colonial imagination. All the figural intricacy
which Rosemond Tuve has uncovered in George Herbert's imagery appears as well in the children's rhymes of *The New England Primer*—
"Zacheus he/Did climb a tree/Our Lord to see"—as in the mature verse.
Joseph Thompson's lines, "A louely Cluster on a uine I saw/ . . .
Climbing the sun side of an house of prayer," praise Jesus as ladder-tree,
vine-grapes, and Son-church.[11] Peter Bulkeley's elegy to Thomas Hooker
is more complex still:

193

> To sinners stout he was a son of dreadful thunder.
> When all strong oaks of Bashan us'd to quake . . .
> He clave the rocks, they melted into tears.

A complete analysis of the symbols would entail pages of biblical exegesis. For example: the "son of thunder" is a figure of Christ; the woods
of Bashan are the enemy grounds through which the chosen Israelites
passed before entering the promised land; the "rock he clave" alludes,
through the "typical" Moses, to Jesus' blood, the waters of baptism, the
"delivery of us . . . through the Red Sea [of sin]" and "the rock whence
the store of blessings issues evermore"; and Hooker's "tears" evoke a configuration of the "tears of Jeremiah, of Christ entering Jerusalem, and
of Christ at Gethsemene."[12] Such involved patterns inform much of New

---

10 In Green's *Commonplace Book, Proceedings of the Colonial Society of Massachusetts,* XXXIV (1938), see, for example, p. 221 (on "baptisme & ye Lords-supper") and
p. 205 (on Christ in the "offices of a prophet of a priest & of a king"). An important
instance of Eliot's use of typology is his *Harmony of the Gospels* (Boston, 1678),
where see esp. his remarks on the *"return of Jesus out of Egypt to Israel the Church
of God"* (pp. 17 ff.), on the *"sufferings of Jesus Christ in the form of a servant"* (pp.
43 ff.), and on the "Garden" (pp. 66 ff.). Wigglesworth describes his fight against pride
in the following terms (*Diary, Proceedings of the Colonial Society of Massachusetts,*
XXXV [1946], 423-25):
> I retain a Sodom within the temple . . . [and may therefore sink] in the red sea. . . .
> [My] grievous sin . . . provokes god to lead me through a howling wilderness of
> fiery temptations. . . . . [I turn from the] rock of my salvation . . . [and remain in]
> dalliance with strange lovers and [have] shut christ my Lord out of dores.

11 "Zacheus," in *The New England Primer* (Boston, 1727; first published c. 1689);
Thompson, "The Amiable uirgin memorized," in *Handkerchiefs from Paul,* ed. Ken-
neth B. Murdock (Cambridge, 1927), p. 10. Cf. Tuve's *A Reading of George Herbert*
(Chicago, 1952), pp. 56-59, 83-86.

12 Bulkeley, "On . . . Hooker," in Nathaniel Morton, *New England Memorial,* in
Chronicles of the Pilgrim Fathers, ed. John Masefield (New York, 1910), pp. 158; Tuve,
Herbert, pp. 116, 56, 35. Peter Bulkeley is another New England divine whom Miller
expressly names, along with Hooker, as a detester of typology ("Roger Williams,"
p. 37).

England verse, from its anagrams and acrostics[13] to some of its finest imaginative efforts. Edward Taylor's constant typologizing—not only in his thirty "meditations on types" but in most of his lyrics[14]—represents a technique which was shared, to varying degrees, by Anne Bradstreet, Philip Pain, John Wilson, Benjamin Tompson and others; and which may be seen as the creative expression of a theological mode which they, like George Herbert, were "brought up on."[15]

194

The controversy, then, between Williams, the heretic, and John Cotton, the spokesman for the orthodoxy, took place within a culture thoroughly familiar with typology. Indeed, to all appearances it was Cotton who interjected the latter into the debate. We do not have Williams' first letter; but Cotton, who characteristically answers his opponent point by point, never hints in his reply that figural interpretation was at issue. "Two stumbling blockes (I perceive by your letter) have turned you off from fellowship with us," he writes. "First, the want of fit matter of our church. Secondly, disrespect of the separate churches in England under afflictions, who doe our selves practice separation in peace" (*CL*, p. 15). Both accusations stem from Separatist thought. The first concerns the vexed problem of the validity of a "visible church" which, as Calvin taught, could never "be wholly pure in its membership . . . [since] the

13 Thus John Wilson sees "Job" in "Joseph Brisco," and discovers parallels also to Josiah, Jonah and Joseph, all of whom, like Job, are types of Christ. *Handkerchiefs from Paul*, ed. Murdock, pp. 83-84.

14 A separate essay would be needed to examine Taylor's use of typology. A convenient index, however, is offered by Tuve's examination of Herbert's use of types. Virtually all of the figures she notes appear, many recurrently, in Taylor's poems. Three random examples: thorns-vine-grapes (p. 56: I, 37); garden-cabinet-jewels-music (pp. 141 ff.: I, 40); blood-Ark-Jordan (p. 126: II, 78). (References are first to the page number of Tuve's *Herbert*, and, following the colon, to the number of the series and of the "meditation," as given in Donald E. Stanford's edition of *The Poems of Edward Taylor* [New Haven, 1960].) Taylor's use of typology is too obvious for his critics to have bypassed entirely but it has never been adequately explored, and some illuminating analyses, especially Norman Grabo's *Edward Taylor* (New York, 1961), seem to me to suffer from this inadequacy. Ursula Brumm has recently provided an interesting survey of the subject (*Die Religiose Typologie im Amerikanische Denken* [Leiden, 1963], pp. 49-72), but, following Miller (see her Introduction and pp. 33 ff.), she begins her discussion only with the end of the seventeenth century and so fails to present Taylor in his immediate European and American context.

15 Tuve, *Herbert*, p. 28. A few representative samples: in *New England's Memorial*, William Bradford's "Verses" (pp. 173-75) and Benjamin Woodbridge's elegy on Cotton (pp. 166-67); in *Handkerchiefs from Paul*, ed. Murdock; John Wilson's poem to Norton (pp. 92-97); in Anne Bradstreet's *Works*, ed. John H. Ellis (Gloucester, Mass., 1962): "The Flesh and the Spirit" (p. 384); in Pain's *Meditations*, ed. Leon Howard (San Marino, Calif., 1936): *Meditation 55* (p. 32); in Benjamin Tompson's *Poems*, ed. Edward J. Hall (Boston, 1924): "Remarks on . . . WILLIAM TOMPSON" (pp. 106-7).

mystery of God's grace would conceal hypocrites among the saints."[16] In this regard, Williams recalls that in "the Church of the Jewes . . . if a person uncleane by a dead body, touch holy things, those holy things become uncleane unto him," and deduces that no "Churches [may] . . . any more be accounted churches, as doe receive such [unregenerates] amongst them" (*CL*, pp. 21, 18).

The second accusation is one of hypocrisy. Williams wanted to know why, since the New Englanders were in fact "practising separation here," they were "preaching and printing against it" as dogma (*CL*, p. 24). Neither charge involves more than Calvinist logic and neither touches directly upon the relation between magistrate and minister in the state. Though Williams was already known for resorting to "allegoryes . . . figures and flourishes," he seems not, significantly, to have found these crucial in first presenting his grievances.[17]

Cotton's answers affirm the "middle way" in both matters, and the affirmation rests, in part, on the meaning of certain types. Concerning church membership, he feels that Williams is demanding too high a standard. Moreover, he is misreading his prooftext: "the touch of the dead body did type out . . . fellowship with dead [i. e., unregenerate] works . . . or dead persons . . . or dead world"; hence, the dichotomy was not simply between saints and sinners, but between those who sincerely desired salvation, though still sinful, and those who turned willfully to Satan's world (*CL*, pp. 22-23). As for Separatism, Cotton replies mildly that though New England tolerates and even respects Puritans of that conviction, he thinks them rather extreme. "The errours of men," he admits, such as those who hold with the Church of England, "are to be contended against . . . [with] the sword of the Spirit," yet it would be sheer "Butchery, to heale every sore in a member with no other medicine but abscission from the body" (*CL*, p. 25). If, however, Williams persists in his opinions despite "all reasonable remonstration," he should remain true to his conscience and leave the colony. In an uncustomary flash of sarcasm, apparently prompted by his opponent's self-righteous manner, Cotton asks, "What should the Daughter of *Zion* doe in *Babell*? why should she not hasten to flee from thence?" (*CL*, p. 14).

In his rejoinders, Williams generally bypasses the issues of Separatism

---

16 Leon Howard, "The Puritans in Old and New England," in *Anglo-American Cultural Relations in the Seventeenth & Eighteenth Centuries*, Fourth Clark Library Seminar (Los Angeles, 1958), p. 6; cf. *CL*, p. 19. See further Edmund S. Morgan, *Visible Saints* (New York, 1963), pp. 20-32; and Ziff, *Cotton*, pp. 212 ff.

17 John Winthrop's letter to Endicott (1934), in *Winthrop Papers*, ed. Allyn B. Forbes (Boston, 1943), III, 147. It is notable, however, that in this letter, which lists Williams' grievances (pp. 146-49), Winthrop neither speaks of typology as a basis of disagreement nor refers to the question of the magistrate's power in matters of conscience.

and "fit membership," or more accurately, he incorporates them into the
overall distinction between church and state—a distinction built upon
the figurative ramifications of the "spiritual sword," "Babel" and the
"dead body." His thesis may be briefly stated: Cotton was defending a
civil judgment by way of types that had been fulfilled in Christ and so
applied exclusively to the realm of the spirit. Those very types, therefore, demonstrated that the magistrate had no right to banish a heretic,
or in any form to interfere in questions of conscience. The Hebrew law
concerning "dead bodies" pertained only to the "Nationall Church of the
Jewes, with all [its] . . . shadowish typicall Ordinances . . . [which]
it pleased the most holy to take away" when "at his so long typed out
coming, [He] . . . erected his *Spiritual Kingdom* of *Israel*, appointed
Spiritual Officers, Punishments, &c." (*WL*, p. 72; *BT*, p. 2; *YM*, p. 43).
In short, reference to the Israelite ordinances should remind us that since
Christ all theological matters concern solely the universal, "invisible"
church. Errors of conscience might warrant excommunication, but never
corporal punishment. How, then, could Cotton speak of banishment as
the flight from Babylon? "If he call the Land *Babel* mystically . . . how
can it be *Babel*, and yet the Church of Christ also?" Are not "*Gods* people . . . mingled amongst the *Babylonians*, from whence they are called
to come out, not *locally* . . . but *spiritually* and mystically to come out
from her sins and *abominations*"? Furthermore, banishment expressly
contradicts the concept of "the sword of the Spirit." The latter "anti-
typed and abolished" the Israelite magistrate's powers:

196

> *Gideon's Sword* [is now] . . . the sharpe two-edge sword in the mouth
> of Christ . . . the holy word of God. . . . Master *Cotton* knows that
> . . . his [Christ's] *kingdome* was not earththly [sic], and therefore his
> sword cannot be earthly . . . must he not grant that the material
> Sword of the *Church of Israel* [i.e., the Israelite magistrate's authority
> in religion] types out the *spiritual sword* of *Christ Jesus* . . . cutting
> off offenders *spiritually* [and not in any physical sense] . . . ? (*WL*,
> pp. 56-64; *BT*, pp. 65-66, 419-21; *YM*, pp. 186, 276-77)

These arguments, reiterated *ad tedium*, form the substance of Williams'
radicalism. They derive from a popular method of biblical exegesis and
are expressed with a mixture of rage and bafflement that so eminent a
typologist as John Cotton should disagree.

To the general assumptions Cotton does accede. "*Canaan* was *Typical*
. . . Christs Kingdom is spiritual" (see *YM*, pp. 73, 43). But he refuses
to abandon the literal parallel between the biblical chosen people and
the children of Israel in New England. Williams, as we have seen, maintains that the events and laws of Israel, having found completion in the
New Testament, were without exception purely moral and ceremonial,

and thus, in their entirety, "dead" for all practical purposes. It is with
this sweeping and unequivocal judgment, rather than with the approach
itself, that Cotton takes issue. There remains, for him, a crucial qualification to be made: though Christ fulfilled the Hebrews' "ceremonial
duties," He "never abolished a National Civil State nor the judicial laws
of Moses" (*BTW*, pp. 68, 126). If such a state adopted the True Religion—if it agreed to "submit . . . to the lawes of his [God's] word"—
then it has "as much Truth and reality of holinesse, as *Israel* had. And
therefore, what holy care of Religion lay upon the Kings of *Israel* in the
Old Testament, the same lyeth now upon Christian [magistrates] . . .
to protect . . . the Churches" (*BTW*, pp. 92, 105).   197

Indeed, Cotton continues, the Christian Israel holds all the greater
right to such vigilance, precisely because it adheres to the New Testament, which brought to light the meaning of the Old. "I see no reason,"
he cries, "why the chast and modest Christian Church should any more
spare and pity a spirituall Adulterer, that seeks to withdraw her from
her spouse to a false Christ, than . . . an Holy Israelite was to spare
and pity the like Tempters in the dayes of old" (*BTW*, p. 144). Should
not the "Magistrates Sword," in the New Canaan even more than the
Old, "be called the Sword of God as the Sword of warre"? (*BTW*, p. 104).
The fact that the gospels offer no precepts "for the *breach* of *Civill Justice*" by no means signifies that Christianity has absolved its ties with
the world; it requires us rather to "fetch . . . [our] *Rules* of *Righteousness* . . . from *Moses* and . . . the Prophets, who have expounded Him
[Christ] in the Old-Testament" (*BTW*, p. 178). Understanding the virtuous Israelites, that is, as Christ's shadows, we should see in their theocracy a "patern . . . *for Magistrates* power *in spiritual* cases" whereby
the Mosaic code is performed "*out of Faith*" in Christ (*YM*, p. 172; cf.
BTW, pp. 61-64). Otherwise, Cotton warns, we invert typological reasoning and give Israel precedence over the Church:

> [The Hebrew] Law . . . provided an effectual punishment against
> . . . offenders . . . *that all Israel might heare, and feare, and doe no
> no more presumtuously.* . . . But so doth not Excommunication [as
> opposed to banishment]. . . . Is the figure [thus] become more power-
> full, and effectuall, then the substance? the shadow, then the body?
> the type, then the Antitype? . . . And if spirituall Babylon have now
> so farre prevailed against the Church of Christ, as that they have rooted
> it up from the face of the earth, then what is become of the promise of
> Christ; *The gates of Hell shall never prevaile against it?* (*CR*, pp. 69-
> 70, 72)

Against such blasphemy, Cotton proposes that the acts both of Israel and
of New England are simultaneously literal and spiritual. On the former

level, the biblical theocracy provides the eternal pattern of civil justice; spiritually, Canaan as the Promised Land prefigures Christ. And in this double capacity Israel becomes a model for the New England church-state, a temporal, local entity which yet embodies the nature of the anti-type.

This argument has a pragmatic strain, certainly, but as in Williams' case its substance is typological. Perhaps the best summary of the difference between the two men comes from Williams' pen. Throughout the polemic, he states, he has tried to "draw away the *curtaine* of the *shadow*" in order to show that "spiritual *signs* and *wonders*" of the Bible have no relevance to what "hath literally [occurred since Israel in] . . . any nation in the *whole world*"; Cotton, on the other hand, mingling "*Heaven and Earth*, the *Church* and *worldly state* together . . . [would] propose the rich and peacable, victorious and flourishing National State of the *Jewes* as the Type of the . . . Nation and Kingdome of *Christ Jesus*" (*YM*, pp. 181, 403). Acutely, Williams infers the consequences of this parallel. By asserting Canaan's literal significance, his opponent is implying a typology of contemporary history:

> Mr. *Cotton* . . . would make that comming forth of *Babel* in the anti-type . . . to be *locall* and *materiall* also [i.e., as well as mystical] . . . but . . . if *Babel* be *locall* now, whence Gods people are called, then must there be a locall *Judea*, a Land of *Canaan* also, into which they are called. . . . Mr. *Cotton* having made a locall departure from Old *England* in *Europe*, to New *England* in *America* . . . doth he count the very Land of *England* literally *Babel*, and so consequently *AEgypt* and *Sodome* . . . and the Land of new England, *Judea Canaan?*
> (*WL*, p. 76)

The query suggests that the New England minister is in his way a more adamant separatist than the heretic, and Cotton, in direct reply to the accusation, tries to avoid political embarrassment by an ambiguity.[18] But he retains to the end his basic premise: that "in those words, *Come out of Babel, my People*, locall separation be intended" (*CR*, p. 145; see also pp. 78-79), and that Israel is "fulfilled" in the New World Christian theocracy.

In sum, the conflict stood between two views of typology, which might be called the allegorical and the historical modes. Williams stresses the spiritual progress of the Church, arguing that the meaning of "the whole *Church* of *Israel*, *Roote* and *Branch*, from first to last . . . [is] *figurative* and *Allegorical*" (*YM*, p. 450). In this view, the events of the Old Testament signify a-temporal states of soul, as in Herbert's lines,

---

18 "Some other godly men might finde more favour and exemption from Babylonish corruptions in the midst of *England*, than I was suffered to doe" (*CR*, p. 145).

I did toward Canaan draw, but now I am
Brought back to the Red sea, the sea of shame;

or in Bunyan's story of Christian's pilgrimage from "Egypt," through a "wilderness" of temptations, to "the Land that Flows with Milk and Honey."[19] Cotton proclaims the literal-spiritual continuity between the two Testaments and the colonial venture in America. In effect, he posits an historic movement in which New England—Israel's antitype (by way of Christ)—becomes in turn a preview of the New Jerusalem. Though he never says so as explicitly as does Williams, he is delineating a form of typology which links past, present and future in a developmental historiography.

199

The foundations for this approach, and for that of Williams, had been laid long before the seventeenth century, in the writings of Augustine and Eusebius. Augustine's strict differentiations between the City of God and the City of Man, as Robert W. Hanning observes, "denies the applicability of typological exegesis to the public, social life of men." Since the progress toward Christ takes place apart from earthly vicissitudes, Augustine sees all "types fulfilled in the continuing life of Christ in Christians," and restricts their use to "the development of the Christian (or a-Christian) personality." His method had a powerful effect upon later generations; it was not, however, entirely dominant. Professor Hanning notes further that, directly before Augustine, Eusebius developed a diametrically opposite approach. In his *Ecclesiastical History* of Rome —a work which proved "extremely influential" upon subsequent Christian historiography from Orosius through the Middle Ages—the Empire itself, the City of Man, becomes a "type of the eternal order . . . in a 'horizontal' . . . view of history which binds together Israel and the earthly Christ through an elaborate network of typological correspondences . . . [wherein] Constantine is the new Moses; his army, the new Israelites seeking the new promised land . . . [and] Maxentius is a new pharoah. . . . Israel has been succeeded by Rome, which provides universal evidence . . . of the role of Christ whose reign is shortly to begin."[20] The striking resemblances between these divergent outlooks and those underlying the New England controversy do not necessarily point up any direct connections. They do serve to demonstrate that typology lends itself, with equal force, both to "vertical" and to "horizontal" analysis. To claim that the "illuminations of typology are outside all log-

19 George Herbert, "A Bunch of Grapes," ll. 6-7, in *Works*, ed. F. E. Hutchinson (Oxford, 1941), p. 128; John Bunyan, *The Pilgrim's Progress*, ed. James B. Wharey (Oxford, 1960), p. 158.
20 *The Vision of History in Early Britain* (New York, 1966), pp. 36, 26, 29, 32, 38, 42.

ics of [historic] progression"[21] accounts for only one possibility of the technique, and overlooks the grounds of Cotton's reasoning.

It overlooks, too, the impact of the Reformation upon biblical exegesis, as this is reflected in the methodological impasse in the controversy. Williams, it will be recalled, insists on an absolute separation of the literal and the spiritual, charging that Cotton writes as though "the *letter* . . . [is] yet in force, and *Christ Jesus* the *mysticall* and *spirituall King* of *Israel* is not yet come" (*YM*, p. 154). Cotton, upholding the interrelationship of the literal and the spiritual, claims that Williams' one-sided outlook "transform[s] all the Scripture into an Allegory" (*BTW*, p. 180). His suspicion of allegory echoes that of the leading Reformers, but in neither case does this denigrate the authority of typology. The distinction between allegory and typology is well known; one attempts "to 'spirit away' their [the Scriptures] historical character," the other to present "a definite event in its full historicity," so that the event "was no . . . mere representation . . . but participated in the object which it symbolized . . . [and thus] *was* what it represented."[22] In rebelling against the former method, Luther and Calvin were simply demanding a proper use of the *figura*. "In all figures and types," Luther explains, "there must be some [actual] similarity which underlies them and brings the two objects into correspondence."[23] Elijah, for instance, prefigures John because the text reveals mystical *and* historical resemblances between the two men; whereas the notion that the bread allegorically "signifies" Christ's body outrageously contradicts our actual sense both of the bread and of the body. Far from renouncing typology, these principles were meant to rescue it from the complexities of medieval interpretation.[24] Accordingly, as Victor Harris has demonstrated, "After the Reformation . . . with the attempt to avoid open allegorizing, there was a greater proliferation of types, [and] the 'literal' Old Testament prefigurings . . . [became] the established device for relating Scriptural history."[25]

It was a device which in some important ways tended toward the Eusebian "horizontal" view. First, in refusing "to jettison the historical state-

21 Miller, "Roger Williams," p. 17; see also pp. 11, 18.

22 Erich Auerbach, *"Figura,"* in *Scenes from the Drama of European Literature* (New York, 1959), pp. 36, 54; K. J. Woollcombe, "The Biblical Origins and Patristic Development of Typology," *Essays on Typology* (Naperville, Ill., 1957), pp. 40, 74.

23 *Confessions Concerning Christ's Supper*, in *Luther's Works*, ed. Helmut T. Lehmann (Philadelphia, 1961), XXXVII, 262.

24 As Frederic W. Farrar remarks, quoting Luther, they wanted to discard the medieval multi-level "monkey-game" while retaining the principle of "the reference of all Scripture to Christ." *History of Interpretation*, Brampton Lectures for 1885 (New York, 1961), pp. 328, 332.

25 "Allegory to Analogy in the Interpretation of Scriptures," *PQ*, XLV (1966), 5-6, 10-11.

ment," Renaissance Protestants rejected, or minimized, the validity of all
abstractly spiritual renderings and proposed in their place a fusion of
"heaven and earth." Samuel Mather writes that types "are not bare Allegories" as the "Popish interpreters" contend, but "a true Narration of
Things really existent and acted in the World, and are literally and historically understood." Almost a century before, William Whitaker similarly asserted that the Catholics divide textual meaning

> into two species; the historic and literal, and the mystic or spiritual
> . . . and allegorical. . . . We affirm that there is but one genuine
> sense of scripture . . . [which includes both species, for] a type is a   201
> different thing from an allegory. . . . When we speak of the sign by
> itself, we express only part of its meaning; and so also when we men-
> tion only the thing signified: but when the mutual relation between
> the sign and the thing signified is brought out, then the whole com-
> plete sense [is revealed]. . . . The Jews [for instance] were punished
> when they sinned: therefore, if we sin in like manner, we shall bear
> and pay God similar penalties. . . . [Or again:] the *Son* . . . denotes
> [both Christ and] the people of Israel. . . . Hereupon emerge not differ-
> ent senses, but one entire sense.[26]

Clearly, Williams falls in the wrong camp by these criteria, and (though
in other respects he was a far more thoroughgoing Calvinist than either
Whitaker or Samuel Mather) also by those of John Calvin. According
to the Genevan,

> The Scholastic dogma by which the difference between the sacraments
> of the old and the new dispensation is made so great, that the former
> did nothing but shadow forth the grace of God . . . must be altogether
> exploded. . . . Whatever . . . is now exhibited to us in the sacra-
> ments, the Jews formerly received in theirs — viz. Christ, with his spir-
> itual riches. . . . Those wretched sophists are perhaps deceived by the
> extravagant eulogiums on our signs which occur in ancient writers: for
> instance, the following passage of Augustine: "The sacraments of the
> old law only promised a Saviour, whereas ours give salvation." . . . Not
> perceiving that these and similar figures of speech are hyperbolical,
> they too have promulgated their hyperbolical dogmas. . . . [But] Au-
> gustine means nothing more than . . . if he had said, "Those figured
> him when he was still expected, ours now that he has arrived, exhibit
> him as present." . . . In both there is an exhibition of Christ, but in
> ours it is more full and complete.

[26] Harris, "Allegory to Analogy," pp. 3 ff.; Mather, *Figures or Types*, pp. 128-30;
Whitaker, *A Disputation Concerning Scripture, Against the Papists*, ed. William Fitz-
gerald (Cambridge, 1849), pp. 403-7, 409. Cf. Increase Mather, *The Wicked Man's Portion* (Boston, 1675), pp. 22 ff.

Calvin does not disavow Augustinian typology (which retained, in fact, a strong imaginative hold throughout the seventeenth century in descriptions of the individual Christian life), but his bias against pure spiritualization easily leads, as in Whitaker's case, to an interest in the social, public nature of types. It does not seem entirely accidental that during the period Eusebius' history, as "rendered" by Hanmer (in English), Bildius (in Latin), Hedio (in German) and many others, became widely influential.[27]

This tendency found further support in the literalist millenarianism inspired by Luther and other Reformers. Typology, we know, not only looks backward from Christ to the Old Testament, but forward from the New Testament to the New Adam. In Augustine and Origen this form of "figural prophecy" is purely spiritual: "the appearance of Christ" becomes "a new promise of the end of the world," "a shadow of the kingdom to come";

> Christ's Passion brings about the overthrow of the world of devils, but it is still required that every individual make this victory personal to himself. Each of us carries within himself the Jericho of his own idols. Under the leadership of Jesus, head of the army, the Jericho must be overthrown . . . and the New Jerusalem established.[28]

With Luther, however, the concept of the Second Coming takes on an immediate and worldly significance. In his attempt to explain away the long reign of the Papacy, he discovered in the Book of Revelation prophecies of the present Protestant tribulations which lay embedded in the Old Testament figures but which, at the time of John the Divine, remained still unfulfilled. Thus "he revived the old Hebraic conception of a chosen people valiantly holding out against increasingly heavy persecutions, but destined to enjoy a glorious triumph at the very end," proposing a development from Canaan through the apostolic churches to the Reformation, and explicitly calling the Israelities a figure of the German

---

27 *Institutes of the Christian Religion*, tr. Henry Beveridge (Grand Rapids, Mich., 1953), II, 507-8, 510-11 (cf. Increase Mather, *First Principles* [Boston, 1675], pp. 3 ff., and Cotton's *Some Treasure Fetched Out of Rubbish* [London, 1660], esp. the section explaining why "the signs . . . [of] his Covenant are not bare, naked empty shadows," pp. 43 ff., 16-18); C. A. Patrides, *The Phoenix and the Ladder* (Berkeley, 1964), p. 49. A full list of the translations of Eusebius' *Ecclesiastical History* is in the British Museum Catalogue. Meredith Hanmer's English edition (1577) ran through six printings by 1661; there were five separate Latin translations in the sixteenth century (of which Bildius' work alone had four editions), and by 1600 the work appeared in at least five European languages.

28 Auerbach, *"Figura,"* p. 41; Danielou, *Origen*, tr. Walter Mitchel (New York, 1955), p. 170, and *From Shadows to Reality*, tr. Wulstan Hibberd (Westminster, Md., 1960), p. 280.

people as a new Army of Christ.[29] This conjunction of the prophetic-chiliastic viewpoint with historical typology reappears in Puritan writings throughout the seventeenth century, particularly in "the countless . . . interpretations of the Johannine Apocalypse, naturally focusing on the Day of Wrath, but mindful of the linear nature of history . . . as well." Thomas Brightman, for example, in an often-quoted work on Revelation, speaks of the "bare types" through which "many things were foretold that should come after," since "the continual race of the whole church . . . could not be [fully] understood out of former types." And in a companion work, Arthur Dent employs the "perfect" number seven "for a *type*" (of Israel, Christ and "primitive" Christianity) to prophesy about the outcome of the Reformation.[30]

203

In early New England where the orthodoxy intensely shared the millenarian hope, anticipating its advent in America itself,[31] the method is especially pronounced. In his treatments of Revelation and Canticles, Cotton follows Luther in delineating the "three periods" of the *"prophetical history* of the estate of the Church." So, too, Peter Bulkeley's *The Gospel Covenant* employs the "captivity of the Jews . . . as a resemblance and type . . . to the state of the Church under the tyranny of Antichrist" which has chiliastic implications "for the present" time; John Eliot's *Christian Commonwealth* points out various types in Daniel which *"clearly foreshew* [that] . . . *that stone Christ, by his faithful Instruments* [in America], *shall overthrow* . . . Satan"; and Samuel Mather, in a more theoretical discussion, enlarges upon "the *work* of the *Type*, which is to *shadow forth* or represent . . . *future good things."* More emphatically still, Richard Mather begins his "Apology" for the New England Way by announcing the return "of the Gentiles . . . from Pagan, Antichristian, Babylonish, or Jewish bondage and captivitie," and then explains:

[29] Ernest L. Tuveson, *Millenium and Utopia* (Berkeley, 1949), p. 27; Charles L. Sanford, *The Quest for Paradise* (Urbana, Ill., 1961), pp. 49-50, 79-80.

[30] Patrides, *Phoenix and Ladder*, p. 47; Brightman, *A Relation of the Apocalypse* (Amsterdam, 1611), pp. 168-69; Dent, *An Exposition Upon the Revelation* (Amsterdam, 1611), pp. 1-6. That this combination of prophesying and typologizing relied on the historic-literalist method of typology is attested to, for example, by William Perkins, *The Art of Prophecying*, tr. T. Tuke (London, 1607), p. 30, *et passim;* and by William Guild who devotes the last third of his typological treatise, *The Harmony of all the Prophets* (London, 1626), to explaining events from Titus to the Second Coming (pp. 39-56).

[31] See Alan Heimert, "Puritanism, the Wilderness, and the Frontier," *New England Quarterly*, XXVI (1953), 380-81; Sanford, *Quest for Paradise*, pp. 83, 89-90; and Edward K. Trefz, "The Puritans' View of History," *Boston Public Library Quarterly*, IX (1957), 115-20. In addition to the many works cited by these critics, an essential example of the influence of Luther's millenarianism in New England is Thomas Parker's *Visions . . . of Daniel* (London, 1646).

For as in some passages in the Scripture were never fully accomplished
. . . so many things that literally concerned the Jewes were types and
figures, signifying the like things concerning the people of God in
these latter days . . . [in their] returne . . . from Romish slavery to
the true Sion. . . . And this may be added further, that this seemes not
onely to be meant of the private or personall conversion of this or that
particular Christian, but also further, of the open and joynt calling of
a company, because it is said, they shall come, the children of Israel
. . . and . . . their saying shall not be, *Let me joyne, &c.* but in the
Plurall number, *Let us joyne our selves unto the Lord,* so noting joyning of a company together in holy Covenant with God.[32]

204

This interest in millenarian prophecy, which accorded with the general
Reformation attitude to biblical exegesis, undoubtedly contributed to
Cotton's argument.

Undoubtedly also his argument reflects his particular social circumstances. The resemblances in the thought of Augustine and Williams
on one hand and of Eusebius and Cotton on the other suggest the effect
of public commitment on the theology of history. Like Augustine,[33] Williams was bitterly disappointed with the state; Cotton, like Eusebius,
thought himself part of a great collective endeavor. In this endeavor the
New England theocrats attempted to join two seemingly incompatible
doctrines: the national covenant, by which a group of men enter voluntarily into a pact with God, and the covenant of grace, by which God
mysteriously determines to redeem certain individuals. Perry Miller has
shown how, increasingly through the seventeenth century, colonial ministers mitigated the harsh Calvinist meaning of grace in order to allow
for a social purpose under rational control.[34] Cotton's typological out-

---

[32] Cotton, *Exposition of Canticles,* p. 79; Bulkeley, *The Gospel Covenant* (London, 1646), pp. 2-3; Eliot, *The Christian Commonwealth* (London, 1659), "Preface" (p. A4 verso); Samuel Mather, *Figures or Types,* p. 52; Richard Mather, *An Apology of the Churches in New-England for church-government* (London, 1643), pp. 1-2. In his In-troduction to his brother's *Figures or Types,* Nathanael Mather writes (p. iv) that *"their* [the Hebrews'] *Institutions and OURS agree, the one being a . . . darker Adumbration, the other a more lightsome . . . Image of the same Things. . . .* [Thus] *our Institutes* [are] *Antitypes to theirs."* And in a similar vein, John Wilson's "Song of Deliverance" (in *Handkerchiefs From Paul,* ed. Murdock), calls the Israelites' vic-tory over Pharoah's army a "type of Englands bliss,/ saved from Spanish fury," for
. . . what is there [in the Old Testament] to Israel committed,
Hath a more large and general extent,
And to our present times may well be fitted. (p. 28)
[33] See Robert L. P. Milburn, *Early Christian Interpretations of History* (New York, 1954), p. 82. Needless to say, I am suggesting not a simple cause-effect relationship be-tween social engagement and typological outlook, but some degree of interaction between the two.
[34] "Preparation for Salvation in Seventeenth-Century New England," *JHI* (1943), IV, 253-86.

look implies yet another solution to the dilemma. The national covenant emphasized the Lord's promise to Abraham, which materialized in
the Israelite state; after the Hebrews' apostacy, the promise was renewed,
this time *in aeternum*, by Christ to His Church. The renewal antitypes
the earlier agreement; historically, it establishes a developmental connection between two elect communities. Seen in this double aspect, the New
World theocracy becomes a collection of saints whose public contract reflects the progress of human history and by the same token is mystically
foreordained, like the covenant of grace. It resembles the latter also in
that the chosen nation and the chosen individual are one in Christ as
antitype. The Incarnation is foreshadowed both by a succession of the
elect and by God's people as a whole, regarding whom He tells Moses:
"Say unto Pharoah, Thus saith the Lord, Israel is my son, even my first-
born: and I say unto thee, Let my son go." [35] This correspondence
between Israel and the "new Adam" (and by extension between the
"new Israel" and the "second Adam") can be made to serve, from the
standpoint of historical typology, as an implicit justification of the New
England doctrine of a "visible" church-state.

205

In the controversy itself, Cotton does not refer to the problem of the
covenants (as does Richard Mather, in the work cited above). But he
does so in other treatises, where he links the "charter to Paradise" with
the public covenants of Noah, Abraham, Isaac and Moses, in effect uniting the "personal conversion" of the "particular Christian" with the
"joynt calling of a company." [36] And in view of the nature of Williams'
attack, this consideration may well have influenced Cotton's defense of
the state.

Two other, more practical considerations seem to be involved. One of
these is legal and political. In combating Anglicanism, the emigrants
also revolted against many aspects of the English code of laws and looked
perforce to the Bible for new guidelines.[37] Since the latter were not to
be found in the gospels (as Cotton explained to Williams), they turned
to the Old Testament—presupposing of necessity a direct continuity between the Israelite and Christian communities. This line of reasoning
structures many explications of various points in civil and religious be-

[35] Exod. 4:22-23 (cf. Hosea 11:1). References to the Bible are to the King James Version, unless otherwise indicated, though they have been checked with the Geneva translation which was generally used by Puritans up until the mid-seventeenth century.
[36] For example, *God's Promise to His Plantations* (London, 1630), pp. 4 ff. and *A
Treatise of the Covenant of Grace* (London, 1659), pp. 3, 101 ff., 197-98. Cf. Increase
Mather, *The Times of Men* (Boston, 1675), pp. 17 ff.
[37] See Herbert W. Schneider, *The Puritan Mind* (Ann Arbor, Mich., 1961), pp. 20-
21. The critics of the New England state often castigated this turning to biblical precedents for legal procedure; e. g., John Childe, *New Englands Jonas in Tracts . . . of
the colonies in North America*, ed. Peter Force (Cambridge, 1844), V. no. 3, 16-17 ff.

havior; most comprehensively, it is evident in the Cambridge Platform (the central doctrine of the theocracy), which presents the "form or pattern of [Mosaic] Government" as being "soe perfect, as . . . able to make the [Christian] man of God . . . thorough-ly furnished vnto every good work," on the basis of numerous correlations between the Hebrews' precepts and those of St. Paul.[38]

Another such immediate factor was the emigrants' physical experience. They had left a corrupt land, crossed a "vast sea" and sought to establish a Holy Commonwealth in a wilderness inhabited by hostile heathen tribes. Were they not, obviously, an Israel *redivivus?* It seems well-nigh inevitable that the Puritan leaders should have understood these correspondences to be "providential," that even without a suitable theology of history at hand they should have sustained and encouraged the settlers by picturing them as the long-awaited Remnant which was to make the desert bloom like the rose. One cannot distinguish here between theory and fact, but to some measure at least these exigencies of the American Puritan enterprise stand behind Cotton's rationale.

Cotton's polemic, integrating as it does these varied elements, is a central formulation of the colonists' mission in the New World. As such, it offers a summary of their first statements of purpose, and adumbrates, both in concept and in expression, the later New England histories. "The building of our Churches in these ends of the world," writes Cotton in a characteristic passage,

> is the raising up of . . . the Arke of *Noah*. . . . For as there was in old *Babel,* sundry of Gods *Israel* . . . so will there be in new *Babel* sundry of Gods chosen people. . . . Unto whom as the Lord sent his Angels to hasten *Lot* out of *Sodome* . . . so he hath sent and will send the voyce of his Messengers to hasten his people . . . out of new *Babel* (as he did out of old) before that sodaine destruction fall upon the City. (*CR,* pp. 229, 143-44)

The allusion to Babylon unmistakably carries the implications perceived by Williams; together with "Noah's ark," it invokes the configuration, discussed above, of the Jordan crossing, the Church of Christ and New England's national covenant. All this is reinforced by the image through which Cotton identifies America. The "ends of the world" is a traditional figure of the New Zion; in William Guild's words, it means the final

---

38 *A Platform of Church Discipline* (Cambridge, 1649), p. 1. Along these lines, Increase Mather deals with the question of church membership by way of the Israelites who "prefigure" the Puritan children raised "within" the theocracy and of the Hebrews' "Temple . . . [which] was a Type . . . signifying the *visibility* of the *Church." A discourse . . . of Baptism* (Boston, 1675), pp. 8, 32-33.

Calling of the Gentiles . . . according to Noahs wish, and the Promise made to Abraham.

Aske of me, and I shall give thee the Heathen for thine inheritance, and the ends of the earth for thy possession [Ps. 2:8; cf. I Sam. 2:10, Luke 1:46-55]. . . .

They that dwell in the wilderness shall kneele before him [Ps. 72:9; cf. 72:8, 98:3].

I will give thee for a Covenant of the people, and for a light of the Gentiles . . . that thou mayst be my salvation, to the end of the world [Isa. 42:6, 49:6; cf. 45:20-25, 43:1-6].

Behold I will bring them from the North country, and . . . leade them by the Rivers of water in a straight way wherein they shall not stumble; for I am a Father to Israel [Jer. 31:8; cf. Zech. 9:9-15].[39]

207

It is with these meanings in mind that Cotton Mather relates "the Considerable Matters, that produced and attended the . . . COLONIES . . . erected in those *ends of the earth*," depicting the Puritan emigration as "the Church of our Lord . . . now victoriously sailing unto the . . . NEW ENGLISH ISRAEL . . . [having had] the same causes for departure [from England] as the Israelites out of Egypt . . . [and] their father Abraham had for leaving the Chaldean territories . . . [and] the primitive Christians [had for] . . . flying idolatry and heathenish corruption." Cotton Mather was a third-generation American; in the previous two generations, colonial historians had written in almost identical terms:

When England began to decline in Religion, like lukewarme Laodicea [Rev. 3:16] . . . in this very time Christ . . . raises an Army . . . for freeing his people from their long servitude . . . [before He

---

[39] Guild, *Moses Unvailed* (London, 1626), pp. 41-47 (references are to the Geneva Bible). Cotton explains the apocalyptic meaning of "the ends of the earth," and the other images cited above, in his *Exposition Upon . . . Revelation* (London, 1656), pp. 122-23, *et passim*. An early application of these concepts to the New England church-state appears in John Winthrop's famous lay-sermon, "Christian Charitie. A Modell Hereof," especially in the connections it makes between Abraham and the Macedonians (p. 78); between the "Cases" in Deuteronomy for which "Christ was a generall rule," "Adam in his first estate" seen in the light of the gospels, and Ezekiel's prophecies (pp. 81-86); and, at the end, between the Gentile "remnant" and the Israelites (p. 93). (References are to the edition of Edmund S. Morgan, in *Puritan Political Ideas* [New York, 1965].) In Winthrop's key concept of the colony as a "city set upon a hill," the meaning of "hill" relates to Sinai and Pisgah (Exod. 34:2, Deut. 34:1), the Mount from which Christ preached, the Mountain of His Transfiguration, and the Mount Zion of the redeemed remnant (Matt. 5:1, 17:1, Rev. 14:1; cf. Matt. 4:8 and Acts 21:13). The "city" as metaphor extends to passages in the Old Testament (e. g., Ps. 48:1, 8; 87:38) and the New (e. g., Eph. 2:19), implying a link between the national covenants of Israel and New England; all of which is made explicit in a striking passage of Richard Mather's *Apology*, pp. 12-13.

would bring upon their enemies a] sudden and unexpected destruction. . . . The little remnant remaining [He carries to America in
order to] . . . create a new Heaven, and a new Earth in, new Churches,
and a new Common-wealth together [Joel 2:32-3:17; Isa. 11:1-11; Rev.
21:1] . . . and make his miraculous deliverance famous . . . to the
end of the World.

•   •   •   •   •

208

This Colonies Foundation was not laid, by . . . [British] Princes,
Peers or Lords. . . . It was an incomparable Minute . . . parallel to
that of the *Father of the Faithful* [Abraham], who upon a Divine
Call, left Kindred, [and] Country. . . . [When the emigrants had
crossed the ocean] with Noah's Dove [they] . . . found rest for the
Soles of their feet [Mal. 4:3], and marched forth from their Floating
Arks. . . . [Thereupon] they *Sang the Song of Moses and of the Lamb*
[Rev. 15:3], whom they had in this Voyage followed, and now paid
their Vows to God to Serve him . . . in this remote End of the
Earth.[40]

The distinctive characteristics of these descriptions appear in sharper
focus if (with Cotton's phrases in mind) we place the New England histories alongside their immediate predecesssors, the early promotional accounts of the colony, written mainly to elicit settlers and supplies. In a
typical tract of this kind, Francis Higginson minimizes the perils of the
ocean passage, presents the "Wilderness" from a naturalist's viewpoint
("much abound[ing] with Snakes and Serpents of strange colours and
huge greatness"), and portrays the Indians as "natural men" with "curious" customs. In an appendix, Thomas Graves adds: "Vines doe grow
here plentifully laden with the beggest Grapes," comparable only to those
"of *Hungaria*."[41] In the later histories, such observations take on the
symbolic proportions of historical typology—of events pertaining to
"Gods *Israel* . . . in their March through the Wilderness into the Land
of *Canaan*, not many years after their Departure from *Egypt*, their *House
of Bondage*." The emigrants—in flight from an "England ripe . . . for
the slaughter" and imminently to "be brought down to hell"—cross the
Atlantic under the guidance of "Jehovah . . . [their] exact Pilot." The
wilderness serpents they encounter become the temptations of the Israelites and of Christ; the battles with the Indians, "the Seed of the Serpent,"

[40] Mather, *Magnalia*, I, 25, 43, 48, 166; Edward Johnson, *Wonder-Working Providence of Sions Saviour in New England, 1628-1651*, ed. J. Franklin Jameson (New York,
1952), pp. 23-25, 151; Joshua Scottow, *A Narrative of . . . the Massachusetts Colony*
(Boston, 1694), in *Massachusetts Historical Society Collections*, 4th ser., IV (1858),
292, 286-87.
[41] *New Englands Plantation* (London, 1629), in *Proceedings of the Massachusetts
Historical Society*, LXII (1929), 215-18.

are "Wars of the Lord" fought by a "wandering Race of Jacobites" who
are also "Souldiers of Christ"; the "assaults" of the heretics and witches
("Snakes . . . in the tender grass" that would destroy "this Eden") are
the same that Satan inflicted upon Christ, "producing a most horrible
anguish in his mind . . . [which] made . . . a figure in his conflicts
for us." Fed in their hardships by "divine manna" (cf. Exod. 16:14 ff.
and Matt. 4:11), the settlers transform the wilderness, miraculously, into
a Garden of God. For Graves, the vines and grapes are simply material;
Roger Williams uses them as types in order to contrast "the *Gardens* of
Christs Churches" with "the *Wilderness* . . . of the world" (WL, p. 108).
Johnson, Scottow and Mather, like Cotton, invoke them in both senses,
as literal-prophetic figures. Their histories depict the church-state as "this
Vineyard of the Lord" filled with "goodly branches of Christs vines," as
"Christs Garden" whose "clusters of *rich grapes*" were "sweeter . . . than
the Grapes of *Eschol* were to Israel of old."[42]

209

In all three histories, too, the flowering of the wilderness is set directly
against the backdrop of the millennium. New England, writes Edward
Johnson, has

> not only the Lords promise to Israel, but to his only Son Christ Jesus;
> Lord, hast thou not said, *Ask of me, and I will give thee the Heathen
> for thine inheritance, and the uttermost ends of the earth for thy posses-
> sion;* and now Lord, are not these [the American churches] the Churches
> of Christ which thou hast planted for his [Christ's] possession . . . [?]
> Then . . . the time of the Lords arising to have mercy upon Sion is come,
> yea his appointed time is at hand. . . . Mr. John Cotton, among many
> others . . . hath declared some sudden blow to be given to this blood-
> thirsty monster. . . . [And indeed] the overthrow of Antichrist, and call-
> ing of the Jews . . . in all likelihood is very suddenly to be performed.

42 Scottow, *Narrative*, pp. 285, 289, 293, 295; Johnson, *Wonder-Working Providence*,
pp. 62, 82, 118, 126, 148, 234, 244; Mather, *Magnalia*, I, 163, 347; II, 447. The American
Puritan attitude to England varies through the century, of course, and generally remains rather circumspect; nonetheless, the implications of the colonists' typological
view is manifest in all the histories. It may be well to note here that it is mainly in the
interests of economy that I deal only with these three historians, who (as I indicate
above) represent three New England generations. The same typological structure underlies (to varying degrees) the other New England histories. This holds true not only
for the writings of men like Increase Mather, but even for William Bradford's *History
of Plymouth Plantation*, though it records the "pilgrimage" of a group of Separatists
rather than the progress of a colony. For example: a) Europe resembles Babylon, Egypt
and "the highplases in Israell" (e. g., pp. 25, 29, 45-46, 79); b) the wilderness "temptations" are compared to those of Christ and of the Israelites (e. g., pp. 88, 137, 156); c)
the colony itself is many times referred to as a new "state of Israel"; and d) the millenarian implications, though relatively subdued, form an intrinsic part of the story
(e. g., pp. 29, 97, 364). The references to Bradford's *History* are from the edition of
William T. Davis (New York, 1959).

. . . [For this] poor remnant of Gods people . . . the glorious harvest of our Lord Christ . . . is hard at hand.

More than half a century after Johnson's *Wonder-Working Providence of Sions' Saviour,* Cotton Mather repeated its predictions with equal fervor. Quoting in part from the sermons of Nicholas Noyes, he announces that "the *reigning* of the saints a thousand years [becomes] within the last few sevens of years nearer to accomplishment. . . . [There is] a REVOLUTION AND A REFORMATION at the very door [cf. Matt. 24:33 and Mark 13:29], which will be more wonderful than any of the deliverances yet seen by the church of God from the beginning of the world."[43]

210

Mather's forecasts are intrinsic to the very texture of his narrative, as is also the case with Johnson and Scottow. He recreates in Phip's victory over the natives, for example, the Hebrews' entrance into the promised land, in which the Indian leader becomes Og, the Israelites' enemy prefigured by "the serpent, Python" (a type of Satan), and Phips is described as Joshua, antitype of Apollo who destroyed Python and a figure in turn of "Christ . . . that 'SUN of righteousness' [see Mal. 4:2]"; and, on this basis, he concludes that "all the *serpents* . . . have found themselves engaged in a fatal enterprise." It is no less an event than the climactic onslaught of "the *devils* and the *damned*" which was shadowed forth by the War in Heaven and now signifies the proximity of the New Jerusalem. Neither Johnson nor Scottow could rise to this height of figural sophistication; but the difference between them and Mather is only one of degree. All three historians depend on the same method, and all three present a similar vision of New England. Alan Heimert has pointed out that the Puritans formed their concept of the wilderness out of their actual experience, and Kenneth Murdock has noted in their "allegories and parallels" an attempt at "assuaging their loneliness in a 'howling desert.' " [44] No doubt these elements played their part, but the largest factor, the framework of their historiography, lies in the *Weltanschauung*

---

[43] Johnson, *Wonder-Working Providence,* pp. 238-39, 268, 30, 255 (cf. Scottow, *Narrative,* e. g., pp. 301-2); Mather, *Magnalia,* I, 330-31; II, 653-54, 578-79; I, 46. The critics of the American Puritan state were, like Williams, quick to recognize the nature of this general outlook. Thus Thomas Morton sarcastically records Joshua Temperwell's Atlantic crossing as "a more miraculous thing . . . than it was for the Israelites to goe over Iordan drishod," and his arrival in America as that of "all the 12. Tribes of new Israell come" to "take full possession" of "the Land of Canaan" (*New English Canaan,* in *Tracts,* ed. Force, II, no. 5, 108). His reference is to Isa. 11:10-16, which describes how "the remnant of his people" shall "go . . . drishod" over another "Egyptian sea," and establish the New Jerusalem.

[44] Mather, *Magnalia,* II, 566; Heimert, "Puritanism, the Wilderness, and the Frontier," *passim;* Murdock, "Clio in the Wilderness: History and Biography in Puritan New England," *Church History,* XXIV (1955), 234-35.

consciously set forth as early as *The Bloody Tenent Washed* and prevalent in a considerable body of the literature from the diaries to the jeremiads.[45]

The "linear" emphasis did not, of course, preclude the use of Augustinian typology, if the areas of application—public and personal—remained distinct. Augustine's protégé, Orosius, adhered to his master's teachings though his *Historia* "restates and expands the premises" of Eusebius; and for their part the New Englanders never forgot that, in terms of the individual's journey to salvation, Canaan *was* a shadow of heaven and "the world an howling wilderness . . . as those Arabian deserts were."[46] The two methods sometimes appear separately and sometimes alongside one another in the same work.[47] Frequently, however, they are juxtaposed in a deliberate effort (intimated earlier) to identify the exemplary colonist with the community. This technique stands out most dramatically in the biographies and elegies. It appears in the elegy on Hooker, quoted above, where the quaking "oaks of Bashan" relate at once to the accomplishments of the individual (as allegory) and to the collective body of New Englanders (as history). In general, it manifests itself in the Puritan habit of combining history and hagiography.[48]

211

---

45 For example, Wigglesworth records in his *Diary* (p. 383) that "Coming through the wilderness we were overtaken with a great and dreadful tempest . . . and about 40 [trees] I suppose we see in our way. . . . I thought how good it was to have this great god for a mans friend." The conjunction of the number forty, the "wilderness," the "tempest" and divine assistance unmistakably reveals a typological pattern imposed on this experience (e. g., see Thomas Taylor, *Christ's Combat and Conquest* [London, 1618], p. 20). Perhaps the most striking and sustained instance in the diaries of such a pattern appears in Cotton Mather's analyses of his speech difficulties and of his efforts to overcome them (*Diary*, ed. Worthington C. Ford, *Massachusetts Historical Society Collections*, 7th ser. [1911], VI, 49-70, 188-207, 311-40). The jeremiads are closely bound up with Puritan historiography and, in fact, form an intrinsic part of every New England history, from Bradford to Mather. In a sense, indeed, the jeremiads are a logical extension of historical typology (see Hanning, *Vision of History*, p. 29, and Auerbach, "Figura," pp. 40-41; and cf. Sanford, *Quest for Paradise*, p. 83, and Trefz, "Puritans' View of History," pp. 130-34); and their general outlook, like that of the histories, is formulated in Cotton's polemic: "*Hierusalem* was counted a faithfull Citie, and the Nation Holy, by Priviledge of their Covenant: yet [it] . . . was alwayes a City of the provocation of Gods wrath. . . . Where more hath been given, the more will be required of the Lord" (*CR*, p. 131; see also pp. 155-56 and cf. *YM*, p. 486). For a comprehensive statement of this view, see Cotton's *Gods Mercie mixed with his Justice* (London, 1641), pp. 3-10, 32-35, 54-57, 67-68, 104-6.

46 Thomas Taylor, *Christ Revealed* (London, 1635), pp. 158-59; regarding Orosius, see Hanning, *Vision of History*, pp. 37-42.

47 Nathaniel Morton, for example, in *New England's Memorial*, uses Canaan and the wilderness as historical types (e. g., pp. 36, 43, 63, 226), yet he also writes that his work will help the reader in "his journey through the wilderness of this world, to that eternal rest . . . in the heavenly Canaan" (p. 6).

48 This connection between the two forms may be seen in the close resemblance between the pattern of the histories (as suggested above) and the "unvaried formula" which Reginald E. Watters finds in Puritan biographies: "regeneration . . . dedica-

Johnson writes of one settler that "Christ crowned . . . [his] head/ In Wilderness to manage his great War,/ 'Gainst Antichrist"; of another that he "Undaunted . . . [does] not allow . . . men to wast/Christs vineyard heere"; of still others that, being "Christ's Soldiers," their work shows that "The day's at hand, down falls that man of sin." Do these figures concern the solitary Christian's conquest of Satan, or that of the church-state? Obviously, the answer is both; the private pilgrimage lights up the social reality and vice versa: each provides a proof of the other. This "People of Israel," Johnson says, were determined to "gather together as one Man, and grow together as one Tree." Joshua Scottow, who organizes his narrative around the saintly life of John Cotton, writes of the whole enterprise that "the Body of this People was animated as with one soul." And Cotton Mather asserts that "In one Eliot, you see what a people it is" that inhabits New England, portraying its founders as being microcosmic Gardens of God while building the narrative upon figures of conversion, baptism and Christ's triumphant agon in the wilderness.[49]

This harmony between historical and allegorical typology brings out the furthest implications of John Cotton's answer to Roger Williams. It enlists the heretic's exegetical method as support for the theocracy and binds all aspects of the New England venture—physical and theological, individual and communal—into a comprehensive vision. Its distinctive blending of the notions of representative men and a "chosen" country, whereby one signifies (or should signify) the other, may be seen as an essential part of the Puritan legacy to American literature. At any rate, Cotton's use of typology, as it conforms to, suggests and perhaps influenced that of his contemporaries and successors, attests to an imaginative force in American Puritan writing which has too often gone unrecognized. Perry Miller has described the New England mind as a kind of logic-machine run by the principles of the Ramist dialect and oiled by rigid pedantry. "As Cotton Mather said proudly of John Cotton, his 'Composures all *Smelt* of the *Lamp*,' and so also, by deliberate intention, did those of every New England preacher in the seventeenth century."[50]

tion . . . persecution . . . flight to New England . . . installation in a church there . . . godliness of life," and, finally, ascension to the heavenly Jerusalem ("Biographical Technique in Cotton Mather's *Magnalia*," *William and Mary Quarterly*, II [1945], 155). William R. Manierre notes the general use of typology in biographies by Cotton Mather and other New England divines in "Cotton Mather and the Biographical Parallel," *American Quarterly*, XIII (1961), 157-60.

[49] Johnson, *Wonder-Working Providence*, pp. 107, 44, 194, 60; Scottow, *Narrative*, p. 287; Mather, *Magnalia*, I, 527. For representative examples of Mather's typological method as it combines allegorical and historical typology, see I, 398 (individual as colony); I, 398 (exodus as conversion); I, 529 (sea-crossing at baptism); II, 447 (witchcraft and Christ's agon).

[50] *New England Mind: The Seventeenth Century* (Cambridge, 1954), p. 352. The reference is to Mather's *Magnalia*, I, 254.

This viewpoint, which until recently has dominated our literary appreciation of the period,[51] shapes his presentation of the Williams-Cotton controversy. The actual terms of contention, however, understood within their proper context, indicate the emotion and creative vitality behind much of the literature. They indicate, too, that Mather may conceivably have meant by "lamp" not only the candle by which his grandfather read his Ramus, but also the Lamp which is Christ. And if so, Miller's statement would be accurate in a sense quite different from that which he intended. Mather would then be pointing to the full scope of Cotton's studies, by reference to what his uncle classifies as the "Lamp . . . [which] shines in the Candlestick . . . [as] doth the Ministry in the Church,"[52] and even beyond this, perhaps, to the golden candlestick that symbolizes the biblical Israelites, the early Christian church and the Jerusalem of the Gentiles (e. g., Exod. 25:31, Rev. 1:12, Zech. 4:2).

213

By this "lamp," indeed, John Cotton and his fellow congregationalists expounded their venture in America. It is the "light of the world" to which Winthrop and others allude when they speak of New England as a "city set on a hill" (see Matt. 5:14-15), and by which Mather himself characterizes John Cotton in particular—one of "our *burning and shining lights*" in "the first candlestick set up" in Boston—as well as the colony at large: "behold, ye European Churches, there are golden Candlesticks (more than twice times seven!) in the midst of this 'outer darkness': unto the upright children of Abraham, here hath arisen *light in darkness* [see Ps. 112:4; Matt. 8:12, 22:13, 25:30]."[53] Edward Johnson describes it as the "bright light" which has "rid Christ's Temple" from the "smoke" of Williams' and others' heresies; its "shining" rays, he con-

---

[51] Thus Kenneth B. Murdock writes that Ramus' influence led the New England Puritan writers to view "the created universe" as a strictly "logical structure" (*Literature and Theology in Colonial New England* [New York, 1963], pp. 63-64); Roy Harvey Pearce finds Edward Taylor's poetry wanting because it "reflects . . . the very logic of orthodox New England culture, the logic of Peter Ramus" ("Edward Taylor: The Poet as Puritan," *New England Quarterly*, XLIII [1950], 40-41); and Charles Feidelson blames the entire failure of American Puritan literature on its dependence upon "the Ramist scheme" (*Symbolism and American Literature* [Chicago, 1959], p. 86). The recent contributions toward a revaluation of American Puritan literature are summarized and enlarged upon in an important essay by Norman S. Grabo, "The Veiled Vision: The Role of Aesthetics in Early American Intellectual History," *William and Mary Quarterly*, XIX (1962), 493-511.

[52] Samuel Mather, *Figures or Types*, p. 391. The candlestick is typologically represented in the singular ("a note of unity") and in the numbers seven ("a note of perfection") and ten ("a note of multitude"). John Bunyan, *Solomon's Temple Spiritualized* (Hartford, 1802), p. 74.

[53] *Magnalia*, I, 245, 25, 27. Mather sustains this figure of New England's *"golden Age"* (I, 27) through all seven books of his Church History (e. g., I, 79, 585; II, 8). Winthrop's image of the colony recurs, for example, in Johnson's *Wonder-Working Providence*, p. 29.

tinues, reveal that on the American Strand the "ratling bones together run . . . of Israels sons long dead," and thus "Jerico's high walls" have fallen again, proclaiming the death of "Dagon" and the approaching "Resurrections Day."[54] Most movingly of all, Edward Taylor hails the Lamp, in a long Meditation, as the "bright Lanthorn . . . Endungeoning all Darkness underground" and "imparadising" those upon whom it shone.[55] His image here extends, typologically, to the "lamp" of the Mosaic "law" and of the Gentiles' "salvation" (Ps. 119:97-112; Isa. 62:1, 11-12); explicitly, it refers to the "Sun of righteousness" acclaimed by Malachi, in the chapter where this last of the Hebrew prophets heralds the new chosen people:

214

> For, behold, the day cometh, that shall burn as an oven. . . . But unto you that fear my name shall the Sun of righteousness arise with healing in his wings; and ye shall go forth, and . . . tread down the wicked . . . under the soles of your feet. . . . Remember ye [therefore] the law of Moses my servant, which I commanded unto him in Horeb for all Israel, with the statutes and judgments. (Mal. 4:1-4)

54 *Wonder-Working Providence*, pp. 203-4. Dagon is Satan, the old Dragon; Jericho "is the type of the world," especially as the Devil's kingdom, and its fall is a familiar figure of "the end of the world" (Daniélou, *Shadows to Reality*, p. 276); for the implications of "ratling bones," see Ezek. 37: 7.

55 "Meditation [68 (A)]. Mal. 4. 2. The Sun of Righteousness, etc.," 11. 3, 5, 57, in *Poems*, ed. Stanford, pp. 202-3. In connection with the biblical quotations below, cf. Scottow's reference (and its context) to the "Soles of their [the settlers'] feet," and Mather's use of the "SUN of righteousness" above.

Isaac Backus and the Separation of Church and State in America

WILLIAM G. McLOUGHLIN*

THE role of Isaac Backus (1724-1806) and the Separate Baptists in the development of the American tradition of separation of church and state has not yet been given its due. Yet any careful evaluation of this tradition must acknowledge that neither the position of Roger Williams nor that of Thomas Jefferson and James Madison adequately defines it. The basic premises of Williams' position were far too Puritan in theology and too anti-institutional in polity to be typical, while the basic premises of Jefferson's and Madison's position were far too rationalistic and anticlerical. Or, to put it another way, Williams was too great a perfectionist about religious purity while Jefferson and Madison were too indifferent, if not hostile, toward revealed religion to be entirely representative of the American approach to church-state relationships.[1]

215

In the secular mood of the twentieth century the United States Supreme Court has drawn heavily upon Jefferson and Madison in its increasingly rigid interpretation of the "no establishment" clause of the First Amendment, but throughout the nineteenth century most Americans firmly believed that the United States was a Protestant nation and that as such its laws and customs should conform to the will of the evangelical majority.[2]

A professor at Brown University who is interested in the history of religion in America, Mr. McLoughlin is the author of *Modern Revivalism: Charles Grandison Finney to Billy Graham* (New York, 1959). He delivered this paper in a different form as one of the Warren Lectures Series in American Religious History at the Harvard Divinity School, April 10, 1967.

[1] Perry Miller seems to me quite right in arguing that Williams came to his final position "because he was driven by religious passion and not because he was mollified by the religious indifferentism of a Jefferson. He preached liberty of conscience not because he thought it the least destructive or most economical way for men to live together, but because of a vision which for him was a never-ending ecstasy. He did not look forward to a free society as the goal of human endeavor; instead he looked down on it, in pity and sorrow, seeing in freedom only a preliminary requirement for the Christian pilgrimage." (*Roger Williams: His Contribution to the American Tradition* [Indianapolis, 1953], 27-28; see also Edmund S. Morgan's excellent new study *Roger Williams: The Church and the State* [New York, 1967] which amplifies and in places corrects Miller's view.)

[2] James Bryce captured the prevailing view of Americans on this question in the nineteenth century when he said, "The matter may be summed up by saying that Christianity is in fact understood to be, though not the legally established religion, yet the national religion." (Quoted in *Church and State in American History*, ed. John F. Wilson [Boston, 1965], 154.) By the increasing rigidity of the Court's interpretation, I mean in contrast to the nineteenth-century American attitude described by Lord Bryce. Since 1948, I recognize, many strict Separationists feel that the Court has permitted considerable breaching of the wall of separation.

1392

Since the Baptists and the Methodists were the most widespread and numerous denominations in that century, it seems essential to include their evangelical theory of Separationism in any attempt to define that tradition. It is hardly logical to expect that the views of a seventeenth-century Calvinistic Seeker like Williams or an eighteenth-century deistic Episcopalian like Jefferson or Madison would accurately represent the views of these evangelical pietists. The Methodists, who were still part of the Anglican Church during the Revolution, produced no spokesman for their views on this tradition during its formative period. But the Baptists found in Backus a most energetic and eloquent one. In his long, active career and his trenchant tracts he provided a dedicated, effective leadership for eighteenth-century sectarian pietism that entitles him to rank with Williams, Jefferson, and Madison as a key proponent of this fundamental tenet of the American democratic faith.

216

Backus was born in 1724, the son of a well-to-do farmer and a member of one of the most distinguished Congregationalist families of Norwich, Connecticut. Baptized as a child into the parish church of his parents, he grew up without ever questioning its orthodoxy or its practice of the halfway covenant. But after his conversion, under the New Light preaching of James Davenport and Eleazar Wheelock in 1741, he began to notice how many of the church's members were not really visible saints. And when the parish minister would not agree to exclude such reprobates from communion, Backus and several of his relatives, together with a large number of the most respectable people in his congregation, left the parish church and formed a Separate church in Norwich in 1745.[3] A year later Backus felt called to become an itinerant New Light preacher, and in 1748 he was ordained pastor of a Separate church in Middleborough, Massachusetts. In 1751, after two years of spiritual doubt, he adopted antipedobaptist views and was rebaptized by immersion. He then tried to conduct his Separate church on open communion lines for five years. Finding this impossible, he dissolved the Separate church in 1756 and organized the First Baptist Church of Middleborough on closed communion and evangelical Calvinist principles. He remained pastor there until his death in 1806, devoting himself tirelessly to itinerant evangelism, denominational consolidation, and the fight to overthrow the established system of the Congregational churches in New England.

[3] For a discussion of the Separate or Strict Congregational movement in New England, see C. C. Goen, *Revivalism and Separatism in New England, 1740–1800* (New Haven, Conn., 1962). It should be noted that on the whole most of these Separates favored Separationism; the latter is a modern shorthand term for the principle of separation of church and state (or voluntarism), which has no specific relationship to the Separate movement.

The history of separation of church and state in Massachusetts from 1692 to the Great Awakening, so ably told by Susan Reed in her neglected monograph on this subject,[4] is a story of how the Quakers, Baptists, and Anglicans fought, each in their own way, to establish their right to exemption from paying compulsory religious taxes for the support of the Standing or Congregational churches. But in this early period it was the Quakers and Anglicans who carried the main thrust of the movement. The Baptists played a secondary role, fighting mainly for the preservation of their privileged position in the town of Swansea. The Anglicans, of course, did not oppose religious taxation out of any commitment to the principle of voluntarism. They frankly coveted the privileged position of the Congregationalists. The Quakers, while committed to voluntarism, rested content after 1729 when the Massachusetts General Assembly granted exemption from paying religious taxes to all members of their persuasion who could prove that they were bona fide Quakers.

217

The Baptists did not come forward to lead the fight for voluntarism until after the Great Awakening. Their theory of Separationism evolved slowly and painfully during the years 1748–1773. But the place to begin a discussion of their views is in the year 1739, just before the Great Awakening began. At that time the Massachusetts ecclesiastical laws stated that three kinds of dissenters were to be tolerated as persons exempted from supporting the establishment: "Anabaptists," "Quakers," and "Churchmen." All three terms had pejorative overtones indicating that the weight of public opprobrium was cast so heavily against joining one of these "dissenting sects" that even the opportunity to evade the high costs of religious taxation seldom persuaded a man to do so except out of the strongest conscientious scruples.

The law required anyone who claimed to be a member of the Anabaptist or Quaker "persuasion" to provide a "certificate" signed by his minister stating that he did regularly attend and contribute money to that church; the minister and two leading members of that church or congregation had to swear that such persons were "conscientiously of their persuasion," not simply tax dodgers.[5] The Standing Order considered this, and rightly so, a most generous arrangement. Compared to the status of dissenters in those colonies where the Anglican Church was established or

---

[4] Susan M. Reed, *Church and State in Massachusetts, 1691–1740* (Urbana, Ill., 1914).
[5] The requirements for signatures on the certificates varied from time to time, but throughout most of the century three signatures were required. (See *The Acts and Resolves, Public and Private, of the Province of the Massachusetts Bay* [21 vols., Boston, 1869–1922], II, 714.) Anglicans were also required to obtain similar certificates, but this did not entitle them to tax exemption; it merely gave their minister claim to their religious taxes for his support.

to those in England, the dissenters of Massachusetts were indeed far better off. Due credit has not been given to the Congregationalists of "the Glacial Age" for the advance they made toward toleration by these laws—albeit the advance was made grudgingly and under strong pressure from England.[6] Many Congregationalists, however, resented the fact that dissenters received this special tax exemption, especially since every exemption to a dissenter raised the tax burden for the rest of the community. Hence local authorities often made it extremely difficult for dissenters to obtain certificates, and the term "certificate man" was one of scorn and resentment throughout the eighteenth century.

218

Because the tax exemption laws in Massachusetts were temporary and had to be renewed approximately every five years, and because some Baptists complained that they were not fairly administered, a committee of the leading Baptists in the vicinity of Boston, under the leadership of James Bound and Joseph Callendar, was organized in the 1730's to negotiate with the General Court over revision and improvement of the laws. In 1739, when the exemption law of 1734 was about to expire, the legislature consulted with this group and permitted it to submit a bill on the subject. It is significant that this group, describing itself as "Agents for the people called Baptists," told the General Court that they found the tax exemption system satisfactory in principle, but wished that it could be a permanent rather than a temporary law. They said, however, that they would be satisfied if the current law were extended for ten years. Their petition humbly thanked the court for the exemption system which "hath been much to the relief and comfort of the said people called Baptists, as well as an honourable Characteristick of the mildness, moderation and Christian Spirit of the Legislators."[7]

The Great Awakening, however, produced a wholly new kind of Baptist in Massachusetts (and throughout the country) who was not so humble or acquiescent. These Baptists were known colloquially as the "new Baptists" or the "Separate Baptists." They began as radical New Lights converted during the Great Awakening; finding that the Old Lights were successfully thwarting their reforms, they separated from the Standing

[6] See Reed, *Church and State in Massachusetts,* for the pressure Anglicans and Quakers were able to bring upon Massachusetts from England. In 1739 there were only nine Baptist churches in Massachusetts with perhaps three hundred members, most of them in the area of the old Plymouth Colony around Swansea and Rehoboth.

[7] Massachusetts Archives, Ecclesiastical, XII, 96, 127, Massachusetts Archives, Secretary of State's Office, Massachusetts State House, Archives Office, Boston. It appears that the legislature, fearing tax dodging, was preparing to revise the tax exemption law so that Baptists and Quakers would have to pay religious taxes like the Anglicans and then have these taxes turned over to their own ministers. Hence the Baptist agents may simply have been settling for the lesser of two evils.

Order and eventually adopted antipedobaptist views. Over 125 such separations occurred in New England, but to their dismay the Separates discovered that the General Assembly declined to recognize them as bona fide dissenters. The legislators argued that the Separates had no distinctive marks as a persuasion or denomination to differentiate them from the Congregational churches of the establishment; to grant them the same tax exemption privileges as had been granted to Anabaptists, Quakers, and Churchmen would, therefore, lead to utter confusion and the total breakdown of the prevailing system.[8] Consequently the Separates found themselves saddled with double taxation: they had to support their own churches and those of the Standing Order as well. And if they were so adamant as to refuse to pay taxes to support the Standing Order, they were imprisoned or had their goods distrained and sold at public auction.[9] Under this pressure the Separate movement gradually disintegrated, and, of the 125 Separate churches existing in 1754, only about a dozen remained by 1776.

Meanwhile many of the Separates moved from their original position of "Strict Congregationalism" into the position of antipedobaptism. The theological reasons for this shift are complex, but suffice it to say that the question of infant baptism had always been one of the most awkward and inconsistent aspects of New England Congregationalism; the Puritans professed to believe that a church should be made up only of visible saints admitted to communion upon profession of their faith after conversion. But this left undefined the role that those baptized in infancy were to play in the church when they came of age if they had not yet become visible saints. The Separate movement began in large part out of a reaction against the halfway covenant and Stoddardeanism which were efforts to solve this problem but which, in the eyes of the new pietism of the Great Awakening, had only made it worse.

There was a certain logical consistency therefore in moving from the Separate position to the antipedobaptist position and arguing that a voluntaristic church of visible saints could only mean a church in which adult, professed believers should be granted the seal of baptism and the privileges

---

[8] The Standing Order was of course correct in its view that to grant tax exemption to Separates whose doctrines and practices differed from that of the established churches only in the intensity of their pietistic fervor would have destroyed the ecclesiastical system. Baptists, Quakers, and Anglicans could be tolerated and given tax exemption only because they were so few. But if 125 towns and parishes were divided into competing Congregational factions of almost equal size, most would not have been able to provide adequate support for both. The Separate movement had to be crushed.

[9] Backus himself was threatened with jail for this reason in 1748, and four years later his mother and brother were imprisoned in Norwich, Connecticut, for refusing as Separates to pay religious taxes. (See W. G. McLoughlin, *Isaac Backus* [Boston, 1967], 22, 49.)

of church membership. As the Separate movement began to crumble from
outside pressure by the civil authorities, it simultaneously disintegrated
internally from the dissensions arising among those moving into the antipedobaptist camp. Naturally there were many in the Standing Order who
looked upon this movement as an effort by the Separates to claim the
right of tax exemption granted to Anabaptists. But few pietists were so
hypocritical as this, and fewer would have been willing to bear the double
onus of being schismatics and Anabaptist "certificate men" just to "wash
away their taxes" by immersion.

220   Anyone reading the diaries and letters of men like Backus who made
this painful transition from Separate to Baptist between 1749 and 1756 will
soon be convinced of the tortuous trial of conscience involved. Backus in
fact said that he at first opposed the idea of antipedobaptism because he
thought the devil was tempting him and his Separate brethren by offering
them an easy way out of persecution. Like most Separates, Backus was
ready to go to jail rather than pay religious taxes to support the Standing
Order, but he was not ready to let his fear of jail lead him into religious
error.[10]

The evolution of Backus' First Baptist Church of Middleborough from
strict Separate to open communion Separate to closed communion Baptist
principles in the years 1748–1756 was typical of many such transitions
throughout the province. And it was from the new evangelistic drive of
these Separate Baptist churches that the Baptist denomination in New
England derived its vigor and growth in the late eighteenth century.
Backus, who quickly became a leading spokesman for these Separate
Baptists, was aware of the evolutionary development of his own views.
Writing in 1781 he said, "I was such a dull scholar in Christ's school
that I was thirty-two years in learning a lesson of only six words, namely,
'One Lord, one faith, one baptism.' "[11] By this he meant that having started
his spiritual life as a pedobaptist New Light in 1741, he then took ten
years to evolve to the position of antipedobaptism, five more years to
acknowledge the truth of closed communion, and then seventeen more
years to decide that he could no longer acquiesce in the New England
system of tolerated tax exemption for dissenters. It is important to keep in

[10] The diary, letters, and other papers of Backus, which are now being edited for a letter-
press edition under a grant from the National Historical Publications Commission, are owned
principally by Andover Newton Theological School, Newton Center, Massachusetts. The best
proof that the Standing Order feared tax dodging among the Separates was the new tax exemption law of 1754 that was designed specifically to exclude the "new Baptists" from the tax
exemption privileges of the old Baptists. It proved impossible, however, to maintain the distinction, and the law did not function as expected.
[11] Isaac Backus, *Truth Is Great and Will Prevail* (Boston, 1781), Appendix, 7.

mind the evolutionary and often pragmatic development of the Baptist position on church and state if we are to distinguish it from the more ideological and consistent positions of Williams, Jefferson, and Madison.

While Backus fought vigorously for the right of Separates and then of Separate Baptists to be exempt from compulsory support of the Standing Church and ministry, his early efforts were limited to broadening the definition of a bona fide dissenter to include the new Baptists, whom the legislature tried to classify as Separates, and to increasing the effective and honest administration of the tax exemption laws for Baptists. Liberty of conscience and freedom of religion represented for him, and for most Baptists prior to 1773, essentially a self-centered and denominationally oriented goal rather than an absolute or clearly enunciated principle. Nowhere did Backus argue on behalf of dissenters in general, as Williams and Jefferson so often did; nor did he join forces with other dissenting groups to work for separation on an interdenominational basis.[12] Always the Baptists worked with and for the Baptists. If their principles had a broader application, that was secondary to them, and it is as misleading to read our current theory into them as into the principles of Williams or Jefferson. Like all radical reformers, the Separate Baptists occasionally exalted their immediate personal claims into broad abstract principles. But in practice their goals were limited, their practices expedient. For example, they showed little concern for other new dissenting groups that arose in New England after the Great Awakening; in the opinion of the Separate Baptists, the Universalists, Shakers, Sandemanians, and Methodists were merely corrupt and dangerous heretics, not allies against the establishment. One of the most noted Separate Baptists, a minister who worked closely with Backus for the abolition of compulsory religious taxes, Valentine Rathbun, actually tried to persuade the people of Pittsfield in 1781 to banish all Shakers from that town.[13] Nor is there a word in all of Backus' published or unpublished writings concerning the famous lawsuit of 1783–1786 by which John Murray, the founder of the Universalists in America, won toleration and tax exemption for his sect in Massachusetts. Backus was positively vitriolic in his tracts attacking Universalists, Shakers, and Methodists, all of whom he considered as dangerous heretics to a Christian commonwealth as the Puritans had considered the Munsterite Anabaptists

---

[12] The one exception to this occurred in 1774 when the Baptists accepted an invitation by some leading Quakers in Philadelphia to join them in a protest to the Continental Congress. But this joint endeavor was limited to the one specific occasion, and it was prompted by the ulterior motives of the Quakers who hoped to thwart the radical efforts of the Congress by injecting this divisive note. (See McLoughlin, *Isaac Backus,* 128–32.)

[13] The motion supported by Rathbun in the town meeting at Pittsfield in 1781 is quoted in J.E.A. Smith, *History of Pittsfield* (2 vols., Boston, 1869), I, 454.

to be. He did not specifically urge their persecution, but neither did he urge their toleration. The same implacable hostility was displayed by nineteenth-century Baptists and Methodists against Mormons, Catholics, and Christian Scientists.[14]

Nor did Backus argue at first for complete disestablishment of church and state, for that would have committed the Baptists to opposing the established status of the Church of England at home. But the Baptists often found the king to be their strongest bulwark against Massachusetts' persecution, and they did not want to alienate him by attacking the church of which he was the head. It was only under the stimulus of the incipient revolt against England, and after the examples of civil disobedience provided by the Sons of Liberty against the Stamp Act, that Backus finally led the Baptists to adopt an uncompromising attitude against mere religious toleration.[15] It was not until September 1773 that the Baptists of New England finally took a stand for freedom of conscience as a natural or supernatural right and began a campaign of massive civil disobedience by refusing any longer to submit annual certificates of their dissenting persuasion in order to obtain exemption from religious taxes. And even then the line between church and state was drawn specifically in terms of compulsory religious taxation.

Many aspects of Separationism that we now associate with the tradition were still unresolved among the Baptists even at the time of Backus' death. Throughout the nineteenth century, in fact, the Baptists, like other evangelicals and the public at large, were quite ready to use the state to enforce their superior claims against Freemasons or the heathen Indians and Orientals. Francis Wayland, the Baptist president of Brown University, virtually preached a doctrine of religious survival of the fittest in the 1840's, and other evangelicals were still preaching Christian imperialism at the end of the century.[16] Few nineteenth-century evangelicals saw any inconsistency in supporting laws to enforce the Protestant Sabbath or prohibition, laws against blasphemy and profanity, laws against lotteries, gambling, theatergoing, dancing, and, ultimately, against the teaching of evolution. In recent years staunch neoevangelical supporters of Separation-

---

[14] Backus referred to Mother Ann Lee of the Shakers as "a common prostitute" and called John Wesley a Tory and a liar. Of course Williams bitterly attacked the Quakers, and Jefferson was equally hostile toward Calvinists and Catholics, but what Backus lacks is any clear-cut statement that, despite their theological errors, these new dissenters equally deserve religious liberty. Somehow he could not bring himself to include them as true religious believers.

[15] Even as late as the spring of 1775 Backus was urged by many Baptists to be cautious in taking the patriot side lest it lose them the good will of the King. (McLoughlin, *Isaac Backus*, 134.)

[16] See Francis Wayland, *The Elements of Political Economy* (Boston, 1852), 131-32, and Josiah Strong, *Our Country* (New York, 1886), Chap. XIV.

ism have cried out against the decisions of the Supreme Court preventing Bible reading and prayer in the public schools. Certainly Jefferson would have approved of these Court decisions, and so would Williams. But it seems certain that Backus would not. And it is the pragmatic middle ground of Backus on church and state, not the more consistent positions of Jefferson and of Williams, that prevailed in practice throughout most of American history.

As a Baptist Backus might be expected to have drawn upon the work of his illustrious predecessor, Williams, in evolving his pietistic theory of Separationism. Being a contemporary and later a political supporter of Jefferson, he might also have been expected to share some of his views about this matter. But in fact he drew little from either of them and developed his Separationist views on very different grounds. While he shared Williams' Calvinistic theology, he had no use for his Seekerism. While he shared Jefferson's Lockean defense of voluntarism, he deplored his deistic theology. Sidney Mead has rightly pointed out that the positive ideological thrust of Baptist Separationism from Reformation principles was less important in achieving Separationism in America than the practical necessities of the New World situation. But his claim for a "rationalist-pietist alliance" is subject to serious qualifications, especially in New England.[17] The rationalists in New England were Unitarians, and the Unitarians, as Backus knew, were stout defenders of the establishment. Backus evolved his principles and wrote his tracts against the New England establishment before he had even heard of Jefferson or Madison. As for Williams, he had held Baptist views for only about four months in 1639, and his repudiation of their views for the more radical stance of the Seekers made him no authority for the Baptists of New England.[18] His books were a rarity in America, and Backus did not read them until 1773.[19] It is ironic that Backus agreed with most Congregationalists that

223

---

[17] See Sidney E. Mead, *The Lively Experiment* (New York, 1963), 19, 40–44.

[18] Morgan argues that Williams was not, properly speaking, a Seeker (*Roger Williams*, 152). But whether he shared all of the official tenets of this group there still seems no other adequate term for his position after 1639. Williams' famous statement to John Winthrop after having left the Baptist denomination is also worth quoting here: "I believe their practice comes nearer the first practice of our great Founder Christ than other practices of religion doe, & yet I have no satisfaction neither in the authorities by which it [baptism] is done nor in the manner [immersion]; nor in the prophecies concerning the rise of Christ's Kingdome after the desolation of Rome &c." (Massachusetts Historical Society, *Collections*, 4th Ser., VI [1863], 274.)

[19] Backus first mentions reading Williams in his diary, Feb. 2, 1773, Backus Papers: "Met now with some writings of old Mr. Roger Williams which I was very glad of." The first publication in which Backus quoted Williams was his *Appeal to the Public for Religious Liberty* (Boston, 1773), 25–26. For some of the reasons why Backus did not often quote Williams, see Thomas B. Maston, *Isaac Backus: Pioneer of Religious Liberty* (Rochester, N. Y., 1962), 76.

Rhode Island was a poor example of the results of separation of church and state because its religious institutions were so poorly supported; he frankly called that colony "irreligious" and preferred to cite Pennsylvania as a more prosperous and respectable example of the blessings of voluntarism.[20]

But even setting aside the question of direct influence upon Backus of Williams or Jefferson, it is plain that there are striking differences in their respective approaches to the proper relationship of church and state.[21] Granted that all three opposed an establishment of religion that required conformity of conscience and uniformity of worship and that laid taxes upon all citizens for the support of one state church. But this kind of establishment existed nowhere in the American colonies in the eighteenth century. Williams had to fight against total conformity and uniformity in seventeenth-century New England, but neither Jefferson nor Backus faced this situation.[22] What was in existence in most of the colonies by 1750 was a preferred or privileged church that received official aid from the state but that granted broad toleration to dissenters. These dissenters were totally exempt from supporting the privileged Congregational churches in New England after 1730, and the collection of religious tithes was notably lax in the Anglican colonies. The problem of religious liberty consequently was more practical than ideological, especially after 1776. As Mead points out, the pietists and rationalists agreed that social morality and order, not conformity of belief and worship, was the only real church-state issue to be settled.[23] On this point the Unitarians of New England agreed with those latitudinarians in Virginia like George Washington, John Marshall, Richard Henry Lee, and Patrick Henry who believed that a general assessment tax upon all citizens to provide support for the church of the individual's own choice was the only feasible system in a poor

---

[20] Isaac Backus, *Policy as Well as Honesty* (Boston, 1779), 10.

[21] I agree with Miller's statement that "although Williams is celebrated as the prophet of religious freedom, he actually exerted little or no influence on institutional developments in America: only after the conception of liberty for all denominations had triumphed on wholly other grounds did Americans look back on Williams and invest him with his ill-fitting halo." (*Roger Williams*, 29.)

[22] It should be noted here that the Congregationalists of eighteenth-century Massachusetts always denied that their system was in fact an establishment of religion. They defined an establishment in terms of a confessional state in which conformity to a specific creed and ritual was required of all churches supported by law. Congregational churches were autonomous in creed and ritual.

[23] Mead, *Lively Experiment*, 59–70. Mead claims that under voluntarism the churches proved inadequate "to define, articulate, disseminate the basic religious beliefs essential for the existence and well-being of the society"; thus they had to turn the task over to the state via the public schools. I would argue that most nineteenth-century evangelicals saw the schools as merely an adjunct to the churches and placed their faith in revivalism in order to convert the nation to Christian morality and order. They relied, meanwhile, upon the power of moral suasion from the pulpits and the passage of wholesome laws to maintain the well-being of society.

country. Voluntarism was simply inadequate to build sufficient meeting-houses and support sufficient ministers to inculcate the principles of moral-ity and obedience essential to a stable, honest, orderly social system. Williams had faced virtually the same situation in England in 1652 when the tolerant Protectorate also sought to lay religious taxes for the support of a variety of sects.[24]

In opposing the concept of a general assessment tax (Jefferson and Madison successfully, Backus and Williams unsuccessfully) the advocates of voluntarism may seem to have had much in common. Yet a closer examination of their statements on an ideal church and an ideal state indicates marked variations in their fundamental outlooks. Williams, for example, denied that there was any ideal church ordained by God, though he was convinced that the word of God had revealed Calvinism as the true form of orthodox belief.[25] Backus clearly believed that closed com-munion Calvinistic Baptists organized in a congregational polity but united in associations were the ideal "gospel church."[26] Jefferson passion-ately hated Calvinism and the priestcraft and believed that voluntarism would undermine the power of churches, priests, and superstitious creeds and free American minds for a natural theology without ministers or churches;[27] he denied flatly that America was or should be a Christian nation. Backus and the Baptists, like most nineteenth-century evangelicals, were convinced that America was not only a Christian nation but a Protestant one. Backus looked forward to the day when Baptist ministers and evangelists would convert all Americans to antipedobaptism. Williams denied that short of a new revelation or the millennium any form of

225

---

[24] For Williams' opposition to this system, see his *Fourth Paper Presented to Major Butler* (London, 1652).

[25] For Williams' stalwart Calvinism, see Miller, *Roger Williams*, 28. Again I would agree with Miller that Williams never speaks "in the tones of modern liberalism. For him the ideologi-cal issue [of Separationism] is not central: the question is the meaning of Scripture. Were Cotton correct in saying that such-and-such is clearly demonstrable, Williams would have to agree that a good conscience ought to submit and allow the magistrate to help, just as we today believe that a judge can sentence unrepentant thieves." (*Ibid.*, 104.) In *The Bloody Tenent Yet More Bloody* (London, 1644) Williams makes this concession to the Puritans: "Let Master Cotton now produce any such nation in the whole world whom God in the New Testament hath literally and miraculously brought forth of Egypt, or from one land into another, to the truth and purity of his worship—then far be it but I should acknowledge that the seducer is fit to be put to death." (Quoted *ibid.*, 183.)

[26] Backus devoted many of his energies to overthrowing the Arminian, Six-Principle Baptist position that grew up in and around Rhode Island after Williams' death, and he was a strong advocate of associationism for maintaining the good order and orthodoxy of his de-nomination of closed communion, Five-Principle Calvinist Baptists.

[27] It is hardly necessary to reiterate Jefferson's disdain of "the mountebanks calling them-selves the priests of Jesus" and his fear of "the power and the profit of the priests. Sweep away their gossamer fabrics of factitious religion, and they would catch no more flies. We should all then, like the Quakers, live without an order of priests, moralize for ourselves, follow the oracle of conscience, and say nothing about what no man can understand, nor therefore be-lieve." (Quoted in *Thomas Jefferson on Democracy*, ed. Saul K. Padover [Mentor ed., New York, 1954], 177–18.)

church or denomination should be formed; he even denied that God called any men to be ministers, pastors, or evangelists since the days of the Apostles, and hence no man should make his living by preaching the word of God.[28]

Unlike Backus and Jefferson, Williams had an essentially pessimistic and premillennial view of history: the world was in the hands of antichrist and would shortly come to a disastrous Day of Judgment.[29] This was far from the optimistic mood of the rationalist Jefferson or the pietistic Backus, each of whom foresaw the rising glory of America in his own terms. Nineteenth-century Americans preferred the pietistic vision of Backus to the secularistic one of Jefferson. And despite Jefferson's hope that Americans would all be deists by 1830, the fact that Congress in the 1790's supported chaplains in the army, navy, and Congress, that it placed "In God We Trust" on the coins, and happily supported the national days of fasting, prayer, and thanksgiving proclaimed by Presidents Washington and Adams indicates that Backus' vision was the more typical.

If Backus' difference with Jefferson is not obvious enough in these respects, one has only to contrast the bill he proposed for the Massachusetts Constitution of 1780 regarding religious freedom with the statements of Jefferson and Madison on this principle:

As God is the only worthy object of all religious worship, and nothing can be true religion but a voluntary obedience unto his revealed will, of which each rational soul has an equal right to judge for itself; every person has an inalienable right to act in all religious affairs according to the full persuasion of his own mind, where others are not injured thereby. And Civil rulers are so far from having any right to empower any person or persons to judge for others in such affairs, and to enforce their judgments with the sword, that their power ought to be exerted to protect all persons and societies within their jurisdiction from being injured or interrupted in the free enjoyment of this right under any presumption whatsoever.[30]

Jefferson and Madison never defined "true religion" as "a voluntary obedience" to God's "revealed will" in Scripture. They wished to free men's minds

[28] As Williams put it in his *Hireling Ministry None of Christ's* (London, 1652), 4, neither "the Begetting Ministry of the Apostles . . . or the Feeding and Nourishing Ministry of Pastors and Teachers . . . are yet restored and extant." He also denounced here the man who "makes a Trade of Preaching" and who demands "a maintenance" or "explicitly makes a covenant or bargaine" for his salary as a preacher. (*Ibid.,* 8.) Yet Backus, in his *The Liberal Support of Gospel Ministers, Opened and Inculcated* (Boston, 1790), explicitly defended the right of the minister to demand a fair salary from his congregation and even to excommunicate for covetousness any who failed to provide their proportionate share.

[29] For Williams' prediction that the true testimony of God's prophets and witnesses "is probably neer finished" and "the slaughter of the Witnesses, Revel. 11" is about to begin, "After which and their shame three years and a halfe, followeth their most glorious and joyfull Rising," see his *Hireling Ministry,* 2.

[30] The manuscript of Backus' proposed "Bill of Rights" for the Massachusetts Constitution is in Backus Papers; it is printed in Maston, *Isaac Backus,* Appendix C, 121–23.

from superstition and to measure true religion in terms of the universal laws of nature. As Mead points out, "Religion was defined as one's 'opinion'" in Jefferson's bill for religious freedom.[31] For him the Bible was neither more nor less God's revealed will than the books of Euclid and Isaac Newton. But disestablishment for Backus meant leaving Christ's kingdom free to propagate itself through the evangelistic ministry of the Word and the supernatural grace of the Holy Spirit. Both Jefferson and Backus wanted separation of church and state so that the truth would prevail, but for Backus truth came through the heart by grace while for Jefferson it came through the head by reason.

227

The views of Williams and Jefferson on Separationism have often been expounded, but the manner in which Backus evolved his position and the various inconsistencies in the Baptists' pragmatic approach to this problem in New England need more careful elaboration. Backus first became engaged in the movement for separation of church and state in 1748 when the parish in which his Separate church was located laid a tax to build a meeting-house. Backus and all of his congregation were assessed for this tax to support the established Congregational church, and when the parish refused to heed their request for exemption, Backus called a conference in Attleborough in the spring of 1749 to which he invited the members of four Separate churches in the vicinity. At this meeting a petition to the General Court was drawn up asking that the Separates be granted the same privileges of tax exemption as the Baptists and Quakers. The petitioners pointed out that under the charter of 1691 "liberty of conscience is granted to all Christians except Papists," yet "if we pass not under the denomination of Churchmen . . . or Anabaptists or Quakers or do not worship on the Sabbath with the major part of the town or precinct where we live" then they "imprison some and put some in the stock[s] and also take away some of our goods and chattles."[32]

It is significant that neither in this petition nor in any subsequent petition did Backus and the Separates or Baptists ever state that they wished to have full religious liberty granted to "Papists." Williams in 1655 had specifically stated that "Papists, Protestants, Jews or Turks" should have the same freedom of religion, and the charter of Rhode Island made no ex-

[31] See Mead, *Lively Experiment*, 57. It must be admitted that in the years 1775–1785 Jefferson and Madison tried not to exaggerate but to play down their differences with the pietistic dissenters who supported disestablishment. It was in the years after 1800 that their deism became most pronounced in its hostility toward revealed religion and the priestcraft.

[32] Massachusetts Archives, Ecclesiastical, XII, 626.

ceptions in this regard nor denied any civil privileges to Roman Catholics. But Backus and the Separate Baptists, being children of Puritan heritage, looked upon Catholics the same way the Puritans had looked upon Anabaptists: as dangerous heretics and subverters of civil order. At most Backus held that their peaceable presence might be tolerated, but he saw no need at this time to grant them religious liberty in the form of exemption from religious taxes.

Backus' petition of 1749, limited though it was in its quest for toleration, was not granted by the General Court. Five years later this same petition was again presented by Backus and his brethren, and again it was turned down. So far as I can discover, Backus made no further pronouncements in public on church and state until he published *A Fish Caught in His Own Net* (Boston, 1768). This tract was a polemic in answer to the charges of the Reverend Joseph Fish, the Standing minister of Stonington, Connecticut, that the Separates and Separate Baptists were ignorant fanatics who deserved no countenance by the state. Here Backus first spelled out his theological position against compulsory religious taxation, quoting Biblical texts that he construed to ordain voluntarism and insisting that since Christ's kingdom was not of this world all man-made laws governing ecclesiastical affairs were contrary to divine laws: "For no man can serve two masters." He devoted less than 15 out of 129 pages in this tract, however, to the question of Separationism; most of the work sought to deny Fish's charges that the Separates were heretical in faith and disorderly in practice.

Two years later Backus published *A Seasonable Plea for Liberty of Conscience against Some Late Oppressive Proceedings Particularly in the Town of Berwick* (Boston, 1770). Of the 48 pages in this tract, 3 are devoted to some general statements on liberty of conscience and the remainder to protesting against the censure of some antipedobaptists in the Standing Church of Berwick. Since antipedobaptism was in his eyes commanded by God, it astounded him that a minister should censure a Christian who followed his conscience in adopting this principle. The thought uppermost in his mind here and throughout his writing was that the state, by forcing men to pay to support the false doctrine of pedobaptism, was thwarting or hindering the spread of Gospel truth and aiding in the spread of error.

Finally Backus issued his first and major treatise devoted wholly to the subject of religious liberty: *An Appeal to the Public for Religious Liberty against the Oppressions of the Present Day* (Boston, 1773). It is a strong and forthright statement of the Baptist or pietistic position on Separationism and deserves to rank with Williams' *Bloody Tenent* and Madison's *Remonstrance* as one of the great American expositions of this principle. It owes

228

something to John Locke,[33] a little to Williams,[34] much to Backus' reading of the Bible, but most of all to the historical experience of the Separate Baptists since 1748. This tract may be described as the Declaration of Independence of the Separate Baptists against the ecclesiastical tyranny of the Standing Order, for it was written in order to justify the policy of civil disobedience adopted by the Baptist churches at their annual association meeting that September. At this meeting the delegates from most of the Baptist churches in Massachusetts voted overwhelmingly to refuse any further compliance with the system of certificates and to suffer mass imprisonment if necessary in order to affirm their conscientious objections to compulsory religious taxes.

229

The gist of Backus' argument can be discerned in the five reasons he gave at the conclusion of this tract for the Baptists' decision to oppose the certificate laws:

1. Because the very nature of such a practice [giving in certificates] implies an acknowledgment that the civil power has a right to set up one religious sect above another.
2. Our legislature . . . claims the right to tax us from *civil obligation* as being the representative of the people. But how came a civil community by any ecclesiastical power?
3. Their laws require us annually to certify to them what our belief is concerning the conscience of every person that assembles with us as the condition of their being exempted from taxes to other's [*sic*] worship.
4. The scheme we oppose evidently tends to destroy the purity and life of religion. . . . bringing an *earthly power* between Christ and his people.
5. The custom which they want us to countenance is very hurtful to civil society. . . . when temporal advantages are annexed to one persuasion and disadvantages laid upon another. . . . Not only so, but coercive measures about religion tend to provoke emulation, wrath, and contention.

Backus himself never signed another certificate for any of his church members, but this test of massive civil disobedience was thwarted by the events leading to the outbreak of the Revolution. For the sake of unity most towns ceased to prosecute Baptists when the war began, and after 1778 the problem took an entirely new turn with the drafting of a new constitution for the state. Backus was not able during his lifetime, however, to persuade the people of Massachusetts, or of any other Puritan colony, to abandon the system of compulsory religious taxation. Instead Massachusetts adopted a general as-

---

[33] What it owes to Locke derives from his *Letters concerning Toleration* and not from his *Second Treatise on Government*, for in this tract Backus specifically repudiated the contract theory of government, another fact that highlights his divergence from the thought of Jefferson and Madison.

[34] He quotes two short paragraphs from *The Bloody Tenent Yet More Bloody*. Backus, who rediscovered Williams' forgotten works, quoted him sparingly, and other writers on Separationism in this period almost never mention him.

sessment system in 1780 very similar to the one Patrick Henry proposed in Virginia several years later.

There is not space here to pursue the historical account of this problem. The point I wish to stress is that Backus and the Baptists of eighteenth-century New England thought primarily of religious liberty in terms of ending compulsory religious taxation and not in terms of a high wall of separation. In order to indicate how fuzzy the line between church and state remained for Backus and the Baptists, a few examples may be cited.

230
In 1766 in South Brimfield the Separate Baptists came to constitute a majority of the parish, and as such they were able to block the election of any minister of the Standing Order as the settled pastor of the parish. To resolve this problem the Congregationalists joined with some of the leading Baptists and agreed to vote for their pastor, James Mellen, as the Standing or official minister and to pay his salary by taxing all the property owners of the parish. Mellen accepted this proposal and was elected. Religious taxes were assessed for his support; those who refused to pay them, some of whom were Baptists, were arrested and taken to jail. The opponents of this scheme, however, fought back by taking the matter to court where they succeeded in proving that Mellen was not entitled to be a parish minister because he lacked a college degree or approbation by the Standing ministers of the county, which the law required for all parish ministers.[35] In 1770 Mellen's church, which considered itself Baptist, apologized to the other Baptists in the province for having agreed to allow their minister to be elected parish minister.

Backus, it must be said, deplored the whole incident, but obviously even the issue of compulsory religious taxation was not so clear-cut to many Baptists as some of their historians would have us believe. If Mellen had won his case, perhaps Baptists elsewhere would have tried to emulate "the South Brimfield Plan." The truth is that many Separate Baptists agreed with the Congregationalists that voluntarism simply was not an adequate method of providing support for religious worship. Backus himself admitted that the Baptists were frequently unable or unwilling to provide sufficient freewill offerings to build a meetinghouse or to pay a decent salary to their ministers.[36] One of the leading Separate Baptist ministers of Massachusetts, Ebenezer Hinds of Middleborough, a close friend and associate of Backus, went so far as to petition the legislature in 1788 requesting the civil authori-

[35] Isaac Backus, *A History of New England with Particular Reference to the Denomination Called Baptists*, ed. David Weston (2 vols., Newton, Mass., 1871), II, 143–44.
[36] See *ibid.*, *passim*, and Backus, *Liberal Support of Gospel Ministers*.

ties to force his congregation to pay his back salary.[37] Even though most Baptist ministers engaged in farming or some other trade to supplement their incomes, countless Baptist churches broke up and disappeared in these years because they could not provide subsistence for their minister and his family.

Backus might assert that God would "preserve His church even against the gates of Hell," but the fact was that the Baptists were in feeble circumstances in most New England communities. And being good Calvinists they recognized that human nature was too inherently selfish to part voluntarily with much money even for so good a cause as ministerial support. A secularist, like Jefferson, who ultimately placed his hope for democracy in a tax-supported public-school system, could ignore this problem. Seekers, like Williams, who declared (as Jehovah's Witnesses do today) that all denominations were wrong and all ministers lacked valid ordination, could be equally cavalier about the decay of church institutions; Williams said as much in his famous statement that the civil state would not be affected if all the churches broke up and disappeared.[38] But the Baptists, who insisted, as Backus did, that a true government must be a Christian government in which there was "a sweet harmony" between church and state,[39] had difficulty in refuting the hardheaded, practical arguments used against a voluntaristic system.

231

Another example of the Baptists' willingness to take advantage of state aid for religion in this period can be seen in the history of the town of Ashfield. The Ashfield affair is famous in Baptist history as an example of the worst kind of persecution of the Separate Baptists, and Backus worked hard to persuade the King to invalidate a Massachusetts law of 1768 that made the Baptists in Ashfield responsible for paying support to the parish minister despite the general tax exemption law. Yet part of the resentment against the Baptists in Ashfield stemmed from the fact that in the early years of the settlement of that town, when the Separate Baptists had been a majority of the inhabitants, they had elected one of their brethren, Ebenezer Smith, to be the settled minister of the town and laid claim to the plot of land reserved in all new townships for the first settled minister. They also claimed the right to the income from the plot of land laid aside for the support of the parish church, and they may even have had hopes of raising

---

[37] A copy of Hinds's petition is among the Backus Papers. Hinds also praised the Massachusetts Constitution of 1780 as "the Best Constitution that the Baptist[s] have been under Since the Massachusett[s] Began," although Backus denounced it as making the Baptists' position worse than it had been since 1729. (See Hinds's letter to the Warren Baptist Association, Sept. 3, 1781, *ibid*.)

[38] Quoted in Miller, *Roger Williams*, 117.

[39] See Isaac Backus, *A Fish Caught in His Own Net* (Boston, 1768), 23.

money by taxation for their Baptist meetinghouse. In addition, they claimed
that Smith, as the settled minister of the town, was exempt from paying civil
taxes just as Congregational parish ministers were. The Congregationalists
in Ashfield took the matter to law, however, and the courts ruled that Smith
lacked the qualifications to be a parish minister. Thus the plans of the Baptists were thwarted, and the "persecution" began. But the fact remains that
these Baptists too were not above attempting to derive such benefits from the
state as they could get and from claiming the legal status and privileges of
parish ministers.[40]

232   In the less rigid ecclesiastical systems of Maine, New Hampshire, and
Vermont there are many examples of Baptist ministers who made good their
claims to the ministerial plots in new towns because they were the first settled ministers in these towns. Elias Smith relates several instances in the
1790's where Vermont towns offered him their ministerial plots, and Job
Seamans was actually installed as the settled minister of New London, New
Hampshire, in 1788, and for several years he permitted the town to lay
taxes for his support.[41] Backus disapproved of Seamans' being paid by
taxation, but there is no record of his opposing the granting of ministerial
plots to Baptists who were the first settled ministers in new towns.

After 1790 the Baptists, like other dissenters in New England, began to
claim the right to use the parish meetinghouses and to share proportionately the income from the town's ministerial lands. There were numerous
lawsuits involving such claims, and in many towns the Baptists were permitted to use the town meetinghouse for a certain number of Sundays each
year in proportion to the number of their adherents in the parish. It all
seemed perfectly just to the Baptists; since public tax money had built the
meetinghouses and since the ministerial plots were a public provision for
the support of religion, why should they not receive their fair share?[42]

But of all the issues on which the Baptists found themselves most bitterly divided in the latter part of the century, that of seeking incorporation
by the legislature was the most hotly contended. The principal purpose of
incorporation was obviously to compel Baptist congregations to provide
adequate compensation for their pastors. Baptist leaders like Hezekiah
Smith, one of the wealthiest men in Haverhill, flatly disobeyed the resolution

[40] For the Ashfield case, see Frederick G. Howes, *History of the Town of Ashfield* (Ashfield, Mass., 1913), and *Acts and Resolves*, IV, 1036 ff.
[41] For Smith, see *The Life, Conversion, Preaching, Travels and Suffering of Elias Smith*
(Portsmouth, N. H., 1816) 205, 206; for Seamans, see Backus, *History of New England*, ed.
Weston, II, 537–38.
[42] The result of this was often ludicrous as four or five denominations tried to divide up
the fifty-two Sabbaths among themselves. Gradually after 1810 the towns decided that the
town hall should be a wholly secular or civil building and that each denomination, including the Congregationalists, should build its own house of worship.

of the Warren Baptist Association in seeking incorporation for the church of which he was pastor in 1793.[43] Many other Baptist ministers did the same during the next forty years. The legislative records reveal that over forty Baptist churches had obtained legislative acts incorporating them by 1810.[44] Some incorporated Baptist churches in the 1790's and early 1800's sued their own members in court and distrained their goods for failing to pay their duly assessed share of the minister's salary.[45] The Congregationalists doubtless enjoyed the spectacle and delighted in seeing the Baptists admit the failings of voluntarism. Backus, let it be said, bitterly opposed incorporation, pointing out that the right of the legislature to incorporate some churches implied its right to deny incorporation to others. But his arguments were not always heeded.

233

Though Backus was consistent in opposing the actions of Baptist elders like Mellen, Ebenezer Smith, Seamans, and Hezekiah Smith, he was nevertheless far from having a clear-cut position on the precise line to be drawn between church and state. For example, he sided with the majority of the Baptists in the Warren Association in 1791 in voting to petition Congress (along with the Congregational clergy) for the establishment of a federal commission to license the publication of all Bibles in the United States. It never occurred to him that the right to license carried with it the right not to license.

Backus similarly praised the Constitution of Massachusetts because it required a religious oath of all officeholders: "No man can take a seat in our legislature till he solemnly declares, 'I believe the Christian religion and have a firm persuasion of its truth.' "[46] Many Baptists disagreed with Jefferson, Madison, and Williams that religious liberty should include the right to hold office even for Jews, Mohammedans, deists, atheists, and infidels.[47] Backus

[43] For an account of the confrontation between Hezekiah Smith and Backus on this matter, see *Life . . . of Smith*, 233–34. Another reason often given to justify incorporation of a Baptist church was that a series of court decisions after 1780 ruled that unincorporated dissenting churches in Massachusetts could not claim exemption from religious taxes. But most Baptist ministers found other ways around these decisions than by incorporation.

[44] It should also be pointed out that some confusion in the constitutional clauses over tax exemption implied that only an incorporated church or congregation could obtain the religious taxes paid by its members under the new general assessment procedures. The courts were not consistent about this, however.

[45] "The society at Haverhill was incorporated and from this it spread till cattle and horses were taken by force to pay baptist ministers for preaching." (*Ibid.*, 234.)

[46] Isaac Backus, *A Door Opened for Equal Christian Liberty* (Boston, 1783), 12. Backus later applauded the fact, however, that the federal Constitution prohibited any such oath of office for federal officeholders.

[47] The man who succeeded Backus as the leading spokesman for the Massachusetts Baptists, Elder Thomas Baldwin of Boston, stated in the Massachusetts Constitutional Convention of 1820 that "He was willing that parishes should have power to tax all persons within their limites who are not enrolled in any other [religious] society." That is, he was willing that persons who belonged to no church or congregation should be taxed to support the parish church. (*Journal of Debates and Proceedings of the Convention* [Boston, 1853], 422.)

defended test oaths requiring Roman Catholics to forswear their spiritual allegiance to the pope before they could assume public office or, as he put it, to "disclaim the principles which are subversive of a free government."[48]

Similarly it never seems to have occurred to him that the inculcation of the Westminster Confession in the public schools of New England was in any way an infringement upon the rights of parents to bring up their children in their own religious faith. Backus, being a strict Calvinist, firmly believed that the Westminster Confession contained the only true interpretation of Scripture. To him the banning of religious training from the public schools of New England would have been the greatest wickedness—though he did not, of course, care to have infant baptism taught in those schools.[49]

Backus and the Baptists were also strong believers in the necessity of the so-called Puritan blue laws, which punished persons for profanity, blasphemy, or profanation of the Sabbath. In an unpublished sermon written some time after 1784 he praised and quoted a tract by a Baptist minister of London in which it was "deemed a kind of persecution by connivance when, for want of putting the laws into execution against Sabbath breaking, our magistrates permit the profane to disturb them that fear God in their closets and families."[50] He went so far as to condone the actions of his grandfather who, as justice of the peace in Norwich, had condemned two members of the seventh-day sect called Rogerenes to be whipped in 1725 because they were apprehended traveling through his jurisdiction on the Sabbath.[51]

And of course Backus saw nothing wrong with laws requiring public adherence to his own puritanical conceptions of morality: laws against gambling, card playing, dancing, and theatergoing. There is an amusing entry in his diary at the time of the burning of the Grand Theater in Boston in 1798. Backus had noted earlier that this theater had opened in direct violation of the laws against stage plays in Boston, and when it burned to the ground just as the company was preparing a grand spectacle of the de-

234

[48] Backus, *Truth Is Great*, 33.

[49] See *Life . . . of Smith*, 119–23, for an interesting example of the way in which public-school teachers imposed the Westminster Confession on all children even against the will of parents. Backus has no recorded statement on this issue.

[50] This manuscript sermon, entitled "The Man of Sin Revealed," also quotes a sermon by Benjamin Wallin, a Baptist minister in London, dated Oct. 9, 1774, 31–32, in which Wallin bemoans the fact that a recent "petition, signed by a great number of respectable persons, for some further check to the horrid impiety [of Sabbathbreaking] not barely failed of success but was treated with derision [by Parliament]." Wallin complained that "little regard is now paid to a day once held sacred through the nation, the pollution of which is an inlet to all manner of disorder and wickedness and proves fatal to millions." Backus agreed. (See Backus Papers.)

[51] "I saw a Book writ by John Bolls of New London Printed 1734 in the latter end of which was set down 2 Copies of a record from under my grandfather Backus's hand of his punishing said Bolls and Sarah Colver 2 Quakers on July 26, 1725 for their traveling on the day before, which was Lordsday. . . . Both were whipt for breach of Sabbath, which they called Persecution." (Backus' unpublished diary, Aug. 4, 1754, *ibid.*)

struction of Sodom and Gomorrah, Backus wrote that this was "a plain testimony against mocking God."[52]

The Baptists were also perfectly willing that the state, through its chief magistrates, should require certain days of fasting, thanksgiving, or prayer to be observed throughout the year, thereby turning weekdays into Sabbath when everyone was supposed to stop work or travel, close his business, and resort to religious worship in the meetinghouses. Backus regularly read the governors' proclamations of such days from his pulpit and observed them in his church. This was part of the harmony between church and state about which he and Jefferson would have violently disagreed. Jefferson and Madison, as Presidents, pointedly refused to issue fast and thanksgiving day proclamations as Washington and John Adams had done.[53]

There is some difficulty in finding a quotation in all of Backus' forty-two published works and his many unpublished letters and papers in which he directly and forthrightly opposed the law requiring compulsory church attendance by all citizens on the Sabbath. His only reference to this was published in a tract of 1783 when he said that he and his brethren did not necessarily agree with the law, but, he added, "we have had no controversy with our rulers about this matter."[54] If Backus, who was among the most radical of the Baptists on this subject, did not wish to push such a controversy, it seems clear that most of his brethren probably agreed with the Standing Order that such a law was essential to the good order of a Christian commonwealth.[55]

There is no neat way to sum up the respective contributions of Backus, Williams, Jefferson, and Madison to the development of the American tra-

235

---

[52] Backus' unpublished diary, Feb. 11, 1798, *ibid.*

[53] It is not clear whether Backus opposed the payment of chaplains by the state and federal legislatures though in 1793 he did express displeasure with the United States Senate for paying five hundred dollars each to two episcopal bishops for this purpose. (See Isaac Backus, *Testimony of the Two Witnesses* [Boston, 1793], 46.)

[54] *Id., A Door Opened*, 6.

[55] Some historians consider John Leland a more radical exponent of Separationism among the Baptists than Backus; others more or less equate the views of the two men. In my opinion Leland was too eccentric to be typical of the Baptists, especially of those in New England. Leland spent his most productive years in Virginia where he imbibed much of the spirit of the most radical dissenters, and his views of Separationism were decidedly nearer to those of Jefferson and Madison than to those of Backus. His eccentricity can be indicated by the fact that after his return to New England to settle in Cheshire, Massachusetts, in 1792 he refused to perform the Lord's Supper in his church because it seemed to him an empty ritual. (See the records of the Cheshire Baptist Church, Pittsfield Athenaeum.) Like Madison and Jefferson, Leland wanted a high wall of separation between church and state, opposing not only public fast and thanksgiving days but even laws against dueling, lotteries, or for the enforcement of the Sabbath. In sharp contrast to Backus, who believed that America was and should be a Christian nation, Leland stated, "The notion of a Christian commonwealth should be exploded forever." (*The Writings of John Leland*, ed. L. F. Greene [New York, 1845], 107.) Leland became a scandal among the New England Baptists when, after Backus' death, he opposed the foreign mission movement, the Sunday-school movement, and the effort to persuade Congress to prohibit the delivery of mail on Sundays.

dition of separation of church and state. Williams, it would appear, was the least influential of the four and probably the least representative, for few Americans since 1750 have been pessimistic premillennialists, Calvinist typologists, and anticlerical Seekers. Jefferson and Madison spoke for a rationalist-humanist element in American thought that has become increasingly influential in the twentieth century but that throughout most of our history has been the view of a small minority. But Backus probably represents most adequately the evangelical view of Separationism—the "sweet harmony" of a Christian nation—that has predominated. Historians would do well to re-examine his position and to give it its rightful place in future evaluations of this notable tradition.

236

PURITANISM AND SCIENCE:
The Anatomy of a Controversy*

By Richard L. Greaves

Despite the assertions of Max Weber and R. H. Tawney, the theological tenets of Protestantism played no major role in fostering the rise of modern scientific thought in the sixteenth and early seventeenth centuries. The earliest great breakthroughs in scientific thought occurred in Catholic rather than in Protestant territories. Yet by the end of the seventeenth century Protestant rather than Catholic lands had become the center of scientific advancement. Certainly after the 1630's the cultural environment in Protestant countries was more conducive to scientific progress than it was in Catholic areas, largely because of the restrictive effects of the Counter Reformation.[1]

Scholars like Dorothy Stimson, Richard F. Jones, Robert K. Merton, and Christopher Hill have argued that the scientific progress which occurred in Protestant England after the 1630's was in part due to the role played by religious factors. *Prima facie* there would seem to be a strong case for accepting their contention that there was something inherent in Puritanism which facilitated the acceptance and development of scientific thought–though not its actual rise. There were, for example, a comparatively large percentage of men with Puritan backgrounds engaged in the work of the "Invisible College" in London and the Royal Society in the earliest stages of its organization.[2] There was also a more concerted effort during the Restoration to teach the

237

*I would like to express my appreciation to the National Endowment for the Humanities for a grant which made much of this research possible, and to Provost Richard Schlatter for his assistance and encouragement.

[1]Theodore K. Rabb, "Religion and the Rise of Modern Science," *Past & Present,* 31 (July 1965), 376-443. For the more traditional view, S. F. Mason, "The Scientific Revolution and the Protestant Reformation," *Annals of Science,* IX (1953), 64-87, 154-75.

[2]Statistical analyses have been made by Dorothy Stimson, "Puritanism and the New Philosophy in 17th Century England," *Bulletin of the Institute of the History of Medicine,* III (May 1935), 321-334, and *Scientists and Amateurs: A History of the Royal Society* (New York, 1948); also Robert K. Merton, "Science, Technology and Society in Seventeenth Century England," *Osiris,* IV (1938), 360-632. Perceptive criticisms of the analyses have been made by M. M. Knappen, *Tudor Puritanism* (Chicago, 1939), 478; James Conant, "The Advancement of Learning during the Puritan Commonwealth," *Proceedings of the Massachusetts Historical Society,* LXVI (1936-41), 29-30; and Rabb, "Puritanism and the Rise of Experimental Science in England," *Cahiers d'Histoire Mondiale,* VII (1962), 50ff.

scientific subjects (especially medicine) in the Dissenting Academies than in the universities.[3] Furthermore, the open and effective introduction of the new scientific thought in the English universities occurred in the Commonwealth period.

My purpose here is to examine the possible ways in which Puritanism might have aided in the acceptance and development of scientific thought. Puritanism was fundamentally a religious movement; all its other characteristics were derivatives of religious convictions. Puritans sought the reformation but not the destruction of the state church. Theologically they were Calvinists—either moderate or strict[4]—who stressed the inner working of the Spirit. In their epistemology they were not rationalists, though they retained rationalism in the religious sphere and subordinated it to faith and empiricism. They were less radical than the sectaries,[5] who were anti-liturgical, anti-professional, and, in their religious epistemology, anti-rational and anti-intellectual. Sectarian theology, strongly dominated by an emphasis on the Spirit, embraced everything from Calvinism to Antinomianism to mysticism and even Arminianism. Considerable dispute has arisen as to whether or not there was something inherent in the religious ideology of these men which significantly aided in the acceptance of modern scientific thought.

I

There were seven principal values purportedly shared by Puritans and scientists, thus giving rise to the idea that Puritanism provided an inducement to scientific work: (1) the utilitarian spirit; (2) a concern for the welfare of society; (3) a belief in progress; (4) opposition to authoritarianism and a corresponding belief in free inquiry; (5) opposi-

[3]Phyllis Allen, "Medical Education in 17th Century England," *Journal of the History of Medicine & Allied Sciences*, I (Jan. 1946), 142. Cf. Irene Parker, *Dissenting Academies in England* (Cambridge, 1914); and Robert K. Merton, "Puritanism, Pietism, and Science," *Science & Ideas*, ed. A. B. Arons and A. M. Bork (Englewood Cliffs, 1964), 246-47. Merton's article originally appeared in the *Sociological Review*, XXVIII (Jan. 1936). As reprinted by Arons and Bork, it has been updated with a useful Bibliographical Postscript by Dr. Merton.

[4]See Richard L. Greaves, "John Bunyan and Covenant Thought in the Seventeenth Century," *Church History*, XXXVI (June 1967), 151-69. Such a definition of Puritanism would, admittedly, exclude Milton, John Goodwin, *et al.* These men were imbued with most Puritan principles, though their deviation from Calvinism did not leave them wholly within the Puritan fold.

[5]I would fully agree with Christopher Hill when he notes that "there is a sense in which even the most radical sectaries descend from the undifferentiated Puritanism of pre-1640." "Puritanism, Capitalism and the Scientific Revolution," *Past & Present*, 29 (Dec. 1964), 90. Cf. Geoffrey F. Nuttall, *The Holy Spirit in Puritan Faith and Experience* (Oxford, 1946).

tion to Scholasticism; (6) stress on systematic, disciplined labor; and (7) reliance on the empirical method (which will be discussed in section II).

(1) That Puritans placed a premium on knowledge which was utilitarian is commonly recognized. That scientists likewise sought such knowledge is a hotly disputed contention, as is the possible derivation of the utilitarian spirit of both groups from a common source–Francis Bacon. Equally problematical is the matter of relating what might have been utilitarian to a scientist to what was utilitarian for a Puritan. Assuming for the moment that scientists were utilitarian, the kind of knowledge they must have sought after was scientific knowledge applicable to technological problems. Puritans, on the other hand, had as their foremost concern the discovery of knowledge which was utilitarian in the metaphysical sphere. They were concerned with the workings of the Divine with man through the covenant scheme, or with the proper composition of a church, or with more effective means of preaching the Gospel to God's elect. Puritanism was thus metaphysical in nature, whereas scientific utilitarianism (if it existed) was materialistic.

239

Certainly not all seventeenth-century scientists were motivated by utilitarian ideals. The virtuosi in England, as W. E. Houghton has demonstrated, were not.[6] The classical scientific experiments, as Hugh Kearney has pointed out, were not particularly utilitarian. Yet Kearney, in criticizing Hill's concept of science, cites only non-Puritan scientists to substantiate his point–Pascal, Kepler, Galileo, Mersenne, Descartes, Harvey, and Newton.[7] Unquestionably those men were motivated fundamentally by intellectual curiosity and sought (as did the virtuosi) knowledge for its own sake. Yet the scientists that are relevant are those who were seemingly attracted from science to Puritanism, or from Puritanism to science. Such scientists would, according to Stimson, Merton, Jones, and Hill, include the Wadham College group at Oxford. These men were mostly mathematicians, and, according to Kearney and Leo Solt, regarded science more as an abstract intellectual activity than something undertaken for essentially utilitarian ends.[8] Wilkins, though, at the very beginning of his treatise *Mathematicall Magick* (1648), wrote: "Our best and most divine

[6]"The English Virtuoso in the Seventeenth Century," *Journal of the History of Ideas*, III (Jan. 1942), 51–73, and III (April 1942), 190–219.

[7]"Puritanism and Science: Problems of Definition," *Past & Present*, 31 (July 1965), 108.

[8]Kearney, "Puritanism, Capitalism and the Scientific Revolution," *Past & Present*, 28 (July 1964), 94; and Leo F. Solt, "Puritanism, Capitalism, Democracy, and the New Science," *American Historical Review*, 73 (Oct. 1967), 23.

knowledge is intended for action; and those may justly be accounted barren studies which do not conduce to practice as their proper end."[9] Wilkins, in fact, was interested in the application of the principles of physics to utilitarian purposes, including the preservation of the spoken word for later playback, a windmill-driven carriage, and the creation of submarines, airplanes, and engines. Ward, speaking for the Wadham group, informed John Webster that "it is a real designe amongst us, wanting only some assistance for execution, to erect a Magneticall, Mechanicall, and Optick Schoole, furnished with the best Instruments; and Adapted for the most usefull experiments...."[10] The Wadham group was not simply concerned with knowledge for its own sake; they were clearly interested in its utilitarian application.

240

Both Richard Jones in his *Ancients and Moderns* and Christopher Hill in his *Intellectual Origins of the English Revolution* have attempted to demonstrate the impact of Baconianism on Puritanism. Their arguments have recently been challenged by Rabb and Kearney. Rabb is clearly correct in observing that in the 1620's and 1630's Puritans—with a possible exception or two, such as Bishop Williams—did not evince any particular interest in the utilitarian philosophy of the former Lord Chancellor. The interval between the publication of Bacon's views and their acceptance by Puritans possibly indicates, as Rabb contends, that "there was no natural union between Puritanism's supposed practical bent and the Lord Chancellor's utilitarianism."[11] Yet it must be remembered that in the context of the 1620's and 1630's it would have been difficult for most Puritans to have embraced publicly the philosophy of a man with no reputation of friendship towards Puritans. Considerations of domestic diplomacy and politics would have served as a cautionary bar to temper the outright acceptance of views closely akin to their own but enunciated by a political and religious enemy. As H. Trevor-Roper so aptly put it, Baconianism's "courtly Jacobean clothes, its patrician elegance, its metropolitan urbanity and scepticism, its traces of the galleries and aviaries of York House, the gardens and fishponds of Gorhambury ..."[12] at first made it less than palatable to Puritans. But conditions had changed by 1640. James and Bacon were long dead, and the Puritans were caught up in a revolution. For that revolution they needed a comprehensive philosophy. As it was enunciated by Comenius, Hartlib, and Dury, Baconian-

[9]Quoted in Hill, *Intellectual Origins of the English Revolution* (Oxford, 1965), 85.
[10]*Vindiciae Academiarum* (Oxford, 1654), 36.
[11]*Cahiers d'Histoire Mondiale*, VII, 60. Cf. Rabb, *Past & Present*, 31 (July 1965), 115-17.
[12]"Three Foreigners and the Philosophy of the English Revolution," *Encounter*, XIV (Feb. 1960), 7.

ism met their need, and the two decades of prior hesitation were forgotten.

Kearney has attempted to show that the utilitarian ideology of the Puritans was a heritage from Ramus rather than Bacon. "When Pym and the Puritan party invited Comenius to England in 1641," Kearney wrote, "they were turning to a continental Ramist, reared in the Ramist centre of Herborn, and a man whose *Janua Linguarum* stressed a utilitarian and simplified approach to the study of languages in the spirit of Ramus."[13] Although Kearney has added a needed corrective to the picture by reemphasizing the importance of Ramist views, he pays too little heed to the influence of Bacon on Comenius' thought, also greatly influenced by the German Baconian Wolfgang Ratke's *Address to the German Princes*. Comenius himself later read Bacon's *Novum Organum* while still in his twenties. After he was driven from Bohemia by the Catholic forces in the Thirty Years' War, he found refuge at Leszno in Poland, where he spent further time studying Bacon's works. Copies of those works were sent to him by Samuel Hartlib, then in England. Thus, although Comenius was reared in a Ramist center, he immersed himself in the writings of Bacon. Kearney admits that Comenius found Bacon's utilitarianism appealing, but he implies that this was only the effect of seeing ideas similar to those of Ramus in Bacon. The point remains, however, that although Ramist thought may have helped prepare the ground for the acceptance of Baconianism by the Puritans in the 1640's and 1650's, it was Bacon to whom they primarily turned for inspiration, not Ramus. The weakness in demonstrating parallel value-complexes in Puritans and scientists with respect to utilitarianism lies in the differing concepts of utility, not in a lack of utilitarian values on the part of the Wadham College group or the lack of a relevant connection between Bacon and Puritanism.

(2) Merton, Stimson, and Jones have all argued that Puritans and scientists both valued the public good—the welfare of society. Because science had utilitarian value, it could contribute to that welfare, and was therefore an object of common interest. "Science was to be fostered and nurtured," in Merton's words, "as leading to the domination of Nature by technological invention."[14] There are two obstacles to accepting this whole line of argument. First, the welfare which a scientist might seek through the technological application of scientific data was material welfare; the kind of welfare which was of pre-

241

---

[13]*Past & Present*, 28 (July 1964), 96.

[14]Merton, *Science & Ideas*, 236; Stimson, *Scientists and Amateurs*, 34; Jones, *Ancients and Moderns: A Study of the Background of the Battle of the Books* (St. Louis, 1936), 88, 122.

dominant concern to a Puritan was spiritual welfare, with which
scientific knowledge and technological advancement were not concerned. Second, "the good of the many" included by Merton as a
dominant tenet in the Puritan ethos would be—at best—far inferior
in Puritan thinking to the good of the elect. In other words, furthering
the social welfare of the many by technological progress is not the same
as furthering the spiritual welfare of the elect. The former was of concern to at least some scientists; the latter, to thoroughgoing Puritans.

(3) A third value allegedly shared by Puritans and scientists was a
belief in progress, originating, according to Jones, in Bacon's thought.
The Norwegian scholar, Maren-Sofie Røstvig, argues that this belief
in progress was the basis of the Puritans' approval of science for its
utilitarian value.[15] Such an assumption, however, cannot be justified
unless it can be demonstrated that the Puritans forsook their chiliastic
beliefs in the seventeenth century and replaced them with the concept
of a progressively improving society which would one day usher in the
blissful millenium. Quite the contrary, the Puritans had no such hope.
The deterministic philosophy coupled with their knowledge of God's
past dealings with man made any hope of progress futile. Rather than
expect a gradual ascent into a better world, they viewed the end of
history as an apocalyptic event in which the concept of progress played
no role. Puritans substantially infused with Baconian ideology might
have moderated their views to include a role for progress, but these
men would have been atypical Puritans.

(4) Puritans and scientists are also said to have shared the ideal of
libre examen and an opposition to authoritarianism. Both emphasized
a critical spirit and the right of private judgment as opposed to blind
reliance on authority.[16] The resulting congeniality was, however, more
apparent than real. Like Lutheranism and Genevan or Scottish Calvinism, the role of private judgment was sharply curtailed by a theocratic authoritarianism which remained unbroken until the revolutionary Independents of the 1650's produced an element of religious
toleration. Presbyterianism was anti-authoritarian only as long as the
authoritarianism was not of its own variety. Independency, on the other

[15]Jones, *Ancients and Moderns*, 121-22; Røstvig, *The Happy Man: Studies in the
Metamorphoses of a Classical Ideal, 1600-1700* (Oslo, 1954), I, 55.

[16]Merton, *Science & Ideas*, 257; Stimson, *Bulletin of the Institute of the History of
Medicine*, III, 325. A recent historian of education traces what he feels to be Puritanism's
emphasis on intellectual freedom back to Bacon. Obviously unaware of the political
views of the Presbyterians and Baxter (among others), he writes: Bacon's "insistence on
the necessity for intellectual freedom, coupled with his faith in the potential equality of
all men in affairs of the mind, made it easy for the Puritans to bring his philosophy into
line with their own democratic views." William Boyd, *The History of Western Education* (6th ed.; London, 1952), 269.

hand, gradually saw fit to adopt a more liberal course, and one which more nearly approached the supposed Protestant ideal of *libre examen* and the duty as well as the right of private judgment. In Puritanism as a whole, however, no such tendency was universally perceptible. Too many held the attitude which underlies this piece of advice from Baxter to his fellow ministers:

> It is most desirable that the Minister should be of parts above the people so far as to be able to teach them and awe them and manifest their weaknesses to themselves. . . . See that you preach . . . some higher points that stall their understandings. . . . Take up some profound questions (such as the Schools voluminously agitate) and . . . make it as plain as you can, that they may see that it is not your obscure manner of handling, but the matter itself that is too hard for them, and so may see that they are yet but children that have need of milk.[17]

243

This is not the advice of a man who desires to foster free inquiry and develop private judgment; it is far removed from the Renaissance spirit characterized by an intellectual curiosity and awareness which was conducive to the growth and development of modern science.[18]

(5) It has also been noted that both Puritans and scientists shared a distrust of Scholasticism. The Puritans, concerned about emphasizing Scripture in their preaching, were suspicious of using Scholastic ideas. The scientists, concerned about developing a fundamentally empirical science, were suspicious of relying on the deductive conclusions of Scholastic scientists. Such a shared attitude, according to Richard S. Westfall, made it easier for scientists—steeped in the Calvinist and anti-Scholastic ideas of the Puritan preachers—to accept the mechanical conception of nature.[19] In this sense, therefore, Puritanism helped to foster the acceptance and spread of new scientific ideas. Once again, though, the argument is based on an implicit leap from the scientific to the religious realm. Puritans indeed had little patience with the religious dogma of Scholasticism, yet their own view of the material universe was, as Perry Miller has demonstrated, heavily colored by Scholastic ideas. "While condemning scholastic doctrines of the church and of salvation . . . [the Puritan] was accepting scholastic premises in physics and astronomy, the scholastic theory of the four elements or the four causes, the distinctions between potentiality and act or essence and existence, the theory of motion, the description of human psychol-

---

[17]*Gildas Salvianus, The Reformed Pastor* (2nd ed., 1657), 464–66, quoted in Richard Schlatter, "The Higher Learning in Puritan England," *Historical Magazine of the Protestant Episcopal Church*, XXIII (June 1954), 187.

[18]Cf. Rabb, *Cahiers d'Histoire Mondiale*, VII, 65.

[19]*Science and Religion in Seventeenth-Century England* (New Haven, Conn., 1958), 5.

ogy. . . ." The Puritan also accepted Scholastic physiological theory and the Scholastic concept of the nature of human reason.[20] These were some of the very areas under attack by the scientists. Although both Puritans and scientists were critical of various aspects of an almost monolithic Scholasticism, they criticized quite different areas.

(6) Puritans and scientists did share the ideal of systematic, disciplined, methodic labor.[21] The ends for which such labor was undertaken varied: the scientist labored to discover new knowledge; the Puritan labored because the elect were encouraged to do good works. The scientist labored because he was intellectually curious or because he wanted to better society, or both; the Puritan labored because of a psychological compulsion to prove to himself and to others that he was a member of the elect. The methodical labor of the Puritan was evident even in his preaching, though various other Protestants approached the task of sermon-making with almost similar precision. The ideal was to follow diligently a systematic, methodic plan. John Wilkins published such a plan in his *Ecclesiastes, or, a Discourse concerning the Gift of Preaching as It Falls under the Rules of Art* (London, 1646). Convinced that method, matter, and expression were three "chief helps" in the art of preaching, he planned the sermon with as much systematic care as a scientific experiment. Undoubtedly this was in part due to the fact that its formulator was a scientist, yet the basic format may be perceived in the Puritan sermons of the period. Wilkins undoubtedly produced this plan after studying such sermons, though the method was obviously already in use before he so graphically expressed it. Too much emphasis must not be placed on this similarity in method, however, for the Quakers, whose ranks included scientists (e.g., the botanist Thomas Lawson)[22] rejected such methodical preparation in preference to total reliance on the movings of the Spirit.

Puritan methodicalness was also evident in their better theologians. There was no room for a haphazard, imprecise theology; hence from Ramus, Puritans such as William Ames and Alexander Richardson adopted the concept of technometria (or technologia). As it was applied to theology, technometria meant that theology was made visual as well as methodical—a sort of pictorial anatomy of Puritan doctrine. With diagrammatical precision, a theologian who accepted the principle of technometria could give his writings a logical clarity visible to the eye as well as to the mind.[23] Technometria required intellectual discipline

---

[20] *The New England Mind: The Seventeenth-Century* (Boston, 1961), 100, 105.

[21] Merton, *Science & Ideas*, 236.

[22] See Arthur Raistrick, *Quakers in Science and Industry* (New York, 1950).

[23] See Keith L. Sprunger, "Technometria: A Prologue to Puritan Theology,"

and orderliness as intense as that required of a scientist in the empirical sphere.

II

Not only has the shared value-complex of methodical labor been pointed to as a possible link between Puritanism and science, but the actual methodology itself used by Puritans and scientists has also been alleged to have strikingly marked similarities. Hill, continually stressing Baconianism as a common tie between Puritanism and science, has argued that the Puritan insistence on firsthand religious experience as opposed to reliance on human traditions compares closely with the Baconian emphasis on personal observation and experience. More specifically, Hill contends that "the quest for personal religious *experience*, to which so many Puritan diaries and spiritual autobiographies are dedicated, is closely akin to the experimental spirit in science."[24] John Dillenberger cites the Puritans' experiential and practical approach to Biblical study as being similarly related.[25] Merton too had earlier pointed to this experimental spirit in Protestantism in general and Puritanism in particular as being a factor which aided in the acceptance and development of the new empirically-based science. But Merton carefully qualified his thesis with this observation: "It may very well be that the Puritan ethos did not directly influence the method of science and that this was simply a parallel development in the internal history of science, but it is evident that through the psychological compulsion toward certain modes of thought and conduct this value-complex made an empirically-founded science commendable rather than . . . reprehensible or at best acceptable on sufferance." As a result, Merton contended, talented minds were directed into the scientific fields rather than into more traditionally esteemed professions.[26]

Other attempts have been made to find parallels with the experimental method in science in various aspects of Puritanism. Puritan martyrology and biography, it is suggested, provide such a parallel to the extent that they were case histories read in the Baconian spirit as empirical data indicating the *modus operandi* of the Spirit in man. The church relation used especially by Puritans in New England as a means to ascertain the validity of a man's religious experience purportedly provides yet another parallel. Such a test was so "scientific," in fact, that it has been called a forerunner of the modern Rorschach test.[27]

245

Journal of the History of Ideas, XXIX (Jan.-March 1968), 115-22.

[24]*Intellectual Origins of the English Revolution*, 113; and *The Century of Revolution: 1603-1714* (Edinburgh, 1961), 180.

[25]Dillenberger, *Protestant Thought and Natural Science* (New York, 1960), 128-29.

[26]*Science & Ideas*, 241, 238-39.

[27]R. P. Stearns and D. H. Brawner, "New England Church 'Relations' and Con-

Criticism of these attempts to parallel the experimental method in science with the experimental method in religion have concentrated on the fundamental disparity of the subject matter and the very nature of the respective inquiries themselves. It may legitimately be questioned whether or not the alleged similarities in methodology are only superficial. Clearly the empirical method in science is based not only on the observation of physical phenomena but also on the measurement and evaluation of those phenomena under rigidly controlled conditions reproducible at a later date and by qualified, impartial personnel. The empirical method in religion, on the other hand, must of necessity attempt to evaluate substantially metaphysical phenomena related by untrained and not impartial experiencers of those phenomena to others hardly less partial, even if more trained. Nor can religious phenomena ordinarily be examined under rigidly controlled conditions subsequently reproducible almost at will. The problem is neatly summed up by Solt: "The empirical approach of science involves the observation of physical objects and their arrangement in some kind of regularity; the experimental approach of Puritanism involves the metaphysical confrontation of an anxious pilgrim with the overwhelming power of God's Holy Spirit or divine grace."[28]

Keeping in mind, however, the different objects of empirical analysis, the different degrees of objective, rational examination, and the impossibility of subjecting spiritual data to scientific measurement, the fact remains that both Puritans and scientists valued a methodology which was preeminently empirical and inductive rather than fundamentally deductive. Puritans sought with great intensity for empirical data which would satisfy the psychological compulsion to assure themselves of being members of the elect. Their search lacked the objectivity characteristic of scientific investigation—but then a man of seventeenth-century England did not believe his eternal destiny was involved with his acceptance of the Tychonic or Copernican or Ptolemaic theories. In science there could be objectivity; in religion there could not. And although there could be no subjection of spiritual data to scientific measurement, Puritans strove mightily to analyze their spiritual experiences in the light of Biblical criteria, the past experiences of the saints and martyrs, and the contemporary standards of Puritan faith and morality. They valued an empirical methodology in religion as much as the advocates of the new science did in their field. What has never been conclusively demonstrated, however, is a *conscious* aware-

---

tinuity in Early Congregational History," *American Antiquarian Society* (April 1964), 39–40, 29, 32. Their argument is marred by the untenable assumption that pneumatology is a science, though it was regarded as such in the seventeenth century.

[28]*American Historical Review*, LXXIII, 25.

ness on the part of Puritans and/or scientists that such a parallel in methodology existed.

One further aspect of methodology calls for comment. Apart from the thought of the Cambridge Platonists, the Cartesians, and the Leibnizians, the combination of empiricism and rationalism, with the latter subordinate to the former, was basic to the new science. It was also, as Merton pointed out, common to Puritanism as well.[29] Rather than contrasting the working of the Spirit in believers with the dictates of reason, Puritans sought to juxtapose them. The experiential knowledge revealed by the working of the Spirit was, nevertheless, regarded as superior to mere rational knowledge—not because of its nature but because of its clarity. As Samuel Rutherford put it, experiential knowledge obtained by the revelatory work of the Spirit came as if a man were reading a book by sunlight, whereas knowledge obtained by the use of reason alone came as if a man were reading the same book by candlelight. Still, experiential knowledge was definitely to be subjected to rational analysis,[30] even as empirically-derived scientific data was to be subjected to rational analysis.

247

The force of the methodological parallel diminishes somewhat when it is remembered that various sectaries (or radical Puritans) were interested in the new science and yet adamantly rejected any attempted juxtaposition of spiritual data with rational data in the religious sphere. John Webster, Thomas Lawson, and Gerrard Winstanley—all thoroughgoing sectaries—were interested in the new science, but wished to abolish rationalism in religion rather than even retain it in a subordinate position to empiricism. If the subordination of rationalism to empiricism was sufficiently important to be a motivating factor to interest Puritans in the new science, then the rejection of that relationship by the sectaries should have been a strong hindrance to their acceptance of the new science. But it was not. A number of sectaries were interested in empirical science, including not only Webster, Lawson, and Winstanley, but also Noah Biggs, William Dell, Francis Bampfield, William Penn, George Starkey, and William Sprigg.[31]

---

[29]*Science & Ideas*, 238.

[30]Rutherford, *A Survey of the Spirituall Antichrist* (London, 1648), Pt. I, 52. Cf. Nuttall, *The Holy Spirit in Puritan Faith and Experience*, 47.

[31]Webster, *Academiarum Examen* (London, 1654); Lawson, *A Mite into the Treasury* (London, 1680); Winstanley, *The Law of Freedom in a Platform* (London, 1652); Biggs, *Mataeotechnia Medicinae Praxeos* (London, 1651); Dell, *A Testimony from the Word*, published as an appendix to *A Plain and Necessary Confutation* (London, 1654); Bampfield, *Bayīth Hachemoth. The House of Wisdom* (London, 1681); Penn, *No Cross, No Crown* (London, 1669); Starkey, *Natures Explication and Helmont's Vindication* (London, 1657); and Sprigg, *A Modest Plea for an Equal Common-Wealth against Monarchy* (London, 1659).

III

One of the most intriguing problems raised in the debate over the relationship of Puritanism and science involves the possibility of shared or similar philosophical beliefs and assumptions. No quarrel can be made with Hill's observation that the discovery of scientific truth was delayed by old ideological concepts.[32] The problem is in deciding what role—if any—Puritanism played in breaking down these traditional ideological concepts and replacing them with concepts more conducive to scientific progress. Although this particular problem calls for further research, three basic philosophical beliefs and assumptions have been asserted as common to Puritanism and science—beliefs and assumptions which countered old ideological concepts not conducive to scientific advancement. These are: (1) belief in immutable law and/or predestination; (2) opposition to hierarchicalism; and (3) belief in a plurality of worlds.

S. F. Mason has steadfastly argued that the theological doctrine of predestination prepared the way for the philosophy of mechanical determinism. The God of Calvinism governed in accordance with decrees decided upon at the very beginning of the creative process, and not, as the God of medieval man had done, by the delegation of powers to subordinate spiritual beings of increasingly inferior rank. The original decrees were the laws of nature, hence the Calvinist's universe, according to Mason, was orderly and predeterminate. Mason proceeded to cite Preston and Baxter to substantiate his thesis.[33] Yet Baxter, while an adherent of the theological doctrine of predestination, was opposed to a mechanical interpretation of the universe.[34] Certainly in his case, there was no acceptance of mechanical determinism in science because of a prior acceptance of predestinarian dogma. Mason did point to Wilkins as one of the first men "to perceive the congruity between Calvinist theology and the new theories of modern science. . . ."[35] Wilkins, however, like his fellow Oxford scientists, was not a strong Calvinist at all, but was more inclined to gravitate toward the rationalistic views embraced by the Cambridge Platonists and the Anglican latitudinarians.[36]

----

[32]"William Harvey and the Idea of Monarchy," *Past & Present*, 27 (April 1964), 68.

[33]"Science and Religion in 17th Century England," *Past & Present*, 3 (Feb. 1953), 31-32.

[34]Dillenberger, *Protestant Thought and Natural Science*, 132.

[35]*Past & Present*, 3 (Feb. 1953), 30.

[36]Cf. Solt, *American Historical Review*, LXXIII, 21. For the tendency of most scientists in seventeenth-century England to accept a moderate or latitudinarian position in religion, see B. J. Shapiro, *Past & Present*, No. 40 (July, 1968), 16-41.

Merton more plausibly contends that the idea of immutable law became part of the general intellectual milieu as the result of the influence of both scientists and Puritans. The general intellectual milieu, then, and not Puritanism *per se*, "enhanced the continued prevalence of conceptions characteristic of the new science."[37] The degree of importance attached to Puritanism as a contributing factor to this environment, and the degree to which that environment was actually a factor in the acceptance and development of the new science, remain unanswered—and perhaps unanswerable—questions.

Richard Westfall, working with similar assumptions, suggests that the influence of immutable law conceptions affected not only science but Puritanism also. The God of Calvinism "in his remote majesty" was seen as resembling "the watchmaker God of the mechanical universe, suggesting that the Calvinist tenor of English theology helped to make the mechanical hypothesis congenial to English scientists." Thus far, Mason. But Westfall also reminds his readers of the very significant fact that the mechanical conception of the universe forced at least certain elements of Christianity to accommodate their beliefs to the newer conception of nature.[38] Puritanism's predestinarian emphasis on immutable law may have helped foster the acceptance and development of scientific thought; certainly the mechanistic nature of that thought played a significant role in fostering the rise of deist thought in the Church of England. It is, therefore, rather ironic that Puritanism with its God of involvement in human affairs may have been indirectly responsible for the development of a school of theological thought which removed God from such involvement and relegated him to the role of a creative prime mover alone.

A second philosophical belief purportedly shared by Puritans and scientists was an opposition to the hierarchicalism which had been a dominant motif in both medieval science and medieval theology. Protestantism in general adopted an anti-hierarchical stance when it emphasized the direct relationship between a believer and God, doing away with the absolute necessity of mediation by a hierarchy of priests, saints, and Mary. The development of the idea that God rules the uni-

---

[37]*Science & Ideas,* 242. Rabb criticized Merton on the grounds that the doctrine of predestination was no more "similar or reassuring to the scientist's belief in immutable laws than the Catholic belief in a precise, unvarying dose of purgatory for a given sin" (*Cahiers d'Histoire Mondiale,* VII, 57). There were, however, two very significant differences between predestination and specific purgatorial punishment for a sin, which undermine Rabb's criticism. First, purgatorial punishment could be remitted; predestination and immutable law could not. Second, man could control purgatorial punishment through the accomplishment of good works or the purchase of indulgences; he could do nothing to alter the decrees of predestination.

[38]*Science and Religion in Seventeenth-Century England,* 5.

verse directly through previously-established decrees rather than indirectly through subordinate spiritual beings also had anti-hierarchical implications. Science, too, was undergoing a reaction to the
hierarchical motif. Copernicus rejected the notion that angelic beings
moved the planets. His heliocentric theory "abolished the seven
heavens and established an equality of the earth with other planets
under the sun." Harvey was another scientist who undermined the
medieval hierarchical principle. Not only did he abolish the hierarchy
of heart, liver, and brain in the human body, but he also rejected the
notion that the blood contained vital spirits responsible for its motion.[39]

250   Several problems immediately present themselves. First, opposition
to hierarchicalism in science began in Catholic states, not in Puritan or
even Protestant England. Second, neither Protestantism in general nor
Puritanism in particular completely succeeded in abolishing hierarchicalism in church government or in their theories of the ministry. The
radical Quakers did, but certainly the Presbyterians and the Anglicans
did not. The Baptists were more opposed to hierarchicalism in religion
than either of the latter groups, yet one looks in vain for Baptist involvement in or substantial support for the new science. Third, no evidence has so far been brought forth which actually establishes a link
between anti-hierarchicalism in religion and anti-hierarchicalism in
science. At best one can say only that such feelings in both spheres contributed to the cultural and intellectual environment, which in turn
made it more facile for Puritans to embrace science and scientists to
embrace Puritanism.

Closely related to the purported sharing by Puritans and scientists
of anti-hierarchical principles is Mason's argument that both also
shared a belief in the plurality of worlds. Both, in other words, believed
that the moon and possibly the planets of our solar system were inhabited. This belief, according to Mason, "carried implications which
ran counter to the concept of hierarchy, for it gave weight to the notion
that the earth and the heavenly bodies were of the same qualitative
nature, and were not graded in status, since they supported the same
creatures."[40] The best known example of the expression of the concept
of the plurality of worlds in a man who was both Puritan and scientist

[39]Hill, *Past & Present*, 27 (April 1964), 54, 67; Mason, *Past & Present*, 3 (Feb.
1953), 30, 32. For a critique of Hill's interpretation of Harvey's thought, see Gweneth
Witteridge, "William Harvey: A Royalist and No Parliamentarian," *Past & Present*,
30 (April 1965), 104–109. Hill successfully defends his interpretation in "Science,
Religion and Society in the Sixteenth and Seventeenth Centuries," *Past & Present*, 31
(July 1965), 97–103.
[40]*Past & Present*, 3 (Feb. 1953), 38.

was John Wilkins' *Discovery of a World in the Moon* (London, 1638). Mason's argument is merely an extension of the anti-hierarchical argument, and is open to some of the same objections. In addition, belief in a plurality of worlds was hardly a cardinal tenet of either Puritanism or science. If both accepted the belief as widely as Mason indicates, it proves only that they shared a belief in something which was incidental to them both.

IV

Advocates of the Puritan-science thesis point to a number of Puritan attitudes particularly conducive to the development of scientific interest. The first of these attitudes was the encouragement of the study of nature *ad gloriam Dei* and as a means for obtaining further knowledge of God and increasing man's reverence for him. Merton goes so far as to argue that "perhaps the *most directly effective element* of the Protestant ethic for the sanction of natural science was that which held that the study of nature enables a fuller appreciation of His works. . . ." Haller more cautiously and realistically observes that Puritans were generally interested in nature only insofar as it was a revelation of divine providence, and even then a revelation secondary to that contained in Scripture.[41] Catholics, too, however, could and did view the natural world as a means of divine revelation which could be studied *ad gloriam Dei*. There has been no evidence adduced to show that such an attitude was more characteristic of Protestantism than of Catholicism, or of Puritanism than of other Protestant groups.

A second Puritan attitude suggested to be conducive to scientific development was a strong interest in that which was profitable. Jones and Stimson, writing in the Weber-Tawney tradition, assumed that the profit desired by the Puritans was of a materialistic, financial nature. Jones wrote: "Certainly no part of the population was more interested in the increase of wealth and the improvement of their material welfare than the 'godly men' [i.e., the Puritans]." Jones and Stimson argued that science was welcomed by the Puritans because its knowledge could be put to use not only for general utilitarian purposes but also for monetary gain. Science was, in Stimson's words, "a profitable, leisure-time activity."[42] With respect to this argument there are two points which must be made. First, engagement in scientific endeavor primarily for monetary purposes is an idea quite foreign both to the

251

---

[41]Merton, *Science & Ideas*, 239 (italics mine; cf. 233-35, 240); Haller, *The Rise of Puritanism* (New York, 1938), 302. Cf. Stimson, *Scientists and Amateurs*, 34, and *Bulletin of the Institute of the History of Medicine*, III, 326; and Dillenberger, *Protestant Thought and Natural Science*, 129-30.

[42]Jones, *Ancient and Moderns*, 280; Stimson, *Scientists and Amateurs*, 34.

spirit of early modern science and to the scientists themselves. They may have hoped that their discoveries would be beneficial to the welfare of mankind, but personal profit was not a basic motive. Second, what was really profitable for a Puritan was not material gain but that which tended to the salvation and spiritual progress of himself and his fellow men.

Another Puritan attitude conducive to interest in science, according to Stimson, was intellectual curiosity. Science appealed to the Puritan intellect, hence Puritans devoted time to its study.[13] A careful reading of Puritan tracts does not, however, lead one to believe that Puritans were fundamentally curious people. The curious man is a "doubting Thomas," not a man exhorted at every turn to have faith in the divine providence. Puritans were exhorted to study the Bible, but not to be curious about its teachings—including those touching on scientific matters. Baxter was critical of the scientific spirit—the spirit of curiosity—because he thought it endangered Christianity.[14] John Cotton permitted scientific study, but he warned that scientific knowledge was not always certain, and that the study of science was an unsatisfying occupation which did not lead to happiness.[15]

A fourth Puritan attitude said to be conducive to scientific interest was the obligation of concentrating intensively upon secular activity as opposed to leading an ascetic life. The Puritan was extolled to be industrious, not lazy; to expend physical energy in the pursuit of truth, not to be idle or simply contemplative.[16] Even a cursory reading of Puritan tractate literature will reveal this basic attitude. But it is also found in non-Puritan literature as well.[17] Furthermore, there is nothing inherent in such an attitude which would direct a man to science; he might just as easily engage in commercial or political activities, in education or poor relief, in farming or numerous other secular activities.

Puritan regard for science as a means to control a corrupt world is cited by Merton as another attitude which helped to foster the development of science. Finding in Puritanism an asceticism which expressed itself in the world rather than in the cloister, Merton sought to discover "the significance of the active ascetic drive which necessitated the study of Nature that it might be controlled."[18] The Puritan indeed

---

[13]*Scientists and Amateurs*, 34.

[14]*The Arrogancy of Reason against Divine Revelation Repressed* (London, 1655).

[15]*Briefe Exposition . . . upon . . . Ecclesiastes* (London, 1654), in *The Puritans*, ed. Perry Miller and Thomas H. Johnson (New York, rev. 1963), II, 729–31.

[16]Merton, *Science & Ideas*, 236–37, 241; Jones, *Ancients and Moderns*, 112–13.

[17]E.g., Timothy Hall Breen, "The Non-Existent Controversy: Puritan and Anglican Attitudes on Work and Wealth, 1600–1640," *Church History*, XXXV (Sept. 1966), 273–87.

[18]*Science & Ideas*, 257; cf. 233.

sought to control a corrupt world, but it was not, however, the world of nature which occupied his attention. The world which necessitated control was a moral one in which the forces of the "old man" wrestled with those of the sanctified "new man." It was not the natural world of material objects which demanded the constant attention of the vigilant, but the natural desires and whims which lured the elect with their fiery temptations. When the Puritan looked at the world, he saw it as a spiritual battleground rather than an unknown materialistic phenomenon calling for controlled empirical investigation.

Stimson has suggested that the uprightness of character and the concern for godliness which characterized the Puritan attitude toward life resulted, especially in the Restoration period, in a wariness of the theater and singing, causing men to turn to science for "recreation and refreshment in worthwhile channels. . . ." Science could draw their attention and interest because it was both respectable and exciting.[49] Even if it could be demonstrated that the scientists of the Restoration era had an aversion to singing and the theater, it is difficult to see just why such an aversion should lead them to science rather than to other endeavors. Furthermore, those who pursued scientific interests for "recreation and refreshment" were the virtuosi, and they were interested in science because of the sheer intellectual delight it gave them and not because of any religious compulsion. They should not, moreover, be regarded as a Puritan group.[50]

253

V

A connection between Puritanism and science has been found by a number of modern scholars in the philosophy and program of education embraced by Puritans. The Puritans, according to the general theme of this argument, believed in a practical, utilitarian education, and supported experimental science because it was in keeping with the spirit of this belief.[51] They embraced Baconian-Comenian views on education, which stressed the inherent worth of both empiricism and utilitarianism. The application of these criteria to the academic curriculum resulted in a de-emphasis on classical and Scholastic studies and the granting of an important role to the natural sciences. Jones, who dealt with this argument at length in his *Ancients and Moderns*,

[49]*Bulletin of the Institute of the History of Medicine*, III, 325-26, 334. For a discussion of the Puritan attitude toward music, see Percy Scholes, *The Puritans and Music in England and New England* (London, 1934); and Richard L. Greaves, "Music at Puritan Oxford," in a forthcoming issue of *The Musical Times* (London).

[50]Cf. Houghton, *Journal of the History of Ideas*, III, 51-73, 190-219.

[51]Cf. Merton, *Science & Ideas*, 245; and Phyllis Allen, "Scientific Studies in the English Universities of the Seventeenth Century," *Journal of the History of Ideas*, X (April 1949), 238.

regarded the selection of education by the Puritans as "the most direct and fundamentally efficacious method of establishing the new science. . . ." Jones distinguished between fanatics who sought to destroy the universities and the saner, more influential Puritans who sought to reform education by eliminating theology from the curriculum, abolishing or modifying humanistic studies and traditional methodology, and introducing experimental science and technology. As representatives of the latter, saner group, Jones singled out John Dury, John Hall, John Webster, William Petty, John Wilkins, and Noah Biggs.[52]

It cannot be doubted that education played an important role in the development of modern science. Irene Parker long ago demonstrated the importance of the Dissenting Academies in this development.[53] The work of the Wadham College group at Oxford in the 1650's is well known. More recently Mark Curtis has undertaken to present a more balanced account of the role of the universities in this development in the pre-1640 period. Through their formal training, Curtis asserts, university-trained men were prepared to recognize new facts of significance and relate them to prior notions. They were also trained to think systematically, which enabled them to give serious attention to new theories and work out their logical implications. More especially, Curtis contends, higher education fostered the development of science through extra-statutory studies. Bishop Sprat's tribute to the universities calls attention to the debt of science to education, even to the point of characterizing them as, in Curtis' words, "principal causal factors in the rise of the new philosophy." Sprat had noted that it was the universities which had cherished and revived the study of science. Curtis' main point, which he perhaps overemphasizes, is the valid criticism that Stimson in particular has overlooked the possibility that the formal academic training of the predecessors of the Royal Society may have been very instrumental in influencing them to develop scientific interests as well as in making them competent to undertake scientific research.[54] There was nothing specifically Puritan in the nature of this academic training.

Too much emphasis can be given to this role of the universities, for from them came many who opposed the new science. Indeed, even within their walls were conservative opponents and disinterested individuals.[55] John Wallis, a graduate of Emmanuel College, Cambridge (B.A., 1637; M.A., 1640), recalled in 1697 that "mathe-

[52]*Ancients and Moderns*, 280, 120.
[53]*Dissenting Academies in England* (Cambridge, 1914).
[54]*Oxford and Cambridge in Transition* (Oxford, 1959), 247-49.
[55]Cf. Rabb, *Past & Present*, 31 (July 1965), 113.

matics . . . were scarce looked upon as academical studies [at Cambridge and Oxford], but rather mechanical; as the business of traders, merchants, seamen, carpenters, surveyors of lands, or the like; and perhaps some almanac-makers in London. . . . For the study of mathematics was at that time more cultivated in London than in the universities."[56] There was, in fact, no chair of mathematics at Cambridge until 1663. Not until the purge of Oxford in 1648-49 did that university have a Savilian Professor of Astronomy (Seth Ward) who was a full-fledged advocate of the Copernican theory. Ward's predecessor, John Greaves, was a Ptolemaic. Chemistry was quite ignored at Oxford until the Prussian scholar Peter Sthael was invited there to lecture in 1659. Medical studies at the universities were mediocre at best; men went to Padua or other continental schools if they were able. The London College of Physicians was more advanced in medical knowledge than either of the two universities.[57]

255

The role of university-trained Puritans in opposing scientific progress was largely ignored by Jones. His distinction between the saner Puritans and the radicals was badly drawn and virtually meaningless. There was, certainly, a lunatic fringe bent on the destruction of the universities. Their arguments were even contemplated by the Nominated Parliament. There were also radical Puritans or sectaries who favored the reform but not the abolition of the universities. They advocated the elimination of theology from the curriculum, as a perusal of the writings of Webster, Dell, Winstanley, and the Quaker reformers[58] will reveal. Contrary to Jones, however, there were Baconian-minded educational reformers who did *not* advocate banishing theology from the academic curriculum. Wilkins certainly did not. In his prefatory epistle to Ward's defense of the universities from the criticisms of Webster, Dell, and Hobbes, Wilkins argued that although the theology taught by the universities did

not exceed the sphere of those common gifts which meer naturall men are capable of, yet is it of such singular use to enable a man to speake distinctly unto severall points, to confirme truth, to cleare up difficultyes, answer doubts and consequently to help in the worke of informing others: That I am not able to imagine any reason, why an eminent ability in this kind might not be sufficient to make a man capable of a civill degree, as well as skill in any other faculty.[59]

Dury did not exclude religion from his proposed educational reforms either.[60]

[56]Quoted in Hill, *Intellectual Origins of the English Revolution*, 64.

[57]Allen, *Journal of the History of Medicine & Allied Sciences*, I, 115-43.

[58]See Richard L. Greaves, "The Early Quakers as Advocates of Educational Reform," to be published in *Quaker History* in 1969.

[59]Epistle to Ward's *Vindiciae Academiarum*, 4.

[60]*The Reformed School* [London, 1649?], 52-60.

Conservative Puritans were much less interested in science and educational reform. Even Christopher Hill took note of the fact that the Independents were "more favourable to science and less attached to Aristotle than Bishops or Presbyterians. . . ."[61] It is an injustice to accuse, as Kearney does, the Independents intellectually of having a violent hatred of the universities and of the use of learning in religion.[62] John Owen and Thomas Goodwin, to cite only two leading Independents, served as Vice-Chancellor of Oxford and President of Magdalen Hall, Oxford, respectively. Cromwell himself did not regard higher education as a prerequisite for the ministry, but neither did he disparage the value of learning in religion.[63] Religion was to play an important role in his proposed foundations at Durham and Oxford. The Independents tended to be critics of the universities on religious or educational grounds, but they were substantially in favor of their reformation. The radical critics were sectaries such as Webster, Dell, Lawson, Penn, and Winstanley, and even they offered suggestions for reform. Their principal opponents were conservative Puritans, though Ward and Wilkins—because of their university positions—were forced to defend the universities from the sectarian critics even as they reformed Oxford from within. Harvey, too, had no liking for Webster, though the latter admired him.[64]

The Presbyterian Thomas Hall was a typical conservative Puritan in his educational views. He regarded mathematics, chemistry, optics, and geography as inferior "arts." Ethics, logic, and physic were superior.[65] In 1656, Francis Osborne observed that the gentry (a group with fairly strong Puritan associations) kept their sons at home rather than allow them to be polluted with "the black art" of mathematics.[66] Two years earlier Ward had complained that the sons of the gentry came to Oxford expecting to receive a gentlemanly education, not to study chemistry, agriculture, or natural philosophy.[67] It is quite probable that conservative Puritan preachers were cautioning their congregations against the potential dangers of science. John Cotton was certainly doing it in New England. Baxter thought the study of natural science as well as the humanities unsuited to young minds not

256

---

[61]*Past & Present*, 27 (April 1964), 66.

[62]*Past & Present*, 28 (July 1964), 94.

[63]Cf. *The Letters and Speeches of Oliver Cromwell*, ed. S. C. Lomas (London, 1904), II, 180, 334, 539. Cromwell had mystical tendencies. See George Drake, "The Ideology of Oliver Cromwell," *Church History*, XXXV (Sept. 1966), 262.

[64]Hill, *Past & Present*, 27 (April 1964), 61.

[65]"Histrio-Mastix. A Whip for Webster," published as an appendix to *Vindiciae Literarum* (London, 1654), 214-15.

[66]Hill, *Intellectual Origins of the English Revolution*, 55.

[67]*Vindiciae Academiarum*, 50.

yet accustomed to view all endeavors with an eye to salvation. Although he respected Comenius and Dury, he did not recommend their educational treatises with their emphases on empiricism and utilitarianism.[68] The Presbyterian Edward Leigh, in his *Treatise of Religion & Learning* (London, 1656), defended the traditional emphases in education on classical, linguistic, and theological studies against the Baconian criticisms of Webster. Milton, whose Arminianism made him less than a full-fledged Puritan, similarly stressed classical and linguistic studies, and took only incidental note of science.[69]

What concerned the Puritans more than anything else with respect to education was the place allotted to religion. Before 1640 the Puritans "had the desire for a 'learned' ministry but not for a general program of scholarly or scientific research."[70] Even after 1640, the promotion of godliness and piety was of foremost concern in their philosophy of education, a characteristic that continued in the Dissenting Academies of the Restoration era. Joseph Sedgwick, a Puritan apologist for education and an opponent of Dell, asked: "What are the Universities appointed for but to fit men thence for the work of the Ministry?"[71] Oxford and Cambridge, according to Thomas Hall, were "Nurseries for the Church," hence he called not for the intensification of scientific studies, but for a closer working relationship between the church and the universities. In the collegiate halls young men were to receive both theological knowledge and a general education which "helps to civilize us, and to mollifie the harshnesse, and mitigate the fierceness of our natures. . . ."[72] There is nothing here which would indicate an incitement to intellectual curiosity and scientific study. Rather, the product of such an educational philosophy would be pious gentlemen.

The fact remains, nevertheless, that the Puritan purge of Oxford commencing in 1648 did bring new men into the University who aided considerably in the development of science. The changes at Oxford were primarily made, however, because of religious and political considerations, not to improve instruction and research in the sciences.

257

---

[68]Richard Schlatter, *The Social Ideas of Religious Leaders, 1660-1688* (London, 1940), 45. For Baxter's association with Dury, see Geoffrey F. Nuttall, *Richard Baxter* (London, 1965), 74-76.

[69]See, e.g., his tract *Of Education* (London, 1644). Cf. *Paradise Lost*, X, 122-25; and also Dora Neill Raymond, *Oliver's Secretary: John Milton in an Era of Revolt* (New York, 1932), 252.

[70]Knappen, *Tudor Puritanism*, 480.

[71]*A Sermon. Preached at St. Marie's in the University of Cambridge May 1st, 1653* (London, 1653), 12.

[72]*An Apologie for the Ministry* (London, 1660), 56-57; *The Pulpit Guarded* (London, 1651), fol. Bl *verso*; and *Vindiciae Literarum*, 27.

Cromwell himself was in all likelihood interested in the technological aspects of science primarily because of the practical applications to warfare and navigation. Adequate military posture and a mercantile policy demanded continuing technological improvements. Furthermore, when, in the 1650's, Cromwell called on men with scientific interests to serve him in various capacities, he was not expressing a particular interest in science. As Rabb notes, "Cromwell's personal use of men such as Pell, Dury, Petty, and Wallis was due more to his eye for ability (Wallis, for instance, happened to have an extraordinary talent for decoding), and his brother-in-law's [Wilkins'] influence, than to any conscious preference for scientists."[73]

258   Education did play an important role in the development of science in England in the seventeenth century, but Puritanism itself was involved only incidentally. There was nothing inherent in the Puritan philosophy and program of education which was particularly conducive to science. The Baconian-Comenian philosophy *was* conducive to science, but it was embraced neither universally nor solely by Puritans. Various Anglicans and sectaries were equally imbued with that philosophy of knowledge and education, which led them to scientific interests as well.

VI

Both advocates and critics of theories proposing a relationship between Puritanism and science have increasingly been approaching a common ground: the role of revolutionary ferment in the development of science and the relationship of Puritanism to that ferment. Awareness of this relationship existed in an incipient stage in the writing of Stimson and Jones. In 1935 the former wrote: "The Protestant Revolt in its challenge to the authority of the Pope had aroused a spirit of challenge in other fields besides church affairs. . . ."[74] Yet Stimson's concern was not with revolutionary ferment but with inherent tendencies in Puritanism which might have produced an interest in science. Jones was aware of the reforming spirit shared by Bacon, the scientists, and Puritans,[75] but he, too, sought a more direct connection between Puritanism and science.

The nucleus of Hill's argument has been the revolutionary connection. In Protestantism, Hill argues, there was a "dissidence of dissent" ready to burst out in Protestant countries as soon as circumstances were propitious. When this happened in England in 1640, there

[73]*Cahiers d'Histoire Mondiale*, VII, 62.
[74]*Bulletin of the Institute of the History of Medicine*, III, 323.
[75]*Ancients and Moderns*, 91-92.

resulted a new and invigorating intellectual atmosphere conducive, among other things, to scientific development. Then, in the 1650's, "former royalists [e.g., John Collop and Walter Charleton] had to accept that their opponents' doctrines had been justified by the God of Battles, and they too began to approach these doctrines with more open and receptive minds."[76] Apart from the fantasy implicit in the idea that scientists would accept new theories because their religious and political opponents had won a civil war, Hill is on solid ground in pointing to the revolutionary potentialities in Protestantism which could, when they erupted, infest an entire intellectual atmosphere.

Hill's most intensive attempt to illustrate this point involves the changing thought of Harvey. Like his medieval predecessors, Harvey at first accepted the notion of the sovereignty of the heart and of the motion of the blood in a circle, which he viewed as an analogy in the scientific realm of monarchical sovereignty in the political realm. In 1649, the same year in which Harvey's monarch was executed and the monarchy itself abolished, Harvey dethroned the heart, emphasized the blood, and relegated the heart to the instrument responsible for the blood's circulation. The treatises *De Circulatione Sanguinis* (1649) and *De Generatione Animalium*, which followed in 1651, are both regarded by Hill as republican in their implications. Since Hill finds no evidence that Harvey deliberately suppressed his true views in 1628 because of such implications, he concludes that the development of Harvey's thought was "assisted by the political events of the sixteen-forties." They provided the scientist with the "sharp jolt" needed to get him "to contemplate the possibility of dethroning the heart." Since the Puritans played such a major part in the republican revolution, they were consequently responsible in this sense for scientific development.[77]

Unlike Merton, Stimson, and Jones, Hill has placed more emphasis on the role of revolutionary ferment as the key to the relationship between Puritanism and science than on attitudes inherent within Puritanism itself. Of Protestantism in general he writes: "What mattered for the development of science was not so much protestant doctrine (though this might contribute something) as the breaking of clerical monopoly control. . . ." Because Protestantism diminished or ended the power of priests it served as a liberating force, enabling educated lay opinion to prevail over the stultifying monopolies of the professionals.[78] This was especially true of the 1640's and 1650's, bringing

259

---

[76]*Past & Present*, 29 (Dec. 1964), 89; and 31 (July 1965), 102.

[77]*Past & Present*, 27 (April 1964), 54-72. See the criticism of Gweneth Whitteridge (*ibid.*, 30, 104-109) and Hill's reply (*ibid.*, 31, 97-103).

[78]*Past & Present*, 27 (April 1964), 71-72.

about a fresh intellectual climate conducive to progress in scientific thought.

Rabb, one of the sharpest critics of the Puritan-science thesis, has stated that the encouragement of science was the result of the revolution, not of Puritanism. The essence of his argument is that the stimulus given by Puritans to science "was not due to any inherent *Puritan* tendency, but rather to the *revolutionary's* natural adoption of the convenient, ready-made and *Baconian* philosophy." Rabb will not admit that Puritanism was a main factor or a tangible cause of the increased concern with science, *but*—and here he is nearly in agreement with Hill—"the Puritans were important because they led a twenty-year revolution, during which their benign approval, acquiescence and occasional but hardly conscious encouragement helped to spread more quickly the growing interest in science."[79]

260

Revolutionary ferment as an important factor in the rise of science was recognized by Bishop Sprat in the seventeenth century itself. In his *History of the Royal Society* he wrote: "The late times of Civil War, and confusion, to make recompense for their infinite calamities, brought this advantage with them, that they stirr'd up mens minds from long ease, and a lazy rest, and made them active, industrious and inquisitive: it being the usual benefit that follows upon Tempests, and Thunders in the State, as well as in the Skie, that they purifie, and cleer the Air, which they disturb."[80]

There is a relationship between Puritanism and science, but *not* a direct one. The mediating link is revolution. To the extent that Puritanism was responsible for and participated in the Great Rebellion, it was indirectly a factor in the development of modern science. There was nothing inherent in Puritanism itself which was of significant import to foster scientific interest, but there were beliefs inherent in Puritanism which led the saints to revolt. At the same time, Puritanism was not a major stumbling block to scientific progress—the work of Merton, Jones, Stimson, and Hill clearly proves that much. Scientists, like capitalists, perhaps tended to find attitudes expressed in Puritanism more akin to their own than the basic attitudes of Anglicanism. In either case, the similarities in attitudes which did exist would not have been sufficiently pronounced to provide basic motivation to pursue either science or religion. That motivation. has to be found elsewhere.

Eastern Washington State College.

[79]*Cahiers d'Histoire Mondiale*, VII, 64, 63, 65-66.
[80]Quoted in Jones, *Ancients and Moderns*, 228-29. For a stimulating discussion of the parallel between political and scientific revolutions, see Thomas S. Kuhn, *The Structure of Scientific Revolutions*, 91-109.

Notes and Documents

New England Anglicanism: A Genteel Faith?

Bruce E. Steiner[*]

THE word "Anglican," when mentioned in the context of eighteenth-century New England, connotes a rather definite group
of associations. To the historian it means wealth; it means an
urban setting, lavish living, merchants, aristocracy. This configuration
is not the product of detailed investigations of economic or social status.
It results instead from brief—but, given the construction of the writer's
argument, important—accounts in such studies as Carl Bridenbaugh's
major works, John C. Miller's explanation of the origins of the Anglo-
American conflict, and Alan Heimert's interpretation of New England's
post-Great Awakening religious structure.[1] It is fostered, too, by textbooks and by the casual comments of other scholars.[2] Is it an accurate
picture? Does the label "genteel" adequately characterize a religious
body grown by the era of the Revolution to 25,000 persons[3] and 74

261

[*] Mr. Steiner is a member of the Department of History, Ohio University. An
earlier version of this paper was read before the Organization of American Historians
in Dallas, April 1968.
[1] Carl Bridenbaugh, *Cities in the Wilderness: The First Century of Urban Life in
America, 1625-1742* (New York, 1938), 259, 263, 419-420; Carl Bridenbaugh, *Cities in
Revolt: Urban Life in America, 1743-1776* (New York, 1955), 139, 152-154, 355; Carl
Bridenbaugh, *Mitre and Sceptre: Transatlantic Faiths, Ideas, Personalities, and Politics,
1689-1775* (New York, 1962), 212-214; John C. Miller, *Origins of the American Revolution* (Boston, 1943), 192-197; Alan Heimert, *Religion and the American Mind from
the Great Awakening to the Revolution* (Cambridge, Mass., 1966), 51, 170-171, 255,
362-364.
[2] Oscar T. Barck, Jr., and Hugh T. Lefler, *Colonial America* (New York, 1958),
384-385; H. Richard Niebuhr, *The Social Sources of Denominationalism* (New York,
1929), 146-147; Lawrence H. Gipson, *The British Empire Before the American Revolution,* X (New York, 1961), 23; William H. Nelson, *The American Tory* (Oxford,
1961), 13; Charles W. Akers, *Called Unto Liberty: a Life of Jonathan Mayhew, 1720-
1766* (Cambridge, Mass., 1964), 60, 82, 168-169, 178, 181.
[3] For a discussion of the data upon which this estimate is based, see Bruce E.
Steiner's Samuel Seabury and the Forging of the High Church Tradition: a Study in
the Evolution of New England Churchmanship 1722-1796 (unpubl. Ph.D. diss., University of Virginia, 1962), I, 72-74.

functioning congregations? Answers to these questions must be based on a combination of literary and statistical evidence.

Anglican churches in seaboard urban centers form a natural grouping and a convenient starting point: it was in a port town, at Boston in 1686, that organized Anglicanism began in New England. Boston's eighteenth-century churchmen did include many men in comfortable circumstances and some men of wealth. Such were the proprietors of Trinity Church, the members of which reportedly paid one-fifth of the town's poor rate in 1748, or of King's Chapel, whose rector noted in 1762 that Anglicans—less than one-quarter of Boston's population—held one-third of its taxable property.[4] The 1771 tax assessment list confirms these assertions of large holdings. Whereas 30 per cent of all owners of Boston real estate had properties worth more than £30 a year, 66 per cent of King's Chapel proprietors who were property owners fell in this category, as did every officer of Trinity who appears on the tax list.[5] That list and other records, notably those of the Loyalist Claims Commission, likewise indicate the mercantile origins of much of this wealth.[6] Yet, arguing against any thesis that Anglicanism was *the* religion of fashion in Boston is the fact that just four members of the Brattle Street Church, which in 1772 erected an edifice as magnificent and costly as King's Chapel,[7] held over £41,000 of the £104,000 that Bostonians had at interest in 1771 as compared to less than £3000 loaned by all the Chapel's Boston proprietors.[8] Or, again, to shift the compari-

---

[4] Sir Harry Frankland to an unnamed uncle, Dec. 13, 1748, in William S. Perry, ed., *Historical Collections Relating to the American Colonial Church*, III (Hartford, Conn., 1873), 424; Franklin B. Dexter, ed., *Extracts from the Itineraries and Other Miscellanies of Ezra Stiles* (New Haven, 1916), 100-101; and Henry Caner to Thomas Secker, Dec. 23, 1762, in Perry, ed., *Historical Collections*, 487.

[5] Henry W. Foote, *Annals of King's Chapel*, II (Boston, 1896), 321-329; Jeffrey W. Brackett *et al.*, *Trinity Church in the City of Boston, 1733-1933* (Boston, 1933), 203-204; see Boston tax assessment list of 1771, Massachusetts Archives, State House, Boston. About 80% of this list, which is arranged according to Boston's 12 wards, is extant; the missing sheets include all the entries for ward 11 and some entries for wards 3, 7, and 12.

[6] E. Alfred Jones, *The Loyalists of Massachusetts: Their Memorials, Petitions, and Claims* (London, 1930), 5-6, 12-17, 44-45, 55-56, 105, 117-118, 130-135, 159-160, 167, 179-181, 187-191, 212, 238, 270, 279-280, 283-285.

[7] Foote, *Annals*, 116, 341; Samuel G. Drake, *The History and Antiquities of Boston from Its Settlement in 1630, to the Year 1770* (Boston, 1856), 520n.

[8] Boston tax assessment list of 1771, Mass. Archives. The four members of the Brattle Street Church were John Hancock with £11,000 at interest; his aunt, Madam Lydia Hancock, with £10,000; John Erving, Sr., with £15,000; and James Bowdoin,

son to Trinity: the collections for sufferers from the great fire of 1760 yielded £3500 old tenor at Brattle Street, while Trinity Church, with a congregation of about the same size and somewhat more remote from the flames, produced little more than £1000.[9]

Clearly, then, the merchants of King's Chapel and Trinity did not occupy a social and economic eminence by themselves; indeed, it seems quite possible that the largest and most secure Boston fortunes were to be found elsewhere. Moreover, King's Chapel, if not Trinity, had a sizeable group of people of a low economic status. Between Easter 1756 and Easter 1757 the parish expended £400 old tenor on its poor; regular accounts of money paid to poor parishioners survive from this date to the Revolution.[10] Finally, when assessing the overall status of Boston's churchmen, one must consider the case of Christ Church in the shabby North End district, whose congregation, except for the fact that it was urban, consistently violates the genteel stereotype. Almost from the date of its opening in 1723 there were complaints of this church's comparative poverty.[11] In this case, too, the tax assessment list of 1771 supports the literary evidence. Of Christ Church proprietors with real estate only 15 per cent—as compared with the figure of 30 per cent given earlier for all owners of Boston real estate—had properties valued at more than £30 a year.[12] The proprietors on the list break down by occupation as seven traders of small to middling rank, some of them mere shopkeepers; five sea captains; a tidewaiter in the customs; a physician, a distiller, and

263

Erving's son-in-law, with £5120. For their Brattle Street connections, see Clifford K. Shipton, *Sibley's Harvard Graduates* (Cambridge, Mass., 1933-), XI, 195, 201-202, 518-519, XII, 152; Ellis L. Motte *et al.*, eds., *The Manifesto Church. Records of the Church in Brattle Square, 1699-1872* (Boston, 1902), folding plate, opposite p. 40, of the meetinghouse's ground plan and list of proprietors, *ca.* 1773.

[9] Dexter, ed., *Itineraries of Ezra Stiles*, 101, 120.

[10] Foote, *Annals*, 184. See also, Caner to the Society for the Propagation of the Gospel Secretary, July 18, 1775, Henry Caner Letter Book (copy), Archives of the Episcopal Diocese of Connecticut, Trinity College, Hartford, Conn.; Caner to the S. P. G. Secretary, Jan. 14, 1776, in Perry, ed., *Historical Collections*, 584.

[11] David Dunbar to Edmund Gibson, Dec. 11, 1729, Fulham Palace Manuscripts, Massachusetts, Box 2, No. 80 (copy), Library of Congress; Caner to Richard Terrick, Feb. 3, 1766, Caner Letter Book; Francis Shaw and Thomas Ivers to the S. P. G. Secretary, Jan. 29, 1767, in Perry, ed., *Historical Collections*, 528-529.

[12] The most complete list of Christ Church proprietors for this period is one dated 1774, Society for the Propagation of the Gospel Manuscript, B 22, no. 97. This manuscript and all other S. P. G. collections hereafter cited are copies in the Library of Congress.

a tavernkeeper; many artisans—a tailor, a silversmith, a carpenter, a housewright, a brazier, a cabinetmaker, a blacksmith, an oarmaker, and a painter; and also five men whose precise occupations are not determined but who seem to have been artisans or mariners.[13] And this was the elite of a congregation whose rank and file included great numbers of common sailors.[14]

In the other Massachusetts seaports the situation more closely resembled that of Christ Church than of King's Chapel or Trinity. "Large but many of them poor and illiterate" was a typical description of St. Michael's, Marblehead.[15] Its usual vestryman of the years 1767 to 1775 was the middle-class captain of a fishing vessel, a man who owned his own seven-man schooner, his house, and another dwelling.[16] "Some of the young people of the best families in the Town"—almost all Congregationalist—did attend St. Michael's during that period; this fact, plus the actual conversion of one such person, encouraged the rector to report in 1770 that his church "bids fair to make the richest and most respectable congregation in the Town."[17] For the time being, however, the lower-class element dominated: two-thirds, possibly three-fourths, of the men whose children were baptized in 1771 and who appear on the fragmentary assessment list of that year had no taxable property of any sort.[18]

[13] This list is derived from the data of the assessment list and from a variety of other sources, including four volumes of the Boston Registry Department, *Records Relating to the Early History of Boston* (Boston, 1876-1909), X, XIX, XX, and XXIX; and also "Assessors' Taking Books' of the Twelve Wards of the Town of Boston, 1780," in *The Bostonian Society Publications*, IX (1912), 9-59.

[14] Timothy Cutler to the S. P. G. Secretary, Nov. 28, 1726, in Perry, ed., *Historical Collections*, 205; Caner to Terrick, Feb. 3, 1766 (draft), Caner Letter Book.

[15] Joshua W. Weeks to the S. P. G. Secretary, June 21, 1765, in Perry, ed., *Historical Collections*, 517. See also, William Shaw to the S. P. G. Secretary, Jan. 13, 1715/16, *ibid.*, 117; answers of David Mossom to queries of the Bishop of London, 1724, *ibid.*, 149-150; George Pigot to the S. P. G. Secretary, May 7, 1736, *ibid.*, 314; wardens and vestrymen of St. Michael's, Marblehead, to the S. P. G. Secretary, Dec. 5, 1749, S. P. G. MS, B 17, no. 78; Ebenezer Miller to the S. P. G. Secretary, Oct. 16, 1751, S. P. G. MS, B 19, no. 26.

[16] Marblehead tax assessment list of 1771, Mass. Archives; Records of St. Michael's Church, Marblehead (copy), I, 77, 86, 89, 100, 112, 122, 131-132, 139-140, 147-148, Essex Institute, Salem, Mass.

[17] William McGilchrist to the S. P. G. Secretary, June 27, 1769, in Perry, ed., *Historical Collections*, 547; Joshua W. Weeks to the S. P. G. Secretary, Apr. 2, 1770, *ibid.*, 549. The convert was Joseph Hooper, son of "King" Robert Hooper; for Joseph Hooper, see Jones, *Loyalists of Massachusetts*, 165-166.

[18] The baptisms are in Records of St. Michael's, Marblehead, III, 76-77. The extant

At nearby St. Peter's, Salem, the typical churchman was also of the lower class. At least twenty-nine of forty-six men who signed a subscription for a Society for the Propagation of the Gospel missionary's salary in 1736 and who appear on a tax list of that year belonged in this category.[19] Literary evidence reinforces the statistical: in 1743 one S. P. G. correspondent noted that of fifty families adhering to the church, sixteen were "its chief support, the rest thro' their poverty (however willing) being unable to yield any assistance."[20] The proprietors of pews—always the most substantial group in any congregation—were characterized in 1747 as "neither numerous nor wealthy."[21] By 1772 they were numerous,[22] but real wealth was represented at St. Peter's only by the port's collector and a Harvard-educated lawyer.[23] None of Salem's principal merchants was a proprietor, and while there were many middle-class owners of pews, half the proprietors—on the evidence of Salem's tax lists of 1770 and 1771—were men in poor circumstances.[24]

265

---

sheets of the 1771 tax assessment list include the entries of 19 of the 38 men whose children were baptized in that year. In a few cases 2 or 3 men of the same name appear on the assessment list; the uncertainty as to the proportion of propertyless fathers results from an inability to determine which persons in these instances were the men mentioned in the list of baptisms.

[19] Harriet S. Tapley, "St. Peter's Church in Salem before the Revolution," *Essex Institute Historical Collections*, LXXX (1944), 246; Salem county levy of 1736 in the Salem tax lists, 1734-1741 (copy), B560-B615, Essex Institute. A tax of £1 is taken as the dividing line between the lower and middle classes, this sum being two and one-half times that paid by a ratable poll with no taxable property.

[20] Charles Brockwell to the S. P. G. Secretary, Mar. 25, 1743, S. P. G. MS, B 11, no. 61.

[21] William McGilchrist to the S. P. G. Secretary, Apr. 22, 1747, S. P. G. MS, B 15, no. 12.

[22] The list of proprietors of 1772 is in Tapley, "St. Peter's Church," 347-352.

[23] Among the St. Peter's proprietors was William Browne, a very rich Congregationalist, whose pew probably was purchased for his wife, the daughter of Gov. Joseph Wanton of Rhode Island, an Episcopalian. Originally of Salem's First Church, Browne was a founding member of the North Church in 1772. Shipton, *Sibley's Harvard Graduates*, XIII, 552; subscription for the North Church meetinghouse, Salem, begun Sept. 18, 1771, Essex Institute; *A Catalogue of the Members of the North Church in Salem* (Salem, Mass., 1827), 12.

[24] See Salem tax list of 1770 and the Salem tax assessment list of 1771, Mass. Archives. The leaders of Salem's mercantile community were Francis Cabot and Benjamin Pickman—both active in the founding of the North Church—and Richard Derby. They had, respectively, £6200, £4100, and £6020 in trading stock; 450, 563, and 415 tons of shipping; real estate worth £80, £147, and £159 per annum; and, in the 1770 list, personal estate and faculty of £638, £580, and £757. David Britton, the wealthiest merchant among St. Peter's proprietors, had £1180 in trading

To the east, Queen's Chapel, Portsmouth, and St. Paul's, Falmouth, boasted a larger proportion of local wealth and in the former instance, where that wealth was joined to political power, a definite aristocracy. Among the 73 founders of Queen's Chapel in 1734 were New Hampshire's lieutenant governor, 6 members of the Council, 8 Harvard graduates, and a third of the small group—made up of 6 per cent of Portsmouth's taxpayers—whose rate bill ran as high as a pound.[25] The presence of this element was a matter of frequent comment. In 1774, for example, the rector of Christ Church, Boston, wrote that the Portsmouth congregation, though smaller than his own, was "much genteeler, and more opulent."[26] The prosperous, however, did not occupy all the seats of Queen's Chapel. The tax list locates a full third of its founders in the port's large lower class.[27] As for St. Paul's, Falmouth, while its original members of 1765 included 2 men who were probably the richest in Maine,[28] there was, nevertheless, ample reason for the generous bequest which one of them made to its poor: of 105 adult male worshippers in 1771, at least 46, on the evidence of the church's tax list, were persons of limited means.[29]

266

stock; 150 tons of shipping; real estate worth £20 a year; and, in 1770, personal estate and faculty of £130. Persons having £30 or less in personal estate and faculty in 1770 are considered members of Salem's large lower class; 10 of the 51 St. Peter's proprietors appearing on the tax list had no taxable personal estate and but £10 in faculty, the lowest figure the assessors assigned an able-bodied man.

[25] See "A list of Masters of Familys of Portsmouth in his Majests: Province of New hampshire in New England who has signified their Desire of Joyning the Church of England," S. P. G. MS, A 25, no. 166-167; Shipton, Sibley's Harvard Graduates, V, 156-166, VI, 113-133, 221-231, 240-242, 328-330, 341-342, VII, 278-279, VIII, 634; Portsmouth province levy of 1734, Early Portsmouth Town Records (copy), XV, 302-322, New Hampshire State Library, Concord.

[26] Mather Byles, Jr., to the S. P. G. Secretary, June 14, 1774, S. P. G. MS, B 22, no. 89.

[27] Defined as those persons who paid a province tax of 8/ or less; the largest Portsmouth taxpayers paid £2:5. In 1741 Capt. Christopher Rymes bequeathed £20 currency to the poor of Queen's Chapel; another of the Chapel founders, Theodore Atkinson, dying in 1779, left £200 sterling, the interest to be laid out in bread to be distributed each Sabbath to impoverished members. Nathaniel Bouton et al., eds., Documents and Records Relating to the Province of New Hampshire (Concord, N. H., 1867-1943), XXXIII, 29; Timothy Alden, "An Account of the Several Religious Societies in Portsmouth, New-Hampshire from Their Establishment," Massachusetts Historical Society, Collections, 1st Ser., X (1809), 59.

[28] The brothers Samuel and Francis Waldo, for whom see Shipton, Sibley's Harvard Graduates, XI, 322-325, XII, 214-218; Jones, Loyalists of Massachusetts, 285-286.

[29] St. Paul's tax list of 1771, St. Paul's Episcopal Church Record Book, 1764-1791 (unpaged), Maine Historical Society, Portland. The individuals classified as poor

The congregations of the southern New England ports present much the same picture as those of Massachusetts, New Hampshire, and Maine, that is, an occasional wealthy parish among a larger number of less affluent ones. In Rhode Island wealth was represented by Trinity Church, Newport, whose members fitted the Anglican stereotype perfectly. In 1750, when Newport had 7 churches of 4 denominations, the men of Trinity furnished 32 of the 72 signers of a merchants' petition.[30] Ten years later, although comprising only 17 per cent of the town's taxpayers, they made up 45 per cent of the small elite who owned half its taxable property. Heavily overrepresented also among the upper middle class, the congregation included almost no families from the lowest echelon of Newport society.[31] In the other Rhode Island ports, however, the balance tipped in the other direction. Attending St. Michael's, Bristol, in 1762 were three of the town's seven wealthy men; on the other hand, the church's proportion of the upper middle class was considerably smaller than its proportion of the total population and its share of the poorer inhabitants much larger. Whereas 55 per cent of the other taxpaying families (mainly Congregationalists) paid a tax larger than a pound, only 41 per cent of the Anglicans did so.[32] Evidence that includes a 1760 tax list indicates a similar pattern at King's Church, Providence.[33]

267

---

are those who were relieved of any tax or who paid between 1/ and 8/. Help in interpreting the church's tax structure (the tax was a levy voluntarily submitted to in order to raise part of the rector's salary) is provided by the notice of its members in an "Account of Losses sustained at Falmouth, in October 1775," William Willis *et al.*, eds., *Documentary History of the State of Maine* (Portland, Me., 1869-1916), XIV, 305-310.

[30] "A List of the Adult males belonging to Newport Church [1750]," S. P. G. MS, B 18, no. 57-58; "Petition to the King, relative to bills of credit," Sept. 4, 1750, John R. Bartlett, ed., *Records of the Colony of Rhode Island* (Providence, 1856-1865), V, 311-313.

[31] "Families of Chh. of England, Newport Jany. 10, 1760," in Dexter, ed., *Itineraries of Ezra Stiles*, 15-17; Newport tax list of 1760, Office of the Secretary of State, State House, Providence. The elite—10% of the taxpayers—paid a tax of £10 or more; the upper middle class includes those who paid a tax of more than £2 but less than £10.

[32] "Families Attendg. Chh. in Bristol, Janry. 5, 1762" and "Families in Bristol, Janry. 1, 1762," in Dexter, ed., *Itineraries of Ezra Stiles*, 32-39; Bristol tax list of 1760, Office of the Secretary of State, State House, Providence. The wealthy elite and the upper middle class are defined as at Newport; the 1760 tax lists of both towns represent their portions of the colony levy authorized by the June Assembly of that year.

[33] Providence tax list of 1760, Office of the Secretary of State, State House, Providence; John Graves to the S. P. G. Secretary, Mar. 5, 1760, S. P. G. Journals,

In Connecticut, too, despite the presence of a few wealthy men, the seaport churches consisted mainly of persons of modest rank and fortune. John Still Winthrop, possessor of the proudest name and greatest house in the colony, was a member of St. James's, New London, in 1759; so was a wealthy Irish merchant; so were men of the lower class, some 41 per cent of the congregation.[34] A survey of the families of Trinity Church, New Haven, in 1762 yields a merchant, two customs officials, two shopkeepers, ten artisans, eight sea captains, a waggoner, two men who were probably laborers, three obscure widows, and six other men, artisans or mariners.[35] What the probate and land records reveal of the group's economic status amply documents the rector's assertion of 1763 that more than half his people were "in low circumstances."[36] The composition of Christ Church, Norwich Landing, in the 1770's was identical: "mostly Shop-Keepers, Seafairing-Men, Mechanicks, and Tradesmen, with some few Merchants."[37] Complaints that "those who conform in this Town,

268

XIV, 306; vote of the congregation of King's Church, Providence, Nov. 5, 1760, S. P. G. MS, B 22, no. 104.

[34] Samuel J. McCormick, ed., *The Rev. Samuel Peters' LL. D. General History of Connecticut* (New York, 1877), 121; Judson P. Wood, ed., *The New Democracy in America. Travels of Francisco de Miranda 1783-1784* (Norman, 1963), 123; *New-London Summary, or the Weekly Advertiser*, Aug. 3, 1759; New London county levy of 1759, New London County Historical Society, New London; Records of St. James's Church, New London, 1725-1874, I, 37-50, Connecticut State Library, Hartford, from which the list of members is compiled. In interpreting New London's county levy and the Connecticut grand lists hereafter cited, Grant's definition of the lower class as persons with lists of £1-£29 is utilized. See Charles S. Grant, *Democracy in the Connecticut Frontier Town of Kent* (New York, 1961), 95-96, for his discussion of the economic class structure—lower, lower middle, and upper middle—characteristic of most Connecticut towns which, unlike New London, had no really wealthy inhabitants.

[35] "Episco. Families within Compact Part of N. Haven [1762]," in Dexter, ed., *Itineraries of Ezra Stiles*, 49-50. The list of occupations is derived from the probate materials cited in n. 36 and from a miscellany of such sources as the following: New Haven *Connecticut Gazette*, 1756-1762; the Wadsworth map of New Haven of 1748, reproduced by the New Haven Colony Historical Society; Penrose R. Hoopes, *Connecticut Clockmakers of the Eighteenth Century* (Hartford, 1930), 70-73; American Loyalists: Transcript of the Manuscript Books and Papers of the Commission of Enquiry, XII, 17-42, 357-362, New York Public Library.

[36] File Papers of the New Haven Probate District, and New Haven Register of Deeds, XI-LIV (copies), Connecticut State Library; Solomon Palmer to the S. P. G. Secretary, July 26, 1763, in Francis L. Hawks and William S. Perry, eds., *Documentary History of the Protestant Episcopal Church* (New York, 1863-1864), II, 42.

[37] John Tyler to the S. P. G. Secretary, Oct. 3, 1782, S. P. G. MS, Connecticut, 1635-1782.

are too commonly of the Poorer Sort" find confirmation in a 1751 tax list which shows that two-thirds of the Anglicans at the Landing were of the lower class.[38]

The eleven congregations considered thus far, plus Christ Church, Middletown, and St. Paul's, Newburyport, were the only ones in urban locations. Urban churches, then, numbered only thirteen in the total of seventy-four. While they tended to be larger, they still included only a third of New England's Anglican population.[39] Urban churchmen were thus in the minority, and that minority, if the foregoing analysis is correct, cannot be characterized as exclusively a mercantile elite. If a few congregations contained a considerable number of wealthy gentlemen, there was a large body of poor men in almost all of them.

The two out of three New England Anglicans who lived in rural areas in 1774 were for the most part inhabitants of Connecticut and by contemporary descriptions were generally farmers.[40] Artisans, together with an occasional physician, lawyer, shopkeeper, or merchant, made up the remainder.[41] In terms of the occupations of their members, these rural churches were of two sorts: those in the villages, where the artisan element was strong, and those isolated in the countryside and consisting chiefly of farmers. Stratford, where in 1707 organized Anglicanism first appeared in Connecticut, supplies examples of both types. Christ Church, the original congregation, situated in Stratford village, was early described as composed for the most part of "poor tradesmen."[42] Probate inventories, extant for thirty-three of its adult members buried between 1725 and 1774, reveal that two-thirds of this group were in non-agricultural occupations and also support the claim of their relative poverty. Sixty per cent of the estates inventoried had a value of less than £200 sterling; indeed, more than a third came to less than £100. Only three

269

[38] Tyler to the S. P. G. Secretary, May 5, 1772, S. P. G. MS, B 22, no. 233; Chelsea Society's grand list of 1751 and the lists of Anglicans living in the Society in that year, Ecclesiastical Affairs, 1st Ser., VIII, docs. 352-353, Connecticut Archives, Connecticut State Library.

[39] This estimate is based upon the sources cited in Steiner's Samuel Seabury, I, 72-74, and upon the reports of the S. P. G. missionaries in the 1760's and early 1770's, most of which are in S. P. G. MS, B 22, and B 23.

[40] See McCormick, ed., Peters' General History of Connecticut, 169; Tyler to the S. P. G. Secretary, Oct. 3, 1782, S. P. G. MS, Conn., Photsts.

[41] This pattern emerges from a study of the Anglican faculty—or, for the post-Revolutionary period, assessment—entries in the grand lists cited in n. 53, 55, 56, and 58.

[42] Samuel Johnson to the S. P. G. Secretary, June 2, 1731, in Hawks and Perry, eds., Documentary History, I, 146.

men had real and personal property worth as much as £1000, and none of the three was really wealthy.[43] A notation of Ezra Stiles underlines the fact that the families of Christ Church did not constitute a local elite. Stiles found that although Christ Church in 1768 included 31 per cent of the population residing within the limits of the First Society, the Anglicans possessed "above a Quarter and not a Third of the [grand] List."[44]

A few miles inland, in Stratford's agricultural section of Ripton, the pattern was somewhat different. Probate inventories survive for twelve of the fifteen adult males whose burials are recorded in the register of St. Paul's, Ripton, between 1756 and 1775. Only one of these individuals left less than £200 sterling; still, half of the total number, possessing estates valued at between £274 and £348, also were small property owners. St. Paul's did include two men of wealth with estates as large as those of many a King's Chapel proprietor. Wealth in rural Connecticut did not, however, necessarily imply genteel living. Farmers like their small-property owning brethren, these men had almost no luxury goods. Wealth for them meant additional acres.[45]

The correspondence of the S. P. G. contains many references to the economic status of such village and country congregations. Until 1785 the Society was their financial mainstay, furnishing most of the support of all but one rural rector throughout New England. The letters and petitions that these clergymen forwarded to London occasionally depicted a church as having a reasonably affluent membership. Thus Edward Winslow described the membership of St. Paul's, Wallingford, in 1760 as consisting of "a very considerable number of substantial persons," while in 1772 he characterized the small Bridgewater congregation as "of good repute, and in comfortable circumstances."[46] More typical

[43] Register of burials 1725-1774, Records of Christ Church, Stratford, Conn., 1722-1932 (copy), I, 40-42, 125-129; and File Papers of the Fairfield Probate District, Connecticut State Library. These inventory totals—as is the case with those cited in n. 45—are restatements of the original figures, which were given in old tenor or, later, in lawful money.

[44] Dexter, ed., Itineraries of Ezra Stiles, 268-269.

[45] Register of burials 1756-1775, Records of St. Paul's Church, Shelton (Ripton), Conn., 1755-1907 (copy), II, 150-151, Connecticut State Library; and File Papers of the Fairfield Probate District. The wealthy individuals were Joseph Blackleach (d. 1756) with an estate of £3640 sterling, including more than 1800 acres, and Samuel Shelton (d. 1775), with about 2000 acres and a total estate of £3846 sterling.

[46] Edward Winslow to the S. P. G. Secretary, Jan. 2, 1760, in Hawks and Perry, eds., Documentary History, II, 5; Winslow to the S. P. G. Secretary, July 1, 1772, in Perry, ed., Historical Collections, 564.

of Connecticut churches, however, were such reports as the following: Greenwich and Stamford (1751), "many whose circumstances Are So Indigent that I Am Obliged to Remit their Taxes"; Fairfield (1738), "generally poor"; Norwalk (1762), "many poor people"; Redding and Newtown (1749), "My parishioners are poor"; Ridgefield (1744), "generally of small Estates"; Derby and Oxford (1762), "not a few of them under low circumstances"; Simsbury (1768), "the greater part of my people are very indigent"; Litchfield (1747), "our abilities . . . we confess are small"; Guilford, North Guilford, and Killingworth (1767), "generally poor"; and, finally, Waterbury, Westbury, New Cambridge, and Northbury (1773), "many of them, poor."[47] In Rhode Island, Massachusetts, and Maine the story was the same: Narragansett and Warwick (1747), "the greatest Part . . . are Poor"; Taunton (1766), "low in the World"; Scituate (1738), "most of us are poor and low"; Dedham and Stoughton (1769), "Generally poor"; Braintree (1774), "most of them but in slender circumstances"; Pownalborough (1761), "very poor"; Georgetown (1771), "in general, very poor"; and Gardinerstown (1773), "chiefly very poor."[48]

271

Although it is true that the persons making these statements were intent upon convincing the S. P. G. that they were worthy objects of its bounty, there is no reason to suppose that they misrepresented the situation. If such had been the case, if the rural congregations had, in fact, been in a condition to support their pastors, surely Congregational critics of the Society's expenditures in New England would have constantly emphasized this point. They did not do so—indeed, Ezra Stiles,

[47] Letters and petitions all addressed to the S. P. G. Secretary: Ebenezer Dibble, Apr. 2, 1751, S. P. G. MS, B 19, no. 35; Caner, Nov. 22, 1738, Caner Letter Book; Jeremiah Leaming, Nov. 29, 1762, S. P. G. MS, B 23, no. 240; John Beach, Apr. 1, 1749, in Hawks and Perry, eds., Documentary History, I, 253; Ridgefield Anglicans, Mar. 28, 1744, S. P. G. MS, B 13, pp. 339-340; Richard Mansfield, Dec. 9, 1762, S. P. G. MS, B 23, no. 266; Roger Viets, June 25, 1768, in Hawks and Perry, eds., Documentary History, II, 125; Litchfield Anglicans, Apr. 7, 1747, S. P. G. MS, B 15, nos. 7-8; Bela Hubbard, Jan. 30, 1767, in Hawks and Perry, eds., Documentary History, II, 107; James Scovil, June 1, 1773, S. P. G. MS, B 23, no. 349.

[48] Letters and petitions addressed to the S. P. G. Secretary: James MacSparran, Feb. 25, 1746/47, S. P. G. MS, B 14, no. 35; John Lyons, July 3, 1766, S. P. G. MS, B 22, no. 173; Scituate Anglicans, Jan. 22, 1738, in Perry, ed., Historical Collections, 320; William Clark, Sept. 25, 1769, S. P. G. MS, B 22, no. 139; Edward Winslow, Jan. 1, 1774, in Perry, ed., Historical Collections, 565; Jacob Bailey, Mar. 26, 1761, S. P. G. MS, B 22, no. 59; William W. Wheeler, July 10, 1771, ibid., no. 241; Jacob Bailey, Oct. 4, 1773, ibid., no. 67.

surveying the Anglican churches of Connecticut in 1773, declared that, with the possible exception of Christ Church, Stratford, there was not one of them "able to maintain its Minister."[49] Had Stiles consulted his "Itineraries," he perhaps would have mentioned instead St. Paul's, Wallingford. His observations confirm the S. P. G. report of its prosperity, showing that its families had an average list of £79—a very high mean assessment—in the grand list of 1761.[50] At the same time, he recorded that the Derby church, which supposedly included a large number of the poor, had only its proportional amount of the town's taxable property: one-third of the total population, the Derby Anglicans had in 1761 one-third of the total value of the grand list.[51] A remark by another observer likewise makes plausible the assertion that the Simsbury congregation was poor. In 1766, when their ratio to the Congregationalists was "nearly as one to three," Simsbury churchmen had only one-quarter of the taxable property in a town where the average list for all families was perhaps half the Wallingford Anglican figure.[52]

Such Connecticut grand lists as have survived document in a more precise fashion the picture offered by the S. P. G. correspondents. Unfortunately there are no lists for certain key Anglican centers—Fairfield and Norwalk, for example. Still, lists extending into the 1780's and 1790's exist for a variety of towns and for both village and country congregations.

These tax records, whether of the pre- or post-Revolutionary years, reveal a remarkably consistent pattern. Not only do they show a high percentage of Anglican taxpayers at lower economic levels, but they also demonstrate generally a larger proportion of Anglicans than Congregationalists at these levels. (See Table 1)

New England's Anglican congregations, in short, cannot be viewed as assemblies of aristocrats. If the stereotype of gentility and of lavish living is applicable to a few urban congregations—and generally to only a part of their membership—it is totally inaccurate in rural areas. Both

[49] Franklin B. Dexter, ed., *Literary Diary of Ezra Stiles* (New York, 1901), I, 360.
[50] Dexter, ed., *Itineraries of Ezra Stiles*, 137.
[51] *Ibid.*, 30.
[52] Roger Viets to the S. P. G. Secretary, June 25, 1776, in Hawks and Perry, eds., *Documentary History*, II, 91. This letter puts Simsbury's grand list at £23,944; for an estimate of the total number of families then in the town, compare Viets to the S. P. G. Secretary, Dec. 26, 1763, and June 25, 1768, S. P. G. MS, B 22, nos. 368 and 380.

TABLE I

PERCENTAGE OF CONNECTICUT ANGLICAN AND
CONGREGATIONALIST TAXPAYERS CLASSIFIABLE AS POOR

Town	Year	Percentage of Poor Anglicans	Percentage of Poor Congregationalists
Stamford[83]	1738	36	27
Newtown[84]	1739	28	11
Guilford (First Society)[85]	1758	50	32
Guilford (First Society)[85]	1774	64	38
Guilford (North Society)[85]	1774	36	34
Milford (First Society)[86]	1768	43	28
North Haven[87]	1787	41	44
Redding[88]	1790	59	46
Litchfield[89]	1795	52	41

273

[83] Stamford's grand list of 1738 (copy), Stamford Historical Society, Stamford, Conn. Anglican polls of Greenwich and Stamford under the care of James Wetmore, 1738, Eccles. Affairs, 1st Ser., X, doc. 325, Conn. Archives. Several petitions to the S. P. G. and various town records help to identify the Stamford men in the latter list.

[84] Newtown's grand list of 1738 (copy), in Jane E. Johnson, *Newtown's History and Historian Ezra Levan Johnson* (Newtown, Conn., 1917), 214-217; Anglican polls of Newtown, Redding, and Ridgefield under the care of John Beach, 1738, Eccles. Affairs, 1st Ser., X, doc. 329, Conn. Archives. Again, S. P. G. petitions and local records facilitate the correlation of the grand list and list of polls.

[85] Guilford First Society's grand lists of 1758 and 1774, and North Society's grand list of 1774, Yale University Library, New Haven, Conn.; Miscellany of Christ Church, Guilford, Conn., 1744-1801 (copy, unpaged), Connecticut State Library, from which a list of Anglicans living in the First Society in 1758 has been compiled. When names found in the Christ Church Miscellany and in the Records of St. John's Church, North Guilford, Conn., 1749-1868, I, 1-18, 39, 46, 64-70, 75-79, in Connecticut State Library, are correlated with the grand lists of 1774, it becomes evident that a "C" placed beside an entry was used by the listers to identify churchmen.

[86] Milford First Society's grand list of 1768, Connecticut State Library; Records of St. Peter's Church, Milford, Conn., 1764-1869 (copy), I, 1-19, also in Connecticut State Library, and from which a list of Anglicans living in the First Society in 1768 has been compiled. The percentages of Congregationalists in the lower economic class living in Milford, in Guilford's First Society both in 1758 and 1774, and in Newtown and Stamford were almost certainly smaller than the figures given in the text. Because of the makeup of the grand lists, it has not been feasible in these cases to identify and eliminate from consideration taxpayers who were nonresidents. Since nonresidents' taxable properties appear in general to have been small, the inclusion

literary and statistical evidence converge to present a very different picture. They show that New England Anglicanism in its area of greatest numerical strength—the farm community and the rural village—was in good part a lower class movement.

---

in the Congregational column of all non-Anglican taxpayers inflates to some degree the numbers of Congregational poor.

[57] Grand lists of North Haven's Congregational and Episcopal Societies of 1787, Benjamin Trumbull Papers, Yale University Library.

[58] Grand lists of Redding's Congregational and Episcopal Societies of 1790, in Redding Town Meetings, 1767-1817, Including Town Tax Lists, 1784-1815, 142-147, Connecticut State Library.

[59] Grand lists of Litchfield's Congregational and Episcopal Societies of 1795, Litchfield Town Office Building, Litchfield, Conn. Men in the Congregationalist lists owned and Litchfield's only coach, its 4 riding chairs, all of its silver plate, 32 of its 34 clocks, 36 of its 38 silver watches.

Perry Miller's Rehabilitation of the Puritans:
A Critique

GEORGE M. MARSDEN

In the era between the Civil War and the Depression the mythical character called the "American Mind" was troubled. All was well during the day when prosperity and success faced him at every turn, but at night he would sometimes dream of his childhood and awake feeling strangely uneasy. His analyst explained that this tension was the product of latent guilt feelings and suggested for therapy that he read himself to sleep with recent studies of the oppressive effects of Puritanism on young national minds. Turning to these works, the "American Mind" found that the analyst had been quite right. The source of the guilt feelings, he discovered, was an irrational phase of his development called the Reformation. This phase had been dominant when he lived in New England (he since had moved to the Midwest), but he was assured that the latest scholarship had discovered its influence to be harsh, grotesque, superstitious, narrowminded, illiberal, and worst of all intolerant.[1] The problem was, one expert informed him, that this era "was unleavened by the spirit of the Renaissance."[2] Another observed that the Reformation attitudes were a "subtle poison" flowing thorugh the veins of the entire social organism.[3] Still another implied that the "splendor of the Renaissance" had been delayed three hundred years by Reformation intolerance.[4] Convinced that the open-mindedness of the Renaissance was healthier than the irrational bigotry of the Reformation, the "American Mind" of this era began to feel easier about his past. He resolved to tolerate everyone, except of course his more conservative enemies whom he damned as "Puritan."

By the 1930s, however, Puritan baiting was becoming less and less entertaining. Living Puritans were becoming scarce, and the novelty of abusing Puritans of the past was wearing off. Then while American intellectuals, led by historians Samuel Eliot Morison and Kenneth Murdock, were cautiously considering allowing dead Puritans back into their club, Perry Miller confronted them in 1939 with the evidence that the Puritans were the most respectable of charter members. In *The New England Mind: The Seventeenth Century* he presented the startling assertion "that the reason later generations ceased

275

---

1. See, for example, Brooks Adams, *The Emancipation of Massachusetts* (Boston: Houghton, Mifflin and Co., 1887), p. 42; James Truslow Adams, *The Founding of New England* (Boston: Atlantic Monthly Press, 1921), p. 174; and Vernon Parrington, *The Colonial Mind 1620-1800* (New York: Harcourt, Brace and Co., 1927), pp. 15, 29.
2. Parrington, *op. cit.*, p. 5.
3. J. T. Adams, *op. cit.*, p. 66.
4. Brooks Adams, *op. cit.*, pp. 1-2.

Mr. Marsden is associate professor of history in Calvin College, Grand Rapids, Michigan.

marching to the Puritan beat was simply that they could no longer
stand the pace."⁵ In one stroke the last had been made first in American intellectual history. Paradise was regained.

Perry Miller's restoration of the Puritans is now so thoroughly
accepted that it may be evaluated critically without seriously endanger-
ing the reputation of either the Puritans or of Miller himself. Almost without a doubt Miller was the greatest American intellectual
historian of our era; yet no historian is immune from the prejudices
of his age. As Carl Becker has observed, "All historical writing, even
the most honest, is unconsciously subjective, since every age is bound,
in spite of itself, to make the dead perform whatever tricks it finds
necessary for its own peace of mind."⁶ It is possible, therefore, to discover in Miller's portrait of the Puritans aspects which reflect the
values of twentieth-century America as much as those of seventeenth-
century New England.

In his most comprehensive work, the *New England Mind,* Miller
begins his rehabilitation of the Puritan image by emphasizing Puritan piety. Critics prior to Miller had usually been most impressed by
the rigor of Puritan *action* and had played the trick of evaluating
the Puritans in terms of their acts in the spheres of politics, economics,
and personal morality. Miller, on the other hand, observes that the
action was only secondary in the Puritan scheme of things, and was
worthless to the Puritan without the profound piety which was its
source. Puritan piety, he says, was "one more instance of a recurrent spiritual answer to interrogations eternally posed by human existence." New England's founders were (perhaps like Kierkegaard
or Kafka, it seems suggested) confronted with "an urgent sense of
man's predicament." Their piety was not so much "Calvinist" (a
term of opprobrium in twentieth-century America) as "Augustinian"
(a term of approbation).⁷

Though Miller's portrayal of "The Augustinian Strain of Piety"
in the *New England Mind* is itself impressive, it is overshadowed by
his extensive and penetrating analysis of the Puritan intellect. By restoring the respectability of Puritan thought Miller answers the earlier critics most effectively, destroying their caricatures of the Puritans as narrow-minded obscurantists who made careers out of retard-
ing the Renaissance. In Miller's works it is always clear that the
Puritans were "spokesmen for what we call the Renaissance."⁸ The
inhabitants of seventeenth-century New England were not "as they

5. Perry Miller, *The New England Mind: The Seventeenth Century* (Boston: Beacon
   Press, 1939), p. 59 (hereafter cited as NEM). References in the text to *The New
   England Mind* all refer to this volume and not to the admirable sequel, *The New
   England Mind: From Colony to Province* (Boston, 1953).
6. Carl Becker, *The Heavenly City of the Eighteenth-Century Philosophers* (New Haven:
   Yale University Press, 1932), p. 44.
7. NEM, p. 4.
8. NEM, p. ix. Cf. Perry Miller and Thomas H. Johnson, eds., *The Puritans* (New York:
   Harper Torchbooks, 1963), I, p. 19 (from Miller's introduction).

are often pictured, merely dogmatic Calvinists," but rather "disciples of Erasmus and Colet."[9] Far from being irrational bigots, they were rationalists who precipitated a modification of Calvinism by gradually escalating the estimate of the capabilities natural to man. They were humanists who championed the latest intellectual fashion. "The fundamental fact concerning the intellectual life of the New Englanders is that they ranged themselves definitely under the banner of the Ramists." The "method" of Petrus Ramus "is a testimony to the importance of logic for the Renaissance mind."[10] It is a "typically Renaissance product" which "cleared away the rubbish of scholasticism." It is "the logic of a *Humanist*."[11]

Such emphases on previously neglected aspects of the quality of Puritan intellect and piety have much that legitimately commends them to a twentieth century audience. Yet when Miller deals with the *content* of Puritan religion his otherwise excellent account involves a subtle trick played on the Puritans themselves in order to win sympathy for them in the mid-twentieth century. In the foreward to the *New England Mind,* while attempting "to advertise his impartiality," he acknowledges his own point of view. "I wholeheartedly admire the integrity and profundity of the Puritan character," he writes, "but . . . I am far from sharing in its code or from finding delight in its every aspect."[12] Unquestionably both Miller and many twentieth century readers find little delight in certain aspects of Puritan belief, and although Miller seldom presents any aspect of Puritanism inaccurately, he consistently weights his presentations in slight ways that will minimize such unattractive aspects of Puritan religion. To illustrate how these subtle modifications misrepresent the actual character of Puritanism, this study will consider the types of modifications that Miller consistently makes in four areas, Puritan biblicism, doctrinal formulations, emphasis on the place of Christ, and their Calvinism, and then illustrate how the modifications in each of these four areas contribute to a basic distortion of one of the most crucial of Puritan concerns, their doctrine of the covenant.

One aspect of Puritan thought which Miller seems to find particularly uninviting is its biblicism. Although he clearly states that the most basic source of Puritan ideas was the Bible,[13] he also goes out of his way to avoid suggesting the stereotyped conclusion that their biblicism amounted to "a brutal authoritarianism."[14] Accordingly, Miller almost never acknowledges the direct scriptural antecedents of specific Puritan concepts. The biblical arguments which were at the heart of nearly every Puritan statement are simply ignored.

9. *Puritans*, pp. 24, 21.
10. NEM, p. 116.
11. *Puritans*, pp. 30, 36.
12. NEM, p. viii.
13. As, for example, NEM, pp. x, 20; *Puritans*, pp. 43-4.
14. NEM, p. 65.

The result of these omissions is the occasionally quite misleading impression that the Puritans invented concepts which in fact they took directly from Scripture. In one of Miller's characteristic arguments that the Puritans were "carrying the frontiers of reason to the very boundries of faith," he states, "Here was indeed a triumph in the justifying of God's way to man! Natural knowledge, such as all men can attain, cannot make a man holy, but it can at least render him inexcusable, and God is exculpated from the charge of injustice for his condemnation."[15] He neglects to mention, however, that this ingenius doctrine is precisely one of the arguments of Paul in Romans 1 and 2. The same applies to several references to the law as "school-master." Miller suggests that the Puritans devised this idea in order to soften the demands of the law, viewing God "not so much as a mail-clad seigneur as a skillful teacher."[16] Yet it turns out that both the phrase (school-master) and its application are borrowed directly from Galatians 3.[17]

278

Granted that the biblical source of Puritan ideas is a commonplace observation and that Miller's exposition of extra-biblical influences is a valuable counterbalance to previous accounts; it is nonetheless not entirely accurate to write the intellectual history of the Puritans with only passing mention of the most important source of their ideas. The men who created the New England mind insisted on the principle of *Scriptura sola*. They were painstakingly scrupulous to avoid reading their own ideas into Scripture. Unquestionably, they did not always succeed; but doubtless also, they did succeed in a great many instances. Yet Miller seems to assume the Puritans were very seldom strictly guided by biblical precedents. He betrays this assumption, for instance, when he says, "For the content of their belief, for the meanings which they read into Scripture or the principles they deduced from it, the Puritans both in England and New England drew freely upon the stores of knowledge and the methods of thinking which were then available to educated men."[18] His implication is that Puritans normally either read meanings into Scripture or derived from its principles that were controlled by current intellectual fashion. Accordingly, readers of the *New England Mind* are likely to come away with the impression that the most important characteristics of the Puritan intellect were reverence for reason and particularly Ramist logic.[19]

15. "The Marrow of Puritan Divinity," *Errand into the Wilderness* (New York: Harper Torchbooks, 1964), p. 78; cf. p. 82. This essay was originally published in *The Publications of the Colonial Society of Massachusetts* for February 1935 (hereafter cited as "Marrow").
16. NEM, pp. 397, 384; "Marrow," pp. 69, 82.
17. For other examples see NEM, p. 384 where Miller gives no hint that the concept of man's "debt to the law" is taken from Galatians 5:3; NEM, p. 40 where Genesis 1:28, the source of the "cultural mandate" (a standard Calvinist concept) is not mentioned; and the discussion on the covenant, below.
18. NEM, p. 89.
19. Miller does present a convincing argument for the case that Puritan confidence in reason had the *potential* for undermining the biblical norm. See, for example, NEM, p. 73.

While it is certainly important to recognize that New Englanders "read
the Word of God in the light of Ramus,"[20] it is very unlikely that the
cautious Puritan exegetes would *characteristically* have allowed the
lamp of Ramist logic (which after all was primarily a common sense
method of arranging arguments)[21] to obscure the light of revelation.

A second aspect of Puritan thought with which Miller and most
mid-twentieth century readers have little patience is that of doctrinal
formulations. Although Miller observes that systematic organization
was an "obsession" with the Puritans,[22] he seldom presents the precise theological formulas which strictly defined the limits of their inquiries. Never does he deal with their creeds at any length (compare,
for example, Williston Walker's *Creeds and Platforms of Congregationalism*). While he does discuss at some length such basic concepts
as God, sin, regeneration, and especially the covenant of grace, he
fails to define clearly other standard Puritan doctrines such as unconditional election, limited atonement, effectual calling, adoption, justification, sanctification, union with Christ, and perseverance of the
saints. There is, of course, some merit in sparing modern readers
the burden of mastering these concepts and their intricate interrela-
tionships. Miller intentionally avoids "dealing with the verbal propositions through which the ideas were embodied in the technical hand-
books," seeking rather "to understand the connotations behind these
beliefs "without resorting to sanctimonious and hackneyed phrases."[23]
The result is commendable. He reads far more between the lines than
anyone previously had imagined, and with rare exceptions his insights are astute. Nonetheless, the drawbacks of this neglect of systematic doctrine must be acknowledged as well.[24] Most significantly,
a detailed account of the Puritan mind with little regard for the detail of their finished theological system seems to suggest that their
methods were more important than their results.

The lack of emphasis on the place of Scripture and doctrine suggests that Miller realized that the Puritans could not be rehabilitated
in the mid-twentieth century unless they were dissociated as far as
possible from their exclusively Christian emphases. This suspicion
receives further confirmation when we realize that Miller all but
ignores the most crucial aspect of any Christian system—that of the
person and work of Christ. Other than in quotations from the sources,

279

20. NEM, p. 124.
21. Cf. Miller's own statement to this effect, *Puritans*, p. 29.
22. NEM, p. 95.
23. NEM, p. 10.
24. Occasionally, it simply obscures the precision of Puritan thought. On p. 54, NEM, for
instance, Miller invents the term "imperfect regeneration" to describe what is clearly
the process of sanctification. In another place he virtually denies that the Puritans
held to the dual character of the transmission of original sin as *both* inherited depravity
and judical imputation of guilt ("Marrow," p. 81). Cf. the "Savoy Declaration,"
VI, 2, 3, where this distinction is scrupulously maintained, Williston Walker, *Creeds
and Platforms of Congregationalism* (New York: Charles Scribner's Sons, 1893), pp.
367ff.

Christ is seldom mentioned except incidentally in relation to other teachings. At least, one hardly comes away from any of Miller's accounts
with the feeling that Christ was even theoretically central in the Puritan system. Yet Miller makes no apologies for this omission. He
even goes so far as to suggest that the Reformation was perhaps more
engrossing to the Puritan mind than was the appearance of Christ.[25]
Admittedly the Puritans were deeply engrossed in the intellectual battles of the Reformation; but if the doctrine of Christ was not often
a subject of their disputations, it is only an indication that here was
one area of almost universal agreement. Puritan sermons, the heart
of their intellectual activity, abound with so many references to Christ
that their sincere evangelical emphasis on the love of Christ is unmistakable.[26] Perhaps for this reason the importance of Christ to the
Puritans is so patent that it requires only passing mention. Yet it is
difficult to present a balanced portrait of the Puritan mind with little regard for the author and finisher of their faith.

By minimizing Scripture, systematic doctrine, and the role of
Christ, Miller in effect seems to be engaging in a kind of demytho-
logizing, or more properly "de-Christianizing," of Puritanism. This
process is not by any means a fully developed thesis, but it is an undeniable subtle tendency.

Far more explicit, thoroughgoing, and misleading is Miller's attempt to dissociate the Puritans from a currently much less reputable
aspect of their heritage—their Calvinism. Earlier historical critics had
given John Calvin a very bad press. Miller, in response, attempted
to place the Puritans in a more favorable light by asserting that "Simon-
pure Calvinism is a much more dogmatic anti-rational creed than
that of the Congregational parsons of Massachusetts."[27] As David
Hall of Yale has recently pointed out, Miller simply accepted his predecessor's characterizations of Calvin's God as an arbitrary despot
and then presented the Puritans as though they had lessened the severity of Calvin's system. Hall shows further that this provided a
means of dramatizing the development of the Puritan intellect by suggesting that their most original contributions were efforts to make
Calvin's "unpredictable deity" rational and comprehensible.[28] Miller
claims that Calvin demanded that his disciples "contemplate, with
steady, unblinking resolution, the absolute, incomprehensible, and
transcendent sovereignty of God; he required men to stare fixedly and

25. NEM, p. 467; cf. p. 45, where he claims that they "minimized the role of the Savior in their glorification of the Father." It is, of course, true that the sovereignty of God played a major role in their thinking, but it does not follow therefore that they "minimized" the doctrine of Christ.
26. Cf. H. Richard Niebuhr, The Kingdom of God in America (New York: Harper Torch-books, 1959), p. 94.
27. Puritans, p. 57.
28. David D. Hall, "The Puritans versus John Calvin: A Critique of Perry Miller, The New England Mind." Unpublished paper delivered at the Meeting of the American Historical Association, December 30, 1967. I am indebted to David Hall for furnish-ing me with a copy of this fine paper and for some useful advice and encouragement.

without relief into the very center of the blazing sun of glory."[29] On the other hand, the Puritans, while retaining some essential affinities to Calvin, reputedly transformed God into "a kindly and solicitous being."[30] "The God of the whirlwind" was changed to "the gentle father sorrowing for his lost children."[31] Miller is correct in maintaining that the Puritans viewed God (as Scripture does also) in many roles, not only as the hidden deity or mail-clad seigneur, but also as the benevolent father or skillful teacher. He is simply wrong, however, in supposing that Calvin did not view God in all these same ways.[32]

The fact of the matter seems to be that although Miller apparently read and comprehended nearly everything the Puritans wrote, he either knew or cared very little about Calvin. This may be illustrated in an astonishing way by examining his references to Calvin in "The Marrow of Puritan Divinity" and the *New England Mind*. In more cases than not his notes on Calvin are substantial misrepresentations.[33] In emphasizing the Puritan doctrine of judicial imputation of Adams' sin, for instance, Miller notes, "There is no suspicion of the legal imputation theory in Calvin (see *Institutes*, II, i, 7-8)."[34] When we do see the *Institutes* we find that, although Calvin does not describe imputation in precisely the same terms as the Puritan "federal" theologians, he clearly both suggests and maintains that the transmission of sin is judicial as well as a natural inheritance. "Christ himself, the heavenly judge," says Calvin, "declares, in the most unequivocal terms, that all are born in a state of pravity and corruption." And the "sin of Adam renders us obnoxious to the Divine judgment."[35] Miller in another case, in explaining the Puritan doctrine (from Romans 1 and 2) that the light of nature makes man "inexcusable for a neglect of God's laws," asserts that the entire "direction" of this argument "had been condemned in Calvin in so many words."[36] The passage cited from the *Institutes* (II, ii, 4), however, turns out to have nothing to do with the doctrine of inexcusability (which Calvin elsewhere explicitly defends), but rather is an attack on Pelagianism —a doctrine that was anathema to every self-respecting Puritan.[37] In

281

29. "Marrow," p. 51.
30. "Marrow," p. 64; cf. p. 93.
31. NEM, p. 397.
32. See, for instance, John Calvin, *Institutes of the Christian Religion*, Henry Beveridge, trans., 2 vols. (Grand Rapids, Mich.: William B. Erdmans, 1957), Book III, Chapter xx, Sections 36-40 on the fatherhood of God; II, vii, 11, and II, ix, 5 on God's skill as a teacher; and cf. Calvin's denial that God acts with the "caprice of a tyrant," III, xxiii, 2. (Hereafter Beveridge translation will be cited unless otherwise indicated).
33. Discounting duplications, Miller cites Calvin's work ten times in these studies. Of these, eight misrepresent Calvin in some substantial way. The only one of Calvin's work ever cited is the *Institutes*.
34. "Marrow," p. 81n.
35. *Institutes*, II, i, 6, and II, i, 8; cf. II, i, 5.
36. "Marrow," p. 82 and 82n.
37. Here again the confusion on this point is created by Miller's speaking of a *potential* of Puritan doctrine as though it were an actuality. His misleading observations on the implications of inexcusability seem all the more strange in the light of his mention in a previous note that inexcusability "is a good Calvinist doctrine." ("Marrow," 78n).

a similar instance Miller makes the remarkable suggestion that John
Preston's view of natural man's remaining rational abilities was closer
to that of the deist Lord Herbert of Cherbury than to Calvin. "Calvin," says Miller, "is arguing for the utter incapacity of nature, relieved by occasional grants of power bestowed at the mere pleasure
of an arbitrary sovereign."[38] Even in the passage noted (*Institutes*, II,
ii, 12-17), however, Calvin makes it perfectly clear that the depraved
mind is not devoid of reason. "The human mind, however much fallen
and perverted from its original integrity, is still adorned and invested
with admirable gifts from its Creator," he says. Moreover, "it appears that one of the essential properties of our nature is reason,
which distinguishes us from the lower animals."[39] An even clearer
case of distortion is Miller's argument that men in 1600 demanded
greater assurance of salvation than did men in 1550. "Calvin," he
says, "had wisely advised caution in promising positive assurance, since
predestination takes place in the inmost recesses of divine wisdom. . . ."[40]
He then quotes a statement from Calvin which refers solely to the
doctrine of election in general and not to the question of assurance,
even though in the very same section Calvin states that *only* in the
doctrine of election do we find "any sure ground of confidence" in
our salvation.[41] On the same subject, while describing Calvin's supposed unblinking acceptance of predestination and his condemnation
of speculations on the question, Miller cites a passage where Calvin
is merely warning against such inquiries *going beyond Scripture* and
is himself introducing a fifty-page exposition of the doctrine.[42] Similarly, Miller supports his claim that Calvin simply left it a mystery
why men should do good works if grace is irrespective of works, by
referring to a section of the *Institutes* on man's depravity;[43] he neglects
to mention, however, two other passages where Calvin explains the
very issue at length.[44] In all these cases it is clear that the trick Miller
plays in the interest of refurbishing the Puritan image is not on the
Puritans themselves, but on the most influential of their immediate
predecessors.

The extent to which each of the foregoing aspects of the re-

Even in this previous note, however, Miller claims incorrectly that in Calvin, natural
man's knowledge of natural law had "no validity for any further regulation of life"
(i. e. further than showing their inexcusability), whereas Calvin says, "Nothing, indeed,
is more common, than for man to be sufficiently instructed in a right course of conduct by natural law;" *Institutes*, II, ii, 22.
38. "Marrow," pp. 75, 75n; cf. NEM, pp. 186-7.
39. *Institutes*, II, ii, 15, and II, ii, 17. In each of the above instances Miller does sense
differences in nuances between Calvin and the Puritans. The present analysis is not
intended to deny that there were such differences. It does, however, point out that
Miller exaggerates them to the point of distortion.
40. NEM, p. 370.
41. *Institutes*, III, xxi, 1. In this, as in the example that follows, Calvin warns only against
speculations into the divine mysteries that go *beyond* Scripture. Cf. III, xxiv, 4, for a
more complete statement on election as the primary ground of assurance.
42. "Marrow," p. 51; cf. *Institutes*, III, xxi-xxv.
43. *Institutes*, II, ii, 1; cited in NEM, p. 367 and in "Marrow," p. 54.
44. *Institutes*, II, v, 1-7; III, xxiii, 9-14.

habilitation process controls Perry Miller's account of the New England
mind can best be demonstrated by a consideration of his treatment of
the covenant of grace, a concept that he correctly maintains played a
crucial role in Puritan thought.

The covenant of grace, according to Miller, was the Puritan divines' most ingenious stratagem for resolving the dilemma of maintaining human responsibility in a deterministic system, and hence
the major component in their "revision of Calvinism."[45] Miller therefore repeatedly presents the covenant as though it were part of a conscious plot by Puritan ministers to promote morality. "The divines,"
he says, "had to discover some more explicit grounds on which to
plead the necessity of works." The covenant was "an extremely subtle
. . . device within the framework of predestination for arousing human activity." It was "a juridical relationship slyly substituted for
the divine decree."[46]

In fact, however, it seems that Miller has slyly substituted his
plot for the actual development of the covenant doctrine. First of
all, he minimizes the extent to which the concept of the covenant of
grace was derived directly from Scripture.[47] He does acknowledge,
but only in the appendix to the *New England Mind,* that the covenant
"is found in the Old Tesament in a sense not too remote from that
in which they took it."[48] Nonetheless Miller clearly considers such a
biblical precedent almost incidental to the Puritans' motives for accepting the covenant teaching. It is of course possible that he is correct in suggesting that the covenant became popular in the sixteenth
and seventeenth centuries because of the appeal of contractualism to
the spirit of the age and because of its usefulness in explaining man's
responsibilities to a sovereign God. The simpler explanation, and the
one the Puritans themselves would have given, however, seems far
more probable. The covenant doctrine was emphasized primarily because it was discovered to be a central biblical concept. It was emphasized in the sixteenth and seventeenth centuries (rather than in
some previous era) because the Protestant Reformers studied the
whole Scripture intensively and demanded that it all be taken seriously
and, whenever possible, literally. This was particularly important with
regard to the Old Testament, which since the time of Augustine had
been frequently allegorized and seldom studied systematically and

283

45. NEM, p. 396.
46. NEM, p. 368; NEM, p. 394; "Marrow," p. 73.
47. With regard to the social covenant Miller acknowledges the scriptural origins more
prominently (NEM, p. 399). Here his contention that is was designed primarily to
encourage obedience to the government is more satisfactory than is the same argument
with regard to the covenant of grace, since in the social covenant the complicating feature of the gracious work of Christ is removed. The development of the Congregationalist church covenant, for which there is less biblical precedent, presents the best
case for showing that the Puritans simply made a logical (probably Ramist) extension
of the concept to another sphere.
48. NEM, p. 502. Cf. "Marrow," p. 61, where Miller describes how the covenant was
given to Abraham.

where the idea of covenant (*berith*) appears hundreds of times. It is hardly surprising, therefore, that the Puritan interpretation (which, incidentally, included the New Testament explanations as well) resembled the biblical interpretation. The development of the covenant doctrine was basically one more instance of the Protestant recovery of biblical teaching. That this is the case is supported by the fact that the covenant doctrine began to appear in numerous places almost as soon as the Reformation had begun. Zwingli, Oecolampadius, Bullinger, Bucer, Tyndale, and several lesser figures developed early formulations of the concept.[49] The connections among these as well as their connections with the Puritans are not entirely clear. But a major part of the explanation is most likely that they all read the same source.

284

Miller's second offense in his treatment of the covenant of grace is that in the course of his argument he inadvertently demolishes the precision of Puritan systematic theology. Anxious to dramatize the Puritan pastors' zeal to prevent moral laxity, Miller claims that "the final outcome in all New England preaching of the covenant theory was a shamelessly pragmatic injunction. It permitted the ministers to inform their congregations that if any of them could fulfill the Covenant, they were elected."[50] Such statements, he contends, were designed to promote morality because faith was impossible without performance, and the performance required was stated in the moral law.[51] His implication is that New England ministers were informing their congregations that if they tried to fulfill the moral law they would contribute something to their salvation. But this would be the exact opposite of what the Puritans actually said about the covenant of grace. The covenant was of *grace* precisely because it could not be *fulfilled* by good works. There had been a "covenant of works" with Adam; but when Adam fell this was replaced by the covenant of grace. Repeatedly the Puritans maintained that faith (which is not a work but a gift of grace) is the only requirement of this new covenant, and that man can do no work to *fulfill* its terms.[52] True, they did say that there is no faith without good works. But to say that works proceed from faith or that faith without works is dead is hardly

49. Leonard J. Trinterud, "The Origins of Puritanism," *Church History*, 20 (1951), 39-41; Jens G. Moeller, "The Beginnings of Puritan Covenant Theology," *Journal of Ecclesiastical History*, 14 (1963), 46-54; and Everett H. Emerson, "Calvin and Covenant Theology," *Church History*, 25 (1956), 136-7.
50. NEM, p. 395, and "Marrow," p. 88.
51. NEM, p. 396.
52. See, for instance, Walker, *Creeds and Platforms of Congregationalism*, the "Savoy Declaration," VIII, 3: ". . . the covenant of grace; wherein he freely offereth unto sinners life and salvation by Jesus Christ, requiring of them faith in him, that they may be saved . . . ." And XVI, 5: "We cannot by our best works merit pardon of sin, or eternal life. . . ." Notice also that men's "ability to do good works is not at all of themselves, but wholly from the Spirit of Christ. . . ." XVI, 3.
    On faith as a gift of grace, see "Savoy Declaration," XIV, 1. Miller neglects this aspect when he suggests that the covenant is "a *quid pro quo*, an 'if I believe' necessitating a 'you have to save me,'" rather than involving "irresistable grace, unexpected and undeserved." "Marrow," p. 71, cf. NEM, p. 389.

new with the Puritans.

The ambiguity Miller permits regarding Puritan covenant doctrine is closely related to his minimization of the place of Christ in their thinking. If we are to believe the Puritans' own statements, the gracious work of Christ is central for understanding the covenant of grace; yet Miller mentions this aspect only in passing.[53] According to the Puritans, the covenant of grace was fulfilled by Christ alone. Though the requirements of the moral law were an integral part of the covenant, no man after Adam's fall could hope to keep those requirements. Christ, however, by his perfect obedience and sacrifice had perfectly kept the law and thus satisfied God's justice.[54] Seen in this light, the covenant adds relatively little as a means of urging good works. It is a contract which God graciously offers to men, and it does demand obedience. But since man cannot fulfill his side of the contract, it augments the incentive to obey God only slightly. The only incentive provided derives from the relation of the covenant concept to the idea that the works of regenerated men will be graciously accepted and rewarded despite their manifold imperfections.[55] Nevertheless, man's duty to keep God's law as well as God's condescending love in accepting men's unprofitable works can be (and often has been) preached just as effectively without any explicit reference to the covenantal relationship.[56]

285

Miller's mistreatment of the Puritan emphases concerning the covenant seems relatively slight compared to his abuse of Calvin's doctrine. In this historical trick Calvin is clearly the straight man. Calvin, who reputedly "made hardly any mention of the covenant," is said to "turn in his grave" as the Puritan theologians made the covenant "the foundation for the whole history and structure of Christian theology."[57] "The horrified ghost of Calvin shuddered" as he beheld "his theology twisted into a spiritual commercialism."[58] Though picturesque, this portrait of Calvin is an inaccurate caricature. We can quickly see how remarkably inaccurate it is by comparing Calvin's own statements on the covenant to the supposed Puritan modifications of Calvinism. From several recent studies of Calvin's doctrine it can be shown not only that Calvin knew much of the covenant but that he developed its implications concerning the unity of Scripture, God's soverignty, and man's responsibility in very nearly the same ways as did the Puritans.

53. NEM, pp. 377, 382, for example.
54. "Savoy Declaration," VIII, 5.
55. "Savoy Declaration," XVI, 5, 6; cf. VII, 1. Miller does mention this aspect (NEM, p. 387), but he does not follow its implications in his subsequent analysis (e. g. NEM, p. 395).
56. In the "Savoy Declaration," for instance, the covenant is never mentioned in the chapter on "Good Works," and the primary ground for urging obedience is simply that God demands it.
57. "Marrow," p. 60.
58. NEM, p. 389.

Though the covenant is not prominent in the *Institutes*, it does appear and plays an important role in the defense of the continuity of the administration of grace in the Old and the New Testaments and in the corollary argument for infant baptism (based on continuity of circumcision and baptism as covenantal signs).[59] Calvin says, for instance, "The covenant of all the fathers is so far from differing substantially from ours, that it is the very same; it only varies in its administration."[60] Thus when Miller pictures the reformer turning in his grave as William Ames announces that since Abraham there has been one covenant, "yet the manner . . . of administering this new Covenant, hath not alwayes beene one and the same . . . ," Miller is failing to recognize that in this very instance, "Ames is merely quoting Calvin, as every Calvinist theologian did."[61]

286

Calvin's fullest exposition of the implications of the covenant of grace for understanding God's sovereignty and man's responsibility is found in his sermons on Deuteronomy, preached in 1555 and 1556. These sermons leave no doubt that Perry Miller was mistaken in supposing that the Puritans contrived the covenant concept in order to circumscribe the sovereignty of Calvin's God or to transform "the hitherto stern Deity" into a "condescending," "kindly and solicitous being." In support of this argument Miller quotes from John Preston, "how great a mercie it is, that the glorious God of Heaven and . . . he the Creator, and we but the creatures; and yet he is willing to enter into Covenant, which implyes a kinde of equality between us."[62] But compare Calvin:

> The creatures do see that the living God abases himself so far as to be willing to enter into treaty with them, as if he should say, Come, let us see at what point we are: indeed there is an infinite distance between you and me. I might command you what seems good to me without having anything further to do with you . . . yet . . . I am willing to govern you, and you shall be as my little family. . . . I am here ready to enter into covenant with you, and to bind myself to you.[63]

The mutuality of this covenant is likewise clear in Calvin's sermons. He says, for instance, "There must be this mutual bond between us, that since God binds himself so to us, we must also submit ourselves wholly to him."[64] Miller presents an almost identical passage from

59. See the excellent treatment of these subjects by Anthony Hoekema of Calvin Theological Seminary, "The Covenant of Grace in Calvin's Teaching," *Calvin Theological Journal*, 2 (1967). Hoekema argues that "for Calvin the covenant idea is the thread which ties salvation history together," and provides documentation for this from seven separate sections of the *Institutes*; pp. 136-139.
60. *Institutes*, II, x, 2 (John Allen translation).
61. Moeller, "Puritan Covenant Theology," p. 49n; "Marrow," p. 69 Miller claims incorrectly that "The beginnings of this conception are to be found in Ames, and it was probably his chief contribution to the system."
62. "Marrow," p. 64.
63. Quoted in Hoekema, "Covenant . . . in Calvin," p. 142 from *Corpus Reformatorum*, XXVI, 242, trans. Arthur Golding, *Sermons of Master John Calvin upon the Fifth Book of Moses called Deuteronomie* (London, 1583), pp. 179-180.
64. Quoted in Hoekema, "Covenant . . . in Calvin," p. 145 from Golding, *op. cit.*, p. 913b. See Hoekema, pp. 140-144, for further examples of Calvin's teachings on the above points.

John Preston's comments on Genesis 17, claiming that such condescension of God, amounting to "mutual obligation," is another Puritan invention. Here Miller's note reads, "The innovation of this theology upon the theology of Calvin becomes apparent when its interpretation of Biblical texts is compared with him. Calvin, for instance, finds no such proposal in Genesis, XVII . . . ."[65] Had he turned to the more obvious source than the *Institutes,* he would have found that Calvin in his *Commentary* on Genesis 17 represents God as saying, "whereas I owe thee nothing, I condescend graciously to engage thee in a mutual covenant."[66]

Calvin also used the covenant of grace to urge man's moral responsibilities in a way almost identical with that which Miller attributes to Puritan ingenuity. Miller claims that Calvin "simply disregarded" the problems in motivation implicit in *unconditional* election, whereas the great achievement of the Puritans was their resolution of such problems by developing a "conditional covenant."[67] However, as Anthony Hoekema in his fine study of Calvin's covenant teaching observes, "Calvin did not hesitate to speak of conditions of the covenant."[68] Already in the *Institutes* Calvin, speaking of God's rejection of some men, says, "For the condition had been laid down that they should faithfully keep God's covenant which they faithlessly violated."[69] In his sermons on Deuteronomy he elaborates on such moral obligations regarding the elect:

> For this reason we must be aroused and spurred on by his promises to serve him. Thus we see how the conditional promises shall not be in vain in respect to us, namely, when they are referred to the freely bestowed goodness of God, where he receives us though we are not worthy to be so received. . . .[70]

Surely this is precisely the emphasis which Miller thought was so novel with the Puritans. Moreover, it makes clear what was clear also to the Puritans (but not consistently so in Miller's account of them), that God accepts the good works of the elect not because they fulfill the conditions of the covenant, but in spite of the fact that they do not. The conditions of the covenant "are real, but not meritorious."[71] Only with this balance, which the Puritans following Calvin maintained, could they avoid the Arminian implications which Miller reads into the covenant of grace.

It must be admitted, of course, that Calvin was not a covenant theologian in the sense that Ames or Preston was. The covenant doc-

287

---

65. "Marrow," p. 61n.
66. *Commentary on Genesis,* Calvin Translation Society edition (Edinburgh, 1847), p. 444; cf. Moeller, "Puritan Covenant Theology," p. 49, and Hoekema," Covenant . . . in Calvin," p. 143.
67. NEM, p. 395; cf. "Marrow,' p. 88.
68. Hoekema, "Covenant . . . in Calvin," p. 155. Hoekema's study makes no reference to Miller.
69. *Institutes,* III, xxi, 6 (Battles translation).
70. Quoted in Hoekema, "Covenant . . . in Calvin," p. 147 from Golding, *op. cit.,* pp. 923-24. See Hoekema, pp. 144, 155-161 for numerous other examples of how Calvin developed this doctrine, together with a valuable exposition.
71. Hoekema, "Covenant . . . in Calvin," p. 155.

trine is not conspicuous in much of his work. Furthermore, he did not
extend the terminology to concepts such as the "covenant of works,"
the "covenant of creation," the "covenant of nature," or the "church
covenant."[72] Nevertheless, there is sufficient evidence to support Hoekema's contention that, although the covenant of grace was not the one
all-controlling principle in Calvin's theology, it was (at least by the
time of the Deuteronomy sermons) "the key to Calvin's understanding of the God-man relationship."[73]

The question of whether the Puritans received their basic notions
of the covenant directly from Calvin or from somewhere else remains,
despite several competent studies of the subject,[74] a moot point. One
reason may be that by the Puritan era the covenant idea was already
so generally disseminated that it could have been found almost anywhere. A further explanation suggests itself as well. Since Calvin
developed the implications of the covenant doctrine in his Deuteronomy
sermons preached during 1555 and 1556, and since this was the very
time that a considerable number of the Marian exiles were in Geneva, is it not possible that some of those Englishmen tutored in covenant doctrine from Calvin's pulpit carried the teaching, nearly full
grown, back to Elizabethan England?[75]

Whether or not the covenant doctrine was derived directly from
Calvin, it is abundantly clear that with regard to the covenant of
grace and its uses the teachings of New England's Puritans were consistent with those of the Genevan reformer.

At the end of these critical remarks it is important to point out
that the vast majority of what Miller says about the Puritan mind
still stands. The *New England Mind* remains one of the great master-
pieces in American intellectual history. Its flaws are few and, except
for those concerning Calvinism and the covenant of grace, are matters of emphasis that add as much as they detract. In almost every
case Miller at least *mentions* those aspects of Puritanism that do not
fit the main themes of the drama he is portraying. Miller's excellence
resided in his ability to read between the lines and then to translate
seventeenth century statements into twentieth century meanings. The
result is a shift in balance. When Miller dwells extensively on what
is between the lines, the contents of the lines themselves often become
buried in the middle of paragraphs. When he interprets Puritan thought
for his contemporary audience, concepts which the Puritans themselves considered most essential are lost among the riches of the comments of the twentieth century observer.

72. Cf. Trinterud, "Origins of Puritanism," p. 48.
73. Hoekema, "Covenant . . . in Calvin," p. 140; cf. p. 134.
74. See especially, Trinterud, "Origins of Puritanism"; Moeller, "Puritan Covenant Theology"; and Emerson, "Calvin and Covenant Theology."
75. This suggestion would be supported by Moeller's evidence of the influence of the Genevan Bible of 1560 in disseminating covenant views in England; "Puritan Covenant
Theology," p. 57.

The quality of Miller's rehabilitation of the Puritan image should not be taken lightly either. His work was a revision, and like all revisions errs somewhat in the other extreme. Certainly Miller played fewer historical tricks on the Puritans than did his American predecessors. His contribution to both understanding and appreciating Puritanism is invaluable. He does, however, restore the Puritan image at the expense of important aspects of Puritan theology and religion. When we remember, as Miller has demonstrated, that the Puritans were tough-minded men of the Renaissance, let us recall also that they were uncompromising Christians and (in the twentieth century view) bigoted Calvinists. As for the thesis that the covenant of grace represented a revision of Calvinism, Miller has created a myth that has been so elegantly presented and widely repeated that it will be difficult to destroy.

289

Will and Intellect in the New England Mind

T HERE was probably more debate at seventeenth-century Harvard on the nature of the will than on any other topic in moral philoso-phy. At least thirty commencement *theses* and *questiones* before 1700 directly or indirectly pertained to this problem, and, repeatedly, antithetical positions were taken, evidence in itself of the vitality of the subject. This fact alone calls for some attention to the details of the controversy. Beyond that interest, a study of the will in its relation to the intellect and the appetites brings one promptly into the midst of some complicated problems of moral psychology, and it is possible to show in this context that there were important connections between these seventeenth-century debates and the more familiar eighteenth-century notions of moral psychology, such as were current, for example, during the Great Awakening.

The difficulty in our time in treating the subject of will is not only the typical one common to terms that have multiple and confused meanings —such as, for example, "reason" or "nature"—but that, in addition, the meanings of "will" that are particularly relevant to understanding the issues in the seventeenth century are now archaic. It is hard to say what is in the popular mind at present, but most of modern psychology seems to do quite nicely without any concept of the will at all. So profoundly has human psychology and psychological theory changed that talking about will is something like talking in medical physiology about bodily humors and the four elements.[1] What can the notion of will as "rational appetite" mean today, what personal or introspective reference do we have to it? There is hardly a surviving verbal echo of the idea. Similarly,

* Mr. Fiering is Editor of Publications, Institute of Early American History and Culture. He is indebted to Ms. Carol Esler of Williamsburg, Va., and Mr. John Mazaitis of Georgetown University for Latin translations, and to Mr. Mazaitis and Professors Thomas McTighe of Georgetown University and William Frankena of the University of Michigan for critical readings of an early draft of this article.

[1] There are signs of some change, however, especially among the psychotherapists. See, for example, Leslie H. Farber, *The Ways of the Will: Essays toward a Psychology and Psychopathology of Will* (New York, 1966); and Rollo May, *Love and Will* (New York, 1969).

the will, in the nominative, as the faculty of choice or decision, is remote from modern connotations of "will." Under these circumstances it is not surprising the whole subject has not received the careful attention it truly deserves if we are to be faithful to seventeenth-century concerns.[2]

The central problem at seventeenth-century Harvard was not the famous one of free will versus determinism as it occurs in either of its classic forms. Insofar as the free will problem was essentially a theological debate, such as that which took place between St. Augustine and Pelagius, or Luther and Erasmus, or Calvinists and Arminians, it was a relatively dormant issue in New England where the doctrine of predestination by free grace and man's "inability" were undisputed dogmas. The other classic form of the problem of free will, that which was provoked by the assertion of the determinist hypothesis based not upon God's sovereignty but upon the law of natural causation in all known phenomena, found its modern expression in English thought principally in reaction to the writing of Thomas Hobbes and did not reach New England until almost the end of the century, thus playing no role in the period we are presently examining. In fact, on the broad matter of human freedom there was considerable unanimity before the rise of naturalistic determinism. Everybody, including Calvin, believed that man was free enough to be held responsible before God for his sins and before other men for his crimes. It was a truism passed on from virtually all of the ancient moralists as well as the schoolmen that praise and blame implied some degree of moral autonomy. Beyond that consensus there was little need to go. Man was held to be self-actuating and spontaneous, a voluntary creature exempt to some degree at least from the bonds of

291

---

[2] In my discussion of will I have been most instructed by Thomas E. Davitt, S.J., *The Nature of Law* (St. Louis, 1951); Anthony Levi, S.J., *French Moralists: The Theory of the Passions, 1585 to 1649* (Oxford, 1964); E. Gilson, *La Liberté chez Descartes et la Théologie* (Paris, 1913); Vernon J. Bourke, *Will in Western Thought: An Historico-Critical Survey* (New York, 1964), a useful book which is not entirely reliable; and Archibald Alexander, *Theories of the Will in the History of Philosophy* (New York, 1898), which studies only the few major figures, most of whom were not key influences on American thought in our period. With regard to early American thought, the theory of the will before Jonathan Edwards has hardly been studied at all. In his 100-page introduction to Edwards's *Freedom of the Will*, Vol. I of *The Works of Jonathan Edwards* (New Haven, 1957), Paul Ramsey refers to almost nothing in the 17th century and accepts the widely-held assumption that Edwards's interest in the will dated from his reading of Locke. But Locke himself was writing in the context of the great 17th-century debate concerning the will.

nature which controlled all the rest of the creation. With the angels and God Himself man was ordinarily moved not by "coaction," to use the terminology of the time, but by "counsel." Or, in other words, freedom was characterized simply by the absence of constraint or compulsion in behavior, a condition which was not in any way diminished by the exercise of rational choice.

What then was at the core of the controversy which for fifty years agitated the brains of the tiny group of scholars and tutors passing through the college in Cambridge, Massachusetts, and the minds of similar classes of men at other university centers in the West? Broadly speaking, the challenging question was not whether or not man is free but wherein his freedom lies. In response to this question there was a choice of only two general answers. It was clear that man's freedom was somehow part of his higher faculties, that is, part of his rational soul rather than his animal or his vegetative soul, for if freedom could be traced to his animal soul (also called the sensitive soul), then the animal kingdom, too, would share in this privileged liberty, which was unthinkable and contrary to accepted observation. Animals by definition were dominated solely by material appetites. With the field narrowed down then to the rational soul, within that focus there were two possibilities only, corresponding in emphasis to the two faculties of the rational soul: freedom as exclusively an act of the will, or freedom as an act of both intellect and will in inseparable unity. Here was the nub of the problem with surprising ramifications in many directions.

Before looking at the content of this debate and some of its corollaries, it will be clarifying if we devote a few words to a description of those elements in the psychological theory of the time to which nearly all parties agreed and make some effort to provide the rationale for this psychology so that it does not remain insuperably alien. Too many history books simply refer to something called "faculty psychology" which everybody is supposed to know is bad, and this serves as an end to any further explication. Frequently, too, in this connection, John Locke's well-known critique of "faculties" is cited, as though *all* past psychological reasoning was easily discarded following upon his magic words and thereby a neat line drawn between old-fashioned and modern. But Locke was addressing himself here, as in several other famous arguments in his *Essay Concerning Human Understanding,* to the common abuses in late scholastic philosophy rather than to the best scholarly way of thinking,

292

which in many of its parts was not so far from his own ideas. Indeed, in this area of the faculties, Locke was close enough in 1690 to the traditional psychology taught at Harvard in 1650 to be easily used as an excellent example of the inherited teaching regarding the general powers of the rational soul: "This, at least, I think evident,—That we find in ourselves a power to begin or forbear, continue or end several thoughts of our minds, and motions of our bodies, barely by a choice or preference of the mind ordering, or as it were commanding, the doing or not doing such or such a particular action. This power which the mind has thus to order . . . or to prefer . . . is that which we call the *Will*."[3]   293

The other power of the mind which Locke recognized was the intellect, or what he usually called the understanding. Of course, in his analysis of the precise acts of the understanding he diverged from tradition, but it is significant that in accordance with centuries of earlier speculation he conceived of understanding and will as the sole rational faculties. His complaint was against the hypostatization of the faculties, such that "this way of speaking of *faculties* has misled many into a confused notion of . . . distinct agents in us," each with "their several provinces and authorities," and able to "command, obey, and perform several actions, as so many distinct beings." But he ended by affirming what was in fact the standard view: "Faculty, ability, and power . . . are but different names of the same things,"[4] a matter which was clear enough in an age of Latin scholarship when *facultas* meant just that: ability or power and no more. Two Harvard commencement *theses* from 1675 and 1684 respectively said as much: "The faculties of the rational soul are distinguished from the soul only notionally," and "Intellect and will are the soul as understanding and as willing."[5]

There was then nothing mysterious about faculties, nor is there anything intrinsically abhorrent in them. Locke in the Cartesian manner

---

[3] *An Essay Concerning Human Understanding,* ed. Alexander Campbell Fraser (New York, 1894), Bk. II, chap. xxi, 5.

[4] *Ibid.,* 6-21.

[5] "*Facultates animae rationalis Ratione tantum differunt ab Anima*"; "*Intellectus & Voluntas sunt anima intelligens & volens.*" In Appendix B to *Harvard College in the Seventeenth Century,* II (Cambridge, Mass., 1936), Samuel Eliot Morison has reprinted virtually all of the surviving printed copies of the commencement broadsides to the year 1708. The two *theses* cited here, however, are from a manuscript booklet in the Harvard University Archives, Cambridge, Mass., which contains a valuable selection of early *theses* (there is another booklet of *quaestiones*), most of which are not in Morison.

founded the faculty of will on internal experience; it is a power, he
said, that we find in ourselves. This explanation, however, is hardly
enough to account for the immutability for centuries of the picture of the
mind as having principally the dual powers of intellect and will. The
strength of this model probably depended, in fact, rather little upon recurrent introspection or observation. Its strength lay instead in its
congruence with a series of other unquestioned distinctions. It was a
commonplace that the intellect responded to the truth, whereas the will
responded to goodness, and thus logic and ethics could be distinguished
along these lines, the former concerned with the well-ordering of the
intellect toward truth, and the latter the well-ordering of the will toward
good. Thus, the great ideal ends of man, the true and the good,
unknown to the beasts, were capable of realization through man's possession of a rational soul which had these two special powers. There
was also a parallel between the powers of intellect and will and the
rational functions of reasoning and choosing. The will (*voluntas*)
which is directed to the good makes choices (*arbitria*) in relation to its
end, in a similar fashion as the intellect reasons to its special end of
truth. At the same time God also, by analogy, had these two powers
of intellect and will. From the creature's point of view, the first made
His laws intelligible, and by the second He determined all things.

The distinction made frequently in modern writing between thought
and action continues to some extent the idea behind the division into
intellect and will. Of course, there are important differences too, particularly in that the term "action" lacks a teleological overtone that was
nearly always present in the idea of will up to the seventeenth century.
But as in the distinction between thought and action, it was generally
held that the will was blind—the phrase itself reappears constantly—or
at least purblind; whereas, on the other hand, intellect was passive, in
the sense that it was incapable in itself of sponsoring motion.[6] Thus,
independent deficiencies or limitations made intellect and will comple-
mentary and unitary. Both were needed for the wholesome functioning
of man's higher soul.

In St. Thomas Aquinas, who was very well known in early seventeenth-century philosophy and was cited occasionally in student notebooks that have survived from Harvard in this period, the rational

[6] There was also an active side to intellect—its ability to abstract intelligible
species from material phenomena.

294

faculties of will and intellect are described in a unified way that might well have satisfied Locke.[7] Will and intellect "include one another in their acts," Thomas wrote, "because the intellect understands that the will wills, and the will wills the intellect to understand."[8] Or, in different terms, Thomas said, "truth and good include one another; for truth is something good, otherwise it would not be desirable; and good is something true, otherwise it would not be intelligible." Thus, when the mind apprehends an object, it has the power both of considering it as true and willing it as good, but never one entirely without the other.[9] In the physiological work of William Ames, the seventeenth-century Puritan theologian most highly esteemed in New England, there is a similar gloss: "Intellect and will differ neither from the rational soul nor from one another essentially, but only differ formally or by a formal notion, namely, with respect to intrinsic operation. Will is intellect as external, for the purpose of possessing and making what it knows. Intellect is will as immanent, for the purpose of understanding."[10]

295

Other examples could be given of this widely accepted analysis that will and intellect were simply two facets of the one characteristic of the higher soul, namely, reason.[11] But there is more to be said about the will,

[7] St. Thomas Aquinas is referred to and quoted in several places, for example, in John Holyoke's notebook of 1662-1663, a manuscript in the Harvard University Archives. Solomon Stoddard owned a couple of works by Thomas when he was a graduate student at Harvard in 1664. See Norman S. Fiering, "Solomon Stoddard's Library in 1664," *Harvard Library Bulletin*, XX (1972). In 1682 Noahdiah Russell bought from the Harvard Library some duplicate copies of works by Thomas Aquinas, as did Cotton Mather. See the fragment from Russell's diary, "Copy of the Diary of Noahdiah Russell, Tutor at Harvard College, Beginning Anno Dom. 1682," *New England Historical and Genealogical Register*, VII (1853), 57; and Clarence S. Brigham, "Harvard College Library Duplicates, 1682," Colonial Society of Massachusetts, *Publications*, XVIII (1917), 409-417.

[8] Fathers of the English Dominican Province, trans., *The "Summa Theologica" of St. Thomas Aquinas*, IV (London, 1938), Pt. I, Q. 82, art. 4.

[9] *Ibid.*, Pt. I, Q. 79, art. 11.

[10] The notebook of William Partridge, from 1686, in the Beinecke Library, Yale University, New Haven, contains a section entitled "Gulielmi Amesii Theses Physiologica" from which this quotation is taken. See n. 14 below.

[11] Thus, Bishop Edward Reynolds, in his *Treatise of the Passions and Faculties of the Soule of Man* (1640), states that understanding and will together may be called by the one name of "Reason." See *The Works of Edward Reynolds* (London, 1679 [orig. publ. 1658]), 633. Reynolds's treatise was widely dispersed in New England. See, for example, Evan Evans, "Literary References in New England Diaries 1700 to 1730" (Ph.D. diss., Harvard University, 1934), 149; and Worthington C. Ford, *The Boston Book Market, 1679-1700* (Boston, 1917), 74.

particularly in its guise as rational appetite. In the traditional view, if man had not a faculty of will, he alone in all the creation would lack a natural inclination to an appointed end. Every animal and every plant had inbuilt instincts, appetites, or tendencies that led them unfailingly to perform their special vital duties and functions on earth. Man, too, had animal appetites to guide him to preserve his body and to reproduce himself. These lower ends, however, did not encompass all of his purposes. On the other hand, his intellect which was clearly capable of *knowing* ideal values could not of itself *desire* them. But in the will was found that exclusive appetite which sought what was true for higher beings alone. Only man had a rational appetite added to sensitive appetites, that is, a will, and this trait was roughly analogous to the role of instinct in lower animals. Such reasoning comprised the background of the dictum, repeatedly expressed in scholastic philosophy, that no person can will evil as evil. The will is always directed toward what appears at the time to be good.

296

In anticipation we should note that when this meaning of the will as the appetite directed toward the rationally conceived good was finally abandoned, the term "will" itself lost a good deal of its former usefulness in philosophical anthropology. What was left was still the idea of the will as an elective faculty, man's *proairetic* power in Aristotle's terms, but this power was easily absorbed into the purely intellective functions of comparison and judgment. And for the rest, that is, the need to account for the active or conative side of human nature, the passions or affections of the sensitive appetite were sufficient. Thus, Thomas Hobbes's famous definition of the will as simply the "last appetite in deliberating" denied, in effect, that there was any such thing as a uniquely rational appetite.

It is clear from both the long-enduring status of the will as one of man's specific rational faculties and from its comparatively rapid downfall as a viable concept in the seventeenth and eighteenth centuries that the idea of the will was almost as much a cosmic as a psychological unit; in its history is reflected the most profound changes in outlook about man's place in the universe.

Enough has been said now to enable us to consider in greater detail the controversy at Harvard over the relation of will to intellect. For this purpose we can begin with the more established view by quoting from a notebook kept in 1686 by a Harvard student named William Partridge,

who was most likely a sophomore at the time of writing. Partridge's
notes were extracted, probably indirectly, from the Aristotelian natural
philosophy text of Henricus Gutberleth (d. 1635), a teacher at Herborn
in Germany.[12] There was nothing unusual about using textbooks seventy
years old, nor was there anything anomalous in finding a discussion of
the will treated under natural philosophy, which undertook to study man
insofar as he was part of the natural world. In the seventeenth
century, when the ordering of the disciplines was quite different than
at present, opinion on the will may be gathered, indeed must be, from
work on theology, on moral philosophy, and on natural philosophy.   297
According to William Ames, will was the last subject studied in natural
philosophy or physics, and the first to be studied in theology. Partridge
begins with a definition in Latin, which may be translated as follows:
"Will is a human disposition by which man freely desires the good
known by the intellect."[13] Then follows a scholium in English:

Even as the understanding is occupied in the knowledge of good and
bad; so the will is busied in desiring of that which is good, but known
by the understanding, whence the rational appetite is called, whereby it
is differenced from the sensitive appetite, which proceeds not from the
understanding, but from the sense. for the understanding shows to the
will, what is to be embraced and what is to be rejected: then the will
desireth and governeth those inferiour faculties, to wit, the sensitive
and locomotive appetite. Moreover the good which the will desireth
is either good really or apparently, for as the understanding judgeth,
so the will desireth: Sometimes it judgeth that good which is
evil . . . ; so the will [*in that case*] desireth what is part of man's
misery. here the rule is: the error of the will follows the error of the
judgment. Oftentimes likewise the vehemency of the appetites anticipates
and obscures the judgment of the understanding, . . . so that a man
runs to evil with violence. . . . To the will is opposed the aversation
of evil known by the understanding, [which] for the sake of teaching
we may call nilling. from volition and nolition ariseth an intellectual
affection [*i.e., a disposition*] whereby a man is moved and excited to

---

[12] Partridge heads this section "Henrici Gutberleth philosophia naturalis Liber
primus, qui est de corpore naturali, in genere." This probably refers to Gutberleth's
Physicae, hoc est, naturalis philosophiae (Herborn, 1613).
[13] "*Voluntas est hominis affectio, quâ quod homo intellectu cognovit bonum,
liberè appetit.*"

follow after that which is good, and to avoid that which is evil, [*as these are*] known to be such by the understanding.[14]

This, as I have said, was the common and more established view of the relation of will to intellect. The understanding shows to the will what is to be embraced or rejected. As the understanding judges, so the will desires. The will is itself never culpable in the case of moral error, since it invariably follows the judgment of the intellect. But because of the misjudgment of the intellect it may unwittingly choose the apparent rather than the real good. The will as the rational appetite ought to govern the lower sensitive appetites, though it may happen that unruly, vehement, sensitive appetites, or passions, will carry one forward independently of intellect and will, anticipating and obscuring rational judgment. It should be noticed, too, that the standard concept of the technical opposite to willing and volition, namely nilling and nolition, suggests the degree to which many of the psychologists of the time were quite free of a reification of the will and were thinking in terms of function and power more than psychic entities.

298

This example from Partridge is neither complete nor especially precise, but it does give a rough picture of what may be broadly termed the *intellectualist* position.[15] It was the most common opinion in the seventeenth century and the centuries preceding. It had the support of Thomas Aquinas behind it, as well as that of figures like Cardinal Cajetan (d. 1534), who did a major commentary on Thomas, and Robert

---

[14] Partridge graduated in the class of 1689 at Harvard and died four years later. See John Langdon Sibley, *Biographical Sketches of Graduates of Harvard University*, III (Cambridge, Mass., 1885), 416-417. Partridge's notebook, partly in Latin and partly in English, is exceptionally legible and contains excerpts from three logic systems: Charles Morton's, Downame's Ramist logic, and the Legrande-Brattle logic. It is of some interest that this notebook came into the hands first of Timothy Edwards, who succeeded Partridge at Harvard by a couple of years, and then of his famous son, Jonathan Edwards, whose autograph appears several times in the book with the dates 1718, 1719, and 1720, along with a few pages of unreadable notes. It may also have been owned by Jonathan Edwards, Jr., in 1751. The notebook is in the Beinecke Library.

[15] The term "intellectualism" may also be used to denote a theory of the relation of intellect to the passions and affections, which is a closely related but not identical concept. A great deal of clarity is added to discussions of 18th-century psychology as well as 17th when the casual use of the term "rationalism" is sharply curtailed and kept for specific purposes in metaphysical and epistemological theory. As a *psychological* term "rationalism" has little use beyond that which is already better served by the term "intellectualism."

Bellarmine (d. 1621), the great seventeenth-century Catholic polemicist, all of whom were highly respected by and influential upon both Protestant and Catholic scholars.[16] Among the Protestant theologians themselves, a number of influential figures like Theodore Beza, Girolamo Zanchi, Johann Piscator, and Johann Gerhard were also intellectualists.[17] A particularly important representative of a subtle type of intellectualism in the seventeenth century was the Scots theologian John Cameron (d. 1625), who taught mostly in France.[18] Of four moral philosophy texts used at Harvard in the seventeenth century that I have reviewed, only one is directly opposed to the intellectualist structure. Two others state unconditionally that there can be no willing without a prior judgment of the intellect.[19] In another notebook kept by a Harvard student in the seventeenth century, the point is made effectively with a quote

299

[16] See Davitt, *Nature of Law, passim*, on Cajetan and Bellarmine. An eloquent defense of intellectualism, defined more broadly than usual, is Father Pierre Rousselot's *The Intellectualism of Saint Thomas* (London, 1935). Rousselot makes intellectualism into a metaphysical doctrine, however, which might better be termed "rationalism"! He defines intellectualism as "the doctrine which places the supreme value and intensity of life in an act of intellect, that sees in this act the radical and essential good, and regards all things else as good only in so far as they participate in it." (p. 3) There has been considerable controversy about the degree and nature of Thomas's intellectualism.

[17] Matthias Nethenus, Hugh Visscher, and Karl Reuter, *William Ames*, ed. and trans. Douglas Horton (Cambridge, Mass., 1965), 183, 202, n. 155. This work is a compilation by Horton of three widely-dispersed works about Ames. Reuter is dealing in these sections with the intellectualist conception of *faith* to which Ames was opposed, not the psychological issue in particular. He also mentions Keckerman, and Maccovius, Ames's colleague at Franeker. The psychological issue is treated directly on p. 258. See also Robert P. Scharlemann, *Thomas Aquinas and John Gerhard* (New Haven, 1964), 161. In Brian G. Armstrong, *Calvinism and the Amyraut Heresy: Protestant Scholasticism and Humanism in Seventeenth-Century France* (Madison, 1969), there is some useful information on the intellectualism of the controversial French theologian at Saumur Academy, Moïse Amyraut (d. 1664), but Armstrong does not understand the history of this psychological theory, its significance in theology, or its future development, and the concept of intellectualism never emerges as anything distinct from something known vaguely as "rationalism."

[18] Cameron's ideas are presented in a biased context in Armstrong, *Calvinism and Amyraut Heresy*, 42-70, where there is also a bibliography.

[19] The four works are: Theophilus Golius, *Epitome Doctrinae Moralis. Ex decem libris Ethicorum Aristotelis ad Nicomachum collecta* (1592); Eustache de Saint Paul, *Ethica* from his *Summa Philosophiae quadripartita, de rebus Dialecticis, Ethicis, Physics, et Mathematicis* (1609); Franco Burgersdicius (Burgersdyck), *Idea Philosophiae Tum Moralis, Tum Naturalis* (1631); and Adrian Heereboord, *Meletemata Philosophica* (1654).

from the English bishop Robert Sanderson (d. 1663): "All voluntary
actions are done with some deliberation, more or less; because it is the
nature of the will to Consist with the Understanding in Every act, else
it would be Irrational and bruitish."[20] Without its counterpart in intellect
the will becomes simply a brute desire and is indistinguishable from
sensitive appetite.

The commencement *theses* and *quaestiones* from early Harvard summarized the intellectualist theory in the form of a Latin axiom that was
constantly repeated: *"Voluntas determinatur ab ultimo Intellectus practici Judicio"* (The will is determined by the last judgment of the
practical intellect). These words appear in some form in 1666, 1671,
1678, 1686, and 1692, and we have only a remnant of what may have
existed. The great virtue of this theory was that it grounded human
conduct in reason, that is, it demanded at once that (1) all moral decision and action be accountable in terms of intelligible ends or reasons,
and also (2) that reason be, to use the Stoic term, the *hegemonikon* or
the ruler of the soul.[21] The latter proposition followed from the former. If
reason alone was capable of participation in the divine mind and of
discovering moral norms, whether these norms were considered to be,
as in Aristotle, the proper mean between the extremes, or some other
standard of intelligible good, then this unique capability of reason, that
of knowing the universal good, entitled it to rule in the soul. And, perhaps, it was also such thinking that led to the firm conviction that in

[20] John Hancock's Commonplace Book, 1687 to 1751?, Houghton Library,
Harvard University. Hancock graduated A.B. from Harvard in 1689 and was the
grandfather of the famous signer. The quote is from an edition of Sanderson's
sermons. In an anonymous tract spawned by the Puritan revolution, *The Ancient
Bounds, or Liberty of Conscience* . . . , the intellectualist thesis on the relation of
will to intellect is used as the basis of a defense of liberty of conscience: "Now
this liberty of trying and judging [religious doctrines] is in vain if there be not
a liberty of profession; and to hinder this were a most tyrannical usurpation over
that connection which God hath made between the act of the understanding and
the will, whereby *voluntas sequitur dictamen intellectus,* and to put asunder what
God hath joined together, and indeed to violate the law of God and nature. A man
cannot will contrary to the precedent act of judgment; he wills weakly without an
act of judgment preceding. To force a man to a profession or practice which he
wills not, nay, which he nills, is to offer unto God a sacrifice of violence on the
part of the compulsor, and an unreasonable service on the part of the compelled,
and therefore necessarily unacceptable." A. S. P. Woodhouse, ed., *Puritanism and
Liberty* . . . (Chicago, 1951), 259.
[21] On the stoic term *hegemonikon,* see Vernon J. Bourke, *History of Ethics*
(Garden City, N. Y., 1968), 35-37.

fact reason did always rule in some fashion, even in the case of error or wickedness, when it mistakenly chose the lesser or partial good.

Intellectualism has, of course, the strongest ties with classical philosophy, and it has been suggested that not until the Patristic era is there to be found anything contrary. The only states of mind which Plato and Aristotle recognize "as immediate antecedents of bad acts," writes the philosopher Henry Sidgwick, "are (1) predominance of irrational impulse overpowering rational judgment or prompting to action without deliberation, and (2) mistaken choice of evil under the appearance of good." Now Sidgwick also notes that this intellectualism involved the classical moralists in a rather uncomfortable and unwelcome determinism, for it established that all action was "'necessitated'—as Plato expressly says—by causes that lie in time before the bad volition."[22] But, as we have noted, it was the universal opinion that moral responsibility entailed some kind of freedom, so there was here the possibility of a troublesome inconsistency.

Whatever the case may be with the ancients (and the exact nature of Aristotle's intellectualism in particular) by the thirteenth century A.D., shortly after the recovery of the bulk of the Aristotelian texts, intellectualist moral psychology was already causing some disturbance within the Church. In the famous condemnation of 219 propositions by the bishop of Paris in 1277, which counted certain of the teachings of Thomas Aquinas among its objects for censure, the doctrine that "the will necessarily pursues what is firmly held by reason, and that it cannot abstain from that which reason dictates," was expressly cited for heterodoxy.[23] This move was one of the stimuli behind the development in the thought of John Duns Scotus and others of an important rival theory of action, that which attributed to the will a self-determining power. The best known example of the reasoning of this school is the famous case of "Buridan's Ass," placed equally between two equally desirable bales of hay between which there is no intellectual foundation for choice. In such an instance, it was argued, unless one is to remain paralyzed with

301

[22] Henry Sidgwick, *Outlines of the History of Ethics* (New York, 1886), 69. Aristotle has been most closely studied in this regard by James Jerome Walsh, *Aristotle's Conception of Moral Weakness* (New York, 1963). Walsh warns against "easy generalizations about 'Greek intellectualism'" but interprets Aristotle as an intellectualist, as did Sidgwick.

[23] Ralph Lerner and Muhsin Mahdi, eds., *Medieval Political Philosophy: A Sourcebook* (Glencoe, Ill., 1963), 335-354, is the only printing in English of these propositions.

indecision forever, an arbitrary will must take the initiative. An ass lacking rational faculties could not solve this problem, the Scotists said, but a human will could. Here one finds the origins of a concept of free will which implies not only the freedom of the agent from constraint or impediment in action but also a freedom from determinism or necessity.[24] The significance for our purposes of this school of thought, which might be called *scholastic voluntarism*, lies in its vigorous rejuvenation in sixteenth- and seventeenth-century Jesuit theology, and its entrance into the philosophical melee between Protestants and Catholics over the nature of the will. About scholastic voluntarism in the seventeenth century and its influence on the philosophy of mind in America we will have more to say shortly.

302

But there was still another alternative to Aristotelian and Thomist intellectualism, one with different roots and different results than the scholastic. It did not grow out of opposition to determinism; on the contrary, it was closely associated with it. We have mentioned that it is sometimes asserted that the development of an alternative to intellectualist moral psychology had to wait until the Patristic period. The original inspiration for its appearance at that time, it is said, lies in the striking lament of St. Paul in Rom. 7:14-28:

What I do is not what I want to do, but what I detest. But if what I do is against my will, it means that I agree with the law and hold it to be admirable . . . the will to do good is there, the deed is not. The good which I want to do, I fail to do; but what I do is the wrong which is against my will; and if what I do is against my will, clearly it is no longer I who am the agent, but sin that has its lodging in me.

I discover this principle, then: that when I want to do the right, only the wrong is within my reach. In my inmost self I delight in the law of God, but perceive that there is in my bodily members a different law, fighting against the law that my reason approves and making me a prisoner under the law that is in my members, the law of sin. Miserable creature that I am, who is there to rescue me out of this body doomed to death?[25]

Certainly by the time of St. Augustine there is present a psychology of the will that is of quite a different character than the prevailing

[24] See Bourke, *Will*, 21, 85.
[25] Quoted from *The New English Bible*. See Alexander, *Theories of the Will*, 84: "For the first time in the history of thought, Paul presents from a subjective point of view the conflict of a man between two moral alternatives."

ancient pagan view. But it is a curious fact that in the seventeenth
century, when the intellectualist model was challenged, it was usually
neither in the name of Paul nor Augustine. Strangely, it was rather
the Latin poet, Ovid, whose words were constantly recalled. In the *Metamorphoses* (VII, 20) the author has the dramatic heroine Medea proclaim: "*Video meliora proboque; Deteriora sequor*" (I see and approve
the better course; I follow the worse). Ovid was here only imitating
the anguished cry of Medea in Euripides's great tragedy, but it was
Ovid's lines that were quoted in hundreds of ethics and physics treatises
in order to illustrate a main difficulty with the intellectualist schema.[26]
I am personally convinced that the Augustinian challenge to intellectualism did have essentially Judeo-Christian roots and that the use of
Ovid or Euripides was primarily a matter of convention and convenience, a point which perhaps will become evident further on. On the
other hand, it is worth noting that E. R. Dodds in his important study
The Greeks and the Irrational has indicated that the internal conflict
of Euripides's Medea was already a subject of controversy among the
ancient Stoics and that Euripides was almost certainly engaged in a
conscious effort to refute the Socratic theory that virtuous behavior was
identical with right knowledge.[27] The gist of what may be called the
Medean paradox (or St. Paul's similar dilemma) is, of course, that much
experience seems to testify to a human capacity for deliberate, conscious
choice made contrary to the continuously known higher good, or in
other words, testifies to the existence of an independent and sometimes
perverse will.

The Medean paradox or the example of Paul's dilemma could be
argued away, however, for they were more in the nature of problems
than doctrines. Through an intricate analysis of "velleity," "volition,"
"intention," and other such psychological phenomena, the intellectualists
were able to maintain their position. As the Leyden professor Franco
Burgersdyck wrote in a text preferred at Harvard, the battle in the soul

[26] A curious example is Benjamin Franklin's "Silence Dogood" Letter, No. 14,
printed in the *New-England Courant* (Boston), Oct. 8, 1722, where Franklin excerpts from *The Spectator*, No. 185, a long passage which contains a reference to
"that trite Passage which we see quoted in almost every System of Ethicks, . . .
Video meliore proboque/Deteriora sequor." Leonard W. Labaree *et al.*, eds., *The
Papers of Benjamin Franklin*, I (New Haven, 1959), 44.
[27] (Berkeley and Los Angeles, 1951), 186-187, 239-240, and particularly the
footnotes.

expressed typically in the *Video meliora* . . . does not take place between a rebellious will and the judgment of the intellect, or because of a departure of the will from the judgment of the intellect, but from a conflict or "fluctuation in the intellect when the intellect disapproves of the thing absolutely considered but approves of it relatively or with its circumstances. . . ." The will is divided, but the foundation of the division is in the intellect. Sometimes such a conflict was described as "woulding" to do the best, but "willing" to do the lesser.[28]

304   The most enduring and persistent antagonist to intellectualism in Western thought has been the Augustinian teaching concerning the will, the influence of which is seen in St. Anselm and St. Bernard before Scotus. The Augustinian teaching was probably more powerfully at work in the Christian anthropology of the seventeenth century than at any other time before or since, affecting equally Catholic and Protestant circles. In this doctrine the will is not identifiable as a rational appetite at all, except possibly in some perfected state of humanity. Nor is the will easily confinable to a particular operation of the rational soul; instead, it comes to be almost synonymous with the inner essence of the whole man, the battleground of God and the devil. The personal drama of salvation is enacted in the will, and on the will's ultimate orientation depends one's entire fate with God. The biblical term "heart" was used almost interchangeably with will in this sense, and the terms "love" and even "soul" itself are also substituted for it. Thus Augustine calls a "right will" "good love" and a "wrong will" "bad love," and insists that man's salvation hangs alone on the quality of his will or love, or, in other words, on the fundamental disposition of his heart.[29] It is love misdirected, not intellectual misjudgment, that is considered the source of moral evil in man, and in most respects the distinction between will and affections is obliterated. The sin of concupiscence which to some extent dominates all men is expressed in a rebellious will, the primary failing of which is its rejection of the dictates of right reason and revelation. In the same vein,

[28] Burgersdyck, *Idea Philosophiae Moralis* (1623), 65, 141, 310, 313; Burgersdyck, *Idea Philosophiae Naturalis* (1622), 99-100. See also Heereboord, *Meletemata*, 100, 108, 472-489, 692, 712.
[29] *The City of God against the Pagans*, IV, trans. Philip Levine (Cambridge, Mass., 1966), Bk. XIV, chap. vii; XII, i-iii, vi-ix. For a well-argued view, however, that the Augustine of the Jansenists and the Protestant pietists of the 17th century was not the real Augustine, see Nigel Abercrombie, *The Origins of Jansenism* (Oxford, 1936).

here is Luther in his exchange of letters with Erasmus on the will using an image taken directly from Augustine and which was also used by Calvin: "The human will is like a beast of burden. If God rides it, it wills and goes whence God wills. . . . If Satan rides it, it wills and goes where Satan wills. Nor may it choose to which rider it will run, nor which it will seek. But the riders themselves contend who shall have and hold it."[30] Obviously, Luther was not claiming that the will is free, except in its relation to any other of man's psychological powers or faculties. Its dependency is not on the intellect but on God. In this conception the will is not only rebellious to reason's control, but it is also by its nature not necessarily selective of the rationally apparent good. For there are perverse or demonic wills, too. In fact, without the assistance of divine grace, all wills are that way.

305

As was the case with intellectualism, from the first decade of Harvard until the end of the century there were commencement *theses* and *quaestiones* which upheld the voluntarist position, usually quite simply, by the negative assertion, "The will does not invariably follow the last dictate of the practical intellect," from which statement alone, however, it is impossible to tell whether it is scholastic or the quite different Augustinian voluntarism which is being affirmed.[31] The related *thesis* presented in 1647, 1677, and 1682, "*Voluntas non potest cogi*" (The will cannot be coerced), is much more clearly aligned with the Jesuit school, and a thesis of 1691, "*Indifferentia est de essentia liberi arbitrii*" (Indifference is the essence of free choice), extraordinarily so. The so-called "liberty of indifference" was the battle cry of the followers of the Jesuit theologian Luis de Molina (1535-1600) in opposition to both the intellectualism of the broadly defined Thomist school and the divine determinism of the Protestants. The several propositions at commencements, always in the negative, concerning the *scientia media,* the intermediate knowledge by which God knows future contingent events, also reveals the notice taken at Harvard of Molinism. But it was one thing for a Protestant college to take notice of Jesuit theology and another to defend it. More typical of Harvard certainly was the opposite opinion on the liberty of indifference expressed in the negative response of Timothy Edwards to his Master's *quaestio* in 1693, "*An indifferentia sit de Essentia liberi Arbitrii?*"

[30] Ernst F. Winter, trans. and ed., *Desiderius Erasmus and Martin Luther, Discourse on Free Will* (New York, 1961), 112; John Calvin, *Institutes of the Christian Religion,* ed. John T. McNeill, trans. Ford Lewis Battles (Philadelphia, 1960), Bk. II, chap. iv, 1.
[31] Aug. 9, 1653, and 1658, 1676, 1683, 1691.

Augustinian or pietistic voluntarism was unmistakably in evidence at the commencement of 1658 when Gershom Bulkeley, who later became a renowned physician in Connecticut, took as his Master's degree *quaestio* a slight variant of the famous proposition we have already mentioned: "*An Voluntas semper sequatur ultimum dictamen intellectus practici?*" (Whether the will invariably follows the last dictate of the practical intellect?) and answered in the negative. We do not have his full statement, but appended to his *quaestio* on the printed commencement broadside for that year is a Latin verse which runs as follows in literal translation:

306

How many times does it happen that a prince will spurn the dictates of his council, and though he sees the better way, follow the worse? Who would say that the cause of the angels' fall was the dictate of the mind? . . . Or who will tell me [*that a bad dictate was*] the cause of Adam's fall? There was in him no error of the intellect. There was no demon who was not a demon before; nor is there any error in the mind without sin. Therefore, it is the imperious will that drives one into vice, and when the mind offers good advice, the will says, "I don't like it; reason is against it." When will puts itself in reason's place, should you not rather call it nill? Therefore, the will does not invariably follow the dictates of the mind, but resembles Medea more than the deity.[32]

The implication of the last line is that only in God is there perfect integrity of intellect and will. Man's sinful nature is primarily a matter of perverse will, not intellectual error.

In manuscript there are several significant lengthier voluntarist statements from early Harvard, but they are best approached only after some preliminary discussion of contemporary influences on seventeenth-century New England. First of all, Harvard College, like almost every academic center in the West for a good part of the seventeenth century, was heavily indebted to the work of the Spanish Jesuit Francisco Suarez (d. 1619), the impact of whose writing in his own time is only now being adequately recognized.[33] Paul Dibon has called him the undisputed master of the art of disputation in an era when nearly all philosophical instruction

[32] Morison, *Harvard College*, II, 595.
[33] See José Ferrater Mora, "Suárez and Modern Philosophy," *Journal of the History of Ideas*, XIV (1953), 528-547; Paul Dibon, *La Philosophie Néerlandaise au Siècle d'Or: L'enseignement philosophique dans les universités à l'époque précartésienne, 1575-1650* (Paris, 1954), 42; William S. Morris, "The Young Jonathan Edwards: A Reconstruction" (Ph.D. diss., University of Chicago, 1955); Gerard

took this form. As it happened, Suarez was a proponent of the liberty of indifference. There is no mistaking Suarez's weight in New England. Most of the textbooks specifically mention him, and the *Ethica* of Eustache de Saint-Paul, which was used at Harvard, argued the Molinist voluntarist case in accordance with him. If you argued for liberty of indifference in the seventeenth century, directly or indirectly, you were probably following Suarez; if you argued against it, directly or indirectly, you were probably arguing against Suarez.[34]

No doubt more important than Suarez, however, was the influence of William Ames, who himself borrowed freely from the Spanish metaphysician on certain points. Ames treated the question of the relation of will and intellect at length in *Conscience with the Power and Cases thereof,* which first appeared in Latin in 1630 and in English translation in 1643. According to Ames, conscience is a rather complex human endowment. But its most important characteristic in relation to the matter at hand is that it is not in any sense a separate faculty. It is rather a reflexive power of the intellect by which *synteresis* (or universal natural law) in all men turns in upon the self and judges whether actions are licit or illicit. The dictates of conscience may sometimes precede and accompany our actions and sometimes follow them. Now this raises what Ames himself calls "a hard question." "How can a man do any thing against the dictate of Conscience which goeth before, or accompanieth his action?" For "it seems to many," Ames writes, that the will "cannot will or nill any thing, unless *reason* have first *judged* it to be willed or nilled; neither can it *choose* but *follow* the *last practicall judgement,* and do that which *reason* doth dictate to be done: and by consequent, the *will* cannot move against the determination of *conscience.*" But to this difficulty, Ames states confidently, there are answers "so cleare that no man can question it."[35]

When Perry Miller in *The New England Mind: The Seventeenth Century* quoted this passage from Ames, he inadvertently left out Ames's

307

Smith, ed., *Jesuit Thinkers of the Renaissance* (Milwaukee, 1939). Leon Mahieu, *Francisco Suarez, sa philosophie et les rapports qu'elle a avec sa théologie* (Paris, 1921), written from a Thomist point of view, is a very useful exposition of Suarez's thinking. Suarez's *Disputationes Metaphysicae* (1597) was in many early American libraries.

[34] Suarez's position is thoroughly treated in Thomas Mullaney, *Suarez on Human Freedom* (Baltimore, 1950), and also more briefly in Davitt, *Nature of Law.*

[35] Ames, *Conscience,* Bk. I, chap. vii.

opening phrase, "it seems to many," and then incorrectly attributed the intellectualism in the passage to Ames himself, remarking that the English theologian "wrote this doctrine deep into the New England tradition, and founded the whole ethical system upon it."[36] But the contrary is emphatically the case. Ames was one of the leading figures in opposition to the intellectualist theory. One of the consequences of Miller's reading is an illogical severance of eighteenth-century evangelicism from seventeenth-century Puritan thought.

308   Ames states his case in eight propositions which I have rearranged and condensed. He is not consistent in his answers, for part of his argument is an attempt to preserve the concept of will as rational appetite despite its separateness from intellect, while in other places he implicitly rejects this notion altogether. To take the latter view first, which is the one that mainly concerns us, he makes the point that if the will necessarily follows the judgment of the understanding, "then there should (in proper speaking) be no sin of *malice,* distinct from those sins which are committed through ignorance, or passions." "But," he observes, "it is manifest, that this kind of sin is found in Devils, and likewise in some men." It is not necessary that an error of judgment precede an evil act. In short, there can be a bad will which rejects the lead of reason. Secondly, if the will necessarily follows the understanding, then in regeneration, that is, the creation of the new man by divine grace, "the will it selfe need not be internally renewed" but the mere "inlightening of the Understanding would be sufficient," which is "repugnant to Faith and Godlinesse." The implications of intellectualist thinking are, it is suggested here, that a certain degree of education might suffice for salvation, or that a minister could just as well preach to the head as the heart.

Finally, along these same lines, Ames advances the significant idea

---

[36] (New York, 1939), 248. On p. 250, Miller also underestimates the importance of the problem of intellect and will in 17th-century New England, holding it was "largely academic." But strangely, a few pages further on, he correctly notes that "the deliberate errancy of the will, as against the informed reason," was an emphasis "greater among the Puritans than among many other Protestant communions," refers to Augustinian and Scotist influences, and even quotes Ames to this effect. (pp. 260, 285) Miller's final thought seems to be that the issue was one between the physicists, that is, natural philosophers, and the theologians, which may be correct in the particular case of William Ames's own indecision but is not generally true. Miller also falls into the crucial error of confusing the question of the independence of the will in relation to intellect with the problem of the freedom of the will in relation to divine decrees. (p. 285)

that the will can "turne away the understanding" from the consideration of any object which it is apprehending and judges to be good at
the moment, and turn it instead toward the consideration of either
another object or to an earlier consideration and judgment of the same
object. "By reason of this commanding power, the *Will* is the first
cause of unadvisednesse, and blameworthy error in the understanding,"
for this influence of the will by which it draws away the understanding
from that which it has judged to be good "it doth by its owne inclination," without any prior judgment that it should do so.[37] This case, we
may remark, is an especially clear instance of both the scholastic and
the Augustinian theory of the will combining to break through the
Thomist scholastic structure, a process which was going on generally in
the seventeenth century.[38] Ames was inspired in the most fundamental
way by the Augustinian tradition; at the same time he made use of the
brilliant dialectics of the Jesuit Suarez to put down the intellectualists.
It should be noted, too, that the activity of the will as described here by
Ames is hardly to be differentiated from that of the passions or affections of the sensitive appetite in its power to sway the reason according
to its inclination. Ultimately this theory of the will would connect with
several other strands of thought more or less independent of it and
give rise to the so-called sentimentalist school in eighteenth-century
ethics which had a notable career in American letters.

There is another series of arguments in Ames which throws light
on his position. Here a traditional scholastic distinction is relied upon,
that between the specification and the exercise of an act. The specification of an act is roughly identical to the intellectual substance of it,
or its description, and the exercise to the choice of acting or not acting at
all, regardless of the substance. In terms of freedom, the liberty of
specification in action was a liberty of contrariety, or the liberty to do
something different; the liberty of exercise was a liberty of contradiction,
or the liberty simply not to do anything in a particular case. The
seventeenth-century Thomists (leaving aside the question of how true
they were to their mentor) adhered to a liberty in the will of exercise
but not of specification. The Suarezians, or the Molinists and the Jesuits
in general, held that the will had liberty in both specification and
exercise. This doctrine necessarily gave will a certain amount of cogni-

309

---

[37] Ames, *Conscience*, Bk. I, chap. vii.
[38] This is one of the main themes in Anthony Levi's superb study, *French Moralists*.

tive as well as active power. Ames disagreed to the extent that he was willing to admit that the intellect must supply the object or the specification of an act, since the will is blind, but he held with the voluntarists that "in regard of *exercise* or act of willing, it moveth both it selfe, and the understanding with the rest of the faculties." This same principle of liberty was expressed in the common voluntarist belief that the will had the power of suspending action. As Ames puts it, "The *Will* can at pleasure *suspend* its act about that which is *apprehended* and *judged* to be good; without any *foregoing act of judgment* that it should do so; for if to *suspend* an act, and to leave off acting, an act of judgment be necessarily required; then to suspend that judgment, another judgment is requisite; and to suspend that, another, and so *in infinitum*."[39] In other words, every time we stop or start to think (which is itself an action) or to act outwardly, a special judgment of the intellect is not necessary and it would be absurd to assume so.

Ames's defense of this limited freedom in exercise, or freedom to suspend, was a more moderate stand than his other points about the power of the will actually to undermine rational judgment, though he shows no awareness of the entirely different presuppositions upon which he is arguing, or that, in fact, the radical Augustinian voluntarism which he also espoused vitiated all his other reasoning about the relation of will to intellect. However, even the sole ability to suspend action, we should note, is a considerable power for the will in ethical situations where timing may be of the essence.[40]

The inconsistency evident in Ames in this area illustrates, I think, how much the radical suggestions he makes in favor of a nonintellectual will were dictated not by philosophical conceptions but by Puritan religious sensibility. This sensibility insisted on a dichotomous struggle between good and evil in the soul which swept the intellect along rather than was guided by it. The will was in a sense no more than a symbol for the interiority of this struggle which encompassed the whole man and over which he had little intellectual control.

The detachment of the will from the intellect as argued by Suarez

[39] Ames, *Conscience*, Bk. I, chap. vii.

[40] It may be of incidental interest to note that Locke in his *Essay* considered the power to suspend action "the great privilege of finite intellectual beings" and the only freedom that man has that makes any sense. Bk. II, chap. xxi, 53. Locke did not doubt, on the other hand, that will follows the last judgment of our reason, a fact which he called, as did Descartes and Burgersdyck 50 years earlier, a "perfection of our nature" rather than a fault. *Ibid.*, 48-49.

310

undoubetdly provided support for Ames. But the Protestant emphasis
on the radical dependence of the will on God is not found in Suarez,
who considered this idea a Lutheran heresy. The Jesuit theologian upheld the independent freedom of the will even from divine coaction,
arguing that the relation of God's will to human action is solely a matter
of concurrence. The human will accedes to God's grace through its own
disposition only and without constraint.[41]

It is significant with regard to how Ames was understood by his
contemporaries that Adrian Heereboord, Burgersdyck's successor at Leyden, mentions Ames along with Suarez as a proponent of voluntarism,
a school of thought which both Heereboord and Burgersdyck firmly
rejected. At his own University of Franeker in Holland, Ames also
tangled on this issue with his colleague Johann Maccovius, who believed
that "the will always and necessarily follows the judgment of thought." In
Adam, according to Maccovius, sin first established itself in his understanding and will followed. In redemptive regeneration the process is
the same: "God's light enlightens the understanding of man and through
it first allows virtue to stream into the soul." But Ames believed that the
will "is an immediate and original creation of God." A modern com-
mentator has astutely pointed out that Ames's voluntarism was directed
against two distinct enemies: firstly, "scholastic intellectualizing for the
pleasure of it," among the majority of orthodox Reformed theologians,
and secondly, "moralizing in the Enlightenment vein on the part of the
Remonstrants" or Arminians.[42] Augustinian voluntarism combated the
first by making the intellect relatively impotent to effect personal religious
reform, and the second by making the *carnal* will relatively impotent
to cooperate. What was left, designedly, was only God and the devil.
It has, perhaps, not been sufficiently appreciated in American historiog-

311

---

[41] See Mahieu, *Suarez*, 506-507, 236-240, 453-468.
[42] Reuter, *Ames*, ed. Horton, 258ff. On Ames's reputation as an Augustinian
voluntarist in relation to his contemporaries, see also Ernst Bizer, "Reformed
Orthodoxy and Cartesianism," *Journal for Theology and the Church*, II (New
York, 1965), 20, 63. For an illustration of the background to an intellectualism like
that of Maccovius, see Heiko Oberman, *The Harvest of Medieval Theology: Gabriel
Biel and Late Medieval Nominalism* (Cambridge, Mass., 1963), 164-165. Oberman
finds that the predominant thinking in the scholastic tradition, even among the
nominalists, supported the maxim: *"Cognitio radix et fundamentum omnium
virtutum."* "Reason or knowledge, not good will, is the root and foundation of
all virtues," and the primary task of the Church is to "provide the Christian people
with the proper information about God which necessarily leads to moral improvement."

raphy that Ames's program was revolutionary within reformed Protestantism and even within Puritanism itself, which in the course of the
sixteenth and seventeenth centuries had become deeply scholasticized and
intellectualized.

If we are to see the true situation in the seventeenth century, we must
recognize that the controversy within Protestantism had at least three
sides, excluding Molinism which very few Protestants if any could possibly accept, however much they may have borrowed arguments from
Suarez. A preliminary sketch might look as follows. There was first of
all a perfectly orthodox Protestant scholasticism characteristic of Theodore Beza and the majority of Reformed theologians after him which
preferred to accept a moderate Thomist-type intellectualist framework
in psychology. These men represented a cautious middle group which
would not be hasty to abandon the central learned tradition built on
stable and tested Aristotelian foundations. Secondly, there was a "liberal"
group with perhaps a remote tendency toward moralism and Pelagianism, for whom intellectualism was a central doctrine which suited
an outlook broadly rationalist in direction. They could be called "illumi-
nationists" insofar as they stressed the importance of intellectual enlightenment as a precondition of both faith and morals, but they fell short of
Pelagianism in that they denied the natural man could merit salvation.
John Cameron was one of the most influential of these men. To call
this group "humanist" as opposed to scholastic, as does Armstrong in
his study of Amyraldism in France, does not seem sufficiently precise,
but the suggestion is helpful. Evidence of the French debate arousing
interest in America may be found in an address by Increase Mather to
Harvard students near the end of the seventeenth century: "We find
also in the word *Amyraldus, Arminius redivivus* (Arminius restored to
life): for the followers of Amyrault, sometimes called New Schoolmen
and Methodists, profess little or nothing but what they have learned
from the Arminians."[43] Finally, there were the Augustinians, or "reformed pietists" according to the designation of Ernst Bizer, who found
the intellectualist theory theologically unacceptable and were therefore
opposed to the Protestant scholastics on technical grounds but still

312

[43] Quoted by Cotton Mather, *Magnalia Christi Americana*, II (New Haven,
1820 [orig. publ. London, 1702]), 17. The problem with the term "humanism"
is illustrated by the case of St. Francis of Sales, a pioneer Augustinian psychologist
at the opposite pole from Cameron, who is classified by Levi, *French Moralists*,
into a group called "devout humanists."

could join with them (and did) to combat the liberalism, moralism, Cameronianism, Amyraldism, or Arminianism of the second group. The great danger to which the Augustinian voluntarists were themselves subject was above all a fideism which divorced the religious life from both reason and natural morality.[44] The Catholic counterpart of this third movement within Protestantism was of course Jansenism, and this, too, had its effect in New England through the ardent propagation of the *Augustinus* by the English dissenter Theophilus Gale, whose *Court of the Gentiles* (1669-1678), which was as well known to the New Enland clergy as almost any other book one could name, was in good part devoted to an admiring exposition of Jansen's thought.[45]

313

Reasoning such as Ames's, which contained some combination of scholastic and Augustinian voluntarism, was common enough in Puritanism in the second half of the seventeenth century. A similar confused division occurred in Edward Reynolds's *Treatise of the Passions*, for example, a well-known work in psychology from the same period. And in John Flavel's *Pneumatologia* (1685) there is another curious blend. Flavel, the author of the famous *Husbandry Spiritualized*, touches on several possibilities in the course of his exposition and seems to become increasingly radical. The understanding "is the noble leading Faculty of the Soul" and serves to direct and guide us in life. It is rightly called by philosophers the *tò egemonikon* "because the Will follows its practical Dictates," but it does not rigorously enforce its dictates "for the Will cannot be so imposed upon." The understanding gives the will only "a directive Light . . . pointing, as it were, with its Finger, at what it ought to chuse, and what to refuse." The will, too, is "a very high and noble Power of the Soul," to which the understanding bears the same relation "as a grave Counsellor doth to great *Prince*." The will cannot be compelled and forced; "Coaction is repugnant to its very Nature."

---

[44] See Levi, *French Moralists*, 324, concerning fideism.
[45] Gale could well be called the English Jansen. Bourke, *Will in Western Thought*, fails to say a word about Jansenism. Gilson, *Liberté chez Descartes*, contains a good deal of material on the intellectual background of Jansen's ideas and especially emphasizes the anticipation of Jansen's theory of liberty by the little-known figure Guillaume Gibieuf (d. 1650). Abercrombie, *Origins of Jansenism*, has valuable insights into 17th-century Augustinianism but overlooks Gibieuf completely and stresses the work of the Flemish Catholic theologian Michael Baius (d. 1589). A good sense of the Augustinian/intellectualist rift in the 17th century is given in the Zaharoff lecture by Antoine Adam, *Sur le problème religieux dans la première moitié du XVIIᵉ siècle* (Oxford, 1959); and in Levi, *French Moralists*.

All of this would seem to be in accordance with a scholastic voluntarism. But Flavel reveals that the will has other limitations and other
sources of guidance. The will can "open or shut the Hand or the Eye
at its Pleasure, but not the Heart." For whatever the decrees of our
subjective will, God's intercession must also be recognized. It is as
though there were two wills in Flavel's analysis, one that follows the
judgments of the intellect and another which can only obey the judgments of God. Thus, for example, "the Will commands the Service of
the Tongue, and chargeth it to deliver faithfully such or such Words."
But when the will comes "to do its Office, the Tongue faulters, and contrary to the Command of the Will, drops some Word that discovers
and defeats [its] Design." A different power has interceded. The will
has not the same command over the inner man as it has over the outer.
It is true that "it can oftimes perswade the Understanding and Thoughts
to lay by this or that Subject and apply themselves to the Study of
another," but when a man's evils are set before his eyes through God's
work on the soul prior to conversion, "fain would the carnal Will
disengage the Thoughts from such sad Objects ... but all to no purpose."
And when Satan is tempting the regenerate man with "hellish Suggestions," though the "sanctified Will opposes itself to them," it has no
more success than the carnal will. The sanctified will no more than the
carnal can control the "Thoughts of the Heart." But for all this, the will
"is a noble Faculty, and hath a vastly extended Empire in the Soul of
Man: It is the Door of the Soul, at which the Spirit of God knocks for
Entrance; when this is won, the Soul is won to Christ; and if this stand
out in Rebellion against him, he is barr'd out of the Soul, and can have
no saving Union with it."[46]

[46] *Pneumatologia. A Treatise of the Soul of Man* . . . (1685), in Flavel, *The
Whole Works of the Reverend John Flavel* (Edinburgh, 1731), I, 283-284. Flavel's
confusion is apparent when he comes to discuss conscience, which he calls the
"Chief *Counselor, Guide* and *Director* in all. . . . Bodily Members are but Instruments, and the Will itself as high and noble a Faculty, or Power as it is, moveth not,
until the Judgment cometh to a Conclusion, and the Debate ended in the Mind."
(p. 346) It will be remembered that it was precisely over the relation of conscience
to will that Ames found it necessary to break with the intellectualists. Yet Flavel
expressly follows Ames on other matters relating to conscience. One of the best
and most interesting discussions of the relation of will and intellect in the late
17th century may be found in the exchange of letters between the young John Norris
of Bemerton and the distinguished Platonist Henry More. Norris argued the intellectualist position. From this exchange of letters it is clear that More has not,
in general, been correctly interpreted on the subject of the will. This has some significance because of his great influence in America. See John Norris, *The Theory*

We are now better prepared to examine closely the voluntarist treatment of the will in several student notebooks from early Harvard. "An explication of certain rules in Logick," copied by John Stone in 1653, the year of his graduation, is thoroughly Amesian in thinking but may have been taken from one of the manuscripts of the work of the Cambridge professor Alexander Richardson which were floating about in Puritan circles in old and New England.

Stone begins his report on the will with the comment that "the will is the last thing handled in physicke and the first in theologie, whereof it is the subject; and whose scope it is . . . to close with the chiefe good." Then there is an analysis of "cause by councell," which establishes the freedom of rational creatures. The portion relevant to the relation of will and intellect is as follows: 315

After a man understands a thing fully, he chuses or refuseth; the understanding finds out things and presents to the will (which setts as queen) to know her majesties pleasure; some question whether the will or the understanding be the superior faculty, but the will is the supreame, for it hath the casting and determining vote, all the rest are for this, the outward senses are for the inward, and the inward for the understanding (according to that rule nihil est in intellectu quod non prius fuit in sensu), and the understanding is for the will, as an antecedent of her actions, and as a pilote to guid and direct her . . . and [as an] attendant to beare the candle and lanthorne before her: and both understanding and will for god; the will is above the powere of any seconde cause, it cannot be compelled by any; men may force the hand to work and the feet to walk, and the tongue to confesse, but they canot the will to act because the proper act of the will is to elect; it is a contradiction to say it may be compelled to elect . . . the will hath power and dominion over its own actions: voluntas prout uti voluntati. A man can will to will and chuse to chuse, and this liberty is as inseparable from the will as light from the sun.[47]

In this analysis the will is the supreme faculty of the soul because it is

and Regulation of Love . . . To which are added, Letters Philosophical and Moral between the Author and Dr. Henry More (London, 1694). See also the important discussion in John Owen, Πνευματολογία or, _A Discourse Concerning the Holy Spirit_ . . . (London, 1674).

[47] This material is in Abraham Pierson's "Notes of Lectures attended at Harvard College," a manuscript notebook in the Beinecke Library, which has a variety of items in it by different hands.

within the will that the decisive movement takes place which determines man's final relation to God. As Ames had said, "The will is the true subject of theology since it is the true beginning of life and of moral and spiritual action." And further, because the will cannot be compelled, even by force of logic as is the case with the intellect, it is the center of that free choice by which man determines his eternal condition.[48] The will is the apex of the soul; or better, the free act of willing is the climactic movement of the soul, since the dispute with the intellectualists here is not simply over the power of rival faculties so much as over which faculty best represents what is in the end the quintessential element in both faith and virtue. On this level it is far too narrow a category to speak of Puritan or even Protestant moral concerns. As Eugene Rice has shown, in the Italian Renaissance figures Petrarch and Salutati there is a similar conviction that "the will is nobler than the intellect and that love, which is the action of the will, is nobler and more perfect than contemplation or vision, the act of the intellect." And Rice comments, "This emphasis on the will and love is a traditional characteristic of those medieval thinkers who kept their Augustinian fervor undampened by Aristotle's intellectualism. For Anselm, Bernard, the twelfth-century Victorines, Bonaventura, and Scotus it was a position which, they felt, guaranteed the possibility of enthusiasm and kept high the temperature of piety."[49]

Perhaps the most extreme voluntarist statement in a student notebook from seventeenth-century Harvard is found in the commonplace book of John Leverett, who was to become Harvard's most distinguished president in the colonial period. The entry dates from about 1680, twenty-

316

[48] William Ames, *The Marrow of Theology*, ed. and trans. John D. Eusden (Boston, 1968), Bk. I, chap. iii, 206; II, ii, 4-8. See also Thomas Hooker, "A True Sight of Sin," in Perry Miller and Thomas H. Johnson, eds., *The Puritans* (New York, 1938), 293-294: "The will of man [is] the chiefest" of all God's workmanship. The body is for the soul, "the mind to attend upon the will, the will to attend upon God, and to make choyce of him, and his wil." The Law is "the rule" of God's "Holy and righteous will, by which the will of *Adam* should have been ruled." "By sin we justle the law out of its place," and say we will be ruled "by mine own wil and led by mine own deluded reason."

[49] Eugene F. Rice, Jr., *The Renaissance Idea of Wisdom* (Cambridge, Mass., 1958), 36-37. In the case of Ficino, whose work was at the height of its influence in the 17th century, there is a development in his thinking from intellectualism to Augustinian voluntarism, or a gradual identification of will with love. See Paul Oskar Kristeller, *The Philosophy of Marsilio Ficino* (New York, 1943), 269-276. Or in the 17th century, see Pascal's *Pensées* (Paris, 1770), 580: "God prefers rather to incline the will than the intellect."

five years later than Stone's notes.[50] "Some make Intellectus to be nobilior voluntate," Leverett begins, but this may be proved false by the following reasons:

1. Because the rule of the understanding is Logick, but the rule of the will is divinity: Divinity is more excellent being last art of all, and to which all the rest are subordinate. 2. The subject of the will is bonum, and of the understanding verum; so much is the will better than the understanding; yea the proper object of the will is god himself, because he is summum bonum, but he is not the subject of understanding, for our reason cannot comprehend him. 3. The will is the end of every act ab extra or of things unto us; and the beginning of every act ab Intra, or proceeding from our selves. Every thing is received from the outward sense, from then convey'd to the inward, and thence to the understanding, then to the affections, and last of all to the will, which embraceth it or refuseth it, and the act of the will is the end of all the former acts. 4. When I do any thing intra, the will is the beginning of the act, and shee like a Queen first comands, I will have this or that done; then Reason thinkes of means to this end, and those being found, the power doth put the thing in practice; and hence is drawn a similitude to express the mistery of the Trinity: that the father should be compared to the will, for that he is the beginning of the action; the Son Reason, for to him is given the dispensation of things, and here is the wisdome of his father; the HG to the power of executeing things for he is the perfecter of every Act, and is called the power of the most high.

317

To this analysis of the supremacy of the will Leverett adds what at first appears to be a twist. "Some think that Voluntas non cogitur [i.e., will cannot be forced] but 'tis not always true. men wrong themselves often times, and sin compelleth the will. It is not I, but Sin in me, [sayeth] Paul." But this concluding remark simply verifies what we have already stressed was characteristic of pietistic voluntarism. The will is not uncoerced with respect to the power of God and Satan, but only with respect to the other faculties of the soul.

The most intriguing suggestion in Leverett's student notes—which were probably gathered in preparation for a disputation—is the placing of the will absolutely first in what he calls acts *ab intra*, commanding the reason like a queen to think of means to the end it desires. Here

[50] Leverett's manuscript commonplace book is at the Massachusetts Historical Society, Boston.

is the will in control of both specification and exercise, with the reason reduced to an ancillary function, or, we might say, a pragmatic function. It is not a very great leap from this kind of voluntarism to David Hume's famous dictum, and Francis Hutcheson's earlier, that the reason is and only ought to be the slave of the passions, although there are several notable steps in between. Leverett's description of the relation of will to intellect can be traced back to Suarez at least, who held explicitly that "the intellect can only *show* the necessity of an act. It cannot confer it. Only the will can *confer* necessity" or moral obligation. And Suarez himself was building upon the distinction between indicative and imperative law initiated centuries earlier by Scotus.

318

There have also fortunately survived from Leverett's papers two formal statements in Latin regarding the will. The first, on the topic "Indifference is not of the essence of freedom," is dated October 3, 1680, and thus was written only a couple of months after he received his bachelor's degree, perhaps as part of an academic exercise.[51] The second, in the form of a *quaestio,* is dated July 20, 1683, and headed: "Whether the will follows the last judgment of the intellect?" Leverett responded in the negative to this.[52] The notes in English from his commonplace book that I have already quoted may have fallen in time of composition somewhere between these two statements in Latin which appear toward the end of the same commonplace book. In the first exercise the central argument is that liberty and necessity are not entirely incompatible, and therefore one does not have to speak of indifference in order to have liberty. Like Calvin, Leverett held that there is a kind of *"voluntaria necessitas,"* a voluntary necessity which is consistent with freedom. Through divine concursus "everything, but especially morals, are brought about by . . . necessity and harmony, by a necessary harmony or a harmonious necessity." When divine concursus necessitates the will it does so with "the greatest harmony, complete fitness, and supreme sweetness."

The compatibility of the will with both freedom of a sort and harmony

[51] The dates of Harvard commencements are reported in Albert Matthews, "Harvard Commencement Days, 1642-1916," Col. Soc. Mass., *Pubs.,* XVIII (1917), 309-384.
[52] According to the manuscript, President John Rogers moderated at the occasion: "Moderante D. Praeside J. R. discussa fuit haec Quaestio." Rogers was not inaugurated as president until Aug. 14, but he had been in Cambridge since May. *Ibid.,* 371. This *quaestio* was not the one Leverett chose for his M.A. ceremony that same summer.

is apparent from the following facts, Leverett continues: the will adheres to the highest good when grasped as such, and this is most necessary. But still it is free "because it is the most perfect human act (*quoniam perfectissimus est actus humanus*)." Secondly, the saints and glorified angels are necessarily determined to the one good, but they are free in the choice of it. "Suarez most acutely agreed that the obedience of the saints and glorified angels is necessary though free." Thirdly, Christ's obedience was most free, "otherwise it would not be meritorious," but still his obedience was most necessary. Finally, God himself, the freest of agents, is "most necessarily determined in his acts. For all his acts, with respect to their origin and principle, are identical with his essence, and so external and unchangeable." It is not deniable, Leverett continues, that extrinsic compulsion is inconsistent with liberty. But intrinsic, spontaneous liberty "such as arises from the effective influence of the first cause and last end, God, is connatural with both the essence and existence of freedom." And from this it follows that indifference is not in any way connatural with, let alone essential to, freedom. 319

The last section of Leverett's argument concentrates on a rather complicated analysis of indifference, including not only the distinction between specification and exercise, but also passive and objective indifference, active and subject indifference, absolute and conditioned indifference, and actual and habitual indifference, all of which it would not be profitable to explore in detail here. Leverett's aim in this document was to refute the Molinist theory of grace rather than to answer the intellectualists. The liberty of suspension might be admitted when it was a question of the rule of intellect versus the rule of will, that is, purely a natural psychological matter. It might be used, as in the case of Ames, to demonstrate the independence of willing from intellectual domination. But no orthodox Protestant could attribute to the will the liberty of receiving or rejecting God's mercy. It is in this context that we are able to understand Leverett's remark, toward the end of this piece, on the liberty of suspension: "Indifference to acting or not acting is not essential to freedom. For the Will cannot suspend its act of adherence to the final end when grasped as such. . . . The beatific vision allows of no suspension of acts to the extent that they are love of God and happiness in him." This disputation, then, expressing an opinion on the perfect compatibility of necessity and liberty (when properly understood), in terms precisely like those in Calvin's *Institutes,* was directed to the free will debate and in that area was opposed to scholastic voluntarism.

But in July 1683, in response to another *quaestio,* Leverett delivered
an unambiguous voluntarist statement. This document is highly illustrative of the nature of the controversy as it existed in seventeenth-century
America. It deserves some attention. Leverett opens his discussion with
the comment that the dispute among philosopher-theologians (*"Philos-
ophico-Theologos"*), both in the past and recently, on the question of
whether the will is determined by the last judgment of the intellect is a
"serious" and "not unmerited controversy." He then outlines the historic

320   positions. Both sides in the issue have "legions" of followers as well as
"aristocrats in the republic of letters" doing battle. Among them, Leverett writes, "are the defenders of the absolute power and dignity of the
will as queen of the microcosm. These deny that will in any way follows
the last dictate of the intellect—not even in its specification, let alone in
its exercise." The opposition, on the other hand, "fearing . . . that this
mistress . . . might assume despotic control for herself, so limit her power
. . . that they maintain that the will does not act except at the bidding
of the last dictate of the intellect. So much so, that according to them, the
will is determined by the last judgment of the practical intellect not
only in specification but even in exercise." Accordingly, "lest the truth
suffer in such a sharp clash of many men equally learned, some of the
scholastics desirous of making peace, endowed the will with a kind of
mixed monarchy. According to them, the will's inferiors in power
neither despise nor hate her, but like a queen beloved of faithful subjects,
she holds the scepter among them. Yet because there is safety in an
abundance of advice, the intellect is called into council. It is the first of
the will's privy advisors; she does not often act without the intellect's
advice. But she is not so bound by its last dictate that she cannot suspend
her actions and even sometimes originate actions contrary to its last
decree."

Leverett's stance amidst these possibilities is as follows. He does not
deny, he states, the will's dependence upon the intellect for its specification, even in the will's freest actions. For the will cannot will without an
object proposed by the intellect. "In this sense philosophers say the will
is not carried into the unknown, and the poet says, '*Ignoti nulla Cupido,*'"
there can be no desire for something unknown.[53] But, Leverett adds,

---

[53] This famous phrase, also from Ovid, was often cited in the context of the
closely related controversy which cannot be explored here over whether love or
knowledge must precede in human response to God or the world. Although there
can be no love for what is not known, as Ovid said, neither can there be knowl-

dependence is not the same as determination by the last dictate of the intellect. For in the acts of the will there is no need of a practical judgment; "simple apprehension of the object (*apprehensio objecti simplex*) is enough." There are, in effect, indeliberate acts of the will, which is clear in the case of infants and the insane. The apprehended good possesses all the conditions required in an object of the will. The rational appetite, i.e., the will, no less than the sensitive appetite, is aroused through the simple apprehension of the object. The same kind of choice independent of the last dictate of the intellect can occur when there are two goods presented, either of which is to be chosen. "The intellect judges speculatively that the one is a false the other an authentic good, and then judges practically that the authentic good is to be preferred to the false. But the will, in its freedom, can choose the false good, abandoning the authentic, however much the intellect may judge that the authentic is to be preferred practically, and act in accordance with those words of Medea, 'I see the better and approve; but I follow the worse.'" Those who act against their conscience, Leverett says, when they know what they are doing is prohibited, are clear examples of the will actually rejecting the practical judgment.

321

Leverett's conclusion is firm and definitely aligns him with the voluntarists. The will in its exercise may move not only itself but also the intellect. Even in specification, the will is limited only by what has been "previously apprehended" by the intellect, not by what is last judged. Inevitably, we see, the will is given some degree of independent cognitive power to replace its lost reliance on the intellect. Leverett cites also in his conclusion the common example of the first sin of angels and man, which if it required an error of intellect to occur would have meant that they suffered a penalty of sin before the first sin. According to the common belief, before the first sin the practical judgment was fully, clearly, and innately informed of the moral law. Therefore, it was not an intellectual error which came first but a disobedient act of will. Gershom Bulkeley had used the same argument earlier. Finally, Leverett states, the will like the intellect can err, and if the will necessarily followed the judgment of the intellect, then in the regeneration of man there would be no need for the will's inner renewal through grace

edge without a desire (i.e., a love) to know. Thomas Aquinas put knowledge first. Jansen, Pascal, and William Ames put love first. For some discussion, see Levi, *French Moralists*, 32-33, 326; and Kristeller, *Philosophy of Ficino*, 273-276.

(*intrinsice et in sese renovaretur per gratiam*)*;* the illumination of the intellect would be sufficient for everything. "But this is farther from faith and piety than I am from the truth when I maintain that the will does not always follow the last dictate of the intellect."

One of the most pregnant incidental suggestions in Leverett's description of the will was his reference to its power of "simple apprehension of the object," which takes place without intellectual assistance. The will responds to the moral good alone without the aid of any other faculty. But an analysis of the significance of this teaching in relation to both its antecedents and its eventual convergence with the "moral sense" of the eighteenth century, which was allied to the affections of the soul, would go beyond the scope of our subject.

There is one additional problem that requires clarification regarding the controversy over will and intellect at seventeenth-century Harvard. This has to do with the relation of the doctrine of regeneration and reprobation to psychological theory. The question may always be asked, to which of the three possible states of man does a psychological theory of the faculties apply: the natural man, that is, Adam before the Fall,[54] the fallen man, or the redeemed man? With respect, for example, to the famous lament of St. Paul, quoted earlier, it was a standing dispute for centuries, and presumably still is, whether Paul was describing a condition before or after regeneration. It has been suggested, but I think incorrectly, that the intellectualist position was applied to the hypothetical condition of man before the Fall, and to a lesser degree to the regenerate soul, whereas voluntarism, i.e., the rebellious will, was peculiarly the accurate teaching when man was considered in a degenerate state.[55] There is a great deal of evidence in support of this assumption in Puritan literature and outside of it. Thus, Bishop Edward Reynolds, following John Cameron, lists among the curative psychological effects of regeneration the irradiation of "the mind and judgment with heavenly light" and "an act of *spiritual inclining and effectual determining the will of man* to embrace the *ultimate dictate* of a *mind* thus enlightened." And in another well-known psychological study, *The Passions of the Minde in General*, by Thomas Wright, first published in 1601, the author describes

[54] See Oberman, *Medieval Theology,* 47ff; and Scharlemann, *Aquinas and Gerhard,* 47-71, regarding the state *"ex puris naturalibus,"* which is the condition of man without infused grace, the hypothetical condition between *"in culpa"* and *"in gratia."*

[55] Miller, *Mind,* 250.

322

how that "bitter Apple which edged all mens teeth" troubled our wills "with tempests and wicked inclinations," even though it is "connatural" for the will to follow the rule of reason and prosecute virtue and honesty. It was thus only by a kind of "vicious miracle," namely the Fall, that the will behaves contrary to nature.[56]

However, it must be stressed that there was no necessary relationship between intellectualism and the psychological theory of regeneration and voluntarism and the psychological theory of corruption. Everybody agreed, it is true, that in the fallen state the ideal harmony of the faculties was profoundly disordered, that in Adam's soul before his sin such a harmony had existed, and that the action of divine grace on the soul in sanctification brought about some restoration of this primitive harmony. But within this consensus there continued to be latitude for different concepts of the exact nature of the harmony or disharmony in the soul. In fact, here one finds quite a variety of beliefs. After all, God's being is perfect, yet He was understood by intellectualists and voluntarists in contrary ways. Concerning the condition of man in the corrupt state, the intellectualists still tended to argue that the basic problem was not the carnal will, though that may enter in, but the darkness of the rational judgment, its failure to supply the will with the right guidance upon which it depends. At the critical moment when the will is hesitant to follow the direction of conscience, for example, the understanding should step in with additional considerations of the ultimate consequences of the will's rebellion, but this it neglects to do. And thus it abandons the will to its blindness. Such an analysis comports well with Burgersdyck's intellectualist interpretation of the Medean paradox mentioned above. The principal failure evident in man's corrupt state, according to this view, is a failure of understanding. Thus, there was no insurmountable inconsistency between intellectualist psychological theory and the degenerate soul. On the other hand, it was not difficult to interpret the redeemed or even the perfect state of the rational soul in voluntarist terms. The issue accommodated itself to many existing religious categories; it was not constitutive of them.

Indeed, both kinds of will, will as love and will as intellect, are necessary activities of the soul and an excess of either leads to pathology.

323

---

[56] Reynolds, *Works,* 583, 635, 769; Wright, *Passions,* 2d ed. (London, 1630), 319.

Men must be sufferers as well as actors, patients as well as agents, help-less lovers as well as potent willers, and an incapacity in either of these abilities means personal disaster.[57] The historic philosophical debate over the nature of the will usually took place within the boundaries of psychological health and was for the most part a matter of emphasis, but emphasis is never a negligible matter.

It can be established then that coexisting with theological quarrels, and relatively independent of the question of the freedom of the will in its classic forms, there existed in seventeenth-century New England a deep-running debate concerning psychological models, which in the end may be assessed as a debate based ultimately on temperamental preferences. With regard to the present historiographical controversy over the degree of intellectuality of the New England "mind," it is helpful to realize that the Puritans themselves disputed about how "intellectual" they were or wanted to be. A recent commentary by Robert Middlekauff suggests that the Puritan's experience of feeling and his expression of it was nearly always rather controlled by the intellectual structure of his religious belief and practice, and that this form of control "should be regarded as one of the determinants of Puritan character." A false and antiquated dualistic conception of psychological experience which divides intellect and emotion, Middlekauff adds, in any case "obscures the connections of emotion and intellect" and thereby obscures "the unity of the psychic process itself." But any reconstruction of the Puritan psyche, Middlekauff concludes, must recognize that the intellect is preeminent.[58]

It is questionable, however, that a controversy of this nature can ever be resolved in favor of one side or the other. It is enough to understand

324

[57] For brilliant discussion of these points, in terms which closely parallel the 17th-century issues, see the works cited in n. 1 above and Eugen Rosenstock-Huessy, "Hitler and Israel, or On Prayer," *Journal of Religion*, XXXIV (1954), in Rosen-stock-Huessy, ed., *Judaism Despite Christianity* (University, Ala., 1969), 179-194, which discusses the meaning of the prayer, "Thy will be done."

[58] Robert Middlekauff, "Piety and Intellect in Puritanism," *William and Mary Quarterly*, 3d Ser., XXII (1965), 457-470, is concerned with the relationship of in-tellect and feeling in Cotton Mather, Samuel Sewall, and some others in 17th-century New England. One difficulty is that of relating the history of psychological theory to the actual human psychology of an age and place. It is sometimes for-gotten that these interact reciprocally to some degree. An influential theory alters human experience and behavior. On the historiographical controversy, see Michael McGiffert, "American Puritan Studies in the 1960's," *ibid.*, 3d Ser., XXVII (1970), 50-54.

that the seventeenth-century debates run smoothly into certain eighteenth-century issues and were part of the universal clashing motifs of "heart" and "head" in Western culture and in American literature in particular. Puritan voluntarists were not romantics, or even "evangelicals" in the later sense. But there are important and demonstrable connections between certain elements in the psychological theory of some Puritans and eighteenth-century preromanticism, sentimentalism, evangelicism, and related phenomena. This general historical relationship is rarely brought out. One exception is Walter Jackson Bate's lectures of twenty-five years ago, *From Classic to Romantic*. But Bate also fails to make some essential distinctions. Duns Scotus, he writes, "sought to demonstrate that the will is not dependent on knowledge but, on the contrary, is completely free and directed of itself to the good. But with the will thus deprived of a rational guide, the followers of Scotus were not exactly sure how the will was to know the good; and from this uncertainty ultimately stemmed both the social and empirical determinism and the emotional individualism, unified in origin but diverse in direction, which largely tended to replace rationalism in European moral and aesthetic thought. . . . The will, left rudderless in the empirical world, was increasingly discovered to be determined by material circumstances." The obvious example of this tendency is, of course, Hobbes, for whom the will was governed, as Bate says, "by the chain of events and forces of the empirical world."[59] What Bate left out, however, is the variety of voluntarism we have seen in William Ames, in which it is not the empirical world which ultimately dominates the "will" but spiritual forces greater than the objects in this world.

By the same token, it is often not recognized that Pelagianism and Arminianism are intimately related to the intellectualist theory, although there has always been a completely orthodox intellectualist tradition in reformed Protestantism, too. In fact, sometimes the reverse is thought, that voluntarism is conducive to a Pelagian potency of will,[60] a confusion which is due to the failure to distinguish between Molinist liberty of

[59] *From Classic to Romantic: Premises of Taste in Eighteenth-Century England* (Cambridge, Mass., 1946), 49-52. On p. 22 Bate writes that the removal of reason from control over the will "was to plunge European philosophy, by the close of the eighteenth century, into a disunity which was without parallel in its entire history, and from which it has shown no genuine sign of emergence."

[60] Miller, *Mind*, 285, seems to make this error.

325

will and the Augustinian liberty which subordinates the will to either divine or satanic influence. But if this confusion between the will as independent of the dictates of intellect and the will as "free" is unscrambled, then it becomes readily evident that intellectualism can lead rather easily to a belief in salvation by effort and endeavor, whereas the pietistic voluntarist can only wait on divine grace for redemption. If the will is corrupt, controlled by Satan and unmanageable in its concupiscence or self-love, then only a redeeming love from outside can turn it around toward God. The function of the ministry of the church is to reach the heart or the affections, opening the way with God's assistance for a new will to enter. Intellectualism, on the other hand, may encourage human pride in knowing the way and in the natural man's sufficiency for virtue and even salvation. This pride was historically supported by the fact that the remaining intellectual endowment of man after the Fall was of impressive magnitude, as the pagan philosophical achievement proved. The Natural Law tradition of morality survived all of the assaults of the Reformation, which meant that intellectualism had available an advanced and well-established notion of human ability. If, then, is added to these factors the intellectualist belief in a perfectly tractable will which is obedient to the dictates of the understanding, it is evident the prerequisites are there for considerable confidence in what effort and striving by itself can achieve. All that must be watched for in the struggle to live a pious life is, as with the ancient pagans, error in the understanding and unbridled passions.

By extending these arguments a little it will be seen that the divisions in American thought during the Great Awakening of the 1740s between evangelicals, so-called "old Calvinists," and incipient liberal "Arminians"[61] were partly a carry-over from the debates of the seventeenth century and in some respects continuous with them, though this connection has not been observed before to my knowledge. There were some indispensable intermediate steps, too, that is, developments in moral psychology (especially in the theory of the passions) which took place between Descartes's treatise on the passions and the work of the Scottish

[61] See the excellent clarifying article by Gerald J. Goodwin, "The Myth of 'Arminian-Calvinism' in Eighteenth-Century New England," *New England Quarterly*, XLI (1968), 213-237. But Edwards may have meant by Arminianism something like Cameronianism.

moralist Francis Hutcheson which cannot be explored here, but even without these essential steps it is remarkable how close the correspondence is between the seventeenth-century Augustinian voluntarist position and the ideas of Jonathan Edwards, and the seventeenth-century intellectualist position and the ideas, for example, of Edwards's opponent, Charles Chauncy. Edwards completely identified the will with the affections or passions, that is, treated the will as though it were itself simply a generalized name for the affections of the heart. This was also Ames's position and that of a number of others in the seventeenth century and before. "Ames feels the kinship between feeling and will to be so close at their deepest point that they are at times for him interchangeable terms."[62] And Edwards then stressed that "the informing of the understanding is all vain, any farther then it *affects* the heart." Like St. Augustine and Ames, Edwards emphasized that our loves and hates, which are the basic actions of the will, are beyond rational control. "The soul wills one thing rather than another, or chooses one thing rather than another, no otherwise than as it loves one thing more than another. The Scripture often teaches that all true religion summarily consists in the love of divine things. And therefore that kind of understanding or knowledge, which is the proper foundation of true religion, must be the knowledge of the loveliness of divine things." It is that knowledge which is the "proper foundation of love," and inseparable from love. "It is not speculation merely that is concerned in this kind of understanding: nor can there be a clear distinction made between the two faculties of understanding and will, as acting distinctly and separately, in this matter."[63] That Edwards means something far different from the old scholastic unity of intellect and will is apparent.[64] "There

327

---

[62] Reuter, *Ames*, ed. Horton, 190. See Jonathan Edwards, *Religious Affections*, ed. John E. Smith, *The Works of Jonathan Edwards*, II (New Haven, 1959), 96, 106, and *passim*. The development of the theory of the passions in Britain and America in the 17th and 18th centuries is a complicated story in itself which rightly belongs in juxtaposition to the theory of the will and intellect. But none of the most important literature illustrative of this history has been included here. For a concept of will as love like Edwards's or Augustine's, see Vivian de Sola Pinto, *Peter Sterry: Platonist and Puritan, 1613-1672* (Cambridge, 1934), 136.

[63] Jonathan Edwards, *Some Thoughts Concerning the Present Revival of Religion in New-England* . . . (Boston, 1742), 8, 9; Edwards, *Religious Affections*, ed. Smith, 271-272, 96, 106.

[64] Jay Wharton Fay, *American Psychology Before William James* (New Bruns-

is a distinction to be made between a mere notional understanding, wherein the mind only beholds things in the exercise of a speculative faculty; and the sense of the heart, wherein the mind don't only speculate and behold, but relishes and feels. . . . The one is mere speculative knowledge; the other sensible knowledge, in which more than the mere intellect is concerned; the heart is the proper subject of it, or the soul as a being that not only beholds, but has inclination, and is pleased or displeased." What Edwards is talking about here is not a conative function of intellect so much as a cognitive function of the will conceived of in the broadest possible sense, that is, where it verges into the meaning of "heart."[65]

328

Edwards was, of course, completely familiar with Ames's work as well as that of figures like the Scottish theologian Samuel Rutherford (d. 1661), Theophilus Gale, John Owen, and other exponents of Augustinian voluntarism. He was also devoted to the *Theoretico-Practica Theologia* of Petrus van Mastricht (1630-1706), his favorite work in theology. Mastricht, a professor at Utrecht, was himself much influenced by Ames. Reuter calls Mastricht "hardly more than the expositor of Ames," and Mastricht stated in the preface to the second Latin edition of *Theoretico-Practica Theologia:* "I have followed the system of the renowned Ames as is laid down in his *Medulla* and his *Casus Conscientiae* which seem so helpful and clear to me that I neither desire nor need any other in its stead."[66] In 1770 in the midst of the controversies over the Edwardsean theology in America a brief section of Mastricht on the topic of regeneration was translated into English and published in New Haven, Connecticut. A good part of this small volume (which also contains a valuable appendix of statements from various authorities before and after Mastricht who shared his views) concerns the relation of will and intellect, and particularly the question of whether divine regeneration is a *physical* process in the will or simply a matter of intellectual illumination and *moral* suasion. Mastricht emphasizes that it is the whole man that is regenerated—intellect, will, and affections—but the point at issue is whether there is a supernatural

wick, N. J., 1939), misinterprets Edwards's psychology, which he thinks is Aristotelian and scholastic because Edwards speaks of only two rational faculties, understanding and will.

[65] Edwards, *Religious Affections,* ed. Smith, 266ff.

[66] Reuter, *Ames,* ed. Horton, 145-146, 177.

physical change in the will. It is true, Mastricht responds to the Arminians and Cameronians, that the will "doth naturally follow the *last*
dictate of the practical understanding," but, he adds, "only when the
understanding, in its last dictate, judgeth agreeably to the *inclination*
of the will. ... If we should make the absurd supposition of the *understanding's* being most clearly enlightened, and yet the *will* not renewed,
the will would not follow the practical judgment, because in that case
the understanding would not dictate agreeably to [the will's] propensity.
... It is therefore in this spiritual propensity of the will, that the seeds
of all those graces, which are necessary to salvation are contained."[67]

329

Directly connected with this conclusion is the question of whether
the action of God in regeneration is moral or physical, and whether
"the physical operation," which Mastricht of course accepts, affects the will
"immediately." The Pelagians and the Socinians, according to Mastricht,
"allow nothing but a moral *action* or agency of God in regeneration,
in which he *teacheth* what is to be done, and by motives persuadeth to the
doing of it." They deny any "physical operation" of God in the process.
Next to them are the "Semi-Pelagians, together with the Jesuits and
Arminians," who allow "some *physical* agency of God in regeneration.
... But, as they restrain the depravity, arising from sin to the *inferior*
faculties of the soul, or at most, to the understanding, so they allow the
physical agency of God, only with respect to these faculties: while,
as to the *will* or free will of man, they hold only to a *moral agency.*"
Mastricht thinks the Semi-Pelagian reservation on this point grows out
of a fear that a physical action on the will would vitiate freedom. The
Cameronians among the reformed "allow indeed a physical operation
upon the *will;* but that only by the *medium* of the understanding,
which God, in regeneration so *powerfully enlightens,* and convinces,
that the will cannot but follow its last practical dictate." This was
also the position of Bishop Reynolds as we saw above. Finally, the orthodox Reformed group, to which Mastricht himself adheres, considers
the physical operation of God immediately upon the will to be the essential principle in regeneration, an operation which directly "begets in
the will a new *propensity* toward spiritual good."[68]

[67] Peter van Mastricht, *A Treatise on Regeneration ... Extracted from his System of Divinity, called Theologia theoretico-practica* (New Haven, 1770), 26-27.
[68] *Ibid.,* 35-38.

The anonymous editor and translator of this volume of Mastricht was in the Edwardsean camp. In a twenty-page appendix he added the words of a dozen other authorities, Charnock, Twisse, Flavel, Witsius, Ames, Rutherford, and so on. From Rutherford's anti-Arminian tract of 1636, *Exercitationes apologeticae pro gratia divina,* the editor extracted the telling comment: "If the last judgment of the understanding necessarily and of itself determined the will, grace would become mere suasion . . .; to remove the darkness of the mind and instruct it in what it is ignorant of would be sufficient, *which is the grace of Pelagians.*"[69] And in a footnote to Mastricht's seventeenth-century text on the relation of will and intellect quoted above the editor introduced the eighteenth-century comments of Jonathan Edwards from his *Enquiry into . . . Freedom of Will* (1754) in support of Mastricht:

330

In some sense, the will always follows the last dictate of the understanding. But then the understanding must be taken in a large sense, as including the whole faculty of perception or apprehension, and not merely what is called reason or judgment. If by the dictate of the understanding is meant what reason declares to be the best . . . , it is not true, that the will always follows the last dictate of the understanding.[70]

It was Edwards's contention that the dictate of reason, the intellectual factor, was just one thing "put into the scale" which is considered in "the compound influence which moves and induces the will."[71] The image of the scales or the balance is the preeminent model for the theory of volition in Edwards's *Freedom of Will,* and the scales are tipped not by *reasons* but by what Edwards called "motives," a catch-all term deliberately chosen to allow for the direct physical action of God on the will (including heart and affections) as well as the direct action of many other imponderables and variables, or second causes, by which God directs human destiny. As one of Edwards's earliest critics, James Dana, pointed out in his *Examination of . . . Edwards's "Enquiry,"* the great Calvinist in his *Enquiry* had in fact skirted the whole question

[69] *Ibid.,* Appendix, n.p.
[70] Ed. Ramsey, 148.
[71] *Ibid.* The interpretation of James Carse, *Jonathan Edwards & the Visibility of God* (New York, 1967), 60, that Edwards held that "the *cause* of a man's action is the same as his *reason* for that action," is incorrect.

of what human motives were, that is, of what caused one action rather than another or what was really behind our willing this rather than that,[12] but he did establish certainly that practical intellect could not be the sole determinant of will and that in consequence regeneration was not solely or even primarily a matter of intellectual persuasion.

On the other hand, the intellectualist opponents of the revival, like Chauncy, also reiterated some ancient arguments: "Is it reasonable to think," Chauncy asked, "that the *Divine SPIRIT*, in dealing with Men . . . would give their *Passions* the *chief* Sway over them? Would not this be to invert their Frame? . . . One of the most *essential* Things necessary in *new-forming* Men, is the Reduction of their *Passions* to a proper Regimen, i.e. The Government of a *sanctified Understanding.* . . . *Reasonable* Beings are not to be guided by *Passion* or *Affection*, though the Object of it should be GOD. . . . The plain Truth is, an *enlightened Mind*, and not *raised Affections*, ought always to be the Guide of those who call themselves Men." And Chauncy made perfectly clear how differently from Edwards he understood the nature of the will. "There is the Religion of the *Understanding* and *Judgment*, and *Will*, as well as of the *Affections*; and if little Account is made of the *former*, while great Stress is laid upon the *latter*, it can't be but people should run into Disorders."[73] The will for Chauncy remains a rational appetite. All of the disputants in the Great Awakening debate were relying on well-established older arguments, some of which we have not exposed here; but of them the voluntarist/intellectualist debate of the seventeenth century was possibly the most central.

It may be of some interest to notice the position of Edwards's grandfather and predecessor in the pulpit at Northampton, Massachusetts, Solomon Stoddard. Although Stoddard had a small reputation as a revivalist himself in the early years of the eighteenth century, he adhered to the psychological theory predominant among the antirevivalists of later years, a matter which came into the open twenty-five years later when Edwards published a direct refutation of Stoddardeanism, his *Humble*

331

[12] James Dana, *An Examination of the late Reverend President Edwards's "Enquiry on Freedom of Will"* (Boston, 1770). See Ramsey's introduction to Edwards, *Freedom of Will*, 19.
[73] Charles Chauncy, *Seasonable Thoughts on the State of Religion in New-England . . .* (Boston, 1743), 324, 326-327, 422.

Inquiry into the Rules of the Word of God, Concerning the Qualifications Requisite to a Compleat Standing and full Communion in the Visible Christian Church.[74] "The Nature of Man is such," according to Stoddard, "that the Will always follows the last dictates of the Understanding; the Will it self is a blind faculty, and it follows the direction of the Understanding. When once Men have a Spiritual Sight of the glory of God, they can do no other but serve him." By "sight" here Stoddard seems to mean an intellectual vision. "Light and Life go together. Before Men know God it is impossible that they should love him, for they are strangers to the reason and foundation of love. . . . But when their eyes are opened and they see the glory of God, they would act against their Nature if they did it not." In answer to this old scholastic problem of which must come first in human response to an object, love or knowledge, Stoddard has chosen knowledge. Ames had given, in opposition to this opinion, the example of prayer, which he said must first come out of love without preceding knowledge of the object. Finally, Stoddard concludes this section: "The excellency of the object is the foundation of the duty, and when that reason is seen, [men] are under a necessity to do it. . . . The sight of the glory of God will necessarily draw forth holy Actions."[75] Edwards's answer, based on the difference between "assent" and "consent," summarizes the differences between him and Stoddard well: To own the covenant, Edwards said, "is to profess the Consent of our Hearts to it; and that is the Sum and Substance of true Piety. 'Tis not only a professing the Assent of our Understandings, that we understand there is such a Covenant, or that we understand we are obliged to comply with it; but 'tis to profess the Consent of our Wills." And the assumption Edwards makes is that inner consent does not necessarily follow intellect assent.[76]

The editors of an excellent collection of documents relating to the Great Awakening make the point rightly that "the central conflict of the Awakening was thus not theological but one of opposing theories

332

[74] (Boston, 1749).

[75] Solomon Stoddard, *Three Sermons Lately Preach'd at Boston* (Boston, 1717), 71-74. See also Thomas Schafer, "Solomon Stoddard and the Theology of the Revival," in Stuart C. Henry, ed., *A Miscellany of American Christianity* (Durham, N. C., 1963), 348, n. 88, where Schafer notes that Edwards followed Mastricht not Stoddard on the matter of intellect versus will.

[76] Edwards, *Humble Inquiry*, 28-29.

of the human psychology."[77] It is certainly a mistake, however, to consider Edwards's psychological theory a reformulation of Locke and therefore modern, and Chauncy's theory outmoded. This is true only in the sense that Augustinian voluntarism fed into the rising tide of romanticism which was yet to reach its full height. Moreover, the direct influence of Locke's *Essay Concerning Human Understanding* on the American mind in the first half of the eighteenth century has been almost as much exaggerated as the influence of his treatises on government. The Great Awakening issue was not one between old and new, but rather a recurrence of the perennial opposition of head and heart, both sides of which have found able supporters in every age.

333

[77] Alan Heimert and Perry Miller, eds., *The Great Awakening: Documents Illustrating the Crisis and Its Consequences* (Indianapolis, 1967), xxxix.

The Renaissance of Sacramental Piety in Colonial New England

E. Brooks Holifield*

IN 1690 Cotton Mather, disturbed by the "Paucity" of sacramental manuals in New England, published *A Companion for Communicants*, a series of discourses on the nature and purpose of the Lord's Supper, along with instructions on preparing for *"that Holy* Ordinance."[1] The publication was a notable event, for it marked the first time that any sacramental meditation was ever printed on New England presses, which had been pouring forth religious treatises continuously since 1639. The book portended a transition in the development of New England piety; it was the first of many sacramental manuals to be printed in the colonies.

Sacramental meditations provide a singular insight into the changes in the New England religious sensibility during the late seventeenth and early eighteenth centuries. They reflect the emergence of an evangelistic sacramental piety, oriented around practical and pastoral concerns, intended to evoke conversions and to fill the churches with regenerate visible saints. They also reveal a remarkable preoccupation with the dilemmas of overly scrupulous Christians who failed to come to the sacrament for fear that they were unworthy. In fact, the meditations suggest that concern for the scrupulous as well as dismay over the indifferent established the immediate context of the celebrated Stoddardean controversy. Furthermore, the meditations demonstrate that by the beginning of the eighteenth century, sacramental piety was becoming a highly visible and significant part of New England religious life.

For over two decades Cotton Mather was the sole New England minister to publish a sacramental manual. In 1711, however, Ebenezer Pemberton, pastor of the Old South Church in Boston, arranged for the posthumous publication of Samuel Willard's *Some Brief Sacramental Medi-*

---

* Mr. Holifield is a member of the School of Theology, Emory University.

[1] Cotton Mather, "Preface," *A Companion for Communicants: Discourses Upon the Nature, the Design, and the Subject of the Lords Supper; with Devout Methods of Preparing for, And Approaching to that Blessed Ordinance* (Boston, 1690), n.p.

tations, which Willard had written for his own edification while he was the teacher at Old South. Three years later, Cotton Mather published *A Monitor for Communicants,* which was eventually reprinted four times. In 1724 Benjamin Wadsworth, the new president of Harvard College, published *A Dialogue Between a Minister and his Neighbour, About the Lord's Supper,* and in 1728 Benjamin Colman, minister at the Brattle Street Church, published twenty of his sacramental discourses in London.[2]

The New England ministers were unable to satisfy the demand for meditations by themselves. In 1700 Bartholomew Green, the Boston printer, published *The Young Mans claim unto the Sacrament of the Lords Supper,* a popular manual on preparation by the English Presbyterian John Quick, and the work went through two editions. In the same year, Green printed a *Treatise Concerning the Lord's Supper,* written by another English Presbyterian, Thomas Doolittle. This work underwent three reprintings in New England within three decades. The Mathers reported that "Many Hundreds" of Doolittle's manuals were sold in the colonies.[3] Eight years later Green's press produced an edition of John Flavel's *Sacramental Meditations Upon divers Select Verses of Scripture.* Within four years this Presbyterian manual was also reprinted. In 1715 the Boston printers Fleet and Crump reissued the *Sacramental Exercises* of Jabez Earle, another English Presbyterian, who lived to see his book reprinted twice in New England. Then in 1716 and again in 1723, Fleet and Crump reprinted *The Communicants Companion* by Matthew Henry, and in 1718 James Franklin printed *A Familiar Guide to the Right and Profitable Receiving of the Lord's Supper,* by still another English nonconformist minister, Theophilus Dorrington.[4] During the same period books of sacramental meditations printed outside the colonies were also selling in New England bookstores. According to Increase Mather in 1708, "Many of

335

[2] Benjamin Colman, *Some of the Glories of Our Lord and Saviour Jesus Christ, Exhibited in Twenty Sacramental Discourses* (London, 1728).

[3] Increase and Cotton Mather, "A Defence of Evangelical Churches," in John Quick, *The Young Mans claim unto the Sacrament of the Lords-Supper: Or the Examination of a Person approaching to the Table of the Lord* (Boston, 1700 [orig. publ. London, 1691]), 62.

[4] Quick, *Young Mans Claim;* Thomas Doolittle, *A Treatise Concerning the Lord's Supper* (Boston, 1727 [orig. publ. London, 1665]); John Flavel, *Sacramental Meditations Upon divers Select Verses of Scripture* (Boston, 1708 [orig. publ. London, 1689]); Jabez Earle, *Sacramental Exercises: Or, The Christian's Employment, Before, At, and After the Lords Supper* (Boston, 1715 [orig. publ. London, 1707]); Matthew Henry, *The Communicant's Companion: Or, Instructions and Helps For the Right Receiving of the Lord's Supper* (Boston, 1716 [orig. publ. London, 1704]); Theophilus Dorrington, *A Familiar Guide to the Right and Profitable Receiving of the Lord's Supper* (Boston, 1718 [orig. publ. London, 1695]).

the Lords People in New England" were reading treatises on the sacrament by Richard Vines, Jeremiah Dyke, Stephen Charnock, and Daniel Rogers, all English Puritan divines.[5]

This was the milieu in which Edward Taylor, New England's finest Puritan poet, wrote his poetical meditations on the Lord's Supper in connection with sermons delivered in his Westfield parish.[6] This was also the setting in which the Boston layman Samuel Sewall tried to arrange for the sacrament to be so scheduled in the four Boston churches that the city could enjoy the "Great Priviledge and Honor" of having "the Lord's Supper administered in it every Lords Day."[7] Neither the lay nor the clerical enthusiasm for the sacrament represented any marked change in New England's reverence for the Lord's Supper. Earlier in the seventeenth century, Thomas Shepard and Michael Wigglesworth had given evidence in their diaries of an intense sacramental devotion, as had the merchant Robert Keayne, who in 1653 bequeathed to his son as a "special gift" a manual that he esteemed "more precious than gold," having read through it, by his own testimony, hundreds of times.[8] Never before, however, had the religious leaders of New England cultivated this piety as in the waning years of the seventeenth century and the early decades of the eighteenth. The transition was reflected most clearly in the volumes printed on New England presses: in the first fifty-one years of printing,

[5] Increase Mather, "An Advertisement, Directed to the Communicants in the Churches of New England," in Doolittle, *Treatise Concerning the Lord's Supper*, n.p. See Richard Vines, *A Treatise of the Institution, Right Administration, and Receiving of the Sacrament of the Lord's Supper* (London, 1657); Jeremiah Dyke, *A Worthy Communicant: or a Treatise, Shewing the Due Order of Receiving the Sacrament of the Lord's Supper* (London, 1636); Stephen Charnock, *The Works of the late learned divine Stephen Charnock*, eds. Edward Veal and Richard Adams, II (London, 1699); Daniel Rogers, *A Treatise of the Two Sacraments of the Gospell Baptisme and the Supper of the Lord*, 2d ed. (London, 1635).

[6] Edward Taylor, *The Poems of Edward Taylor*, ed. Donald E. Stanford (New Haven, Conn., 1960); Taylor, *Christographia* (1701-1703), ed. Norman S. Grabo (New Haven, Conn., 1962). See also Taylor, *Treatise Concerning the Lord's Supper* (1694), ed. Grabo (East Lansing, Mich., 1966).

[7] Samuel Sewall, *Diary of Samuel Sewall* (Massachusetts Historical Society, *Collections*, 5th Ser., V-VII [Boston, 1878-1882]), VI, 138. Hereafter cited as Sewall, *Diary*.

[8] Bernard Bailyn, ed., *The Apologia of Robert Keayne: . . . The Self-Portrait of a Puritan Merchant* (New York, 1965), 28. Reprinted from Colonial Society of Massachusetts, *Publications*, XLII (Boston, 1964), 243-341. See also Edmund S. Morgan, ed., *The Diary of Michael Wigglesworth, 1653-1657: The Conscience of a Puritan* (New York, 1965). Reprinted from Col. Soc. Mass., *Publications*, XXXV (1951), 311-444. Thomas Shepard, Diary, New York Public Library, New York; and Shepard, Sacramental Sermons, 1647-1648, American Antiquarian Society, Worcester, Mass.

not one sacramental meditation issued forth; in the subsequent thirty-eight, New England printers produced twenty-one separate editions of manuals. Though partly a response to controversies over admission to the Lord's Supper, most of the manuals were products of piety, not of polemic, and continued to appear long after controversy had diminished.[9]

The sudden preoccupation with the Lord's Supper was prompted in part by the change in baptismal practice brought about by the Synod of 1662. That synod encouraged New England churches to baptize and accept into "half-way" membership the children of unregenerate New Englanders who had themselves been baptized in the colonial churches as infants. In line with earlier New England tradition, the synod still required evidence of a specifiable experience of regenerating grace for admission into full church membership and participation in the Lord's Supper. But most ministers apparently assumed that an ever-broadening host of regenerate communicants would emerge from the ranks of these baptized halfway members and their children.[10]

To the profound disappointment of the godly, however, the baptized seemed to be surprisingly resistant to the promise of grace sealed by their baptism, and being unregenerate, they failed to seek access to the Lord's Supper. Increase Mather complained in 1711 that there were "many thousands of Children born in *New-England*" who had never sought to receive the Lord's Supper.[11] His son Cotton lamented over the *"Multi-*

337

---

[9] For example, John Quick's sacramental manual was still being printed in New England in 1728, without the polemical introduction by Increase and Cotton Mather that had accompanied its first New England publication during the controversy over admission to the sacrament. Since I deal here solely with sacramental piety, I should point out that many of the later New England ministers believed in a strong Calvinist doctrine of the sacramental presence. See Samuel Willard, *Some Brief Meditations, Preparatory for Communion at the Great Ordinance of the Supper* (Boston, 1711), 19-20, 23; Willard, *A Compleat Body of Divinity, in Two Hundred Expository Lectures on the Assembly's Shorter Catechism* (Boston, 1726), 865-876; and Taylor, "Preparatory Meditations," *Poems,* ed. Stanford, 136, 238, 245, 251. See also Donald E. Stanford, "Edward Taylor and the Lord's Supper," *American Literature,* XXVII (1955), 172-178; and Norman S. Grabo, "Edward Taylor on the Lord's Supper," *Boston Public Library Quarterly,* XII (1960), 22-36. Cotton Mather frequently sounded flatly Zwinglian, but on occasion he too expressed a Calvinist view of the presence. See Mather, *Companion,* 21, 60, 67, 138-139.

[10] See, for example, Cotton Mather, *Companion,* 72. The term "half-way membership" was coined by a later generation of ministers who disagreed with the action of the 1662 synod.

[11] [Increase] Mather, *An Earnest Exhortation to the Children of New England, To Exalt the God of their Fathers* (Boston, 1711), 32.

tudes, and *Quantities"* of New Englanders who did "daily turn their Backs upon the Table of the Lord Jesus."[12]

[When I see] whole *Scores* of *People* going away from the Table that has the *Bread of Life* upon it; then, *The Fire Burns, my Heart is hot within me,* and I cannot Suppress the just indication of my Sorrowes at so Unchristian a practice in those that will yet be called *Christians.*[13]

In some towns, according to Solomon Stoddard, there were "scarce five or six" young people who would "attend the Lords Supper."[14]

The ministers reacted with an evangelistic sacramental piety. If the hearts of the baptized were unmoved by the benefits promised by baptism, they could yet be broken and humbled with an appropriately ominous reminder about baptismal obligations and eucharistic duties. So the ministers began to publish and import sacramental manuals addressed to two different audiences: "*Mainly* to Communicants" already qualified for communion, but "not only to them."[15] Cotton Mather, for example, wrote his *Companion for Communicants* partly to assist faithful visible saints to prepare themselves for the Lord's Supper, but he was equally concerned to instruct, admonish, and exhort unregenerate baptized Christians in the hope that they might find the grace to approach the Lord's table. "Every Christian," he said, had "the Duty of *Self-Examination* incumbent on him," and he advised the unregenerate as well as the presumably converted to "set apart a time for due and deep thoughts" on their readiness for the sacrament.[16]

For those who were already communicants, the instructions of the manuals were precise, detailed, and rigorous. Cotton Mather told them that "there should be a Time, with us, which we may call, *A Preparation for the Sacrament.* And We should oftentimes count a *Whole Day,* but enough to be so laid out."[17] During this period of introspection, the communicant was to examine the condition of his soul, the rectitude of his

338

---

[12] Cotton Mather, *Companion,* 62.

[13] *Ibid.*

[14] Solomon Stoddard, *Three Sermons Lately Preach'd at Boston* (Boston, 1717), 107.

[15] Cotton Mather, *Companion,* 101. See also *ibid.,* 3-4, 62-80.

[16] *Ibid.,* 84, 78. See also Cotton Mather, *A Monitor for Communicants: An Essay to Excite and Assist Religious Approaches to the Table of the Lord: Offered by an Assembly of New-English Pastors, unto their own Flock, and unto all the Churches in these American Colonies,* 3d ed. (Boston, 1715), 9-11.

[17] Cotton Mather, *Companion,* 95.

beliefs, and the quality of his relation to God and man. Mather's manual
was primarily an exercise in spiritual cartography, guiding the communicant into the difficult terrain of the soul and describing the landmarks
he should expect to find there. Was his knowledge of Christian doctrine
competent and his belief orthodox? Did he yield a full intellectual assent
and a cordial consent to the whole Word of God? Did he rely on Christ
alone? Did he exalt Christ above all creatures? Did he desire above all
things to be conformed to Christ and to look upon sin as the worst of all
evils? Had he placed his chief happiness in acquaintance and fellowship with God? Did he desire the prosperity of his neighbors and endeavor to return good for evil? Was he convinced of his own sinfulness?
Did his conviction produce contrition and did that in turn issue in confession? Did he possess a *"sense* of Truth," so that he could *"Tast and
See,* that *the Lord is Good?"*[18] Page after page, by the sheer force of
repetition and the thoroughness of their demands, the meditations compelled the sincere communicant to purge himself of impurity and to
approach the sacrament with humility and sanctity. In Mather's words:

339

There ought to be a very Industrious and Conscientious *Preparation* in
us, for that *Fellowship* with the Lord Jesus, which the Holy Spirit will
then afford. . . . Thus would I say, *You are to Sanctify yourselves, that
you may come to the Sacrament.* If *Joseph* judg'd it proper for him to
cleanse and change himself, before his going in before the King of *Egypt,*
how much more ought we to get our selves well *fitted* when we are going
in unto the King of *Heaven!*[19]

The sacramental meditations differed in tone and emphasis. Cotton
Mather's were intensely subjective and preoccupied with analyzing the
dispositions of the soul. Samuel Willard displayed greater interest in the
objective data of the Christian tradition, devoting most of his manual to
reflections on such matters as the sufferings and obedience of Christ, the
necessity of vicarious satisfaction for sin, the holiness and righteousness
of God and His redeeming love, and the concurrence of the Persons
of the Trinity in the work of salvation.[20] Willard, however, shared with
Mather a zealous concern for worthy communion: "If I have obstructed
my Spiritual frame, by carnal and vain thoughts or actions, and come

[18] *Ibid.,* 95-128.
[19] *Ibid.,* 95-96.
[20] Willard, *Meditations,* 90-169.

rushing to this Ordinance without any fore-preparation for it, how shall I shew that due respect to Christ that I ought?"[21]

To the second audience that the manuals addressed—unregenerate absentees from the Lord's Table—the ministers posed a difficult dilemma. They directed the unregenerate to consider, first, that absence from the sacrament was a positive sin. Baptism obliged a man to procure the grace sufficient for communion at the Lord's Supper. Cotton Mather reminded the absentees:

340

> The *baptised* are under *bonds,* to do *all things whatsoever the Lord Jesus has Commanded.* And is not *This* one of *Those Things?* Do not think now to mock the God of Heaven, by something that Looks like a *Renewal* of your *baptismal Covenant,* without seeking the *Supper* of the Lord.[22]

Neglect of the Lord's Supper by the baptized was decried as *"a continual breach of their vow made to God in Baptism."*[23] Furthermore, those who absented themselves from the sacrament were guilty of more than breaking their baptismal covenant, however serious that might be. To abstain was blatantly to dishonor God; it was a *"Scarlet,* and a *Crimson* Sin." The ministers accused the absent of disobedience to the commands of Christ, disrespect toward the remembrance of a dying Friend and Saviour, and disdain for the welfare of their neighbors, whom they were leading astray into a life of neglect and indifference. *"In a word,* Look and see, whether you can find any thing among the worst of men to *Equalize,* and so to *Justify,* the *Iniquity* of this Omission."[24]

At the same time that they decried abstention from the Lord's Supper, the ministers insisted that saving faith was a prerequisite for worthy communion. Unworthy, faithless communion was a dangerous presumption, Samuel Willard warned; it created "the risque of . . . Damnation."[25]

> If I do not partake in this Ordinance, according to the nature, worth, dignity, and excellency of it, I shall so far bring myself under this guilt: and how many ways may I thus do? What watchfulness, then, and what care had I need to use in this regard? If I am not in Christ by a true and living Faith, I must inevitably partake unworthily. This Ordinance is a

[21] *Ibid.,* 51. See also Benjamin Wadsworth, *A Dialogue Between a Minister and his Neighbour, About the Lord's Supper* (Boston, 1724), 46.
[22] Cotton Mather, *Companion,* 68.
[23] Wadsworth, *Dialogue,* 61.
[24] Cotton Mather, *Companion,* 63-69.
[25] Willard, *Meditations,* 49.

Seal of the Covenant, and if I am not in Covenant with God, what right have I to the Seal of it?[26]

"There are those," he said, "to whom this Ordinance may become a Seal of their Damnation."[27] Willard's warning was echoed in all the sacramental manuals read in New England. Cotton Mather insisted that only a man who possessed *the Graces of a Regenerate Christian* could partake without danger,[28] and he said in 1700 that he wrote his *Companion for Communicants* mainly to show "the Importance of *probable Regeneration,* as a *Qualification* for the Subjects of *Sacraments.*"[29]

The ministers recognized that their repeated warnings created a dilemma for the unregenerate:

341

In fine, There is no escaping or avoiding of Great Sin without *coming to the Table of the Lord.* It is a sin to *come unworthily* to, but it is also a sin to *stay unworthily* from, that Blessed Ordinance. *Neither* of these things must be done; to choose either of them, is, *As if a man should flee from a Lion, and a Bear should meet him.*[30]

Precisely such a dilemma, they thought, was the perfect "inducement . . . to constrain sinners to conversion."[31] The "main design" of the invitation to the Lord's Supper, said Edward Taylor, was to bring men "out of a state of sin into a state of grace."[32]

The proliferation of sacramental manuals with such warnings after 1690 might seem to indicate a declining religion in late seventeenth-century New England. Certainly New England had its share of obtuse and indifferent sinners. Cotton Mather complained that absentees from the Lord's Table were often simply *"not willing to be at the pains of Getting and Keeping good Terms between God and their own Souls."*[33] Therefore, it might appear that the manuals were essays in spiritual rehabilitation, attempts to attract and discipline the indifferent with the promise of a sacramental feast, and to terrify the recalcitrant with reminders of the ominous consequences of shunning the Lord's Table.

[26] *Ibid.,* 49-50.
[27] *Ibid.,* 41.
[28] Cotton Mather, *Monitor,* 17-18.
[29] Increase and Cotton Mather, "Defence of Evangelical Churches," in Quick, *Young Mans Claim,* 56.
[30] Cotton Mather, *Companion,* 78. See also Wadsworth, *Dialogue,* 57.
[31] Taylor, *Treatise,* 143.
[32] *Ibid.,* 21.
[33] Cotton Mather, *Companion,* 78.

Though partly true, such an explanation for the sudden appearance and continued popularity of the manuals is insufficient, for the ministers made it quite clear that the manuals were intended to comfort and assure the scrupulously pious as much as to scold and threaten the impious. Cotton Mather acknowledged in his *Companion for Communicants* that "the most common and usual objection with which men Apologize for their not coming to the *Lords Supper*" was their fear that they were *"not fit for the Supper of the Lord"* because of their belief that it was *"a dangerous thing to come unworthily thereunto."*[34] Fourteen years later, when he wrote his *Monitor for Communicants*, the situation was unchanged: "The common *Apology* made for this Omission is; *I am afraid; I shall come Unworthily; and by doing so, I shall Eat and Drink Judgment unto my self."*[35] The year Mather published his *Monitor*, an association of ministers meeting at Dedham unanimously endorsed the manual precisely because they found it well adapted to bring to the Lord's Supper those *"Children of the Covenant"* who were convinced of "their *Unfitness* and *Unpreparedness* for it."[36] Benjamin Wadsworth directed his *Dialogue Between a Minister and his Neighbour, About the Lord's Supper* to a similarly conscientious audience. In his preface, Wadsworth observed that "one particular Objection often insisted on" by noncommunicants in New England was *"the danger of unworthy receiving, in not discerning the Lord's Body."*[37] The "neighbour" of Wadsworth's dialogue expressed his fearfulness of unworthy communion at the outset: "Because those who in this Ordinance *eat and drink unworthily do eat and drink Damnation to themselves,* I'm so startled and frighted thereby, that I dare not come."[38] A large part of the dialogue was devoted to assuaging such anxieties.

Having set out to purify sacramental communion, the Puritan ministers had succeeded almost too well. Cotton Mather told John Richards that many baptized, presumably sincere potential communicants in Boston's Second Church were inhibited by their "Doubts and Fears."[39] In an appeal for closer relations with English Presbyterians in 1726, Mather acknowledged that such scrupulosity was common in the colony:

According to this, that many of those who in their *Adult Age,* are ad-

---

[34] *Ibid.*, 76.
[35] Cotton Mather, *Monitor,* 5.
[36] *Ibid.*, 23.
[37] Wadsworth, *Dialogue,* ii.
[38] *Ibid.*, 2, 68.
[39] Cotton Mather to John Richards, Dec. 14, 1692, Mass. Hist. Soc., *Collections,* 4th Ser., VIII (1868), 399.

mitted unto *Baptism*, do not presently also come unto the *Lord's Supper*, it seems rather owing to their *own chusing* to stay till they are more satisfied in their *Qualifications,* than from the Churches refusing to admit them, should they desire it.[40]

Ministers who otherwise disagreed violently about sacramental issues testified with one voice to the prevalence of an extreme conscientiousness about the sacrament. Solomon Stoddard complained about men neglecting the Lord's Supper from "Meekness of Conscience, fearing whether they have liberty to come."[41] Edward Taylor agreed that some persons abstained because of fear and doubt. While recognizing that other sinners lived in "total neglect" of the sacrament,[42] he devoted his longest description of the New England absentee to the earnest Christian who was guilty of the sin of abstention:

343

What a lamentation is this! Persons professing the gospel, religious in their lives, knowing in the concerns of religion and the things of God, orderly walkers in their conversation, attending God's worship public in assemblies, private in their families, secret in their closets, and filled with experiences of God treating of them in His Word, yet miserably neglecting this wedden supper. Oh! what a lamentation is this! Certainly they fall under rebuke from our doctrine for their neglect.[43]

Taylor testified that "several Congregational churches" had "admitted persons into a full state, that have desired the church's forbearance with them, as to the Lord's Supper till they have had more light as to their own fitness for it; and it hath been granted."[44]

The fearful introspection of the New England communicant emerged clearly in Samuel Sewall's diary. Sewall joined the church in 1677 with hope that God would "communicate himself" in the sacrament, but he was "afraid that because I came to the ordinance without belief, that for the abuse of Christ, I might be stricken dead." Sewall considered fleeing from the meetinghouse. But he feared that such a course would

[40] Cotton Mather, *Ratio Disciplinae Fratrum Nov-Anglorum: A Faithful Account of the Discipline Professed and Practiced; in the Churches of New-England* Boston, 1726), 86.
[41] Stoddard, *Three Sermons,* 108. See also Stoddard, *The Inexcusableness of Neglecting the Worship of God, Under a Pretence of being in an Unconverted Condition* (Boston, 1708), 25.
[42] Taylor, *Treatise,* 20.
[43] *Ibid.,* 24.
[44] *Ibid.,* 122, 186ff.

leave him unfit for the next sacrament, and he "thought it would be strange for me who was just then joined to the Church, to withdraw, wherefore I stayed." Even then, Sewall could "hardly sit down to the Lord's Table," so terror-stricken was he. The entire experience was painful; after Sewall convinced himself to receive the sacrament, his hopes that Christ would proffer "some glimpse of himself" were disappointed, and although he was not "stricken dead," he did not record his first communion with any sense of joy.[45] One purpose of the sacramental manuals was to comfort the Samuel Sewalls of New England.

344

As a consequence of this mixture of indifference and extreme scrupulosity among potential New England communicants, the problem of admission became extremely complex, particularly in view of New England's traditional restriction of the Lord's Supper to converted visible saints. The complexity appeared most prominently in Cotton Mather's sacramental meditations, since he was more concerned to preserve the New England tradition than were Willard, Wadsworth, or Colman. Mather required of communicants a credible expression of saving faith,[46] but for a defender of a rigorous tradition, he also exhibited remarkable generosity to potential communicants whenever their search for grace seemed to prove disappointing. He told them, first, that a little earnest effort would probably bring them safely to the table: "Immediately set upon doing your parts for the *preparing* of your selves: Who knows, what God may *work in you, both to Will and to Do?*"[47] Second, he suggested that anyone sufficiently motivated to follow his program of preparation possessed enough faith to benefit from communion. Any man who truly desired grace, he said, was qualified to receive the Lord's Supper, since *"the Desires of Grace are Grace."* Any man who sincerely grieved at his lack of faith could experience the benefits of communion: "You *have* what you *Groan* to have."[48] And the sacrament, he said, required only a modicum of grace: "If there is but the *least Grain* of *Grace* in your Souls, God has made a glorious provision for it and the *Holy Supper* is part of that provision."[49] Mather's doctrine was not revolutionary. The celebrated ministers of New England's first generation—Thomas Hooker, John Cotton, Thomas Shepard—had never required perfect assurance of salvation from communicants.[50] Those ministers, however, had

[45] Sewall, *Diary*, V, 46-47.
[46] Cotton Mather, *Companion*, 29.
[47] *Ibid.*, 78.
[48] *Ibid.*, 131.
[49] *Ibid.*, 130.

not pleaded with the doubtful to advance a claim for the sacrament. Mather was pleading.

To judge that a minimum of grace was sufficient to ensure beneficial communion was not to address directly the question of admission. On that matter, the authors of the meditations appealed again to the scrupulous. Not only was the barest minimum of grace sufficient, but also the most ambiguous perception of that grace entitled a claimant to approach the Lord's Table. The Mathers believed that grace was discernible, but they required of communicants no infallible assurance of saving grace. Indeed, they required no assurance at all.[51] It was enough merely to hope: "If you have any preponderating *Hopes* that you *have* these Things, or cannot fairly and justly Pronounce the *Sentence,* that you *have them not;* You may and should come."[52] There was no need to be "*fully Sure of Sincerity.*"[53] In fact, a suitable communicant might entertain "many *Fears*" about the genuineness of his faith; Cotton Mather urged the doubtful and wary to "Run some *Hazard* and *Venture,* out of Obedience to the Lord Jesus Christ."[54] At Second Church in Boston, Mather required of communicants only a profession of faith, showing their knowledge and belief, and a statement of "hope," oral or written, that the "*Grace* of God" had quickened their souls.[55]

While holding to the formal requirements established by the first generation, Mather tried to relax them just enough to attract potential communicants who feared the consequences of unworthy reception. He noted with approval the generosity with which the New England churches evaluated communicants:

Whatever might seem too *strict* and *hard* in the demands of these Churches formerly, is now *generally* Relaxed and Abated; the Churches generally require no more at the Admission of any to their communion, than any *Godly Man* would be willing to come up unto.[56]

[50] See, for example, Thomas Hooker, *A Preparative to the Lords Supper,* in *The Paterne of Perfection Exhibited in Gods Image on Adam* (London, 1640), 350, 369-372; John Cotton, *The Way of the Churches of Christ in New England* (London, 1645), 5, 73.

[51] Cotton Mather, *Companion,* 131. See also Increase and Cotton Mather, "Defence of Evangelical Churches," in Quick, *Young Mans Claim,* 53.

[52] Cotton Mather, *Monitor,* 17. See also Increase Mather, *Dissertation,* 84; and Taylor, *Treatise,* 121.

[53] Cotton Mather, *Monitor,* 6.

[54] Cotton Mather, *Companion,* 132.

[55] *Ibid.,* 76.

[56] *Ibid.,* 75-76.

For Mather, the sacrament was a promise and a demand directed to all baptized adults, an occasion to convert the sinful and to convince the wavering that their rightful place was within the community of the redeemed.

This attempt to combine rigor and generosity in a rejuvenated sacramental piety formed the immediate background of the celebrated controversy that erupted following a 1677 sermon by Solomon Stoddard in Northampton. Stoddard shared the Mathers' zeal for the conversion of the sinful as well as their eagerness to resolve the dilemma of the excessively conscientious, but he thought prevailing New England doctrine and practice ill designed both for conversion and the persuasion of the conscientious. He charged that the inability to resolve the problem lay precisely in the misguided effort to combine rigor and laxity.

346

To begin with, the attempt to be rigorous—to restrict the Lord's Supper to the regenerate—was based on the entirely false supposition that the church could identify the saved. Stoddard believed that the absence of a "certain rule given in the Scripture to the guides of the Church" ensured that the ministers would always lack *"certain knowledge who have Sanctifying Grace."*[57] But Stoddard also found inadvisable the generosity with which the Mathers defined conversion; he did not think it wise to encourage conscientious absentees from the Lord's Supper to enter the circle of the presumably regenerate on the basis of an ambiguous perception or an anxious hope of saving grace.

Such laxity was no real solution to the problem of scrupulosity—a problem which worried Stoddard as much as the Mathers. Almost all of Stoddard's comments on the Lord's Supper in his first major published work, *The Safety of Appearing,* were directed to conscientious absentees:

[57] Stoddard, *Inexcusableness,* 14. Stoddard did not, as is sometimes asserted, think that "the heart of the problem was that no man could know certainly that he was sanctified," despite the claim to that effect in Grabo, ed., "Introduction," *Treatise,* xxvii. Like other New England ministers, Stoddard assumed that it was "the duty of hypocrites to discover their hypocrisy" and "of Saints to discover their Sincerity." Stoddard, *An Appeal to the Learned: Being a Vindication of the Right of Visible Saints to the Lords Supper, Though they be destitute of a Saving Work of God's Spirit on their Hearts: Against the Exceptions of Mr. Increase Mather* (Boston, 1709), 9. He thought that this might be a temporary problem. See Stoddard, "All such as do make a Solemn Profession of their Repentence . . . ," bound with Edward Taylor Manuscripts, n.p., Boston Public Library, Boston. Men were capable of perceiving grace in themselves; Stoddard's main point, however, was that no man could identify with certainty sanctifying grace in *another* man.

Attend the Sacrament of the Lord's Supper: the great design of this
Ordinance is for the strengthening of Faith ... herein the hearts of Gods
people have had peculiar establishment, some when in a discouraged
condition are backward to come to this Ordinance, the Devil has a great
hand in it, to keep them from that which is the means of help: they are
afraid that they shall eat and drink judgment to themselves; but God
no where requires a faith of assurance in those that partake of that
Ordinance.[58]

He acknowledged that his 1707 sermon on *The Inexcusableness of Neglecting the Worship of God* was written "to answer a case of Conscience, and direct those that might have Scruples about Participation of
the Lords-Supper, because they had not a work of Saving Conversion."[59]
Stoddard simply did not believe it helpful to advise the overly scrupulous
to come to the Lord's Supper on the basis of some "probable hope" that
they might be converted:

347

If these persons be told that this Ordinance be only for Converted persons,
yet if they after serious Examination have hopes that they are Converted,
they may and ought to come; That will not satisfy their tender Consciences: they will say, *We may have such hopes and yet not be Converted.*[60]

To tell the merely hopeful that they should venture and dare to present
themselves for communion was to turn "Sacrament days which should be
days of Comfort" into "Days of Torment."[61]

The generosity of New England practice actually stood in the way of
conversion. The "conversion of sinners," Stoddard said, "lyes much upon
the heart of God."[62] It lay upon Stoddard's heart, too. He was against
encouraging men to think of themselves as sanctified on the basis of a
vague perception or a mere hope of grace, for:

[58] Stoddard, *The Safety of Appearing at the Day of Judgment, In the Righteousness of Christ: Open and Applied* (Boston, 1687), 338.
[59] Stoddard, *Appeal*, 2-3. I therefore do not accept the view of James Walsh,
"Solomon Stoddard's Open Communion: A Reexamination," *New England Quar-
erly*, XLIII (1970), 107, that Stoddard was no longer sympathetic to the "scrupu-
ous" in 1707. But on other points I am in agreement with Walsh.
[60] *Ibid.*, 88.
[61] Solomon Stoddard, *The Doctrine of Instituted Churches Explained and Proved
from the Word of God* (London, 1700), 22.
[62] Edward Taylor, Some notes of the said Mr. Stoddards touching the Lords
Supper as a converting Ordinance, Taylor MSS, n.p.

Many that judge that Persons should be Converted before they come to the Sacrament, do run into a great fault, viz. they perswade Persons that they are Converted before they are: they are zealous against mens coming to the Lords-Supper in an Unconverted condition, yet advise and incourage such persons to come under a notion that they are Converted.[63]

By making men "believe that they are Godly before they be," such advice and encouragement was likely "to prove a mighty impediment" to genuine conversion.[64] The Mathers insisted that Stoddard was too demanding, that there was too great an *"Exactness, in his Thoughts about a Work of Regeneration."* If a minister were compelled to apply "the *Judgement of Severity*" proposed by Stoddard, there would "not be in a whole Town, *Regenerate* Persons enough, to make a *Church,*" whereas the Mathers' own *"Judgment of Charity* would find a considerable Number."[65] Stoddard, however, thought that the Mathers' charity would produce complacent communicants, blind to the danger of their unregenerate state and satisfied with a mere hope of conversion.

New England's admission policies also stood in the way of conversion, Stoddard thought, because they excluded many who might benefit from the Lord's Supper. To keep men of godly conversation away from the Lord's Supper was to hold them out of "the way of conversion."[66] In place of New England's traditional sacramental orthodoxy, Stoddard preached that the Lord's Supper itself was a converting ordinance to which all moral and orthodox Christians should be admitted.[67] His doctrine was hardly original, for he was introducing into New England a precept about which English Puritans had been debating for half a century.[68] By emphasizing the converting efficacy of the sacrament, Stoddard simultaneously resolved to his own satisfaction the dilemma of the scrupulous and indicated his own concern for conversion.

Stoddard held a lower doctrine of the sacramental presence than was characteristic of the sacramental renaissance in New England. He criticized his fellow ministers for implicitly overestimating the Lord's Supper

[63] Stoddard, *Inexcusableness*, 20-21.
[64] *Ibid.*
[65] Increase and Cotton Mather, "Defence of Evangelical Churches," in Quick, *Young Mans Claim*, 46, 47.
[66] Some notes of the said Mr. Stoddards, Taylor MSS, n.p.
[67] Stoddard, *Appeal*, 47.
[68] See E. Brooks Holifield, The Covenant Sealed: The Development of Puritan Sacramental Doctrine in Old and New England, 1570-1720 (unpubl. Ph.D. diss., Yale University, 1970), 202-243, 384-389.

348

by "crying it up above all Ordinances both of the Old and New Testament."[69] At the same time, he helped to intensify New England's concern for the sacrament. Stoddardeanism was important, among other reasons, because it both stimulated and reflected the colony's increasing interest in sacramental matters.

In 1734 the sermons of Stoddard's grandson, Jonathan Edwards, sparked an outburst of religious excitement at Northampton, and for a decade New England was shaken by religious revivals. Edwards and his fellow revivalists were unhappy with the new sacramental practices. They rejected Stoddard's admission policies; they demanded of communicants a credible profession of saving faith; and they denied that the Lord's Supper was in any sense a converting ordinance.[70] At the same time, Edwards was clearly no proponent of the evangelistic sacramental piety espoused by Cotton Mather. He believed with Mather that communion was a religious duty, but he would not plead with the scrupulous to apply for admission on the basis of a mere "hope." He wanted candidates who could "judge themselves truly and cordially" to be pious disciples of Christ by their possession of genuine saving faith, and he thought it far more important to exclude hypocrites than to lure overly conscientious saints into church membership with sacramental evangelism.[71] Indeed, the Great Awakening and its aftermath severely inhibited the expansion of sacramental piety. New England printers, who had produced twenty-one editions of communion manuals between 1690 and 1738, printed only eight between 1739 and 1790.[72] Whatever else it may have been, the Awakening was also a repudiation of the sacramental renaissance.

349

[69] Stoddard, *Appeal*, 53.
[70] See Jonathan Edwards, *An Humble Inquiry into the Rules of the Word of God, Concerning the Qualifications Requisite to a Complete Standing and Full Communion in the Visible Christian Church, The Works of President Edwards*, IV (New York, 1830). For a typical Edwardsean treatment, see Joseph Bellamy, *That There is But One Covenant, Whereof Baptism and the Lord's-Supper are Seals, viz. The Covenant of Grace* (New Haven, Conn., 1769).
[71] Edwards, *Humble Inquiry*, IV, 293, 341, 348, 369, 416-417.
[72] See Charles Evans, *American Bibliography: A Chronological Dictionary of all Books, Pamphlets and Periodical Publications Printed in the United States of America from the Genesis of Printing in 1639 Down to and Including the Year 1820*, II-VIII (New York, 1941).

"An Appeal to the Learned":
The Mind of Solomon Stoddard

LucasPaul R. Lucas

SOLOMON Stoddard, minister of the First Congregational Church of Northampton, Massachusetts, from 1669 to 1729, is considered one of the most important ministers of early New England, and the reasons for his importance are fixed firmly in the minds of students of the period. It is generally believed that by 1700 his personality, ecclesiology, and theology dominated the laymen and clergy of western Massachusetts and much of Connecticut. Moreover, it is argued that among a clergy obsessed by church discipline, and especially Congregationalism, Stoddard's Presbyterian-like "Instituted Church" with its "converting" ordinances and open communion represented a radical alternative to the Puritan "New England Way" and did much to cause its destruction. Finally, it is believed that Stoddard, grandfather of Jonathan Edwards, formulated many of the evangelical notions which led to the Great Awakening.[1]

The flaws in this portrait are many. The idea that Stoddard dominated the Connecticut Valley stemmed from the research of Perry Miller, the scholar most responsible for modern interest in Stoddard.[2]

footnote* Mr. Lucas is a member of the Department of History, Indiana University, Bloomington.

[1] Some of the more important treatments of Stoddard are Perry Miller, "Solomon Stoddard, 1643-1729," *Harvard Theological Review*, XXXIV (1941), 277-320, as well as his *The New England Mind From Colony to Province* (Cambridge, Mass., 1953), hereafter cited as *From Colony to Province* (I have used the 1961 paperback edition published by Beacon Press); Edmund S. Morgan, *Visible Saints: The History of a Puritan Idea* (New York, 1963); Norman Pettit, *The Heart Prepared: Grace and Conversion in Puritan Spiritual Life* (New Haven, Conn., 1966); Robert G. Pope, *The Half-Way Covenant: Church Membership in Puritan New England* (Princeton, N. J., 1969); Thomas A. Schafer, "Solomon Stoddard and the Theology of the Revival," in Stuart C. Henry, ed., *A Miscellany of American Christianity: Essays in Honor of H. Shelton Smith* (Durham, N. C., 1963), 328-361; and James P. Walsh, "Solomon Stoddard's Open Communion: A Reexamination," *New England Quarterly*, XLIII (1970), 97-114. Some of the ideas presented in this article were outlined in Paul Lucas, "The River Gods: Mr. Stoddard's Valley, 1650-1730" (a paper delivered at the meeting of the American Historical Association, Dec. 30, 1967, Toronto, Canada).

[2] For example, see Miller, "Solomon Stoddard," *Harvard Theo. Rev.*, XXXIV (1941), 277-285, and Miller, *From Colony to Province*, 231-245.

However, neither Miller nor anyone else has offered any evidence to support this contention. Miller relied on Increase Mather's suspicions[3] and J. R. Trumbull's *History of Northampton*.[4] Trumbull, while arguing that "Stoddardeanism" swept the Valley, offered no documentation, only the common assumption of other nineteenth-century chroniclers of Valley ecclesiastical history.

Another flaw is the apparent discrepancy between doctrine and discipline in Stoddard's thought, the gap between his evangelicalism and his allegiance to a presbyterial Instituted Church. This discrepancy emerges in the attempts of commentators to prove compatibility. For example, Thomas A. Schafer, who has offered the most cogent analysis of Stoddard's ties to the Awakening, emphasizes his contributions to evangelical doctrine, especially his theory of conversion. Schafer attempts to tie Stoddard's doctrinal stance to his Instituted Church by speculating that his notion of communion was but a small part of his general scheme for preparing sinners for grace. Yet Stoddard thought otherwise. In his *The Doctrine of Instituted Churches Explained and Proved from the Word of God* (1700) he described the Instituted Church as the only way to salvation and contended that Christ "instituted" the ordinances of the church for conversion, not simply for preparation.[5]

351

From another vantage point James Walsh views Stoddard solely as a champion of discipline. He argues that Stoddard was a Presbyterian, and a rather ordinary one at that, who offered the parish way as a solution for the decline of religion in New England. To fill the churches, he rejected the binding covenants and restrictive membership policies of Congregationalism and opened church doors to all professing Christians. Walsh suggests that Stoddard did not really believe in "converting" ordinances or a sacramental church. Similarly, he places little credence in Stoddard's evangelicalism. Yet Schafer provides abundant evidence that Stoddard sought to revive religion and win souls through gospel preaching, not Presbyterian discipline.[6]

[3] Miller, "Solomon Stoddard," *Harvard Theo. Rev.*, XXXIV (1941), 299.
[4] (Northampton, Mass., 1898-1902).
[5] Schafer, "Solomon Stoddard," in Henry, ed., *Miscellany of American Christianity*, esp. 328-335, 340; Stoddard, *The Doctrine of Instituted Churches Explained and Proved from the Word of God* (London, 1700), 1-8, 18-22.
[6] Walsh, "Stoddard's Open Communion," *NEQ*, XLIII (1970), 106-114. Walsh should be compared to E. Brooks Holifield, "The Renaissance of Sacramental Piety in Colonial New England," *William and Mary Quarterly*, 3d Ser., XXIX (1972),

Among modern students only Miller wrestled with the apparent
discrepancy in Stoddard's thought, and he tried his best to explain
it away.[7] In seventeenth-century New England, Miller wrote, Stoddard
was unique. Although a Presbyterian, his premises reflected American
experience rather than European ideology. He was our first empiricist,
"announcing a new era, free from the past and self-reliant; he was
arguing from facts and not from theories, concerned with results and
not with dogmas."[8] Anticipating his analysis of Edwards, Miller asserted that Stoddard's theology and ecclesiology grew from the reality
of life in the Connecticut Valley, not from abstract speculation. Stoddard's revolution, he wrote in a 1941 article, "was a product of his
character and his background. He was spokesman for the frontier, for
the Connecticut valley, against Boston and Cambridge."[9] He repeated the
argument in *The New England Mind From Colony to Province*. "I am,
of course, speculating," he mused, "but the impression of Stoddard's
personality is so vivid that one cannot help seeing in his doctrine the
reflection of his surroundings; to these, rather than to any European
or English influence, must be attributed his so-called 'Presbyterianism.' "[10]
Stoddard, he went on, appealed "not to the Bible or nature, or even
to reason, but to the lessons of history in western Massachusetts. . . . The
New England mind dearly loved logic, but Stoddard's was a new kind
of dialectic, the premises shot out of his experience like bullets from a

352

33-48. Holifield argues that the dismay of many clergy in the late 17th and early
18th centuries over the failure of the "scrupulous" and the "indifferent" to attend
the Lord's Table resulted in what he calls a "renaissance" of an "evangelistic sacramental piety." He notes correctly the importance of Stoddard's influence in that
renaissance.
   [7] Pettit, *Heart Prepared,* esp. 205, detects a major discrepancy but does not pursue it. While analyzing Stoddard's position on preparation as outlined in *A Guide
to Christ. Or, The Way of directing Souls that are under the Work of Conversion*
(Boston, 1714), as well as Stoddard's relationship to other New England prepara-
tionists, he writes that "although Stoddard had discarded experiential relations as
the requisite for church membership and had extended communion to sinners, this
practice did not alter his notion of conversion." The implication is that it should
have. Pope, *Half-Way Covenant,* 253, also notes an inconsistency in Stoddard's
thought and suggests, as though unaware of the significance of his statement, that
Stoddard changed his mind on certain important matters of theology. As the reader
follows the argument of this article that significance should become clear.
   [8] Miller, "Solomon Stoddard," *Harvard Theo. Rev.,* XXXIV (1941), 318.
   [9] *Ibid.,* 281.
   [10] Miller, *From Colony to Province,* 257.

musket."[11] Increase Mather, Miller concluded, "could never understand how much of an empiricist Stoddard had become."[12]

New England society changed rapidly, outgrowing the stultifying conformity of the New England Way and the New England Mind. Experience was the new guide to social utility and Stoddard was its spokesman. Thus, for Miller, Stoddard's Instituted Church and his evangelicalism were compatible because they came from experience, "the lessons of history in western Massachusetts." Yet Miller's argument rang hollow even to his own ears. Evangelicalism coincided with the democratic, leveling tendencies of the frontier. It eschewed discipline, undercut authority, damaged institutional order, and paved the way for a new scheme of things. But Stoddard's Instituted Church was another matter, for it seemed out of step with frontier life. The Instituted Church emphasized discipline, order, and authority centered among the few rather than the many. In fact, in most respects it seemed more like the outmoded New England Way than any "new dialectic." Miller sensed the problem, but he could not resolve it.[13]

353

The key to understanding Solomon Stoddard is not to be found in New England Congregationalism, Old World Presbyterianism, frontier "experience," or frontier democracy. Nor is it fair, or sensible, to view him solely as an actor in the historian's saga of the rise, reign, and fall of the New England Way. Stoddard's complaint went far beyond New England Congregationalism to the whole of the Protestant Reformation, in which New England represented but one isolated outpost. As he often wrote, he was a soul-winner, an evangelical, and he rejected not only New England's, but also the Reformed tradition's, seventeenth-century preoccupation with church discipline. That was Stoddard's significance for his time, a fact overlooked by most modern scholars.[14] He was a lonely but vocal colonial exponent of doctrine over discipline. His sympathies always lay with the early reformers, the propounders of doctrine, never with the later reformers, the architects of church discipline. He, alone among New England's clergy, disagreed with

[11] *Ibid.*, 277.
[12] *Ibid.*, 280.
[13] Miller, "Solomon Stoddard," *Harvard Theo. Rev.*, XXIV (1941), 299-314; Miller, *From Colony to Province*, 231-265, 276-287. See also Walsh's appraisal of Miller in "Stoddard's Open Communion," *NEQ*, XLIII (1970), 97-100.
[14] One who flirted with that notion was Joseph Haroutunian, *Piety versus Moralism: The Passing of the New England Theology* (New York, 1932), 197-198.

Thomas Hooker's admonition that the Protestant Reformation proceeded in two stages, one doctrinal and one disciplinary.[15] For Stoddard
the latter was an aberration, an insult to divine and earthly intelligence.

Coming of age at a time when it was generally believed that
religion in New England was dying, Stoddard blamed the prevailing
polity, Congregationalism. But he went much farther, noting that religion
waned in all Protestant areas, a fact he attributed to an obsession with
discipline. No Presbyterian, he rejected all forms of church government that purported to represent the pattern of the primitive Christian
church. In their stead, and as an antidote to spiritual decline, he offered
his Instituted Church, a sacramental church neither Protestant nor
Catholic, but rooted in his own peculiar and solitary conception of the
meaning of scripture and the evolution of God's plan for mankind.

Consequently, for much of his life Stoddard was a maverick, revered
personally but opposed by nearly everyone, including the members of
his own church. The notion of the "pope" of the Connecticut Valley is
a myth. Stoddard's influence, and it was considerable, stemmed from
his personality, not from his theology or ecclesiology. His Instituted
Church, while it generated much controversy, accomplished little more,
and, contrary to legend, he never controlled either the clergy or the
laity of the Valley.

In the last fifteen to twenty years of his life, however, Stoddard
underwent an intellectual transformation of startling proportions, a fact
which has also eluded modern scholarship. He did not alter his allegiance to soul-winning or his violent hostility to discipline and its particularly onerous New England form, Congregationalism, but he changed
his tactics. He scrapped the Instituted Church with its institutionalized
salvation, heaped abuse on the churches of New England for their
preoccupation with church discipline, and chose the role of evangelical
preacher. As a result, in his last years he developed a following among
clergy he had not had before and played an important role in bringing about the Great Awakening.

Stoddard presented the Instituted Church to New England in 1700
with the London publication of his first and only comprehensive treatise
on church polity, *The Doctrine of Instituted Churches*. Although brief,

[15] See Thomas Hooker, *A Survey of the Summe of Church Discipline* (London,
1648), Introduction, A2-A4.

354

it contained the essentials of his position and showed quite clearly that he was at odds not only with the New England Way but with some of the main tenets of Reformed thought. While the Reformation sought the revival of primitive Christianity, Stoddard rejected all attempts to model polity on the supposed nature of the early Christian church. The Congregational tradition held that the authority of Christ passed to the early congregations of Rome, Antioch, and elsewhere as autonomous units. Hence, the true church was a congregation of true believers in which decisions were made by the members. Presbyterians contended that Christ's authority passed to the Apostles, who formed the first consistory of elders. The modern clergyman, they argued, was the descendant of those early "ministers" and possessed ultimate authority in Christ's visible church.

Stoddard also sought purity, but he denied that it was to be found only in the primitive church. God's church, he believed, formed a continuum from Old to New Testaments, and if one wished the restoration of the "pure" church, one looked first at the polity of God's church among the ancient Israelites. According to Stoddard, the church of Israel represented an Instituted Church created, or instituted, by God for the salvation of men. But what form did that salvation assume? According to Stoddard's exegesis, God made a covenant with the Israelites that if they lived according to His law they would be saved. Christ's death, however, changed the rules for salvation, for in death Christ atoned for the sins of men; to be saved, a man had only to accept Christ as his savior.

In Stoddard's view, man was, of course, powerless to effect his own salvation, for that was the province of the Almighty. Stoddard emphasized instead the process whereby grace was conveyed from God to man through the ordinances of the Instituted Church. They were Christ's legacy and, as a consequence, the real historical significance of primitive Christianity. Christ died to redeem mankind and provided the means of redemption in the ordinances of baptism, prayer, scripture, preaching, censure, and the Lord's Supper.

This, then, represented the heart of Stoddard's complaint against the churches of New England and much of the Reformed tradition as well. Too much time was wasted in speculation about the precise form of the primitive Christian church, for the significance of early Christianity was doctrinal not disciplinary. New England's failure was obvious:

Prevailing theories concerning "pure" churches and the sacraments as only "Seals" of the Covenant of Grace caused God's anger and the country's decline, so that New Englanders starved for lack of spiritual nourishment.

Stoddard's conception of the Instituted Church represented an amalgamation of Old Testament form and New Testament function. The church of Israel was a national church comprising only the Jewish nation. In Christ, God extended his rule and benefits to all men. However, he retained the form of the church of Israel, changing only the rules for salvation. While adherence to the moral law had been sufficient justification for the Jews, a nation of believers, God now confronted a multitude of unbelievers who knew nothing of His power or His law. Obviously, new means were required for their salvation. The Jewish church had existed primarily as a vehicle for divine worship. The new church was that and much more. Its purpose was evangelistic, the saving of sinners, for whom God sacrificed His Son, then "instituted" his church—through the ordinances—to convey the message and the gift to the world.[16]

Unfortunately, Stoddard sounded occasionally as though he favored universal redemption, that his Instituted Church was, in truth, meant for all, and that no man could or would be barred from admission. In reality, although he often implied it, he did not mean it. His argument would have made much more sense had he stated that Christ died for all "visible saints," for that was his intent. In discussing the "fit matter" for church membership, he always made it clear that membership and the sacraments were intended only for visible saints.

By the standards of most New England Congregationalists, however, Stoddard's definition of a visible saint was so broad and loose that, by comparison, his communion did appear to be "open" to almost anyone. His definition proceeded directly from his analysis of the function of the Instituted Church. There were three churches, he argued. The invisible church encompassed the elect. The visible or "catholic" church included all who professed "the true faith in Christ." These made their sainthood visible through a blameless life and a sincere desire to close

[16] Stoddard, *Instituted Churches*, 1-5, 22, 25-28; see also Increase and Cotton Mather's analysis of Stoddard's position, "A Defence of Evangelical Churches," introduction to John Quick, *The Young Mans Claim unto the Sacrament of the Lords-Supper. Or, the Examination of a Person approaching to the Table of the Lord* (Boston, 1700 [orig. publ. London, 1691]).

with Christ, not through church membership or proof of regeneration. Thus, it was possible for a man to be a visible saint and not a member of any particular congregation.

The third church was the Instituted Church, which provided the institutional means for the dissemination of grace. The basic purpose of that church was obvious: to bring all professing Christians to the ordinances so that they might be saved. Thus, for Stoddard, no obstacles should be placed in the path of professing Christians, or visible saints, desiring union with the institutional church.[17] He rejected New England's efforts to insure church purity through tests of regeneration. The ordinances lay open to all who wanted and could qualify for their benefits, and a man who thought himself a reprobate had as much right to them as the man who believed himself a saint. The reasons for this were twofold. First, Stoddard found no warrant in either Testament for any practice limiting membership to proven regenerates. Second, he believed that although a minister could aid in the search for "signs" of redemption, no external test could be devised to determine the condition of something so intangible as the human soul. Moreover, an over-zealous attempt to separate wheat from chaff violated the nature and function of the Instituted Church. Men desired membership because they sought the church's saving ordinances, and any attempt to keep them out for reasons other than immorality or ignorance of Christian doctrine represented a denial of the meaning of Christ's death.[18]

357

[17] In his chapter on Stoddard in *From Colony to Province,* Miller was correct in asserting that Stoddard differed from most New England divines in that his God was more Old Testament than New. However, Miller was wrong in arguing that Stoddard upheld a capricious, irrational God. Stoddard's God was perhaps more terrible than the God of most of his colleagues, yet he was still bound by the "law," and although above it, agreed to abide by it (the binding Covenant of Grace and Christ's atonement). Stoddard, *The Safety of Appearing at the Day of Judgement, In the Righteousness of Christ: Opened and Applied* (Boston, 1687), 205. If anything, Stoddard's notion of God made the Deity a very rational being. Stoddard believed that God's plan for man was perfectly clear and understandable and represented an unbroken chain from creation to the present. Although all-powerful, God acted rationally and man could easily interpret His plan as it was revealed in history. This was Stoddard's message in both *Safety of Appearing* and *Instituted Churches.*

[18] Stoddard, *Instituted Churches,* 5-6, 18-19, 22. Stoddard did not leave the decision to seek membership to chance. Although most ordinances existed only for visible saints, the "Scandalous" were not ignored. They were to be impelled to reform and seek membership through another ordinance, enlightened preaching. Stoddard dwelt very little on preaching in his early treatises, although his Northampton revivals or "harvests" were common knowledge. However, from occasional remarks

Thus, Stoddard could not accept the Congregational doctrine of the autonomous congregation as a community of saints drawn together out of society to worship God and celebrate the sacraments, bound together and to God by a covenant. The particular church, he argued, was a manifestation of the visible catholic church, and membership in one church constituted membership in all churches. For Stoddard, as for Presbyterians, a particular church was an institution whose "members were bound" by the appointment of God to assemble in one place in a constant way for the celebration of "Publick Worship." The church's importance lay in the dispensation of the sacraments. Particular churches were appointed by God as places where members of the universal catholic church came together to celebrate the sacraments.

358

In the absence of a binding covenant, the authority of the particular church came from its membership in the national church. Stoddard believed that the church of ancient Israel had been a national unit. God had made a covenant with the Jews and that relationship applied to the Christian church as well. Each Christian nation was in covenant with God, promising obedience to Him in return for His blessing. Consequently, as in the case of the Jewish church, spiritual authority and power flowed from God through the national covenant to the ruling body of the national church and from there to particular churches.

The Congregational doctrine of independent churches seemed to Stoddard "too lordly a principle." The experience of New England proved to him that the implementation of such a principle led to ecclesiastical anarchy with congregations working constantly at cross purposes. The Instituted Church, as he portrayed it, had but a single purpose—the salvation of sinners. To accomplish its mission, it needed effective coordination of the activities of local churches through a centralized governing body. The "light of nature" suggested to Stoddard that the Church of Scotland most resembled the Old Testament model and God's will.[19]

---

it is known that he envisioned preaching as primarily an educative function designed to instruct the sinner in Christian doctrine and morality, thus qualifying him for church membership. Later, however, Stoddard altered radically his conception of the preaching function, giving it a position of preeminence in the process of conversion. Simultaneously, he deemphasized the saving power of other ordinances, especially the Lord's Supper. See pp. 288ff. and n. 78. See also *ibid.*, 22-25, and Stoddard, *The Inexcusableness of Neglecting The Worship of God, Under a Pretence of being in an Unconverted Condition* (Boston, 1708), 27.

[19] Stoddard, *Instituted Churches*, 7-8, 25-29.

Here Stoddard showed his indebtedness to Samuel Rutherford, the Scottish Presbyterian whose books he had read and admired while a student and tutor at Harvard. Stoddard asserted that ultimate authority in the national church should be vested in a synod composed of all the elders of the churches, or, if the country were too large, of a few elders representing all the churches. The power of that national synod was both specific and pervasive. It would have full authority in the determination and dissemination of sound doctrine and in the fight against error and heresy. It would judge complaints and impose ecclesiastical censures when necessary. It would also oversee the training and placement of ministers, appointing groups of elders to examine each prospective minister to determine proper qualifications.

To facilitate the government of particular churches, Stoddard urged the division of the national church into provinces, each controlled by a body of elders immediately subordinate to the national synod. In turn, each province was to be divided into a number of classes, bodies composed of elders whose duties were to implement, on the local level, the decisions of the national synod.[20]

Turning to the polity of the local church, Stoddard wrote that the minister and ruling elders had complete authority in matters of doctrine and discipline. These officers formed a "presbytery" with total control over church affairs, total because the minister's power came from God through the national covenant and the hierarchical structure of church government. But Stoddard, like New England's Presbyterians, could not totally escape Congregational theory. The brethren, he concluded, were not without rights. They had the authority to choose their ruling elders and thus had considerable power in church affairs.

The pastor administered the sacraments of the church and decided who would be admitted to them and who would not. Baptism lay open to any person who was a visible saint. Membership in a particular church was not a prerequisite, nor was it necessary for the applicant to be the child or grandchild of a member. The prerequisites for communion were much the same. A prospective member need only be a visible saint, that is, to "walk blamelessly" and "profess faith in Christ." Yet Stoddard did have another condition: prospective communicants were to have knowledge of the principles of religion. This latter qualification barred infants from the Table.[21]

[20] *Ibid.*, 29-32.
[21] *Ibid.*, 12, 18-22.

This was the core of Stoddard's "Presbyterianism." His attacks on restrictive membership requirements, church covenants, and congregational government, and his advocacy of open communion, converting ordinances, synodical government, and national churches were tied together neatly in a package labeled the Instituted Church. Was the Instituted Church also the church of New England's Presbyterians? Was Stoddard their spokesman, or was he a maverick whose views were peculiarly his own? Edward Taylor, who knew Stoddard well, favored the latter explanation. He and Stoddard maintained a friendly but serious argument over church discipline throughout the last three decades of the seventeenth century, and no one understood the significance and meaning of the Instituted Church better than the Westfield clergyman. In a 1687 letter Taylor commented on Stoddard's desire to open the Lord's Supper to "all above fourteen years of age, that live morally, and hav[e] Catechisticall knowledge of the Principalls of Religion," and on his views on polity in general. Taylor argued that Stoddard's position reflected the thoughts of no other New England clergymen and represented a dangerous apostasy likely to lead to the pollution of the churches. Yet, while he labeled Stoddard's scheme as new to New England, he recognized precedents in the history of Reformed thought, although, as he cautioned, "you [have] so few of the Non-Conformists for you, and therefore it is a thing well to be suspected."[22]

Boston's Increase Mather disagreed with Taylor, at least at first. As Miller points out, Mather believed that Stoddard led and spoke for a horde of Valley Presbyterians, especially after the protracted debate between the two at the synod of 1679 when Stoddard defended the "Broad Way" or Presbyterian approach to church membership and seemed to have so many clerical supporters.[23]

Mather still thought so in 1700 when, only a few months before the appearance of Stoddard's *Instituted Churches,* he published a lengthy expository defense of New England Congregationalism entitled *The Order of the Gospel.*[24] This was a general attack on the views held by the founders of Boston's Brattle Street Church and, to a lesser extent, by Stoddard. The Brattle Street Church had been formed without many of the traditional trappings of Congregational churches, including

[22] Edward Taylor to Solomon Stoddard, Feb. 13, 1687/8, Edward Taylor's Notebook, Massachusetts Historical Society, Boston.
[23] Miller, "Solomon Stoddard," *Harvard Theo. Rev.,* XXIV (1941), 299-302, and Miller, *From Colony to Province,* 231-247.
[24] (Boston, 1700).

a covenant, and Mather denounced such innovations as dangerous to the safety and purity of New England's churches.[25] He assumed that the views of the Brattle Street founders and Stoddard were identical, listed and refuted their "dangerous" innovations in church polity, and blamed Presbyterians for the worldly and profane attitude of the people and for what he saw as New England's general decline. Religion would thrive again, he concluded, only when unsound doctrine—Presbyterian doctrine—was driven out.[26]

But when Mather read *The Doctrine of Instituted Churches,* his notion of the relationship of Stoddard to the Presbyterians quickly changed and he endorsed Taylor's view that, despite its Presbyterian-like quality, Stoddard's ecclesiology was unlike that of any other New England divine. To counter the *Instituted Churches,* Mather rushed into print a treatise written some years before by an English Presbyterian, John Quick, offering a different view of the nature of the sacraments.[27] In his introduction, which was longer than Quick's text, Mather warned the reader of the peril lurking in the hinterland of Massachusetts. Stoddard endangered the "Happy Union" of the New England churches, he announced, and represented a force more pernicious than all the Presbyterians combined. Compared to the Northampton cleric, the Brattle Street group was harmless. Obviously something Mather read in the *Instituted Churches* had taken him by surprise.[28]

361

[25] There is considerable debate over whether the Brattle Street Church (1698) was intended to be a Presbyterian or an Anglican church or neither. Most scholars have argued for Anglicanism. See, for example, Clifford K. Shipton, *Sibley's Harvard Graduates,* IV (Cambridge, Mass., 1933), 122-123. Miller, *From Colony to Province,* 240-260, does not opt for either label. Instead he sees the church as the result of a conspiracy of wealthy Boston merchants, who could no longer tolerate the stultifying qualities of the New England "Mind," against the protectors of "orthodoxy," the Mathers. Miller believed that the founders of Brattle Street, including Benjamin Colman, were linked with Stoddard as the representative vanguard of a "Yankee" society which recognized that the "New England Way" no longer conformed to the demands of life in the bustling, acquisitive society of early 18th-century New England.

[26] Mather, *Order of the Gospel,* 1-8.

[27] Quick, *Young Mans Claim.*

[28] Increase and Cotton Mather, "Defence of Evangelical Churches," introduction to Quick, *Young Mans Claim,* 9-11. Herein, the elder Mather argued that his *Order of the Gospel* ought to be construed as an answer to Stoddard and that he meant it as such. Yet it seems apparent from his argument in the "Defence" that much of what Stoddard wrote took him by surprise. Why else would he have appended a 62-page treatise to Quick's pamphlet, if he had said all that was necessary in the *Order of the Gospel?*

What surprised him was Stoddard's rejection of so many of the principles of the Protestant Reformation and his obvious interest in seeing the "Enclosures about the Churches demolished, and whatever distinguishes them from the wide and wild World Extinguished."[29] Stoddard rejected what Mather considered the basis of the Reformation: the attempt to distinguish saints from reprobates so as to create churches composed solely or largely of God's elect. For centuries, Mather argued, "Papists" had polluted Christian doctrine with unsound notions while filling their churches with known unregenerates. The Reformation had sought to undo that tangle by studying the New Testament for sound doctrine and practice and by imitating the practices of the early Christian churches. Mather supported this effort and he believed that Congregational doctrine and discipline flowed from it. Stoddard appeared alien to that tradition, for he sought no primitive church in the pages of the New Testament. Instead, he argued that the discipline most reflecting God's wishes was the church of the Israelites, a comprehensive, corporate, national church which made only a token attempt to distinguish saints from reprobates and which, to Mather's eye, differed little from the corrupt Roman Catholic church Protestants had repudiated.

362

Thus, for Increase Mather, representing New England's Congregationalists, Stoddard posed a significantly greater threat to New England than did the Brattle Street group or Presbyterianism in general. The latter challenged New England's ecclesiastical system as Mather saw it but did so within the framework of Reformed ecclesiology. Stoddard questioned one of the major themes of the Reformation, the search for the primitive New Testament church. "We shall not concern our selves," Mather announced, "with his Doctrine, *That Elders have not only power over their particular Churches, but also over others;* and his Essay to Erect *Provincial* and *National* Churches, (and these must Consist only of the *Clergy*) as of *Divine Right*." Instead, he concentrated on Stoddard's scriptural model for the Instituted Church, the Old Testament church of the Israelites. "We see now the *Fault* of our *Platform of Church discipline,*" he concluded: "*Tis too much compiled out of the books of the New Testament!*"[30]

While asserting that the Instituted Church ran contrary to Reformed doctrine, Mather also declared that the Jewish church was not the national church Stoddard portrayed it to be. In one concise paragraph,

[29] Mather, "Defence of Evangelical Churches," in Quick, *Young Mans Claim,* 10.
[30] *Ibid.,* 24, 27.

Mather touched on both his ecclesiological and his historical objections
to Stoddard's position. "To tell us," he wrote, "That the Constitution
of the Church of *Israel,* and of the *Synagogues* as particular Churches
under it, in the Land of *Canaan,* is an Instituti[o]n for the Churches of
the *New Testament,* will rather Astonish than satisfy *Considerate
Christians.* . . . But almost all [t]he *Traditions* that we have about the
Church Government of the *Synagogues,* are ei[t]her the Fabulous, or at
best, uncertain Reports of the *Talmuds,* which were not in being, till
several Hundreds of years after our Saviour."[81]

363

The use of the Jewish church as a model for reformed Christian
churches was but half of Stoddard's argument. Stoddard claimed that
the requirements for man's salvation had changed since the days of the
Israelites from conformity to the Law to faith in Christ's atonement, and
from that he drew the inference that Christ had instituted the ordinances
for the transmission of saving grace. Once Mather understood the
context from which Stoddard argued for his notion of converting ordinances, he hammered at the theme that Stoddard's position was "Papist"
and, although asserted by a few early Lutherans, was rejected by
Protestants because of its similarity to Catholicism.[82]

Mather buttressed his attack with evidence that no major Protestant
group accepted Stoddard's position. He cited the *Heads of Agreement*
as proof that neither Congregationalists nor Presbyterians deviated
from the doctrine of the "Seals."[83] He used Samuel Rutherford as further
proof of Presbyterian rejection.[84] Even the Church of England, which in
many respects conformed to Stoddard's notion of a national church,
kept unregenerates from the Lord's Table. The opposition of New
England's Congregationalists was well known, and he doubted that
New England Presbyterians would be any more sympathetic. For Mather,
Reformation polity represented an attempt to recreate primitive Christianity. Reformed theology sought the same end, rejecting the institutionalized salvation of Catholicism for the more personalized view of
the confrontation of God and man without earthly mediators. Stod-

[81] *Ibid.,* 26.
[82] *Ibid.,* 43-50, 59-60.
[83] According to the doctrine of the "Seals," the Lord's Supper was a commemoration or "Seal" of the Covenant of Grace between God and man. Therefore, it
was argued that admission to the Supper ought to be restricted to known regenerates.
[84] Mather hints that Samuel Rutherford once flirted with the notion of "converting" ordinances.

dard's polity and divinity came close to the institutionalized salvation of the "Papists." Thus, Mather rejected Stoddard because Stoddard questioned the Reformation.[35]

Reading the *Instituted Churches* may have convinced Mather that Stoddard's ecclesiology was unlike that of other New England Presbyterians, but it did not convince him that Stoddard was a maverick. The close temporal proximity between the formation of the Brattle Street Church and the appearance of Stoddard's treatise seemed more than coincidence. Mather linked the two and assumed the worst. An unholy alliance had formed between Stoddard and the Presbyterians, an elaborate plot hatched in the Connecticut Valley and directed toward New England Congregationalism. Had not Stoddard said as much in his treatise? Had he not blamed New England's woes on her congregational polity and warned that he would not be silent until the polity he espoused was enshrined as New England's discipline? Consequently Mather treated Stoddard's work as the war cry of New England Presbyterians, most of whom were located in the Connecticut Valley. He assumed, as did other ministers, that since Stoddard's was the first "Presbyterian" tract to appear from the pen of a New England minister he spoke from a broad and solid base of power. How could he dare attack the Bay establishment unless he could count on the support of the clergy and laity of the Valley? Thus Mather filled his preface to Quick's treatise with dire warnings of the "*Presbyterianism* that runs down *Connecticut* River." He attacked Rutherford, whom he saw as fashionable among the younger Valley clergy, and reminded them that one of their forebears had thoroughly refuted Rutherford. "You our Brethren in the Colony of *Connecticut*," he warned, "that Exceed all the rest of New England, for proclaiming your Indisposition to the *Order* wherein your Churches have so long flourished, will above others attend; Because t'was *Rutherford* that was against your *Thomas Hooker*, . . . whom though he were (with your leave) the greatest man that ever your Colony saw, yet now the most Raw Youths among you can . . . Confute him!"[36]

If Mather hoped to provoke a Presbyterian rejoinder, he did not have to wait long, for soon after the publication of Quick's *Young Mans Claim* a lengthy treatise entitled *The Gospel Order Revived*[37] appeared in Boston. The pamphlet, published anonymously in New York, repre-

[35] *Ibid.*, 43-46.
[36] *Ibid.*, 30-31.
[37] (New York, 1700).

sented the thoughts of three clergymen: Benjamin Colman of Boston's Brattle Street Church, Simon Bradstreet of Charlestown, and Timothy Woodbridge of Hartford's First Church.[38]

The purpose of *Gospel Order Revived* was to defend a tradition—New England Presbyterianism—against Increase Mather on the one side and Stoddard on the other.[39] Its authors disagreed completely with Mather's interpretation of New England's ecclesiastical position and could accept neither his view of New England orthodoxy nor his characterization of Presbyterian "innovators." Moreover, they sought to dissociate Presbyterianism from Stoddard. They rejected his Instituted Church, and they wanted New England and the world to know that they, not Stoddard, spoke for New England's Presbyterians. They agreed with Stoddard on many questions of polity—membership requirements, rule by elder, and particular church covenants—but the discipline they espoused was New Testament, not Old. They sought, like Mather, the essence of primitive Christianity, and they abhorred Stoddard's emphasis on the Old Testament Jewish church and his argument for institutionalized salvation through converting ordinances.

Mather's mistake, the authors argued, was in assuming their views were identical to Stoddard's. Nothing was further from the truth. They

365

[38] The authorship of this important piece remains in doubt. That Colman was the prime contributor seems to be generally accepted, but his coauthors are more difficult to identify. The American Antiquarian Society, Worcester, Mass., possesses a copy that was Increase Mather's own. On the front Mather identified the authors as Colman, Simon Bradstreet, and "T" Woodbridge, suggesting Timothy Woodbridge of Hartford.

[39] Miller assumed that *Gospel Order Revived* was written only to defend the Brattle Street Church and that Colman, the author, had the support of the merchant-founders of that church. However, several manuscripts contained in the Colman Papers, Mass. Hist. Soc., indicate that considerable disagreement existed between ministers and laymen over the correct form of church polity. One letter in particular suggests that the founders intended to form an Anglican church. J. Nelson to Benjamin Colman, May 20, 1699, Colman Papers, I. Yet Colman was a Presbyterian, and several of his later letters suggest that he sought to mold the church into a Presbyterian church but was frustrated by the "Congregationalism" of the land. See esp. Colman to Robert Wodrow, Dec. 9, 1717, in Niel Caplan, ed., "Some Unpublished Letters of Benjamin Colman, 1717-1725," Mass. Hist. Soc., *Proceedings*, LXXVII (1965), 107. This would tend to lend credence to the supposition that the *Gospel Order Revived* was a purely ministerial undertaking, devoid of the conspiratorial aspects suggested by Miller (see n. 25). It also indicates a possible explanation for the authors' decision to turn the treatise into a general defense of New England Presbyterianism while ostensibly only defending the "innovations" of Brattle Street.

accepted Quick's denunciation of Stoddard's conception of the Lord's Supper. Stoddard did not speak for all Presbyterians—Connecticut or otherwise—but only for himself. "Had the Attestation, . . ." they concluded, "been only to recommend the following Treatise of the excellent Mr. *Quick*'s to our perusal and Practice, no Minister in *New England,* that calls himself a *Presbyterian,* but would chearfully subscribe it; but we believe few would considerate in its Reflections on the Reverend Mr. *Stoddard,* or favour that worse Report, That *under the Umbrage of the Name of* Presbyterians *some would bring in Innovations, ruinous to our Churches, and contrary to the Doctrine and Spirit of Mr.* Quick's *Book.*"[40] No doubt the last line was received gloomily in Northampton.

366

Colman, Bradstreet, and Woodbridge did not dwell as much on their differences with Stoddard as on those with Mather, but they did not have to. They had made their point, and lengthy refutation of the Northampton divine would only have weakened their position. Yet Stoddard's Instituted Church sufficiently resembled Presbyterianism that to ignore him would be construed as tacit approval by Congregationalists like Increase Mather. So, in refuting Mather's *Order of the Gospel* and his use of the *Young Mans Claim,* they also rejected any affiliation with Stoddard. They might endorse parish organization, open communion, and rule by elders in the local church, but they wanted it understood that New England's Presbyterians did not accept Stoddard's interpretation of the meaning of the Reformation. He was not their spokesman, nor did they consider him one of them. So far as they were concerned, his sacramental church placed him outside the pale of Reformed ecclesiology.[41]

The pamphlet warfare between Stoddard and Mather continued for the rest of the first decade of the eighteenth century, and Mather gained the support of numerous lesser known New England clergymen who published treatises attacking Stoddard's Instituted Church. Curiously, Stoddard, the supposed "pope" of the Connecticut Valley, could find no one to come to his defense. The literature was all in opposition. Nothing more was heard from the authors of *Gospel Order Revived,* nor did any other New England Presbyterian enter the fray. Through Colman, Woodbridge, and Bradstreet, Presbyterians obviously felt they had distinguished their views from Stoddard's innovations and Mather's distortions of New

[40] Colman *et al., Gospel Order Revived,* 39.
[41] See *ibid.,* ii-viii, 11-27, for the essence of the authors' Presbyterianism.

England's ecclesiastical history. Having accomplished that they withdrew—and watched.[42]

This evidence, while damaging to Stoddard's assumed historical significance, does not destroy it. To assess the true strength of Stoddard's ecclesiology one must scrutinize the clergy and brethren of the Connecticut Valley, for if Stoddard's views swept that region, extant records would reveal it. But they do not, at least not in Connecticut, where few ministers endorsed Stoddard.[43] Most of Connecticut's clergymen were Congregationalists of various hues, while a minority were Presbyterians, although not sympathetic to Stoddard. If any sizeable support existed for the Instituted Church in Connecticut, it would have emerged in connection with the synod of Connecticut churches at Saybrook in 1708, for that meeting took place during the Stoddard-Mather debate. But no such support was evident.[44]

367

[42] The important publications in the controversy are listed in Miller, "Solomon Stoddard," *Harvard Theo. Rev.*, XXXIV (1941), 303-304. Holifield, "Sacramental Piety," *WMQ*, 3d Ser., XXIX (1972), 33, characterizes the debate as an important event in the emergence of sacramental piety among New England's clergy. While this was true, it represented only a portion of the debate. Behind Stoddard's affirmation of converting ordinances lay his idea of the Instituted Church and his attack on Reformed ecclesiology. This was more than enough to prompt Mather, Colman, Woodbridge, Bradstreet, and others to write rejoinders.

[43] I have searched the libraries of both Connecticut and Massachusetts for any evidence linking Connecticut clergymen to Stoddard's views and found practically nothing. Only two may be connected to Stoddard with any certainty. Gurdon Saltonstall of New London—Governor Saltonstall after 1707—supported Stoddard in his Sermon Preached before the First Church of New London, Dec. 26, 1703, "Sermons of Gurdon Saltonstall," Mass. Hist. Soc. Stephen Mix of Wethersfield, Stoddard's son-in-law, made a request in his will that all his daughters receive copies of Stoddard's works (see Sherman W. Adams and Henry R. Stiles, *The History of Ancient Wethersfield Connecticut* [New York, 1904], I, 330-332) and partially endorsed Stoddard in his *Extraordinary Displays of the Divine Majesty and Power* (New London, Conn., 1728), 29.

[44] The best discussion of the Saybrook synod and Platform remains Williston Walker, *The Creeds and Platforms of Congregationalism* (Boston, 1960 [orig. publ. New York, 1873]), 495-516. Another competent discussion of the Platform is M. Louise Greene, *The Development of Religious Liberty in Connecticut* (Boston, 1905), 134-146. The movement for a Connecticut synod and platform of discipline coincided with a similar movement in Massachusetts led by, among others, Increase Mather, who in 1705 circulated a series of proposals for a platform among the Bay Colony churches. The proposals, however, generated little interest and no synod resulted. In *From Colony to Province*, 264-266, Miller observes that the Saybrook Platform, "although borrowing much of its language from the *Proposals,* institutionalized the ecclesiastical theories of Solomon Stoddard." However, he offers no evi-

In preparation for the synod the general court instructed each county to collect the desires of member churches and present a platform of discipline for consideration by the synod. Led by Timothy Woodbridge, Hartford and Fairfield counties, the centers of Presbyterianism in Connecticut, called for synodical rule and the adoption of a Presbyterian constitution. All other counties endorsed some form of Congregationalism. The representatives, meeting in the summer of 1708, worked in a remarkable spirit of compromise and with little disagreement endorsed the theological position of the *Heads of Agreement* of 1691, the joint declaration of London Congregationalists and Presbyterians. There was more argument on a confession of faith. The Presbyterians favored the Westminster Confession while the Congregationalists preferred the Savoy Confession of 1658. After some debate the Presbyterians gave in.[45]

The real struggle occurred over the issue of church government as the representatives perused the drafts presented by the counties. Presbyterians tended to favor Woodbridge's plan, while Congregationalists drifted toward the plan circulated by Nicholas Noyes of New Haven County. The majority preferred the New Haven plan, "but some Clauses were put into it, in Conformity to Mr. Woodbridge of Hartford and some others, who were inclined to the Presbyterian Side."[46] The resulting plan of church government became part of the Saybrook Platform. A general council or synod of all the churches was to meet yearly to discuss common problems and to make recommendations, although no substantive powers were assigned to the body. The plan envisioned the creation of county councils to determine cases of discipline and render decisions in church disputes, as well as "associations" of ministers to license and regulate the clergy and "consider and resolve questions and cases of Importance which shall be offered by any among themselves or others."[47]

---

dence for this conclusion. On the contrary, there is every indication that the Massachusetts "Proposals" and the Saybrook Platform were nearly identical in both language and content, and that neither reflected the assumptions of Stoddard's Instituted Church.

[45] Walker, *Creeds and Platforms*, 438-502, and J. Hammond Trumbull and Charles J. Hoadly, eds., *The Public Records of the Colony of Connecticut . . .* (Hartford, Conn., 1850-1890), V, 51.

[46] The passage is from the Ezra Stiles MS, Yale University Library, New Haven, Conn., and is quoted in Walker, *Creeds and Platforms*, 501.

[47] Walker, *Creeds and Platforms*, 505. The Platform's section on church government is to be found on 502-506.

Nothing in the records of Saybrook suggests the influence of Solomon Stoddard or his Instituted Church. None of the conclusions of the synod, except for the yearly synod and area associations, was even remotely similar to Stoddard's, and the associations received considerably less authority than Stoddard wanted. The Presbyterians at Saybrook, among whom Stoddard ought to have been influential, followed their own leaders, especially Woodbridge, and pursued a course conforming to the intent of the authors of the *Gospel Order Revived,* not the *Instituted Churches.*[48]

369

Similarly, there is no evidence that Stoddard had influence among the laymen of Connecticut's churches. No Connecticut church adopted a polity conforming to Stoddard's or endorsed his notion of converting ordinances. Presbyterianism in general was treated suspiciously by the laity. Some churches did follow practices similar to those proposed by Stoddard but to attribute them solely to his influence is unwarranted.[49]

One such practice was "open communion," which is often assumed to have been a Stoddardean innovation. Stoddard's view that any man or woman above the age of fourteen years could be admitted to the

[48] The existence of an independent "Presbyterian" faction in Connecticut in 1708 is ably documented by Walker, *Creeds and Platforms,* 495-516. Its leader was Timothy Woodbridge, not Stoddard. Presbyterians formed a solid minority of the Connecticut clergy as early as 1660, antedating the arrival of Stoddard in the Valley by a decade. For a discussion of the emergence of Connecticut Presbyterianism, see Pope, *Half-Way Covenant,* 75-95, and Paul R. Lucas, "Presbyterianism Comes to Connecticut: The Toleration Act of 1669," *Journal of Presbyterian History,* L (1972), 129-147. For a recent analysis of the Saybrook synod and Platform, see Richard Bushman, *From Puritan to Yankee: Character and the Social Order in Connecticut, 1690-1765* (Cambridge, Mass., 1967), 150-155.

[49] This conclusion is based on extensive research among extant church records available in manuscript or on microfilm at the Connecticut State Library, Hartford. The notion of Stoddard's influence is predicated largely on the number of clergymen and churches in Massachusetts and Connecticut in the late 17th century apparently sharing his view on an open communion. Scholars have assumed that the idea originated with Stoddard, but, as Pope suggests and my research bears out, it was common to Presbyterians and some Congregationalists long before Stoddard. Stoddard was not innovating but adopting a familiar belief. The innovative elements in Stoddard's ecclesiology were twofold: (1) his peculiar interpretation of the relationship of Old and New Testaments, and (2) his attempt to link open communion to "converting" ordinances. Thus, for documentation of Stoddard's influence, I have scanned church records not for evidence of open communion, for that would be meaningless, but for attempts to link open communion and converting ordinances. I have found no such evidence, except in Stoddard's own church. See Pope, *Half-Way Covenant,* 251-258, and Lucas, "Presbyterianism Comes to Conn.," *Jour. Pres. Hist.,* L (1972), 140-145.

church and to the Lord's Supper if morally upright and possessing sound knowledge of Christian doctrine was adopted by the Northampton church in 1690.[50] The Windsor church of John Warham had dropped the same practice in 1647.[51] The First Church of Hartford adopted it probably in the 1660s and continued it at least until the death of Woodbridge in 1730. In the Hartford area it became known as "Mr. Woodbridge's Way," although it antedated the beginning of his ministry. Hartford's adoption of an open communion had nothing to do with Solomon Stoddard or his converting ordinances. The Hartford church continued to endorse the doctrine of the "Seals" and, despite Woodbridge's Presbyterianism and his opposition to such practices, maintained "Half-Way" and "Full Communion" designations for members as well as zealously guarding the governing rights of the membership.[52]

370

The ecclesiastical records of the churches and clergy of the Connecticut Valley of western Massachusetts, while scant, do not support the supposition of Stoddard's intellectual dominance over the area, although they do attest to the power of his personality. In the early years of his ministry he was surrounded by hostile Congregational ministers. Besides the opposition of Edward Taylor, Stoddard faced one of the oldest and ablest of the Valley clergy, John Russell of neighboring Hadley. Russell, who had led the migration of Connecticut families from Wethersfield, Windsor, and Hartford to Hadley in the 1650s, was once labeled a "Presbyterian" by those of Wethersfield who disliked both his views on ministerial authority and his advocacy of the "broad

[50] Entry dated "1690," Edward Taylor's Notebook.

[51] See the Windsor "Creed and Covenant," adopted Oct. 23, 1647, and Rev. Henry Rowland's brief illuminating history of the Windsor church in Windsor Church Records, III, Conn. State Library. See also Henry R. Stiles, *The History of Ancient Windsor, Connecticut* (New York, 1859), 172-173, and George L. Walker, *History of the First Church in Hartford, 1633-1883* (Hartford, Conn., 1884), 429-431.

[52] Woodbridge's method for admitting new members is described in the records of the First Church of Wethersfield, II, Jan. 2, 1703, Conn. State Library. The date of its adoption is not known, since the Hartford records do not go back earlier than the beginnings of Woodbridge's ministry in 1684. There is no record of a change of the practice under Woodbridge, thus suggesting that it antedated him. Most likely it stemmed from the 1650s or 1660s, for it is known that Samuel Stone, Hooker's colleague, endorsed a position identical to the later practice. See Stone, "Against a Relation of Experience" (n.d.), Notebook of Joseph Gerrish, 1697, Mass. Hist. Soc., which was partially responsible for a violent controversy in the church in the 1650s and 1660s. The controversy is outlined in G. Walker, *Hartford*, 150-180. See also Records of the First Church of Hartford, X, Accounts and Records, 1685-1772, Conn. State Library.

way" in admitting new members. In 1679 he and Stoddard attended the
founding of Taylor's Westfield church and, after witnessing the public
professions of religious experience of the seven "pillars" of that church,
Russell called it the most ludicrous display he had ever seen, and Stoddard concurred. But Russell was no Presbyterian and no supporter of
Stoddard's views, as he made clear in a 1681 letter to Increase Mather.
He reported on Stoddard's activities and expressed his disgust not only
for Stoddard but for all who deviated from the doctrine espoused by
the synod of 1662. "Our good Brother Stoddard," he wrote, "hath bin
strenuously promoting his position concerning that right which persons sound in the doctrine of faith, and of (as he calls it) a holy
Conversation, have to full Communion." He thought it was time for
the members of the synod of 1662 to defend their fourth proposition
"for the securing of the churches: from pollutions by unprepared ones
incroaching upon full Communion in the Lord's Supper and voting. . . .
the doctrine of those propositions in the Synod 62 doth tend in the end
of the worke . . . to shake and undermine the fundamentall doctrine
and practise of the Congregationall way, viz. that visible Saints are only
matter of a church of Christ."[53]

371

The clearest indication of the ecclesiastical views of the clergymen
closest to Stoddard comes from the scattered remains of the Hampshire
Association of churches, an organization formed largely at Stoddard's
instigation in 1714. Six ministers drew up the proposal for its creation:
Stoddard, John Williams of Deerfield, William Williams of Hatfield,
Isaac Chauncey of Hadley, Daniel Brewer of Springfield's First Church,
and Nathaniel Collins of Enfield. The wording of the document indicated that all of the men favored Presbyterianism, although not necessarily Stoddardeanism. The rationale for the existence of the Association
was Presbyterian, particularly the concluding sentence: "we judge it our
duty, to be subject to a Council of the County, until there be some
Superiour Council set up in the Province unto which we may appeal."[54]

[53] John Russell to Increase Mather, Mar. 28, 1681, "The Mather Papers," Mass.
Hist. Soc., Collections, 4th Ser., VIII (1868), 83-84. The story of Russell's problems
with the church in Wethersfield may be found in Adams and Stiles, Wethersfield,
I, 159-163. Russell's reactions to the relations of experiences by the Westfield members is recounted in John H. Lockwood, Westfield and its Historic Influences,
1669-1919 . . . (Westfield, Mass., 1922), 114-117.
[54] Northampton Church Records, I, Dec. 9, 1714, Forbes Library, Northampton,
Mass.

Yet no evidence links any of these ministers to Stoddard's Instituted Church. This was true even of William Williams, who, next to Stoddard, was probably the most widely known minister in western Massachusetts in the early eighteenth century. His extant writings—a few sermons and letters—give no hint of sympathy for Stoddard's position, only that he was a Presbyterian. Moreover, he was the sole Valley minister to publish a treatise during the Stoddard-Mather debate. That treatise, while devoted largely to the nature of the Lord's Supper, was no defense of Stoddard, for Williams made it clear that he did not believe in converting ordinances.[55]

The extant records of the churches of the Valley do not manifest any sympathy for Stoddard's Instituted Church or, for that matter, Presbyterianism. Several churches refused to join the Hampshire Association even though it did not vest in a ministerial organization the kind of power Stoddard called for in the *Instituted Churches*.[56] The Hampshire Association imitated the associations created by the Saybrook Platform. Although its constitution upheld the Presbyterian conception of a covenanted national church and suggested that individual churches ought to bow to higher ecclesiastical authority, it contained no provisions to make such authority effective.[57] Yet lay opposition to the Association caused dissension and, even among churches whose ministers assented to the Association, one resisted participation. Nathaniel Collins of Enfield faced the loss of his pastorate because of his support. His flock refused to allow him to serve communion, complained bitterly of the quality of his preaching, and criticized him for involving them in the Association.

The controversy in Enfield, which lasted from 1714 to 1718, created the first test for Stoddard's "ecclesiastical council" and provided a barometer of the real influence of the Northampton clergyman in his own area. In 1714 a body of representatives from neighboring churches

[55] Williams's conception of the Lord's Supper is outlined in *The Danger of Not Reforming Known Evils Or, The Inexcusableness of a Knowing People Refusing to be Reformed* (Boston, 1707). See also Williams, *The Honour of Christ Advanced by the Fidelity of Ministers and their being received as sent by Him* (Boston, 1728).

[56] Missing from the list of original churches were, for example, Westfield, West Springfield, and Northfield.

[57] The charter of the Association made no mention of any machinery for the enforcement of decisions of the council and gave no evidence that local churches were being asked to surrender their sovereignty. Northampton Church Records, I, Dec. 9, 1714.

met but failed to find a solution. The next year the matter went to the Association, where the controversy was studied and a scathing letter sent to the church. "We do not understand," the letter read, "that Mr. Collins has given any occasion of grievance. Several persons belonging to other places, who have occasionally heard him abroad and at home have given an Account that his preaching hath been profitable and worthy to be accepted and some of your (selves) that remain unfaithful have given testimony that his preaching has mended."[58] The church had asked for a council the preceding year, the letter continued, but had ignored its advice. Now the church sought another council but, obviously, just to promote its own position. Angrily, the Association told the church to settle its differences with Collins immediately.[59]

373

Three years later the dispute still continued. The Association had failed to find a solution, and in a bitter letter to the church Stoddard, John Williams, and William Williams indicated that the only alternative was for Collins to go elsewhere, an obvious admission that the church had won and the Association had lost in its initial attempt to assert "Superiour power over particular Congregations." The letter read as follows:

Brethren

In answer to your letter of July 29th, we judge that the church of End-field have had no cause of such dissatisfaction these many years, But have cause to reflect upon themselves, having manifested an unpeaceable and disorderly Spirit and layed God much temptation before Mr. Collins; . . . the discord is grown to so great a height, and rejects all remedies, so that it proves an overbearing discouragement and impediment to Mr. Collins in his worke, and a great hindrance to the peoples edification and the edification of their children, we judge it not unwarrantable for Mr. Collins to lay down his work, in that place, hoping that God will make provision for him that he may be more serviceable in another place.

Sol: Stoddard
John Williams
William Williams[60]

Collins left Enfield soon after.

[58] Hampshire Association to the Enfield Church, 1715, Forbes Library.
[59] Ibid.
[60] Hampshire Association to the Enfield Church, Aug. 20, 1718, Gratz Collection, American Section, "American Colonial Clergy," Box 25, Historical Society of Pennsylvania, Philadelphia.

The failure of Stoddard's Hampshire Association to resolve amicably the Enfield dispute reflected the true extent of Stoddard's influence over the churches of the Connecticut Valley. Although Stoddard was personally revered, even feared, his idea of the Instituted Church fell on deaf ears. Nor was his own church a significant exception, for he had only slightly greater success with his own congregation than with neighboring ones. His attempts to remold his church into a model of the Instituted Church were quietly and consistently resisted throughout his pastorate, although, because of his personal influence, he achieved some success and retained the good will of his flock.

374

The First Church of Northampton had been formed in 1661. Stoddard arrived in 1669 as replacement for the first minister, Eleazer Mather, who had died the same year. The church had been organized under Mather's watchful eye, and its polity reflected his Congregationalism. But in 1667 Mather became bedridden with a serious illness and was unable to continue his pastoral duties. The church used his absence as an opportunity to change certain aspects of its polity that the brethren disliked. The church underwent what it called a "reformation," designed to bring its practices into conformity with the prevailing opinions of the country. The "reformation" ended shortly before Stoddard assumed the pulpit.[61]

Northampton's reformation centered on the adoption of the Half-Way Covenant, which Mather had opposed. In addition, the church adopted a new and enlarged church covenant which spelled out in greater detail the obligations of members. The covenant stressed the congregation's duty toward the children of the church and established provisions for their care and edification. Also, the church sought to extend its watch to persons baptized in the Northampton church who remained nonmembers. These persons were allowed to enter a special "state of education" where they could be disciplined and catechized until such time as they could meet the requirements for full communion. The church approved a new profession of faith defining the nature of the Lord's Supper according to the doctrine of the "Seals," and reaffirmed its traditional position on admission to communion. All prospective members were required to make a "relation of experience" designed to reveal the "special worke of Gods Grace" to the assembled members.[62]

[61] Trumbull, *Northampton*, I, 70-105, 214-215.
[62] Northampton Church Records, I, Jan. 9, Feb. 16, and Feb. 22, 1668.

Stoddard began to agitate for changes in the church's constitution soon after his arrival. After his ordination in 1672 he achieved some success when the church agreed to a significant liberalization of membership requirements by allowing children of the church almost automatic membership upon reaching adulthood. "Such as grow up to adult age in the church shall present themselves to the Elders," the church affirmed, "and if they be found to understand and assent unto the doctrine of faith, not to be scandalous in life, and willing to subject themselves to the government of Christ in this Church, shall publickly own the Covenant and be acknowledged members of this church."[63] This was a momentous decision for a church which had shown so much concern four years earlier to bring its practices into conformity with the general practices of the country. In one day a significant group of potential members was released from the obligation of relating an experience of conversion before the congregation.

375

Stoddard probably hoped for more. If he did, he was disappointed, for the polity of his church remained unchanged for the next eighteen years. During that time he no doubt placed his entire church in a "state of education," urging them to accept the reforms he so ardently proposed.[64] Finally, in the winter of 1690 he offered two motions to the church. First, he called for the abolition of a public confession of religious experience in order "to bring all to the Lords Supper that had a knowledge of [the] Principles of Religion, and not Scandalous by open Sinfull Living." Second, he asked the church to approve his contention that the Lord's Supper was a converting ordinance. Stoddard won the first motion and the public profession—a church practice for thirty years—was abolished. The second motion lost by a small majority; the younger members supported Stoddard while the older ones, including the ruling elders, voted against him.[65]

Stoddard's dream of an Instituted Church was not to be realized. The church retained its covenant as well as a half-way status for baptized adults not reared in the town. Members continued to be designated as being in "full communion," and the brethren retained an equal voice with the minister in matters of doctrine and discipline, a situation

[63] Ibid., Nov. 5, 1672.
[64] See, for example, Russell to Increase Mather, Mar. 28, 1681, "Mather Papers," Mass. Hist. Soc., Colls., 4th Ser., VIII, 83-84; see also Edward Taylor to Solomon Stoddard, Feb. 13, 1687/8, Edward Taylor's Notebook, and Stoddard's reply of June 4, 1688, in Taylor's Notebook.
[65] Entry dated "1690," Edward Taylor's Notebook.

inconsistent with Stoddard's beliefs. Moreover, the church never gave official sanction to his notion of the Lord's Supper as a converting ordinance although Stoddard had one final victory. In 1714, the forty-fifth year of his pastorate, the church endorsed the formation of the Hampshire Association and acknowledged the validity of a national church in covenant with God, one in which local congregations recognized that in some areas their powers gave way to those of "ecclesiastical councils." Also, the church agreed to bring all baptized persons in the town under the discipline of the church regardless of whether they had ever owned the covenant.[66] By that vote the Northampton church endorsed a form of Presbyterianism familiar to New England. It was not, however, "Stoddardeanism."

376

At seventy-two, some men might have been content with a small victory, but not Stoddard. Too devoted to his private struggle, he never considered either surrender or armistice. Always the strategist, he recognized that any objective could be approached from different directions just as he knew the value of masking intentions before the eyes of opponents. Therefore he was not above an occasional display of intellectual trickery, such as a public affirmation of something he did not believe or a public denial of something he did believe.

Stoddard's early career documented his elusiveness. All available evidence, for example, suggests that the thought and activity of the young Stoddard led directly to the *Instituted Churches*, yet he consistently disguised his intentions to all but a few persons. He let it be known that he favored an open communion, although he never revealed the Instituted Church which lay behind it. He let men consider him a Presbyterian favoring a Presbyterian view of the sacraments and church admission, not the purveyor of strange doctrine.

In 1687 he published his first book, *The Safety of Appearing at the Day Of Judgement, In the Righteousness of Christ,* in which he endorsed an open communion and stated clearly that the sacraments possessed no saving power but existed primarily to facilitate the preparation of sinners for grace. For that reason and no other, he wrote, he kept only immoral or openly "scandalous" persons from the Lord's Table.[67] Yet, four years after the publication of *Safety of Appearing,*

[66] Northampton Church Records, I, Dec. 9, 1714.
[67] Stoddard, *Safety of Appearing,* 119-125, 175-180.

Stoddard asked his church to endorse the Lord's Supper as a converting ordinance. How many previous attempts he had made is unknown. By his own admission, however, and the implications in Edward Taylor's notebook, the attempts must have been numerous and spread over many years.

Stoddard's craftiness, his occasional attempts at subterfuge, and his skill as a polemicist not only confused contemporaries but have baffled modern scholars as well. Thus it is not surprising to find that students have missed his most important alteration in form, the decision to abandon the Instituted Church around 1708. Attracting little support from any quarter, lay or clerical, and attacked from press and pulpit, Stoddard published a treatise entitled *The Inexcusableness of Neglecting The Worship of God, Under A Pretence of being in an Unconverted Condition.* In it he returned to the position of *Safety of Appearing,* arguing that he had never meant that any ordinance, least of all Communion, existed primarily for conversion. Rather, he continued, the sacraments were intended mainly for preparation, although it was possible that in attending the Table a sinner could be converted. Concerning Communion, on which much of his debate with Mather had centered, he argued that it was no more than a "Memorial of Christs Death."[68]

As he had in 1685, he again urged that open communion was necessary because of the importance of the ordinances in preparatory work. But rather than admit a change of heart, he simply stated that he had been misconstrued by critics who punished anyone daring to "depart from the ways of our Fathers . . ."[69] He continued the same refrain the next year in another pamphlet, *An Appeal to the Learned . . . ,*[70] and then he stopped. He wrote no more on the Instituted Church.

Why he stopped is the object of considerable historical debate. Some students have argued that he defeated Increase Mather and, knowing it, retired. Others, believing the laments of *Inexcusableness* and *Appeal to the Learned,* have ventured the opinion that Stoddard grew tired of being

[68] Stoddard, *Inexcusableness of Neglecting The Worship,* 11-12, 16-17, 25-27. Cf. Stoddard's argument in *Instituted Churches,* 22, where he states emphatically that all ordinances, and especially the Lord's Supper, exist primarily for conversion.
[69] Stoddard, *Inexcusableness of Neglecting The Worship,* Preface.
[70] Stoddard, *An Appeal to the Learned. Being A Vindication of the Right of Visible Saints to the Lords Supper, Though they be destitute of a Saving Work of God's Spirit on their Hearts: Against the Exceptions of Mr. Increase Mather* (Boston, 1709).

misunderstood and misconstrued and simply gave up.[71] In a way he did, but not for these reasons. Stoddard had lost and knew it, and, although he continued to press his own church for reforms for a time, he was eager to extricate himself from further public debate. *Inexcusableness* and *Appeal to the Learned* were designed to allow him an honorable retreat.

Although he lost a battle, he retained his intense desire to reach New England's unconverted, as well as his hostility to church discipline, especially Congregationalism. He saw continued signs of religion's decay and, as always, he blamed New England Congregationalism and the Reformed mentality which had fostered it. Too long a frontier minister to be foiled by adversity, Stoddard developed a new plan for New England's redemption.[72] In 1718, he explained his decision to drop the Instituted Church in a blistering little pamphlet entitled *An Examination of the Power of the Fraternity.*[73] *An Examination,* a savage attack on Congregationalism and the Cambridge Platform, sounded typically Stoddardean, but it was not. He wrote it to confess publicly a serious error in judgment. For decades he had assumed that New England Congregationalism represented the collective thoughts and actions of the clergy, so, in seeking reform, he had attempted to alter the thinking of his colleagues. Few had accepted his program, but many had come to agree that change was necessary and had worked actively to bring it about. Their efforts, and his, had reached fruition in such devices as the Saybrook Platform and the Hampshire Association.

In retrospect, Stoddard lamented, they achieved nothing, for the real power in the churches lay with the brethren, and they resisted every attempt at reform, no matter how innocuous. The brethren, Stoddard

[71] Miller suggested that Stoddard won the argument: *From Colony to Province,* Chap. 17. Walsh supports Stoddard's contention that no one understood his position. See "Stoddard's Open Communion," *NEQ,* XLIII (1970), 111-112.

[72] Stoddard's continuing concern for the unconverted as well as his fear of impending doom for New England is ably demonstrated in *The Efficacy of the fear of Hell, to restrain Men from Sin* (Boston, 1713), 5-10. The elements of his new plan for reaching the unconverted were sketched in two sermons bound with *Efficacy.* These sermons, undated, were delivered during a revival in Northampton. One was entitled "Minister's had need have the Spirit of the Lord upon them, in order to the reviving of religion among the people." The other was "To Preach the Gospel to the Poor."

[73] Appended to Stoddard, *The Presence of Christ with the Ministers of the Gospel* (Boston, 1718).

argued, were the true paladins of Congregationalism, although it was not the Congregationalism of clergy, synods, or the Reformed tradition. Rather, it masked the very godlessness he and others had labored so long to destroy. The brethren were hypocrites, claiming to protect their rights and privileges in God's name while seeking only self-interest. They labeled all existing practices and beliefs traditional and therefore sacrosanct, and resisted reform even when shown how, in the name of the "power of the fraternity," their recalcitrance contributed to the collapse of true religion.[74]   For the first time, Stoddard drew a sharp distinction between lay and clerical conceptions of a congregational polity. The former, not the latter, constituted the real enemy. The Instituted Church foundered not as a result of Increase Mather's logic but because of the ignorance and hostility of the laity. Smug and secure in their churches, fearful of change in any form, the brethren cloaked worldliness in the guise of Congregationalism while arguing that no alteration in either doctrine or discipline was possible without the approval of the fraternity—approval the fraternity never granted.

379

The brethren rationalized the "power of the fraternity" with constant appeals to the Cambridge Platform, and Stoddard turned his fury on that document and its creators. "The mistakes of one Generation," he announced, "many times become the calamity of succeeding Generations. The present Generation are not only unhappy by reason of the darkness of their own Minds, but the errors of those who have gone before them, have been a foundation to a great deal of Misery." The Platform was contrary to the "experience" of the churches in that it was written "before they had much time to weigh those things . . . and some of their Posterity are mightily devoted to it, as if the Platform were the Pattern in the Mount." And what was the "experience" of the churches? A century of life in New England demonstrated that the "community" was unfit to judge and rule in the church. The brethren lacked both understanding and wisdom, for few had "read or studied." "If the Multitude were to be judges in Civil causes," Stoddard warned, "things would quickly be turned up-side down."[75]

Stoddard offered "practical" objections to the Platform as well, evidently assuming that laymen would respond to that approach. He devoted his energies to refuting specific arguments against clerical rule,

[74] Ibid., 1-3.
[75] Ibid., 1-2, 11.

repeating a litany he had uttered for half a century. He chided those willing to let elders act only as "moderators" of meetings. To those who feared "corrupt" elders he replied that lay power was a poor defense against corruption since corrupt rulers always indicated a corrupt people. He spoke also of those who feared rule by elder because it tended to "exalt the Minister or debase the Brethren." In that, he added sarcastically, there was no more danger than in "the confining of Preaching to the Minister."[76]

380

More than ever Stoddard blamed New England's preoccupation with church discipline for the sad state of religion. By 1718 he believed he possessed a clearer understanding of the problem, and it was far worse than even he had imagined. Buttressed by the Cambridge Platform, clerical Congregationalism had wrought a social revolution. The brethren, blindly following the dictates of deluded minds, used the Platform to justify godless ways and protect them from all clerical attempts at reform. Trapped by ancient rhetoric, the clergy continued to seek a solution in discipline, little realizing that synodical decisions paled before the "power of the fraternity." Stoddard was just as critical of his own thinking. His Instituted Church, an alternative to Congregationalism and Presbyterianism, had been aimed at clerical ears. That it had generated no enthusiasm meant little, for he realized now that, even had he won hosts of ministerial supporters, the fraternity would have stopped him, just as it had in Northampton. Thus, perhaps sadly, Stoddard wrote the epitaph for his sacramental church.

To destroy the grip of the brethren on the structure of the churches, to resurrect clerical authority, and to reach New England's ever-growing multitudes of unconverted, Stoddard adopted a new tactic and gave it theological justification. By his own claim one of New England's most successful soul-winners, Stoddard measured his ministerial experience to find the secret of his success. His own personality, he decided, was the key. Not that he attributed any special power to his own efforts—for whatever he possessed was God's—but he had been the agent in the conversion of many souls and, he concluded, whatever he had done must have been right in the sight of God.

The position that Stoddard now adopted was not so much new as an elaboration of skeletal ideas presented in *Safety of Appearing*. The gospel was the sole means to conversion. Before conversion, however,

[76] *Ibid.*, 7, 14-15, 16.

every sinner underwent preparatory work, although that work had no saving power in itself. Preparatory work proceeded in two stages, humiliation and contrition, and its progress was aided by the ordinances of the church: baptism, preaching, the Word, Communion, and the like.[77]

His new evangelicalism was patterned on this outline, although in a considerably modified form. Searching his own experience in Northampton, he decided that God most often used the ordinance of preaching as the vehicle for the dispensation of grace.[78] Thus he concluded that if religion in New England languished it did so primarily because of the low quality of ministers and their lack of training in the workings of the Spirit, often due to their own unconverted state. Also, it languished because of the pathetic state of preaching and the shortage of "powerful preachers."[79]

Simply stated, Stoddard's plan involved little more than an attempt to upgrade the quality of ministers by conveying to them what he, in his success, had learned of the true nature of the ministerial function. What he passed on by book and pamphlet between 1713 and 1729 were his secrets. In *A Guide to Christ* he explained the workings of the Spirit and the "varieties of religious experience" and offered to young clergymen his wisdom and expertise in guiding sinners through preparatory work. In the same book he emphasized the absolute necessity of a converted ministry, arguing that no one could understand another's travail until he had followed the same path. Only six years earlier he had

381

---

[77] Stoddard, *Safety of Appearing*, 119-125; his argument should be compared with his *Guide to Christ* (1714), Preface, 3-23, and *The Nature of Saving Conversion, and the Way wherein it is Wrught* (Boston, 1719), 81-83, for obvious similarities.

[78] This is the essence of *Guide to Christ*. Throughout the sacramental phase of his career Stoddard emphasized that preaching was meant primarily to edify those not able to qualify as visible saints, while other ordinances were to prepare and convert professing Christians. Thus, in downgrading the converting power of some ordinances, he enlarged and enhanced the meaning and scope of gospel preaching. See, for example, *Inexcusableness*, 27, and n.18 above.

[79] Stoddard's argument, repeated often between 1713 and 1729, may be gleaned from several of his writings. In addition to *Guide To Christ* and *Efficacy*, see *Presence of Christ, The Defects of Preachers Reproved* (New London, Conn., 1724), and *The Duty of Gospel-Ministers to preserve a People from Corruption* (Boston, 1718). The most concise statement I have found of his position is the sermon, "Minister's had need have the Spirit," given around 1712, printed with Stoddard's *Efficacy* and also appended to the 1816 edition of *Guide To Christ* (Northampton, Mass.), 157-175.

written that a converted ministry was not really necessary to do God's work.[80]

In the writings of his last years, Stoddard developed his conception of "powerful preaching," including the proper use of emotionalism and the fear of damnation. Schafer and others have noted its distinctive characteristics.[81] Stoddard stressed constantly the correct manner of preaching—his manner. The gospel, while the only means of conversion, seemed most "efficacious" in the hands of the experienced and converted minister of the Lord who developed its truths in the manner used by Stoddard. Such a message was not novel in New England, for it invoked images of Shepard and Hooker, as well as an earlier Stoddard.[82] Yet for the aged warrior it represented a real breakthrough, for it suggested a tactic that would simultaneously reach the unconverted, raise the level of ministerial importance by making clergy vital in conversion, and provide a lever to unhinge the "power of the fraternity" and diminish the importance of church discipline in the minds of both clergy and laity.

Meanwhile other Valley clergymen began to share Stoddard's contempt for ecclesiastical discipline and synodical decisions. As their writings suggest, they flocked to his new plan. The Word was the only source of salvation, and it was most "efficacious" when applied by the "powerful preacher." The ministry must be upgraded, not by formal education, but through experience of the workings of the Spirit and practice in guiding souls through preparation. Suddenly, as never be-

382

[80] Stoddard, *Guide To Christ*, XXI. Cf. his argument in *The Falseness of the Hopes of Many Professors* ... (Boston, 1708), 16.

[81] Schafer, "Solomon Stoddard," in Henry, ed., *Miscellany of American Christianity*, esp. 333-335, 340-342, is outstanding in this regard and, while devoted largely to analyzing his theory of conversion, takes notice of Stoddard's belief in the efficacy of emotional preaching and the proper presentation of the Word. Schafer's article, while generally excellent, should be followed by Pettit's discussion of Stoddard as a preparationist in *Heart Prepared*, 200-207, which displays a keener understanding of the position of Stoddard in the evolution of the notion of preparation for grace in New England.

[82] Stoddard paraphrased Hooker when he wrote, "The word of God is an hammer, and men must smite with strength to make the nail enter, or the rock to break. If the word of God be preached in a dull dead way, it is not like to have much efficacy." "Minister's had need have the Spirit," in *Guide to Christ* (1816), 159. See also the sermon following, "To whom is the gospel to be preached?," 163-169, 176-183. Other passages illustrating Stoddard's doctrine of minister and Word are quoted by Schafer, "Solomon Stoddard," in Henry, ed., *Miscellany of American Christianity, passim.*

fore, ministerial writings discovered Paul as the archetype of the powerful preacher and agent of conversion. He was described as an itinerant
evangelist, dispensing the Word and bringing souls to Christ. Paul had
argued, the evangelicals believed, that there were two principal ingredients
in conversion, minister and Word. Properly handled, they were devastat-
ing.[83]

As Stoddard hoped, the Connecticut evangelicals' emphasis upon
gospel preaching led them to open hostility toward Congregational
discipline. Their intent was to create a "Great Awakening" and, to
facilitate its coming, they advocated an itinerant, evangelical ministry.
The realization of this ideal began haltingly in efforts like Stoddard's
Hampshire Association's establishment of weekly public lectures around
1712 in which members exchanged pulpits and gave "reforming sermons" designed to stimulate religious revivals.[84] In the 1720s the practice became more informal and subject to abuse by laymen who travelled
about posing as trained clergy. Ultimately, of course, the trend toward

383

[83] Stoddard's evangelicalism was matched by that of his colleague at Hatfield,
William Williams, in *The Great Salvation Revealed and Offered in the Gospel*
(Boston, 1717). Like Stoddard, Williams based his treatise on Paul's letters,
emphasized the role of minister and gospel in conversion, and issued a call for a
ministerially inspired "revival." Other examples of Williams's evangelicalism are
found in *A Painful Minister The Peculiar Gift of the Lord of the Harvest* (Boston,
1717), *The Great Duty of Ministers To Advance the Kingdom of God* (Boston,
1726), and *The Honour of Christ*. In Connecticut one of the most ardent advocates
of the new evangelicalism was Eliphalet Adams of New London. Adams's arguments closely paralleled those of Stoddard and Williams, exalting the power and
authority of the minister because of his central position in the conversion process.
Adams's commitment to Pauline theology was complete, his zeal for revival an
obsession. See esp. *A Sermon Preached at Windham* . . . (New London, Conn.,
1721), *The Work of Ministers, rightly to Divide the Word of Truth* (New London,
Conn., 1725), and *Ministers Must take heed to their Ministry, to Fulfil it* (New
London, Conn., 1726). There were also other treatises on the new evangelicalism
published by ministers of lesser note. These include two by Jonathan Marsh of
Windsor, *An Essay, To Prove the Thorough Reformation of a Sinning People is
not to be Expected* . . . (New London, Conn., 1721), and *The Great Care and
Concern of Men Under Gospel-Light* . . . (New London, Conn., 1721); an ordi-
nation sermon by Isaac Chauncey of Hadley entitled *The Faithful Evangelist, Or the
True Shepherd* (Boston, 1725); also Samuel Whitman of Farmington, *Practical
Godliness the Way to Prosperity* (New London, Conn., 1714); and John Woodward
of Norwich, *Civil Rulers are God's Ministers, for the Peoples Good* (Boston, 1712).

[84] The reference to the Hampshire County Weekly Lecture is from Warham
Williams, Journal, 1712, Mass. Hist. Soc. A Hartford County Weekly Lecture
began soon after and is discussed in G. Walker, *Hartford*, 268-270.

an itinerant ministry would find fruition in the career of George Whitefield.

Evangelicals continually looked for signs of an "Awakening." In the 1720s, revivals and mass conversions or, in the ministerial rhetoric, great "outpourings of the Spirit" appeared frequently. In 1721, for example, Eliphalet Adams of New London traveled to Windham, Connecticut, to mark a revival in that community and praise the minister whose preaching brought it about. He told a throng that revivals, although still widely scattered, were no longer uncommon and that a "great Awakening" appeared imminent.[85]

384

Adams, of course, was correct, although it is doubtful whether the results were those intended or expected by the clergy. In Norwich, for example, evangelicalism only added fuel to the deep-seated personal and institutional antagonisms already present in church and community, especially those between church and minister, church and town, and brethren and brethren. Instead of reviving religion and restoring ministerial authority, revivalism in Norwich resulted in the destruction of the church.[86] In Northampton where Stoddard's grandson and successor, Jonathan Edwards, gave revivalism an intellectual justification far superior even to Stoddard's, Edwards's reward was missionary work among the Indians.

The pattern in Norwich and Northampton was the pattern of the Great Awakening in New England.[87] The institutional cement of many churches—Stoddard's lay Congregationalism—cracked, although the result was not so much heightened religiosity as social and ecclesiastical chaos. A plethora of new sects emerged and anticlericalism remained, as did the trend toward secularism or "worldliness." Moreover, the fragmenting effects of the Awakening appeared in secular institutions, disrupting traditional patterns of authority, weakening institutional relationships, and, some have argued, creating fertile ground for a revolutionary mentality.

Had he lived, Stoddard would have decried the results as loudly as

[85] Adams, *Sermon at Windham*, ii-iv.
[86] See J. M. Bumsted, "Revivalism and Separatism in New England: The First Society of Norwich, Connecticut, as a Case Study," *WMQ*, 3d Ser., XXIV (1967), 588-612.
[87] An exception to the pattern of disruption is noted and analyzed by James Walsh, "The Great Awakening in the First Congregational Church of Woodbury, Connecticut," *ibid.*, XXVIII (1971), 543-562.

any. Yet New England's traditional preoccupation with discipline suffered irrevocable harm, and revivalism and evangelicalism became permanent features of American religious history. Solomon Stoddard, New England's often lonely pioneer advocate of doctrine over discipline, deserved much of the credit although the irony of his final victory would not have escaped him. A persistent foe of Reformed ecclesiology, his most effective weapon proved to be Reformed theology. Long the champion of the institutional church, Solomon Stoddard nearly brought about its demise.

385

Notes and Documents

Perry Miller: A Note on His Sources in
The New England Mind: The Seventeenth Century

C ARL Bridenbaugh's declaration in 1940 that "as the Bible was the ultimate authority of the Puritans, so *The New England Mind* must be a Sibylline Book for students of American history, litera-ture, and thought" has become a truism over the past three decades.[1] Perry Miller's work has retained this enduring influence partly because it in-spired many other scholars to activity; a mere survey of the literature re-lated to Miller's work in the single decade of the 1960s has constituted a lengthy article.[2] Some monographs, like Edmund S. Morgan's *The Puritan Dilemma*, have expanded upon themes suggested in *The New England Mind*.[3] Other books, such as Norman Pettit's *The Heart Prepared*, Robert G. Pope's *The Half-Way Covenant*, and T. H. Breen's *The Character of the Good Ruler*, have amended *The New England Mind* to some extent but are still within what might be called the Millerite tradition.[4] Only David D. Hall's recent book, *The Faithful Shepherd*, departs appreciably from Miller's work, reasserting the Cal-vinistic and reformed traditions of Puritan thought.[5] Even the behavioral

---

* Mr. Selement is a doctoral candidate at the University of New Hampshire.
[1] Review of Perry Miller, *The New England Mind: The Seventeenth Century*, in *American Historical Review*, XLV (1939-1940), 889.
[2] Michael McGiffert, "American Puritan Studies in the 1960's," *William and Mary Quarterly*, 3d Ser., XXVII (1970), 36-67.
[3] *The Puritan Dilemma: The Story of John Winthrop* (Boston, 1958).
[4] Pettit, *The Heart Prepared: Grace and Conversion in Puritan Spiritual Life* (New Haven, Conn., 1966); Pope, *The Half-Way Covenant: Church Membership in Puritan New England* (Princeton, N. J., 1969); Breen, *The Character of the Good Ruler: A Study of Puritan Political Ideas in New England, 1630-1730* (New Haven, Conn., 1970).
[5] *The Faithful Shepherd: A History of the New England Ministry in the Seventeenth Century* (Chapel Hill, N. C., 1972). Hall's differences with Miller can be found in his essay, "Understanding the Puritans," in Herbert J. Bass, ed., *The State of American History* (Chicago, 1970), 330-349. George M. Marsden's

historians, such as John Demos, Philip Greven, Kenneth Lockridge, and Darrett Rutman, who devote themselves to the very social history which Miller insisted failed to deal with the "fundamental themes" of New England's history, attempt to relate their work to Miller's intellectual history.[6] All of this demonstrates the significant impact that *The New England Mind* has made on colonial historians in the last thirty-five years.

Another reason why Miller's work has retained its vitality, and remained the only new synthesis of the Puritan mind, involves his reputation for exhaustive research. The "unprecedented thoroughness" of *The New England Mind* and its use of "material almost entirely unfamiliar" have led scholars to believe that Miller meticulously and chronologically "read everything written by Puritans in England or New England in the seventeenth century."[7] As recently as 1966 Morgan asserted that during the 1930s Miller "systematically read everything written by New Englanders in the seventeenth century along with the bulk of writings by English Puritans," which supplied the basis for *The New England Mind.*[8] After thirty-five years, however, it seems necessary to inquire: What exactly were Miller's sources? How did he use them? Did he really define the whole of New England's mind?

Unfortunately Miller obstructed most historians from scrutinizing the materials he used by abandoning conventional documentation, eschewing print, and depositing his footnotes in Houghton Library of Harvard University.[9] The relative inaccessibility of the footnotes seems to have discouraged historians from carefully analyzing them. Perhaps

---

"Perry Miller's Rehabilitation of the Puritans: A Critique," *Church History,* XXXIX (1970), 91-105, also reveals some of the shortcomings of Miller's analysis and suggests alternative approaches to the history of Puritanism.

[6] Demos, *A Little Commonwealth: Family Life in Plymouth Colony* (New York, 1970); Greven, *Four Generations: Population, Land, and Family in Colonial Andover, Massachusetts* (Ithaca, N. Y., 1970); Lockridge, *A New England Town, the First Hundred Years: Dedham, Massachusetts, 1636-1736* (New York, 1970). Rutman's *American Puritanism: Faith and Practice* (Philadelphia, 1970) is a recent effort to "bridge the gap" between the intellectual historians who study New England "as a Puritan *idea*" and the social historians who study New England "as a *society*" (vi).

[7] See Edmund S. Morgan, "Perry Miller and the Historians," *Harvard Review,* II (1964), 54, 58, and the following reviews of *The New England Mind:* W. E. Garrison in *Christian Century,* LVII (1940), 575, and Marjorie Nicolson in *New England Quarterly,* XIV (1941), 377. Cf. Alan Heimert, "Perry Miller: An Appreciation," *Harvard Rev.,* II (1964), 43-44, and the following reviews: Merle Curti in *Social Studies,* XXXI (1940), 37; Edmund S. Morgan in *The Boston Transcript,* Oct. 19, 1939; J. H. Shera in *Library Quarterly,* X (1940), 304.

[8] Edmund S. Morgan, "The Historians of Early New England," in Ray Allen Billington, ed., *The Reinterpretation of Early American History: Essays in Honor of John Edwin Pomfret* (San Marino, Calif., 1966), 52.

[9] Two reviewers criticized Miller for his decision not to publish the footnotes: John M. Mecklin in *American Journal of Sociology,* XLVI (1940-1941), 111, and William W. Sweet in *Journal of Religion,* XX (1940), 290-292.

this accounts for the widespread belief that Miller read, comprehended, and utilized all or, at least, the overwhelming majority of New England materials. Actually, the converse is closer to the truth. Miller utilized a limited and extremely selective number of authors in formulating his version of the New England mind.

According to Miller, the seventeenth century included the opening decades of the eighteenth. Therefore his New England sources could have been selected from any published or unpublished materials by any New Englander between the years 1620 and 1730. One can estimate, being careful to avoid duplication, from the 1,063 works written by Harvard graduates up to the class of 1690 and listed in John Sibley's *Biographical Sketches of Graduates of Harvard University,* the 399 titles to be found in Joseph Sabin's *A Dictionary of Books relating to America,* and an additional 44 titles catalogued in Charles Evans's *American Bibliography* that there are at least 1,506 published New England sources available to the colonial historian.[10] To the list of published treatises must be added town, colony, and church records, creeds, laws, unpublished diaries, letters, sermons and sermon books, poems, histories, scientific journals, Latin exercises, legal briefs, even medical prescriptions, and Harvard theses.[11] To what extent did Miller exploit this enormous mass of material?

To define the intellect of the first part of the century, from 1620 to 1660, Miller relied on but nineteen authors and eighty-five literary sources.[12] Although not an overwhelming quantity of materials and failing to fulfill rigorous standards for a definitive study, his selections, if sufficiently representative, might possibly have reflected accurately the thought of the period. But fully forty-seven of the eighty-five sources were the works of just three New England ministers—Thomas Hooker, John Cotton, and Thomas Shepard. One must question whether three ministers adequately reflected the thought of a complicated forty-year period, one which saw the very founding of the New England Way. Does this body of material encompass the subtle variations even among "orthodox" ministers? What of the dissenters? Miller cited Roger

388

[10] Clifford K. Shipton, *Sibley's Harvard Graduates: Biographical Sketches of Those Who Attended Harvard College* (Cambridge, Mass., 1933-); *Joseph* Sabin *et al., A Dictionary of Books relating to America from its Discovery to the Present Time* (New York, 1868-1936); Clifford K. Shipton, ed., *Evans's American Bibliography: A Chronological Dictionary of All Books and Pamphlets and Period- icals Printed in the United States of America from ... 1639 ... to ... 1820* (New York, 1903-1955).

[11] For Harvard theses see Samuel Eliot Morison, *The Founding of Harvard Col- lege* (Cambridge, Mass., 1935), 438-440, and *Harvard College in the Seventeenth Century* (Cambridge, Mass., 1936), 580-638.

[12] All statements regarding Miller's footnotes are based on a study of the volumes deposited at Houghton Library, Harvard University, Cambridge, Mass.

Williams once, ignored the writings of the Antinomians, and left
Baptist literature untapped. What of Plymouth's contribution? What of
merchants, farmers, and civil leaders whose lives, while deeply religious,
involved more than formal religion? Rutman has correctly argued that
"we cannot simply assert that the ministers' ideas were Puritan ideas
equally ascribable to ministers and laymen."[13] Miller did not have to
write his history "from the bottom up," but it would seem that he could
have based his work on a broader foundation of source materials.

Miller's use of sources from the second part of the century, between
1660 and 1730, was on a par with that for the first part. He employed
138 writings by forty-one authors. Although the variety in this seventy-
year period appears larger, three clergymen accounted for 56 percent
of the sources. Can Increase Mather, Cotton Mather, and Samuel Willard
legitimately represent an even larger New England population? Quakers
besieged the commonwealth during this period, complicating the problem of dissenters, but Miller cited only one Quaker work, Thomas
Maule's *Truth held forth and maintained*.[14] Peter Folger's *A Looking
glass for the Times* was the only Baptist tract considered.[15] In short,
considering the ever-expanding complexity and diversity of New England,
Miller's overriding dependence on three clergymen for documentation
seems blatantly inadequate. Miller's foundation is perhaps too limited
for definitive statements.

In sum, Miller rested his case largely on the opinions of six clergymen.
Out of a total of 223 sources cited, written by sixty colonials, Hooker,
Cotton, Shepard, Increase Mather, Cotton Mather, and Willard accounted
for 56 percent of Miller's documentation. The common notion that
Miller formulated *The New England Mind* from an exhaustive canvass
of sources seems questionable. Morgan's repeated assertion that Miller
"read everything written by New Englanders in the seventeenth century"
may be correct, but from Miller's documentation it is obvious that he
neglected to incorporate such comprehensive reading into *The New
England Mind*.[16] Miller, in fact, used only 15 percent of the published
materials located in Sibley, Sabin, and Evans, and very few unpublished
materials.

The distribution of Miller's quotations from the 223 literary sources
further confirms the limited basis from which he generalized. Although

389

[13] Rutman, *American Puritanism*, 32.
[14] *Truth held forth and maintained according to the testimony of the Holy
Prophets, Christ and his Apostles . . . With some account of the judgments of the
Lord, lately inflicted upon New England by witchcraft . . .* ([New York], 1695).
[15] *A Looking glass for the Times, or the former spirit of New England revived
in this generation . . .* (Boston, 1676).
[16] Morgan, "Historians of Early New England," in Billington, ed., *Reinterpretation of Early American History*, 52.

he quoted colonial sources 996 times, Hooker, Cotton, Increase Mather, Cotton Mather, Willard, and Shepard account for 678 quotations. The ministers can be divided into two clusters, according to the number of times Miller cited each individual. Willard (203), Hooker (182), and Cotton (161) formed the most important group. These three ministers alone supplied 55 percent of Miller's quotations. Increase Mather (56), Shepard (45), and Cotton Mather (31) constituted a supporting group and another 13 percent of Miller's citations. In essence, Miller took 68 percent of his quotations from six ministers.

Miller broadened the narrow scope of his source material only in his discussion of logic where he cited a variety of Harvard theses.[17] In drawing on the theses, primarily in chapters five and six, Miller prevented his treatment from becoming merely an exposition of predominantly European sources. Yet, even counting the citations to Harvard theses, he still drew 57 percent of his documentation from European authors. Only 17 percent of the citations were from Miller's usual ministerial sources. Consequently, if Miller's documentation is an accurate reflection of the clerical interest in logic, one can legitimately ask how important it was to New England thought. European philosophy, although essential as intellectual heritage, cannot directly reveal New England ideology. Harvard theses were strictly academic exercises and, according to Samuel Eliot Morison, "are open to various interpretations, and must be used with caution."[18] Thus, although Miller broadened his source material to some extent, his reliability is questionable because of the heavy reliance on European scholars and Harvard students.

Miller's discussion of logic is also an excellent example of the flexibility and literary license he permitted himself in documentation and the construction of arguments. He combined Renaissance authors, sixteenth- and seventeenth-century English writers, Harvard theses, and

390

---

[17] Miller cited Harvard theses 8 times in chapter four, 32 times in chapter five, 44 times in chapter six, 12 times in chapter seven, 9 times in chapter nine, 3 times in chapter eleven, and 2 times in chapter twelve. Out of a total of 110 citations he used at least 88 to develop his arguments regarding logic and epistemology. Consequently, to treat the theses statistically as equivalent to Miller's other literary sources, which provided the foundation for his volume, would have distorted the actual basis he utilized for his work. Because the theses constitute a sort of special additional source for one subject of the volume, they have been omitted from the above statistics. It is difficult to deal fairly and statistically at the same time with the theses. On the one hand, their inclusion would affect the citation figures very little— a matter of reducing 68% to 61%. On the other hand, to add 100 theses to the 223 literary sources would change the source material percentage (six clergymen most frequently cited) from 56% to 37%. Such a reduction would be deceptive for one additional reason to those already indicated. Footnotes to Harvard theses quite often included four or more theses for one citation, which even further limited the amount of material actually incorporated from them into the text. For all of these reasons the Harvard theses have been treated as a special category.

[18] Morison, *Harvard in the Seventeenth Century,* I, 161.

Puritan divines in one mammoth hodgepodge of complexity. He disregarded chronology throughout the entire analysis, quoting anyone, regardless of time or place, who happened to illustrate a particular point. Thus, in one short paragraph he invoked Petrus Ramus, Ramus's supporters, one of Ramus's enemies, William Brattle, and one of the *Theses Technologicae* of 1719 to develop an argument.[19] In another paragraph he quoted Ramus, a Harvard thesis of 1687, an earlier thesis, Alexander Richardson, George Downame, Samuel Stone, and Samuel Mather.[20] Such passages illustrate Miller's disregard for historical development and setting, and reflect his assumption that men writing in 1544 and 1719, whether in Europe or America, belonged to an identical intellectual milieu.

This assumption was fundamental to Miller's scholarship. Departing from the historian's usual, more cautious technique of citing selected individuals as representatives of an intellectual community or movement, he asserted that "the first three generations in New England paid almost unbroken allegiance to a unified body of thought, and that individual differences among particular writers or theorists were merely minor variations," concluding that the literature of New England could be treated as if it were the product of "a single intelligence."[21] What did Miller mean by such statements? He certainly knew about the existence of Antinomianism, the quarrels over the half-way covenant, the differences regarding church polity, dissenters like Williams or Samuel Gorton, the Separatists of Plymouth, and such sectarians as Baptists and Quakers. Miller simply could not have meant that all New England ministers, to say nothing of laymen, were in absolute agreement. Instead, he seems to have meant that an "orthodoxy" prevailed in New England, encompassing a majority of the ministers. If such an orthodoxy was the focus of Miller's work, it becomes logical for him to argue that it was "a matter of complete indifference or chance that a quotation comes from Cotton instead of Hooker, from Winthrop instead of Willard" because "all writers were in substantial agreement."[22] Such reasoning might explain Miller's limited source materials. He may have invoked Hooker, Cotton, and Willard as spokesmen for "orthodoxy."

The error in Miller's approach lay in his failure to inform readers, either in the title, preface, text, or conventional footnotes, that he was dealing with a select group of ministers. Consequently, everything about *The New England Mind*—from its title to Miller's assertion that "were I to supply a footnote indicating the exact source of every direct

[19] Perry Miller, *The New England Mind: The Seventeenth Century* (New York, 1939), 124-125.
[20] *Ibid.*, 128-129.
[21] *Ibid.*, vii.
[22] *Ibid.*, ix.

quotation or the inspiration for many remarks which are not literal citation, I should republish the complete bibliography of early New England, with various additions, not merely once but many times over"—projects the impression that it speaks for all New Englanders, giving credibility to those who indict Miller for his monolithic treatment of the region's intellectual history.[23] As an alleged survey of New England thought, his account fails to deal adequately with the intellectual diversity that existed among New England thinkers.

392

John Woodbridge, Jr., a Harvard graduate and minister at Killingworth, Connecticut, is an example of a Puritan preacher opposed to the views of Miller's "representative" clergymen. Woodbridge's objection to the New England Way involved the matter of church polity. He informed Richard Baxter, an English divine revered by contemporaries on both sides of the Atlantic, that controversies plagued New England over "whether the Church of Christ upon earth is to consist in Independent and particular Species or no." Woodbridge's Presbyterianism led him to believe that "the Church Consists not of Congregations as specificall or Individuall parts of the whole (as the Ramists call Individuum Species) as Petrus is Part of Homo; But as Integrall parts as manus is pars Corporis."[24]

In a subsequent letter to Baxter, Woodbridge also volunteered his own version of New England's mind. He characterized the region as quite diverse in its ideology, dividing the country into "four quarters, vid: Road Island . . . , Plimouth Colony, the Massachussets, and Connecticot." Rhode Island he deemed the "Sinke into which all the Rest of the Colonyes empty their Hereticks." Plymouth was more acceptable but still "oversprinkled with Brownisme" and "threds of Anabaptisme." Woodbridge did not perceive uniform orthodoxy even in Massachusetts where "three formes of Disciplinarians" existed: the rigid independents, the more moderate ones who abided by the decisions of church councils such as the synod of 1662, and those "Presbyterianly addicted." Connecticut, Woodbridge happily reported, had "waded farthest out of Independency"; out of some twenty-two Connecticut towns there were twelve ministers inclined to Presbyterianism.[25]

Church polity might seem insignificant and something that ministers could differ over without serious effects on other aspects of their thought. Such was not the case with the Reverend Mr. Woodbridge. His Presbyterianism led him to a different procedure for admitting com-

[23] Ibid.; cf. McGiffert, "Puritan Studies in the 1960's," WMQ, 3d Ser., XXVII (1970), 40-42.
[24] John Woodbridge, Jr., to Richard Baxter, Oct. 14, 1669, in Raymond Phineas Stearns, ed., "Correspondence of John Woodbridge, Jr., and Richard Baxter," NEQ, X (1937), 565-566.
[25] Woodbridge to Baxter, Mar. 31, 1671, ibid., 573-576.

municants. He examined the candidates "concerning their knowledge and proficiency in the way of life, of the understanding of the Nature of the Sacrament, and the Qualifications of every Communicant," and if he found "them not deficient before the Sacrament," he declared to the church that "there is nothing Appearing why they should not partake with us in that holy feast." Woodbridge thus deviated from the practice of public testimonies of one's personal conversion experience—so important to Miller's Puritans. He even denounced the idea that "every brother be allowed a feeling of his [the prospective communicant's] pulse and smelling of his Breath and handling of his neck and hands lest he shoud prove a smooth supplanter," adding that "'tis extreame[ly] difficult (it being so pleasing to Naturall pride) to make men vomit it up."[26]

393

Giles Firmin, a participant in the Hutchinsonian synod, is another example of a Puritan cleric who differed from Miller's ministers on an important point of dogma. Firmin found the doctrine of preparation, as taught by Hooker in *The Soules Humiliation* and Shepard in *The Sound Beleever*,[27] unacceptable because of the intense anxiety it caused conscientious Christians. According to Firmin, Hooker and Shepard taught that Christians had to experience "strong convictions, such dreadful legal terrors, deep sorrows and humblings" as a normal part of the conversion process. Firmin admitted that the divines "put in a few words to ease troubled souls" who failed to achieve such upheavals but concluded that those people "very inquisitive after the soundness" of their conversion were unsatisfied and often deeply troubled. The solution, Firmin insisted, was to inform the sincere seeker that "it is the duty of all the sons and daughters of Adam, who hear the Gospel preached, and Christ offered to them, to believe it, or receive Christ, be they prepared or not prepared."[28] Such a "liberal" view was, of course, agreeable to Woodbridge but unacceptable to the "rigid independents" of Massachusetts.

The views of other Puritans connected with New England further indicate that there were variant versions of what ought to constitute the true "city upon a hill." Thomas Lechford, who published *Plain Dealing: or, Newes from New-England* as a result of his visit to the colonies, judged that "congregational independent government" had "no sound ground in Scripture" and was "unfit" for England, Ireland, or any other populous nation.[29] Thomas Parker, teacher of the Newbury congre-

[26] *Ibid.*, 577.
[27] Hooker, *The Soules Humiliation* (London, 1637), and Shepard, *The Sound Beleever. Or, A Treatise of Evangelical Conversion* (London, 1645).
[28] *The Real Christian, or a Treatise of Effectual Calling* (London, 1670), 2.
[29] *Plain Dealing: or, Newes from New-England* (London, 1651), 160.

gation, expressed his reservations concerning Congregationalism in a letter to the Westminster Assembly, which found its way into print as *A True Copy of a Letter written by Mr. Thomas Parker*. He admitted anyone to church fellowship who was not "extremely ignorant or scandalous."[30] John Warham, of Windsor, Connecticut, went one step more, suggesting that "the visible church may consist of a mixed people, godly, and openly ungodly."[31] James Noyes, a student of William Ames and Parker's colleague at the Newbury church, confessed in his *The Temple Measured* that he was "in some things coincident with the judgement of the Reverend Presbyters in New England, in some things consenting with the reverend Assembly in England, and in some things distant from them both."[32] Simon Bradstreet, Woodbridge's uncle, rightly concluded that those who "professe the Congregationall way are not all alike minded in some necessary and essentiall points of Church Government."[33]

394

Certain other conceptual differences became apparent in the banishment of Williams, in the Antinomian Controversy, and in the debates over the half-way covenant. Pope has demonstrated that considerable controversy surrounded the adoption of the half-way covenant. He depicted a divided clergy and a divided laity, joining at different times and places in diverse combinations in their acceptance and rejection of the covenant. Clergymen debated clergymen. Laymen argued with each other. Laymen both supported and resisted clergymen. Schisms plagued many of the churches, and even a "new orthodoxy" emerged from the debates.[34] Such intellectual variations divided members of the Puritan community and in the case of the Antinomian Controversy disrupted the normal social and political patterns. Yet Miller's work, proceeding from his assumptions, made no allowances for such differences. Williams and John Wheelwright definitely do not fit into Miller's scheme, just as Woodbridge, Firmin, Lechford, Parker, Noyes, and Bradstreet are exceptions, and either Thomas Shepard, Jr., or John Davenport, depending on how one views the half-way covenant, seems unable to maintain his "orthodoxy." For Miller, controversial and minority figures—Folger, who was originally orthodox enough to satisfy Cotton Mather but even-

[30] *A True Copy of a Letter written by Mr. Thomas Parker, a learned and godly Minister in New-England unto a Member of the Assembly of Divines now at Westminster; declaring his Judgment touching the Government practised in the Churches of New England* (London, 1644).
[31] Samuel Fuller to William Bradford, June 28, 1630, in "Governour Bradford's Letter Book," Massachusetts Historical Society, *Collections*, 1st Ser., III (1794), 74.
[32] *The Temple Measured, or a Brief Survey of the Temple Mystical, which is the Instituted Church of Christ* (London, 1647), quoted in John Gorham Palfrey, *History of New England*, II (Boston, 1860), 172.
[33] Simon Bradstreet to Richard Baxter, Feb. 5, 1671/2, in Stearns, ed., "Woodbridge Correspondence," *NEQ*, X (1937), 583.
[34] Pope, *Half-Way Covenant, passim.*

tually turned Baptist, Quaker Maule, the Hutchinsons, Williams, William Bradford, and Edward Winslow from the Plymouth stream—were irrelevant to the mainstream of New England thought or beyond the scope of his "orthodoxy." Yet without Separatists, Baptists, Seekers, Antinomians, Quakers, Gortonists, and the other varieties of sectarians, Miller's is a pale shadow of New England's complicated mind. Such groups truly lived in New England, a fact which requires any comprehensive intellectual history of the region to analyze their philosophies and possible influences, and a prima facie case for their contribution to the intellectual development of the area is easily made. "Orthodoxy" produced much of its literature in response to their speculations. The pamphlet warfare between Cotton and Williams is a ready example. The work of John Allin of Dedham is another, for Allin advocated the half-way covenant because its rejection would "give great Advantages to the *Antipædobaptists*" and "tend much to their Encouragement and Encrease, to the Hazard of our Churches."[35] With regard to Plymouth, Larzer Ziff has argued that Miller underestimated the importance of its influence on the "ecclesiastical establishment" of Massachusetts Bay; Rutman has subsequently supported Ziff's conclusion in *Winthrop's Boston,* recognizing the value of Plymouth church as a "model" to emigrating Puritans.[36]

395

The monolithic treatment of the Puritan mind fails, too, to recognize that thought changed and evolved. Even the second volume of *The New England Mind,* subtitled *From Colony to Province,* which traces the changes in thought that were "hardly perceptible to the actors themselves," occurred "inside" the intellectual framework erected in *The New England Mind: The Seventeenth Century.* For Miller the 'massive structure of logic, psychology, theology stands apparently untouched."[37] But there are both continuity and change in history, and neither of these elements can be ignored or sacrificed. Rutman noted the importance of historical circumstances in the literature of the early period, writing that "each [ministerial] pamphlet was written at a moment in time, for a specific purpose, aimed at a specific audience by a specific person with a specific point of view."[38] Theological conceptions and their

---

[35] Williston Walker, ed., *The Creeds and Platforms of Congregationalism* (Philadelphia, 1969 [orig. publ. New York, 1893]), 249n. John Eliot's *A Brief Answer to small book written by John Norcot, against Infant Baptism . . .* (Boston, 1679) is et another example.

[36] Larzer Ziff, "The Salem Puritans in the 'Free Aire of a New World,'" *Huntington Library Quarterly,* XX (1957), 380-384; Darrett B. Rutman, *Winthrop's Boston: Portrait of a Puritan Town, 1630-1649* (Chapel Hill, N. C., 1965), 8, 285.

[37] Perry Miller, *The New England Mind: From Colony to Province* (Cambridge, Mass., 1953), ix.

[38] Rutman, *Winthrop's Boston,* 289.

practical applications altered from generation to generation. Cotton Mather, for example, emphasized piety in a way quite foreign to John Winthrop or Bradford. Benjamin Colman and others of his generation looked to the dissenters in England, such as Edmund Calamy and Matthew Henry, for intellectual inspiration rather than to the theologians of the *"good old Puritans,"* like Richard Sibbes and John Preston.[39] Even within the life of a single minister one finds change, particular ministers reversing their positions with the passage of time. Cotton realigned himself with the majority opinion after the Antinomians were exiled. Increase Mather switched his position regarding the half-way covenant. In brief, the contention that Puritan thought remained basically static between 1630 and 1730 is a hypothesis instantly suspect. Robert Middlekauff has departed from such an approach in *The Mathers: Three Generations of Puritan Intellectuals, 1596-1728,* distinguishing the respective intellects of the Mathers and defining the nuances in each of their generations.[40] Likewise, Breen in *The Character of the Good Ruler* has argued that there was "simply no single or uniform Puritan response to political questions"; not only was there a "rich variety of responses" but "each generation conducted its own dialogue about the character of the good ruler."[41]

Although Miller sensed the omission of evolutionary progression in his work, admitting that "the topical method of this volume has inevitably falsified certain perspectives; it has most notably obscured the chronology of the situation," his followers today tend to argue that the differences among Puritans pertained to issues rather than concepts.[42] Yet, because they are manifestations of broader ideological differences, issues can seldom be divorced from concepts. When Puritans debated the relationship of sanctification and justification within the context of the Antinomian Controversy, the formulation of the doctrine of salvation was ultimately at stake. Furthermore, the dispute involved hermeneutical and exegetical principles whose role should not be underestimated in theological controversy. Those who emerged with the accepted version of the Bible and the resultant theology formulated a new orthodoxy. Pope clearly acknowledges such a process when he declares that the deaths of Richard Mather, Jonathan Mitchel, and John Allin "symbolized the end of one era and the opening of a new one in which the half-way covenant became part of Massachusetts orthodoxy."[43]

[39] White Kennett to Benjamin Colman, Mar. 13, 1716/7, in Mass. Hist. Soc., *Proceedings,* III (1920), 75.
[40] (New York, 1971).
[41] Breen, *Character of the Good Ruler,* viii.
[42] Miller, *New England Mind: The Seventeenth Century,* 490.
[43] Pope, *Half-Way Covenant,* 184.

What is apparent from a careful examination of Miller's sources is that he defined in exhaustive detail the works of a select number of ministers which he alleged—but never attempted to prove—were representative of an orthodoxy pervading not just Massachusetts but all of New England. It is also obvious from the examples presented here and those to be found in the work of Breen, Hall, Middlekauff, Pope, Rutman, and others that any orthodoxy in New England was very tenuous and jeopardized by a host of dissenters. The best that can be said, it would seem, is that some ministers were striving for one orthodoxy while other orthodoxies were being sought by other ministers.

This analysis of Miller's sources, although cast in a critical format, is not intended to discredit his work. Miller was brilliant and hard-working. Most important, he revived interest in a subject which had been laid aside, and challenged a generation of scholars to study seriously New England's intellectual history. This note is itself yet another "spin-off" from his work. But it is critically important that students of Puritanism know the sources he used, their implicit bias, and what they reveal about Miller's conception of the New England Mind.

397

Congregational Clericalism:
New England Ordinations before the
Great Awakening

J. William T. Youngs, Jr.*

O N October 28, 1724, a young man named Ebenezer Parkman was ordained in Westborough, Massachusetts, and thereby became a member of the Congregational clergy. Parkman's ordination —an occasion to which he refers in his diary as "my Solemn Separation to the Work of the Gospel Ministry"—was carried on with the dignity deemed appropriate to that ceremony in the early eighteenth century. Four ministers presided over his initiation into the clergy: the Reverend Joseph Dorr of Mendon opened the service with a prayer; the Reverend John Prentice of Lancaster preached the ordination sermon; the Reverend William Williams of Weston offered a second prayer; and the Reverend Israel Loring of Sudbury gave "the Right Hand of Fellowship" welcoming Parkman into the ministry. Parkman reported that it had been "truely the Greatest Day I ever Yet Saw."[1] It was natural that Parkman should have been pleased. In a region where Congregationalism was the dominant religion, and in an era when medicine and the law were not yet well-established vocations, the ministers constituted New England's most distinguished professional group. The formal preeminence of the clergy was deceptive, however, for the ministers had developed a definition of clerical legitimacy that obviated the need for public support and tended to create a division between themselves and laymen.

Parkman's "Solemn Separation," although signified by an impressive ceremony, reflected the troubled condition of the clergy in the early eighteenth century. Ordination had changed greatly since the first years of Puritan colonization. In the 1630s it called attention to the minister's position as a member and leader of a fellowship of Christian believers. Almost a hundred years later it had come to celebrate his admission into a different and narrower community, that of the professional clergy. The new ordinations reflected an obsession with the importance of the

---

* Mr. Youngs is a member of the Department of History, Eastern Washington State College.
[1] Francis G. Walett, ed., "The Diary of Ebenezer Parkman, 1719-1728," American Antiquarian Society, *Proceedings*, N.S., LXXI (1961), 117-118.

ministry which can be described as Congregational clericalism. This development was clearly inconsistent with the ideals of the first New England pastors, and it suggests that in the years preceding the Great Awakening the ministers were no longer confident of their ability to command widespread public esteem.

Ordination in the early seventeenth century was a simple service in which a congregation formalized its appointment of a minister. It emphasized the minister's close attachment to his congregation rather than his special role as a clergyman. The best account of an ordination ceremony in the early years of settlement is found in the records of the First Church in Dedham. The members of this church, including its future minister, John Allin, considered the creation of their congregation far more important than the installation of its pastor. The church was formed on November 8, 1638, after nearly a year of preparation. It met during the following winter, admitted new members, and listened to Allin's preaching. Only after the winter was over did the congregation set about choosing and ordaining a minister. The formation of the religious community was of primary importance; the formal installation of a pastor, although desirable, was less consequential.[2]

In 1639 the church elected Allin as its minister and after careful deliberation decided that since the members had the power to choose their minister, they also had the authority to ordain him, "ordination being but a declaration of the same and installing into that office." Upon reaching this conclusion, they asked the advice of the elders of the church in Roxbury, who "confirmed our judgment in that point that the power of the whole worke did belong to us alone under Christ." On April 24, 1639, the ordination ceremony was carried out. Members and ministers of other churches were invited to attend, but they had little to do in the proceedings. The essential steps were taken by members of the Dedham church. Allin preached the sermon; he and two laymen ordained John Hunting as ruling elder; finally, Hunting and two other church members ordained Allin as pastor. The visiting clergymen played no part in the laying on of hands whereby Allin was made minister of the church. Their participation was limited to a favorable testimony made by their representative, Samuel Whiting of Lynn, of "their love and approbation of the proceedings of the church by giving to the officers chosen the right hand of fellowship."[3]

This service was typical of early New England ordination ceremonies. The presence of representatives from other churches indicates that they approved of Dedham's practice. In 1648, moreover, the procedure was en-

399

[2] *The Early Records of the Town of Dedham,* II (Dedham, Mass., 1888), 1-15.
[3] *Ibid.,* 17-18, 20.

dorsed by the Cambridge Platform of Church Discipline. The ninth chapter of the Platform, entitled "Of Ordination and Imposition of Hands," declared that the power of choosing church officers belonged to the particular congregations and recommended that ordinations be performed locally:

> In such Churches where there are Elders, *Imposition* of hands . . . is to be performed by those Elders.
>
> In such Churches where there are no Elders, *Imposition of* hands may be performed by some of the Brethren orderly chosen by the church thereunto. For if the people may elect officers which is the greater, and wherin the substance of the Office consists, they may much more (occasion and need so requiring) impose hands in ordination, which is the less, and but the accomplishment of the other.[4]

400

The records of the Dedham church and the pronouncements of the Cambridge Platform indicate that in the early years of settlement the minister's official standing was entirely dependent upon his relation to an assembly of covenanted Christians. A church could be formed before its minister was chosen; the minister was selected by the congregation; he was given the official character of a clergyman in a ceremony performed by the members of his own congregation; and the ordination sermon was delivered by the new pastor himself. These procedures emphasized the minister's place within a brotherhood of Christian believers rather than his separation to a sacred priesthood of religious leaders.

Within a few years after the drafting of the Cambridge Platform this emphasis would change. By mid-century in most churches the ceremony of ordaining the new minister came to be performed by other ministers rather than by laymen in the congregation.[5] This development radically altered the character of the ceremony. By placing their hands on the minister's head the representatives of the people had symbolized the congregation's choice of one of its members to guide their religious lives. Ordination by other ministers, however, emphasized the young man's initiation into a clerical order. The fact that by the late seventeenth century laymen were generally excluded from the ordination service suggests that the ministers were no longer willing to base their legitimacy so ex-

---

[4] Williston Walker, ed., *The Creeds and Platforms of Congregationalism* (New York, 1893), 216.

[5] David D. Hall, *The Faithful Shepherd: A History of the New England Ministry in the Seventeenth Century* (Chapel Hill, N. C., 1972), 106. Lay ordination was reintroduced by Separatist congregations during the Great Awakening. See C. C. Goen, *Revivalism and Separatism in New England, 1740-1800* (New Haven, Conn., 1962).

clusively on their relationship to the congregations they served.[6]

Although the ministers thus began to play a more active role in the creation of clergymen, this modification of earlier practice did not fully distinguish them as a formal professional class. They were still chosen by the congregations, and their election was commonly regarded as more important than their ordination. In the early eighteenth century, however, the ministers began to claim that clerical status was bestowed by the ordination ceremony, rather than by the people's election. In 1718 Thomas Prince, preaching his ordination sermon, asserted that when ministers are ordained, "the Power of taking Care of Your Souls is *actually* committed to Them: And They do *actually* receive it, and lay Themselves under the most Solemn Vows and Obligations to take Care of Them." In 1729 William Williams, preaching at the ordination of David Hall, declared, "The Election of the Church or People does not Constitute them in their Office or Authorize them to act in it." The people's role in creating the minister came to be so little respected that in 1738 Nathaniel Appleton could warn that "this Priviledge or Liberty of electing their own Pastors, has, on occasion of the Abuse of it by the Church themselves ... been taken away from many of the Churches of our Lord Jesus Christ." Such statements tend to suggest that the ministers believed they should have primary authority in determining who would be admitted to their number.[7]

401

In most cases the people continued to choose their own ministers, but under exceptional circumstances the clergy began to ordain ministers "at large," men who were deemed worthy to preach, baptize, and offer communion, but were attached to no particular congregation. In 1698 Nathaniel Clap was ordained by ministers in Boston to carry on "the work of the Gospel" throughout Rhode Island, which had only one Congrega-

---

[6] In *Faithful Shepherd* Hall describes many other developments in the history of the 17th-century clergy that reinforced the ministers' view of their separate status. For a general treatment of clerical history in the 18th century see J. William T. Youngs, Jr., "God's Messengers: Religious Leadership in Colonial New England, 1700-1750" (Ph.D. diss., University of California, Berkeley, 1970). Many of the changes discussed in this article had roots in the period covered by Hall's excellent study. However, unlike Hall, who stresses the "remarkable continuity" of ministerial history in the first three generations (*Faithful Shepherd*, 270), I have been particularly impressed by the divergence of clerical history by 1720 from the ideals of the first Puritan ministers of New England.

[7] Thomas Prince, *A Sermon Delivered by Thomas Prince . . . at his Ordination* (Boston, 1718), 17; William Williams (of Weston), *The Office and Work of Gospel-Ministers . . .* (Boston, 1729), 16; Nathaniel Appleton, *Superiour Skill and Wisdom necessary for winning Souls . . .* (Boston, 1737), 49. In the early 18th century, through associations and consociations, the ministers sought to determine who should be eligible for the clergy. See Youngs, "God's Messengers," Chap. 8: "Ministerial Associations."

tional church at that time.[8] In the early eighteenth century several other men were ordained ministers at large before setting out as preachers to Indians or to backcountry settlements.[9] Although ordinations of this sort were unusual, the introduction of the practice gives further evidence of the shift in clerical consciousness. A man could now become a minister without having been so designated by any group of laymen.

As the ceremony of consecration by the ministers came increasingly to be regarded as the most significant step in the creation of a clergyman, the ministers attempted to make the event more formal and sought to end the festivity that the service had sometimes occasioned. In his ordination sermon for William Gager in 1725 Eliphalet Adams noted, "I have so often seen such offensive Disorders upon such Occasions as thèse, People seeming to Imagine that it was a Time when they might allow themselves more Liberty." He urged that there "be no rude, Light or Unseemly Behaviour in this Assembly this Day." Of the ordination ceremony itself he said, "The Solemn Separation of any Person to the Work of the Sacred Ministry . . . is a thing so weighty, that Every one who are present as witnesses at such a Solemnity, should come Prepared with the spirit of Piety." At another ordination in the same year John Graham scolded those who might have come to the service "out of a vain Curiosity, or to get an opportunity of a Frolick." He lamented that this is "too too Common with Young Persons on such Occasions." Although large banquets accompanied many ordinations throughout the eighteenth century, objections against frivolity were a natural concomitant of the desire to heighten the dignity of the service.[10]

As ordination came to symbolize the solemn initiation of a novice into a formal profession, the practice of preaching one's own ordination sermon fell into disuse. When clerical power had been thought to flow from the congregation, it had been natural for the new pastor to address his people in his moment of consecration. Thus Allin and other ministers of his time had preached their own sermons. But in the early eighteenth

---

[8] Hall, *Faithful Shepherd*, 222.

[9] Cotton Mather justified this practice for ministers who were to preach in remote areas that were "destitute of *Ordainers.*" Mather, *Ratio Disciplinae Fratrum Nov-Anglorum* (Boston, 1726), 42. It is significant that in such cases, where there was a choice between omitting the church members or the settled ministers from the ordination ceremony, the church members were omitted. For examples of ordinations of this sort see John Langdon Sibley, *Biographical Sketches of Graduates of Harvard University . . .* (Cambridge, Mass., 1873-   ), IV, 183; VII, 570; VIII, 143-144.

[10] Eliphalet Adams, *The Work of Ministers, rightly to Divine the Word of Truth* (Boston, 1725), 1-2; John Graham, *The Obligations which the Profession of the Christian Religion, lays Men under to Depart from Iniquity* (New London, Conn., 1725), 36. There was a celebration after Stephen Williams's ordination in Longmeadow, Mass., in 1716. But Williams later regretted his frivolity, saying, "I fear we were too merry together." Sibley, *Harvard Graduates*, VI, 26.

century, in accordance with the idea that authority passed from minister to minister, this practice became exceptional. Of the first twenty-five sermons that were published after 1716 only five were preached by the new minister himself. In his ordination sermon for John Lowell in Newbury in 1726, Thomas Foxcroft declared that he preferred the old practice. "Truly glad shou'd I have been," he said, "if (pursuant to the Custom, which hath so long obtain'd among us) he cou'd have been prevail'd on to take up the Book at this time, and preach to us his own devout Thoughts and Purposes." But Foxcroft had to admit that the former practice had fallen into disuse; he referred to the "plea's usually advanc'd in this case, against the common Custom."[11] The "common custom" was, in fact, no longer common. In 1728 John Adams preached his own ordination sermon in Newport, Rhode Island, but between 1728 and 1740 all the published ordination sermons were preached by someone other than the new minister himself. In 1729 William Williams said, "The Objections against the *Person* to be Ordained his Preaching his *own Ordination Sermon,* have prevail'd very much against the *late Custom.*"[12]

403

Within a century of the settlement of New England the ordination service thus underwent a series of gradual but significant changes. Ordination came to be performed by ministers rather than by laymen; the ordination ceremony rather than the election by the people began to be regarded as "conveying" the ministerial office; ministers were occasionally ordained without having been chosen by the people of any particular congregation as their pastor; the ordination sermon was preached by older ministers rather than by the man being installed; and finally, in keeping with these other changes, the clergymen began to insist that the ordination day should be regarded as a solemn occasion. These changes indicate that the ministers now regarded themselves as a self-perpetuating body of religious leaders.

In order to understand fully the significance of these innovations, we should recall the cultural climate in which they occurred. Historians generally agree that this was a time of extensive social turmoil in the colonies of Massachusetts Bay and Connecticut. Perry Miller's chapters on the period in *The New England Mind: From Colony to Province* are appropriately titled "The Splintering of Society." John Demos argues that by 1690 familial tensions within New England were so acute that the young girls at Salem Village who falsely accused older women of witchcraft may have been driven by displaced animosities toward their moth-

---

[11] Thomas Foxcroft, *Ministers, Spiritual Parents, or Fathers in the Church of God* (Boston, 1726), 2.
[12] William Williams (of Weston), *Gospel-Ministers,* 2. See also Mather, *Ratio Disciplinae,* 25.

ers. Philip J. Greven, Jr., has shown that by 1750 overcrowding had caused many citizens of Andover to move elsewhere to find land; he concludes that "the ties binding men to their parents and to their families were loosening." Richard L. Bushman demonstrates that in eighteenth-century Connecticut conflicting economic interests divided a once harmonious community into contending factions with the result that "a person's total attachment to any community whatsoever diminished." Timothy H. Breen and Stephen Foster argue that by the 1680s "Massachusetts had changed from a peaceful to a relatively turbulent society."[13] In this atmosphere of contention and fragmentation the ministers developed ordination procedures that emphasized their distinct professional standing.

In addition, the ministers began to suggest that they themselves constituted a peculiarly holy group of men—as if in a society gone wrong they alone embodied the religious life of the community. This development appears in both the dissemination and the content of the ordination sermons. With the growing emphasis on the professional significance of ordination and with the spread of the custom of having experienced ministers do the preaching, ordination sermons acquired new importance. In 1709, for the first time, a New England ordination sermon was published, to be followed by another in 1716, still another in 1717, and seven more the ensuing year. In the quarter century from 1716 through 1740 seventy-eight ordination sermons were published.[14]

Characteristically these sermons were discourses on the ministry—its necessity, authority, and responsibility—and the tenor of the sermons was strongly sacerdotal, quite in contrast to the pastoral emphasis of Allin's ordination text of 1639 (1 Corinthians 3:9): "For we are laborers together with God: ye are God's husbandry, ye are God's building." The actual sermon does not survive, but we may reasonably suppose that Allin dwelt

[13] Perry Miller, *The New England Mind: From Colony to Province* (Cambridge, Mass., 1953); John Demos, "Underlying Themes in the Witchcraft of Seventeenth-Century New England," *American Historical Review*, LXXV (1969-1970), 1311-1326; Philip J. Greven, Jr., *Four Generations: Population, Land, and Family in Colonial Andover, Massachusetts* (Ithaca, N. Y., 1970), 272; Richard L. Bushman, *From Puritan to Yankee: Character and the Social Order in Connecticut, 1690-1765* (Cambridge, Mass., 1967), 72; Timothy H. Breen and Stephen Foster, "The Puritans' Greatest Achievement: A Study of Social Cohesion in Seventeenth-Century Massachusetts," *Journal of American History*, LX (1973), 20.

[14] This figure is based on a count of the ordination sermons listed in Charles Evans, *American Bibliography* (reprint ed. New York, 1941 [orig. publ. Chicago, 1903-1934]), and includes two sermons preached at the ordination of Baptist ministers and one sermon preached at an ordination on Long Island by Congregational ministers. The others were preached in New England for Congregationalist ministers and all were published in New England. There were only three other ordination sermons published in the colonies in this period, one in Pennsylvania and two in New York.

on the community of the faithful, himself included as co-laborer with his fellow saints, rather than on the sacred "separation" of the ministerial office.[15] Although it is impossible to date the change precisely, most of the ordination sermons published before 1740 not only dealt primarily with the ministry, but stressed the peculiar importance of ministers.[16] Daniel Lewes, for example, asserted in 1720 that among the many "offices and employments" of men, *none* [was] of more Importance ... than that of the *Ministry*. Nay, it may with Truth be asserted to be the *most* weighty, awful and important Work that ever mortal Man was employed in."[17] Thomas Clap declared that "the Work of the Ministry is the greatest and most solemn Work and Office that any Men are employed in here in the World."[18] Benjamin Colman argued that the "minister's office distinguishes him from other men," and as "it is the chief End of a *Christian* to glorify God, so it is of a Minister to magnify his Office."[19] Many other preachers echoed these sentiments.[20]

405

The ministers also began to claim a superior sanctity. Solomon Williams held that a good pastor's heavenly hopes were greater than those of other Christians: "The Ministers of Christ who have had greater Advantages by their Gifts and Station in the Church than other Men, if they have faithfully Improved those Advantages ... will have a distinguishing and eminent Reward above other Men."[21] William Shurtleff declared that a minister's life should be more noble than that of his fellows: "Let us labour that our Lives and Actions may be at an equal Distance with our Rank from the common Level. Since we move in such advanc'd Orbs, and are plac'd so much nearer to God than others, let us endeavour to be further remov'd from every Thing that is sinful and impure, and from whatever may be justly accounted mean and low."[22] Magnifying their office with Colman and moving in advanced orbs with

[15] *Dedham Records*, II, 18.
[16] In this period the ministers also discussed their profession in pamphlets about clerical salaries, in funeral sermons, and in general discourses on the ministry.
[17] Daniel Lewes, *Of Taking Heed to, and Fulfilling the Ministry* ... (Boston, 720), 1-2.
[18] Thomas Clap, *The Greatness and Difficulty of the Work of the Ministry* Boston, 1732), 7.
[19] Benjamin Colman, "Preface" to Thomas Symmes, *Ordination Sermon* (Boston, 722).
[20] See William Williams (of Hatfield), *The Great Concern of Christians* ... Boston, 1723), 1; Joseph Belcher, *God Giveth the Increase* ... (Boston, 1722), 24; Appleton, *Superiour Skill and Wisdom*, 36; Nathaniel Henchman, *The Divine Pastor* ... (Boston, 1733), 20; and Ebenezer Pemberton, *A Plea for the Ministers of the Gospel* ... (Boston, 1706), 8.
[21] Solomon Williams, *The Glorious Reward of Wise and Faithful Teachers* Boston, 1730), 10-11.
[22] William Shurtleff, *Gospel Ministers exhibited under the Notion of Stars* ... Boston, 1739), 20-21.

Shurtleff, the clergy tended to identify the religious life of New England with that of their own profession.

It was in this spirit that clergymen not only used the ordination sermon to chastise the people for failure to support their pastors properly, but equated the prosperity of their professional class with the spiritual destiny of the whole community. Thomas Symmes argued that "where the Credit of the Ministry runs low, there may be a Form of Godliness, but there is little of the life and power of it." Thomas Foxcroft compared the minister to a father whose family is included in his own destiny: "As to particular Families, much of their Beauty and Safety is bound up in the wise and good Fathers at the Head of them. Even so learned and faithful Ministers are very much the Strength and Glory of a People." Solomon Williams argued that not only a people's temporal benefits, but their chance for salvation as well, were dependent upon the well-being of their pastor. If you treat your minister kindly, said Williams, "You will not only be the Means of brightning his Reward and Glory in the future World; but will also secure your share in a Prophets Reward, when He shall shine as the brightness of the Firmament, and as the Stars for ever and ever."[23]

Finally, it became customary not to form a new congregation until a candidate could be ordained pastor at the same time. In the seventeenth century many churches had been formed and held services for months or or even years before a minister was ordained to serve them. But in the eighteenth century the formation of a new parish and the ordination of its pastor usually occurred on the same day, suggesting that without a minister there could be no church.[24]

It is evident from all of these developments that the early Protestant ideal, present in the founding of the Dedham church, of a "priesthood of all believers" had all but vanished from the New England of the 1720s and 1730s. In the new ordinations the ministers tended to apply ideals to their own class that had once been associated with New England as a whole. No example of this change is more dramatic than an assertion that appeared in two ordination sermons in 1726. On January 19, 1725/6, at the ordination of John Lowell in Newburyport, Massachusetts, Foxcroft declared that "Ministers are (as Parents in the Family) in a somewhat *elevated* and *conspicuous* Station; they are as a City set on a Hill, which can't be hid." Eight months later on September 14 at the ordination of Nathanael Morril in Rye, New Hampshire, William Shurtleff echoed Foxcroft's words: "The Ministers of Christ should remember that they are in a peculiar manner the *Lights of the World;* that they are as a

---

[23] Symmes, *Ordination Sermon,* 19; Foxcroft, *Ministers, Spiritual Parents,* 12; Williams, *Glorious Reward,* 22.

[24] These generalizations about the timing of ordination and church formation are based on Sibley, *Harvard Graduates, passim,* and Mather, *Ratio Disciplinae,* 3.

City set upon a Hill, which cannot be hid."[25]

When John Winthrop uttered his famous words about the "City upon a Hill" almost a century before, he had intended to describe all of the residents of New England. But now an image that had once evoked the coherent destiny of a whole community was limited to the description of a single profession. In such sermons the preachers seemed to be saying that if New England as a whole would not be a "City set upon a Hill," then the ministers would separate themselves from their people and become the holy community themselves.

In developing this attitude the ministers were responding to forces that affected all of New England. Breen and Foster describe the new society succinctly when they write that "as time passed men increasingly defined the common good in narrow, personal terms."[26] In such a community the ministers acted in a perversely logical fashion by embracing an exalted view of their own importance and by minimizing their dependence upon laymen. In so doing—in defining the common religious good in narrow clerical terms—they may have hoped to secure a stable position among men who were becoming increasingly secular and contentious.

The frailty of their idea of religious leadership would become apparent, however, if spiritually awakened laymen should insist that the minister's worth rested not in his attachment to a professional class, but in his ability to serve the religious needs of his people. In contrast to the tumultuous years of the Great Awakening, when such a revival of lay religiosity did occur, the period in which Ebenezer Parkman was ordained was a time of religious tranquility. But the tensions that would set laymen against ministers a decade and a half later were already apparent in 1724. By considering themselves to be a self-perpetuating body of sacred religious leaders the Congregational clergymen suggested that they did not depend upon laymen for the validity of their ministry. The price that they paid for this exalted view of their status was an uneasiness about their relationship to their congregations. The text of Parkman's ordination illustrates precisely the difficulty of religious leaders who thought of themselves as great servants of the Lord, but who did not expect warm support from their own people. John Prentice chose as his theme 2 Corinthians 12:15: "I will very gladly spend and be spent for you; though the more abundantly I love you, the less I be loved."[27]

407

[25] William Shurtleff, *The Labour that attends the Gospel-Ministry* (Boston, 727), 30.

[26] Breen and Foster, "The Puritans' Greatest Achievement," *JAH*, LX (1973), 20.

[27] Walett, ed., "Diary of Parkman," Am. Antiq. Soc., *Procs.*, N.S., LXXI (1961), 18.

Samuel Hopkins and the New Divinity: Theology, Ethics, and Social Reform in Eighteenth-Century New England

Joseph A. Conforti

THE intellectual stress of the Great Awakening of the eighteenth century was simultaneously divisive and creative. It split New England theologians into contending camps, one of which grew from the teachings of Jonathan Edwards and represented the first indigenously American school of Calvinism. Proponents of the New Divinity, as the doctrines of this Edwardsian party came to be called, attempted to build a complete, consistent system of evangelical Calvinism around such critical issues of the Awakening as the nature of and need for spiritual rebirth, the authenticity of mass conversions, the role of means (prayer, Bible reading, and church attendance) in regeneration, and the coming of the millennium.

In the years after the Awakening, and particularly during his Stockbridge exile (1751-1757), Edwards assumed the task of refining and systematizing the revival's theological implications. His untimely death at the height of his creative power in 1758 left his ambitious project uncompleted. But in the years since the revival Edwards had attracted clerical followers who aided him in his efforts and continued his work.

Edwards's closest friend and disciple was Samuel Hopkins. Born in Waterbury, Connecticut, in 1721, Hopkins graduated from Yale in 1741, studied for the ministry in Edwards's Northampton parsonage, and was ordained at Housatonic (renamed Great Barrington in 1761), Massachusetts, in 1743.[1] Eight years later, when Edwards settled in Stockbridge, Hopkins renewed their friendship and frequently made the thirty-minute horseback ride from Housatonic to the Indian mission. Upon Edwards's death, all of his unpublished papers were placed under Hopkins's care. From 1770 to 1803

Mr. Conforti is a member of the Department of History at Rhode Island College.

[1] On Hopkins see Edwards A. Park, *Memoir of the Life and Character of Samuel Hopkins, D.D.* (Boston, 1854), and Joseph A. Conforti, "Samuel Hopkins and the New Divinity Movement: A Study in the Transformation of Puritan Theology and the New England Social Order" (Ph.D. diss., Brown University, 1975), upon which this essay is based.

Hopkins served the First Congregational Church of Newport, Rhode Island, where his theological concerns became focused on social reform.

In the late 1750s Hopkins and other ministers began to publish tracts and tomes which were designed to complete Edwards's theological work. In so doing, these New Divinity clerics, or "Consistent Calvinists" as they were also called, so radically extended and modified their teacher's ideas that many New Lights, such as the Baptist leader Isaac Backus, claimed for themselves the name of Edwardsians and rejected the New Divinity as a bastardizing of Edwards's thought.[2]

The New Divinity's alterations of Edwardsianism have allowed historians to heap praise on Edwards while belittling the school he helped to found. In this standard view, Edwards marks the apex and the New Divinity the nadir of colonial New England's intellectual history.[3] For some historians, the Consistent Calvinists lacked Edwards's piety; they could rationally grasp his doctrines but could not plumb the depths of the religious experience upon which he based his theology. For others, the New Divinity men lacked not only Edwards's piety but his acumen as well. Their commitment to consistency betrayed intellectual debility. Absorbed in exploring minute and subtle details, they retreated into a rarefied intellectual world and lost contact with social reality. They promoted a "paper war" of religious polemics, created abstract metaphysical systems, and thereby alienated the laity. They discoursed with one another, oblivious to the expanding and changing society around them. In the end, the subtle differences of their discourses and systems became obscure to the participants themselves, and few New Englanders grieved over the passing of the New England theology.[4]

409

[2] See William G. McLoughlin, *Isaac Backus and the American Pietistic Tradition* (Boston, 1967), 184-185.

[3] The classical statement of this view is Joseph Haroutunian, *Piety versus Moralism: The Passing of the New England Theology* (New York, 1932).

[4] In addition to Haroutunian, *Piety versus Moralism*, expressions of the views summarized above may be found in Sidney Earl Mead, *Nathaniel William Taylor, 1786-1858: A Connecticut Liberal* (Chicago, 1942), *passim*, esp. 96; Herbert Wallace Schneider, *The Puritan Mind* (Ann Arbor, Mich., 1958 [orig. publ. New York, 1930]), 222-223; Douglas J. Elwood, *The Philosophical Theology of Jonathan Edwards* (New York, 1960), 154; Edmund S. Morgan, *The Gentle Puritan: A Life of Ezra Stiles, 1727-1795* (New Haven, Conn., 1962), 313-315; Morgan, "The American Revolution Considered as an Intellectual Movement," and Donald Meyer, "The Dissolution of Calvinism," in Arthur M. Schlesinger, Jr., and Morton White, eds., *Paths of American Thought* (Boston, 1963), 18-22, 77-80; Cedric Cowing, *The Great Awakening and the American Revolution: Colonial Thought in the Eighteenth Century* (Chicago, 1971), 197-198; and Stephen E. Berk, *Calvinism versus Democracy: Timothy Dwight and the Origins of American Evangelical Orthodoxy* (Hamden, Conn., 1974), chap. 6. Two exceptions to the views found in these works are Edwin Scott Gaustad, *The Great Awakening in New England* (New York, 1957), 126-140, and Richard D. Birdsall, "Ezra Stiles versus the New Divinity Men,"

In reality, however, Consistent Calvinism was far from simply a body of abstract metaphysical arguments which contemporaries might justly dismiss as intellectually absurd and socially irrelevant. When one focuses on the problem of true virtue and especially on Hopkins's original interpretation of the doctrine of disinterested benevolence, the social context and meaning of the New Divinity come into view. The debate over the nature of true virtue derived from efforts to define authentic spiritual sentiments in light of what many saw as the false piety and emotional excesses of the Awakening. The controversy also had a social dimension; it was in part a response to what the New Divinity men viewed as a crisis in social thought in mid-eighteenth-century New England. Hopkins, for example, was disquieted by the conflict between traditional social values and the behavior of New Englanders in a time of critical change. Like other evangelicals, he inherited a social ethic that stressed corporate obligation, personal restraint, and communal harmony and simplicity. But the economic and demographic expansion of New England during his lifetime promoted acquisitive, egocentric patterns of behavior at odds with those norms.[5]

The doctrinal "paper war" revolving around the problem of true virtue arose from attempts to close the gap between values and experience by formulating new theological legitimations for behavior.[6] With his doctrine of disinterested benevolence, Hopkins endeavored to discredit liberal, Old Light, and even New Light compromises of inherited social thought. In the process he gave evangelical Calvinism an activist social thrust—a development which some historians, most notably Alan Heimert,[7] would lead us to

410

American Quarterly, XVIII (1965), 248-258. For a theological compendium that falls somewhere between the competing interpretations of the New Divinity movement see Frank Hugh Foster, A Genetic History of New England Theology (Chicago, 1907).

[5] Jack P. Greene, "Search for Identity: An Interpretation of the Meaning of Selected Patterns of Social Response in Eighteenth-Century America," Journal of Social History, III (1970), 190-224, esp. 191-205. For other interpretations of this cleavage see Richard L. Bushman, From Puritan to Yankee: Character and the Social Order in Connecticut, 1690-1765 (Cambridge, Mass., 1967), chaps. 12-16; Edward M. Cook, Jr., "Social Behavior and Changing Values in Dedham, Massachusetts, 1700 to 1775," William and Mary Quarterly, 3d Ser., XXVIII (1970), 546-580; and Kenneth A. Lockridge, "Social Change and the Meaning of the American Revolution," Jour. Soc. Hist., VI (1973), esp. 423-424. On the traditional New England social values see Michael Zuckerman, Peaceable Kingdoms: New England Towns in the Eighteenth Century (New York, 1970), and Stephen Foster, Their Solitary Way: The Puritan Social Ethic in the First Century of Settlement in New England (New Haven, Conn., 1971).

[6] On the problem of legitimation in the sociology of religion see Peter L. Berger, The Sacred Canopy: Elements of a Sociological Theory of Religion (New York, 1967), chaps. 2, 7.

[7] Alan Heimert, Religion and the American Mind: From the Great Awakening to the Revolution (Cambridge, Mass., 1966).

believe flowed directly from Edwardsianism and not by way of the New Divinity movement. While in fundamental respects Hopkins was a follower of Edwards, he nevertheless found serious flaws in his mentor's theology. Specifically, Hopkins concluded that Edwards's interpretation of true virtue was deficient on several counts. Not only did it tend toward abstraction, but it mixed ethics with aesthetics, made unnecessary concessions to rational moral philosophers, and did not provide an adequate spur to social action.

Edwards's *Dissertation concerning the Nature of True Virtue* was written in 1755 but did not appear in print until 1765. It provoked responses from Old Light Calvinists who had been carrying on a theological controversy with the New Divinity men for several years. In 1770, for example, William Hart of Saybrook, Connecticut, published his *Remarks on President Edwards's Dissertation concerning the Nature of True Virtue*. Hart intended his work to be a final moderate Calvinist assault on the theology of the Great Awakening. He wanted to demonstrate how the New Divinity as a whole, and particularly Edwards's concept of true virtue, were "wrong, imaginary and fatally destructive of the foundation of morality and true religion."[8] Hart was especially disturbed that Edwards had replaced the biblical God with the abstract metaphysical concept of "Being in general." Furthermore, Hart argued, a penchant for metaphysics and aesthetics had led Edwards to deny that social morality was true virtue and to "involve practical religion . . . in a cloud." Most of Edwards's dissertation was vitiated, Hart suggested, because he had confused aesthetics with ethics.[9]

Such criticism helped clarify for Hopkins the deficiencies in Edwards's ethical theory and convinced him that his own work should be an improvement on, not simply a defense of, Edwards. Hopkins focused on Edwards's interpretation of Being in general as one of the central areas in need of improvement. "True virtue," Edwards began his dissertation, "most essentially consists in benevolence to *Being in general*," and he went on to explain that "I shall not be likely to be understood, that no one act of the mind or exercise of love is of the nature of true virtue, but what has Being in general or the great system of universal existence, for its direct and immediate object." While Edwards seemed to equate Being in general with God, he described an ultimate reality different from traditional notions of the Deity. God was not only "the *head* of the system [of universal being] and the chief part of it,"[10] but the source of all being. Hopkins found this conception of

411

[8] William Hart, *Remarks on President Edwards's Dissertation concerning the Nature of True Virtue* . . . (New Haven, Conn., 1771), 41.
[9] *Ibid.*, 9, 21, 45-46.
[10] Jonathan Edwards, *Works*, ed. E. Hickman (New York, 1843), II, 262, hereafter cited as Edwards, *Works*. The concept of Being in general may be traced back to Edwards's early theological efforts. See, for example, his essay "Of Being" in

Being in general both amorphous and abstract. He attempted to correct Edwards—and thus silence Edwards's critics—by redefining Being in general as "God and our neighbors," that is, God and mankind.

Hopkins was also dissatisfied with Edwards's handling of the subjective nature of true virtue. Love of Being in general, Edwards argued, originated in a "relish," "propensity," or "inclination" of the will or heart. In short, true virtue was essentially a matter of motivation. While natural principles governed the will of an unconverted person, through regeneration an authentic Christian had a benevolent affection implanted in his heart which motivated him to love Being in general.[11]

At this point, critics such as Hart charged that Edwards transformed his analysis into a discussion not of ethics but of aesthetics. To ask what is the nature of true virtue, Edwards wrote, "is the same as to inquire, what that is which renders any habit, disposition, or exercise of the heart truly *beautiful*."[12] The major alteration produced by regeneration, and thus the distinguishing feature of true virtue, Edwards concluded, consisted in a "comprehensive view"[13] of spiritual reality, which the saint relished and loved for its beauty. Edwards's overly aesthetic interpretation of true virtue was another element of his theology which Hopkins undertook to improve.

Both Hopkins and the critics of *True Virtue* saw that Edwards's emphasis on the beatific nature of regeneration militated against worldly action. Edwards left an ambiguous legacy for Christian ethics.[14] In the 1740s he had attempted to counteract a new wave of revival-inspired antinomianism by insisting upon the importance of evangelical activity as a fruit of conversion. But a decade later, New England's religious life had changed dramatically, and the emphasis of Edwards's theology changed with it. A sharp decline in conversions put an end to the antinomian menace. Anti-revival rationalism now posed the major threat to evangelical Calvinism. Indeed, it seemed to Edwards that the spiritual delights of regeneration had been largely forgotten. In this sense, the dominant theme of *True Virtue*—that regeneration

412

Harvey G. Townsend, ed., *The Philosophy of Jonathan Edwards from His Private Notebooks* (Eugene, Ore., 1955), 1-20. The best modern interpretation of the concept is in Elwood, *Philosophical Theology of Edwards*, esp. 22-23.

[11] *True Virtue*, in Edwards, *Works*, II, 261-266.

[12] *Ibid.*, 261. Roland André Delattre, *Beauty and Sensibility in the Thought of Jonathan Edwards* (New Haven, Conn., 1968), offers an excellent analysis of the role of aesthetics in Edwards's theology. See also Clyde A. Holbrook, *The Ethics of Jonathan Edwards: Aesthetics and Morality* (Ann Arbor, Mich., 1973), esp. 104-105.

[13] *True Virtue*, in Edwards, *Works*, II, 262.

[14] This conflict in Edwards's thought between quietism and activism is best revealed in the *Religious Affections*. Holy action is the last of the 12 distinguishing signs of conversion that Edwards discusses. Many of the other signs (4 and 10, for example) are existential states and aesthetic perceptions. Edwards, *Works*, III, esp. 108, 171.

culminates in relishing the beauty of Being in general—was intended as an antidote to rationalist thought.

Edwards's approach, however, placed theological obstacles in the way of evangelical activism.[15] In Hopkins's view, the quietistic emphasis of *True Virtue* made Edwards vulnerable to the charge that he had involved practical religion in a cloud. Edwards's detailed descriptions of the subjective nature of regeneration, when combined with the mystical quality of his concept of Being in general, encouraged passive contemplation and rapt otherworldliness. Through his doctrine of disinterested benevolence Hopkins endeavored to remove the ambiguity in Edwards's theology on the issue of ethics. The cause of religious reform profited from this shift.

When Edwards did discuss social morality in *True Virtue*, he made clear that he was talking about an inferior, secondary order of virtue and beauty. Hopkins found Edwards's analysis of secondary virtue the most deficient part of his ethical theory. In his judgment, it was objectionable in general because it borrowed too much from the views of contemporary moral philosophers whose thought was essentially rationalistic and in particular because it embraced a concept of self-love that was ethically as well as spiritually dangerous.

Religious rationalists in Europe and America—as advocates of what was called natural theology—held that man had the natural ability to understand scripture, judge right from wrong, and attain salvation. Edwards's concept of secondary virtue incorporated the views of such exponents of natural theology as the earl of Shaftesbury and the Scottish philosopher Francis Hutcheson.[16] Responding to the moral cynicism of Thomas Hobbes, Shaftesbury and Hutcheson rested their sanguine hopes for mankind on belief in an innate "moral sense" capable of regulating the behavior of individuals without the need for supernatural grace.[17] Many eighteenth-century moral philosophers

413

[15] Heimert in *Religion and the American Mind* exaggerates the role of evangelical activism in Edwards's theology and in the process creates an overdrawn portrait of the social and political implications of Edwards's thought. As Delattre notes, Heimert's chapter on "The Beauty and Good Tendency of Union" shows an understanding of the place of aesthetics in Edwards's theology, "but he overstates his case for the location of that divine beauty in human community" (*Beauty and Sensibility*, 10-11).

[16] Edwards's *True Virtue* was intended in part to refute Hutcheson's *An Inquiry into the original of our ideas of Beauty and virtue* (London, 1725). In his reply Edwards incorporated aspects of Hutcheson's ethical theory. See A. Owen Aldridge, "Edwards and Hutcheson," *Harvard Theological Review*, XLIV (1951), 35-53, and Clarence H. Faust and Thomas H. Johnson, eds., *Jonathan Edwards: Representative Selections . . .* (New York, 1935), lxxv-xciii.

[17] Conrad Wright, *The Beginnings of Unitarianism in America* (Boston, 1955), chap. 6. On the "common-sense" philosophy see Gladys Bryson, *Man and Society: The Scottish Inquiry of the Eighteenth Century* (Princeton, N.J., 1945), 1-28;

reacted to Hobbesian pessimism by basing the regulation of social behavior on another natural faculty in man—self-love. Not always carefully distinguishing this principle from selfishness, they described it as an inclination to seek one's own happiness and avoid misery. Moses Hemmenway, an Old Light critic of Edwards and the New Divinity who adopted the view of most rational, common-sense philosophers, and of most moderate and liberal Calvinists, defined self-love in reply to Hopkins in 1772 as "that affection or propensity of heart to ourselves, which causes us to incline to our own happiness." Rationalists maintained that self-love did not conflict with the public good. It was a form of enlightened self-interest in which individual happiness was part of the public good. Selfishness, Hemmenway argued, was a much narrower affection; it was "a regard to ourselves and our own good, exclusive of all regard to others or their good."[18] In short, self-love, like man's reason and moral sense, was a natural principle implanted in human nature by God; upon it, both true virtue and social order were established.

414

Edwards countered by arguing that natural principles played an important role on the level of secondary virtue. Not true virtue but an inferior form of virtue resulted from the operation of reason, conscience, moral sense, and even self-love. To Hopkins's disappointment, Edwards agreed with many rationalists that "self-love is a principle that is exceeding useful and necessary in the world of mankind." Self-love may promote social harmony, Edwards asserted, because unregenerate men "are most affected towards, and do most highly approve, those virtues which agree with their interest most, according to their various conditions in life."[19] What Edwards was saying in his attempt to assimilate the natural theology of the rationalists into his ethical theory was that God had provided for the organization of society on the basis of a kind of virtue and beauty inferior to true virtue and its beauty. While the realization of a thoroughly virtuous social order depended upon mass revivalism, the realization of a basically harmonious society did not have to wait for a new Awakening, because natural principles such as reason, moral sense, and self-love were at work in the world. Even though the human race suffered from natural depravity, Edwards reminded the readers of *True*

Douglas Sloan, *The Scottish Enlightenment and the American College Ideal* (New York, 1971), esp. chaps. 3, 4; Henry F. May, *The Enlightenment in America* (New York, 1976), 341-358; and Sydney E. Ahlstrom, "The Scottish Philosophy and American Theology," *Church History*, XXIV (1955), 257-272.

[18] Moses Hemmenway, *A Vindication of the Power, Obligation and Encouragement of the Unregenerate to attend the Means of Grace. Against the Exceptions of the Rev. Mr. Samuel Hopkins . . .* (Boston, 1772), 63. On self-love theorists in the 18th century see Jacob Viner, *The Role of Providence in the Social Order: An Essay in Intellectual History* (Philadelphia, 1972), 62-85, and Wright, *Beginnings of Unitarianism*, 142-145.

[19] *True Virtue*, in Edwards, *Works*, II, 283-299.

Virtue that "the present state of mankind is so ordered and constituted by the wisdom and goodness of its supreme Ruler, that these natural principles for the most part tend to the good of the world of mankind."[20]

To Edwards, secondary virtue established negative moral goodness as the normative ethical condition of natural man. "By negative moral goodness," Edwards wrote, "I mean the absence of true moral evil." Although secondary virtue "be not of the nature of real positive virtue or true moral goodness, yet it has a negative moral goodness, because in the present state of things it is evidence of the absence of that higher degree of wickedness which causes great insensibility or stupidity of conscience."[21] Furthermore, in practice, secondary and true virtue often resembled one another. Trying objectively to differentiate one moral state from the other was comparable, Edwards suggested, to attempting to distinguish between invisible and visible saints. At bottom the difference was not external but resided in the motive or inclination of the heart or will.[22] Thus, he concluded, rationalists were labeling as true virtue what in reality was only secondary virtue.

Hopkins discovered a number of defects in Edwards's concept of secondary virtue. He feared that while Edwards had denied the rationalists' contention that natural man was not capable of true virtue, he had nevertheless conferred theological legitimacy on natural principles. Hopkins was especially alarmed by Edwards's acceptance of self-love. It appeared to him that Edwards's position played into the hands of the rationalists who, by distinguishing self-love from selfishness, were developing a social ethic that was facilitating the transition from communal to individualistic social ethics. The concept of self-love as differentiated from selfishness served as the underpinning of the rationalist clergy's social thought in the second half of the eighteenth century. Their "realistic" social perspective held that the best possible society and the greatest good to the greatest number would result from the operation of self-love, that is, from the individualistic pursuit of happiness.[23] Hopkins's identification of all virtue with disinterested benevolence was an attempt to shore up traditional social thought and block the advance of self-love theories. His radical call for self-denial, in conjunction with his efforts to amend what he saw as the abstract and aesthetic qualities

---

[20] *Ibid.*, 299.

[21] *Ibid.*

[22] *Ibid.*, 297.

[23] Bushman, *Puritan to Yankee*, 278-279. On clerical and lay use of the concept of self-love in economic and social theory at mid-century see J. E. Crowley, *This Sheba, Self: The Conceptualization of Economic Life in Eighteenth-Century America*, The Johns Hopkins University Studies in Historical and Political Science (Baltimore, 1974), 72-73, 91-92; also see Henry W. Sams, "Self-Love and the Doctrine of Work," *Journal of the History of Ideas*, IV (1943), 320-332.

of Edwards's interpretation of true virtue, broadened the theological base for social reform within the New Divinity movement.

In 1773 Hopkins entered the theological paper war over the nature of true virtue with the publication of *An Inquiry into the Nature of True Holiness.* Where Edwards located true virtue in exalted consciousness, Hopkins placed it in elevated social behavior. Consequently, evangelical activism superseded mystical quietism. In one respect, then, Hopkinsianism did indeed liberalize Calvinism—or, as one critic of the New Divinity prefers to put it, moralize Edwardsianism—and looked forward to modern humanized religion.[24] But the weight of theological tradition prevented an easy slide into Enlightenment humanism. The social ideals which Hopkins's *Inquiry* endorsed, for example, were reactionary; that is, the work marshaled old and new theological arguments to reaffirm the legitimacy of New England's communal values against lay desertion and clerical compromise.

Edwards described Being in general as a comprehensive ontological reality, and true virtue as an aesthetic perception of this universal being. Hopkins, on his part, stressed that Being in general was the tangible reality of God and our neighbors. As a result, Hopkins saw true virtue as more an ethical than an aesthetic ideal. Universal benevolence or "love to God and our neighbour, including ourselves . . . or friendly affection to all intelligent beings"[25] constituted Hopkins's definition of true virtue.

On the question of God's moral nature and its relation to true virtue, Hopkins arminianized Edwards's thought. For Edwards, God's glory did not depend upon His benevolence toward His creatures. Although God desired man's happiness, His "goodness and love to created beings is derived from, and subordinate to his love of himself." While self-centered existence was morally reprehensible in man, Edwards argued, it was appropriate in the Deity. God did not exercise disinterested benevolence toward earthly beings; rather, He loved Himself as the "chief part" and source of all being. Though he acted benevolently toward mankind, He was not morally obliged to promote their happiness.[26]

For Hopkins, on the other hand, God's moral nature circumscribed His sovereignty. God was not a self-centered deity but a benevolent governor whose glory depended upon the happiness of mankind.[27] Disinterested be-

---

[24] Haroutunian, *Piety versus Moralism, passim,* esp. 83-84.

[25] Samuel Hopkins, *An Inquiry into the Nature of True Holiness* . . . (Newport, R.I., 1773), 11, hereafter cited as *True Holiness.* Hopkins's phrase "including ourselves" was not an acceptance of self-love. According to him, a man should have a "regard" to himself only as part of Being in general, "so that all his own particular interest is subordinate to that of the whole" (*ibid.,* 24).

[26] *True Virtue,* in Edwards, *Works,* II, 268-270.

[27] *True Holiness,* 53. At times Edwards moved closer to Hopkins's position. See, for example, "Miscellany 3" in Townsend, ed., *Philosophy of Edwards,* 193.

nevolence was His primary moral attribute: "the holiness and perfection of God and his people, consists, so much at least, in disinterested benevolence, that there is no moral perfection without it, in God or the creature."[28] Hopkins joined liberal Arminian Calvinists in linking divine perfection to human happiness. Benevolence was such an important part of God's moral nature that He had always to act in accordance with the moral interests of His creatures.[29]

Edwards would not have recognized his concept of Being in general or the God of his Calvinism in Hopkins's *Inquiry*. On these two points Hopkins had greatly altered Edwards's thought. But Hopkins's most important refashioning of Edwards's definition of true virtue—and his major contribution to an evangelical theology of social reform—dealt with the opposition of disinterested benevolence to self-love. Here he not only parted ways with Edwards but dismissed out of hand the views of the rational moral philosophers. Hopkins refused to give even the slightest theological sanction to the self-interested behavior which he saw undermining New England society, particularly that of Newport.

Hopkins contended that no middle ground such as secondary virtue and beauty existed between true virtue and selfishness. Every human being's heart was filled with either totally self-interested or totally disinterested affections, and a gulf existed between these moral states which only the Holy Spirit could close. Hopkins confidently rejected Edwards's claim that the secondary virtue which natural principles produced was morally and socially valuable even though it fell short of true virtue. He maintained that secondary virtue and the "negative moral goodness" it established in the world were irreconcilably opposed and in no way analogous to the disinterested benevolence of true virtue: "There is, however, a great difference, and opposition in these two kinds of affections; . . . This selfish affection, though extended to the whole community with which the selfish man is connected, is at bottom nothing but love to himself. This is the foundation and center of his love. He in reality loves nothing but himself, and regards others wholly for his own sake."[30] Hopkins created a complete disjunction between true and secondary virtue, because every affection that fell short of disinterested benevolence was rooted in selfishness. He argued, for example, that self-love, far from restraining wickedness, "is the source of all the profaneness and impiety in the world; and of all pride and ambition among men; which is nothing but selfishness acted out in this particular way."[31]

Hopkins's strictures on self-love led ultimately to the most famous tenet

---

[28] *True Holiness*, 45.
[29] For the liberal Calvinists' interpretation of the benevolence of the Deity see Wright, *Beginnings of Unitarianism*, chap. 7.
[30] *True Holiness*, 23.
[31] *Ibid.*, 29.

of his theological system: a regenerate person must be willing to be damned for the glory of God. "He therefore cannot know that he loves God and shall be saved," Hopkins argued in *A Dialogue between a Calvinist and a Semi-Calvinist*, written in the late 1780s and published posthumously in 1805, "until he knows he has that disposition which implies a willingness to be damned, if it be not most for the glory of God that he should be saved."[32] In other words, one could not avoid damnation except by being willing to be damned. Lay and clerical opponents of the New Divinity (and some modern historians as well) tore this doctrine out of context and used it to portray Consistent Calvinism as an absurd system. Hopkins's position becomes intelligible, however, when it is related to the eighteenth-century debate on the nature of true virtue and to the crisis of social thought in New England.

418

After rejecting Edwards's contention that natural principles, including self-love, resembled true virtue and brought secondary virtue into the world, Hopkins reassessed the larger role of self-love in his mentor's theology. Few New Englanders other than Hopkins had access to the unpublished writings of Edwards that supplemented *True Virtue*. In these manuscripts Hopkins found Edwards arguing that self-love not only produced secondary virtue but operated on the level of true virtue. "That a man should love his own happiness," Edwards noted in *Charity and Its Fruits*, written in 1738 (but not published until 1851), "is as necessary to his nature as the faculty of the will is; and it is impossible that such a love should be destroyed in any other way than by destroying his being."[33] Self-love, like the will, was a faculty common to all members of the human race. The converted as well as the unconverted were moved by it to desire their own happiness. The essential difference was that the regenerate, having gained a new disposition of the heart, identified their interest and happiness with love of Being in general. On the basis of this view of self-love, which was grounded in Lockean sensationalism, Edwards found it inconceivable that a person could be willing to be damned. In "Miscellany 530" Edwards stated the matter clearly: "Love to God, if it be superior to any other principle, will make a man forever unwilling, utterly and finally, to be deprived of that part of his happiness which he has in God's being blessed and glorified, and the more he loves Him, the more unwilling he will be. So that this supposition, that a man can be willing to be perfectly and utterly miserable out of love to God, is inconsistent with itself."[34] Regeneration disposed the faculty of self-love to

[32] The *Dialogue* was printed in Stephen West, ed., *Sketches of the Life of the Late Rev. Samuel Hopkins, D.D. . . .* (Hartford, Conn., 1805); quotation on p. 150.
[33] Jonathan Edwards, *Charity and Its Fruits; or, Christian Love as Manifested in the Heart and Life* (New York, 1851), 229.
[34] Townsend, ed., *Philosophy of Edwards*, 204; Holbrook, *Ethics of Edwards*, esp. 56-63.

relish, delight, and seek happiness in eternal harmony with God. While not going as far as theological utilitarians, Edwards did argue that "wicked men do not love themselves enough"[35] or else they would seek their own eternal happiness by avoiding sin.

Hopkins countered by arguing that a Christ-like disposition to self-denial, rather than an inclination flowing from self-love to identify ultimate happiness with Being in general, was the hallmark of true virtue. He rejected all ethical theories that approved self-centered inducements to salvation: "to give up our temporal interest, worldly interest, for the sake of eternal happiness, wholly under the influence of self-love, is as real an instance of selfishness, as parting with all we have now, to possess a large estate next year."[36] Love of God and neighbor, and not the saving of one's soul, became the core of Hopkinsianism. The true Christian must lose himself in a cause higher than his own salvation—namely, the temporal and eternal well-being of others.[37] Thus the most peculiar tenet of Hopkinsiansism, and the one most offensive to the rational mind, reinforced the social activism which his redefinition of Being in general and his criticism of secondary virtue encouraged.

419

Taken together, Hopkins's innovations represented an important shift away from the equivocal theological legacy of Edwards on the issue of worldly action toward an emphatic endorsement of social reform.[38] Where Edwards saw true virtue as essentially a matter of right affections, Hopkins viewed it as right actions. God's moral law, Hopkins concluded, "leads us to consider holiness as consisting in universal disinterested good will considered in all its genuine exercises and fruits, and acted out in all its branches toward God, and our neighbor."[39]

In reinterpreting true virtue as radical disinterested benevolence, Hopkins was not simply responding to Edwards's positions. He was also attempting to furnish a corrective to the increasingly fashionable theological notion of self-love. As in Edwards's theology, self-love in the eighteenth century was

[35] Edwards, *Charity and Its Fruits*, 236.

[36] *True Holiness*, 70.

[37] On this and several other suggestive implications of Hopkins's interpretation of disinterested benevolence see Oliver Wendell Elsbree, "Samuel Hopkins and His Doctrine of Benevolence," *New England Quarterly*, VIII (1935), 534-550.

[38] Heimert detects such a trend toward activism in the thought of Edwards's followers: "Within Calvinist doctrine itself, the 1750's witnessed something of a redefinition of Christian virtue, making 'zeal' a more distinguishing affection . . . than love. The changing emphasis reflected the shift in focus from the heart to the will implicit in the *Religious Affections*" (*Religion and the American Mind*, 311). Such a shift occurred somewhat later than Heimert believes, largely, as I have tried to show, as a result of Hopkinsianism.

[39] *True Holiness*, 41.

at times viewed as a mediating moral state between selfishness and true virtue, and at others as part of true holiness itself. In either case it appeared to the New Divinity men to be a doctrine that promoted and legitimized avaricious, egoistic patterns of behavior. Their apprehensions had considerable justification, for the concept of self-love proved to be an intellectual way station on the road to a full-fledged theory of self-interest. By removing much of the moral obloquy attached to egocentric behavior, it eased the passage from traditional communal ideals to a new ideology of individualism and self-interest. As the rational clergy saw it, the idea of self-love brought about greater coherence between social theory and social reality. At the same time, they argued, it denied the legitimacy of naked self-interest (selfishness) and would create a more stable social order since, in theory at least, self-love would promote the public good. To the structural forces in eighteenth-century New England that encouraged individualistic, self-centered behavior—economic and demographic expansion, and land hunger—the rationalists now added a theoretical argument that may have allowed many people to allay feelings of guilt for having violated social tradition and to rationalize self-interest.[40]

420

To be sure, all of this was not self-evident in the middle of the eighteenth century. Rather, as Richard L. Bushman has pointed out, "the 1750s and 1760s were a period of experimentation in social theory because everyday experience confronted people with the problem" of contriving "a new rationale for the social order . . ."[41] But the New Divinity man perceived present and potential dangers in such experimentation. Liberal and Old Light Calvinists drew their self-love social theories directly from rational moral philosophers like Shaftesbury and Hutcheson. Many New Lights, on the other hand, gave self-love a role in human behavior based upon the views of Edwards in *True Virtue*.[42] It remained for the New Divinity men to

[40] This was particularly true in commercial areas, where, by the 1760s, the crisis in social thought was adjusted and a modified corporate ethic (self-love) was in conflict with naked self-interest (see Crowley, *This Sheba, Self*, 96-97). But as Kenneth A. Lockridge has recently argued, the rural world that spawned the New Divinity clung to an idealized corporate perspective that made even relatively minor social changes seem like "catastrophic alterations of an idyllic and holy past" ("Social Change and the Meaning of American Revolution," *Jour. Soc. Hist.*, VI [1973], 423-424); see also Zuckerman, *Peaceable Kingdoms, passim*. In both commercial and rural New England, the republican ideology of the Revolution, with its emphasis on public virtue and simplicity, heightened the conflict between social theory and social practice, and fired the hopes of evangelicals like Hopkins.
[41] Bushman, *Puritan to Yankee*, 272.
[42] On the use of the concept of self-love by both Old Lights and New Lights see, for example, Samuel Cooper, *A Sermon Preached in Boston, New England, before the Society for Encouraging Industry and Employing the Poor* (Boston, 1753), 2-3, and Thomas Clap, *An Essay on the Nature and Foundation of Moral Virtue and Obligation* . . . (New Haven, Conn., 1765), 13-17.

protest what they saw as theological concessions to selfish social behavior.

To this task Hopkins brought a strong sense of moral urgency. In growing numbers ministers chose "to represent the hopes and fears, joys and sorrows, and all the exercises of the Christian as wholly selfish," he protested, "and treat of all the doctrines and duties of christianity in this light! How common to find arminians, neonominists, professed calvinists, antinomians, or whatever other name they may bear, and however they may differ in other things, all agreeing in this!"[43] The New Divinity men held that self-love ethical theories, whether Edwardsian or Hutchesonian, were contributing to the failure of communal ideals. As Hopkins reasoned, "if no person can renounce his eternal interest, in opposition to a selfish regard to it, there is no such thing in nature as self-denial, or public, disinterested affection."[44] Furthermore, if the new social morality was anchored in egocentricity, then the truly benevolent man was required to battle that false morality in all its social manifestations. Hopkins's theology thus obliged him to oppose the emergent values of commercial Newport; in particular, it inspired his assault on slavery and the slave trade.

Hopkins's repudiation of the new morality derived from his rural upbringing and twenty-five-year pastorate in the backcountry. It was intensified by his experience of the worldly society and mercantile economy of Newport, with its involvement in the slave trade and the production of rum which was used to secure human cargo on the coast of Africa. To the rustic theologian, committed to a simple, even ascetic socio-religious tradition, Newport appeared a symbol of what America was in danger of becoming. Moreover, the behavior of Newport slave merchants underlined the importance of distinguishing secondary virtue from true virtue. In terms of conventional social morality the respectable slave traders, most of whom were practicing Christians, seemed to be virtuous men. Measured against the yardstick of disinterested benevolence, however, their virtue fell far short of love to Being in general. Finally, Hopkins linked his attack on Newport's slave traders and the social order they represented with the Revolutionary struggle against Great Britain.

In the early 1770s Hopkins preached to his congregation on the iniquity of the slave trade, and he published his first important antislavery tract, *A Dialogue Concerning the Slavery of the Africans*, in 1776. The work was dedicated to the Continental Congress, from which he sought reassurance that a 1774 resolution prohibiting the slave trade issued "not merely from political reasons; but from a conviction of the unrighteousness and cruelty of

421

[43] *True Holiness*, 78.
[44] *Ibid.*, 70. For an interesting debate on self-love between Hopkins and a prominent secular leader see the correspondence with Roger Sherman in Andrew P. Peabody, ed., "Hopkinsianism," American Antiquarian Society, *Proceedings*, V (1889), 437-461.

that trade and a regard to justice and benevolence." He urged the delegates
not to divorce politics from morality but rather to promote the moral
regeneration of America and guarantee the success of the Revolution by
"bring[ing] about a total abolition of slavery, in such a manner as shall
greatly promote the happiness of those oppressed strangers, and [the] best
interest of the public."[45]

With the mode of life of Newport's wealthy merchant class undoubtedly
in mind, Hopkins challenged the American people not only to abolish slavery
but also to launch a "thorough reformation" of all "public sins."[46] For
several years he had seen the promise of radical social regeneration held out
by resistance to Great Britain. "The struggle is like to prove fatal to tea
drinking in America which will save much needless expense," he had written
to the Reverend John Erskine in Scotland in 1774, adding that "there is a
hopeful prospect of its putting an end to many other extravagances, unless
accommodation should take place soon."[47] In his *Dialogue* Hopkins urged
Americans to reform all their selfish, profligate ways. By concentrating on
the evil of slavery he did "not mean to exclude other public, crying sins found
among us, such as impiety and profaneness—formality and indifference in
the service and cause of Christ and his religion—and various ways of open
opposition to it—intemperance and prodigality; and other instances of
unrighteousness." Slavery and all the sins of America were "the fruits of a
most criminal, contracted selfishness."[48]

Through the 1780s and 1790s Hopkins remained committed to the
abolition of slavery and the slave trade, and continued to see these evils in the
larger context of a social order rooted in self-interest and extravagance rather
than true virtue.[49] The Revolutionary dedication to simplicity and the public

422

[45] Hopkins, *A Dialogue Concerning the Slavery of the Africans; Shewing it to be the Duty and Interest of the American Colonies to emancipate all their African Slaves* . . . (Norwich, Conn., 1776), iii. Two recent essays briefly analyze Hopkins's antislavery thought and actions. See David S. Lovejoy, "Samuel Hopkins: Religion, Slavery, and the Revolution," *NEQ*, XL (1967), 227-243, and David E. Swift, "Samuel Hopkins: Calvinist Social Concern in Eighteenth-Century New England," *Journal of Presbyterian History*, XLVII (1969), 31-54. Also see Bernard Bailyn, *The Ideological Origins of the American Revolution* (Cambridge, Mass., 1967), 232-241, and David Brion Davis, *The Problem of Slavery in the Age of Revolution, 1770-1823* (Ithaca, N.Y., 1975), 293-299.
[46] Hopkins, *Dialogue Concerning Slavery*, 53.
[47] Hopkins to John Erskine, Dec. 27, 1774, Gratz MSS, Historical Society of Pennsylvania, Philadelphia. For similar hopes and their implications for the Revolution see Edmund S. Morgan, "The Puritan Ethic and the American Revolution," *WMQ*, 3d Ser., XXIV (1967), 3-43, and Lockridge, "Social Change and the Meaning of the American Revolution," *Jour. Soc. Hist.*, VI (1973), 424.
[48] Hopkins, *Dialogue Concerning Slavery*, 52.
[49] For a full discussion of Hopkins's antislavery position in relation to the Revolution and the central themes of this essay see Conforti, "Samuel Hopkins and

good had been abandoned, Hopkins wrote in an antislavery essay in 1787, and Americans were spending their money "for foreign luxuries or unnecessaries, and those things which might have been manufactured among ourselves."[50] The continuing oppression of the blacks became for Hopkins the main sign that the Revolution had failed to reform thoroughly the indulgent self-centered behavior of the American people and to reconstruct the social order on the basis of love to Being in general. Hopkins singled out Newport, where the slave trade had been resumed, as "the most guilty ... of any [community] on the continent, as it has been in great measure built by the blood of the poor Africans, and the only way [for it] to escape the effects of Divine displeasure is to be sensible of the sin, repent and reform."[51] Although Hopkins persevered to the end of his life in supporting the antislavery cause, when the federal constitutional convention prevented congressional interference with the slave trade until 1808, he became pessimistic about America's immediate future and transferred to the millennium his hope for a society held together by self-sacrificing love of God and our neighbors.

423

The idea of disinterested benevolence, as one critic of Hopkins has recently reminded us, was not exclusively of New England origin. Francis Hutcheson, George Whitefield, John Wesley, and the Quakers, for example, all developed notions of benevolence in the eighteenth century that inspired the crusading reformers of the next century.[52] No theories of disinterested benevolence, however, not even that of Edwards, approached the self-denying idealism of Hopkins's views. For this reason, many of New England's future religious reformers, particularly the next generation of young, pietistic, Congregational clerics, would come to see the doctrine of dis-

---

the New Divinity Movement," chap. 8. One important antislavery consequence of his theology was the institution of ecclesiastical sanctions against the holding and trading of slaves in his own church. Under his prodding the church voted in 1784 "that the slave trade and the slavery of the Africans, as it has taken place among us, is a gross violation of the righteousness and benevolence which are so much inculcated in the gospel; and therefore we will not tolerate it in this church" (Jan. 30 and Mar. 4, 1784, First Congregational Church Records, Newport Historical Society, R.I.).

[50] This essay, signed "Crito," appeared in two installments in the *Providence Gazette: and Country Journal* (R.I.), Oct. 6, 13, 1787. It was reprinted under the title "The Slave Trade and Slavery" in *Timely Articles on Slavery by the Rev. Samuel Hopkins* (Boston, 1854), a collection of Hopkins's antislavery writings. The quotation is on p. 619.

[51] Hopkins to Moses Brown, Apr. 29, 1784, Moses Brown Papers, Rhode Island Historical Society, Providence; "The Slave Trade and Slavery," in *Timely Articles on Slavery*, 615.

[52] Lois W. Banner, "Religious Benevolence as Social Control: A Critique of an Interpretation," *Journal of American History*, LX (1973), 25-41.

interested benevolence as a unique contribution of the New Divinity movement.[53]

Far from losing contact with social reality by spinning a metaphysical cocoon around itself, the New Divinity movement, as this analysis of the debate over the problem of true virtue has tried to suggest, was in constant dialogue with the clerical spokesmen for, and the lay representatives of, an emerging secular social order. New Divinity theology struck a responsive chord among certain segments of New England society. The movement increasingly captured the allegiance of aspirants to the Congregational ministry, especially in the years leading up to and following the founding of the predominantly Hopkinsian Andover Seminary in 1808.[54] Moreover, on the lay level, the New Divinity appealed to and was welcomed by congregations throughout rural New England. Thus, surveying the backcountry from his pastorate in Salem in 1813, liberal Calvinist William Bentley reluctantly concluded that Hopkins's "System of Divinity is the basis of the popular theology of New England."[55]

From the vantage point of rural New England, and in light of the region's crisis in social thought, it is interesting to speculate on the intellectual consequences of the New Divinity's triumph. For many pious young men, religious reform provided an outlet for the tension between Christ and culture to which the New Divinity was addressed and which it encouraged. But for most inhabitants of rural New England who supported the New

424

[53] For a recent assessment of the influence of Hopkins and the New Divinity on 19th-century reform see Davis, *Problem of Slavery in the Age of Revolution*, 296. Two 19th-century reformers left glowing testimonies to the influence of Hopkins; see William Ellery Channing to E. A. Park, Feb. 14, 1840, Yale MSS, Sterling Memorial Library, New Haven, Conn., and John Greenleaf Whittier, *Works*, VI, (New York, 1888), 130-140.

[54] By 1792, for instance, Ezra Stiles reported that more than one-third of the Congregational clergy in Connecticut identified themselves as New Divinity men. In the same year, Stiles noted, the Consistent Calvinists claimed to have the allegiance of all new Congregational ministerial candidates in the state. Franklin Bowditch Dexter, ed., *The Literary Diary of Ezra Stiles, D.D., LL.D.*, III (New York, 1901), 463-464. For other evidence documenting the growth of the New Divinity see *ibid.*, 247, 363; *The Diary of William Bentley, D.D.: Pastor of the East Church, Salem, Massachusetts* (Salem, 1905-1914), I, 161, III, 364; West, ed., *Sketches of the Life of Hopkins*, 102-103; Park, *Memoir of Hopkins*, 236-237; Leonard Bacon et al., *Contributions to the Ecclesiastical History of Connecticut* (New Haven, 1861), 240; and Charles Keller, *The Second Great Awakening in Connecticut* (New Haven, 1942), 36-37, 50-52. On Hopkins's influence over the Andover seminarians see Wolfgang E. Lowe, "The First American Foreign Missionaries: The Students, 1810-1829: An Inquiry into their Theological Motives" (Ph.D. diss., Brown University, 1962).

[55] *Diary of Bentley*, IV, 302; see also Foster, *Genetic History of New England Theology*, 1.

Divinity, the conflict between normative values and new patterns of behavior was not so easily resolved. For these people the Second Great Awakening, like the First, may have been a vent for the moral uneasiness that character- ized a continuing crisis of religious legitimation. If this is so, then the New Divinity did not betray its origins in experimental religion by over- intellectualizing the piety of the First Awakening but preserved, for the backcountry at least, the revival's creative tension between social tradition and social practice.

425

THE TYPOLOGY OF
AMERICA'S MISSION

SACVAN BERCOVITCH
Columbia University

THE PURITANS INVENTED THE SACRED HISTORY OF NEW ENGLAND; THE eighteenth-century clergy established the concept of America's mission. In this essay I want to suggest the nature of that development, with special emphasis on the role of the Edwardsean revivals. I use the word *suggest* to stress the limits of my subject. My perspective is a very partial one: partial in its view of Edwards, of Puritanism, of the Great Awakening, and above all, of the social and ideological factors that carried the colonies from revival to revolution. I try to indicate something of the "larger picture" in the course of my analysis, but mainly I focus on questions of rhetoric. My assumption is that (after due allowance is made for all the complexities involved) American culture may be said to have grown in a more or less coherent way toward a modern free enterprise economy, that that growth finds expression in the quasi-figural outlook we have come to associate with manifest destiny and the dream, and therefore that to describe that outlook is (by implication at least) to illuminate some of the controversial connections between Puritan, Yankee, and Revolutionary America.

The connections have been controversial for many reasons. In the interests of clarity, I center my discussion on the rhetoric of millennialism, and specifically Edwardsean "post-millennialism": first, in its relation to New England Puritanism; and second, in its relation to what has recently been termed "civil millennialism." In both cases, historians have emphasized a radical shift in approach. Without denying the fact of change, I hope to demonstrate the ways in which the persistence of language and vision constitutes an underlying unity of design. I need hardly add that to demonstrate is not the same as to endorse.

* * *

Let me begin with the differences in outlook between the Puritan clergy and their Yankee successors. The New England colonists saw their errand into the wilderness as part of the final stage of history. In developing that view, they distorted traditional forms of exegesis, but they were careful to justify themselves by recourse to scripture. They always rooted their interpretations (however strained) in biblical texts, and they appealed to (even as they departed from) a common tradition of Reformed hermeneutics. Their Yankee heirs felt relatively free of such constraints. During the Enlightenment, the meaning of Protestant identity became increasingly vague; typology took on the hazy significance of image and symbol; what passed for the divine plan lost its strict grounding in scripture; providence itself was shaken loose from its religious framework to become part of the belief in human progress. The eighteenth-century clergy took advantage of this movement to shift the focus of figural authority, from Bible history to the American experience. In effect, they substituted a regional for a biblical past, consecrated the American present as a movement from promise to fulfillment, and translated fulfillment, from its meaning within the closed system of sacred history, into a metaphor for limitless secular improvement.

427

These discontinuities, as they have often been called, resulted from a process of extension and adaptation, not of transformation. The Puritan clergy had set out to blur traditional distinctions between the world and the kingdom. Their rhetoric issued in a unique mode of ambiguity that precluded the conflict of heaven's time and man's. "Canaan" was a spiritual state for them, as it was for other Christians; but it was also (in another, but not conflicting sense) their country. They spoke of the mutuality (rather than the coexistence) of fact and ideal. By "church-state" they meant a separation of powers in the belief that in the American Canaan, and there only, the ecclesiastical and the civic order had been made to correspond. And in the course of time the correspondence yielded the secular basis of multidenominational religion and the sacral view of free enterprise economics. Both these developments were rooted in the heterodox tenets established a century before: the moral distinctions between the Old World and the New (as between Egypt and Canaan), the interrelation of material and spiritual blessings, the concept of a new chosen people whose special calling entailed special trials, and above all a mythic view of history that extended New England's past into an apocalypse which stood "near, even at the door," requiring one last great act, one more climactic pouring out of the spirit, in order to realize itself.

Recent scholars have recognized the importance of millennialism to our religious and social history. But by and large they have dated that notion from the Edwardsean revivals, because of what they assumed to be a fundamental theological shift. Technically speaking, the seventeenth-century colonists (like most Protestants of their time) were pre-millennialists. That is, they believed that the descent of New Jerusalem would be preceded and attended by a series of cataclysmic divine judgments and followed by a universal change in all things. Jonathan Edwards, on the contrary, was a post-millennialist; he posited a final golden age within history, and thereby freed humanity, so to speak, to participate in the revolutions of the apocalypse. Students of the Great Awakening have used this distinction to make Edwards out to be a radically innovative historian, the first New World spokesman for an optimistic view of human progress.

428

The distinction is a questionable one. Historians of religion have long noted that pre-and post-millennialism are often present in the same movement, sometimes in the same thinker. And even if we accept a significant difference between the two approaches it is by no means certain that Edwards was our first post-millennialist. David Smith has argued that that honor belongs to the latter-day theocrats (like Samuel Sewall, Cotton Mather, and Joseph Morgan), and if to them, then also, I would maintain, to the first- and second-generation ministers who made the doctrine of the chiliad almost canonical in their church-state. For chiliasm, the belief in an earthly paradise, recasts the apocalyptic hope into something like the Edwardsean idea of progress, especially when it is accompanied, as it was in early New England, by a typological sense of fulfillment. "The flourishing beauty of . . . heavenly grace," said William Hubbard, in an election-day sermon of 1676, "which did so strangely metamorphose the visage of the face of things at first in the world . . . was the verdant lustre . . . that turned [our] rough and barren wilderness . . . into a fruitful Carmel or fragrant Sharon"; and New Jerusalem, in turn, would bring that lustre to a "more brilliant glow."[1] The spiraling process that Hubbard outlines (Creation to Eden, to Canaan, to New Canaan in America, to New Eden) was a commonplace of the New England Puritan pulpit. It calls attention to the implications of the Puritans' eschatology of errand—what we might call their *American* millennialism.

---

[1] David E. Smith. "Millennarian Scholarship in America," *American Quarterly*, 17 (1965), 537 (see also 530, 541–42); William Hubbard, *The Happiness of a People* (Boston, 1676), 61.

For though Hubbard and his colleagues believed the millennium would involve a drastic overturning, that overturning meant "metamorphosis" to them: a change in this world, and most dramatically in their New World. Their errand led not from earth to heaven (like the pilgrimage of the Plymouth settlers), but from lesser to greater glories on the American strand. As they conceived it, New Jerusalem would come not to abrogate their venture, but to complete it. The apocalyptic wonders were for them part of the latter-day "magnalia Christi Americana," and the millennium itself, by extension, part of the country's history. Whereas their European contemporaries expected the millennium to bring secular history to an end, the New England Puritans spoke of the millennium as the motivating force of their errand. America, in their view (like Eden, Canaan, and New Jerusalem), was intrinsic to the progress of the work of redemption. They acknowledged, of course, that New Jerusalem was different and all-too-distant from the New England church-state. But in the eye of prophecy, it was already present for them, as the harvest is implicit in the planting, the glorified in the justified saint, and the antitype in the *figura*. "Though there be in special one grand accomplishment of Scripture Prophecies," said William Adams on a fast-day in 1678, "yet there hath been a glorious accomplishment of it already," albeit a "partile accomplishment . . . wherein those . . . promises are fulfilled in their measure and degree." Adams was not just speaking for the mid-century clergy. With Hubbard, he was making explicit what the orthodox had believed from the start: in transforming the American wilderness, God was providing through their church-state "a type and Embleme of New Jerusalem," "a *First Fruits* of that which shall in due time be accomplished in the world throughout."[2] As the theocracy foreshadowed New Jerusalem, so New Jerusalem would be the Good Old Way written large.

429

This parallel between Edwards and the Puritans reminds us (or ought to) that Edwards himself denied any substantial difference in this respect between himself and his predecessors. We know that he was influenced by Thomas Shepard's *Parable of the Ten Virgins* (1636), and in 1744 he made the legacy clear in complaining about the "slanderous" charges of Charles Chauncy, the leading spokesman for the Old Light orthodoxy. Chauncy had accused Edwards of having "often said that the millennium was already begun"; but the truth was, Edwards wrote, that he had seen the revivals as no more than "forerunners of those glorious times." Even

---

[2] William Adams, *The Necessity of the Pouring Out of the Spirit* (Boston, 1679), 35; James Allin, *New England's Choicest Blessing* (Boston, 1679), 13; Increase Mather, Preface to Samuel Torrey, *An Exhortation Unto Reformation* (Cambridge, Mass., 1674), sig. A₂ recto.

at the peak of his enthusiasm, during the harvests of 1739–41, he had known (and stated in his *Thoughts on the Revival*) "that there would be many changes, revivings and intermissions, and returns of dark clouds and threatening circumstances, before . . . Christ's kingdom shall be everywhere established." Had not Thomas Shepard and all the "fathers"—John Davenport, John Cotton, Richard Mather, and others—spoken in much the same terms about the prospects in store for New England?[3] No doubt such assertions of filiopietism were a source of Edwards' appeal. The New Lights revolted not (as some have said) against paternal authority, but against a generation they thought had betrayed the founding fathers. No doubt, too, Edwards exaggerated his bonds with the past, much as the latter-day Puritans had exaggerated theirs with the theocracy, and as nineteenth-century evangelicals were to exaggerate their loyalty to Edwards. But that sense of continuity was itself part of the myth; the very discrepancy between assertion and fact attests to the persistence of Puritan rhetoric. This does not explain the discrepancy away, of course, and I will return to it later in the essay. But first it seems necessary, in view of current scholarship, to trace the development that Edwards suggests.

430

The crucial link is the emphasis on process. In contrast to European chiliasts, the Puritans and Edwardseans concerned themselves far less with the final event than with the design of gradual fulfillment. For both groups the time was always at hand, but somehow that was of secondary interest. The real issue was the *figural* meaning of the present, which is to say, the union of history and prophecy. What distinguishes Edwards' approach is the greater consistency of its logic. The Puritans' concept of errand, for all its internal coherence, is marred (from the standpoint of historic process) by its pre-millennialism. Their sense of prophetic fulfillment, leading upward from Eden to New Canaan, is blurred (if not undermined) by its reliance on an entirely extraterrestrial agency—some superhuman "shattering of the order of nature." Edwards, by changing the scenario for this last act of the errand, welded the whole progression into an organic human-divine whole. That was his contribution. In cultural terms, it had enormous import for the course of American millennialism. But as a view of history, it simply drew out the implications of the outlook developed a century before. "Though there has been a glorious fulfillment of . . . prophecies already," Edwards wrote in 1740, describing the chiliad in phrases that make the legacy unmistakable, "other times are only forerunners and preparatories to this," as the exodus of Israel

[3] Jonathan Edwards, *The Great Awakening*, C. C. Goen, ed. (New Haven: Yale Univ. Press, 1972), 560, and *Works*, John Erskine, ed. (New York, 1849), 3:316.

from Babylon "typified" the Reformation and the Great Migration. And what the Great Migration meant now seemed to him "gloriously visible." Christ, he announced, will have "the heathen for his inheritance," a "nation shall be born in a day," and Protestant America, climactically, will become another, greater Mountain of Holiness, "Beautiful as *Tirzah,* comely as *Jerusalem,* and terrible as an Army with Banners"—"*Put on thy beautiful garments,* O America, *the holy city!*"[4]

Edwards' conviction that sacred history was reaching its apex in the New World seals his indebtedness to the Puritans. Without forgetting his very considerable borrowings from European thinkers—without forgetting either that his millennialism both antedates and postdates his hopes for the Awakening (and that eventually he may have lost faith in America's mission)—it seems safe to say that, at the height of his fervor, Edwards adopted wholesale the Puritan vision of the New World. For him as for his forebears, the "discovery of America" was not just an event in secular history, the opening of new territories to European Christians. It was the unveiling of some momentous truth, as an inspired exegete unveils the meaning of an obscure passage in scripture. In this hermeneutic sense, Edwards *discovered* America in scripture, specifically in the apocalyptic passage, Isaiah 66:19; and like his forebears, he proceeded to celebrate the golden age of the first planters as the millennial dawn. Given these premises, Edwards' view of the Awakening was a foregone conclusion. English millennialists like Moses Lowman helped him decide on particular apocalyptic dates; German Pietists like August Hermann Francke and English evangelists like George Whitefield heightened his sense of expectancy. But in the main his concept of the Northampton Millennium—including not only his account of things past and present, but also his forecasts of things to come (vast increases in population, ecumenism in faith, great piety, true liberty, general prosperity, and an expansion of scientific, moral, and religious knowledge)—derived from Puritan New England.

431

Especially revealing is Edwards' emphasis on trial. The familiar contrast between the Puritans' "cosmic despair" and the revivalists' "high cosmic optimism" simplifies the attitudes of both groups. As the earlier group had found a way out of despair so, conversely, the eighteenth-century Calvinists found ample opportunity to remind their audiences of the dangers before them—the "cataclysms," the "ferment and struggle," the "mighty and violent opposition" which would precede the overthrow of

---

[4] C. C. Goen, "Jonathan Edwards: A New Departure in Eschatology," *Church History,* 28 (1959), 32; Edwards, *Works,* 1:484–86.

Satan's kingdom. In these latter days, they explained, darkness and affliction were "always to be expected." Like the Puritan Jeremiahs, the
Edwardseans fused threat and promise in making probation their overriding metaphor for the times. If it seemed that God was about "to forsake
this land, and to bring most awful judgments upon it," then there was
cause to rejoice. It was precisely through such a "time of testing" that
Christ's American saints could (as it were) assert their right to make
New England a "heaven upon earth." There are numerous parallels for
such statements in seventeenth-century sermons—most strikingly perhaps,
in the covenant-renewal ceremonies established during King Philip's War
(1674–76). In both the Puritan covenant-renewals and the revivalist con-
certs of prayer, the clergy linked personal salvation and the progress of
the work of the redemption with a unique American enterprise. And in
both cases the ritual was based on the Israelites' covenant renewals under
Joshua and Nehemiah. Then, God had led His people from captivity to
Canaan; now, God was calling upon His people in New England to complete the liberation of the church. According to Cotton Mather, that call
had first been answered by the Great Migration, with the Puritan Ark of
Christ "victoriously sailing round the *globe*," changing geography into
"Christiano-graphy." Exactly a century later, commenting on the Revo-
lutionary period of trial underway in the United States, David Austin confirmed the promise once more in his "Advertisement" to Edwards'
History of the Work of Redemption:

432

> Though to the eye of unbelief, the Ark may seem, now, to be involved in
> tempestuous weather, and soon to be foundered through the probable failure
> of borrowed strength; yet, to the joy of the passengers there are those, who,
> looking through the mists of human or internal jars, do hail the approach of
> MILLENNIAL DAY!
> On the Ocean of the Millennium [our] . . . Ark shall safely and uninterrupt-
> edly sail.[5]

*   *   *

Austin was speaking directly to the fate of revivalism in the eighteenth
century. His scorn for the sceptic's "unbelief" reminds us that since 1742
a growing number of Enlightenment liberals had been heaping contempt

[5] Alan Heimert, *Religion and the American Mind: From the Great Awakening to
the Revolution* (Cambridge: Harvard Univ. Press, 1966), 64, 66; Edwards, *Works*,
1:481, and 3:316 (see also 1:322–24, 469, 486–94, and 3:291, 299, 308–19, 322–24,
410, 417–18, 424, 431–34, 454–61, 492); Cotton Mather, *Magnalia Christi Americana*,
Thomas Robbins, ed. (Hartford, 1853), 1:42–43; David Austin, "Advertisement" to
Jonathan Edwards, *History of Redemption*, Austin, ed. (New York, 1793), iv.

upon "enthusiasts" like himself. But the liberals failed to persuade. Austin's optimism, his sense of the apocalyptic "joy" aboard the American ship of state, recalls the continuing vitality of Edwardsean revivalism. And revivalism remained vital to the culture, I would suggest, because Edwards neither broke with the Puritans nor aligned himself with them, but molded their myth to fit the needs of his own times. From the perspective I have been advancing, his contribution was to make revivalism a force toward independence by making it part of the evolving typology of America's mission. This is (to repeat) a very limited perspective on Edwards' achievement; it reveals the provincialism of a brilliant mind, the capacity of a profound religious thinker to be misled by cultural afflatus into an astonishing arrogance, both on his own behalf and on behalf of his region and continent. Nonetheless, insofar as Edwards' arrogance reflects a set of widely shared beliefs it seems to me to illuminate some salient implications of his thought.

433

    It indicates, first of all, that he drew out the proto-nationalistic tendencies of the New England Way. Edwards inherited the concept of a new chosen people, and he enlarged its constituency from saintly New England theocrats to newborn American saints. In fact, if not in theory, theocracy had meant exclusivism, the literal and direct continuity from elect father to (presumably) elect son. Revivalist conversion opened the ranks of the American army of Christ to every white Protestant believer. Whereas the Puritan covenant renewals called the children of New England to their filial obligations, the Edwardsean concerts of prayer sought to awaken all prospective American saints, North and South, to the state of their souls, the shortcomings of their society, and the destiny of their New World Canaan.

    In effect, Edwards expanded the Puritans' tribal genetics of salvation into a genealogy of the latter-day American church. The second- and third-generation clergy had extolled the emigrants as founding fathers, but they limited the legend perforce to the story of New England. Edwards freed the errand from the confines of regional theocracy. He rendered the legend of the founding fathers the common property of all New World evangelicals, and thus opened the prospect for expanding the Puritan past into a *figura* of the American Way. This accounts for the impression that many scholars have had of the relatively high optimism in the revivalist sermons. The Puritans also described their mission in terms of "Christ's mighty deeds in America." But they were committed to a regionally defined, doctrinally exclusive way of life; and for all their self-assurance they never quite managed to reconcile the restrictive and expansive tendencies of their thought. Edwards had no such conflicts. His view of history, like his evangelicalism, was couched in terms of continuous and indefinite enlargement. He could afford to adopt a post-millennial view because he required no supernatural event to bridge the gap between an "enclosed garden" and the country at large, or between an outmoded past and a world-redemptive future. The New England Way was for him above all a shadow or type of the "union of love" that would knit together, as one city on a hill, all of Protestant America.

For if Edwards abandoned the Puritan belief in theocracy, he none-theless retained the Puritan vision of personal/communal exceptionalism. As Alan Heimert notes, he differed from English revivalists, including Whitefield, by his emphasis on corporate mission. Edwards attacked the Separates for their spiritual pride, and the colonial Establishment for its lax method of church admission. The "middle way" he espoused was, like John Cotton's, an ambiguous union of extremes: it aspired simul-taneously to absolute purity and to a full involvement in this world. In America, Edwards insisted, "the holy community must serve as a type of New Jerusalem" and hence as an earthly "instrument for bringing it into being." The Separates argued (as Roger Williams had against Cotton) that typologically there was a "plain Difference between the World and the Church." Edwards replied (as Cotton had to Williams) that the story of America was intrinsic to sacred history. The aim of the American church, as "a type of New Jerusalem," was not merely "the salvation of individuals, but of society," since the society, in this case, was by defini-tion engaged in "the forwarding of the Work of Redemption."[6]

I invoke the parallel now to stress the change from 1640 to 1740. We have often been told that Edwards' position in the culture was a transi-tional one. Undoubtedly it was, if we add that the transition marked not so much the end of an old order as the unfolding of a new stage of growth in colonial society. According to Perry Miller, Edwards was a modernist in spite of himself—the first American to recast Puritanism into "the idiom of empirical psychology"—and thus a central figure in the movement toward the values of liberal free enterprise. There is a good deal of evidence for this view; but even more to support the case for Edwards the traditionalist—the orthodox Calvinist who sought passionately to curb the threat of modernism by all means at his disposal, including the ideal of christic selfhood. In direct opposition to Locke, he main-

434

---

[6] Alan Heimert, Introduction to Jonathan Edwards' *Humble Inquiry*, in *The Great Awakening*, Heimert and Perry Miller, eds. (Indianapolis: Bobbs-Merrill, 1967), 424; "A Letter from the Ministers of Windham" (1745), in *Great Awakening*, Heimert and Miller, eds., 401; Heimert, *Religion*, 123–24 (citing Edwards and the Separates; see also 125–30).

tained that true individuation was not a self-contained, empirical process but a public and spiritual commitment. Regeneration for him depended on conformity through grace to "a principle of oneness that is manifested . . . as identical multiple units of generic consciousness." What brings together these two sides of Edwards' thought, at least during the period of the Awakening, was his effort to link regeneration to the destiny of the New World. American Protestants, after all, had a special role to play in God's plans. For them above all other peoples, conversion, rebirth, and "generic consciousness" were manifested typologically, through the correspondence (which Edwards never tired of explaining) between personal fulfillment and social harmony. The result, however unintended, was that he went further than his predecessors in adjusting the Puritan vision to the norms of his age. Recent historians of religion have observed that Edwards' "ethics were prudent and flexible applications of the early Puritan tradition to the settled life of mid-eighteenth-century Massachusetts," that his chief followers "tended to espouse a . . . radically egalitarian, libertarian, and fraternal view of . . . social and political life," and that his theology proved flexible enough for them to "empower the theory of a nation."[7] Edwards should not be burdened with all the sins of his disciples, of course; but in this case we cannot entirely dissociate his thought from theirs. By implication, it seems clear, his long labor to wed Calvin and Locke issued in the union of eschatology and self-interest under the canopy of American progress.

435

From this perspective, Edwards' post-millennialism was indeed a major advance upon the Puritan vision. By opening the future to human control, he adapted the belief in process to the needs of an enterprise that had grown beyond the limits of a particular region or religious sect. The Bay theocrats had joined secular to sacred history, and posited a continual increase of material/spiritual blessings. Edwards made the spiral of redemption synonymous with the advance of mankind. In doing so, Cushing Strout has shown, he "provided an exit from the harsh confines of Calvinism [he] expounded and paved the way for . . . new Arminian theologies of belief in the free will and moral strivings." The historical ironies this involved may be more strongly stated. Edwards sanctified a worldli-

---

[7] Perry Miller, *Jonathan Edwards* (New York: W. Sloane, 1949), 62; David Lyttle, "Jonathan Edwards on Personal Identity," *Early American Literature*, 7 (1972), 165; William Clebsch, *From Sacred to Profane America: The Role of Religion in American History* (New York: Harper and Row, 1968), 185; Roland Delattre, "Beauty and Politics: A Problematic Legacy of Jonathan Edwards," in *American Philosophy from Edwards to Quine*, R. W. Shahan and K. R. Merrill, eds. (Norman, Okla.: Univ. of Oklahoma Press, 1977), 21-22; Clebsch, *From Sacred to Profane*, 144.

ness he would have despised and lent support to new ideologies that
linked American striving with scripture prophecy, economic reform with
the work of the spirit, and libertarian ideals with the approach of New
Jerusalem. Thus his use of commercial imagery ("to live unto God . . .
is the business and . . . the trade of a Christian") became a mainstay of
Yankee pietism. Thus his figural view of economics (the increase in
colonial trade "is a type and forerunner" of the time when the whole
world "shall be supplied with spiritual treasures from America") reappears
in countless promotional tracts. And thus the Awakening he inspired, as
Richard Bushman has shown, encouraged "worldly ambition and resistance to [conservative forms of] social authority"—a middle-class
upsurgence that resulted in territorial expansion, "increased economic
opportunities," a "multitude of new traders who called for currency issues," and a rising demand for democratic self-government, all
of this sustained and augmented by the sense that it reflected some grand
providential design—in Edwards' words, "the rising of a New Heaven and
a New Earth in the New World."[8]

436

*   *   *

[8] Cushing Strout, *The New Heavens and New Earth: Political Religion in America*
(New York: Harper and Row, 1975), 113; Edwards, *Works*, 1:10, and *Images or
Shadows of Divine Things*, Perry Miller, ed. (New Haven: Yale Univ. Press, 1948),
102; Richard Bushman, *From Puritan to Yankee: Character and the Social Order in
Connecticut* (Cambridge: Harvard Univ. Press, 1967), 37, 288; Edwards, *Works*, 3:88.
Let me repeat that, here as elsewhere, the effect was something very different from the
intent. Undoubtedly, Edwards differed in many ways from Revolutionary Calvinists,
"like Abraham Keteltas . . . [who] welcomed to the cause of God anyone who would
take up the sword against the anti-christ of British tyranny." The revivalists were
addressing "bands of pious saints," or potential saints, in the hope of "promoting the
kingdom," whereas the radical Whigs were mobilizing citizens for political ends.
(Nathan O. Hatch, "The Origins of Civil Millennialism in America: New England
Clergymen, War with France, and the Revolution," *William and Mary Quarterly*, 31
[1974], 409). Nonetheless, a common pattern may be discerned. The striking cultural
fact is that civic oppression should take the form of Antichrist, while at the same
time the crusade to "drive back the forces of darkness" should assume such specifically
American implications that ministers like Keteltas could see "American society as the
model upon which the millennial kingdom would be based" and vaunt republicanism
as "the cause of . . . heaven against hell" (Hatch, "Origins," 409; Abraham Keteltas,
God Arising and Pleading His People's Cause [Newberryport, Mass., 1777], 30). See
also Robert Middlekauff, "The Ritualization of the American Revolution," in *The
National Temper*, Lawrence W. Levine and Middlekauff, eds. (New York: Harcourt,
Brace, Jovanovich, 1972), 103, and Nathan O. Hatch, *The Sacred Cause of Liberty:
Republican Thought and the Millennium in Revolutionary New England* (New Haven:
Yale Univ. Press, 1977). Regrettably, Prof. Hatch's book appeared too late for me to
use in this essay.

Edwardsean revivalism was only one of several factors in this development, of course. My point is not that it caused later events, but that it
provided a framework for harnessing the Puritan outlook to the conditions
of a new age. Its impact appears, for example, in the revision of the
concepts of Adamic naturalism and *translatio imperii,* "the Westward
course of empire." Traditionally, the return to nature meant a static condition (whether pastoral or utopian); whereas the "Westward course of
empire" implied a cyclical view of history, the recurrent rise and fall of
civilizations. In Enlightenment America, these conflicting views were
absorbed into a wholly progressive outlook, and transformed into alternative modes of cultural affirmation. When colonial writers sang of a New
World paradise, they were not thinking of Adam's garden. They envisioned   437
the new end-time Eden, where a gathering of new Adams would complete
God's grand design. Far from being nostalgic or primitivistic, their paradise was to be the result of a series of reformations in history, and therefore a fulfillment of social as well as spiritual norms. And if by other
standards "Eden," "paradise," and "God's design," as they repeatedly used
these terms, were merely metaphors for secular achievements, for Americans they also served as reminders that here, as nowhere else, the secular
was infused with special teleological meaning.

The same teleology was imposed upon the classical concept of *translatio imperii.* Edwards (following the Puritans) had recast this into a
variation of Daniel's apocalyptic scheme of the "four empires," and by
and large it was the Puritan-Edwardsean version that the eighteenth-
century colonists adopted, transferring their proof-text as they did so from
scripture to the story of America. The westward star of empire meant
much more to them than the movement of civilization from East to West.
It signaled the "complete fulfillment" of "the various ancient prophecies."
It was the morning star heralding the triumphant sun/Son that (in
Edwards' words) would "rise in the West, contrary to the course of . . .
the world." And this holds true for everything that *empire, West,* and
fulfillment evoked in eighteenth-century America. Libertarianism was not
just a better way of life, but "the long-promised glory"; the prospects of
free trade and open competition called to mind the "beauties of IM-
MANUEL'S LAND"; Westward expansion promised the endless bounty of
'the kingdom of the latter days." It was not a matter of attaining innocence, more land and wealth, the refinements of high culture. These were
tangible proof of something greater. Elsewhere, such advances might make
(temporarily) for a good society. In the New World, as a mid-century
English traveller marveled, the "course of empire" entailed a new "idea,

strange as it was visionary," that at some approaching "destined moment
. . . America is to give law to the rest of the world."[9]

I don't know precisely to what extent the Edwardseans were responsible
for that strange, visionary idea. What seems clear is that they sanctioned
the union of sacred history, local progress, and spiritual self-fulfillment, and
so established the terms in which Yankee Americans could usurp the
types of scripture for national ends. In the long view, the Great Awakening,
for all its apparent failure as a religious movement, succeeded in making
the evangelical mode central to the culture. In an immediate sense, its
concept of mission fed into the rhetoric of the French and Indian War.
The result was a triumph equally for English foreign policy and for
American millennialism. Extending the old techniques to accommodate
commercial and territorial aspirations—clothing imperialism as holy war
—the mid-eighteenth-century clergy summoned the colonists to an Anglo-
Protestant errand into the Catholic wilderness. The French were "the offspring of that *Scarlet Whore*"; French Canada "the North American
Babylon"; and the invasion itself a "grand decisive conflict between the
Lamb and beast," preview of Armageddon. From the siege of Louis-
bourg (1745) to the Peace of Paris (1763), all of New England, as
Nathan Hatch has shown, was gripped in "millennial optimism." Hatch,
noting the infusion of new concepts, claims that this "civil millennialism"
marked a radical departure in colonial eschatology. His claim is no more
valid, I believe, than that which has been made for Edwardsean post-
millennialism; but he is right about the mood of the times. Liberals and
revivalists from Massachusetts to Virginia, including Edwards' old antagonist Charles Chauncy, joined in chorus. The downfall of French Canada,
they predicted, would bring a "most signal revolution in the civil and
religious state of things in this world"; victory meant nothing less than
"the accomplishment of the scripture-prophecies relative to the Millennial State."[10]

Significantly, Edwards himself adopted essentially the same view of the
war. From his wilderness exile at Stockbridge he exulted in every hopeful

438

---

[9] William Smith, *Works* (Philadelphia, 1803), 2:170 (see also 2:171–73); Jonathan
Edwards, *Images or Shadows*, 92; Thomas Frink, *A Sermon Delivered at Stafford*
(Boston, 1757), 4–5, and *A Sermon Preached Before His Excellency* (Boston, 1758),
30; Jonathan Mayhew, *A Sermon Preach'd* (Boston, 1754), 34; Michael McGiffert,
The Question of '76 (Williamsburg, Va.: Institute for Early American Life and
Culture, 1977), 10.

[10] John Burt, *The Mercy of God* (Newport, R. I., 1759), 4; Nathaniel Appleton,
A Sermon Preached (Boston, 1760), 36; Samuel Davies, *Sermons on Important Subjects*
(Philadelphia, 1818), 257–58; Hatch, "Origins," 417; Jonathan Mayhew, *Two Dis-
courses* (Boston, 1759), 61; Charles Chauncy, *Marvellous Things* (Boston, 1745), 21.

scrap of news. His "Account of Events Probably Fulfilling the Sixth Vial" —fulfilling, that is, the last of the prophecies before those concerning the advent of New Jerusalem—includes reports culled from a host of local newspapers in Boston and New York. Nothing, it would seem, was too petty, too flagrantly secular or self-seeking, to contribute to his calculations. The capture of French ships, increases in New England's "trade and acquisitions," signs of commercial, military, and moral decline in France, political "distress" in French Canada, the (piratical) seizure of French stores of gold, provisions, merchandise, and armaments—every fact that touched upon the war was pregnant with prophetic meaning, as much an image or shadow of things to come as was any fact of scripture. "The late wonderful works of God in America," Edwards wrote to a Scottish correspondent after the battle of Cape Breton, were hastening the completion of the divine plan. They bespoke "an extraordinary spirit of prayer given the people of God in New England, with respect to this undertaking, more than any public affair within my remembrance." Clearly, "the Most High has made his hand manifest, in a most apparent and marvelous manner . . . it being perhaps a dispensation of providence, the most remarkable in its kind, that has been in many ages . . . and a great argument . . . that we live in an age, wherein divine wonders are to be expected."[11]

439

Edwards' enthusiasm about the French and Indian War is a striking testament to the continuities between revivalist and civil millennialism. But the war contributed in its own right toward broadening the scope of the rhetoric. The revivalists had enlarged the errand to include the visible saints not only of Massachusetts but of all the English colonies. The established clergy from 1745 to 1763 went further still. In mobilizing the "patriotic inhabitants of Protestant America," they associated "our Sion" with "our Colonies" in a wholly secular sense. The basis of their plea was not only religion but specifically the civic traditions of Anglo-America— not only Protestantism, that is, but English libertarianism. To some extent, this issued in a heightened sense of loyalty to "the mother country." Britain was the source of colonial liberties, and the writings of this decade continually celebrate that legacy. But as Paul Varg has observed, they also speak over and again of *America* and *Americans,* and increasingly they extol "the founding fathers, who left England" in order to enjoy "the blessings of freedom" in a "New Canaan of *Liberty.*" *A Canaan of Liberty!* The phrase offers a convenient index to the growth of the myth.

[11] Jonathan Edwards, *Apocalyptic Writings,* Stephen J. Stein, ed. (New Haven: Yale Univ. Press, 1977), 254–57, 267, 261, 449, 459.

The Puritans had justified the errand by reference to the Israelite exodus. Eighteenth-century Americans justified both the Israelites and the Puritans by reference to their own progress. And having done so, they invoked the example of the Bay emigrants in order to inspire their countrymen to still greater deeds. "Liberty was the noble errand of our fathers across the Atlantic"; they "set the seas and skies, Monsters and savages, Tyrants and Devils at Defyance, for the sake of liberty." So adapted and revised, the legend of the Puritan founders belonged unequivocally to all white Protestant colonists. As "the children of *Israel* [were] led out of *Egypt*," cried Theodorus Frelinghuysen of New York in 1754, "So [were] our Ancestors brought over from Europe to this land." And as "God Almighty [gave] them the Land of the Heathen," so now He intends to give French Canada to the forces of Protestant America.[12]

The message was repeated steadily through the war years, and it was accompanied, as of old, by the figural rhetoric of probation. During the last, critical stage of the conflict, the ministers tended to mute their threats. But no sooner was peace declared than they resumed the lament in full force. The battles just past, they warned, did not resolve the issue. Far from it: the real crisis had only begun. Like the revivalists, they saw evidence wherever they looked of degeneracy, and the thunder of their moral complaint continued into the Revolutionary era. Popery, corruption, delicacies and luxuries abounding, rampant lust, gaming, idleness, and intemperance—all the "enormities" enumerated by the Synod of 1679 and the sermons of 1740 returned in the orations of the 1760s and 1770s. The cause was independence now, not British-American Protestantism; the social ideal a republic, not an Enlightened monarchy. And of course the enemy assumed another, subtler, and more perfidious form. The English King, rather than the French, was now the instrument of the Scarlet Whore; England rather than French Canada was the modern Babylon; the danger within came from European fashions and royal agents rather than from Indians, Jesuits, or heretics.

And yet the rhetoric, while dramatically enlarged in its applications, has essentially the same structure. Never did the voice of Jeremiah sound more loudly in the land than in the springtime of the republic. It may be the "Will of Heaven," wrote John Adams on the eve of independence,

---

12 David Hall, *Israel's Triumph* (Boston, 1761), 11; Paul A. Varg, "The Advent of Nationalism, 1758–1776," *American Quarterly*, 16 (1964), 180–81; Jonathan Mayhew, *A Sermon Preach'd*, 23; Samuel Cooper, *A Sermon Before Thomas Pownall* (Boston, 1759), 48; Theodorus Frelinghuysen, *A Sermon on the Late Treaty* (New York, 1754), 9; Samuel Haven, *Joy and Salvation* (Portsmouth, N. H., 1763), 28 (see also Matthias Harris, *A Sermon in Lewes* [Philadelphia, 1757], 35–36).

that "Americans shall suffer Calamities still more wasting and Distresses yet more dreadful. . . . The Furnace of Affliction produces Refinement, in States as well as Individuals." That was July 3, 1776. Not long before, he had heard a minister predicting that God would "come with a vengeance" upon the land—and "the whole prophecy," Adams told his wife, "filled and swelled the bosom of every hearer." He knew that in saying this he was not instructing but confirming Abigail in her faith. She herself had comforted him often enough about the ambiguities of God's wrath with His chosen. Both of them realized that, by "the intention of Heaven," it was *through* "all the gloom," by *means of* "blood and treason," that the nation's "deliverance [would] be wrought out . . . as it was for the children of Israel." Declension, doubt, political and economic reversal—as they detailed the afflictions of God's Country it all amounted once again to the "day of Israel's trials." Both of them could endorse the promise, emblazoned in rough print on a Vermont Thanksgiving broadside, that "God would yet make us glad, according to the Days wherein we have been afflicted, and the Time in which we have seen Evil."[13]

441

The Vermont broadside is characteristic of a host of civic as well as clerical writings—treatises, orations, pamphlets—which, having detailed every local iniquity, sound an urgent summons for covenant renewal and concert of prayer. And as Gordon Wood has observed, it was a summons that generated millennial frenzy out of the very process of self-doubt. Increasingly during the 1760s and early 1770s, patriot leaders drew on the image of a "chosen band, removed from the depravations . . . of Europe," going forth to receive "the heathen . . . for an inheritance and these uttermost parts of the earth [for] a possession." Increasingly, they invoked what they construed to be the libertarian legacy of the Puritan founders. And increasingly, they spoke of the emerging conflict for independence in apocalyptic terms. When in 1774 Thomas Jefferson revived the fast-day ritual, he noted with some surprise that "the effect thru' the whole colony was like the shock of electricity, arousing every man & placing him erect." He learned the lesson well enough to return to those rhetorical devices on other important public occasions, from his exhortations during the Revolutionary era to his Second Inaugural Address. Tom Paine must

[13] John Adams, *Adams Family Correspondence*, L. H. Butterfield, ed. (Cambridge: Harvard Univ. Press, 1963–73), 2:28; John and Abigail Adams, *Familiar Letters*, Charles Francis Adams, ed. (New York: Hurd and Houghton, 1876), 306, 403; Thomas Chittenden, broadside, quoted in Mason I. Lowance, Jr., Introduction to *Early Vermont Broadsides*, John Duffy, ed. (Hanover, N. H.: Univ. Press of New England, 1975), xvii.

have learned the same lesson, to judge by his otherwise startling recourse
to that language in *Common Sense*. I refer to his use of biblical precedents,
to his emphasis on providence, and above all to the figural blueprint he
presents for American exceptionalism, with due emphasis on the landmarks
of early New England christianography: a fallen Old World (harboring a
Romish Antichrist), an Egyptian England (in bondage to a "hardened,
sullen-tempered pharaoh"), and a New Canaan charged "by the design
of Heaven" with "the cause of all mankind."[14]

442

No doubt these Enlightenment heroes capitalized on the work of the
"black regiment," that "numerous, learned and respectable body," as
the Revolutionary historian David Ramsay described the New England
clergy, "who had a great ascendancy over the minds of their hearers.
They connected religion and patriotism, and in their sermons and prayers
represented the cause of America as the cause of Heaven." To varying
degrees, most of the leading Revolutionaries—not only the clerics but such
disparate political thinkers as Washington, Hamilton, Sam Adams, David
Humphreys, and Elias Boudinot—responded in similar fashion. Their
appeals for unity, sounded from military camp, scholar's study, and political platform, affirm the same typology of mission: the Hebrew exodus,
New England's errand, America's destiny. Athens and Rome offered a
variety of practical incentives or warnings for the republic. As before,
sacred history provided the controlling metaphors. Recent historians
have reminded us that the first proposals for the Seal of the United States,
submitted by Franklin and Jefferson, featured Moses leading the chosen
people; it might be added that the symbol adopted instead was widely
interpreted in just this way. "If any should be disposed to ask," said
Edwards' disciple David Austin, "what has become of the eagle, on whose
wings the persecuted woman [Rev. 12:14] was borne in to the American
wilderness, may it not be answered, that she hath taken her station upon
the Civil Seal of the United States"? So indeed it was answered (to no
one's surprise) by Samuel Sherwood on the eve of revolution. Invoking
the same text from Revelation, Sherwood proceeded to link this to the
corresponding commemorative and proleptic passages in the Old Testament: "Ye have seen what I did unto the Egyptians, and how I bare you
upon eagles' wings. . . . Now therefore . . . ye shall be unto me . . . an

---

[14] Gordon Wood, *The Creation of the American Republic, 1776–1789* (Chapel Hill:
Univ. of North Carolina Press, 1969). esp. 107–08, 414; David Griffith, *Passive Obedi-
ence Considered* (Williamsburg, Va., 1776), 14; Jacob Duché, *The American Vine*
(Philadelphia, 1775), 26; Thomas Jefferson, *Writings*, P. L. Ford, ed. (New York,
1892–99), 1:11; Thomas Paine, *Common Sense*, N. F. Adkins, ed. (New York: Liberal
Arts Press, 1953), 27, 3, 23.

holy nation" (Exod. 19:4-6), and "shall mount up with wings as eagles" (Isa. 40:31). Then, making explicit the figural import of all three texts, Sherwood announced to his election day audience of May, 1776:

> When that God, to whom the earth belongs, and the fulness thereof, brought his church into this wilderness, as on eagles' wings by his kind protecting providence, he gave this good land to her, to be her own lot and inheritance forever. He planted her as a pleasant and choice vine; and drove out the Heathen before her. He has tenderly nourished and cherished her in her infant state, and protected her amidst innumerable dangers. . . . God has, in this American quarter of the globe, provided for the woman and her seed. . . . He has wrought out a very glorious deliverance for them, and set them free from the cruel rod of tyranny and oppression . . . leading them to the good land of Canaan, which he gave them for an everlasting inheritance.[15]

443

*   *   *

The Church's Flight into the Wilderness was the most popular and inflammatory sermon of 1776, the clerical counterpart of Tom Paine's *Common Sense,* and far more representative than *Common Sense* of what was to become the dominant culture of the new nation. The figural outlook it sets forth is a telling example of both continuity and change. Almost a century and a half before, in the spring of 1630, John Cotton had chosen the same texts (from Exodus, Isaiah, and Revelation) to instruct the *Arbella* passengers about their venture into the New World. But whereas *God's Promise to His Plantations* uses the authority of tradition (the standard view of the eagle as Christ) to justify the venture, Sherwood takes that justification, rather than the tradition behind it, as his authority. Ultimately, he appeals not to church tradition, and not even to the Bible, but to the American experience; and in doing so he virtually reverses the hermeneutic process—turns figuralism inside-out. Sherwood's authority is the country's progress, his text the Puritan past, his exegetical framework the prophecies of America's future. Hence the ease with which he interprets the eagle as the Puritan spirit of liberty, *figura* of the spirit of '76. The radical Whigs, he is saying, are the children of promise, as Joshua was the heir to Moses: it is all one grand spiral of fulfillment from theocracy to democracy. Though he includes the Reformation and forecasts the millennium, as Cotton does, Sherwood describes the main redemptive events in terms of the growth of colonial society. The sacred point of origin is the Puritan settlement; its climax, the impending war of independence.

---

[15] David Ramsay, *History of the American Revolution* (Lexington, Ky.: Downing and Phillips, 1815), 1:243; David Austin, *The Millennium* (Elizabethtown, N. J., 1794), 415; Samuel Sherwood, *The Church's Flight* (New York, 1776), 22-24.

In 1670, celebrating the fortieth year of New England's travails in the wilderness, Samuel Danforth had similarly posited a figural unfolding from the Great Migration toward a new heaven and new earth. But Danforth's pre-millennial view precluded a secular process of fulfillment. Edwards had opened the way for identifying American progress with the work of redemption, but the Great Awakening was only one more landmark in the unfolding drama of the New World. The development of the Anglo-American colonies, as Edwards conceived this, stretched indefinitely into the age of the spirit. For Sherwood and his compatriots, the concept of mission took on a distinct, self-enclosed American form. Drawing out the logic of their forebears to a conclusion undreamt of by Danforth or Edwards (much less by Cotton and Winthrop), they announced that the long-promised, eagerly awaited apocalyptic moment had arrived with the American Revolution. The patriot Whigs, "acting for the benefit of the whole world and of future ages," were sounding the same clarion call "as that of the heavenly host that announced the birth of the Savior." The Revolution, they explained, marked the full and final "accomplishment of the *magnalia Dei*—the great events . . . designed from eternal ages to be displayed in these ends of the earth . . . to the end of time"; the "independence of the United States of America is not only a marked epoch in the course of time, but it is indeed the end from which the new order of things is to be reckoned. It is the dividing point in the history of mankind; it is the moment of the political regeneration of the world." Appropriately, the July Fourth tradition began with an oration of 1778 (delivered in Charlestown, South Carolina) which defined "the Revolution as the beginning of a new age in human history."[16]

We can trace the development of this figural scheme through the patriotic addresses of the Revolutionary and Federalist periods—Nicholas Street's *The American States Acting Over the Part of the Children of Israel in the Wilderness* (New Haven, 1777), Samuel Langdon's *The Republic of the Israelites an Example to the United States* (Exeter, N. H., 1788), Abiel Abbot's *Traits of Resemblance in the People of the United States of America to Ancient Israel* (Haverhill, Mass., 1799). In all of these state-of-the-covenant messages, and countless others like them, such terms as "acting over," "example," and "resemblance" denote a biblical reality

444

[16] Chandler Robbins, *A Sermon Preached at Plymouth* (Boston, 1794), 16, 6–8 (see also Samuel Cooper, *A Sermon Preached Before John Hancock* [New York, 1780], 43–57); Robert Rantoul, quoted in Rush Welter, *The Mind of America, 1820–1860* (New York: Columbia Univ. Press, 1975), 49; Wesley Frank Craven, *The Legend of the Founding Fathers* (New York: New York Univ. Press, 1956), 71.

thrice removed. For the Puritans the errand carried forward the biblical exodus; for Edwards, the revival brought to fruition the Puritan errand; for the Whig preachers, the Revolution unveiled the meaning of exodus, errand, and revival. The flight of Noah, the wanderings of Abraham, the desert march of Israel, the formation of the early church, the revolt of Luther and Calvin against Rome: to all this the Revolution stood as antitype. Like the Incarnation, it marked a qualitative change in the spiral of human history. A new era had begun with the discovery of the New World, and the Revolution confirmed it, precisely as Christ had confirmed the new era of faith. In doing so, He had invoked the authority of scripture, but it was His mission that defined and explicated the prophecies. Such too was the relation between Old and New Israel. Now that the Americans had fulfilled the covenant, their *magnalia Dei* would continue, in the image of the Revolution, "to the end of time."

445

It would be another generation or so before the typology of America's mission could be fully rendered—before Washington could be enshrined as savior, his mighty deeds expounded, his apostles ranked, the Judas in their midst identified, the Declaration of Independence compared to the Sermon on the Mount, the sacred places and objects (Bunker Hill, Valley Forge, the Libery Bell) properly labeled. It would take several decades for the Constitution to be duly ordained (in Emerson's words) as "the best book in the world" next to the New Testament, and for the Revolution to be "indissolubly linked" (as John Quincy Adams put it) with "the birthday . . . of the Savior," as being the social, moral, and political correlative of "the Redeemer's mission on earth" and thus "the first irrevocable pledge of the fulfillment of the prophecies, announced directly from Heaven." But the pattern was well established by the end of the eighteenth century. And fittingly enough, a key figure in its establishment was Edwards' grandson, Timothy Dwight, a leading member of the black regiment, signer of the Declaration of Independence, Enlightenment intellectual, Connecticut wit, libertarian, Calvinist, and patriot Whig. "This great continent," Dwight exclaimed, "is soon to be filled with the praise, and piety, of the Millennium; *here,* is the stem of that wonderful tree whose topmost boughs will reach the heavens."

The period is now on the wing in which "the knowledge of the LORD shall fill the earth as waters fill the sea." . . . Another sun, rolling around the great Centurial year will, not improbably, have scarcely finished his progress, when he shall see the Jew "reingrafted into the olive, from which he was broken off." . . . Think of the manner in which God *bare* your fathers in this land *on eagles wings.* Recal[l] their numerous deliverances. . . . A work, thus begun, and thus carried out, is its own proof, that it will not be relinquished.[17]

Dwight expressed these hopes most fully in his epic poem, *The Conquest of Canäan*, which builds on constant crises and "trials" (backsliding, treachery, holy war) toward a celebration of the New World republic—America, the second "blissful Eden bright," "by heaven design'd." Dwight's hero is Joshua; his subject, the battle for the biblical Canaan. But the action itself, he makes clear, is part of a grand process culminating in the Revolution. The Israelite leader serves by comparison (as harbinger of a "greater dispensation") to reveal Washington as the Christ-like "Benefactor to Mankind," directing a *"more* fateful conflict" on *"new* Canaan's promised shores." Ultimately, that is, Israel's conquest of Canaan finds its vindication, its epic-heroic quality, in what it tells us of America's mission.

446

> To nobler bliss yon western world shall rise,
> Unlike all former realms. . . .
>
> . . . .
>
> Here union'd choice shall form a rule divine;
> Here countess lands in one great system join;
> The sway of Law unbroke, unrivall'd grow. . . .

Some twenty years later, Washington's successor to the role of the American Joshua, John Adams, contemplated the meaning of that more fateful conflict. He decided, in a justly famous passage, that the motives behind the Revolution "ought to be traced back for Two Hundred Years, and sought in the history of the Country from the first Plantations. . . . This produced, in 1760 and 1761, AN AWAKENING and a REVIVAL of American Principles and Feelings, with an Enthusiasm which went on increasing till in 1775 it burst out in open violence."[18] Adams' use of the Great Migration as precursor of the War of Independence is a significant testament to the secular-sacred typology developed through the eighteenth century. Significantly, too, his key terms remind us, whether by intention or not, of the Northampton millennium: *enthusiasm, awakening, revival.**

---

[17] Ralph Waldo Emerson, *Works,* Edward W. Emerson, ed. (Boston: Houghton, Mifflin, 1903–04), 9:199; John Quincy Adams, *An Oration Delivered* . . . (Newburyport, Mass.: Morss and Brewster, [1837]), 5–6; Timothy Dwight, *A Discourse on the National Fast* (New York: J. Seymour, 1812), 54, 55–56, and *A Discourse on Some Events* . . . (New Haven: Ezra Read, 1801), 39–40, 42–43.

[18] Timothy Dwight, *The Conquest of Canäan* (Hartford: E. Babcock, 1785), 1:2–3, 755–57; 10:466, 524–30; John Adams, quoted in Richard J. Hooker, ed., *The American Revolution: A Search for Meaning* (New York: Wiley, 1970), 11–12.

* The themes and ideas discussed in this essay are developed in greater detail in my book, *The American Jeremiad* (Madison: Univ. of Wisconsin Press, forthcoming).

The Radical Ideology of Samuel Gorton:
New Light on the Relation
of English to American Puritanism

Philip F. Gura

S AMUEL Gorton remains one of the most enigmatic characters in early New England history, primarily because his doctrinal link to prominent English radicals has not been sufficently understood. Most historians' accounts of him have fallen into the historical typecasting that either resembles Nathaniel Morton's vituperative description of Gorton as "a proud and pestilent seducer . . . deeply leavened with blasphemous and familistical opinions," or errs in the opposite direction through excessive but oversimplified praise, suggesting that he was an early American advocate of religious freedom second only to Roger Williams in vehemence for the cause. Even so profound a scholar as Perry Miller described Gorton's beliefs merely as "part and parcel" of a "lunatic fringe" of Puritanism in Stuart England.[1]

Because of Gorton's relatively inaccessible prose style—one nineteenth-century historian stated that Gorton's religious discourse "employ[ed] a

Mr. Gura, a member of the Department of English and director of American Studies at the University of Colorado, Boulder, wishes to thank Alan Heimert for fostering his interest in Samuel Gorton. He notes that "this study is an implicit answer to Professor Heimert's question—directed at the author during his doctoral examination—whether Gorton thought that he, Gorton, 'typologized Christ,' and hopes that this response will be belatedly accepted."

[1] For the major historical accounts prior to the 19th century see Nathaniel Morton, *New Englands Memoriall* . . . (Cambridge, Mass., 1669), quotation on p. 108; Cotton Mather, *Magnalia Christi Americana; or, the Ecclesiastical History of New-England*, II (Hartford, Conn., 1820), 436-438; J. Franklin Jameson, ed., [Edward] *Johnson's Wonder-Working Providence, 1628-1751*, Original Narratives of Early American History (New York, 1910), 222-225; William Hubbard, *A General History of New England* . . . , VI (Massachusetts Historical Society, *Collections*, 2d Ser., XV-XVI [1848]), 402-407; and James Kendall Hosmer, ed., *Winthrop's Journal*, "History of New England, 1630-1649," Orig. Narratives of Early Am. Hist., II (New York, 1908), 123-125, 147-150, hereafter cited as *Winthrop's Journal*.

For the favorable 19th-century views see John M. Mackie, "Life of Samuel Gorton, One of the First Settlers of Warwick, in Rhode Island," in Jared Sparks, ed., *Library of American Biography*, 2d Ser., V (Boston, 1864), 317-411, hereafter cited as Mackie, "Life of Gorton"; Lewis G. Janes, *Samuell Gorton; A Forgotten*

dialect utterly incoherent to the uninitiated"—most students have glossed
over his religious opinions and have accepted the simplistic exaggerations of
earlier historians.[2] We are seldom reminded that Gorton's theology was
similar to that of such English Puritan radicals as John Saltmarsh and
William Dell, chaplains in the new model army and men prominent in the
Seeker and Ranter movements of their day; or that while in England in the
mid-1640s Gorton enjoyed great success as an itinerant preacher; or that after
he returned to New England in 1648 he was one of the few men to defend the
Quakers when they attempted to land in Boston in the 1650s. Instead, Gorton
is tossed haphazardly into that murky and seldom-stirred cauldron that
contains such American religious misfits as John Wheelwright, William
Coddington, and Anne Hutchinson, idiosyncratic troublemakers who obstructed the Bay Colony's march to the New Jerusalem but whose political
ideology differed significantly from Gorton's.[3]

448

New England's deepest fears about Gorton stemmed from the ideological
implications of his profoundly held mysticism, and Massachusetts's prolonged
attempts to slander him were part of a pressing need to condemn Gorton's
deviance from the traditional norms of their community. Gorton's actions too
closely resembled those of many "antinomian" radicals in England, and he
threatened to broadcast to the Protestant world that New England's "pure"

Founder of Our Liberties... (Providence, R.I., 1896); Adelos Gorton, The Life
and Times of Samuel Gorton... (Philadelphia, 1907); and Charles Deane, "Notice
of Samuel Gorton," New England Historical and Genealogical Register, IV (1850),
201-220.

[2] Deane, "Notice of Gorton," NEHGR, IV (1850), 211. Robert Emmet Wall,
Massachusetts Bay: The Crucial Decade, 1640-1650 (New Haven, Conn., 1972),
chap. 4, and Larzer Ziff, Puritanism in America: New Culture in a New World
(New York, 1973), 95-99, freshly examine Gorton's New England career, but
neither explicates his theological affinities.

[3] While my analysis of Gorton's thought suggests his connections to English
radicalism, his association with "antinomian" elements in America cannot be
neglected. When he first moved to Rhode Island, he lived among many of those who
had been exiled from Boston because of their connections to the Hutchinsonians, and
an analysis of his supporters reveals many of them to have had close sympathies with
the exiles. See John Gorham Palfrey, The History of New England during the Stuart
Dynasty, II (Boston, 1865), 121-122, n. 3. George Arthur Johnson in "From Seeker to
Finder: A Study in Seventeenth-Century English Spiritualism before the Quakers,"
Church History, XVII (1948), 299-315, briefly mentions Gorton's connection to
English "Spiritist" groups, and Rufus M. Jones notes that "there was much more of
the Seeker type of dissent in the American colonies than most historians have
reckoned with" (Mysticism and Democracy in the English Commonwealth [Cam-
bridge, Mass., 1932], 100), but no one has since followed up these hints. See also
James Fulton Maclear, " 'The Heart of New England Rent': The Mystical Element
in Early Puritan History," Mississippi Valley Historical Review, XLII (1956), 621-
652, and Geoffrey F. Nuttall, The Holy Spirit in Puritan Faith and Experience
(Oxford, 1946).

Congregational polity offered a fertile spawning ground for the chaos threatening England during the civil wars. He brought into dangerously close focus not only the questions of the political jurisdiction of magistrates and the proper use of ordinances but also the more basic issue (also faced by the colonists' brethren in England) of how Puritans committed to a Congregational or "Independent" ecclesiastical polity could control behavior that stemmed from a fervent mystical faith—what Emery Battis calls the "inherent Jacobinism of Protestant theology" that produced a "revolutionary dynamic . . . irrepressibly particularistic and anti-authoritarian."[4]

Claiming victory over Gorton, the New England Puritans could more confidently march to the synod at Cambridge in 1648 and proclaim with Nathaniel Ward that "all Familists, Antinomians, Anabaptists, and other Enthusiasts shall have free Liberty to keepe away" from the American strand.[5] The colonists dramatically announced that, despite the military successes of the new model army and the increasing toleration for Christian sects in England, New England would not become the mirror image of old. The "New England Way" became possible only when the Puritan colonists comprehended the newly formalized doctrinal boundaries of their church-state, boundaries that precluded anyone's turning the world upside down in the way sought by Gorton and many English Puritan radicals. But, given the New England Puritans' hyperbole when dealing with their enemies, it should come as no surprise that the historian who penetrates to the marrow of Gorton's theology discovers not a dangerous and immoral troublemaker but rather a man who, more than any other New Englander, was in step with the religious politics of his times and whose history illuminates the complexity of the relationship of American to English Puritanism.

449

A sketch of Gorton's New England career demonstrates how violently the Massachusetts Puritans reacted to anyone whose behavior deviated from the standards set by their own ministers, especially if that behavior seemed antinomian in its tendencies. Born about 1592 in Gorton, England, an area near Manchester which, from the 1580s on, was known as a Puritan stronghold, Samuel Gorton eventually found his way to London, where he engaged in the respectable middle-class trade of a clothier.[6] The motive for

[4] Kai T. Erikson, *Wayward Puritans: A Study in the Sociology of Deviance* (New York, 1966), 11; Emery Battis, *Saints and Sectaries: Anne Hutchinson and the Antinomian Controversy in the Massachusetts Bay Colony* (Chapel Hill, N.C., 1962), 254-255.

[5] Nathaniel Ward, *The Simple Cobler of Aggawam in America . . .* (1647), ed. P. M. Zall (Lincoln, Neb., 1969), 6.

[6] Mackie offers the best biography of Gorton, but the outlines of his career are summarized in Kenneth W. Porter, "Samuell Gorton: New England Firebrand," *New England Quarterly*, VII (1934), 405-444. Invaluable is William R. Staples's

his removal to the Puritan colony is unknown, but in 1636/7 he arrived in Boston, at the height of the troubles with Anne Hutchinson and her followers. Remaining apart from the immediate controversy, Gorton, by 1638, was within the boundaries of the Plymouth patent, having left Boston—at least so William Hubbard and Cotton Mather would have us believe—because he was dunned for one hundred pounds by the agent of a Londoner from whom he had solicited such an advance before coming to New England.[7]

A more plausible explanation for the brevity of his stay in Boston is that he recognized the direction in which the ministerial winds were blowing. If Gorton sensed that his religious beliefs were similar to those held by the beleaguered Hutchinsonians and did not want to risk bringing the wrath of the synod on himself as well, he was wise to remove to more peaceful Plymouth. But as much as he tried to stay clear of those not likely to tolerate his peculiar religious opinions, once he began acting on the Word as it was revealed to him he was bound for trouble. Nathaniel Morton's account sets the tone for later reports. Though harboring little affection for Gorton, Morton still admitted that upon Gorton's first coming to Plymouth there was hope that he would be "a useful instrument"; but all too quickly Gorton showed himself "a subtle deceiver, courteous in carriage to all, at some times (for his own ends) but soon moved to passion." His passions raised by difficulties over his wife's serving woman (whom the Plymouth authorities threatened to banish when "nothing was laid to her charge, only it was whispered privately that she had smiled" in the Sabbath meeting), Gorton was not long in condemning Plymouth's government.[8]

edition of Gorton's *Simplicities Defence against Seven-Headed Policy* ... (1646) (Rhode Island Historical Society, *Collections*, II [1835]), hereafter cited as Gorton, *Simplicities Defence*, which provides extensive annotation to Gorton's life as well as to his treatise. Early Puritanism in the Manchester area is discussed in R. C. Richardson, *Puritanism in North-West England: A Regional Study of the Diocese of Chester to 1642* (Manchester, 1972), chap. 1. For Roger Brearley and the Grindletonians, who were active nearby and who held views similar to Gorton's, see Christopher Hill, *The World Turned Upside Down: Radical Ideas during the English Revolution* (New York, 1972), 65-69; Jones, *Mysticism and Democracy*, chaps. 3, 4; and n. 39 below. Ronald A. Marchant, *The Puritans and the Church Courts in the Diocese of York, 1560-1642* (London, 1960), 40-41, also describes Brearley's activities.

[7] Documentary evidence suggests that the first time Massachusetts heard criticism of Gorton was in a letter from Roger Williams to John Winthrop, Mar. 8, 1641, in Edward Winslow, *Hypocrisie Unmasked: By a true Relation of the Proceedings of the Governour and Company of the Massachusets against Samuel Gorton* ... (London, 1646), 55, and in Deane's "Notice of Gorton," *NEHGR*, IV (1850), 201-221. In this letter the term "familist" is first used in connection with Gorton.

[8] Morton, *New Englands Memoriall*, 108-110. Gorton's side of the story is told

The animosity soon displayed toward Gorton was caused by more than his uncivil behavior in his defense of the woman, for the Plymouth records charge him not only with "misdemeanours in the open Court, towards the elders, the Bench, and [with] stirring up the people to mutynie in the face of the Court," but with heresy as well. It was rumored that Gorton had already begun "to sow such seeds . . . whereby some were seduced," and among those whom he influenced was none other than the wife of Ralph Smith, the colony's minister; she frequented Gorton's home for daily prayer and told her neighbors "how glad she was that she could come into a family where her spirit was refreshed in the ordinances of god as in former dayes." The scenario was all too familiar, especially since Gorton, like Anne Hutchinson, was engaged in lay preaching that alienated the community from the settled ministry. Not about to risk more dissension—or the further embarrassment of Smith—the elders tried Gorton for religious and civil insubordination. Charging him with preaching (among other things) "no more happiness than this world affords," they banished him from the patent.[9]

451

By 1639 he reached the newly established settlement of Aquidneck (later Portsmouth) where William Coddington, John Clarke, and others forced out of Massachusetts in the Antinomian controversy had joined the Hutchinsonians.[10] But Gorton soon upset the political alignment of that infant colony, and Coddington, from the outset suspicious of Gorton's religious eccentricities, moved swiftly against him. Thomas Lechford, who had his own bones to pick with New England, described the proceedings with precious understatement. "They began about a small trespasse of swine," he noted, but "it

in a letter sent to Morton, June 30, 1669, in Peter Force, ed., *Tracts and Other Papers . . .*, IV (Washington, D.C., 1847), No. 7, hereafter cited as Gorton to Morton, June 30, 1669. Winslow gives Plymouth's version and reports that the woman had uttered "unworthy and offensive speeches" shortly after arriving in the colony (*Hypocrisie Unmasked*, 67).

[9] Nathaniel B. Shurtleff, ed., *Records of the Colony of New Plymouth . . .*, I (Boston, 1855), 105; Gorton to Morton, June 30, 1669, 7; Morton, *New Englands Memoriall*, 108. Complicating events, Gorton rented half of Smith's house; once Smith was aware of Gorton's highly regarded meetings he sought to evict him, against the terms of the agreement on which Gorton had leased the home.

[10] A minority party—headed by the Hutchinsonians and strengthened by Gorton and a band of supporters who had moved with him from Plymouth—ousted Coddington from his "judgeship" during his absence from the settlement. Coddington moved to the southern tip of the island and established Newport; and, after his new base of power was consolidated, he acted to unite the island settlements under one government, a task aided by friction between Gorton and Hutchinson. Gorton, *Simplicities Defence*, 3; Charles M. Andrews, *The Colonial Period of American History* (New Haven, Conn., 1934-1938), II, 8-10. For an economic and sociological analysis of the Rhode Island settlements in the 17th century see Carl Bridenbaugh, *Fat Mutton and Liberty of Conscience: Society in Rhode Island, 1636-1690* (Providence, 1974).

is thought some other matter was ingredient." Indeed it was, for after Gorton refused to acknowledge the authority of the local government in a trespassing complaint, he behaved as he had at Plymouth, calling the town's magistrates "great asses" and its judges "corrupt," and taunting Coddington with the words, "all you that are for the King, lay hold on Coddington!" For this seditious behavior—Mather sarcastically pointed out that Gorton had affronted "what little government they had"—he was whipped and banished from the area.[11]

Matters went no better in Roger Williams's settlement of Providence, where Gorton again became embroiled in disputes. Within a few months of Gorton's arrival, the usually mild-mannered Williams wrote an exasperated letter to John Winthrop, complaining that Gorton, "having foully abused high and low at aquedneck, [was] now bewitching and bemadding poor Providence." Besides censuring "all the Ministers of this Countrey," he was "denying all visible and externall ordinances," and his opinions seemed to be spreading, for "all most all suck in his poyson as at first they did at aquedneck."[12] Then, on November 17, 1641, Gorton's name was brought officially to Governor John Winthrop's attention in a petition from thirteen inhabitants of Providence, who requested aid in settling the disputes Gorton had complicated. They "counted it meet and necessary to give . . . true intelligence of the insolent and riotous carriages of Samuel Gorton and his company," who had "no manner of honest order of government, either over them or amongst them" and who taunted, threatened, and assaulted those who sought to resist their "lewd, licentious courses." Faced with this unusual complaint (the settlement was not within his jurisdiction), Winthrop acted cautiously, replying that the Bay "could not levy war, etc. without a General Court," and "except they [the petitioners] did submit themselves to some jurisdiction, either Plymouth or ours, we had no calling or warrant to interpose in their contentions." Then in September 1642 the petitioners formally subjected themselves to the authority of Massachusetts Bay and so solicited its protection.[13]

Having recently battered down the Antinomians, Massachusetts now was presented with an opportunity not only to drive a wedge into the plantations

452

---

[11] Thomas Lechford, *Plain Dealing: or, News from New-England* . . . (London, 1642), III (Mass. Hist. Soc., *Colls.*, 3d Ser., XXIII-XXIV [1833]), 97.

[12] In Providence the difficulties were over land boundaries. For a description of the near-battle that resulted from Gorton's presence see Mackie, "Life of Gorton," 336. Williams to Winthrop, Mar. 8, 1641, in Winslow, *Hypocrisie Unmasked*, 55. Janes, *Samuell Gorton*, 35n, questions the letter's authenticity because its tone seems inconsistent with Williams's usual graciousness.

[13] This petition is found in its entirety in an appendix in Gorton, *Simplicities Defence*, 191-194. See also *Winthrop's Journal*, II, 53-54. It is important to note that Roger Williams was not among the signers of this document.

begun as refuges for those seeking that "soul-liberty" New England Congregationalists so distrusted, but also to secure a strategic window on Narragansett Bay, facing the Dutch plantations to the south. Winthrop soon issued
a warning for the Gortonists to halt further agitation among the inhabitants
of Providence.[14]

Gorton's patience—never his prominent virtue—became strained, and
he sent the Bay Colony an immoderate reply unequivocally refusing compliance with their directive. He objected to the Bay Colony's attempt to
enlarge its jurisdiction without the consent of a majority of the inhabitants,
for by English law "neither the one nor the other [that is, neither William
Arnold and the other petitioners nor the Bay Puritans] . . . have power to
enlarge the bounds, by King Charles limited" to them. He claimed that
Massachusetts betrayed the true intent of its actions by its willingness to
honor the request for aid from men like William Arnold whom it once had
banished from its society because they had been associated with Anne
Hutchinson. "We know very well," he argued, "that it is the name of Christ,
called upon us which you strive against, whence it is that you stand on tiptoe
to stretch yourselves beyond your bounds, to seek occasion against us. . . .
We know, before hand, how our cause will be ended, and see the scale of
your equal justice turned already, before we have laid our cause therein."[15]
Gorton declared that his band would not capitulate to the Bay's jurisdiction,
for they had "wronged no man" and "will not be dealt with as before; we
speak in the name of our God, we will not; for, if any shall disturb us . . .
secret hypocrites shall become open tyrants, and their laws appear to be
nothing else but mere lusts, in the eyes of all the world." Hurling a final
insult, Gorton maintained that if any people thought his words "unchristian"
it was because their magistrates had kept them "ignorant of the cross of our
Lord Jesus." Gorton accused the Puritan leaders of setting up their own
cross, "Seighnirim," signifying "horror and fear," and he dared tell Winthrop that this was the cross the governor held and taught and by which he
thought to be saved.[16]

By his unrestrained sarcasm Gorton openly challenged the Puritans to
persecute him as they had the Antinomians, but his only defense was the
location of his settlement beyond the boundaries set in the Massachusetts
charter. To insure his safety—and because of bitter feelings in Providence—
Gorton moved even farther south, finally purchasing a piece of land called
Shawomet (later Warwick), where he felt secure from any intrusion by
Massachusetts. But to his immense surprise and consternation the Mas-

453

[14] Gorton, *Simplicities Defence*, 52-54.
[15] *Ibid.*, 61-62, 68. For an analysis of the European-Indian relationship in Rhode
Island during this period see Francis Jennings, *The Invasion of America: Indians,
Colonialism, and the Cant of Conquest* (Chapel Hill, N.C., 1975), 262-272.
[16] Gorton, *Simplicities Defence*, 83.

sachusetts magistrates soon summoned him and his followers to Boston on the complaint of two Indian sachems who claimed that he had seized their land unjustly. Urged on by Gorton's enemies (one of the Providence petitioners acted as the Indians' interpreter in Boston), both sachems had appeared before the authorities, submitted to the jurisdiction of Massachusetts, and asked aid in recovering the property they claimed was swindled from them. Having lost their quasi-legal hold on Gorton when he moved from Providence, and outraged at the numerous heresies and blasphemies in his letters to them, the Massachusetts magistrates took the opportunity to strike.[17] An expeditionary force led by Edward Johnson captured the Gortonists after a duplicitous attempt at negotiations and brought them to Boston for trial as heretics and enemies to civil government.[18]

454

Unable to reach a verdict from the available evidence, the magistrates made Gorton answer in writing, under penalty of death, a set of doctrinal and hermeneutic questions.[19] Just as he had done before Coddington at Aquidneck, Gorton claimed that, before any such penalty could be carried out, he should have recourse to an appeal to England. But the Puritans' patience had worn thin: they told him "never [to] dream or think of any such thing," for no appeal would be granted. Storing this threat for later use against them, Gorton complied without further resistance. Surprisingly, Winthrop then told him that, after studying his responses, the court was "one with him in those answers" and asked only that he retract his earlier insults to the colony. But Gorton refused, claiming that all he had previously written to them agreed with the present documents. Astounded by this insolence, an irate Joseph Dudley proclaimed that "he never would consent to it whilst he lived, that they were one with him in those answers," and he

[17] *Ibid.*, 91. The Arnolds were trading with the Indians in the immediate area and evidently wanted to establish their legitimacy among the natives. The Gortonists' land had been purchased from Miantonomo, supposedly the head sachem of the area, and the minor sachem, Socconocco, had signed the deed with him. There is still dispute over whether Miantonomo was the chief in that area; further, Socconocco claimed that he had been forced into signing the deed. See Jennings, *Invasion of America*, 262-272. Andrews, in *Colonial Period of American History*, II, 14, and 24, suggests that the Arnolds may have been interested in maintaining the power of the minor sachems in the area because they themselves had purchased land from them.

[18] The disputed deed of land is found in Gorton, *Simplicities Defence*, 253-255. See *ibid.*, 92-94n, and Palfrey, *History of New England*, II, 123, for a discussion of the legitimacy of Miantonomo's claim.

[19] See Gorton, *Simplicities Defence*, 119-135, for an account of the trial. While the Gortonists were imprisoned, Nathaniel Ward came to their window and urged them to renounce their errors, assuring them that it would be no embarrassment. As an example he cited the case of John Cotton, "who ordinarily preacheth that publicly one year, that the next year he publicly repents of, and shews himself very sorrowful for it to the congregation" (*ibid.*, 122n). Evidently Cotton was still smarting from his about-face in the Antinomian controversy.

moved the court to vote on whether the Gortonists should be executed for heresy.[20]

Their lives were spared by a few votes but, instead of being freed as innocent, they were sentenced to wear irons and to do hard labor in towns surrounding Boston. The populace, however, was "much unsatisfied" with the punishment dealt out to Gorton and his followers, and within a few months the General Court, without any further testimony, overturned the Gortonists' sentences, freeing them to return to Shawomet and setting the stage for their leader's voyage to England to bring complaint against Massachusetts.[21] In England, Gorton found opportunity to publish his theological doctrines for a public including many prominent people sympathetic to the ideology he represented.

455

When Gorton's doctrinal and polemical writings are juxtaposed with his unsettling behavior in New England, there is substantive proof that the reputation that had followed him throughout the Narragansett settlements was rooted in doctrines that closely paralleled those of certain prominent English radicals. For although none of his treatises was published until he returned to England in the mid-1640s, the implications of the theology later outlined in such works as *An Incorruptible Key, composed of the CX. Psalme* . . . (1647), *Saltmarsh returned from the Dead* . . . (1655), and *An Antidote against the Common Plague of the World* . . . (1656) already were evident in his dealings with the Bay Colony, Plymouth, and Rhode Island authorities, suggesting that prior to his initial removal to New England he may have imbibed his "heresies" from some of the same sources as his English counterparts. Gorton's central idea was also held by such members of the complex "antinomian" culture in England as John Saltmarsh, William Dell, and William Erbury, and later became the keystone to Quaker theology. He argued for an essential divinity in all human beings, a divinity that was defined by the Holy Spirit's presence and that precluded any arbitrary distinctions (be they religious or political) between saints and sinners. For Gorton, as for many other seventeenth-century mystics, conversion consisted in the true and full apprehension of this indwelling divinity and a willingness to follow its dictates against human authority. Though not a Seeker, Ranter, or Quaker, Gorton strongly maintained the all-sufficiency of the Holy Spirit in the true Christian, a concept that exempted the believer from obedience to mankind's perverse and troublesome laws, whether they stemmed from the English Parliament or the Massachusetts General Court.[22]

[20] *Ibid.*, 125, 132.
[21] *Ibid.*, 134-135, 147.
[22] Hill, *World Turned Upside Down*, is a good introduction to the radical spiritualists in England. Also see Maclear, " 'Heart of New England Rent,' "

During the time of Gorton's trial in Boston the question of his guilt had revolved around not only his civil insubordination but also his doctrinal understanding of the process of regeneration and Christ's role in freeing man to receive the Holy Spirit, a subject that had been at the heart of the Antinomian controversy.[23] Winthrop noted that after one of John Cotton's sermons Gorton desired "leave to speak" and openly pronounced that "if Christ lived eternally, then he died eternally." He further remarked that Christ had been "incarnate in Adam" and had been the "image of God wherein Adam was created." Christ's "being born after of the Virgin Mary and suffering" was, then, but "a manifestation of his suffering, etc., in Adam." To these heretical suggestions that the image of Christ had been present in Adam and so was present in all his descendants, Cotton, who had been using "all due pains to *charm* these *adders*, with convincing disputations," replied that a true Christian had to believe that the death of Christ was the cause of "our redemption, whereas the fall of Adam was . . . but the cause of our condemnation." Intent on showing how through Christ's death God was reconciling *all men* to Himself (and not just "imputing their sins"), Gorton countered that, when Christ died, the image of God died just as His image had died in Adam's fall.[24]

Gorton stubbornly maintained that "Christ was incarnate when Adam was made after God's image" because God could have but one image. In human terms "that image was Christ," and "this making of Adam in that image was the exinanition [humiliation, abasement] of Christ." Further, Gorton understood that God Himself was unknowable, making Christ the only rational object of worship; or, as he later put it, "the Father was never knowne nor is he knowable but in Christ." Man's spiritual contact with God was made through His Son, and since man's literal ancestor, Adam, had been formed in the image of God (that is, Christ was "present" in him), so could the Holy Spirit, through Christ's sacrifice, be present in and available to all

456

MVHR, XLII (1956), 621-652; Johnson, "From Seeker to Finder," *Church History*, XVII (1948), 299-315; Nuttall *Holy Spirit*; Leo Solt, *Saints in Arms: Puritanism and Democracy in Cromwell's Army* (Stanford, Calif., 1959); and A. L. Morton, *The World of the Ranters: Religious Radicalism in the English Revolution* (London, 1970).

[23] See Jesper Rosenmeier, "New England's Perfection: The Image of Adam and the Image of Christ in the Antinomian Controversy," *William and Mary Quarterly*, 3d Ser., XXVII (1970), 435-459. Rosenmeier's sketch of Cotton's position on Christ's role in the process of regeneration suggests that Cotton was closer to Gorton's beliefs than to such ministers as Thomas Shepard, for Cotton stressed that when Christ's image was engraved on the soul there was not merely a return to Adam's innocence but a discovery of a new and richer holiness caused by the indwelling of the Holy Spirit.

[24] See *Winthrop's Journal*, II, 145, and Mather, *Magnalia*, II, 436-437, for accounts of the disputation.

believers, enabling them to be justified not through works, but through faith: "That doctrine which ties the death of Christ to one perticuler man in one time and age of the world, as being the scope and intent of God's will concerninge the death of his son in the salvation of the world, that doctrine falsifies the death of Jesus Christ, and sets men upon the law of workes in the ground and matter of their salvation, by which law no man is justified." Gorton expressed the same sentiment later in his life in a letter to John Winthrop, Jr., in which he maintained that "to hold that Christ Jesus was not exhibited in the Church from the beginning, is a point of [the] soules disease and sicknesse . . . [for if He] was in purpose and promise in the begining, but not actually [in existence] till some thousands of years after; [this belief] idolizeth the Lord to be like a corruptible man." If men understood the true meaning of God in Christ, they would discover the inherent divinity of all mankind—what Gorton termed "the equal nearness of the divine spirit to [both] the sinner and the saint." Through this spiritual union, all believers in Christ partook of the perfection of God Himself. In the very same act of the Son of God descending into the world and becoming a finite man, man himself was raised to a state of dignity equal to that of the Son of God.[25]

457

Such doctrine argues Gorton's spiritual connection to certain English Puritan radicals (especially to some of Oliver Cromwell's chaplains in the new model army), whose conceptions of free grace were quite similar. For example, John Saltmarsh, one of the most prominent preachers in the army, in his *Free Grace; Or The Flowings of Christs Blood Freely to Sinners* (London, 1646) offered a clear exposition of what the doctrine of free grace meant to the group known as "Seekers." He proclaimed that one should not "serve the *oldnesse* of the Letter . . . but the *newnesse* of the Spirit," and that because of Christ's sacrifice all Christians were no longer "under the Law, but under Grace." His comrade-in-arms William Dell spelled out the political implications of such doctrines. Maintaining that once a man understood the meaning of salvation through Christ he became a new being, and that "it is not I that live, but *Christ* that lives in me," Dell convinced his soldiers that if they were true saints nothing could stand in the way of their

[25] Hubbard, *General History of New England*, VI (Mass. Hist. Soc., *Colls.*, 2d Ser., XV-XVI [1848]), 403; Janes, *Samuell Gorton*, 88-89, 96, quoting from Gorton's unpublished "A Running Commentary on the Lord's Prayer," manuscript in the possession of the R.I. Hist. Soc., Providence; and Gorton to John Winthrop, Jr., Sept. 11, 1675, in Mass. Hist. Soc., *Colls.*, 4th Ser., VII (1865), 607. This last contains four letters from Gorton to Winthrop, Jr., a correspondence initiated by Gorton because he had heard of Winthrop's reputation as a physician and was seeking aid in curing the "paine of the stone in the bladder" (*ibid.*, 603); see also Gorton, *An Incorruptible Key, composed of the* cx. *Psalme* . . . (London, 1647) for extended treatment of Gorton's conception of Christ."

uprooting England's carnal government.[26] Similarly, men like Gorton, Salt-marsh, and Dell believed that Christians who placed too strong an emphasis on outward ordinances at the expense of an experience of the Spirit (for example, magistrates like those at Aquidneck and Boston, as well as King Charles) were forcing people to live by the wisdom of men rather than by faith in Christ and had no true sense of the freedom the saint possessed.

Gorton's contempt for the New England Puritans' magistracy and its attempts to prescribe matters of faith and belief stemmed from similar doctrinal premises. Believing in the liberty Christ's presence offered man-kind, Gorton was dismayed that even the inhabitants of the City on the Hill subjected themselves "to the hand or skill of the devised ministrations of men," as though God "made man to be a vassal to his own species." Rather than ushering in the millennium by listening to the voice of God, the New England Puritans were merely establishing another worthless set of "idols," best evidenced by their ridiculous concern with turning "the juice of a poor, silly grape . . . into the blood of our Lord Jesus" through the "cunning skill of their magicians," an act that effected no lasting change in the character of its participants and that suggested that New England's polity was becoming just another arm of Antichrist. The New England saints always had "some fast to keep, some Sabbath to sanctify, some sermon to heare, some Battel to fight, some church to constitute, some officers to raise up"; and they erroneously believed that such issues had to be settled before they took "God upon his word, *that we are complete in Christ.*" Winthrop and his fellow-colonists, as well as many persons in England, depended on the contrived ordinances of man and not on the Lord; and when their idolatry was threatened by the likes of Anne Hutchinson or Roger Williams, they could "never rest or be quiet" until they had put the witness "under a bushel," that is, "bounded and measured the infinite word of God" according to their own "shallow, human, and carnal capacities."[27]

458

[26] See John Saltmarsh, *An End of One Controversie . . .* (London, 1646), and *Free Grace; or the flowings of Christ's Blood freely to Sinners* (London, 1645); and William Dell, *The Crucified and Quickened Christian . . .* (London [1652?]), in *Several Sermons and Discourses of William Dell* (London, 1709), esp. 342-343. For good accounts of these and others of the "antinomian" Puritans see Solt, *Saints in Arms;* Morton, *World of the Ranters;* Maclear, " 'Heart of New England Rent,' " *MVHR,* XLII (1956), 621-652; Johnson, "From Seeker to Finder," *Church History,* XVII (1948), 299-315; and Nuttall, *Holy Spirit.*

[27] Gorton, *Simplicities Defence,* 263, 268, 270, and *An Incorruptible Key,* 73. That magistrates should have power only in matters of civil concern was a posi-tion espoused equally vociferously by Williams and was the reason for his initial banishment from Massachusetts. In England such ideas were more common, espe-cially among the "Seekers" in the 1640s and 1650s. See Maclear, " 'Heart of New England Rent,' " *MVHR,* XLII (1956), 621-652; Johnson, "From Seeker to Finder," *Church History,* XVII (1948), 299-315; and Hill, *World Turned Upside Down,* 148-149, 153-154.

But while New England Puritans "contended" and made "great stirre" about such outward displays of piety, and while "the life and spirit of the Gospel" lay "buried under humane ordinances and carnall traditions," the voice of the Holy Spirit was every day revealed to Gorton and his followers. It offered a higher calling than the Puritans' legalisms, which "tend[ed] only to the carriage of one man toward another" and neglected those "principles of divinity . . . tending to faith toward God in Christ." If Christ were a "sufficient King and Ruler in his Church," Gorton maintained, "all other Authority and Government erected therein is superfluous, and as a branch to be cut off." Sounding a note as militant as any uttered by Saltmarsh or Dell, Gorton warned Massachusetts that "if you put forth your hands to us as a countryman, ours are in readinesse for you . . . [but] if you present a gun, make haste to give the first fire, for we are come to put fire on the earth . . . and it is our desire to have it speedily kindled."[28]

This intense belief in the animating presence of the Holy Spirit fostered more than a suspicion of the religious forms and ordinances instituted by governments, for Gorton's ideology also supported an anti-authoritarianism that threatened the social hierarchy adhered to by most New England Puritans. To Gorton, the equality of all men was so literal a fact that deference to a hierarchical system—be it civil or religious—denied the true priesthood of all believers. He criticized the Massachusetts Puritans because they had to have men "be honorable, learned, wise, experienced and of good report" before they could rule, but they did not realize that, to be judged honestly, a man had to be brought before his spiritual peers. Edward Winslow, sent as New England's agent to present its case against Gorton in London in 1646, insisted that to preach free grace as Gorton did was to offer an inconceivable political liberty. He feared that if "the administration of Justice and judgement belongs to no office, but to man as a Brother, then to every Brother, and if to every Brother, whether rich or poore, ignorant or learned, then every Christian in a Commonwealth must be King, and Judge, and Sheriffe, and Captain."[29]

But this was precisely Gorton's point and the reason for much of his uncivil behavior—for example, his addressing Winthrop as the "great and honored Idol General . . . whose pretended equity in distribution of justice unto the souls and bodies of men, is nothing else but a mere device of man." After studying such brash statements, Winslow correctly, if sarcastically, reported that Gorton meant that "to be a Brother, and consequently a

459

---

[28] Janes, *Samuell Gorton*, 93; Gorton, *Incorruptible Key*, 2. The Gortonists' belief that the Holy Spirit was present in every man led to some shocking pronouncements; after Gorton's whipping at Aquidneck "some of his faction said, Now Christ Jesus has suffered" (Deane, "Notice of Gorton," *NEHGR*, IV [1850] 221).

[29] Winslow, *Hypocrisie Unmasked*, 44, paraphrasing Gorton's *Simplicities Defence*, 71-72.

coheire in Christ, is a higher sphere than to be a civill Officer." Moreover, Winslow well understood where such doctrines led: when in 1649 he republished his *Hypocrisie Unmasked* (1647), New England's defense of its actions against Gorton, he had it printed with a new title page aimed directly at Englishmen already suspicious of such radical ideas: it could be purchased under the title of *The Danger of Tolerating Levellers in a Civil State.*[30] Later, in *Saltmarsh returned from the Dead,* Gorton further clarified his democratic beliefs. "The ground of these particular and nominal religons, (as Independent, Presbyterian, Anabaptist, Papist, Generallist, for they all stand on one root) is [that] they limit and infringe the grace of the Gospel" and so disregard the universality of the Holy Spirit. Similarly, Dell, in his *The Way of True Peace and Unity in the True Church of Christ,* proclaimed that, while "according to our first Nativity" men are born into different stations and religions, "yet according to our new or second birth, whereby we are born of God, there is exact equality . . . [and] all have the same faith, hope, love."[31] As envisioned by Gorton and Dell, the Kingdom of God on earth was based on spiritual and political equality.

460

Gorton's anticlericalism was equally pronounced. As one recent critic correctly asserts, Gorton recognized the allegiance between the "Puritan reliance on learning and Puritan social control" and held that any community built on a formal church covenant and supporting an educated, paid ministry was a form of Antichrist—a belief held by many left-wing Puritans during the English Civil Wars, including Dell and William Erbury, the Welsh Puritan radical who linked clergymen and lawyers as the "chiefest oppressors" of the age.[32] Answering Morton's attack on him in *New Englands Memoriall . . .* (1669), Gordon expressed sharp disapproval of the ministry's status as a privileged class. He maintained that, although Morton

[30] Winslow, *Hypocrisie Unmasked,* 28. Palfrey, *History of New England,* II, 211n, mentions the variant title page.

[31] Gorton, *Saltmarsh returned from the Dead . . . The Resurrection of James the Apostle, out of the grave of Carnall Glosses, for the Correction of the Universall Apostacy . . .* (London, 1655), introduction. Dell, *The Way of True Peace and Unity in the True Church of Christ* (London, 1651), in *Several Sermons,* 266. Given this doctrine, there is also the possibility of a connection, still unexplored, between Gorton and such prominent Levellers as John Lilburne. See Hill, *World Turned Upside Down,* 86-95 and chap. 7; and H. N. Brailsford, *The Levellers and the English Revolution,* ed. Christopher Hill (London, 1961).

[32] Ziff, *Puritanism in America,* 95. Christopher Hill, *Antichrist in Seventeenth-Century England . . .* (London, 1971), offers a good summary of the ways in which the epithet "Antichrist" was understood among Gorton's contemporaries. For the radicals' distrust of university education see Solt, *Saints in Arms,* 92-95, and Leo F. Solt, "Anti-Intellectualism in the Puritan Revolution," *Church History,* XXV (1956), 306-316. See also William Erbury, *The Lord of Hosts; or, God guarding the Camp of the Saints . . .* (London, 1648), and Dell, *Christ's Spirit a Christian's Strength . . .* (London, 1651).

had termed him nothing but "a Belcher out of Errours, . . . I would have you
know that I hold my call to preach . . . not inferiour to the call of any
minister in the country . . . [I have not] bin drowned in pride and ignorance
through Aristotle's principles and other heathen philosophers, as millions are
and have bin, who ground the preaching of the Gospell upon humane
principles to the falsifying of the word of God." His call to preach the Word
was "as good as the Degrees in Schooles" or any authorized by bishops,
elders, or the "call of a people"; and though never formally ordained, he
"doubted not *but there hath bin as much true use made of languages . . . for
the opening of Scripture in the place where I live, as hath bin in any church
in New England."* To require a more formal "call" than that of the Holy
Ghost was to institute another of those crass "idols" which Massachusetts   461
leaders were so intent on fabricating to augment their power. Speaking to
some "praying Indians" who had wandered to Shawomet, Gorton elaborated
his sentiments. He argued that, while New England Puritans "teach that you
must have Ministers," these church officers "cannot change men's hearts,
God must do that, and therefore there is no need of Ministers."[33] Since true
religion depended on a unique personal experience of the Spirit, formal
training in language, arts and sciences, and divinity was superfluous; any man
could address others from his own experiences, and under the true dispensation no external education could reform one's life as Christ could.

Gorton resented the charge that he denied life after death and that his
preaching of the doctrine of universal salvation encouraged hedonism. He
stoutly maintained that there was "not a man[,] woman[,] or childe upon the
face of the earth that will come forth and say that ever they heard any such
word[s] come out of my mouth."[34] On the contrary, he was "farre from
understanding" John's message that Christ died for the sins of the whole
world in the "sense of the generallists," because they "exterpate[d] and
roote[d] out" Christ's role in the work of redemption.[35] They denied any
more "Divine or eternall nature th[a]n is in the elements or beginnings of all
earthly and transitory things" and, because of this incipient pantheism, were

---

[33] Gorton to Morton, June 30, 1669, 14, for Gorton's defense of his right to
preach. For the account of his debate with the Indians see Henry Whitefield, ed.,
"A Farther Discovery of the present state of the Indians in New England (1651)," in
Mass. Hist. Soc., *Colls.*, 3d Ser., IV (1834), 135-137.
[34] Gorton to Morton, June 30, 1669, 9.
[35] *Ibid.* By "generallists" Gorton probably meant such people as Gerard Winstanley and Richard Coppin, men who were known as "Ranters" among their
contemporaries in the 1640s and 1650s and who believed that all mankind would
eventually be saved because a benevolent God could not torture his creatures to
eternity. For Winstanley and Coppin see Hill, *World Turned Upside Down*, 138-147,
177-179; also n. 44 below.

prevented from being witness to an "eternall power manifest in that which in it selfe is temporary," that is, the power of the Holy Spirit.[36]

Further, the subtlety by which Gorton maintained his innocence in the face of the New England Puritans' charge that he rejected the usual meaning of the word "eternal" involved his belief that once the soul was touched by the spirit of God it *already* was in eternity, a point of doctrine which had been spread in England by such men as the spirit-mystic John Everard. To Gorton as to Everard (who had translated works of such Continental mystics as Nicholas of Cusa and Sebastian Franck), righteousness was in itself eternal life, and sin eternal death and punishment. A penalty was not assessed arbitrarily at some future time but was rather the natural and inevitable result of evil action. Such doctrine, Gorton declared, "as sets forth a time to come, of more worth and glory than either is, or hath been, keeps the manna till tomorrow, to the breeding of worms in it." Heaven was a condition of the soul *on earth,* and the divine spark of regeneration implied the immediate and eternal destruction of evil as well as the salvation of good, opening the way for man's final perfection in this life. "The righteousness of God is of eternal worth and duration," he maintained, "but the one and the other [courses of life] being wrought into a change at one and the same time, thence comes the capacity of an eternall life and eternall destruction." Or, as Everard suggested, men who are estranged from Christ crucify Him anew in their own hearts and so "live in Hell . . . in the very condition of Devils and Reprobates," while a "good man hath God in him, and he seeth, knoweth, and believeth it."[37] Heaven and hell were psychological conditions, and morality was to be upheld because it made one feel spiritually healthy. "Whose oxe or whose asse have I taken[?]" Gorton asked rhetorically when Morton accused him of leading a "sordid" life. "Or when and where have I lived upon other men's labours and not wrought with mine owne hands for things honest in the sight of men[?]"[38] Possession by the Holy Spirit ruled out such immoral activities.

Viewed against the background of English Puritan radicalism, then, Gorton's theological doctrines, as well as his "political" activity in New

[36] Gorton to Morton, June 30, 1669, 9.
[37] Gorton, *Saltmarsh,* "Dedicatory Epistle." Mackie, "Life of Gorton," 393-394, has a succinct analysis of Gorton's understanding of eternity. Also, cf. Janes, *Samuell Gorton,* 98-101, and the Indians' account in Whitefield, ed., "A Farther Discovery," in Mass. Hist. Soc., *Colls.,* 3d Ser., IV (1834), 136. For John Everard see William Haller, *The Rise of Puritanism* . . . (New York, 1938), 207-212; and John Everard, *The Gospel-Treasury Opened* . . . (London, 1657), for a compendium of his mystical writings (pt. 1, 35-37, pt. 2, 27, for the quotations here). It should be noted that Everard's translations were published by Giles Calvert, who printed one of Gorton's tracts; see n. 44 below.
[38] Gorton to Morton, June 30, 1669, 12.

England, appear less eccentric than some historians have suggested. More-over, his behavior while he was in England from 1644 to 1648 suggests that his main importance—like that of many of his spiritual brethren among the Seekers, Levellers, and Ranters—lay in his public support of those doctrines that would later be embodied in the enduring form of Quakerism.

Even though an emphasis on the doctrine of the indwelling and guidance of the Holy Spirit was common in the hortatory works of such Independent Puritans as Richard Sibbes, John Cotton, and John Preston, Gorton and his counterparts seem to have been influenced by more underground sources, perhaps by the enclaves of Familists found in certain parts of England from the 1580s on, or by the preaching of such men as Roger Brearley or Everard, who after 1618 was preacher of St.-Martin's-in-the-Fields near London and who drew large crowds of both "mechanicks" and gentry with his stress on the power of the Holy Spirit.[39] From any of these sources Gorton could have absorbed the germs of the doctrines he later developed in his theological tracts. Though concrete evidence of such formative influences is lacking—for he rarely mentioned any theologians by name and it is impossible to reconstruct the details of his life before he moved to New England—once he returned to London there is substantial proof of his link to certain English sectaries, especially to those who became the spiritual midwives of the early Quaker movement.

463

Gorton found an England profoundly changed in the eight years of his absence, a change most noticeable in the increased toleration championed by some parliamentary leaders, who required broad support to continue the war against the king. Probably sensing how closely allied many of his doctrines were to those of the sectaries, Gorton quickly contributed his own thoughts

---

[39] See Maclear, " 'Heart of New England Rent,' " *MVHR*, XLII (1956), 621-652; and Nuttall, *Holy Spirit*. Also see Sibbes, *The bruised reede and Smoking flax* . . . (London, 1630); Cotton, *Christ the Fountaine of Life* . . . (London, 1651); and Preston, *The breast-plate of faith and love* . . . (London, 1630). For Brearley and the Grindletonians see n. 6 above. Brearley denied the significance of formal ordination, emphasized the spirit over the letter of the Bible, and claimed the possibility of perfection in this life, as did some Familists. Even the New England saint, Thomas Shepard, admitted that in his youth he had almost fallen into the snares of the comforting Grindletonian heresy; see his "Autobiography," in Michael McGiffert, ed., *God's Plot: The Paradoxes of Puritan Piety, Being the Autobiography and Journal of Thomas Shepard* (Amherst [Mass.], 1972), 42. On John Everard see Maclear, " 'Heart of New England Rent,' " *MVHR*, XLII (1956), 629; Haller, *Rise of Puritanism*, 207; Hill, *World Turned Upside Down*, 149; and Rufus M. Jones, *Studies in Mystical Religion* (London, 1923), chap. 18. It is important to remember that Gorton was termed a "familist" not only by Winthrop, Morton, and Hubbard, but also by Williams (see n. 7 above), who conceivably would have been more tolerant of religious eccentricities and would not have used the term in the same pejorative way as the others.

to the revolutionary movement. And, as Edward Winslow astutely pointed out in a letter to Winthrop, an "evill . . . long feared concerning Gorton" was coming true: he was quick to find a "potent friend" among the radicals. His *Simplicities Defence against Seven-Headed Policy* and *An Incorruptible Key, composed of the CX. Psalme* assured his passage into the world of the radical Puritans.[40]

Simplicities Defence is primarily a historical narrative of Gorton's troubles with the New England Puritans, but many of its internal documents—copies of his correspondence with Massachusetts—contain political and theological discourse that marked him as sympathetic to the ideas of certain English sectarians. Besides suggesting that New Englanders paid little attention to English law, his complaints against the magistrates' repression of religious opinions not consonant with their own would find many sympathetic ears and would cast further doubt on New England's claim to be the beacon for the course of Protestantism in the home country. Moreover, Gorton's report of the strict social hierarchy maintained in the colony would have aroused the ire of anyone associated with the democratically oriented Leveller movement, which was just becoming organized: with Gorton's documentary evidence they could point to Massachusetts as an example of how restrictive a system Independents would establish in England if they assumed power there.[41] *An Incorruptible Key* further defined Gorton's radical beliefs. For while this treatise was an explicit answer to John Cotton's exposition of the same psalm, it also clarified Gorton's belief (akin to that of Saltmarsh and Dell) that, while possessing power in civil matters, magistrates had no right to meddle in affairs of conscience.[42]

Further evidence of his active involvement with English radicalism in the

[40] Edward Winslow to John Winthrop, June 1646, in Mass. Hist. Soc., *Colls.*, 4th Ser., VI (1863), 181-183. In a letter of May 19, 1977, Stephen Foster has suggested that "the potent friend" could have been Sir Henry Vane or Cornelius Holland, among the radicals, or possibly the earl of Warwick. The Puritan colonies were already under simultaneous attack by Robert Childe, who accused them of being high-handed and virtually autonomous states; see Miller, *Orthodoxy in Massachusetts*, 298-306.

[41] On John Lilburne and the Levellers see Hill, *World Turned Upside Down*, 86-95, and Brailsford, *Levellers and the English Revolution*, ed. Hill, 620. Jones's *Mysticism and Democracy* is important to an understanding of the relationship between radical religion and politics in this period; also see J. C. David, "The Levellers and Christianity," in Brian Manning, ed., *Politics, Religion, and the English Civil War* (London, 1973), 225-251.

[42] Cotton's preaching on the subject had not given "satisfaction to all that heard him upon it," and several of Gorton's followers had encouraged him to publish his own interpretation. Staples, in his introduction to Gorton's *Simplicities Defense* (p. 15), gives a generous excerpt from *Incorruptible Key* which contains the gist of Gorton's argument.

mid-1640s is furnished by two other tracts which he sent to England in the 1650s, several years after his return to his plantation at Warwick. One of these, *Saltmarsh Returned from the Dead*, took its inspiration from the prominent new model army chaplain, who had died in 1647. The subtitle is an indication of how highly Gorton regarded Saltmarsh: *The Resurrection of James the Apostle . . . for the Correction of Universal Apostasy, which cruelly buried him who liveth yet.* The last phase may be a veiled reference to Saltmarsh's return to the army during a severe illness ("as one risen from the grave") to berate its officers for not acceding to the populist demands of the Levellers as presented in their *The Case of the Army Truly Stated* (1647).[43] Gorton's volume was printed by Giles Calvert, whose shop was a center of radical activity in London and who "came nearest to uniting the radicals in spite of themselves" in the years before the Restoration.[44] Calvert had published Everard's translations of the Continental mystics (including the founder of Familism, Henry Nicholas) and scores of tracts by such people as Saltmarsh, the Digger Gerrard Winstanley, and many early Quakers. Given Gorton's political orientation, it seems entirely probable that he had met Calvert—or at least men of his circle—during his stay in England, and that they had reinforced his own radicalism.

In *An Antidote Against the Common Plague of the World*, sent to London from Warwick in 1656 with an apology that its contents were so unsophisticated because of the privations of life "in this rude, incumbring and way-less wilderness," Gorton again invoked Saltmarsh, this time as one who had "ascended into the throne of Equity, for the Arraignment of false interpretours of the Word of God." He dedicated this tract to none other than "His Highness, Oliver, Lord Protector," whom he praised as one whose "spirit profoundly looks into . . . that only weighty and great change [in the world, that] which concerns the life and death, humiliation and raign of the Son of God." Primarily a commentary on the twenty-third chapter of Matthew—a condemnation of the scribes and Pharisees who threatened to shut out the Word of God—the volume is significant because it offers proof

[43] The whole episode concerning the Levellers' failure (after the Putney Debates) to persuade the army to back their democratic and tolerant measures is discussed in Solt, *Saints in Arms*, chap. 1, but more completely in Brailsford, *Levellers and the English Revolution*, ed. Hill, 143-309. See also Saltmarsh, *Wonderful Predictions Declared in a Message . . .* (London, 1648).

[44] On Calvert see Hill, *World Turned Upside Down*, 301-302; Norman Cohn, *The Pursuit of the Millennium: Revolutionary Millenarianism and the Mystical Anarchists in the Middle Ages*, rev. ed. (London, 1970), 309-310, 317; Morton, *World of the Ranters*, 98, 106, 132-133; Altha Terry, "Giles Calvert's Publishing Career," *Journal of Friends' Historical Society*, XXV (1930), 45-49. On Winstanley and the Digger movement see George H. Sabine, ed., *The Works of Gerrard Winstanley . . .* (Ithaca, N.Y., 1941).

465

that Gorton, who by his own admission never actually met Cromwell, had been deeply stirred by that leader, especially by "the reports which I have heard [and] the things which I have seen, that have proceeded from your lips." Gorton admitted to having "sensibly felt, and tasted off " similar thoughts, particularly those concerning his distaste for the insincerity evidenced in most of the commonly accepted preaching of England and America.[45] In dedicating such a book to Cromwell, Gorton placed yet another seal on the testament of his own radical ideology, even though by 1656 Cromwell had been abandoned by the remnants of the Levellers and the Fifth Monarchists.

466 Given what we know of Gorton's beliefs, he is best understood as a member of the complex radical community that defined itself around the "spiritist" doctrines of many preachers in the new model army in the 1640s. There is even evidence that while in England, Gorton had become so well known that his preaching was in high demand. Witness, for example, his declaration that when he was abroad he often had been "perswaded to speake the word of god publiquly in divers as eminent places as any were then in London and also about London and places more remote." He had been given the opportunity to preach to audiences "of all sorts of people and personages under the title of a Bishop or a King" and "in the presence of such as had the title of excellencie"; and he had been "lovingly embraced" wherever he went "in the word [he] uttered," even being entreated for "stay and further manifestation," having an offer of a church and five hundred pounds a year salary if he would remain in London.[46]

Moreover, while not himself a preacher in the new model army, Gorton became so renowned that he was summoned before a committee of Parliament on the complaint of some Independent ministers who charged not only that he preached without proper authority (they said he was not "a university man"), but that many of his sermons were openly blasphemous. To strengthen their case they produced *Simplicities Defence* and then called out Edward Winslow from the crowd "(for there was a multitude of people[,] the place being spacious)" to testify against him. But, acting judiciously, Winslow desired "to be excused[,] for he had nothing to say" concerning Gorton's right to preach in England: his own "businesse" concerned the Bay colony and lay "before another Committee of Parliament." After this

[45] Gorton, *An Antidote against the Common Plague of the World. Or, an answer to a small treatise ... intituled Saltmarsh returned from the dead ...* (London, 1657), sigs. A3ᵛ, A4ʳ, A4ᵛ, 63ʳ.
[46] Gorton, *Incorruptible Key*, Preface; Gorton to Morton, June 30, 1669; Mackie, "Life of Gorton," 380. In the prefatory epistle to *Saltmarsh*, Gorton acknowledges not only his "honored friends in London" but also his "much respected and honored friends in and about Lynne, in Norfolke" (*ibid.*, 407). These are the only hints as to the whereabouts of his preaching in the 1640s.

unexpected setback, the committee declared Gorton fit to preach the gospel; and his cause had been so popular that he was quickly congratulated by many "eminent preachers living remote from London" who had heard his arguments before the committee.[47]

But by June 1648, with the Revolution still not over, Gorton returned to Warwick, leaving behind the excitement of the civil war. Why he returned at that time is not clear; but if, as the available evidence suggests, his doctrines do link him to the English radicals, it is conceivable that his remigration to America was occasioned by the disenchantment many others (most notably Saltmarsh and Dell) felt when the Leveller movement began to experience setbacks in its attempts to reorganize English society. And with Saltmarsh's death, it may have been that Gorton perceived a temporary end to the movement toward increased toleration and democracy with which he was sympathetic, and so chose to return to the settlement at Warwick.[48] It is important that he might have safely returned to New England as early as 1646, after his favorable hearing before the parliamentary commission on plantations, to which he had taken his case against the Massachusetts Puritans. In that year his associate Randall Holden did return to Rhode Island, with safe passage through Massachusetts guaranteed by the earl of Warwick, head of the commission. And earlier, in 1644, Roger Williams had succeeded in obtaining a legal patent encompassing Providence, Aquidneck, and Shawomet, thus making Gorton's home formally part of "Providence Plantations" and safely beyond the reach of the Bay.[49] But through 1647 Gorton chose to remain a part of the radical community in England.

467

Before his death in 1677 he made one last political gesture, again directed at the Massachusetts Puritans, one perfectly consistent with the doctrinal positions he had espoused and defended all his life. When in 1656 four Quakers arrived at Boston and were imprisoned by the authorities, Gorton quickly sent the prisoners a sympathetic letter in which he offered asylum if they "had a mind to stay in these parts." Several missives were exchanged, but before any further plans could be made the captives were returned to England.[50] Gorton himself never formally became a Quaker; indeed, oral tradition has it that when George Fox "came over [to Rhode Island] he went to Warwick to see Gorton" but displayed himself "a mere babe" in theology

---

[47] Gorton to Morton, June 30, 1669, 14-15.
[48] See Morton, *World of the Ranters*, 62-68.
[49] Wall, *Massachusetts Bay*, 150-151.
[50] These letters were first printed as appendices to *An Antidote* but are more easily available in Staples's edition of Gorton's *Simplicities Defence*, 16-19. Gorton's behavior after his return to Warwick was exemplary. He was repeatedly elected a member of the town council and a delegate to the General Assembly of Rhode Island colonies, thus putting the lie to the Massachusetts Puritans' frequent claims that his behavior tended toward social anarchy.

compared to his host. But having absorbed the spirit of toleration when he was in England, Gorton did not allow points of doctrine to prevent his hand from reaching out to people who were persecuted for beliefs that stemmed from the same spiritual fountain as his own. For example, the Quaker Humphrey Norton acknowledged in 1659 that he and other Friends were "well received" by "such as were by the English accounted the basest of men, whom many of them they had barbarously banished . . . [to] Rhode Island."[51] The most important effect of Gorton's experience with the radical ferment in England may well have been in his sympathy for the early Quaker movement in America.

There is still more to be learned about the connection between Gorton— and the Rhode Island dissenters as a whole—and the rise of Quakerism in that area, for the presence of Gorton, as well as of a host of minor figures who in one way or another had experienced some of the excitement of England in the 1640s, may have been significant in encouraging Quakers to settle in Rhode Island.[52] But more important, beyond the immediate lesson to be gleaned from a careful study of Gorton's ideology—that he is best comprehended in the context of English radical spiritualism—historians should be aware that the seriousness of New England's attacks on Gorton is accounted for by the fact that his presence could be construed as proof of the English and Scotch Presbyterians' charge that an Independent or "Separatist" polity gave rise to such aberrant doctrines as his. Thus the true significance of Samuel Gorton becomes apparent when one understands him not just as a belligerent Rhode Island mystic but as a threat to the New England Puritans' self-image and to the representation of that image in England. But that is part of another story, one concerning the ways in which English opinion forced New England Puritans to rethink their metaphorical understanding of the American mission in Protestant history.[53] Before that

468

[51] Excerpted from a statement by an elderly "Gortonist" whom Yale president Ezra Stiles encountered on one of his trips to Providence in 1771. See Gorton, *Simplicities Defence*, 19-20, and Mackie, "Life of Gorton," 380-382. Humphrey Norton, *New England's Ensigne* . . . (London, 1659), is another booklet printed by Calvert.

[52] Maclear, " 'Heart of New England Rent,' " *MVHR*, XLII (1956), 649-652; Johnson, "From Seeker to Finder," *Church History*, 299-315; Nuttall, *Holy Spirit*. Jones claims that "the Quaker invaders of the colonies did find . . . numerous groups of Seekers who risked the dangerous adventure of joining the hated invaders and swelling the ranks of what the early Quakers called 'the seed' of the Church of the Spirit" (*Mysticism and Democracy*, 103-104). Also see Hill, *World Turned Upside Down*, chap. 10.

[53] Sacvan Bercovitch, *The Puritan Origins of the American Self* (New Haven, Conn., 1975), has provided the most profound and detailed exposition of the "corporate selfhood" which New Englanders, especially those of the third generation, tried to preserve.

chapter in the history of the relationship between American and English Puritanism can be written, we have to consider more thoughtfully what it meant for New England to have at its southern borders a man whose closest affinity was to a group of Englishmen whose vision of the City of God was so different from that of John Winthrop.

469

Samuel Gorton and Religious
Radicalism in England, 1644-1648

Philip F. Gura

IN these pages in 1979 I published an assessment of the radical New
England Puritan Samuel Gorton and argued that his chastisement by
the Massachusetts Puritans in 1643 stemmed from their fear that he
and his followers promulgated an ideology similar to that of such
prominent English radicals as John Saltmarsh and William Dell.[1] Though I
knew that Gorton had been a popular figure in England's radical underground between 1644 and 1648, I had not located any sources that
indicated specifically with which groups he was associated. In the course of
research for a book on New England Puritan radicalism, however, I have
uncovered several references that allow me to speak more accurately of
Gorton's place in Anglo-American Puritanism. This evidence, which links
Gorton to London's best-known General Baptist conventicles, verifies my
initial assessment of his radicalism and clarifies his relationship to both the
Levellers and the Ranters, as well as to New England's first Quakers,
whom he heartily welcomed in 1656.

Gorton's whereabouts in England during the time when he was pressing
his complaint against the Bay Colony is pinpointed in the heresiographical
literature of Thomas Edwards, Samuel Rutherford, Robert Baillie, and
Thomas Underhill.[2] Both Edwards and Underhill reveal that, while in
London, Gorton was most often found preaching in Thomas Lamb's
church in Bell Alley off Coleman Street. By 1644, "*Lams* Church" had
become a byword for the most extreme forms of religious radicalism; and,
while Lamb is usually considered a member of the group loosely termed
the "General" Baptists, from descriptions of meetings at his conventicle it

Mr. Gura is director of graduate studies in the Department of English at the
University of Colorado, Boulder. He would like to thank the Charles Warren
Center, Harvard University, for support during 1980-1981, during which time he
was able to continue his research into Anglo-American Puritan radicalism.

[1] Gura, "The Radical Ideology of Samuel Gorton: New Light on the Relation of
English to American Puritanism," *William and Mary Quarterly*, 3d Ser., XXXVI
(1979), 78-100.

[2] The key documents are Edwards, *The Second Part of Gangraena* (London,
1646); Rutherf[o]rd, *A Survey of the Spirituall Antichrist . . .* (London, 1648);
Robert Baylie [Baillie], *A Dissuasive from the Errours of the Time . . .* (London,
1645), and *Anabaptism, the True Fountaine of Independency . . .* (London, 1647); and
Underhill, *Hell Broke Loose: Or, an History of the Quakers both Old and New* (London,
1660).

is clear that adult baptism and Arminian doctrine were hardly the most radical principles espoused by him and his associates. In addition to hearing much talk of "universal Redemption" and "Arminian tenets," for example, visitors to Bell Alley reported lively discussions of free grace, pantheism, and Milton's defense of divorce, as well as of doctrine commonly associated with the Seekers. Moreover, these topics were broached not only by such "illiterate mechanicks" as Samuel Oates and Paul Hobson and women preachers like the notorious Mrs. Attaway, but by members of the congregation themselves, who were encouraged to speak out at the meetings. It was in Lamb's church, according to Edwards, that Gorton "vented" his "desperate opinions," and Underhill heard him, in 1647, declare the irrelevance of church ordinances and officers.[3]

Rutherford, who published the most lengthy attack on Gorton, offers another clue to his activities. Citing Gorton's *Simplicities Defence against Seven-Headed Policy* . . . (London, 1646), Rutherford traced his ideological pedigree to such Antinomians as Robert Towne, John Eaton, and Tobias Crisp, and linked his doctrines to those of such contemporaries as Saltmarsh, Dell, and the General Baptists Paul Hobson and Henry Denne. Further, while he offered no direct evidence that Gorton personally knew any of these men (though Hobson and Denne frequently preached at Lamb's church), Rutherford clearly intended his readers to believe that Gorton was acquainted with one "*R. Beacon*," "a grosse Familist," who he claimed was the author of the prefatory poem to *Simplicities Defence* and from whose "Catechisme" he quoted to justify his condemnation of Gorton's ideas. This presumably was Robert Bacon, a Gloucester nonconformist who moved to London, where, Edwards noted, he became associated with Edward Barber, a merchant-tailor and the organizer of a popular General Baptist conventicle at "his great house in Bishopsgatestreet." It most likely was there that Gorton met Bacon, who himself had been criticized for his "close Antinomianism" and later was attacked by Richard Baxter for spreading this error among Cromwell's soldiers. Or, since several of Bacon's tracts were printed for the same Giles Calvert who issued one of Gorton's works, they may have met at his printing shop and bookstore on Ludgate Hill, an establishment that was a well-known clearinghouse for radical Puritans.[4]

471

[3] Edwards, *Second Part of Gangraena*, 174-175; Underhill, *Hell Broke Loose*, 12-13. For descriptions of activities at Lamb's church see Edwards, *Gangraena: Or a Catalogue and Discovery of Many of the Errours . . . of This Time* (London, 1646), 2d pagination, 23, 31, 35-36, 98, and *Second Part of Gangraena*, 10-11, 2d pag., 113-115; and Baillie, *Anabaptism*, 94, 100-101, 108. For a recent discussion of Lamb and the General Baptists see Murray Tolmie, *The Triumph of the Saints: The Separate Churches of London, 1616-1649* (Cambridge, 1977), 69-84, esp. 75-78.

[4] Rutherford, *Survey*, esp. 183-193; Baxter, *Reliquiae Baxterianae . . .* (London, 1696), I, 41. Bacon's important works were *Christ Mighty in Himself . . .* (London, 1646), *The Spirit of Prelacie, Yet Working . . .* (London, 1646), and *A Taste of the Spirit of God . . .* (London, 1652), all published by Calvert, as was Gorton's *Saltmarsh Returned from the Dead . . .* (London, 1655). Calvert's career is briefly

Other important facts about Gorton can be gleaned from the heresio-graphers. Evidently none other than Roger Williams, for example, with whom Gorton had quarreled in New England, had brought his erstwhile neighbor to their attention. In the late fall of 1645 Williams had given Baillie a copy of a manuscript "Paper" in which he described some of Gorton's opinions and from which Baillie subsequently quoted in his *Dissuasive* when he added to a discussion of Milton's unconventional ideas about divorce Gorton's equally radical notions on the subject. After Baillie had used this document, he passed it on to Edwards, who then was preparing *The Second Part of Gangraena*. Eager to add another heretic to his already lengthy list, Edwards solicited information about Gorton's whereabouts and, in addition to locating him at Lamb's church, discovered that the New Englander was "very great" at the conventicle of "one Sister *Stag*," a woman whose identity is unclear but who, as Christopher Hill has suggested to me, may have been Ann Stag, a brewer's wife. Coupled with Williams's account of Gorton's unorthodox views on marriage, his presence at Stag's meetings suggests that, like many of England's advanced radicals, Gorton was willing to accord women a spiritual and social equality unusual for the time.[5]

472

We thus have missed much by neglecting the details of Gorton's four years at the center of England's radical underground. Most important, his activities at Lamb's church and in other General Baptist conventicles placed him in the same ideological crucible from which eventually was poured the spiritual amalgam popularly known as "Quakerism," for the extant reports about these churches make clear that in the early and middle 1640s they were halfway houses for many Puritans who were moving from Seekerism to the camps of the Levellers and the Ranters, and who finally rested in the radical spiritism of George Fox. The practice of lay exhorting, the strident anticlericalism, a belief in the indwelling of the Holy Spirit in all believers and its supremacy over scriptural law—these Quaker traits or tenets had all been articulated in the General Baptist conventicles of London's sectarian underground.[6]

Though Gorton himself never became a Quaker, the tracts he published

---

discussed in Christopher Hill, *The World Turned Upside Down: Radical Ideas during the English Revolution* (London, 1972), 301-302, and in Norman Cohn, *The Pursuit of the Millennium: Revolutionary Millenarians and the Mystical Anarchists of the Middle Ages*, rev. ed. (London, 1970), 309-310, 317. Tolmie describes activities at Barber's conventicle (*Triumph of the Saints*. 78-80).

[5] Baillie, *Dissuasive*. 116, 145; Edwards, *Second Part of Gangraena*. 174-175. For Milton's ideas about divorce see Christopher Hill, *Milton and the English Revolution* (New York, 1978), 111-139. Gorton's radically egalitarian ideas about women are discussed in Lyle Koehler, *A Search for Power: The "Weaker Sex" in Seventeenth-Century New England* (Urbana, Ill., 1980), 304-309.

[6] See Robert Barclay, *The Inner Life of the Religious Societies of the Commonwealth ...* (London, 1876), 274-307, and Geoffrey Nuttall, *The Holy Spirit in Puritan Faith and Experience* (Oxford, 1946), 13, 122.

during and after his stay in England are replete with passages that illuminate his concern with the same ideas that moved Fox's disciples. Moreover, when in 1656 four Quakers arrived in Boston and were imprisoned for their beliefs, Gorton immediately declared his willingness to offer them asylum if they "had a mind to stay in these parts."[7] There were others in Rhode Island—most notably William Coddington and Nicholas Easton—who were instrumental in introducing Quakerism to New England, but none of these individuals had undergone an indoctrination in English radicalism comparable to Gorton's. To colonists who had grown progressively disenchanted with the Massachusetts Puritans and their restrictive theocracy, Gorton thus represented someone who knew firsthand the exciting possibilities of a more tolerant and democratic ecclesiastical polity. In good measure through him, the "wranglings and disputes" that informed the debates in Bell Alley, as well as the radical ideology of such men as Saltmarsh and Dell, entered the religious discourse of Rhode Island and, eventually, of all New England.

473

[7] See, for example, Gorton, *An Incorruptible Key Composed of the CX. Psalme* . . . ([London], 1647), 3-4, 98, 102, Pt. II, 111, and *An Antidote against the Common Plague of the World* . . . (London, 1657), A-H3^v, esp. G3^{r-v}, 27, 167. Gorton's letters to the Quakers in Boston first were published as appendixes to *An Antidote* but are more readily available in *Simplicity's Defence against Seven-Headed Policy*. ed. William R. Staples (Rhode Island Historical Society, *Collections*. II [Providence, R.I., 1835]), 16-19.

THE
NEW ENGLAND
QVARTERLY

SEPTEMBER 1981

474

By arrangement with the COLONIAL SOCIETY OF MASSACHU-
SETTS, *the editors of* THE NEW ENGLAND QUARTERLY *are
pleased to publish the winning essay of the first*

Walter Muir Whitehill Prize in Colonial History

THE FIRST AMERICAN ENLIGHTENMENT: TILLOTSON, LEVERETT, AND PHILOSOPHICAL ANGLICANISM

NORMAN FIERING

I

IN 1741 the great revivalist George Whitefield published the journal he had kept on his first evangelical tour through New England the preceding year.* Among his most censorious observations were those he recorded on the state of religion at Harvard College, which he had visited in the fall of 1740. Tutors neglect to pray with and to examine the hearts of their students, Whitefield asserted; discipline is at a low ebb; and "bad books are become fashionable. ... Tillotson and Clark are read," Whitefield charged, "instead of Shepard, Stoddard,

---

* A version of this paper was read at the East-Central Region Conference of the American Society for Eighteenth-Century Studies, Williamsburg, Virginia, 8–10 November 1979. The author would like to thank John Crowell for helpful editorial comments on an early draft.

and such like evangelical writers."[1] The derogation of Tillotson in particular, who had died almost a half-century earlier, appears to have been a matter of intense personal significance for Whitefield, as though he measured his religious triumphs with the greatest satisfaction when he knew he had directly overcome the pervasive influence and popularity of this most famous of late seventeenth-century Anglican preachers.

On more than one occasion in his journal, Whitefield took pride expressly in his victories over Tillotson. Thus on 30 March 1740, some months before he got to Harvard, he told of "a tradesman" who, at last having "felt the power of the doctrines of grace," abjectly handed over to the revivalist no less than "seventeen volumes of Archbishop Tillotson's *Sermons,*" of which this poor soul had formerly been much enamored, with instructions that Whitefield was to do with the volumes as he pleased. Given Whitefield's sentiments, only burning would have been appropriate. A few weeks later Whitefield again recorded in his journal with satisfaction the case of the wife of a "wealthy, moral, civilized" South Carolina planter, who once had been "a great admirer of Archbishop Tillotson" but now had "her eyes . . . opened to discern spiritual things" and could no longer put up with "such husks, fit only for carnal, unawakened, unbelieving Reasoners to eat."[2]

475

[1] Whitefield was in Boston in September 1740. *A Continuation of the Rev. Mr. Whitefield's Journal from Savannah, June 25, 1740, to his Arrival at Rhode-Island, his Travels in the other Governments of New England, to his Departure from Stamford for New-York* (Boston, 1741), p. 55. "Clark" is Samuel Clarke (1675–1729), the Boyle lecturer in 1704 and 1705 and a universal genius. Whitefield had in mind Clarke's Arianism, rationalism, and Arminianism, perhaps particularly *The Scripture-Doctrine of the Trinity* . . . (London, 1712) and his many sermons. For Clarke's religious thought, see J. P. Ferguson, *Dr. Samuel Clarke: An Eighteenth-Century Heretic* (Kineton, England: Roundwood Press, 1976).

[2] George Whitefield, *Journals,* Banner of Truth ed. (London, 1960), pp. 404, 438. Whitefield may have influenced other New Lights to focus ritualistically on overcoming Tillotson in particular. The Reverend Jonathan Parsons of Connecticut, in a well-known Great Awakening narrative, referred specifically to how "exceedingly pleased" he was with Tillotson's sermons before he converted to evangelical religion. See Parsons's "Account of the Revival of Religion at Lyme West Parish . . . ," in *The Christian History, containing Ac-*

Undoubtedly Tillotson was in part merely a symbol to Whitefield of what he believed were objectionable tendencies in English and American Protestantism.[3] But the liberal archbishop was more than just an abstraction to be conveniently pilloried—as, for example, it might be said of Spinoza or Hobbes earlier, dangerous writers more cited by alarmed enemies than read by anyone. Tillotson was an extraordinary popular force, a literary phenomenon whose sermons were probably the most widely read works of religious literature in America between 1690 and 1750.[4] Dozens of early American library lists in Congregational New England no less than in the Anglican South testify to the prevailing agreement with Bishop Gilbert Burnet's praise that Tillotson left "the noblest body of Sermons that . . . this nation or the world ever saw" and that he was, as the *Tatler* claimed, "the most eminent and

476

---

counts of the Revival and Propagation of Religion in Great Britain, America, &c. for the Year 1774, ed. Thomas Prince, Jr. (Boston, 1745), pp. 120–25, partially reprinted in *The Great Awakening: Documents Illustrating the Crisis and Its Consequences*, ed. Alan Heimert and Perry Miller (Indianapolis, Ind.: Bobbs-Merrill, 1967), pp. 35–40.

[3] See, e.g., G. R. Cragg, *From Puritanism to the Age of Reason: A Study of Changes in Religious Thought Within the Church of England 1660–1700* (Cambridge: Cambridge University Press, 1950), p. 34: Tillotson "became almost a symbol of the late Restoration period."

[4] This conclusion about the popularity of Tillotson is based on my own survey of dozens of library lists. The conclusion is supported by David Lundberg and Henry May, "The Enlightened Reader in America," *American Quarterly* 28 (1976): 262 ff., and more recently by Richard Beale Davis, *A Southern Colonial Bookshelf* (Athens: University of Georgia Press, 1979), p. 79: "Tillotson was far and away the most popular writer of sermons in the colonial South, as he almost surely was in England." Of the titles that Lundberg and May looked for—a preselected list that included virtually all of the well-known late seventeenth- and eighteenth-century authors exclusive of writers of fiction—Tillotson's "sermons" in various editions was the most widely read "book" in America between 1700 and 1776. Forty-four percent of the 92 library inventories Lundberg and May examined for this period had copies of these sermons. Among Anglican readers the only competitor with Tillotson's sermons in popularity would be *The Whole Duty of Man*, which, as George Whitefield noted (*A Letter from the Reverend Mr. Whitefield to a Friend in London . . .* [Philadelphia, 1740], p. v), was "as much admired and read by the more common, as the Archbishop by the more learned, and polite sort of People." The reading of Tillotson's sermons, however, unlike the *Whole Duty*, transcended denominational divisions.

useful author of the age."⁵ When Tillotson died in 1694, his widow sold the manuscripts of his sermons to a publisher, Richard Chiswell, for £2,500, the largest sum, it is said, ever paid up to that time for the rights to an English book.⁶

The vogue of Tillotson was nothing new in Massachusetts in 1740. If anything, it was on the decline at the time of the Great Awakening. Nearly twenty years earlier, in 1723, an ad hoc visiting committee from the Harvard Board of Overseers, inspired probably by Cotton Mather and chaired by the aged and conservative Judge Samuel Sewall, took as one of its questions for investigation, "What are the books in Divinity, which are most used, more particularly recommended to the students?" The committee found, first of all, that there was no "great recommendation" of any books in divinity and that the students read "promiscuously, according to their inclinations, authors of different denominations in religion." However, the Overseers' report continued, "by some information given, the works of Tillotson, Sherlock, Scott and Lucas, are generally most used."⁷ The committee also noted (undoubtedly with some relief) that on Sundays William Ames and Johan Wolleb (or Wollebius) were still recited—the authors of the most esteemed systems of Calvinist orthodoxy—but it is apparent to

477

⁵ Gilbert [Burnet], Lord Bishop of Sarum, *A Discourse of the Pastoral Care*, 3d ed. (London, 1713), preface. *Tatler*, no. 101. See also *Bishop Burnet's History of His Own Time*, 6 vols. (Oxford: Clarendon Press, 1823), 1:189, 4:135-36, where Burnet has more to say in praise of Tillotson. "He was not only the best preacher of the age, but seemed to have brought preaching to perfection." Tillotson's first published sermon was the famous *Wisdom of Being Religious* in 1664. In 1666 the *Rule of Faith*, a collection of integrated sermons, appeared. In 1671 *Sermons Preach'd upon Several Occasions* was published and subsequently went into many editions. In 1695, the year after Tillotson's death, a fourteen-volume edition of his works, containing 200 sermons, edited by R. Barker, began to appear. In 1696 a different edition of Tillotson's works containing 54 sermons was published. By 1735 a tenth edition of these 54 sermons had been issued.

⁶ Charles Smyth, *Art of Preaching: A Practical Survey of Preaching in the Church of England, over Twelve Centuries* (London: Society for Promoting Christian Knowledge, 1964; orig. publ. 1940), p. 103.

⁷ Josiah Quincy, *The History of Harvard University*, 2 vols. (Cambridge, Mass., 1840), pp. 314-20.

the twentieth-century reader, if it was not to the Overseers, that for rare persuasive power, perspicuity nearly unmatched at the time, and literary merit in general, Ames was no competition for Tillotson, who was a good enough writer to have decisively influenced the prose of both Dryden and Addison,[8] and a shrewd enough thinker to have been praised by David Hume for the elegance, conciseness, and strength of his argument against the possibility of transubstantiation.[9] The *Spectator* could hardly praise enough Tillotson's sermon on "Sincerity towards God and Man." Steele wrote, "I do not know that I ever read any thing that pleased me more" (no. 103), and Addison said of the same sermon, "This subject [sincerity] is exquisitely treated in the most elegant sermon of the great

[8] Tillotson's remarkable literary influence is most fully documented in Louis G. Locke, *Tillotson: A Study in Seventeenth-Century Literature*, vol. 4 in the *Anglistica* series (Copenhagen: Rosenkilde and Bagger, 1954). Although the comment is not to be taken entirely at face value, the dramatist William Congreve testified that he often heard Dryden "own with Pleasure, that if he had any Talent for English Prose, it was owing to his having often read the Writings of the great Archbishop Tillotson" (Locke, *Tillotson*, p. 114). See also, David D. Brown, "Tillotson's Revisions and Dryden's 'talent for English Prose,'" *Review of English Studies*, new ser. 12 (1961): 24–39, and "Dryden's *Religio Laici* and the 'judicious and learned friend,'" *Modern Language Review* 56 (1961): 66–69.

[9] Hume's famous chapter against the possibility of miracles begins: "There is, in Dr. Tillotson's writings, an argument against the *real presence*, which is as concise, and elegant, and strong as any argument can possibly be supposed against a doctrine, so little worthy of refutation...." See David Hume, *The Philosophical Works*, ed. Thomas Hill Green and Thomas Hodge Grose, 4 vols. (London, 1882), 4:88–108. Hume's basic point is that there must be "a uniform experience against every miraculous event," otherwise the event would not be considered a miracle, but uniform experience should thus lead us to doubt the possibility of a miracle in any given case. It is inconsistent to rely on experience in order to prove that experience in some cases is not to be relied on. Tillotson used the same argument against transubstantiation, but not against all miracles, in Sermon XXI (1679) and also in Sermon XXVI, known as the "Discourse against Transubstantiation," as well as in a few other places. Tillotson wrote in Sermon XXVI: "Transubstantiation, if it be true at all it is all truth, and nothing else is true; for it cannot be true, unless our senses, and the senses of all mankind be deceived about their proper objects; and if this be true and certain, then nothing else can be so; for if we be not certain of what we see, we can be certain of nothing." My principal source for Tillotson's sermons has been *Sermons on Several Subjects and Occasions*, 10 vols. (London, 1754), which contains 207 numbered sermons.

British preacher," to which the leading modern authority on the *Spectator,* Donald Bond, notes, "For Addison, as always, the 'great Preacher' refers to Tillotson."[10]

The accuracy of the Harvard visiting committee's information on student reading in 1723 may be inferred from Benjamin Franklin's youthful satire of the college in his fourth "Silence Dogood" essay published in the *New England Courant* in 1722 (14 May), where Franklin intimated strongly that what future ministers learned at the College was primarily how to plagiarize Tillotson in their sermons. Franklin, of course, was bothered neither by the use of Tillotson, whose writings he revered all of his life,[11] nor by the plagiarism, which he considered preferable at a divine service to inferior original compositions, but by the pretense that to preach a plagiarized sermon one needed an expensive Harvard education.[12]

479

10 The *Spectator* quoted or cited Tillotson in nos. 103 (Steele), 293 (Addison), 352 (Steele), and 557 (Addison), and perhaps others. (See Donald F. Bond, ed., *The Spectator,* 5 vols. [Oxford: Clarendon Press, 1965], 4:503, n. 1.) There are long sections in various of Tillotson's sermons that could be lifted out and fitted neatly into the *Spectator* without the least incongruity. It is commonly stated by present-day students of the period that with Tillotson the sermon began its transformation into the genteel philosophical essay such as that at which Addison excelled.

11 For Franklin's essay, see Leonard Labaree et al., eds., *The Papers of Benjamin Franklin* (New Haven: Yale University Press, 1959), 1:14–18. On Franklin's admiration for Tillotson, whom he considered a master of literary style, see Elizabeth C. Cook, *Literary Influences in Colonial Newspapers, 1704–1750* (New York: Columbia University Press, 1912), pp. 25–26. In his "Idea of the English School," published in 1751, Franklin placed Tillotson's name first in a short list of "the best English Authors," along with Milton, Locke, Addison, Pope, Swift, "the higher Papers" in the *Spectator* and the *Guardian,* and the best translations of Homer, Virgil, and Horace and the works of Fénelon (Labaree, *Papers of Franklin,* 4:107). Twenty-two years later, on 6 April 1773, in a letter to Thomas Coombe written from London to America, Franklin thought to send some "new Poetry" and "new Sermons," "the best we have had," he said, "since Pope and Tillotson" (William B. Willcox et al., eds., *Papers of Benjamin Franklin,* 20:142).

12 Anglican authorities did not universally frown upon plagiarism in the pulpit, and Franklin's defense in his *Autobiography* of the Reverend Samuel Hemphill's borrowing—"I rather approv'd his giving us good Sermons compos'd by others, than bad ones of his own Manufacture; tho' the latter was the Practice of our common Teachers"—was not necessarily facetious. Bishop Burnet in *Pastoral Care* (p. 201) wrote: "To all that are not masters of the Body

There can be little doubt that the Harvard faculty in the first half of the eighteenth century was infiltrated by admirers of Tillotson's preaching. The biographer of "Father" Henry Flynt (the celebrated Harvard tutor who remained at the job for a record fifty-five years, from 1699 to 1754) calls Tillotson Flynt's "idol" and describes Flynt's sermons as "pale reflections" of the Anglican preacher's. Flynt constantly lent out Tillotson's works from his large library, although not apparently to undergraduates. Thomas Robie, a tutor from 1714 to 1723, Fellow of the Royal Society and one of the leading scientists in New England, "leaned heavily" on Tillotson when he preached in Cambridge, which was frequently.[13] Such was the appreciation of Tillotson in Calvinist New England that by his notorious remark in 1740 that Tillotson knew no more of true Christianity than Mohammed, Whitefield probably lost

480

of Divinity, and of the Scriptures, I should much rather recommend the using other mens sermons, than the making any of their own." *Spectator* no. 106, written by Addison, also recommended that preachers lacking in literary talent learn to present well the best sermons available rather than attempt to compose their own; it would be "more easy to themselves" and "more edifying to the people." *Tatler* no. 269 expressed the same idea and may have influenced Franklin's "Dogood" essay on plagiarism of Tillotson. Thus we cannot be sure if Franklin was making an accurate observation about the plagiarism of Boston ministers or simply mimicking Addison and Steele. George Whitefield also accused American ministers of stealing passages from Tillotson and hoped that his calling attention to the practice would "prevent our younger Clergy [from] making so free with the Archbishop as they usually do. For now People begin to search his Writings, they will be in more danger of being detected, if they deliver the Arch Bishop's Sermons instead of their own Compositions from the Pulpit" (Locke, *Tillotson*, p. 157, quoting from Whitefield's letter of 27 April 1740, printed in *The New England Weekly Journal* [Boston], 20 May 1740). As late as mid-century charges of plagiarizing Tillotson were still being hurled about. See Lemuel Briant, *Some More Friendly Remarks on Mr. Porter and Company* ... (Boston, 1751), p. 26, and, for an even later instance of plagiarism from Tillotson, *The Diary of William Bentley*, 4 vols. (Salem, Mass.: Essex Institute, 1905–1914), 4:95, entry for 3 May 1812. (I am indebted to William Breitenbach for the last two references).

13 Edward T. Dunn, S.J., "Tutor Henry Flynt of Harvard College, 1675–1760" (Ph.D. diss., University of Rochester, 1968), pp. 174, 229, et passim. This work, which should long ago have been published, is an important contribution to historical understanding of Harvard in the early eighteenth century. On Robie, see Clifford Shipton, *Biographical Sketches of Those Who Attended Harvard College*, Sibley's Harvard Graduates (Boston: Massachusetts Historical Society, 1937), 5:450–55.

more friends on this side of the Atlantic than by anything else he ever said or did.[14] To slander the memory of "the great and good Archbishop Tillotson," as none other than Increase Mather had referred to him years before, was a major offense to New England sensibilities. If old England "had always had such Archbishops" as Tillotson, Mather is reputed to have said, "New England had never been."[15]

That Tillotson's sermons were, from as early as the 1680s, warmly embraced in certain circles in Puritan Massachusetts, albeit never without ambivalence, raises a number of challenging questions. For although Tillotson was from Puritan parentage and married to a niece of Oliver Cromwell's, and although of all the Episcopal hierarchy in London in the late 1680s when Increase Mather was there struggling to reinstate the revoked Massachusetts Bay Charter, it was Tillotson who was kindest and most supportive to Mather, still, no dissenter

481

[14] George Whitefield, Three Letters... (Philadelphia, 1740). The first two letters consist of Whitefield's defense of himself for his remark. In the first he wrote: "My affirming that Archbishop Tillotson knew no more of Christianity than Mahomet, has been look'd upon as one of the most unjustifiable expressions that ever proceeded out of my mouth: For this I am not only look'd upon as a greater monster than ever by my enemies, but also have been secretly despised and censured by some who, otherwise, were my friends" (p. 2). Whitefield's remark on Tillotson was constantly cited against him, in England as well as America.

[15] In a letter that Henry Newman wrote to Benjamin Colman on 24 September 1736, Newman recorded Increase Mather's remark to Dr. William Bates following a dinner party that Mather attended at which Tillotson was present: "If you had always had such Archbishops New England had never been" (W. O. B. Allen and Edmund McClure, Two Hundred Years: The History of the Society for Promoting Christian Knowledge [London, 1898], p. 255). See also Cotton Mather's account of Increase's mission in London in Massachusetts Historical Society Collections, 1st ser., vol. 9 (Boston, 1804), p. 246; Kenneth Murdock, Increase Mather: The Foremost American Puritan (Cambridge: Harvard University Press, 1926), p. 236; and M. G. Hall, ed., "The Autobiography of Increase Mather," Proceedings of the American Antiquarian Society, vol. 71 (Worcester, Mass., 1962), p. 328. Increase Mather's esteem of Tillotson was cited against Whitefield in the evangelist's controversy with the Harvard faculty. See The Testimony of the President, Professors, Tutors and Hebrew Instructor of Harvard College in Cambridge against the Reverend Mr. George Whitefield, and His Conduct (Boston, 1744); George Whitefield, A Letter to the Reverend the President, and Professors, Tutors, and Hebrew Instructor at Harvard College (Boston, 1745); Edward Wigglesworth, A Letter to the Reverend Mr. George Whitefield by way of Reply to his Answer to the College Testimony Against Him and his Conduct (Boston, 1745).

could fail to observe at the same time that Tillotson was a real threat to Calvinist orthodoxy. Only a few years after Tillotson died the prominent deist Anthony Collins referred to him provocatively as "the most pious and rational of all priests" and as the man "whom all English free-thinkers own as their head."[16] Collins was certainly distorting Tillotson for his own ends—or, let us say, reading him very selectively—but the learned in Massachusetts could not but recognize that Tillotson was a thoroughgoing Arminian and a "moralist"— that is, one who preached virtue more than the necessity of redemption by Christ—and there was surely apprehension that he was also a "rationalist," a complex term which I will leave undefined for the moment.

It is no new suggestion that the "liberalization" of Calvinist orthodoxy in New England was promoted by the importation of Latitudinarian Anglicanism such as was embodied in the sermons of Tillotson. This, in fact, seems to have been the prevailing contemporary belief. Recently, however, historians, led by Perry Miller, have concentrated rather on the *internal* forces for change in New England, particularly the working out of the alleged inner logic of covenant theology, which, it is said, ineluctably drove New England religion toward such Arminian doctrines as conditional salvation and an emphasis on the rational foundations of Christianity.[17]

Dealing with one strain of what might be called "enlightened" religious belief, Unitarianism, one of Miller's students, Conrad Wright, took note of the presence of English

482

16 *Discourse of Freethinking* (London, 1713), pp. 69, 171–75. See James O'Higgins, S.J., *Anthony Collins: The Man and His Works* (The Hague: Martinus Nijhoff, 1970), pp. 45–47, 92–93.

17 Miller's point of view is well set forth and then persuasively attacked in Gerald J. Goodwin, "The Myth of 'Arminian-Calvinism' in Eighteenth-Century New England," *New England Quarterly* 41 (1968): 213–37. See also Francis A. Christie, "The Beginnings of Arminianism in New England," *American Society of Church History Papers*, 2d ser., vol. 3 (New York, 1912), pp. 152–72. Cf. e.g., Joseph J. Ellis, *The New England Mind in Transition 1696–1772* (New Haven: Yale University Press, 1973). p. 132: "The covenant theology of New England had always contained within itself the seeds of Arminianism." Since the work of Perry Miller, this has become the standard view, but the whole conception is highly questionable.

Latitudinarian influences on American thought of the early eighteenth century but like his mentor generally backed away from crediting it with too much effect. Local social and intellectual forces were assigned as the main causes, including those deeply embedded within New England Puritanism itself. The covenant theology, Wright said, "began a development which, by magnifying the part played by man in his own salvation, inevitably carried [New England Puritans] farther and farther from strict Calvinism. Had the colonies been entirely cut off from outside intellectual influences, the New England doctrine would still have been transformed under the pressure of insistent social forces."[18]

It may be questioned, however, that local conditions, either intellectual or social, had such a positive effect on the development of religious and philosophical thought in New England at the end of the seventeenth century, except insofar as the primitive or virginal social and political environment provided a relatively open arena for the reception of Old World ideas.[19] During the earliest years of settlement, before the founding generation of English-educated immigrants passed from the scene, Massachusetts is properly regarded as an extension of the homeland. This was the great era of Thomas Hooker, John Cotton, Thomas Shepard, and Richard Mather, when New England was on a par intellectually with old England. Between 1640 and 1660, during the Inter-

[18] Conrad Wright, *The Beginnings of Unitarianism in America* (Boston: Beacon Press, 1966; orig. publ. 1955), pp. 16, 10. The first volume of Miller's *New England Mind* (New York: Macmillan, 1939) is more emphatic on the alleged indigenous causes of the "metamorphosis" of New England Calvinism than is the second volume, *The New England Mind: From Colony to Province* (Cambridge: Harvard University Press, 1953). In the second volume Miller took note of the attractiveness to some New Englanders of those "English theologians, some of them dissenters but most of them Anglicans like Tillotson, who, also recoiling from a century of profitless disputation, were celebrating the gentle charms of reasonable forebearance." However, Miller continued, "We must not forget that the colonial version of this tendency, whatever it owed to foreign influence, acquired its peculiar impetus from the profound consternation arising out of a purely colonial predicament" (p. 249), by which Miller seems to have had in mind political strife and religious factionalism.

[19] Cf. John Murrin, "Anglicizing an American Colony: The Transformation of Provincial Massachusetts" (Ph.D. diss., Yale University, 1966), passim.

regnum, almost one-half of the total college-educated elite of New England returned to England, in nearly all cases permanently.[20] One may take this figure as an indication of the closeness of cultural ties with England before the restoration of the Stuart monarchy.

Following the Restoration, however, and the reimposition of persecutory constraints on the expression of religious dissent in England, Massachusetts withdrew into relative insularity. The province was not entirely isolated, certainly, from intellectual developments in England and on the Continent, especially in Calvinist Holland, but it was cut off from and fearful of the intolerance of the established English church, which from the New England point of view was still the church of Archbishop Laud. In other words, in the twenty-five years from 1660 to 1685 New England was on its own culturally to a degree that it had not been before and would not be again in the colonial period, but it was also intellectually removed from its inevitable cultural capital, London, and thus subject to stagnation.[21]

During this same twenty-five-year period in the homeland, however, amidst the repression and vindictiveness of the reign of Charles II, and partly in reaction to it, a remarkable renewal occurred within the Anglican church. The renewal sprang from a movement as much philosophical as theological, and broad enough—or in contemporary language, "catholick" enough—in spirit to virtually cast into the shadows the former intellectual leadership and vitality of Calvinist ortho-

484

[20] Harry S. Stout, "University Men in New England, 1620–1660: A Demographic Analysis," *Journal of Interdisciplinary History* 4 (1974): 379–400.

[21] The situation is classically described in Perry Miller's essay "Errand into the Wilderness," in *Errand into the Wilderness* (Cambridge: Harvard University Press, 1956). Cf., however, Samuel Eliot Morison, *Harvard College in the Seventeenth Century* (Cambridge: Harvard University Press, 1936), p. 390: "A great deal of nonsense has been written about the 'isolation' of 'provincial' New England after the restoration of the English monarchy in 1660. From the Court of Charles II, and the Restoration dramatists ... Harvard was indeed isolated; but with contemporary movements in science, scholarship, and theology, the College was in constant touch." I think Morison exaggerates here, although the closeness of New England to Holland throughout the Restoration period gave the colony access to the entire European world of letters.

doxy.[22] I am referring, of course, to Latitudinarianism, a label that originally was applied opprobriously to the Cambridge Platonists, most of whom were lapsed Puritans, and later to a wing of the Anglican clergy that included Tillotson and a number of others who, like Tillotson himself, had been raised as Puritans. The tolerant liberality of the Latitudinarians toward minor doctrinal differences within English Protestantism made many of the dissenters, almost overnight, look, and perhaps feel, like narrow-minded sectaries, a transformation of perceptions that occurred not just because the dissenters adhered to *Calvinist* theology, but rather because their point of view in general remained essentially "theological" and Scholastic rather than "philosophical." New England after 1660 found itself, then, in a peculiar situation, furiously and retrogressively clinging to its old ways of covenanted churches and ministry, sectarian intolerance, and Scholasticized learning, while at the same time in England the most exciting intellectual developments pointed, on the contrary, toward an ideal of unified Protestantism on broad principles, a rationalized conception of Christianity allowing for liberty of conscience and tolerance for all but Roman Catholics and Unitarians, and the total dissolution of Protestant Scholasticism as a mode of learning and communication.[23]

485

In the mid-1680s, New England's short-lived backwater

[22] See Cragg, *From Puritanism to the Age of Reason*, p. 30: "Seldom had a reversal of fortune been so complete" as that which affected Calvinist predominancy in England. "Within fifty years Calvinism in England fell from a position of immense authority to obscurity and insignificance."

[23] The literature on intellectual developments in England during this period is extensive, and I can mention here only a few secondary titles of recent vintage that will lead the reader into the subject: Cragg, *From Puritanism to the Age of Reason*; Ernst Cassirer, *The Platonic Renaissance in England*, trans. James P. Pettegrove (Austin: University of Texas Press, 1953); Roland N. Stromberg, *Religious Liberalism in Eighteenth-Century England* (London: Oxford University Press, 1954); Richard S. Westfall, *Science and Religion in Seventeenth-Century England* (New Haven: Yale University Press, 1958); Norman Sykes, *From Sheldon to Secker: Aspects of English Church History 1660–1768* (Cambridge: Cambridge University Press, 1959); Barbara J. Shapiro, *John Wilkins, 1614–1672: An Intellectual Biography* (Berkeley and Los Angeles: University of California Press, 1969).

bubble was forcibly burst by events originating in the homeland, and in the three most fundamental areas of public order—church, state, and university—major changes rapidly occurred. It is the changes in church and university that are of
particular concern here, but these were to an incalculable
degree dependent initially on political events, beginning with
the Crown's revocation in 1684 of the original charter by
which Massachusetts Bay had governed itself for fifty years,
486   an instrument that in the eyes of the Puritans was "a holy
document, sacred evidence of a covenant with God."[24] The
colony's subjugation to royal control for the first time, and
the necessity this humbling brought for political accommodation with both parliamentary and monarchical power in England, gave strength to a moderate religious party in Massachusetts. This party was still overtly Calvinist if measured by the
five points of the Synod of Dort, but it was also open to and
hungry for fresh ideas from overseas and aware of the stifling
parochialism of the old Puritan faction that continued to
conceive of the New England Way, which had been recodified
in 1679, as God's final message to mankind. Although Increase
Mather can hardly be considered a member of the Anglophile
moderates, the *Vindication of New England* (1690), usually
attributed to him, is an example of how the political crisis
with the mother country compelled broader sentiments than
had existed earlier. "The good people of New England,"
Mather wrote, "want not a kindness for the Church of England . . . ; they Believe there are thousands in that Communion with whom they expect Eternal happiness in the
same Heaven. Such renowned names as those of Burnet, Tillotson, etc., are as precious and as valued amongst the people
of New-England, and their Books as much Read and Lov'd
and Liv'd, as with many here at home."[25]

[24] David Lovejoy, *The Glorious Revolution in America* (New York: Harper
and Row, 1972), p. 122.

[25] The politics of this period in Massachusetts are well described in T. H.
Breen's *The Character of the Good Ruler: A Study of Puritan Political Ideas*

It would be absurd to suggest that the mere introduction of the Book of Common Prayer or the founding of the Anglican King's Chapel in Massachusetts in 1686 constituted an "enlightenment" by any definition, for this assumption would mean that Virginia and New York, which had always had Anglican establishments, were enlightened when Massachusetts was still benighted. One cannot equate Anglicanism with enlightenment, and Calvinism with darkness. Late seventeenth-century Anglicanism incorporated a whole range of religious and philosophical positions, more or less progressive or reactionary, enlightened or dogmatic. On the other hand it can be argued, on different grounds, that state-enforced toleration of all Protestant denominations was a step toward enlightenment, and the moderate party in Massachusetts, for philosophical as well as political reasons, certainly welcomed this demand from overseas.

487

II

The most significant evidence of the new liberal spirit in church affairs was not the construction of King's Chapel, an event that meant no more than the highly unwelcome intrusion of episcopacy into formerly exclusive Congregational territory, but the founding of the so-called Brattle Street Church in 1699. The Brattle Church was unqualifiedly Calvinist in the elements of theology yet fundamentally antithetical in character to numerous peripheral—or what the Brattle Church's founders considered peripheral—Massachusetts church traditions. There is no need here to review in detail the well-known principles of the Brattle Street Church, except to note its overcoming of the sectarian spirit in its idea of church membership, its repudiation of the concept that visible church societies of any size or type are covenanted with God, and its assertion that in a church, as in a civil, society, relations among members are governed not by special di-

in New England, 1630–1730 (New Haven: Yale University Press, 1970); see also Miller, New England Mind: Colony to Province. A Vindication of New England is reprinted in Andros Tracts, vol. 6 of Publications of the Prince Society (Boston, 1869), 2:19–78.

vine revelation but by the dictates of morality established in Natural Law.[26]

The founders of this church were all respectable native New England Puritans, but they took their cues from developments in London in the last decades of the seventeenth century, not from the Massachusetts synod of 1679. In their quest for new forms of religious community, they turned with hope toward the various schemes for unification of the English Protestant churches that a number of Presbyterians, Independents, and Anglicans (including, prominently, Tillotson before his death) believed to be a real possibility, particularly in the face of the Papist threat from the Continent and the proven disastrous consequences during the preceding century of allowing doctrinal disagreements to be overstressed. Tillotson was one who had led the way out of the thickets of doctrinal disputes. Factions, he believed, take men away from minding "the more necessary and essential parts of religion." Factions lead people to become overly "concern'd about little speculative opinions in religion, which they always call fundamental articles of faith." But there is no greater heresy in the world, Tillotson maintained, than "a wicked life."[27]

It is not often enough noted that the innovators of the Brattle Street Church were the identical group that more than ten years earlier—that is, beginning in about 1686—had brought about the first major reform of the Harvard College curriculum. In other words, the reforms in church and university not only had (to some degree) a common efficient cause—the forcible opening of the Bay colony by political

488

[26] See *A Manifesto or Declaration, Set Forth by the Undertakers of the New Church* (Boston, 1699), and the explication of this manifesto, *Gospel Order Revived* (London[?], 1700), usually attributed to Timothy Woodbridge, Benjamin Colman, and Simon Bradstreet. There is a large secondary literature on the Brattle Street Church.

[27] Sermon XXXIV, "The care of our souls the one thing needful," preached before the King and Queen on 14 April 1689. Latitudinarians like Tillotson shared with seventeenth-century pietists in New England and elsewhere a concern with practical theology, an emphasis on *living to God* as the primary goal of religion. But Tillotson differed fundamentally from the pietists in so many other areas that the resemblance can only be considered superficial.

means to the full range of English culture of the eighties and
nineties—but also a common inspiration, English Latitudinarianism from Henry More to Tillotson.

A central figure in the curriculum reform and a principal
actor also in the founding of the Brattle Church—both tasks
requiring unusual intellectual leadership—was a man who
published not one word in his lifetime and, in a society dominated intellectually by the ministry, was not even a clergyman.
This figure was John Leverett, grandson of the governor of
Massachusetts in the 1670s. Leverett graduated from Harvard
in 1680 when he was eighteen and was appointed tutor a few
years later, along with William Brattle, whose brother
Thomas donated the land on which the Brattle Church was
built. Although the installation of Leverett and Brattle as
tutors (in 1685 and 1686, respectively) was not a direct consequence of the shift in political power in Massachusetts following the revocation of the colony's original charter in 1684, the
curriculum changes were undoubtedly facilitated by the new
political climate.[28] In nearly every discipline—logic, metaphysics, ethics, and natural philosophy—the Aristotelian-Scho-
lastic inheritance was in large part abandoned. The most important single philosophical influence on academic thought
in Massachusetts for the next thirty years was the Cambridge
Platonist Henry More, whose ethics and metaphysics texts
were favored by Leverett and his circle, and behind More was
the Cartesian revolution.[29] This anti-Scholastic movement was

489

---

[28] The only extended treatment of Leverett is Arthur Kaledin, "The Mind of
John Leverett" (Ph.D. diss., Harvard University, 1965). He is treated also in
John Langdon Sibley, *Biographical Sketches of Graduates of Harvard University* (Cambridge, Mass., 1885), 3:180–98, and in Samuel Eliot Morison's, *Harvard
in the Seventeenth Century* and *Three Centuries of Harvard, 1636–1936* (Cambridge: Harvard University Press, 1936). Dunn, "Tutor Henry Flynt" contains
valuable fresh information on Leverett.

[29] The very first American enlightenment was French, if the advent of
Cartesianism may be thought of as at least a pre-enlightenment. At Harvard, in
addition to the works of the Cartesian renegade Henry More, the end of the
century brought Antoine Arnauld's and Pierre Nicole's *Logique, ou l'art de
penser* (1662), translated into Latin in 1674 and into English in 1685; Jacques
Rohault's physics, which was translated into Latin by Samuel Clarke and published in London with Clarke's Newtonian notes in 1697 and 1702; Nicolas

furthered by the coincidental—or perhaps not so coincidental—arrival in Massachusetts in 1686 of Charles Morton, the
principal of one of the leading dissenting academies near London (Newington Green) and the teacher of Samuel Wesley and
Daniel Defoe, among others. Morton, who emigrated at the
advanced age of sixty, was expected to assume the presidency
of Harvard. Called by his bookseller friend John Dunton "the
Epitomy both of Aristotle and Descartes" and "the very soul
of Philosophy," Morton brought to Boston and Cambridge the
living authority of the metropolis as support for an updated
academic program.[30]

Our knowledge of Leverett's influence at Harvard in this
period comes first of all from the evidence we have of the in-

490

Malebranche's logic and epistemology, *Recherche de la Vérité,* published in
London in two separate English translations in 1694; the work of Antoine
LeGrand in all of these fields; Pierre Gassendi's astronomy; and the unclassi-
fiable general critique of Pierre Bayle, whose *Dictionary* was translated into
English in 1710 but whose influence was felt in periodical literature long
before. All of these works were Cartesian inspired. There are surviving précis
of Henry More's *Enchiridion Ethicum* and *Enchiridion Metaphysicum* prepared by John Leverett for student use that date from 1694 at the latest. William Brattle's manuscript logic, which was circulating in New England before
1690, was based on Arnauld and LeGrand. For additional information on intellectual influences on New England in this period, see my "Transatlantic Republic of Letters: A Note on the Circulation of Learned Periodicals to Early
Eighteenth-Century America," *William and Mary Quarterly,* 3d ser. 33 (1976):
642–60; *Moral Philosophy at Seventeenth-Century Harvard: A Discipline in
Transition* (Chapel Hill: University of North Carolina Press, 1981); and
Jonathan Edwards's Moral Thought and Its British Context (Chapel Hill:
University of North Carolina Press, 1981), chap. 1.

[30] Morton was a key transitional figure in the demise of Scholasticism at
Harvard and in England. In his teaching in England, he was possibly the first
academic anywhere to introduce the vernacular systematically, both in lectur-
ing and as a subject for study in itself, a change of much profounder importance in the history of thought than is sometimes recognized. Morton is treated
authoritatively in the *Dictionary of American Biography* by Wilbur J. Bender
and also in considerable detail in a biographical sketch by Samuel Eliot Morison which prefaces vol. 33 of the *Publications of the Colonial Society of Massachusetts* (Boston, 1940). This volume contains Morton's *Compendium Physicae,*
edited from manuscripts by Theodore Hornberger. None of this biographical
work had the benefit of J. W. Ashley Smith's study of the dissenting academies,
*The Birth of Modern Education: The Contribution of the Dissenting Acad-
emies, 1660–1800* (London: Independent Press, 1954), which discusses Morton's
use of the vernacular. For additional bibliography on Morton, see my *Moral
Philosophy at Seventeenth-Century Harvard,* chap. 5.

troduction of new texts in the traditional disciplines and, secondly, from the later testimony of a few of his students, notably Benjamin Colman, who was brought back by the Brattles and Leverett from a four-year stay in England to be the first pastor of the Brattle Street Church, and Henry Newman, who like Colman had also migrated to England sometime after leaving Harvard in the 1690s but remained there permanently and eventually converted to Anglicanism. In 1712 Colman told White Kennett, then Dean and later Bishop of Peterborough, that in the four years he had spent in England, two years in London and two years preaching at Bath, he did "but grow in the natural inclination" he already had to "the generous principles of an enlarged catholick spirit" originally "cherished in [him]" at Harvard by his "Tutor, Mr. Leverett." Moreover, Colman continued, he had spent twelve weeks in Cambridge (England) and seen Oxford, and "if I am able to judge, no place of Education can well boast a more free air than our little College may."[31]

491

Thirteen years later, in 1725, in another letter to Bishop Kennett, Colman recollected once more the pride he had felt when he was in England in his Harvard education under Leverett:

As for the catholick spirit . . . I hope I may have some pretence to it, and I acknowledge it a very good gift and ornament to a person . . . : But then (My Lord) it is the very Spirit of our College and has been so these forty years past, and if I have ever shone in your Lordship's Eyes on that Account, here I learnt it thirty years since, and when I visited the famous universities and private academies in England [in the 1690s], I was proud of my own humble education here in our Cambridge, because of the catholick air I had there breathed in.[32]

These references to the "catholick spirit" and "catholick air" were virtually code words for devotion to broad church

[31] Ebenezer Turrell, *Life and Character of Dr. Benjamin Colman* (Boston, 1749), p. 122.
[32] Turrell, *Benjamin Colman*, p. 136.

principles such as Tillotson's. Simon Bradstreet, another of Leverett's young disciples and successor to Charles Morton as pastor of the church at Charlestown, was described by an eighteenth-century biographer as follows: "He possessed such a catholick spirit and such liberal views of the gospel dispensation, that some of the more zealous brethren accused him of Arminianism; but the only evidence of this," the biographer continued, was Bradstreet's "fondness for Tillotson's sermons" and his being rather "a practical than a doctrinal preacher."[33] Tillotson was also Colman's favorite writer, or at least the author Colman most often cited in his ninety-odd published sermons and other works, an attachment that, as in the case of Bradstreet, was initially fostered during student days under Leverett.[34] In *A Sermon Preached at the Ordination of Mr. William Cooper* (Boston, 1716), Colman chose Tillotson and Burnet as examples of "Venerable men" in the Church of England whose memories were sullied after their deaths by those who rejected their "spirit of Moderation." Yet these were men, Colman said, "of whom the Age was not worthy; of conspicuous Sanctity, abundant in their Labours, Steddy in their Conduct, of unspotted Integrity, of an Apostolical spirit, and ready . . . to have died either for their Country or for Christ. . . . But their Names must needs live in the History of the Church," Colman continued, "if Truth do not perish from the Earth."[35]

Colman has often been regarded as the embodiment of what we can now call, following Henry May, the "moderate" Ameri-

492

---

[33] Quoted in Clifford Shipton, *Biographical Sketches of Those Who Attended Harvard College,* Sibley's Harvard Graduates (Cambridge: Harvard University Press, 1933), 4:157, from the account of John Eliot (Harvard A.B., 1772), printed in *Massachusetts Historical Society Collections,* 1st ser., vol. 8 (Boston, 1802), p. 75 n. See also, David D. Hall, *The Faithful Shepherd: A History of the New England Ministry in the Seventeenth Century* (Chapel Hill: University of North Carolina Press), pp. 206, 272–73. Bradstreet was a classmate of Henry Flynt's.

[34] Clayton H. Chapman, "Life and Influence of Rev. Benjamin Colman, D.D., 1673–1747" (Ph.D. diss., Boston University, 1948), p. 273.

[35] P. 18.

can enlightenment.[36] "He exemplifies, as well perhaps as any colonial American, the early influence on this side of the Atlantic of the great ideas of the Age of Enlightenment," Theodore Hornberger wrote in 1939, when it was still possible to speak vaguely of a single general "age of the enlightenment." Hornberger noticed particularly Colman's emphasis on such "abstractions" as "Nature, Reason, and Humanity," and Perry Miller assigned to Colman primary responsibility for "bringing to New England a consciousness of 'the Age,' an awareness that the Enlightenment had dawned and provincial imitators of the capital should hasten to become enlightened." Colman "deftly showed by his example," Miller wrote, "that the driving, narrow, controversialism and intensity of the seventeenth century had become bad form." Yet Colman was also perfectly orthodox, and Hornberger rightly insisted on Colman's "careful adherence to the Calvinist system."[37]

493

Another of Leverett's pupils, Henry Newman, moved to England, converted to Anglicanism, and became secretary to the Society for Promoting Christian Knowledge. But Newman retained his love for his native Massachusetts all of his life, and his letters contain some of the best information we have on the state of Harvard College in the last fifteen years of the seventeenth century. When Newman was at Harvard in the 1680s and 1690s, first as an undergraduate, then as a graduate student and for three years as librarian, Leverett and Brattle "recommended to their pupils," Newman recalled in 1714, "the reading of Episcopal authors as the best books to form our minds in religious matters and preserve us from those narrow principles that kept us at a distance from the Church of England." These tutors were dissenters, Newman said, and although he was himself now an Anglican, he "was not ashamed to own that [he] was one of their proselytes." It

[36] Henry F. May, *The Enlightenment in America* (New York: Oxford University Press, 1976).

[37] Theodore Hornberger, "Benjamin Colman and the Enlightenment," *New England Quarterly* 13 (1939): 227–40. Miller, *New England Mind: Colony to Province*, p. 271.

was Newman in fact who arranged to have Leverett and Brattle elected to membership in the Royal Society in 1714, writing to John Chamberlayne on 23 November 1713: "Both these Gent. are the 2 Great Luminaries for Learning in that country, and will I am sure reflect honour upon the [Royal] Society because to my knowledge they have many years since perus'd with delight their Transactions and recommended 'em to their Pupils as the best standards of Natural Philosophy now extant."[38] Some insight into the meaning of Leverett's election to the Society may be gained from the realization that a figure like Tillotson, who certainly had no special competence in natural philosophy, had been an FRS since 1672. His eighteenth-century biographer captured the reasoning of the time: Tillotson had a "love for the real philosophy of nature" and was convinced that the "study of it is the most solid support of religion."[39]

494

The instances cited of Harvard students and faculty appreciating Tillotson despite the theological dangers to which he exposed an orthodox Calvinist can only be explained by reference to the attractiveness at the time of the English churchman's "philosophical" spirit.[40] It became a special kind of compliment at the end of the seventeenth century to describe a person as "philosophical." The term indicated that the object of this praise had gone beyond the narrow categories of Calvinist theology alone, and beyond Scholasticisim, too, and was a student of modern reasoning on diverse subjects. Thus

[38] Leonard W. Cowie, *Henry Newman: An American in London 1708–1743* (London: S.P.C.K., 1956), pp. 8–9, 194–99. *Transactions of the Colonial Society of Massachusetts*, vol. 28 (Boston, 1935): 222–24. Both Newman and Colman, in the letters I have quoted, had a special interest in emphasizing the liberalism of Leverett and William Brattle. They were defending Harvard and New England against the imputation of sectarian intolerance and indirectly defending themselves as well. Yet the letters of Newman and Colman about Harvard under Leverett's tutorship could not possibly be collusive, and they therefore corroborate each other in pointing to the nature of education at Harvard after 1686.

[39] Thomas Birch, *The Life of ... Dr. John Tillotson* (London, 1752), p. 349.

[40] Kaledin, "Mind of John Leverett," p. 143, and Dunn, "Tutor Henry Flynt," p. 185, each remark on Leverett's fondness and admiration for Tillotson's sermons.

Bishop Gilbert Burnet wrote of himself: "I have never found a disposition to superstition in my temper; I was rather inclined to be philosophical upon all occasions."[41] A case similar to Simon Bradstreet's, mentioned just above, is that of Thomas Symmes, who was at Harvard under Leverett between 1694 and 1698. While there he was taken with "the human and lax Principles of the Arminians," his contemporary biographer wrote, but later he recovered his staunch Calvinist doctrines. However, when he died at a young age in 1725, a eulogy described him significantly as "a Person of a Catholick Spirit, Generous Principles, a Liberal Soul," and "a true Calvinist."[42] None of these descriptive phrases was considered incompatible with the others; Symmes was obviously philosophical.

495

By the time Leverett's election to the Royal Society came in 1714, he was no longer a tutor: he was president of Harvard. He had relinquished the tutorship formally in 1697 and moved into politics, although he continued to live at Harvard. After serving for several years as the Cambridge representative in the Massachusetts General Court, in 1700 he was elected Speaker of the House. Thereafter he held all of the important judgeships that were available and served on the Governor's Council. Yet despite this considerable immersion in politics and law (a talent for which Leverett had no doubt inherited from his grandfather), in 1707 he resigned from all posts in order to accept the presidency of Harvard, a position he retained until his death in 1724, the only noncleric to have been president of the institution before the nineteenth century. Thus for nearly forty years, from 1685 until his death, Leverett played a crucial role in New England intellectual life, more immediate and important, possibly, than even, let us say, that played by Cotton Mather, but because Leverett left to posterity only his personal influence on students and no major writings, he

[41] Quoted in Cragg, *From Puritanism to the Age of Reason*, p. 68.

[42] *A Particular Plain and Brief Memorative Account of the Rev. Mr. Thomas Symmes*, published with John Brown, *Divine Help Implored ... A Funeral Sermon ... of the Rev. Mr. Thomas Symmes* (Boston, 1726). See, by Symmes, *A Discourse Concerning Prejudice in Matters of Religion* (Boston, 1722).

remains somewhat in obscurity, known mainly by the devotion he seems to have constantly inspired.[43] When the Harvard Corporation settled on Leverett as president in 1707, thirty-nine ministers in the province, in an extraordinary move, sent an address to the royal governor, Joseph Dudley, that read in part as follows:

496

We humbly take the freedom to acquaint and assure your Excellency, that no person whatsoever could be more acceptable to us in that station.... We cannot but give this testimony of our great affection to and esteem for him;... we are abundantly satisfied and assured of his religion, learning, and other excellent accomplishments for that eminent service [as president], a long experience of which we had while he was Senior Fellow [i.e., tutor] ... [;] under the wise and faithful government of him, and the Rev. Mr. Brattle of Cambridge, the greatest part of the now rising ministry of New England were happily educated; and we hope and promise ourselves ... to see religion and learning thrive and flourish in that society, under Mr. Leverett's wise conduct and influence, as much as ever yet it hath done.[44]

Leverett's accession to the presidency in 1707 put Harvard firmly under the guidance of the moderate group that looked to "philosophy" and Latitudinarianism for inspiration. The main governing body of the institution, the Corporation, had as members, among others, William and Thomas Brattle, Simon Bradstreet, and Benjamin Colman. Another member in 1707 was Ebenezer Pemberton, a Boston minister, student of Leverett's in the 1690s, and a tutor himself between 1697 and 1702. When Pemberton died in 1717 at age forty-five, he left an extraordinary library of about one thousand volumes, the inventory of which could almost in itself serve as a guide to the extent and limits of the first New England enlightenment. Pemberton's library was, of course, preponderantly theological, and most of the books were the classic works of

[43] Only scattered Leverett manuscripts have survived, some in the Harvard University Archives and some at the Massachusetts Historical Society.

[44] The address is printed as appendix 20 in Josiah Quincy, *History of Harvard University*, 1:504–5.

divinity from the Church Fathers through the sixteenth and seventeenth centuries, including reams of Puritan and Calvinist literature. This side of the man does not interest us here, although it is a reminder once more that Leverett and his disciples were perfectly orthodox. What is relevant, however, are, first of all, the many works Pemberton owned representative of the Cartesian revolution: nearly everything that Descartes himself wrote, Legrand's compendium, Arnauld's logic, Nicole's moral essays, Malebranche's *Search After Truth* and many works by the "English Malebranche," John Norris of Bemerton, nearly everything by Henry More, and one volume at least of Bayle's *Dictionary*.

497

Another group of works in this pre-1717 library is representative of the important body of literature that may be called "philosophical Anglicanism," a term that reflects the essential quality of the new thinking more precisely than does "Latitudinarianism." Pemberton of course had the fourteen-volume octavo edition of Tillotson's sermons and the three-volume folio edition of his "Works." But he also had Bishop John Wilkins's sermons and his *Principles and Duties of Natural Religion*, which Tillotson, who was Wilkins's son-in-law, had edited and published posthumously in 1675, and the sermons of Isaac Barrow, the well-known predecessor of Newton as Lucasian Professor of Mathematics at Cambridge, who chose preaching over natural science. Tillotson, as it happens, was also the posthumous editor of Barrow's many sermons. Samuel Clarke's Boyle lectures and sermons were not in this inventory, which is a mystery, for despite his reputed Arianism, Clarke ranks with Tillotson as the most influential of the philosophical Anglicans in America in the first quarter of the eighteenth century, and in fact Clarke had modeled his own sermons after Tillotson's. But another great philosophical bishop, Richard Cumberland, was represented in Pemberton's library in the form of James Tyrrel's *Brief Disquisition of the Law of Nature* (London, 1692), which was an abridgement of Cumberland's seminal Latin treatise on the laws of nature (*De Legibus Naturae*), originally published in 1672

and still thought highly enough of fifty years later to be translated into English and published in its entirety in 1727. And
Pemberton also owned Edward Fowler's *Principles and Practices of Certain Moderate Divines of the Church of England,
Abusively Called Latitudinarians,* published in London in
1670, the earliest work to identify Latitudinarianism as a significant intellectual movement.[45] For the historian to understand this group, I would suggest, plus a few other of Tillotson's predecessors and successors in the Church of England,
such as Benjamin Whichcote, whose funeral sermon was
preached by Tillotson, Gilbert Burnet, Benjamin Hoadley,
and William Wollaston, is to gain an essential understanding
of the major currents of religious and philosophical thought in
New England from 1685 to 1735. Yet this assertion immediately raises additional questions: How does Tillotson, who
was neither a philosopher nor a philosophe, fit into any convincing conceptualization of Anglo-American enlightenments? And if the sequence of enlightenments, or let us say,
the process of enlightenment, may be described as evolving in
New England from various forms of Cartesianism initially,
through Cambridge Platonism and philosophical Anglicanism, what happens then to the endlessly repeated (and rarely
examined) dictum of both textbook and monograph that the
works of John Locke and Isaac Newton typify quintessentially
the fresh breezes from overseas that launch the American enlightenment?

To answer these questions it is necessary first to introduce
briefly two elementary axioms that must serve as prerequisites
to any intelligible discussion of American enlightenments.
First, "enlightenment" refers to only one of several ongoing
cultural movements in the eighteenth century. It is obviously
incorrect to treat the eighteenth century and the enlightenment as though they were synonymous, although it may be
legitimate, if a bit tendentious, to speak of the eighteenth century as the *Age* of Enlightenment, meaning only that the en-

498

[45] Ebenezer Pemberton, *A Catalogue of Curious and Valuable Books* ... (Boston, 1717).

lightenment was a prominent feature of it. In America, for
example, from the mid-seventeenth century to the Great
Awakening there is continuous sustenance of the pietist movement, and this trend can hardly be integrated into any imagin-
able conception of enlightenment, although both the enlightenment and pietism had in common, it should be noted, an
enmity to Protestant Scholasticism, which together in the late
seventeenth century they combined to destroy.

The second axiom is even more elementary, yet still bears   499
reiteration. The enlightenment movement had distinctive
characteristics, or certainly distinctive chronologies, in different countries. Therefore, before one can begin to look at
the enlightenment in America it is essential to clear away the
stereotypes derived from well-known conceptions of the
French, English, and Scottish enlightenments. Anticlericalism
was a large factor in the French enlightenment, for example,
but it has little application to colonial America; the deist controversy in England from Toland to Leland, to mention another instance, caused hardly a ripple in Massachusetts. Finally, even Locke's philosophy and Newton's discoveries were
important in early America only in highly qualified ways, and
neither the *Essay Concerning Human Understanding* nor the
Principia Mathematica may be considered crucial documents
for comprehending the development of thought in America
before about 1735. It was not that Locke's *Essay* was unknown
or the significance of Newton's great work unrecognized, but
in the context of the New England mind—I am using Harvard
here as a microcosm—these celebrated figures were addressing
the wrong problems and, in the case of Locke's *Essay*, certainly, giving too many of the wrong answers. Locke's empiricism and skepticism, his nominalism and positivist tendencies,
and his confused denial of innate ideas, particularly the innate
idea of God, were simply unacceptable in New England.[46] On

46 Cf. Kaledin, "Leverett," pp. 181–86. Much may be learned about the
American reception of Locke's *Essay* from John Yolton's *John Locke and the
Way of Ideas* (London: Oxford University Press, 1956), which reviews the Eng-
lish controversies the work provoked.

the other hand, his essays on toleration, on the reasonableness of Christianity, and on education fit comfortably into the existing preoccupations of Massachusetts intellectuals. As for Locke's accomplishments in what at the time was called logic or method (and now epistemology), meaning the study of how "certain" knowledge may be acquired, the Cartesians had already succeeded in breaking out of the Scholastic obsession with textual authority and fruitless disputation, which was the main point.[47]

500

Although Tillotson and Locke were nearly exact contemporaries (Tillotson was born in 1630, Locke in 1632), it must be remembered that Tillotson was famous and influential by the 1670s, long before Locke, who was not well known until the last decade of the century. The belief occasionally heard, therefore, that Tillotson expressed the spirit of Locke, is highly unlikely if not altogether impossible. It might be truer to the case to argue the reverse position, namely that Locke's writings on religious belief and related matters reflected the spirit of Tillotson. When Tillotson died (on 22 November 1694) Locke wrote in Latin to his close friend Phillipus van Limborch, a professor of divinity at Amsterdam: "Now that that great and candid searcher after truth, to say nothing of his other virtues, has been taken from us, I have scarcely anyone whom I can freely consult about theological uncertainties. Others will make known sufficiently how great a man the English public weal has lost, how great a pillar the Reformed church. I have assuredly lost, to my very great hurt and grief, a friend of many years, steadfast, candid, and sincere."[48]

[47] It is impossible to speak of a single John Locke in America. The *Thoughts on Education*, the *Reasonableness of Christianity*, the *Two Treatises on Government*, and the *Essay* each had an entirely separate career. Ebenezer Pemberton owned the first two of these works only, plus some of Locke's exchanges with Bishop Edward Stillingfleet on the *Reasonableness of Christianity*.

[48] Wright, *Beginnings of Unitarianism*, p. 136, for example, appears to make Tillotson derivative from Locke. E. S. De Beer, *The Correspondence of John Locke*, 8 vols. (Oxford: Clarendon Press, 1979), 5:237–38. Locke's letter is dated 11 December 1694. In 1692 Limborch wanted to dedicate his *History of the Inquisition* to Tillotson and asked Locke to serve as an intermediary. Limborch's dedication is unstinting in its praise of Tillotson.

It is a truism of intellectual history that ideas, new forms of thought, new principles, are rarely adopted in a block, without discrimination or local adaptation. New England intellectuals in 1690 were a deeply religious group to the man, immersed in Protestant Christianity and committed to its defense against the forces of atheism (both practical and theoretical), metaphysical materialism, Epicureanism (which signified both materialism and a universe governed by mere chance), and moral relativism (which Locke's *Essay* appeared to sanction in many respects). But these Puritans were also heirs of a learned pre-Cartesian philosophical tradition, both Scholastic and Humanist, and thus were accustomed to employing philosophy in the service of religion. After Descartes, however, the traditional accommodation between philosophy and theology, which had prevailed since the Middle Ages in university circles, became immeasurably more complicated. The power of autonomous critical and creative reason to serve the cause of Christianity seemed to be enormously enhanced by the Cartesian method, but the destructive potentiality of reason was even more dramatically enlarged. The intellectual leaders of New England in 1690 who might be defined as "enlightened" were not looking for emancipation from ignorance and superstition—they did not consider themselves victims of such things—but for new forms of integration of reason and religion. To be enlightened in New England at this time was simply to care about and believe in the capacity of new philosophies—particularly Cartesian and Neoplatonic—to protect religion against the menace of other misguided philosophies. The alternatives to enlightenment of this sort were not many. Most prominently there was pietism—a retreat into spiritual inwardness and personal experience that constituted a rejection of the emphasis on reasoned defenses and explications of religion. Religion from this point of view must be ultimately self-justifying. There was also the conservative option, which meant attempting to maintain continuity with the past at all costs. For those in this camp the old religion and old authorities served as a shelter against a full encounter with new ideas.

501

These considerations help to explain the appeal of Henry More in the first quarter of the century. He had all the warmth and "heart" of a pietist and the right measure of Platonic mysticism, but he was also a persuasive advocate of the rational foundations of Christianity, a thinker who believed that the existence of "spirit" could be proven as conclusively as that of matter, that Christian ethics were universally true because written in the hearts and minds of all men, and that the study of nature revealed as convincingly as Holy Scripture the existence of an intelligent and benevolent deity. None of these virtues could be found in Locke. As for Newton, what he had to say that was of special value to New Englanders was already being effectively proclaimed by writers in natural theology, such as Robert Boyle and John Ray, whose *Wisdom of God Manifested in the Works of Creation* (1691) was enormously popular in America.[49] New cosmological or scientific facts were not considered important in themselves. The Newton who might be interpreted as giving glorious confirmation to the empirical tradition in science was wholly ignored insofar as that tradition signified the pursuit of natural philosophy independent of religious ideals and goals. In order to understand the first American enlightenment, it is far more important to study the development of philosophical rationalism from Ramus to Samuel Clarke than it is to trace the growth of empiricism.[50] Even a little later, it was the Bishop Berkeley who was the disciple of Malebranche, not of Locke, whom American intellectuals, such as Samuel Johnson of Connecticut, found appealing.

502

[49] It is notable that Ray's *Three Physico-Theological Discourses* (London, 1693) was dedicated to Tillotson. Ray and Tillotson were both influenced by the Cambridge Platonists and shared an admiration for John Wilkins, who was Tillotson's father-in-law.

[50] "Rationalism" is a much abused word that is tossed about in historical studies of this period with such a variety of meanings that it has lost almost all precise significance. It should not be casually equated with, or used as a synonym for, naturalism, skepticism, empiricism, materialism, intellectualism, deism, Lockeanism, or Newtonianism. I am using the term specifically with reference to the revival of Platonic rationalism and to the interplay of this outlook with Cartesian rationalism and Continental rationalism in general, exemplified in such figures as Malebranche and Liebniz.

III

We are better prepared now, perhaps, to consider the question of how a seventeenth-century English bishop, Tillotson, who has hardly been uniformly appreciated by historians of philosophy or ideas, may be reckoned a major influence on the first American enlightenment and in many respects the key figure.[51] By the term "enlightenment" we have in mind certain subtle but far-reaching changes in the status and conception of nature and reason in relation to traditional Christian teaching. Two ideas, both found conspicuously in Tillotson, were basic to the transformation that occurred: first, that nature itself, *including human nature,* is a revelation of God that with certain precautions may be trusted as an independent source of divine truth; second, that religion stands to benefit from the free exercise of rational invention without regard to the authority of the vast literature of Christian con-

503

[51] Certain evaluations of Tillotson seem to have been passed on from history book to history book with little evidence that any of the authors went to the trouble of carefully reading him. The famous French critic Hippolyte Taine remarked on Tillotson's "clearness," "naturalness," and "preciseness" and called him "a kind of father of the [English] Church," but chastised his style: "There is nothing lifelike; it is a skeleton, with all its joints coarsely displayed. All the ideas are ticketed and numbered. The Schoolmen were not worse. Neither rapture nor vehemence; no wit, no imagination, no original and brilliant idea, no philosophy; nothing but quotations of mere scholarship.... At the court of Louis XIV Tillotson would have been taken for a man who had run away from a seminary. Voltaire would have called him a village curé" (*History of English Literature,* trans. H. Van Laun [New York, 1891], 3:99–102). We know, on the contrary, that Voltaire in 1766 called him "le meilleur prédicateur de l'Europe" (the best preacher of Europe) and the only one nearly who has not "deshonoré l'eloquence" by "de fades lieux communs" (worn commonplaces) or by "faux raisonnements" (false reasoning) (Norman L. Torrey, *Voltaire and the English Deists* [New Haven: Yale University Press, 1930], p. 46). It seems unlikely that Taine had read much of Tillotson! Tillotson's sermons were translated into French early in the eighteenth century by Barbeyrac, the much esteemed translator of Pufendorf and Grotius, and there were also several German editions. It is also difficult to comprehend an assessment like Cragg's in *From Puritanism to the Age of Reason* (pp. 10, 82–85): During the Restoration, "many of the influential figures were second-rate in their ability, and made no striking contribution because they had no original insight. Tillotson's ponderous folios are a cogent demonstration that where there is no vision the people perish." Tillotson was certainly not an original or deep thinker, on the order of, let us say, Henry More. But in a history of the Anglican clergy, he would rank in the top ten percent of the whole group.

troversy. Or, to put this last point differently, it came to be accepted that originality of argument and clear reasoning, not rhetorical embellishment or the mustering of citations from old texts, were the proper bases for effective persuasion. Lucidity, common sense, and simplicity—I should say a very deceptive simplicity in the case of Tillotson—became the hallmarks of the new enlightened prose, such as is found in Addison's essays and in Benjamin Franklin. This new mode of religious discourse depended upon the implicit principle, Cartesian in origin, that clear reasoning can stand entirely on its own. Tillotson himself went to great lengths in his sermons to expound the point that certain principles of reason, as well as certain principles of natural religion, are absolute preconditions not only of Christianity but of any religion whatsoever. Without a foundation in reason shared by both God and man, there can be no communication at all between the two.

504

These two doctrines, the revelatory character of nature, particularly human nature, and the autonomy of reason, contained within themselves tremendous power for bringing about decisive change in every area of life. Presented baldly, however, as sometimes they were, they could never have been positively received in New England in 1690. But the new wine came in familiar old bottles, in sermons like Tillotson's; and what, after all, can be safer than a sermon? The peculiar magic of Tillotson lay in the subtlety and shrewdness of the philosophy that was hidden beneath the exterior of ingenuousness and simplicity. I am not suggesting that Tillotson was a skeptic or deist in disguise—far from it—but that his logical intelligence, inventiveness, and perceptiveness again and again carried him unwittingly beyond the limits of his mission as a churchman.[52] Thus, his rational argumentation in the service

52 Gerard Reedy, S.J., in a book review (see n. 59, below) correctly warns against treating Tillotson as some sort of proto-freethinker: "Tillotson is, without a doubt, a moralist; he stresses that one is primarily a Christian by one's moral conduct. Yet we must always qualify this by an awareness of his Trinitarian defenses: he willingly espouses a Christianity that is more than simple ethics, that has a necessary core-dogma, and that cannot be derived ... from and by the natural reason of man" (*Eighteenth-Century Studies* 12 [1978–79]: 239).

of Protestant orthodoxy ended up unintentionally nourishing such characteristic elements of enlightenment as naturalism, skepticism, and utilitarian moralism.[53]

The proof of this claim is best found in the sermons themselves, which are still quite readable today, making allowances of course for the limitations of the genre. Even if one were to dismiss—as mere disarming subterfuge or as a zest for delicious irony—David Hume's crediting of Tillotson with the invention of the essential argument behind Hume's critique of the Christian doctrine of miracles, there are other examples of Tillotson's enduring intellectual influence. In 1690 he preached before Queen Mary a sermon on the doctrine of hell that aroused considerable controversy in its time. It was intended to be a defense of the orthodox teaching that the damned would suffer an eternity of hell torments, but in the course of presenting his own arguments, Tillotson along the way undermined nearly every one of the traditional defenses, providing dangerous ammunition thereby to the opponents of hell's eternity, and even to the opponents of the whole idea

505

[53] Tillotson and his ilk have been unpopular with men of stricter (I would not say greater) Christian faith than theirs—like William Law and Whitefield and high church men in the eighteenth century, the Oxford Movement in the nineteenth century, and neo-orthodoxy in the twentieth (the latter of which strongly influenced Perry Miller)—and at the same time, lacking the philosophical rigor of some of his great successors in the church, like Bishops Berkeley and Butler, he has been ignored by philosophers. Henry May, *American Enlightenment*, p. 14, notes rightly that Perry Miller has prejudiced many readers against Arminianism. It has "been treated somewhat contemptuously by modern American historians, following the lead of Perry Miller. It has often been made synonymous with a smooth and bland avoidance of difficult questions. Actually, like all major religious tendencies, it attracted many kinds of people." For high church reaction against Tillotson in eighteenth-century America, see Samuel Johnson (of Stratford, Conn.) to George Berkeley, Jr., 10 December 1756: "As to Tillotson I have myself been heretofore a great admirer of his sermons, but for these several years have been sensible of the ill effects of them in these parts as well as some others worse than they much here in vogue and done my best to guard against them but as he has long been in possession, it will not do here to speak against him with much acrimony except among Methodists" (Herbert and Carol Schneider, eds., *Career and Writings of Samuel Johnson*, 4 vols. [New York: Columbia University Press, 1929], 2:339). As Norman Sykes has observed, the Latitudinarians, rejected by both high church non-jurors and pietistic Methodists, "have received double for their sins" from critics and historians (*Church and State in England in the Eighteenth Century* [New York: Octagon Books, 1975; orig. publ. 1935]).

of hell. What is remarkable is that fifty years later the reasoning in this sermon was still sufficiently vital to lead Jonathan Edwards to make a special case of refuting it. Moreover, if one carefully follows this debate between the deceased Tillotson and the living Edwards, it is clear that on grounds of logic alone Tillotson had the stronger position.[54] Edwards in fact simply evaded some of the most telling points in Tillotson's critique. In this sermon, as in many others he preached, Tillotson was an advocate of the idea that in God's attention to man the divine attribute of benevolence is constantly active, a notion that the church historian Norman Sykes believes was transmitted to the eighteenth century above all through Tillotson's writings. "Tillotson's sermon on the text, 'And His commandments are not grievous,' became the general theme of his age," according to Sykes.[55]

Tillotson had a faculty for looking at the usual or prescribed conceptual relationships between such things as religion and morals, religion and society, religion and God, and then inverting them. The results, naturally, were unconventional, but more representative, perhaps, of the deepest perceptions of his time than the old formulas.[56] In any case, Til-

[54] *The Works of President Edwards*, 4 vols. (New York, 1879), 4:275. This was not the only time that Edwards took note of Tillotson, whom he called "one of the greatest divines," although Edwards disagreed with Tillotson on nearly everything. Edwards also quoted from Tillotson in his *Discourses on Various Important Subjects* (Boston, 1738), and mentioned him early in his "Catalogue" of reading.

[55] Norman Sykes, "Theology of Divine Benevolence," *Historical Magazine of the Protestant Episcopal Church* 16 (1947): 278–91. See also by Sykes, "The Sermons of Archbishop Tillotson," *Theology* 58 (1955): 297–302, and *From Sheldon to Secker: Aspects of English Church History, 1660–1768* (Cambridge: Cambridge University Press, 1959), pp. 176–81.

[56] One cannot improve on Sir Leslie Stephen's great statement in *History of English Thought in the Eighteenth Century*, 2 vols. (New York: Harcourt, Brace and World, 1962; orig. publ. 1876), 1:v–vi. Stephen refers to Tillotson as the "writer of the seventeenth century who was most generally read and admired in the eighteenth," and then goes on: "The unconsciousness with which men like Tillotson put forward arguments capable of being turned against themselves explains one secret of their strength. If Protestantism was unintentionally acting as a screen for rationalism, rationalism naturally expressed itself in terms of Protestantism. Whatever, that is, was gained by reason was gained by the Protestants. The intellect, though it had broken the old barriers,

lotson evidently believed that Christianity was strengthened as a result of his ingenuity. The theory by which Benjamin Franklin, in the 1730s, was able to reconcile the absolutism of divine moral commandments with earthly prudence—that certain actions are bad not because they are forbidden by revelation, but they are forbidden by revelation because they are "bad for us," and that other actions are good not because they are commanded by revelation but because they are "beneficial to us, in their own Natures"—had already been suggested by Tillotson before Franklin was born in a sermon entitled, "Objections Against the True Religion Answered" (Sermon XXVIII).[57] The law of God, Tillotson wrote, "requires nothing of us, but what is recommended to us by our own reason, and from the benefit and advantage of doing it." This is evident, Tillotson argued, because God commands "nothing but what is much more for our own interest to do it, than it can be for God's to command it." The presumption of that statement is well worth pondering. It was not the only time Tillotson undertook to explain God's reasoning. The basic idea is that since every command must be in the interest of someone, and

507

---

was still, to a great degree, running in the old channels. Content with clearing away the grosser superstitions, it gave fresh life to the central beliefs. The vigour of English theology at this period—and it was the golden period of English theology—is due to the fact that, for a time, reason and Christian theology were in spontaneous alliance."

[57] Leonard Labaree et al., eds., *The Autobiography of Benjamin Franklin* (New Haven: Yale University Press, 1964), p. 115. This idea was widespread in the early eighteenth century. "The morality of actions does not, I think, consist in this," Bolingbroke wrote, "that they are prescribed by will, even the will of God; but in this, that they are the means, however imposed the practice of them may be, of acquiring happiness agreeable to our nature" ("Essay Concerning Authority in Matters of Religion," in *Works* [London, 1754], 4:285, quoted in Charles Vereker, *Eighteenth-Century Optimism: A Study of the Interrelations of Moral and Social Theory in English and French Thought between 1689 and 1789* [Liverpool, England: Liverpool University Press, 1967], p. 116). The great wisdom of God appears in this, Matthew Tindal wrote, that he made "men's misery and happiness the necessary and inseparable consequence of their actions, and that rational actions carry with them their own reward, and irrational their own punishment" (*Christianity as Old as the Creation* [London, 1730], chap. 3). For words almost identical to Franklin's see John Clarke of Hull, *Foundation of Morality* (York, England, 1726), p. 17.

God's commands can hardly be in His own interest, then they must be in the interest of mankind; therefore, it followed, what is not in the evident interest of mankind cannot be a command from God.

In a 1681 sermon (no. XXII) on "The Lawfullness and Obligation of Oaths," which attacked Quakers and other sects that on biblical grounds refused to take oaths (see Matthew 5:33–34), Tillotson, as usual, argued not only from Scripture but from the reason of the thing. He pointed to the "great usefulness of oaths in human affairs, to give credit and confirmation to our word, and to put an end to contestations." That which serves "such excellent purposes, and is so convenient for human society, . . . ought not easily to be presumed unlawful," Tillotson wrote. And then he went a step further, in his peculiar fashion, and introduced a principle that was manifestly dangerous to the foundations of traditional religion and yet one that might also be considered statesmanlike. Those who on scriptural grounds alone reject oaths, he said, run the risk of bringing discredit on the wisdom of the Christian religion, given the evident civic utility of oaths. How can one "vindicate the divine wisdom of our Saviour's doctrine, and the reasonableness of the christian religion," Tillotson asked, and still deny the lawfulness of oaths? For Tillotson, clearly, Christianity was in grave danger when it contradicted social utility and practical wisdom. Tillotson already assumed, perhaps, that in the modern world religion would have to justify itself by its usefulness for earthly human happiness and by its benefits for society. It was a teaching his audience of London merchants was undoubtedly ready for.

Tillotson, indeed, may have been the first modern to suggest that the idea of God is so necessary to society that men would have had to invent Him if He did not already exist. The Christian religion, Tillotson believed, is not only necessary to the welfare of society but is particularly fitted for the support of the needs of men. Religion, he said, "is the strongest band of human society, and so necessary to the welfare and happiness of mankind, as it could not have been more, if we could suppose the Being of God himself to have been purposely designed and contrived for the benefit and advantage of men."[58]

Tillotson was also one of the earliest theological writers to argue that a true conception of the deity must be framed in accordance with the most favorable picture of human nature. "I am as certain," he wrote, that the doctrine of predestined reprobation "cannot be of God as I am that God is good and just, because this [doctrine] grates upon the notion that mankind have of goodness and justice. This is that which no good man would do, and therefore it cannot be believed of infinite goodness." The personal assurance of each believer that, in human terms, God is good and just must outweigh "subtle speculations about predestination and the decrees of God."[59]

509

Many other examples could be given of Tillotson's technique, by which criteria other than those from the traditional legacy of theology were quietly employed to answer the needs of religion, as he saw those needs. The effect in both America and England was a general loosening of the traditional categories of discussion. More kinds of evidence were allowable in debating and defending the fundamental questions of religion, and criteria such as individual reason, common sense, prudence, utility, philosophical analysis, and even biological nature were brought to the task. Tillotson, it may be recalled, like Jean-Jacques Rousseau years later, was a great advocate of breastfeeding by the natural mother of the infant.

This, I foresee, will seem a very hard saying to nice and delicate mothers, who prefer their own ease and pleasure to the fruit of their own bodies. But whether they will hear or whether they will forbear, I think myself obliged to deal plainly in this matter, and to be so faithful as to tell them that this is a natural duty, and, be-

[58] Sermon XXVII, "The Protestant Religion Vindicated from the Charge of Singularity and Novelty," preached before the king, 1680. See David D. Brown, "Voltaire, Archbishop Tillotson, and the Invention of God," *Revue de Littérature Comparée* 34 (1960): 257–61.

[59] See Sykes, "Theology of Divine Benevolence," pp. 278–91.

cause it is so, of a more necessary and indispensable obligation than any positive precept of revealed religion. . . .[60]

The duties instilled by nature! Tillotson could not know what a Pandora's box that was to be, and he urged these duties uncompromisingly again and again. One can imagine consternation in many parts of seventeenth-century America when these lines from the pen of an English bishop were first read:

510

> It plainly appears what place natural and moral duties ought to have in the christian religion; and of all natural duties, "mercy and goodness." This is so primary a duty of human nature; so great and considerable a part of religion, that all positive institutions must give way to it, and nothing of that kind can cancel the obligation to it, nor justify the violation of this great and natural law. . . . The law of mercy and humanity, which is the law of nature, ought not to be violated for the promoting of any positive institution. . . . I had rather never administer the sacrament, nor ever receive it, than take away any man's life about it; because the sacrament is but a positive rite and institution of the christian religion, and God prefers mercy, which is a duty of natural religion, before any rite or institution whatsoever.[61]

The appeal to nature and reason in the context of the Latitudinarian Christian sermon was the primary medium by which New England was eased into the enlightenment; nothing more radical than that. "He who would persuade a man

[60] James Moffatt, ed., *The Golden Book of Tillotson, Selections* . . . (Westport, Conn.: Greenwood Press, 1971; orig. publ. 1926), pp. 140–43. This work is a compendium of snippets from Tillotson's sermons. The best modern study of Tillotson's sermons is Irène Simon, *Three Restoration Divines: Barrow, South, Tillotson: Selected Sermons*, 2 pts. in 3 vols. (Paris, 1967–76), which contains a very thorough introduction, both bibliographical and substantive, and a reprinting of nine of Tillotson's sermons. The review of this work by Gerard Reedy, S.J., in *Eighteenth-Century Studies* 12 (1978–79): 234–41, is an essential supplement to it. The Puritans generally urged breastfeeding of infants but tended to back it up by biblical exegesis rather than the authority of nature. (See R. V. Schnucker, "The English Puritans and Pregnancy, Delivery, and Breastfeeding," *History of Childhood Quarterly* 1 [1974]: 644–50.) One wonders if Tillotson's attitude was affected at all by the interesting fact that he was the first archbishop of Canterbury in a century who was married.

[61] Sermon CIII, "Instituted religion not intended to undermine natural."

or prevail with him to do anything," Tillotson wrote, "must do it one of three ways, either by entreaty or authority or argument." Of these three, Tillotson relied on the third. It is "preposterous," he believed, "to entreat men to believe anything or to charge them to do so" before they are "convinced . . . by sufficient arguments that it is reasonable to do so." "I cannot imagine," he wrote, "how men can do greater disservice to religion than by taking it off from the rational and solid basis upon which it stands" and maintain that "men ought to believe without reason; for this is to turn faith into credulity. . . ."[62]

511

While Tillotson lived, and while John Leverett lived, nature and reason, although indubitably autonomous, could be trusted to be dutiful children in the service of their parent, English Protestantism. It was not long thereafter, however, before they became unruly adolescents, casting the household of comfortable American religious belief into chaos.

[62] Tillotson emphasized rational persuasion, but it would be a mistake to assume that he could not be affecting. William Byrd II, who read Tillotson regularly, wrote in his diary on 7 May 1710: "I read a sermon of Dr. Tillotson's which affected me very much and made me shed some tears of repentence." On 21 May he wrote: "I read two sermons in Tillotson, which edified me very much." (See *The Secret Diary of William Byrd of Westover, 1709–1712*, ed. Louis B. Wright and Marion Tinling [Richmond, Va.: The Dietz Press, 1941].)

The Meeting of Elite and Popular
Minds at Cambridge, New England,
1638-1645

George Selement

IN documenting the forces that shaped seventeenth-century New
England, many twentieth-century historians have focused on intellectual influences. Perry Miller and those inspired by him have ably
defined the region according to the Puritan ideas of publishing ministers,
assigning nonideological factors to lesser roles. A few historians—most
notably Richard L. Bushman, John Demos, Richard P. Gildrie, Philip J.
Greven, Kenneth A. Lockridge, Sumner Chilton Powell, and Darrett B.
Rutman—have emphasized the social dynamics behind the behavior of
New Englanders. Jon Butler has been the most extreme in his departure
from intellectual history, positing that to understand the "marrow of
American religious life" historians "need to move beyond the study of
ecclesiology, theology, and the ministry to recover noninstitutional religious practices."[1]

Generally, these historians have published their research as a contribution to ongoing and collective scholarship, each adding different pieces to
the historiographical mosaic that constitutes the profession's knowledge of
early America. Yet these practitioners of social and intellectual history
have also sparred over methodology. Procedural differences certainly
rankled Miller in 1933, inciting him to remark defensively: "I lay myself
open to the charge of being so naive as to believe that the way men think
has some influence upon their actions." Even in 1959—when intellectual
history in general and Miller's interpretations in particular were in
vogue—methodological issues haunted Miller more than ever. "But those
who strive," he wrote, "to escape all concept of the mind by playing down
the majesty and coherence of Puritan thinking, level a barrage against
early New England infinitely more Philistine—not to say historically
inaccurate—than the comparatively innocent fulminations in the 1920's of
Mencken and James Truslow Adams."[2]

Mr. Selement is a member of the Department of History at Southwest Missouri
State University.

[1] Butler, "Magic, Astrology, and the Early American Religious Heritage; 1600-
1760," *American Historical Review*, LXXXIV (1979), 317-318.

[2] Perry Miller, *Orthodoxy in Massachusetts, 1630-1650* (New York, 1970 [orig.
publ. Cambridge, Mass., 1933]), xxv, xxxiv. Miller's *The New England Mind: The*

In the 1960s a new generation of social historians fulfilled Miller's worst fears. Young Rutman, for example, combatively attacked the work of intellectual historians, writing that Miller at times violated "sound historical method" and that some of Edmund S. Morgan's interpretations were "open to serious question." To correct these established scholars, social historians played down the world of ministerial ideas and defined the region by the "man in the village lane," relying largely on nonliterary sources for documentation. By 1970, however, social historians had earned a respectable, if not prestigious, niche in the profession and consequently were able to labor more compatibly with intellectual historians. In *American Puritanism* Rutman offered a paradigm for bridging the gap between the "two schools of thought . . . , one devoted to New England as a Puritan *idea,* the other devoted to the study of New England as a *society.*" More recently, he has informed me that the approaches of social and intellectual historians were attempts "to bridge the same chasm, simply working from opposite sides." David D. Hall, a leader among intellectual historians, concurs: "There is, and is not, a debate; or rather, different persons might construe the issue, or debate, in various fashions." Even Greven, whose Andover book is the most demographic of the published town studies, has combined in *The Protestant Temperament* the methodologies of both social and intellectual historians.[3]

513

Despite this trend to collegiality and sharing of methods, doubts remain. Rutman again: "At the risk of isolating extremes I will say that too many of my friends persist in ignoring ideas altogether while too many 'ideologues' seem to think Miller's reputation is the only question." As late as 1979, Hall lamented that "the discovery of collective mentality" by social historians "is being used as a weapon against intellectual history." And Greven's reliance on the imaginative interpretation of literary evidence rather than empirical deductions grounded in statistics about class led one reviewer to deem his work "almost perverse." As to the "ideologues" Rutman mentioned, James Hoopes now represents those especially concerned about the "unfortunate impact" on Miller's reputa-

---

Seventeenth Century (Cambridge, Mass., 1939) ranked an impressive eighth in "Preferred Works in American History, 1936-1950"; see John Walton Caughey, "Historians' Choice: Results of a Poll on Recently Published American History and Biography," *Mississippi Valley Historical Review,* XXXIX (1952), 300.

[3] Darrett B. Rutman, *Winthrop's Boston: Portrait of a Puritan Town, 1630-1649* (Chapel Hill, N.C., 1965), 284; "God's Bridge Falling Down: 'Another Approach' to New England Puritanism Assayed," *William and Mary Quarterly,* 3d Ser., XIX (1962), 409; "The Mirror of Puritan Authority," in George Athan Billias, ed., *Law and Authority in Colonial America* (Barre, Mass., 1965), 163; and *American Puritanism: Faith and Practice* (Philadelphia, 1970), vi. Rutman to Selement, Nov. 12, 1981; Hall to Selement, Nov. 15, 1981. Philip J. Greven, Jr., *Four Generations: Population, Land, and Family in Colonial Andover, Massachusetts* (Ithaca, N.Y., 1970), and *The Protestant Temperament: Patterns of Child-Rearing, Religious Experience, and the Self in Early America* (New York, 1977).

tion.⁴ The most striking illustration of the methodological chasm that sometimes divides social and intellectual historians can be seen by comparing the contents of "Special Issue: Approaches and Methods in Early American History" in *Historical Methods*, XIII, No. 1 (1980) with any issue of *Early American Literature*.

This essay seeks to close further whatever gap there still may be between social and intellectual historians by clarifying, as Hall puts it, "the distance that exists between elites or intellectuals and other groups." By comparing the thought and experience of Thomas Shepard, prolific author and minister at Cambridge, with his parishioners' understanding of his ideas, it is possible to measure the degree to which we must not, as Rutman concluded, "ascribe the ministers' Puritanism to the laymen and let it go at that." Or, approaching "the same chasm" from Hall's side, we can determine just how much the rhetoric of clerics was "intrinsic to a collective mentality they shared with ordinary people." Both these scholars have declared this type of investigation to be the "task that lies ahead," and the recent publication of *Thomas Shepard's "Confessions"* by the Colonial Society of Massachusetts offers an excellent opportunity to test the "formulas, the assumptions, that comprise collective mentality in seventeenth-century New England."⁵

Shepard's *"Confessions"* contains relations of faith by fifty-one persons applying for church membership at Cambridge between 1638 and 1645. Its great strength is that Shepard faithfully recorded their testimonies, thus preserving the minds and experiences of his parishioners. He did not revise their public narrations, opting to miss a few words and phrases rather than risk editorial distortions. Of course, many of the laymen, probably testifying without notes and in fear of an embarrassing long pause, were like Nathaniel Sparrowhawk, an affluent landowner, who even after making an average number of points regarding his path to grace admitted: "I cannot remember many things which I cannot now express myself." Ellen Greene, wife of wealthy Percival, spoke only five sentences. In her case, Shepard recorded, "testimonies carried it." These testimonies were character references wherein "one, two, or three, or more of the Brethren speak their opinions of the party . . . and that they are willing . . . for their part, to given him the right hand of fellowship."⁶

⁴ Rutman to Selement, Nov. 12, 1981; David D. Hall, "The World of Print and Collective Mentality in Seventeenth-Century New England," in John Higham and Paul K. Conkin, eds., *New Directions in American Intellectual History* (Baltimore, 1979), 166-167; Christopher Lasch, Review of Philip Greven, *The Protestant Temperament*, *WMQ*, 3d Ser., XXXVI (1979), 291; Hoopes, "Art as History: Perry Miller's *New England Mind*," *American Quarterly*, XXXIV (1982), 14n.

⁵ Hall, "World of Print," in Higham and Conkin, eds., *New Directions*, 166, 177; Rutman, *American Puritanism*, 33; George Selement and Bruce C. Woolley, eds., *Thomas Shepard's "Confessions"* (Colonial Society of Massachusetts, *Collections*, LVIII [Boston, 1981]), hereafter cited as *"Confessions."*

⁶ *"Confessions,"* 64, 118; Thomas Lechford, *Plain Dealing; Or News from New England* (1642), ed. J. Hammond Trumbull (Boston, 1867), 21-22. Sparrowhawk

Other laymen, whose relations end abruptly, even sometimes in mid-sentence, may have been prompted by Shepard, who stopped writing in order to lead them with questions and reminders. After all, these narrations served a didactic function, and Shepard wanted each one to be exemplary for the sake of both the confessor and the congregation. All but four confessions include numerous references to Shepard's theological and experiential models. Thus the relations, when juxtaposed with Shepard's writings, offer an opportunity to compare the thinking of forty-eight laymen with that of one ministerial representative.

Before making that comparison, however, several caveats are in order. Prima facie, the testifiers appear to be common folk—representatives of people in the village lane. They were laymen, except for two heads of Harvard College, Nathaniel Eaton and Henry Dunster, and one ministerial student, William Ames. John Jones was also somewhat exceptional as the Harvard-bound son of a minister, John Jones of Concord. All the other twenty-four men but young Roger Haynes, son of Gov. John Haynes, were farmers who sometimes practiced other trades to supplement their income. The twenty-two women were housewives, save for two maidservants. The literacy rate of the group conforms to what Lockridge found to be typical of first-generation New Englanders.[7]

Yet these Cambridge residents were unrepresentative in significant ways. First, they wanted to be members of a Puritan church and thus do not represent the many secular and dissenting New Englanders.[8] Furthermore, they prepared themselves to be members of a particular congregation, Shepard's flock, and no doubt tailored their confessions to win his approval. Thus their views may have varied from those of laymen influenced by other ministers who, like Thomas Hooker of Hartford, differed with Shepard on points of theology and church admission requirements. Indeed, several collective mentalities may have existed in

mentioned 20 points relevant to Shepard's theology, which is 5 more than the average of 15 (737 responses ÷ 48 laymen). Including biblical references, Sparrowhawk's score of 24 is just below the average of 25 (1,200 ÷ 48). The four who said little in their confessions were Christopher Cane (9 responses), Mrs. Greene (1), Hannah Brewer (5), and John Furnell (5).

[7] Twelve confessors testified in various ways to their literacy, 4 more left books in their wills, 4 others studied or taught at Harvard, an additional 2 signed their wills, and Roger Haynes, because of his social class, must have been educated. Woolley and I were unable to find any data about the literacy of the other 28 candidates except for Nicholas Wyeth, who put his "mark" on his will and thus—by Kenneth A. Lockridge's standard—would have been illiterate. On the basis of this evidence, 18 men (64%) and 5 women (23%) were literate, a finding that parallels Lockridge's estimate that in 1650 60% of the men and 30% of the women in New England were literate (*Literacy in Colonial New England: An Enquiry into the Social Context of Literacy in the Early Modern West* [New York, 1974], 39).

[8] Estimates vary on the number of these non-Puritans; cf. Samuel Eliot Morison, *Builders of the Bay Colony* (Boston, 1930), 339-346, and Rutman, *Winthrop's Boston*, 146-147.

New England based on ideological differences between congregations. The *"Confessions,"* therefore, only documents the degree to which one group of laymen in New England reflected the thought of their pastor, leaving open the question whether New England thought was the "product of a single intelligence."[9]

Even in measuring the degree to which Shepard's parishioners reflected his particular thought, difficulties abound because Shepard's was one of several influences that shaped the minds of these laymen. All of them lived in England before coming to Massachusetts and had heard ministers there. For instance, Nicholas Wyeth, a mason of Mellis in Suffolk, traveled four miles to hear Robert Selby at Bedfield, sixteen miles to listen to Jeremiah Burroughs at Bury St. Edmunds, and twenty miles for a sermon by one Mr. Rogers. Once in the Bay Colony, many listened to and conferred with preachers in other towns. These sermon-gadders made 106 references to such clergymen in their confessions, as compared to only 17 mentions of Shepard. On the surface, this might seem to preclude comparing their ideas with Shepard's, for perhaps other pastors were more important, but several factors prove otherwise. First, when laymen paraphrased these numerous Puritan ministers, they selectively recited points that paralleled Shepard's thought. The laity, therefore, either perceived—or believed that Shepard wanted them to perceive—a doctrinal consensus among the clergy regarding the path to grace. Consequently, the candidates seldom focused on the theological nuances that separated "Puritan" from "Puritan," thereby supporting the cherished ministerial notion that the Puritan brotherhood preached the same about uniting with Christ, using means, and looking for signs. Second, the fact that they might first have heard about conviction from Thomas Jenner of Heddon, Northumberland, heard it again from John Wilson of Boston, and finally listened to Shepard elaborate on it sabbath after sabbath in no way vitiates Shepard's influence. And if they had heard three versions of conviction, the fact that they drew material from such differing accounts only to reinforce Shepard's version further documents the tailoring of their confessions to Shepard's beliefs. Third, that they failed to mention Shepard's name in their testimonies suggests that the congregation recognized Shepard as a prime mover behind these narrations, and sensitivity to his modesty may well have led them to refrain from identifying him. The *"Confessions"* clearly reveals other indications of his influence, such as the many references to the parable of ten virgins, the primary text for Shepard's sermons between 1636 and 1640.[10]

The web of exchange among laymen is also critical to understanding the meeting of popular and elite minds. Thirty-eight (75 percent) of the confessors made a total of 104 references to the influence of laymen in

---

[9] Lechford, *Plain Dealing,* ed. Trumbull, 18-19; Miller, *New England Mind: The Seventeenth Century,* vii. On pluralism in New England see Michael McGiffert, "American Puritan Studies in the 1960's," *WMQ,* 3d Ser., XXVII (1970), 40-42.

[10] *"Confessions,"* 194; Rutman, *American Puritanism,* 36.

their conversion experience: 26 citations to relatives, 54 to godly laymen, and 24 to bad examples. Although Richard Eccles, before moving to Yorkshire, was "brought up in popery" and William Hamlet, a London carpenter, was "brought up ignorantly," others praised their "godly parents" who took "much pain" that their children might "be born again." Sometimes it was the "speech of a sister who said she was going to means and I going from it" that stirred a young heart or, as in the case of Katherine, Mrs. Russell's servant, an aunt: "First I went on in ignorance and had no means of light. So I went to an aunt who did, and where I was made by her to seek the means, praying with us before we went to the word." Still others, like Martha Collins, learned of ministerial ideas through their spouses. "By my husband's speaking," she testified, "I saw my original corruption and miserable condition and so had a hungering after means which were most searching." Such confessions confirm Morgan's emphasis on the importance of the family in transmitting Puritanism to the laity.[11] Yet, it is clear that some became Puritans in spite of their families, others looked to relatives other than parents, and a substantial number (twenty-nine, or 57 percent) mentioned no family member in their relations of faith.

517

People in the community played an even greater role than families in the laity's decisions about converting to Puritanism. In England, where these confessors spent their youth, there was no shortage of "loose company," "bad examples," and "young and rude and wicked" who liked to "scoff" at Puritan clerics, get tipsy, and do "much hurt" to would-be saints. Some confessors, before conversion, joined with the scoffers. "As I grew in years," reported John Stansby, a farmer and clothier in England, "I sought a match for my lust; and herein I have been like the devil not only to hell myself but enticing and haling others to sin, rejoicing when I could make others drink and sin." Others seesawed, embracing the ways and views of those closest to them. Edward Collins of Bramford, Suffolk, for example, learned "fundamentals" from his father's catechizing, then moved to "a gentleman's house, a profane house," where he "contracted much guilt to [his] soul," and next went to "old Mr. Rogers of Wethersfield . . . stayed a year and got some good." Still others, revolted by the wicked from the outset, became stronger in their faith. When William Hamlet heard "God's name blasphemed in old England," he could "not endure" the blasphemers and so "annoyed them." Likewise, Edward Shepard, a mariner in England, reported: "Being sent out to sea I could not continue at means and there I was laughed at because I would not drink and break Sabbath as they used to do. And the Lord in this condition I thought—blessed are you when men revile you and persecute you."[12] More important than the influence of sinners, as twice the number of

---

[11] "Confessions," 115, 125, 82, 62, 188, 39, 99, 130-131; Edmund S. Morgan, *The Puritan Family: Religion & Domestic Relations in Seventeenth-Century New England*, rev. ed. (New York, 1966), 87.

[12] "Confessions," 36, 93, 204, 161, 36, 199, 86, 82, 127, 173.

references suggests, was "godly men's company." Mary Angier of Dedham, Essex, vividly recalled the intervention of a saintly neighbor who spoke "of her condition, coming to her and wishing her to leave the Lord to His own ways, telling her that it may be the Lord would let her see her blindness and hardness and God that way work and that she was God's clay." The neighbor asked Angier "if she sought God in private," causing Angier to confess that she had not done so "for some weeks" and to resolve to "set upon it again." Even more striking is the testimony of John Jones. Though the preaching of his father, John, and Peter Bulkeley, both ministers at Concord, first awakened John, a local shepherd also played a vital role in young Jones's conversion. "Going to the fields to recreate," John met another youth who "used to keep cattle." He often found that shepherd "weeping of catechism" and testifying that "the Lord doth break off soul from sin by contrition and self by humiliation and here showed how the Lord leaves the soul to be wearied in itself and end was to bring off soul from self." Consequently, Jones came to have "some hope the Lord might bring me off self unto the Lord Jesus." Here is a splendid example of a humble shepherd influenced by a ministerial publication—a catechism—who in turn teaches the son of a minister (who later would attend Harvard and become himself a minister) about the doctrines of contrition and humiliation, even using the terms of the clergy. In addition to such encounters, groups of laymen met to discuss Puritan beliefs. While in England, John Stedman, a servant, "was admitted to private societies of saints" where he "found much sweetness." Lay meetings appeared in New England, too: Anne Hutchinson's troubles can be traced to such gatherings at Boston. Lay culture thus was a web of interactions between sinners and saints as each group sought to win converts.[13]

Just as with the influence of ministers other than Shepard, lay witnessing often reinforced clerical preaching in general and Shepard's in particular. John Sill's testimony certainly supports this conclusion: "Some told him of Mr. S[hepard] but he [Sill] thought things could not be so as reports went. Men might admire but it was not so." Despite his "prejudicial opinion," Sill went to hear Shepard, took notes on two sermons, discussed them with others, and one "night in prayer" became "convinced of that sin in being set against" Shepard. The other fifty-three references to godly laymen also reflect Shepard's preaching about preparing for grace by living in harmony with the saints. John Fessenden summarized Puritan preaching on this point as follows: "And hearing how those are drawn to Christ: (1) by word, (2) then by motions of Spirit, (3) examples of saints, (4) sacraments; and so I went in use of means." Hamlet put it more simply: "One thing the Lord supported my heart by was love to the brethren." Shepard's own path to grace, which he must have used as a model for those who conferred with him, conformed to this pattern. "When I did light in

[13] *Ibid.*, 111, 67, 201, 74; Emery Battis, *Saints and Sectaries: Anne Hutchinson and the Antinomian Controversy in the Massachusetts Bay Colony* (Chapel Hill, N.C., 1962), 90-92, 101, 103.

godly company," he recalled, "I heard them discourse about the wrath of God and the terror of it. . . . And this did much awaken me, and I began to pray again."[14] Puritan ideas rang from the pulpit, spread by word of mouth among the laity, and reappeared in the testimonies of candidates for church membership.

But just how much did these Cambridge parishioners embrace Shepard's model of conversion? Their emphasis on feelings or religious experiences reflected Shepard's counsel in two ways. He taught that "a man having a form of this knowledge in his head, he may be able to express such, and make a large confession of his faith, discourse of points of controversy in matters that concern Christ, and justification by Christ, etc., and instruct others, and yet having no more, know not, all this while, what the Lord Jesus is." In contrast to hypocrites of this sort, true saints enjoyed a "shining into the heart," which only Christ "in spite of Satan, reveals to his people." In a word, candidates had to demonstrate that they had truly experienced conviction, compunction, humiliation, and vocation rather than simply display a knowledge of such doctrines. Moreover, their vacillations between despondency and joy paralleled Shepard's ups-and-downs on the way to grace. Elizabeth Olbon, for example, "thought it impossible so poor a creature should be saved" but later "witnessed the Lord's love to her," just as Shepard, according to his autobiography, experienced "strong temptations" to suicide but eventually found "a heart to receive Christ." Perhaps the laity simply modeled their narrations after Shepard's, having listened in private conferences to his account of closing with Christ. But these sequences of anguish and relief were also the practical application of formal Puritan theology. Saints had to sense sin's evil (conviction), tremble in fear and despair for sin (compunction), abandon self-confidence (humiliation), and accept the call of Christ (vocation). Nor was this to occur all at once; these were stages in a process that went on for a long time as the Holy Spirit gradually prepared the elect. It is not surprising, then, that Henry Dunster, a minister who wanted to instruct as well as testify, was the only confessor who divided his relation into a recitation of dogma and an account of "the Lord's personal dealing with my soul."[15]

519

In all, these laymen displayed a remarkable knowledge of Shepard's theology of conversion. They made 1,200 references to salvific doctrines, frequently citing basic tenets like conviction (177) but also mentioning obscurer points like the signs of being under the creature.[16] Furthermore,

[14] "Confessions," 47, 176, 126; John A. Albro, ed., The Works of Thomas Shepard . . . (Boston, 1853), II, 564-565; Michael McGiffert, ed., God's Plot: The Paradoxes of Puritan Piety, Being the Autobiography & Journal of Thomas Shepard (Amherst, Mass., 1972), 41.

[15] Albro, ed., Works, II, 122, 124-125; "Confessions," 40, 41, 156, 161; McGiffert, ed., God's Plot, 43, 46.

[16] Because Eaton, Dunster, and Ames were Harvard men or ministers or both, I have omitted their scores from statistics describing the laity's understanding of Shepard's theology.

the factors of sex, literacy, and wealth made no significant impact on the laity's comprehension and recollection of Shepard's preaching. Men made only a few more references to Shepard's doctrines than did women. The illiterate only slightly excelled the literate, and their performances are skewed quantitatively because of the small number of literate females (one of whom panicked and said little in her relation) and the long confession of Nicholas Wyeth, an illiterate male, who spoke much because of the many questions asked him by suspicious peers. Poorer laymen recalled more of Shepard's theology than did the wealthy, but again the difference is statistically insignificant. Likewise, all combinations of wealth and literacy are inconsequential, especially if categories with fewer than four people are justifiably omitted.[17] The *"Confessions"* documents that Cambridge laymen lived in an oral culture, where ministers transmitted elite ideas through sermons and private counsel to receptive laymen. They in turn passed such notions among themselves by word of mouth. The laity's ubiquitous references to "hearing" this-or-that or so-and-so press home this conclusion.[18]

520

Combining statistical data on lay references to Shepard's doctrines with quotation of the *"Confessions"* favors the perspective of those historians who, like Hall and Rutman, have been laboring "to bridge the same chasm, simply working from opposite sides." Consider election, the first tenet of Shepard's morphology of conversion. Eleven laymen made nineteen allusions to the doctrine and often used proper terminology. Christopher Cane explicitly declared: "And hearing that Christ foresaw all elects' sins past and to come and that they were all charged on Him. Hearing this I thought unless this was for me I was undone." Joanna Sill "found it hard if the Lord should damn her and never show mercy." Yet she was willing "to be content," and Christ ultimately subdued her "cursed will" and enabled her to resolve: "Let Him do what He would." Such statements, and similar ones by Mary Angier, Martha Collins, and the unidentified confessor, indicate that though the question of election troubled a few candidates, it was not, as Perry Miller declared, "driving the

[17] I have omitted Eaton, Dunster, and the anonymous confessor from all calculations about sex, literacy, and wealth. I deem a wealthy parishioner to be one who either came to New England with servants, as in Ellen Greene's case, owned more than 100 acres of land, or left an estate exceeding £200. While the last two criteria may be misleading because the wealth may have been acquired after joining Shepard's congregation, there is no other way to make this estimation. Moreover, New Englanders distributed land in part according to a person's "charge and quality"; thus it is safe to assume that those who acquired large tracts were of the wealthier classes. (See Rutman, *Winthrop's Boston*, 44-45.) John Stedman, a servant to the Rev. Jose Glover, was an exception, but he profited in 1638 from the shipboard death of Glover, who had willed Stedman £50 to venture in land and a store.

[18] I have not bothered to count how many times the laity used the word "hearing," but my impression is that it is one of the most frequently used words in the *"Confessions."*

devout to distraction." Whatever their psychological reaction to the doctrine, clearly 23 percent of the laity embraced—to use Rutman's term—the ideological "gift" imparted by Shepard in his sermons.[19] As to the other 77 percent, their confessions implicitly reflected Shepard's preaching on election. He had taught them that God's election meant that the "number of them that shall be saved is very small." In addition, given his Calvinist position on limited atonement, he had told them that there was a "universal offer to all people where the Gospel comes." This offer was "real" and "free" but "doth not speak absolutely that Christ died for all, and therefore for thee, as the Arminians maintain; but it speaks conditionally; it is for thee, if ever the Lord gives thee a heart to receive that grace there." While no candidate specifically mentioned these tenets, almost all of them recognized that salvation was a matter of God's selectivity. Nathaniel Sparrowhawk's concluding statement was typical: "And the Lord brought to mind the story of withered hand that it was in His power, and I have entreated the Lord to help my unbelief and other things whereby I found my heart enlarged." Likewise, the laity referred to covenant theology, as Shepard recommended, within this context of relying upon God's grace. Sparrowhawk "thought I was cast out of favor of God and yet the Lord made me plead with Him and to remember his covenant."[20] It is certain, then, regarding the main points about election, that those historians are correct who have assumed an approximate equation between the thought of Puritan laymen and their ministers.

521

A similar conclusion emerges from the laity's words on union with Christ, which Shepard expounded as the second step to grace. The candidates alluded 425 times to the key elements of closing with Christ and thereby demonstrated a conceptual understanding of Shepard's preaching on preparation and vocation. But they usually failed to use proper terminology. And whereas Shepard presented his doctrines systematically, the laity randomly mentioned various points—often repeating the same one in different ways and consistently failing to proceed logically from conviction through vocation. Hence a gap existed between candidates and their mentor, as social historians have emphasized, but it was one of vocabulary and logic rather than doctrinal knowledge.

Regarding preparation, laymen rarely employed Shepard's vocabulary of conviction, compunction, and humiliation, but their relations of faith in a hit-and-miss fashion mirror those conceptions. The candidates recalled parts of Shepard's fivefold explanation of conviction most frequently;

[19] Rutman to Selement, Nov. 12, 1981; "Confessions," 59, 52; Miller, New England Mind: The Seventeenth Century, 386; Rutman, American Puritanism, 27. Rather than present all of Shepard's theological views in the text, I have included footnote references to the relevant parts of his sermons that deal with the doctrine under consideration. On election see Albro, ed., Works, I, 54, 325, II, 135, 190, 605.
[20] Albro, ed., Works, I, 55, II, 135, 596-598; "Confessions," 64.

forty-seven of them made a total of 177 references to this initial preparatory step. They first confessed their special sins: sabbath-breaking, worldliness, bad-company keeping, drunkenness, lust, adultery, unbelief, pride, swearing, theft, price-gouging, lying, persecution of Christians, carelessness, and even inordinate love of learning. Next, many acknowledged the punishment they deserved for such evil. Elizabeth Olbon, for instance, spoke of the "bitterness of sin" and for a time considered it "impossible so poor a creature should be saved." Without exception, the laity invoked two of Shepard's three other criteria for true conviction by offering no excuses for their sins and maintaining a vision of their wickedness. Only Roger Haynes, however, mentioned Shepard's third criterion, testifying that "one must be sensible of his oppressed condition" in his heart. Finally, many candidates relied on one of Shepard's practical exhortations, which he included among his elaborations on conviction, to achieve a "true sense and feeling of sin" by deeming themselves miserable, undone, condemned, unclean, vile, foolish, lamentable, and carnal.[21]

Thirty-seven laymen also focused on the three concepts of fear of, sorrow for, and separation from sin associated with compunction, citing Shepard's second preparatory step eighty-one times, though without using his term. Jane Winship, mother of four, was "afraid to die and should forever lie under wrath of God," and Martha Collins feared that only "one paper wall" separated her from hell. As to sorrow for sin, Jane Holmes reported that "my grief was that sin parted between me and God." Similarly, God's wrath and sin "oppressed" the "spirit" of John Trumbull, a mariner and farmer, just as John Fessenden confessed that "sin it was which did oppress." Finally, many like William Andrews, a shipmaster with large landholdings, sought to separate themselves from evil by resolving "against every known sin."[22]

Some candidates did use Shepard's term for the final phase of preparation, and forty reflected their understanding of humiliation with 118 citations. John Jones's remark was typical: "I saw no way but to humble myself before God." Without the term, Mary Angier revealed her humiliation by confessing to "leaving her soul with the Lord, let Him do what He will, and thus the Lord gave her a contentedness of spirit and she saw more sin she never saw." So, too, did those who referred to one or more of the four humbling revelations that Shepard ascribed to the Mosaic law. Thus Edward Hall repented of making "examples and duties" his Christ; Richard Jackson's maid confessed her "original corruption"; George Willows recognized the "deadness of his heart under ordinances and the more he did strive against corruption, the more he was overcome by corruption"; and William Hamlet proclaimed how justly God "might require of all creatures power to fulfill His law." Such basic knowledge of humiliation, as well as of conviction and compunction, demonstrates that

[21] "Confessions," 40, 169; Albro, ed., Works, I, 131; cf. 117-136.
[22] "Confessions," 148, 130, 80, 107, 177, 112; cf. Albro, ed., Works, I, 136-174.

these laymen comprehended, albeit unsystematically and without a technical vocabulary, Shepard's teaching about preparation.[23] Their grasp of vocation, the final stage of uniting with Christ, also documents an approximate equation between popular and elite minds. Again the laity rarely employed Shepard's formal terminology of effectual vocation, revelation, illumination, presumption, rebellion, and justifying faith. But twenty-nine of them in forty-nine references evinced a general knowledge of the concepts of answering God's call and embracing the Holy Spirit without undue confidence or unnecessary hesitation. Robert Daniel testified: "Faith hath been wrought more and Christ more revealed more savingly unto me." More specifically, Mary Angier reported that she had "no faith" but the "Lord did incline her heart hereby to seek help in Him." God and Christ "did tender themselves" to young Barbary Cutter. Similarly, hearing in a sermon on Matthew—probably one of Shepard's series on the parable of the ten virgins—about spiritual marriage, Jackson's maid saw the "king, making suit to a poor silly maid do but give thy consent." Hamlet came the closest to ministerial form and language when he declared, "And after this the Lord discovered Christ and satisfaction and His person and offices and hereby did let forth the glory of Christ into my soul and did draw out my affections out in love to Christ."[24]

To these references to vocation must be added the many biblical allusions to, as William Manning put it, laying "hold on a promise," the act of identifying and accepting God's call in the scriptures. While it is impossible to determine how many of the laity's 463 biblical citations pertained to vocation, because they often quoted the Bible without connecting the passage with any particular tenet, the connection is explicitly made in some cases and implied in others. Edward Collins confessed: "And there I took notice of covenant that it was free and saw promises made to such dispositions to lost to meek and hungry and thirsty and to such as were confessors and forsakers of sin and hence I thought Jesus Christ was mine." Hearing John 5:40 "opened," Edward Hall saw "how freely Christ was offered." And Edward Shepard reported that "one morning considering things, James 4 came to mind—draw near to me and I will draw near to you—me thought the Lord spoke graciously." Laymen drew such promises from the gospels (particularly Matthew and John), Romans, Genesis, Exodus, Psalms, and the prophets, especially Isaiah, Jeremiah, and Revelation. Most laymen, like surveyor-farmer Robert Sanders, cited a combination of Old and New Testament passages: "And much ado I had to live by faith, but hearing those Scriptures—look to me all ends of the earth; and whoever will let him drink of the water of life freely; and so come to Me you that are weary and heavy laden and I will give you rest; and so blessed are the poor in spirit where I saw my emptiness and fullness in Christ to depend on Him."[25]

523

23 *"Confessions,"* 200, 68, 34, 119, 43, 126. Cf. Albro, ed., *Works,* I, 174-190.
24 *"Confessions,"* 61, 67, 90, 120, 126.
25 *Ibid.,* 96, 83, 34, 174, 71; for a breakdown of biblical references see 213.

To avoid sounding Arminian, Shepard and his candidates rarely cited "whoever will" verses without juxtaposing verses like Isaiah 40:29: "He giveth power to the faint; and to them that have no might He increaseth strength." Moreover, laymen acknowledged that only the elect could actually close with scriptural promises, reflecting Shepard's view that the Holy Spirit had to put "a necessity upon them" and "irresistibly" bring them to grace. For instance, Barbary Cutter responded to a question about how she knew that the Lord's biblical promises applied to her by declaring that she was "more sure than if named there because Lord by His Spirit would boote to soul." Jane Holmes even denounced an English vicar she had once met as "an opposer of the truth . . . an Arminian, one that taught free will and opposing openly Puritans." To be sure, the fine distinctions and terminology in Shepard's sermons generally eluded those in the pew, but the laity's heavy reliance on biblical promises documents their conceptual grasp of his definition of vocation as that "gracious work of the Spirit, whereby a humbled sinner receiveth Christ; or whether the whole soul cometh out of itself to Christ, for Christ and all his benefits, upon the call of Christ in the word."[26]

524

Eighteen candidates expressed in twenty-two statements reasonable certainty about closing with Christ. Francis Moore, for one, declared that he "was a new creature and hence was received to mercy," and Nathaniel Sparrowhawk used proper terminology in testifying that "God inclined my heart to close with the Lord." The others, however, never expressed such confidence, and a few, such as John Trumbull, who thought "there might be mercy" but could not tell if he "had seen sin or no," offered no definite evidence of uniting with Christ. But most of the other thirty laymen confessed at least to closing partially with Christ. Some were like Jane Champney, who thought she "should be drawn" to Christ but ended her relation by deeming herself "lost and unsupported." Others were more optimistic, as when Jane Winship doubted "by reason of passion whether any grace" but heard "humble yourself under God's hand" and was "comforted." In part, this vagueness about receiving grace resulted from Shepard's admission practices, for he instructed applicants not to give "extravagant, enlarged discourses of the set time of their conversion, and their revelations, and ill applications of Scripture, which makes such long doings, and are wearisome and uncomely." Having coached and screened these candidates privately, he already deemed them visible saints and thus exhorted them to focus on didactic testimonies "of special use unto the people of God, such things as tend to show, Thus I was humbled, then thus I was called . . . and thus the Lord hath delivered me, blessed be his name, etc." Furthermore, the laity's reluctance to proclaim certainty about salvation may have demonstrated their understanding of a finer aspect of Shepard's preaching on vocation. He had warned them not to clutch Christ presumptuously "before the day and hour of God's glorious and

[26] Albro, ed., *Works*, I, 190-191, 195; "*Confessions*," 92, 76. Cf. Albro, ed., *Works*, I, 190-237, II, 317-323.

gracious call," urging them instead to embrace God's call at the "instant" when the Spirit "fully and freely" offered Christ. If aware of his exhortation, scrupulous laymen would have been hesitant to claim they had fully closed with Christ.[27] In contrast to the laity's high scores on election, union, and closing with Christ, their six references to justification, reconciliation, adoption, and glorification seem to support the contention of those historians who have argued that rank-and-file New Englanders did not have "the wits to comprehend the exquisite theories" of Puritan divines. Indeed, Shepard's parishioners revealed no knowledge of adoption and glorification. But the three who mentioned justification—God's absolution from the guilt of and condemnation for sin—displayed a solid grasp of that concept. John Fessenden said he "came to Him for justification and sanctification," linking the doctrines just as Shepard did in *The Sound Believer*. The unidentified confessor rightly concluded that "it was nothing in us that could procure justification but only laying hold on Christ." John Stedman even pinned the idea to the correct proof text: "heard 2 Corinthians 5:20 treating about justification and calling." Likewise, Mary Parish accurately tied reconciliation—Christ's work of bringing peace and love between God and the saved—to 2 Corinthians 5 as well as connecting the idea with being "enemies" to God in mind, will, and affection. Yet Nathaniel Sparrowhawk, who spoke of "entreating reconciliation," and Barbary Cutter, who associated the doctrine with points relating to conviction and humiliation, clearly misunderstood the term by making it synonymous with the act of uniting to Christ. When compared to the hundreds of accurate responses on other points, four correct statements about justification and reconciliation indicate a significant gap between lay and clerical thought.[28]

525

Yet three considerations about these four doctrines merit attention. Technically, they were beyond the scope of a narration about one's steps to grace—for, according to Shepard, these were divine gifts bestowed by the deity simultaneously (in time) and progressively (in logic) upon the elect at the moment of conversion. Thus candidates could have justifiably omitted them from their accounts of how they united to Christ, leaving aside the results of that union. Six laymen, therefore, simply volunteered more than Shepard required. Furthermore, misuse of terminology does not necessarily establish ignorance of concepts—only of labels, and perhaps not even that. Under the pressure of an extemporaneous speech, Sparrowhawk and Cutter might have only momentarily confused terminology.

Such conclusions gain support from the fact that only sanctification, another gift from God, was pertinent for laymen to highlight. And sixteen

27 "Confessions," 36, 63, 107, 109, 191, 149; Albro, ed., *Works*, II, 631, I, 191; for a fuller analysis of Shepard's admission requirements see "Confessions," 21-24.
28 Miller, *Orthodoxy in Massachusetts*, xxxiv; "Confessions," 177, 207, 75, 137, 63, 90; Albro, ed., *Works*, I, 237, 248.

did make twenty references to this "most sweet and comfortable evidence of thy justification." Eleven, like John Trumbull, demonstrated their knowledge without Shepard's terminology. "Then seeing keeping His commands was an evidence," Trumbull reported, "then I remembered though I was vile yet I did love Sabbaths and saints." The other five either simply employed the term—such as Elizabeth Olbon who "longed after Christ to save and sanctify"—or both used and explained it. Golden Moore's comment was especially insightful: "And hearing we might clear up justification by sanctification which, when I could not find, yet hearing that if I sought to the Lord that He would clear and work it Jeremiah 3:22 this stayed." The laity learned this point well because Shepard in his staunch opposition to the antinomianism of Anne Hutchinson and her followers, who denied that sanctification evidenced salvation, had undoubtedly counseled his flock in private and had educated them in sermons. "Let all those dreams of the Familists," he railed in one long exposition on sanctification, "let them vanish and perish from under the sun, and the good Lord reduce all such who in simplicity are misled from this blessed truth of God."[29] On balance, then, the laity's record on these five doctrines indicates some gap between Shepard and his laymen, but overall their performance suggests that the gap was not a wide one.

Similar ambiguity appears in the laity's failure to mention the perseverance of the saints. Only Francis Moore, having "backslid" into loose company, drunkenness, profaning the sabbath, and resting in ordinances, took comfort in the knowledge that "the Lord was unchangeable in Himself and so in His love." That the other forty-seven candidates ignored this tenet may relate to their assurance about closing with Christ. For the many who were uncertain, their evil acts or base thoughts perhaps indicated to them a false hold on salvation, even hypocrisy, rather than any fall from grace. Recall Jane Winship, who having prepared for Christ and applied promises, still doubted "by reason of passion whether [she had] any grace." As to the eighteen who expressed confidence about closing with Christ, except for Francis Moore, they may not have worried about losing their salvation by sinning. As predestinarians, believing in election and perseverance, such parishioners should have assumed that works could neither merit nor imperil salvation. "None can pluck thee out of Christ's hands, neither sin nor devil," Shepard had told them more than once. Thus, as with such doctrines as glorification, the lack of references to perseverance of the saints does not necessarily prove that laymen were ignorant of Shepard's beliefs.[30]

Less controversial is the laity's comprehension of Shepard's preaching on the "means" because every layman recalled one or more of these practical applications of Reformed doctrine. Shepard exhorted parishioners to come to Christ "by means, the ministry of the gospel; else what need there be any Scripture writ, or gospel preached?" Heeding that

---

[29] Albro, ed., *Works*, I, 258, 257; "*Confessions*," 109, 41, 123-124. Cf. Albro, ed., *Works*, I, 237-274.
[30] "*Confessions*," 36, 149; Albro, ed., *Works*, I, 291.

advice, all forty-eight laymen quoted the Bible, citing it 463 times. To be sure, candidates did not usually link their biblical citations with using means, though some like John Sill did, but they all clearly implied that such scriptures were leading them to grace. The same is true of their numerous references to sermons, and in this case twenty did make a total of forty such links. For example, Mary Angier testified: "Every sermon made her worse and sat like a block under all means."[31]

Equally impressive, thirty-seven laymen made eighty references to Shepard's six means of receiving Christ and the "fullness of his Spirit." Again, they seldom used Shepard's label, but their language paralleled his. He had told them to pray for preparation, "not that prayer can move the Lord to it, but because it is a means appointed of God to execute his eternal purposes of grace." Thus John Stedman "entreated the Lord to help me to pray and so" found God saving him from "gross sin" and convicting him of "hardness of heart." Means two, wrote Shepard, was to be "watchful over your hearts" for sins like pride, loathing of ordinances, despising truths, and contending with God's people. While lay allusions to sinfulness were often expressions of conviction and compunction, some were readily tied to Shepard's words on preparatory means. Nathaniel Sparrowhawk, for instance, said: "When I saw others filled with spiritual good, my soul could not bear it but the Lord hath let me see it: Is thy eye evil because mine is good and may I not do with mine as I list?" Similar parallels exist for the other four preparatory means.[32]

527

The candidates also scored well on three of the remaining four sets of means that Shepard prescribed for coming to grace. Sixteen of them made twenty-two references to his means to "enter Christ's rest." Thirteen alluded nineteen times to the means of making "their calling, and election, and the love of Christ sure." And seven cited the means to be "apprehended of the Lord Jesus." A representative example of their understanding of these dozen means is Barbary Cutter who, having heard Shepard say "bring thy heart to a strait, either to reject or receive him to be thine," remarked: "hearing sin of unbelief to bring heart to strait, either to receive or reject Him . . . so found sweetness." Only John Sill and Sparrowhawk, however, used any of Shepard's four means to cure hypocrisy. Still, scattered as these sixteen means were throughout Shepard's sermons on the parable of the ten virgins, it is remarkable that the laity referred 133 times to them.[33]

Shepard also presented in that series of sermons four sets of signs, which a majority of thirty-five candidates recalled. Twenty-three confessed thirty-one times to having been "married to the law." Edward Collins related: "And question being made when a man rested in duties, I was convinced I was the man." Eleven, like "Old Goodwife" Elizabeth Cutter, who "saw I was a Christless creature and hence in all ordinances

---

[31] Albro, ed., *Works,* II, 521; *"Confessions,"* 66.
[32] Albro, ed., *Works,* II, 563-565; *"Confessions,"* 73-74, 64. Cf. Albro, ed., *Works,* II, 563-568, and *"Confessions,"* 90, 61, 34, 46.
[33] Albro, ed., *Works,* II, 290-292, 77-86, 619, 236-237; *"Confessions,"* 91.

was persuaded nothing did belong to me," reflected fifteen times Shepard's signs of being in league with the creature. Eleven also recognized in fourteen instances certain signs of being "evangelical hypocrites," just as eight made ten identifications of the signs of being "filled with the Spirit of Christ." Typically, laymen did not preface their statements with the label "sign," but their words and thoughts clearly mirrored Shepard's teachings.[34]

No one has ever posited an exact parallel between ministerial and lay thought, though historians who have written of Puritan New England have sometimes come dangerously close.[35] Even Shepard, when delving into the finer points of vocation, justification, and sanctification, expressed apprehension about being "thus large in less practical matters." Most historians have rather assumed that for all practical purposes in writing about the history of ideas there was at least a rough correspondence between lay and clerical thought—a collective mentality. With certain qualifications, *Thomas Shepard's "Confessions"* supports their assumption. Cambridge parishioners grasped remarkably well Shepard's teaching on election, union with Christ, sanctification, the means to close with Christ, and several signs of grace. True, their knowledge was often unsystematic and sometimes cursory, just as their terminology frequently lacked precision, and on less practical doctrines—justification, reconciliation, adoption, glorification, and perseverance—their comprehension was understandably shallower than Shepard's. But despite their omissions, distortions, modifications, and simplifications, the laity reflected their pastor's theology. In sum, though historians ought not cavalierly to "ascribe the ministers' Puritanism to the laymen and let it go at that," they can, with caveats, write the history of ideas as if one or more collective mentalities existed in seventeenth-century New England.[36] This is not to posit a Puritan New England, for dissenters and secular persons fostered rival collective mentalities in the region, but to argue that ministers and their flocks held a theology in common.

---

[34] Albro, ed., *Works*, II, 36-41, 33-36, 199-203, 555-557; *"Confessions,"* 83, 145.

[35] To write of Puritan New England suggests that all New Englanders thought along the lines of the publishing clergy in the region. Edmund S. Morgan apparently holds this notion, declaring in a letter regarding Miller's critics: "If I remember correctly a number of reviews suggested that Miller was talking only about the mind of the ministers, that what was needed was a study of the mind of the common man—in effect that intellectual historians should study the ideas of people who had no ideas of their own. I can remember being astonished myself by some of these reviews, and we talked about them" (Morgan to Selement, Dec. 13, 1982). While the laity's confessions document a heavy reliance on ministerial thought, their relations also suggest these laymen had minds of their own. Recall John Sill who doubted the reports on Shepard and embraced him only after a careful evaluation of his preaching. Moreover, the *"Confessions"* reveals that the laity encountered many secular people—some of whom ridiculed religion in general and Puritans in particular—who had ideas of their own.

[36] Albro, ed., *Works*, I, 170; Rutman, *American Puritanism*, 33.

The publisher and editor gratefully acknowledge the permission of the authors and the following journals and organizations to reprint the copyright material in this volume; any further reproduction is prohibited without permission:

The American Jewish Historical Society; *The New England Quarterly*; *History and Theory*; *The William and Mary Quarterly*; the *American Quarterly*; the American Historical Association for material in the *American Historical Review*; the *Journal of the History of Ideas*; the American Society of Church History for material in *Church History*; *The New England Quarterly*, the Massachusetts Historical Society, and Harvard University for Perry Miller's articles, "The Half-Way Covenant," and "Jonathan Edwards' Sociology of the Great Awakening."

CONTENTS OF THE SET